KU-608-688

New
SCHOOL
THESAURUS

Collins
An imprint of HarperCollins*Publishers*

First Published 2001

© HarperCollins Publishers 2001

10 9 8 7 6 5 4 3 2 1

ISBN 0-00-765932-5

The HarperCollins website address is
www.**fire**and**water**.com

A catalogue record for this book is available from the
British Library.

Corpus Acknowledgments
We would like to thank those authors and publishers who kindly
gave permission for copyright material to be used in the Bank of
English.
We would also like to thank Times Newspapers Ltd for providing
valuable data.

Typeset by Stewart C Russell

Printed and bound in Germany by
Elsnerdruck, Berlin

Contents

BANK of ENGLISH

This thesaurus has been compiled by referring to the Bank of English, a unique database of the English language with examples of over 400 million words enabling Collins lexicographers to analyse how English is actually used today and how it is changing. This is the evidence on which the material in this thesaurus is based.

The Bank of English was set up as a joint initiative by HarperCollins Publishers and Birmingham University to be a resource for language research and lexicography. It contains a very wide range of material from books, newspapers, radio, TV, magazines, letters, and talks reflecting the whole spectrum of English today. Its size and range make it an unequalled resource and the purpose-built software for its analysis is unique to Collins Dictionaries.

This ensures that Collins Dictionaries accurately reflect English as it is used today in a way that is most helpful to the dictionary or thesaurus user as well as including the full range of rarer and historical words and meanings.

Introduction

Collins New School Thesaurus is a vital language and literacy tool for today's students and has been created to meet their needs and aspirations. Through research among teachers, many samples were tested so Collins could establish exactly what features would be considered most helpful, and all those identified have been incorporated in this text.

Collins New School Thesaurus is easy to use. On the outer edge of each page there is a marker highlighting the letter of the alphabet featured on that page. At the top of each page the first and last words entered on the page are clearly shown.

But what exactly has our research uncovered that isn't already featured in any other school thesaurus text? Collins' unique new approach ensures that each entry word is followed by a short explanation of its meaning, which is then followed by an example of real English showing the context in which the word may be used. Furthermore, each synonym given for the entry word is also accompanied by an example showing context – this makes it clearer for the student to see which synonyms can be directly substituted for the entry word, and which involve a slight shift in sense.

Again, unlike most thesauruses, *Collins New School Thesaurus* splits the different parts of speech of a word into separate entries. Therefore, instead of scanning through the synonyms in one entry to find the relevant part of speech, the student will find ❶ **glow** NOUN, as one entry, followed by a second entry, ❷ **glow** VERB. Similarly, literal and figurative senses have been split into separate entries, e.g. ❶ **painful** ADJECTIVE *causing emotional pain*, and ❷ **painful** ADJECTIVE *causing physical pain*.

Collins New School Thesaurus has even more ways to help. The ***Word Power*** features are specially created to further expand the vocabulary of older or keener students. These items give more advanced synonyms for the entry word and also give a suitable antonym where appropriate. For example, at the entry ❶ **lying** NOUN, as well as the synonyms *deceit, dishonesty, fabrication, fibbing* and *perjury*, you will find a ***Word Power*** list showing the more advanced synonyms *dissimulation, duplicity,* and *mendacity*.

We occasionally offer themed lists relevant to the entry word, such as different *shades of red* at **red**, different *types of weather* at **weather**, or different *religions* at **religion**. Again, these lists are specifically introduced to expand the students' vocabulary and to enhance their creative writing skills. Some of these lists have been compiled in accordance with the vocabulary lists established by the National Literacy Trust. Thus, at **grammar**, the student will find a list of pertinent *grammar terms, punctuation terms* at **punctuation**, etc.

Also unique to an alphabetically-listed thesaurus is the detailed index to be found at the end of the book. This lists all the synonyms which appear in the thesaurus and shows which head-words each one appears under, so the student can see at a glance whether a word is a synonym for more than one entry word.

In keeping with Collins's practice of World English coverage, there are many words from Australian, New Zealand, and South African English, as well as some British regional words. This shows the student the diversity of the language and the richness of inter-national and dialect words that they can also draw from.

Another exciting feature of the thesaurus is the Wordgames section, again designed to expand the students' vocabulary and enhance their appreciation of language. There is also a photocopiable Thesaurus Skills workpack to accompany this book, containing dozens of classroom activities to develop thesaurus skills.

Collins New School Thesaurus is relevant, accessible, student-friendly – in fact, it's exactly what you asked us to make it. And it's an indispensable companion to the *Collins New School Dictionary*.

How To Use The Thesaurus

Collins New School Thesaurus is easy to use and understand.
Below are some entries showing the thesaurus's main features,
along with an explanation of what they are.

The entry word — **❷ beauty** NOUN
a good-looking person
EG *a dark-haired beauty*
hunk INFORMAL EG *The Swedish
hunk is back again.* — *Advice on when
to use the
synonym*
stunner INFORMAL EG *the
23-year-old stunner*

❸ blow NOUN
*What the word
means* — something disappointing or
upsetting
EG *Marc's death was a terrible blow.* — *An example of
the word being
used*
bombshell EG *His departure was a
bombshell for the team.*
disappointment EG *My exam
results were a real disappointment.*
Synonyms — **misfortune** EG *a series of
misfortunes*
setback EG *We faced many
setbacks before we got the house.*
shock EG *The news came as a
shock.* — *An example of
the synonym
being used*
upset EG *The defeat caused an
upset.*

*Word Power:
more advanced
synonyms* — | **WORD POWER**
Synonyms
calamity
catastrophe
jolt |

How To Use The Thesaurus

blue NOUN OR ADJECTIVE

Shades of blue:
aqua
aquamarine
azure
cerulean
cobalt
cyan
duck-egg blue
electric blue
gentian
indigo
lapis lazuli
midnight blue
navy
Nile blue
peacock blue
periwinkle
petrol blue
royal blue
sapphire
saxe blue
sky-blue
teal
turquoise
ultramarine

Themed list of words connected with the entry word

❶ blunt ADJECTIVE
having rounded edges
EG *blunt scissors*
dull EG *a dull knife*
rounded EG *rounded edges*
unsharpened EG *an unsharpened pencil*

Each sense of a word is shown as a separate entry

The word's part of speech

WORD POWER
Antonym
sharp

Word Power: antonyms

How To Use The Index

The index helps you find any word in the thesaurus. Below is a section showing how the index is arranged.

Look up a word here to find which entry word it appears in as a synonym

abstain → refuse
abstruse → mysterious
abstruse → obscure
absurd → impossible
absurd → incredible
absurd → irrational
absurd → ridiculous
absurd → silly
absurd → stupid
absurdity → stupidity
abundance → a lot
abundance → wealth
abundant → generous
abundant → rich
abuse → impose on
abuse → harm
abuse → insult
abuse → mistreat
abuse → wrong
abused → oppressed
abusive → offensive
abutment → support
abysmal → awful
abysmal → terrible
abyss → hell
academic → learned
accelerate → hurry
accelerated → fast
accent → emphasis
accent → emphasize
accentuate → emphasize

The arrow directs you to the entry word

If a phrase is given as the synonym's target, you should look under the word shown in bold to find the entry it appears under

If a word appears as a synonym in more than one entry, there is an index reference for each place where it can be found

*New
School
Thesaurus*

abandon VERB
to leave someone or something
EG *His parents had abandoned him.*
desert EG *Medical staff have deserted the city's main hospital.*
jilt EG *She was jilted by her first fiancé.*
leave EG *My husband has left me.*
leave behind EG *He walked out and left behind a wife and two young children.*

> **WORD POWER**
> Synonyms
> forsake
> leave in the lurch

abandon NOUN
lack of restraint
EG *He began to laugh with abandon.*
recklessness EG *the headstrong recklessness of youth*
wildness EG *Her wildness just needed to be channelled properly.*

> **WORD POWER**
> Antonym
> control

ability NOUN
the skill needed to do something
EG *the ability to get on with others*
capability EG *We have the capability of going out and winning.*
competence EG *They have a high level of competence.*
expertise EG *legal expertise*
skill EG *the skill to play at a higher level*
talent EG *a talent for music*

> **WORD POWER**
> Synonyms
> dexterity
> proficiency
> Antonym
> inability

abolish VERB
to do away with something
EG *Their objective was to abolish capital gains tax.*
annul EG *The marriage was annulled last month.*
do away with EG *the proposal to do away with nuclear weapons*
overturn EG *criminals seeking to overturn their convictions*
put an end to EG *efforts to put an end to the traffic in drugs*

> **WORD POWER**
> Synonyms
> quash
> rescind
> revoke

❶ about PREPOSITION
of or concerning
EG *anxiety about his sick son*
concerning EG *documents concerning the estate*
on EG *his book on Picasso*
regarding EG *strict rules regarding the disposal of food*
relating to EG *the rules relating to transfer fees*

❷ about ADVERB
not exactly
EG *The procedure takes about thirty minutes.*
almost EG *Their wages have almost doubled.*
approximately EG *It was approximately three times the size of a domestic cat.*
around EG *The crowd here is around 12,000.*
nearly EG *a tradition going back nearly 20 centuries*
roughly EG *One unit is roughly equivalent to half a pint of beer.*

❶ above PREPOSITION
over or higher than something
EG *above the clouds*
higher than EG *There are no hotels higher than four storeys.*

A B C D E F G H I J K L M N O P Q R S T U V W X Y Z

over EG *the picture over the fireplace*

> **WORD POWER**
> Antonym
> below

❷ above PREPOSITION
greater than a certain level or amount
EG *The death toll will rise above 50.*
beyond EG *I expect to live way beyond 100.*
exceeding EG *a floor area exceeding 50,000 square feet*

❶ abrupt ADJECTIVE
sudden or unexpected
EG *the abrupt resignation of the prime minister*
sudden EG *this week's sudden thaw*
unexpected EG *His career came to an unexpected end.*
unforeseen EG *unforeseen difficulties*

> **WORD POWER**
> Synonyms
> precipitate
> unanticipated

❷ abrupt ADJECTIVE
unfriendly and impolite
EG *He was a taken aback by her abrupt manner.*
curt EG *'The matter is closed,' was the curt reply.*
rude EG *He was frequently rude to waiters and servants.*
short EG *She seemed tense and was definitely short with me.*
terse EG *He received a terse one-line rejection from the Ministry.*

> **WORD POWER**
> Synonyms
> brusque
> unceremonious
> Antonym
> polite

absent ADJECTIVE
not present
EG *absent from work*

away EG *She is away on a busines. trip.*
elsewhere EG *Four witnesses can prove he was elsewhere at the time.*
gone EG *I'll only be gone for ten minutes.*
missing EG *Another 44 passengers are still missing.*

> **WORD POWER**
> Antonym
> present

absent-minded ADJECTIVE
forgetful or not paying attention
EG *Her absent-minded stepfather le, the camera under the carriage seat.*
distracted EG *He seems distracted giving the impression of being elsewhere.*
forgetful EG *She's getting rather forgetful, and living mostly in the past.*
random NEW ZEALAND EG *I'm sorry, I'm a bit random these days.*

absorb VERB
to soak up or take in something
EG *plants absorb carbon dioxide*
digest EG *Fats are hard to digest.*
soak up EG *Stir until the wheat ha soaked up all the water.*
take in EG *A growing tree takes in light and processes it for food.*

abstain VERB
to choose not to do something
EG *The patients had to abstain fron alcohol.*
avoid EG *Heartburn sufferers should try to avoid fatty foods.*
deny oneself EG *I won't deny myself some celebration tonight.*
forgo EG *My wife and I have to forgo holidays now.*
give up EG *She gave up smoking last year.*
refrain EG *He appealed to all factions to refrain from violence.*

> **WORD POWER**
> Synonyms
> desist

forbear
renounce

absurd ADJECTIVE
ridiculous or nonsensical
EG *an absurd waste of money*
crazy INFORMAL EG *It would be crazy to tinker with a winning team.*
illogical EG *his completely illogical arguments*
ludicrous EG *It was ludicrous to suggest that the visit could be kept secret.*
nonsensical EG *He says many diets are harmful and nonsensical.*
ridiculous EG *The programme is too ridiculous to take seriously.*

> *WORD POWER*
> Synonyms
> incongruous
> preposterous

abundance NOUN
a great amount of something
EG *an abundance of wildlife*
affluence EG *Pockets of affluence coexist with poverty.*
bounty EG *autumn's bounty of fruit, seeds, and berries*
plenty EG *Allow plenty of time to get home.*

> *WORD POWER*
> Synonyms
> cornucopia
> plethora
> Antonym
> shortage

abundant ADJECTIVE
present in large quantities
EG *an abundant supply of cheap labour*
ample EG *ample space for a good-sized kitchen*
copious EG *copious amounts of red wine*
full EG *a full tank of petrol*
plentiful EG *a plentiful supply of vegetables*

> *WORD POWER*

Antonym
scarce

❶ abuse NOUN
cruel treatment of someone
EG *child abuse*
exploitation EG *Most human life involves the exploitation of animals.*
harm EG *the harm smokers willingly do to their own health*
hurt EG *The victims suffer mental scars as well as physical hurt.*
ill-treatment EG *the ill-treatment of political prisoners*
oppression EG *the oppression of black people throughout history*

❷ abuse NOUN
unkind remarks directed towards someone
EG *I was left shouting abuse as the car sped off.*
censure EG *a controversial policy which has attracted international censure*
derision EG *He was greeted with shouts of derision.*
insults EG *They shouted insults at each other.*
invective EG *A woman had hurled racist invective at the family.*

❸ abuse VERB
to speak insultingly to someone
EG *He was verbally abused by other soldiers.*
curse EG *We started cursing them under our breath.*
insult EG *I did not mean to insult you.*
scold EG *Later she scolded her daughter for having talked to her father like that.*
slate BRITISH INFORMAL EG *Willis's acting skills have been slated, yet again.*

abusive ADJECTIVE
rude and unkind
EG *abusive language*
disparaging EG *He made some disparaging remarks about the team.*

A
B
C
D
E
F
G
H
I
J
K
L
M
N
O
P
Q
R
S
T
U
V
W
X
Y
Z

A
B
C
D
E
F
G
H
I
J
K
L
M
N
O
P
Q
R
S
T
U
V
W
X
Y
Z

insulting EG *She was charged with insulting behaviour to a police officer.*

offensive EG *The book was seen by many Muslims as being deeply offensive to Islam.*

rude EG *He is rude to her friends.*

scathing EG *He made some particularly scathing comments about the design.*

> **WORD POWER**
> Synonyms
> censorious
> vituperative

abyss NOUN
a very deep hole
EG *He crawled to peer over the edge of the abyss.*

chasm EG *The climbers strung a rope across the chasm and crawled along it.*

fissure EG *The earthquake opened large fissures in the ground.*

gorge EG *The valley narrowed to a gorge with cascading crags.*

pit EG *Eric lost his footing and began to slide into the pit.*

void EG *His feet dangled in the void.*

accelerate VERB
to go faster
EG *She accelerated away from the kerb.*

hurry EG *He shouted at me to hurry.*

quicken EG *Her pulse quickened in alarm.*

speed up EG *It is designed to speed up credit-card transactions.*

> **WORD POWER**
> Antonym
> decelerate

accept VERB
to receive or agree to something
EG *All those invited to next week's conference have accepted.*

acknowledge EG *He was willing to acknowledge her as his child.*

agree to EG *Hours before the deadline, the Chinese agreed to the*
conditions.

concur with EG *I concur with her opinion.*

consent to EG *The Russians consented to the peace treaty.*

take EG *He took the job.*

> **WORD POWER**
> Antonym
> refuse

accidental ADJECTIVE
happening by chance
EG *The fire was accidental.*

casual EG *a casual remark*

chance EG *a chance meeting*

inadvertent EG *She giggled at the inadvertent pun.*

random EG *the random nature of death in war*

> **WORD POWER**
> Antonym
> deliberate

accommodate VERB
to provide someone with a place to stay
EG *a hotel built to accommodate guests for the wedding*

house EG *The building will house 12 boys.*

put up EG *I wanted to know if she could put me up for a few days.*

shelter EG *There were no facilities for sheltering the refugees.*

accommodating ADJECTIVE
willing to help
EG *his polite, accommodating manner*

considerate EG *I try to be considerate to non-smokers.*

helpful EG *The staff in the Newcastle office are very helpful.*

hospitable EG *He was very hospitable to me when I came to New York.*

kind EG *It was very kind of you to come.*

obliging EG *an extremely pleasant and obliging man*

accommodation NOUN
a house or room for living in
EG *Travel and overnight accommodation are included.*
digs BRITISH INFORMAL EG *I was studying and living in digs all round the country.*
house EG *He sold his house in London and moved to the country.*
housing EG *a serious housing shortage*
lodgings EG *At the moment the house provides lodgings for Oxford students.*
quarters EG *the officers' quarters*

accompany VERB
to go somewhere with someone
EG *Children must be accompanied by an adult.*
conduct FORMAL EG *He asked if he might conduct us to the ball.*
escort EG *They were escorted by police to their plane.*
go with EG *I haven't asked my friend to go with me yet.*
usher EG *I ushered him into the office.*

accompany VERB
to occur with something
EG *severe pain accompanied by fever*
come with EG *Stress comes with this job.*
go together with EG *Poverty and illiteracy go together with high birth rates.*

accomplish VERB
to manage to do something
EG *If we'd all work together, I think we'd accomplish our goal.*
achieve EG *Achieving our aims makes us feel good.*
bring about EG *the only way to bring about political change*
complete EG *She has just completed her first novel.*
do EG *Have you done it yet?*
fulfil EG *All the necessary conditions were fulfilled.*
manage EG *40% of children*

managed the required standard in reading.

> **WORD POWER**
> Synonyms
> effect
> execute
> realize

accurate ADJECTIVE
correct to a detailed level
EG *Quartz watches are very accurate.*
correct EG *The correct answers can be found at the bottom of the page.*
exact EG *an exact copy*
faithful EG *a faithful translation*
precise EG *precise sales figures*
right EG *That clock never tells the right time.*
strict EG *He has never been a playboy in the strict sense of the word.*
true EG *a true account of what happened*

> **WORD POWER**
> Antonym
> inaccurate

accuse VERB
to charge someone with doing something wrong
EG *He accused her of having an affair.*
blame EG *The police blamed the explosion on terrorists.*
censure EG *The Stock Exchange took the unusual step of censuring him in public.*
charge EG *Police have charged Mr Smith with murder.*
cite EG *He was banned for 30 days after being cited for foul play.*
denounce EG *He publicly denounced government nuclear policy.*

> **WORD POWER**
> Synonyms
> impeach
> incriminate
> indict

A
B
C
D
E
F
G
H
I
J
K
L
M
N
O
P
Q
R
S
T
U
V
W
X
Y
Z

5

A

accustomed ADJECTIVE
used to something
EG *The manager has become accustomed to abuse of late.*
adapted EG *The camel's feet, well adapted for dry sand, are useless on mud.*
familiar EG *He was very familiar with contemporary music.*
used EG *I'm used to having my sleep interrupted.*

> **WORD POWER**
> Antonym
> unaccustomed

achieve VERB
to gain by hard work or ability
EG *She has achieved her best tournament result for years.*
accomplish EG *halfway towards accomplishing an important career goal*
carry out EG *debate about how such reforms should be carried out*
complete EG *The commission completed this task in March.*
do EG *I have done what I came here to do.*
fulfil EG *The army has fulfilled its objective.*
perform EG *He has not performed his administrative duties properly.*

achievement NOUN
something which someone has succeeded in doing
EG *His presence here is an achievement in itself.*
accomplishment EG *The list of her accomplishments is staggering.*
deed EG *His heroic deeds were celebrated in every corner of India.*
exploit EG *His wartime exploits were later made into a TV series.*
feat EG *A racing car is an extraordinary feat of engineering.*

❶ **act** VERB
to do something
EG *The bank acted properly in the best interests of the depositors.*

function EG *All the computer systems functioned properly.*
operate EG *In the first half he operated effectively in defence.*
perform EG *He performed well in (World Cup match last summer.*
work EG *All sides will work towards a political solution.*

❷ **act** VERB
to perform in a play or film
EG *He acted in 91 films altogether.*
act out EG *It was made using real people to act out the scene.*
perform EG *She performed the role on television twice more.*
play EG *He plays agent Lillian Scully in a spoof of The X-Files.*
play the part of EG *She agreed to play the part of Evita.*
portray EG *His mean, moody looks are perfect for the cynical anti-hero he portrays.*

> **WORD POWER**
> Synonyms
> characterize
> personify

❸ **act** NOUN
a single thing someone does
EG *an act of disloyalty to the King*
accomplishment EG *Winning the tournament would be an incredible accomplishment.*
achievement EG *She was honoured for her achievements as a film-maker.*
deed EG *forgotten deeds of heroism*
feat EG *an outstanding feat of athleticism*
undertaking EG *Organizing the show has been a massive undertaking.*

❶ **action** NOUN
the process of doing something
EG *He had to take evasive action to avoid being hit.*
activity EG *the electrical activity of the brain*
operation EG *It is quite a tricky*

operation.

process EG *the peace process*

① action NOUN
something that is done
EG *He did not like his actions questioned.*

accomplishment EG *sporting accomplishments*

achievement EG *If we can win the league it will be a great achievement for me.*

deed EG *daring and heroic deeds*

exploit EG *the stories of his wartime exploits*

feat EG *prodigious feats of engineering*

actual ADJECTIVE
real, rather than imaginary or guessed at
EG *That is the official figure: the actual figure is much higher.*

authentic EG *music played on authentic medieval instruments*

genuine EG *a store selling genuine army clothing*

realistic EG *a realistic picture of Dublin life*

true EG *The film is based on a true story.*

verified EG *verified reports of serious human rights violations*

adapt VERB
to alter for a new use
EG *Shelves were built to adapt the library for use as an office.*

adjust EG *He had to adjust the driver's seat.*

alter EG *The government has altered the rules.*

change EG *The law needs to be changed.*

convert EG *a table that converts into an ironing board*

modify EG *Our workshop is busy modifying the tanks for desert conditions.*

① add VERB
to put something with something else

EG *Add the grated cheese to the sauce.*

attach EG *Don't forget to attach the completed entry form.*

augment EG *a way to augment the family income*

supplement EG *I suggest supplementing your diet with vitamin A.*

WORD POWER
Synonyms
adjoin
affix
append

② add VERB
to combine numbers or quantities
EG *Banks add all the interest and other charges together.*

add up EG *adding up calories on a calculator*

count up EG *They counted up all the hours the villagers worked.*

total EG *They will compete for prizes totalling nearly £300.*

WORD POWER
Antonym
subtract

addition NOUN
something that has been added to something else
EG *recent additions to their range of cars*

increase EG *a substantial increase in workload*

supplement EG *a supplement to their basic pension*

WORD POWER
Synonyms
addendum
adjunct
appendage

admiration NOUN
a feeling of great liking and respect
EG *I have always had the greatest admiration for him.*

A

appreciation EG *gifts presented to them in appreciation of their work*

approval EG *His son had an obsessive drive to gain his father's approval.*

esteem EG *Their public esteem has never been lower.*

regard EG *He has always been held in high regard.*

respect EG *We all have so much respect for her.*

admire VERB
to like and respect someone or something
EG *All those who knew him will admire him for his work.*

appreciate EG *the need for children to appreciate their mother tongue*

look up to EG *A lot of the younger girls look up to you.*

respect EG *I want him to respect me as a career woman.*

value EG *She genuinely values his opinion.*

> **WORD POWER**
> Synonyms
> esteem
> venerate
> Antonym
> scorn

❶ admit VERB
to agree that something is true
EG *The driver admitted to falling asleep at the wheel.*

accept EG *I accepted the truth of all that Nicola had told me.*

acknowledge EG *Belatedly the government has acknowledged the problem.*

grant EG *The magistrates granted that the RSPCA was justified in bringing the action.*

> **WORD POWER**
> Antonym
> deny

❷ admit VERB
to allow to enter

EG *He was admitted to university after the war.*

accept EG *Stephen was accepted into the family.*

let in EG *Turnstile operators were accused of letting in fans without tickets.*

receive EG *He was received into the priesthood.*

take in EG *The monastery has taken in 26 refugees.*

> **WORD POWER**
> Antonym
> exclude

adult NOUN
a grown-up person
EG *Becoming a father signified he was now an adult.*

grown-up EG *Las Vegas is the ultimate playground for grown-ups.*

man EG *He is now a man of 42.*

woman EG *A woman of child-bearing age.*

> **WORD POWER**
> Antonym
> child

❶ advance VERB
to move forward or develop
EG *Rebel forces are advancing on the capital.*

make inroads EG *They have made impressive inroads in the movie business.*

press on EG *Poland pressed on with economic reform.*

proceed EG *He proceeded down the spiral stairway.*

progress EG *the ability to progress from one step to the next*

❷ advance NOUN
progress in something
EG *scientific advance*

breakthrough EG *a breakthrough in cancer treatment*

development EG *the development of the car*

gain EG *a gain of nearly 10%*

progress EG *signs of progress in his*

reading
step EG *the first step towards peace*

advantage NOUN
a more favourable position or state
EG *We have a competitive advantage.*

ascendancy EG *The extremists are gaining ascendancy.*
benefit EG *For maximum benefit use your treatment every day.*
dominance EG *the battle for high-street dominance*
superiority EG *military superiority*

> *WORD POWER*
> Antonym
> disadvantage

advertise VERB
to present something to the public in order to sell it
EG *Bookmakers cannot advertise on television.*

plug INFORMAL EG *If I hear another actor plugging his latest book I will scream.*
promote EG *What are you doing to promote your new film?*
publicize EG *He never publicized his plans.*
push EG *a publisher who knows how to push a product*

> *WORD POWER*
> Synonyms
> blazon
> promulgate

advertisement NOUN
a public announcement to sell or publicize something
EG *She recently placed an advertisement in the local newspaper.*

ad INFORMAL EG *an ad for a minicab company*
advert BRITISH INFORMAL EG *She appeared in a coffee advert.*
commercial EG *She has turned down a small fortune to do TV commercials.*

notice EG *The request is published in notices in today's national newspapers.*
plug INFORMAL EG *a shameless plug for his new film*

advice NOUN
a suggestion as to what to do
EG *Take my advice and stay away from him!*

counsel FORMAL EG *He had always been able to count on her wise counsel.*
drum AUSTRALIAN INFORMAL EG *What's the drum on this?*
guidance EG *The nation looks to them for guidance.*
opinion EG *You should seek a medical opinion.*
suggestion EG *She made suggestions as to how I could improve my diet.*

❶ advise VERB
to offer advice to someone
EG *The minister advised him to leave as soon as possible.*

caution EG *The researchers caution against drawing general conclusions from this study.*
counsel EG *My advisers counselled me to do nothing.*
recommend EG *We strongly recommend reporting the incident to the police.*
suggest EG *He suggested a visit to the Cezanne exhibition.*
urge EG *We urge that vigorous action be taken immediately.*

> *WORD POWER*
> Synonyms
> commend
> enjoin
> prescribe

❷ advise VERB
to notify someone
EG *I think it best that I advise you of my decision to retire.*

inform EG *My daughter informed me that she was pregnant.*
make known EG *The details will*

A
B
C
D
E
F
G
H
I
J
K
L
M
N
O
P
Q
R
S
T
U
V
W
X
Y
Z

9

be made known by the end of August.

notify EG *The skipper notified the coastguard of the tragedy.*

adviser NOUN
a person whose job is to give advice
EG *The President and his advisers spent the day in meetings.*

aide EG *a former aide to Ronald Reagan*

consultant EG *a management consultant*

guru EG *He became Britain's modern design guru after launching Habitat in 1964.*

mentor EG *He is my friend and musical mentor.*

tutor EG *my college tutor*

affect VERB
to influence something or someone
EG *More than 7 million people have been affected by the drought.*

act on EG *This drug acts very fast on the central nervous system.*

alter EG *The earth's climate appears to have been altered by pollution.*

change EG *It was to change the course of my life.*

impinge on EG *My private life does not impinge on my professional life.*

affection NOUN
a feeling of fondness for someone or something
EG *She thought of him with affection.*

attachment EG *Mother and child form a close attachment.*

fondness EG *his fondness for cats*

liking EG *a liking for flashy cars*

love EG *My love for all my children is unconditional.*

warmth EG *He greeted us both with warmth and affection.*

> **WORD POWER**
> Antonym
> dislike

affectionate ADJECTIVE
full of fondness for someone
EG *She gave me a long and affectionate hug.*

caring EG *a loving, caring husband*

fond EG *She gave him a fond smile.*

loving EG *The children were very loving to me.*

tender EG *a tender kiss*

> **WORD POWER**
> Antonym
> cold

afraid ADJECTIVE
scared of something unpleasant happening
EG *I was afraid of the other boys.*

apprehensive EG *People are still terribly apprehensive about the future.*

fearful EG *Bankers were fearful of a world banking crisis.*

frightened EG *She was frightened of flying.*

nervous EG *Emotionally, he left me a wreck, nervous of everyone.*

scared EG *I was too scared to move.*

> **WORD POWER**
> Antonym
> unafraid

after ADVERB
at a later time
EG *Shortly after, police arrested five suspects.*

afterwards EG *He was taken to hospital but died soon afterwards.*

following EG *We shared so much, not only during the war, but in the many years following.*

later EG *He resigned ten years later.*

subsequently EG *She subsequently became honorary secretary.*

> **WORD POWER**
> Antonym
> before

again ADVERB

happening one more time
EG *He kissed her again.*
afresh EG *The couple moved abroad to start life afresh.*
anew EG *She's ready to start anew.*
once more EG *Rage overcame him once more.*

against PREPOSITION
in opposition to
EG *I am against animal cruelty.*
averse to EG *He's not averse to a drink.*
hostile to EG *countries that were once hostile to South Africa*
in opposition to EG *radio stations set up in opposition to the BBC*
versus EG *Portugal versus England*

against PREPOSITION
in preparation for or in case of something
EG *precautions against fire*
in anticipation of EG *His school was one of several which closed in anticipation of Arctic conditions.*
in expectation of EG *The hotel was being renovated in expectation of a tourist boom.*
in preparation for EG *The army massed troops and guns in preparation for a counter-attack.*

aggressive ADJECTIVE
full of hostility and violence
EG *These fish are very aggressive.*
hostile EG *The prisoner eyed him in a hostile silence.*
quarrelsome EG *He had been a wild boy and a quarrelsome young man.*

> WORD POWER
> Synonyms
> belligerent
> pugnacious
> Antonym
> peaceful

agile ADJECTIVE
able to move quickly and easily
EG *He is as agile as a cat.*
lithe EG *a lithe young gymnast*

nimble EG *He built his career around quick reflexes and nimble footwork.*
sprightly EG *She is alert and sprightly despite her 85 years.*
supple EG *She is as supple as a dancer.*

> WORD POWER
> Synonyms
> limber
> lissom or lissome
> Antonym
> clumsy

❶ agree VERB
to have the same opinion as someone
EG *So we both agree there's a problem?*
assent EG *I assented to the request of the publishers to write this book.*
be of the same opinion EG *All the other players are of the same opinion.*
concur EG *Four other judges concurred.*
see eye to eye EG *He has not always seen eye to eye with his brother.*

> WORD POWER
> Antonym
> disagree

❷ agree VERB
to match or be the same as something
EG *His second statement agrees with facts as stated by the other witnesses.*
accord EG *I cannot support policies that no longer accord with my principles.*
conform EG *It doesn't conform with current building regulations.*
match EG *Attendances do not match the ticket sales.*
square EG *Does that explanation square with the facts?*
tally EG *The figures don't seem to tally.*

A
B
C
D
E
F
G
H
I
J
K
L
M
N
O
P
Q
R
S
T
U
V
W
X
Y
Z

11

agreement NOUN
a decision reached by two or more people
EG *The two countries have signed agreements on fishing and oil.*

arrangement EG *Eventually we came to an arrangement that suited us both.*

contract EG *She has signed an exclusive solo-album contract.*

deal INFORMAL EG *The company recently won a five-year deal to build runways.*

pact EG *He ruled out any formal pact with the government.*

settlement EG *She accepted an out-of-court settlement of £4000.*

treaty EG *negotiations over a 1992 treaty on global warming*

> **WORD POWER**
> Synonyms
> compact
> covenant
> Antonym
> disagreement

❶ aim VERB
to plan to do something
EG *The company aims to sign 1 million customers within five years.*

aspire EG *people who aspire to public office*

attempt EG *He will attempt to win the title for the second year running.*

intend EG *I intend to remarry.*

plan EG *Mr Beach was planning to sue over injuries he received.*

propose EG *And where do you propose building such a huge thing?*

strive EG *He strives hard to keep himself very fit.*

❷ aim NOUN
what someone intends to achieve
EG *Our main aim is to offer a superior product.*

ambition EG *His ambition is to sail round the world.*

goal EG *I have to keep setting goals for myself.*

intention EG *It was always my intention to stay in Italy.*

objective EG *His objective was to play golf and win.*

plan EG *His plan was to acquire paintings by the best artists in Italy.*

target EG *his target of 20 goals this season*

❶ alarm NOUN
a feeling of fear
EG *The cat sprang back in alarm.*

anxiety EG *anxiety about crime*

apprehension EG *I tensed every muscle in my body in apprehension.*

fright EG *The birds smashed into the top of their cages in fright.*

nervousness EG *I smiled warmly so he wouldn't see my nervousness.*

panic EG *There was panic in the streets of the capital.*

scare EG *Despite the scare there are no plans to withdraw the drug.*

> **WORD POWER**
> Synonyms
> consternation
> trepidation
> Antonym
> calm

❷ alarm NOUN
a device used to warn people of something
EG *a burglar alarm*

distress signal EG *The pilot was trying to send a distress signal when the aircraft crashed.*

siren EG *a police siren*

warning EG *A second air raid warning sounded over the capital.*

❸ alarm VERB
to fill with fear
EG *We could not see what had alarmed him.*

distress EG *He is very distressed by what happened.*

frighten EG *The future frightens me.*

panic EG *He was panicked by his wife's behaviour.*

scare EG *Horses scare me.*
startle EG *startled by a gunshot*
unnerve EG *Investors had been unnerved by the country's ailing stockmarket.*

> **WORD POWER**
> Antonym
> calm

alcohol NOUN
a drink that can make you drunk
EG *There wasn't even any alcohol at the party.*
booze INFORMAL EG *clutching a bottle of booze*
drink EG *Too much drink is bad for you.*
grog AUSTRALIAN AND NEW ZEALAND INFORMAL EG *They demanded a bottle of grog.*
liquor EG *I could smell liquor on his breath.*
spirits EG *a voluntary ban on advertising spirits on TV*

alert ADJECTIVE
paying full attention
EG *apprehended by alert security staff*
attentive EG *an attentive audience*
observant EG *an observant policeman*
on guard EG *on guard against the threat of invasion*
vigilant EG *letter bombs intercepted by vigilant post office staff*
wary EG *He kept a wary eye on the dog as he passed the gate.*

> **WORD POWER**
> Antonym
> unaware

❷ alert VERB
to warn of danger
EG *I was hoping he'd alert the police.*
forewarn EG *The guide had forewarned me what to expect.*
inform EG *The patient was not properly informed of the risks.*
notify EG *The passengers were notified of the bomb threat.*
warn EG *They warned him of the dangers of sailing alone.*

❶ alive ADJECTIVE
having life
EG *They kept her alive on a life support machine.*
animate EG *animate beings*
breathing EG *Not only is he still breathing, but he lives right here in New York.*
living EG *The blue whale is the largest living thing on the planet.*

> **WORD POWER**
> Antonym
> dead

❷ alive ADJECTIVE
lively and active
EG *I never expected to feel so alive in my life again.*
active EG *half an hour's physical activity, five times a week, will keep you active*
alert EG *A brisk walk will make you feel more alert.*
animated EG *He becomes animated when talking about his work.*
energetic EG *a vital and energetic man*
full of life EG *She was so chatty and full of life.*
lively EG *Cheryl was a very lively and attractive girl.*
vivacious EG *a vivacious personality*

> **WORD POWER**
> Antonym
> dull

❶ allow VERB
to permit someone to do something
EG *Smoking will not be allowed.*
approve EG *The Housing Minister approved the building of the flats.*
authorize EG *authorized to carry weapons*
let EG *They won't let her leave the*

A B C D E F G H I J K L M N O P Q R S T U V W X Y Z

B
C
D
E
F
G
H
I
J
K
L
M
N
O
P
Q
R
S
T
U
V
W
X
Y
Z

country.
permit EG *Unauthorized personnel are not permitted to enter.*
stand for EG *We won't stand for it any more.*
tolerate EG *I won't tolerate sloppiness.*

> **WORD POWER**
> Synonyms
> brook
> give leave
> sanction
> Antonym
> forbid

❷ allow VERB
to set aside for a particular purpose
EG *Allow four hours for the paint to dry.*
allocate EG *an efficient method of allocating resources*
allot EG *We were allotted just 15 minutes.*
assign EG *the full amount of economic aid assigned for the year*
grant EG *Funding had been granted for the project.*
set aside EG *money set aside for education*

all right ADJECTIVE
acceptable
EG *It was all right but nothing special.*
acceptable EG *We've made an acceptable start, but it could have been better.*
adequate EG *Our accommodation was adequate.*
average EG *I was only average academically.*
fair EG *The overall standard of the entries was fair.*
okay or **OK** INFORMAL EG *The prices here are okay.*

almost ADVERB
very nearly
EG *Over the past decade their wages have almost doubled.*

about EG *I was about nine at the time.*
approximately EG *The family owns approximately 8% of the company.*
close to EG *He spent close to 30 years in prison.*
nearly EG *The beach was very nearly empty.*
not quite EG *It's more than a hill but not quite a mountain.*
practically EG *I've known him practically all my life.*

alone ADJECTIVE
not with other people or things
EG *He was all alone in the middle of the hall.*
detached EG *a 'counter-culture' detached from the rest of the world*
isolated EG *Talking things over in a group meant none of us felt isolated.*
separate EG *They were kept separate from the other prisoners.*
single EG *I get depressed on Valentine's Day because I'm still single.*

aloud ADVERB
out loud
EG *Our father read aloud to us.*
audibly EG *Hugh sighed audibly.*
out loud EG *I tried not to laugh out loud.*

also ADVERB
in addition
EG *He is also an army doctor.*
as well EG *She published historical novels as well.*
besides EG *You get to sample lots of baked things and take home masses of cookies besides.*
furthermore EG *Furthermore, they claim that any such interference is completely ineffective.*
into the bargain EG *The machine can play ordinary cassettes into the bargain.*
moreover EG *They have accused the government of corruption.*

Moreover, they have named names.
too EG *I was there too.*

always ADVERB
all the time or forever
EG *She's always moaning.*
continually EG *Malcolm was continually changing his mind.*
every time EG *You can't get it right every time.*
forever EG *He was forever attempting to arrange deals.*
invariably EG *Their teamwork was invariably good.*
perpetually EG *The two groups are perpetually at loggerheads.*

amaze VERB
to surprise greatly
EG *He amazed us by his knowledge of Welsh history.*
astonish EG *I was astonished by his stupidity.*
astound EG *I am astounded at the comments made by the Chief Superintendant.*
shock EG *She was shocked by the appalling news.*
stagger EG *He was staggered by the sheer size of the crowd.*
stun EG *Many cinema-goers were stunned by the film's tragic end.*
surprise EG *We'll solve the case ourselves and surprise everyone.*

WORD POWER
Synonyms
dumbfound
flabbergast
stupefy
---

amazement NOUN
complete surprise
astonishment EG *They looked at each other in astonishment.*
shock EG *I am still getting over the shock of winning.*
surprise EG *To my surprise, I found I liked it.*
wonder EG *Cross shook his head in wonder.*

WORD POWER

Synonyms
perplexity
stupefaction

amazing ADJECTIVE
very surprising or remarkable
EG *some of the most amazing stunts you're ever likely to see*
astonishing EG *an astonishing display of physical strength*
astounding EG *The results are quite astounding.*
staggering EG *a staggering 17% leap in sales*
startling EG *startling new evidence*
stunning EG *a stunning piece of news*
surprising EG *A surprising number of customers order the same sandwich every day.*

❶ among PREPOSITION
surrounded by
EG *The bike lay among piles of chains and pedals.*
amid EG *a tiny bungalow amid clusters of trees*
amidst EG *His parents were found dead amidst the wreckage of the plane.*
in the middle of EG *a tiny island in the middle of the Pacific*
in the thick of EG *a restaurant built on stilts in the thick of a vast mangrove swamp*
surrounded by EG *surrounded by bodyguards*

❷ among PREPOSITION
between more than two
EG *The money will be divided among seven charities.*
between EG *Proceeds from the auction will be shared between the artists.*
to each of EG *£2,000 to each of the five winners*

amount NOUN
how much there is of something
EG *I still do a certain amount of work for them.*

A
B
C
D
E
F
G
H
I
J
K
L
M
N
O
P
Q
R
S
T
U
V
W
X
Y
Z

expanse EG *a vast expanse of grassland*
quantity EG *vast quantities of food*
volume EG *the sheer volume of traffic and accidents*

ancestor NOUN
a person from whom someone is descended
EG *He could trace his ancestors back 700 years.*
forebear EG *our Victorian forebears*
forefather EG *the land of their forefathers*

> **WORD POWER**
> Synonyms
> precursor
> progenitor

❶ **anger** NOUN
extreme annoyance
EG *She vented her anger at the umpire.*
fury EG *She screamed, her face distorted in fury.*
outrage EG *The decisions provoked outrage from human rights groups.*
rage EG *An intense rage was burning inside her.*
wrath EG *He incurred the wrath of the referee.*

> **WORD POWER**
> Synonyms
> choler
> ire
> pique
> spleen
> vexation

❷ **anger** VERB
to make someone angry
EG *remarks which will anger his critics*
enrage EG *He enraged the government by renouncing the agreement.*
infuriate EG *Peter's presence had infuriated Gordon.*
outrage EG *Customers are outraged by the bank's soaring profits.*

> **WORD POWER**
> Antonym
> calm

angry ADJECTIVE
very annoyed
EG *He gets angry with me if I'm late*
cross EG *She was rather cross about having to trail across London.*
enraged EG *The enraged crowd stoned the car, then set it on fire.*
furious EG *He is furious at the way his wife has been treated.*
mad INFORMAL EG *I'm pretty mad about it, I can tell you.*

animal NOUN
a living creature
EG *He was attacked by wild animals*
beast EG *the threat our ancestors faced from wild beasts*
creature EG *sea creatures*

announce VERB
to make known something publicly
EG *He will announce tonight that he is resigning from office.*
advertise EG *He did not want to advertise his presence in the town.*
make known EG *Details will be made known tomorrow.*
proclaim EG *He loudly proclaimed his innocence.*
reveal EG *They were now free to reveal the truth.*
tell EG *She was relieved that she'd finally told the full story.*

> **WORD POWER**
> Synonyms
> promulgate
> propound

announcement NOUN
a statement giving information about something
EG *There has been no formal announcement by either government*
advertisement EG *an advertisement placed in the local newspaper*
broadcast EG *In a broadcast on*

state radio the government announced its plans.
bulletin EG *At 3.30pm a bulletin was released announcing the decision.*
declaration EG *a public declaration of support*
report EG *Local press reports estimate that at least sixteen people have died.*
statement EG *a short statement by her solicitors*

annoy VERB
to irritate or displease someone
EG *Try making a note of the things which annoy you.*
bother EG *I didn't think it would bother me so much to see Brian again.*
displease EG *Not wishing to displease her, he avoided answering the question.*
get on someone's nerves INFORMAL EG *That song gets on my nerves.*
hack off BRITISH AND NEW ZEALAND SLANG EG *This will just hack people off more.*
hassle INFORMAL EG *Then my husband started hassling me.*
irritate EG *The flippancy in her voice seemed to irritate him.*
plague EG *We were plagued by mosquitoes.*
vex EG *Cassandra was vexed at not having noticed it herself.*

❶ annoyance NOUN
a feeling of irritation
EG *He made no secret of his annoyance.*
displeasure EG *She voiced her displeasure at her treatment.*
irritation EG *He tried not to let his irritation show.*

❷ annoyance NOUN
something that causes irritation
EG *Snoring can be more than an annoyance.*
bore EG *It's a bore to be off sick.*

drag INFORMAL EG *A dry sandwich is a drag to eat.*
nuisance EG *He could be a bit of a nuisance when he was drunk.*
pain INFORMAL EG *The peacocks are a pain - beautiful but noisy.*
pain in the neck INFORMAL EG *Traffic jams are a pain in the neck.*
pest EG *He climbed on the table, pulled my hair, and was generally a pest.*

❶ answer VERB
to reply to someone
EG *I knew Ben was lying when he answered me.*
reply EG *He replied that this was absolutely impossible.*
respond EG *'Mind your manners, lady!' I responded.*
retort EG *Was he afraid, he was asked. 'Afraid of what?' he retorted.*

WORD POWER
Antonym
ask

❷ answer NOUN
a reply given to someone
EG *Without waiting for an answer, he turned and went in through the door.*
reply EG *I called out a challenge but there was no reply.*
response EG *There has been no response to his remarks from the government.*
retort EG *His sharp retort clearly made an impact.*

WORD POWER
Synonyms
rejoinder
riposte
Antonym
question

apathetic ADJECTIVE
not interested in anything
EG *apathetic about politics*
cool EG *The idea met with a cool response.*
indifferent EG *People have become*

indifferent to the sufferings of others.
passive EG *His passive attitude made things easier for me.*
uninterested EG *unhelpful and uninterested shop staff*

> **WORD POWER**
> Antonym
> enthusiastic

apologize VERB
to say sorry for something
EG *I apologize for being late.*
ask forgiveness EG *He fell to his knees asking for forgiveness.*
beg someone's pardon EG *I was impolite and I do beg your pardon.*
express regret EG *Mr Galloway expressed regret that he had caused any offence.*
say sorry EG *I wanted to say sorry to her.*

❶ appeal VERB
to make an urgent request for something
EG *The police appealed for witnesses to come forward.*
beg EG *I begged him to leave me alone.*
call upon EG *Frequently he was called upon to resolve conflicts.*
plead EG *I pleaded to be allowed to go.*
request EG *She had requested that the door to her room be left open.*

> **WORD POWER**
> Synonyms
> entreat
> implore
> pray

❷ appeal VERB
to attract or interest
EG *The idea appealed to him.*
attract EG *What attracted you to research work?*
fascinate EG *Classical music had fascinated him since the age of three.*
interest EG *It was the garden that really interested me.*

please EG *It pleased him to talk to her.*

❸ appeal NOUN
a formal request for something
EG *an appeal for peace*
petition EG *The court rejected their petition.*
plea EG *his emotional plea for help in solving the killing*
request EG *France had agreed to his request for political asylum.*

> **WORD POWER**
> Synonyms
> entreaty
> supplication

❶ appear VERB
to become visible or present
EG *A woman appeared at the far end of the street.*
come into view EG *Nearly fifty gliders came into view to the south of the plateau.*
crop up INFORMAL EG *Problems will crop up and hit you before you are ready.*
emerge EG *The postman emerged from his van soaked to the skin.*
show up INFORMAL EG *He failed to show up at the ceremony.*
surface EG *The same old problems would surface again.*
turn up EG *This is like waiting for a bus that never turns up.*

> **WORD POWER**
> Antonym
> disappear

❷ appear VERB
to begin to exist
EG *small white flowers which appear in early summer*
become available EG *In 1950, legal aid became available in Britain.*
be invented EG *The lawn mower was invented in 1830.*
come into being EG *Fireworks first came into being with the invention of gunpowder.*

come into existence EG *before our solar system came into existence*
come out EG *This book first came out in 1992.*

❶ **appear** VERB
to take part in a show or play
EG *He is soon to appear in two more films.*
act EG *She has also been acting in a sitcom.*
perform EG *He is currently performing in the West End show "Grease".*
play EG *He played Hamlet to packed houses.*
play a part EG *His ambition is to play the part of Dracula.*

❶ **appearance** NOUN
the time when something begins to exist
EG *the appearance of computer technology*
advent EG *the advent of satellite and cable channels*
arrival EG *the arrival of modern technologies*
coming EG *the coming of the railways*
debut EG *the debut of the new channel*
emergence EG *the emergence of pay-per-view TV*
introduction EG *the introduction of the minimum wage*

❷ **appearance** NOUN
the way that a person looks
EG *She used to be so fussy about her appearance.*
bearing EG *a man of iron will and military bearing*
image EG *He urged the rest of the band to update their image.*
look EG *She is so much happier with her new look.*
looks EG *a young woman with wholesome good looks*

WORD POWER
Synonyms
demeanour

mien

❶ **appointment** NOUN
an arrangement to meet someone
EG *She has an appointment with her accountant.*
date EG *I have a date with Wendy.*
interview EG *a job interview*
meeting EG *Can we have a meeting to discuss that?*
rendezvous EG *I had almost decided to keep my rendezvous with Tony.*

❷ **appointment** NOUN
the choosing of a person to do a job
EG *his appointment as manager*
election EG *the election of the government in 1997*
naming EG *the naming of the new captain*
nomination EG *They opposed the nomination of a junior officer to the position.*
selection EG *his selection as a parliamentary candidate*

❸ **appointment** NOUN
a job
EG *He applied for an appointment in Russia.*
assignment EG *my first assignment for The New York Times*
job EG *He's trying for a job in the Civil Service.*
place EG *All the candidates won places on the ruling council.*
position EG *She took up a position at the Arts Council.*
post EG *He has held several senior military posts.*

❶ **appreciate** VERB
to value something highly
EG *He appreciates fine wines.*
admire EG *All those who knew him will admire him for his work.*
prize EG *Military figures made out of lead are prized by collectors.*
rate highly EG *The four-year-old*

mare is rated highly by her trainer.
respect EG *I respect his talent as a pianist.*
treasure EG *She treasures her memories of those joyous days.*
value EG *I value the work he gives me.*

> **WORD POWER**
> Antonym
> scorn

❷ **appreciate** VERB
to understand a situation or problem
EG *I didn't appreciate the seriousness of it at the time.*
be aware of EG *I am well aware of the arguments on the other side.*
perceive EG *to get pupils to perceive for themselves the relationship between success and effort*
realize EG *People don't realize how serious this is.*
recognize EG *They have been slow to recognize it as a problem.*
understand EG *They are too young to understand what is going on.*

appropriate ADJECTIVE
suitable or acceptable for a given situation
EG *Jeans are not appropriate wear for work.*
apt EG *an apt title for his memoirs*
correct EG *the importance of correct behaviour and social niceties*
fitting EG *a fitting tribute to a great man*
proper EG *the proper course for the court to take*
suitable EG *a suitable location*

> **WORD POWER**
> Synonyms
> apposite
> appurtenant
> congruous
> germane
> Antonym
> inappropriate

❶ **approval** NOUN
agreement given to something
EG *The plan will require approval from the local authority.*
agreement EG *The clubs are seeking agreement for a provisional deal.*
authorization EG *We didn't have authorization to go.*
blessing EG *Mr. Ryabov appeared to give his blessing to Mr. Yeltsin's plan.*
endorsement EG *His endorsement has been fervently sought by all the main presidential candidates.*
permission EG *They cannot leave the country without permission.*
sanction EG *The King cannot enact laws without the sanction of Parliament.*

> **WORD POWER**
> Synonyms
> assent
> imprimatur
> mandate
> ratification

❷ **approval** NOUN
liking and admiration of a person or thing
EG *He wanted to gain his father's approval.*
admiration EG *a strategy that is winning admiration from around the world*
esteem EG *Their public esteem has never been lower.*
favour EG *He has won favour with a wide range of groups.*
praise EG *She is full of praise for the range of excellent services available.*
respect EG *We all have so much respect for her.*

> **WORD POWER**
> Antonym
> disapproval

❶ **approve** VERB
to think something or someone

is good

EG *Not everyone approves of the festival.*

admire EG *I admire him for his work.*

favour EG *The opposition parties favour constitutional reform.*

praise EG *He praised the fans for their continued support.*

respect EG *I want him to respect me as a career woman.*

think highly of EG *He thought highly of his brother.*

> *WORD POWER*
> Antonym
> disapprove

approve VERB

to agree formally to something
EG *The court approved the compensation plan.*

authorize EG *to authorize the use of military force*

consent to EG *His parents consented to an autopsy.*

endorse EG *I can endorse their opinion wholeheartedly.*

permit EG *The doorman is not allowed to permit them entry to the film.*

sanction EG *He may now be ready to sanction the use of force.*

> *WORD POWER*
> Antonym
> veto

approximate ADJECTIVE

close but not exact
EG *We believe that an approximate figure of 20% is nearer the mark.*

estimated EG *Our estimated time of arrival is 3.30.*

inexact EG *Forecasting is an inexact science.*

loose EG *a loose translation*

rough EG *a rough estimate*

> *WORD POWER*
> Antonym
> exact

❶ area NOUN

a particular part of a place
EG *a built-up area of the city*

district EG *I drove around the business district.*

locality EG *All other factories in the locality went on strike in sympathy.*

neighbourhood EG *She no longer takes evening strolls around her neighbourhood.*

region EG *a remote mountainous region of Afghanistan*

zone EG *a war zone*

❷ area NOUN

the size of a two-dimensional surface
EG *The islands cover a total area of 625 square kilometres.*

expanse EG *a huge expanse of blue-green sea*

extent EG *the extent of the rain forest*

range EG *a driver's range of vision*

size EG *a country nearly three times the size of ours*

❶ argue VERB

to disagree with someone in an angry way
EG *They argued over the cost of the taxi fare.*

bicker EG *They bickered endlessly about procedure.*

disagree EG *They can communicate even when they strongly disagree.*

fall out INFORMAL EG *Mum and I used to fall out a lot.*

feud EG *feuding neighbours*

fight EG *We're always fighting about money.*

quarrel EG *My brother quarrelled with my father.*

row EG *We started rowing about whose turn it was next.*

squabble EG *The children were squabbling over the remote control.*

wrangle EG *Delegates wrangled over the future of the organization.*

❷ argue VERB
to try to prove
EG *She argued that her client had been wrongly accused.*

assert EG *The defendants continue to assert their innocence.*

claim EG *Statisticians claim that the book contains inaccuracies.*

debate EG *Parliament will debate the issue today.*

maintain EG *He had always maintained his innocence.*

reason EG *I reasoned that if he could do it, so could I.*

> **WORD POWER**
> Synonyms
> controvert
> expostulate
> remonstrate

❶ argument NOUN
an angry disagreement
EG *She got into an argument with one of the marchers.*

barney BRITISH, AUSTRALIAN, AND NEW ZEALAND INFORMAL EG *We had such a barney that we nearly split up.*

blue AUSTRALIAN SLANG EG *He gets into more blues with authority than I do.*

clash EG *clashes between police and demonstrators*

dispute EG *a dispute over ticket allocation*

feud EG *a two-year feud between neighbours*

fight EG *We had another fight about money.*

row EG *Maxine and I had a terrible row.*

squabble EG *a family squabble over Sunday lunch*

❷ argument NOUN
a set of reasons presented for something
EG *There's a strong argument for lowering the price.*

case EG *the case for his dismissal*

grounds EG *facts providing grounds for an unfair dismissal*

complaint

logic EG *The logic is that, without more growth, the deficit will rise.*

reasoning EG *the reasoning behind the decision*

❶ arrange VERB
to make plans to do something
EG *Why don't you arrange to meet him later?*

fix up EG *I fixed up an appointment to see her.*

organize EG *She organized the trip to the museum.*

plan EG *She planned to leave in August.*

schedule EG *Our appointment is scheduled for Tuesday.*

❷ arrange VERB
to set things out in a particular order
EG *He started to arrange the books in piles.*

classify EG *Weathermen classify clouds into several different groups.*

group EG *The fact sheet is grouped into seven sections.*

order EG *The French order things differently.*

organize EG *He began to organize his materials.*

sort EG *The students are sorted into three ability groups.*

> **WORD POWER**
> Synonyms
> array
> systematize

❶ arrest VERB
to take someone into custody
EG *Police arrested five men in connection with the attack.*

apprehend EG *Police have not apprehended her killer.*

capture EG *Her accomplice was captured by Dutch police.*

nick BRITISH SLANG EG *Keep quiet or we'll all get nicked.*

seize EG *Two military observers were seized by rebels yesterday.*

take prisoner EG *He was taken prisoner in 1940 at the fall of Dunkirk.*

❶ arrest NOUN
the act of arresting someone
EG *The police made two arrests.*
apprehension EG *information leading to the apprehension of the killer*
capture EG *He was trying to evade capture by security forces.*
seizure EG *the mass seizure of terrorists*

❶ ask VERB
to put a question to someone
EG *She asked me if I'd enjoyed my dinner.*
inquire EG *I rang up to inquire about train times.*
interrogate EG *I interrogated everyone even slightly involved.*
query EG *He queried whether sabotage could have been involved.*
question EG *He was questioned by police.*
quiz EG *He was quizzed about his eligibility for benefits.*

> **WORD POWER**
> Antonym
> answer

❷ ask VERB
to make a request to someone
EG *We had to ask him to leave.*
appeal EG *The police appealed for witnesses to come forward.*
beg EG *I begged him to leave me alone.*
demand EG *I demanded an explanation from him.*
implore EG *I implored him not to give it up.*
plead EG *She pleaded to be allowed to go.*
seek EG *Always seek legal advice before entering into any agreement.*

> **WORD POWER**
> Synonyms
> beseech

entreat

❸ ask VERB
to invite someone
EG *Not everybody had been asked to the wedding.*
bid LITERARY EG *They all smiled at him and bade him eat.*
invite EG *She invited him to her 26th birthday party.*

assistant NOUN
a person who helps someone
EG *His assistant took over while he went out.*
aide EG *a presidential aide*
ally EG *her political allies*
colleague EG *a business colleague*
helper EG *volunteer helpers*
right-hand man EG *the resignation of the manager's right-hand man*

❶ associate VERB
to connect one thing with another
EG *Poverty is associated with old age.*
connect EG *a common problem directly connected with stress*
couple EG *The papers coupled the Gulf crisis with the problems facing the former Soviet Union.*
identify EG *Candidates want to identify themselves with reform.*
link EG *Liver cancer is linked to the hepatitis B virus.*

❷ associate VERB
to spend time with a person
EG *I began associating with different crowds of people.*
hang out INFORMAL EG *People want to hang out with you for the wrong reasons.*
mingle EG *reporters who mingled freely with the crowd*
mix EG *local youths who want to mix with the foreign tourists*
run around INFORMAL EG *What's he doing running around with a teenager?*
socialize EG *She made little effort*

to socialize with other staff.

> **WORD POWER**
> Synonyms
> consort
> fraternize

❸ associate NOUN
a person known through work
EG *the restaurant owner's business associates*
colleague EG *learning from more experienced colleagues*
co-worker EG *Their Chinese co-workers often worked seven days a week.*
workmate EG *employees who expose dishonest workmates*

❶ assume VERB
to accept that something is true
EG *I assumed that he would turn up.*
believe EG *I believe she'll be back next week.*
guess INFORMAL EG *I guess she thought that was pretty smart.*
imagine EG *You tend to imagine that you cannot put a foot wrong.*
suppose EG *I see no reason to suppose that it isn't working.*
think EG *They thought that they had the match won.*

❷ assume VERB
to take responsibility for something
EG *Mr Cross will assume the role of Chief Executive.*
accept EG *He accepted the role of player-captain.*
shoulder EG *He has had to shoulder the responsibility of his father's mistakes.*
take on EG *Don't take on more responsibilities than you can handle.*
undertake EG *He undertook to edit the text himself.*

❶ attack VERB
to use violence against someone or something
EG *I thought he was going to attack me.*

assault EG *The gang assaulted him with iron bars.*
charge EG *He ordered us to charge.*
invade EG *The allies invaded the Italian mainland at Anzio.*
raid EG *He was found guilty of raiding a bank.*
set upon EG *As the lorry drove east it was set upon by bandits.*
storm EG *The refugees decided to storm the embassy.*

❷ attack VERB
to criticize someone strongly
EG *She attacked the government's economic policies.*
blast EG *He blasted the referee for his inconsistency.*
censure EG *The bank has been censured and fined by the authority*
criticize EG *The regime has been harshly criticized.*
have a go BRITISH INFORMAL EG *If they made a mistake the crowd would have a go at them.*
put down INFORMAL EG *He was always putting me down.*
vilify FORMAL EG *He was vilified, hounded, and forced into exile.*

> **WORD POWER**
> Synonyms
> berate
> lambast *or* lambaste
> revile

❸ attack NOUN
violent physical action against someone or something
EG *a vicious attack on an unarmed man*
assault EG *The rebels are poised for a new assault.*
charge EG *a bayonet charge*
invasion EG *the Roman invasion of Britain*
offensive EG *the government's military offensive against the rebels*
onslaught EG *civilians trying to flee from the military onslaught*
raid EG *a raid on a house by armed police*

attempt VERB
to try to do something
EG *They attempted to escape.*
endeavour EG *I will endeavour to arrange it.*
seek EG *We have never sought to impose our views.*
strive EG *The school strives to treat pupils as individuals.*
try EG *I tried hard to persuade him to stay.*
try your hand at EG *He'd always wanted to try his hand at writing.*

attempt NOUN
an act of trying to do something
EG *one of his rare attempts at humour*
bid EG *a bid to save the newspaper*
crack INFORMAL EG *his third crack at the world heavyweight title*
go INFORMAL EG *My mum suggested I should have a go at becoming a jockey.*
shot INFORMAL EG *We'd like a shot at winning the league.*
stab INFORMAL EG *Several tennis stars have had a stab at acting.*
try EG *That makes the scheme worth a try.*

attitude NOUN
someone's way of thinking and behaving
EG *negative attitudes to work*
outlook EG *behaviour that seems contrary to his whole outlook*
perspective EG *It gave me a new perspective on life.*
point of view EG *Try to look at this from my point of view.*
position EG *What's your position on this issue?*
stance EG *the Church's stance on contraception*

attract VERB
to appeal to or interest
EG *The trials have attracted many leading riders.*
appeal to EG *The idea appealed to him.*
draw EG *The match drew a large crowd.*
entice EG *She resisted attempts to entice her into politics.*
lure EG *They were being lured into a trap.*
pull INFORMAL EG *They have to employ performers to pull a crowd.*
tempt EG *Can I tempt you with some wine?*

> **WORD POWER**
> Antonym
> repel

attractive ADJECTIVE
pleasant, especially to look at
EG *an attractive woman*
appealing EG *a sense of humour that I found very appealing*
charming EG *a charming little village*
fetching EG *a fetching outfit*
handsome EG *a handsome man*
lovely EG *a lovely island*
pretty EG *a shy, pretty girl*

> **WORD POWER**
> Synonyms
> comely
> prepossessing
> winsome
> Antonym
> unattractive

❶ automatic ADJECTIVE
operating mechanically by itself
EG *Modern trains have automatic doors.*
automated EG *highly automated production lines*
mechanical EG *the oldest working mechanical clock in the world*
robot EG *a robot telescope*
self-propelled EG *self-propelled artillery*

❷ automatic ADJECTIVE
without conscious thought
EG *automatic body functions*
instinctive EG *an instinctive reaction*
involuntary EG *involuntary*

muscle movements

natural EG *the insect's natural instinct to feed*

reflex EG *Blushing is a reflex action linked to the nervous system.*

available ADJECTIVE
ready for use
EG *There are three small boats available for hire.*

accessible EG *This information is accessible on the Internet.*

at hand EG *Having the right equipment at hand will be enormously useful.*

at someone's disposal EG *Do you have all the facts at your disposal?*

free EG *There was only one seat free on the train.*

handy EG *Keep your keys handy so you can get into your car quickly.*

to hand EG *Keep your insurance details to hand when driving.*

> **WORD POWER**
> Antonym
> unavailable

❶ average ADJECTIVE
standard or normal
EG *the average American teenager*

normal EG *I am now back to leading a perfectly normal life.*

regular EG *He's just a regular guy.*

standard EG *the standard price of a CD*

typical EG *A typical day begins at 8.30.*

usual EG *This isn't the usual kind of mail-order catalogue.*

❷ average
on average ADVERB
for the most part
EG *Men are, on average, taller than women.*

as a rule EG *As a rule, the fee is roughly equal to the savings you have made.*

generally EG *A glass of fine wine generally costs about £4.*

normally EG *Normally, the transport system carries 50,000 passengers a day.*

typically EG *In America, estate agents typically charge 5-6% of the sale price.*

usually EG *In good condition, these models usually fetch up to 300 dollars at auction.*

❶ avoid VERB
to make an effort not to do something
EG *We economists always try to avoid giving a straight answer.*

dodge EG *dodging military service by feigning illness*

duck out of INFORMAL EG *ducking out of the post-match press conference*

fight shy of EG *She fought shy of confronting her critics.*

refrain from EG *Mrs Hardie refrained from making any comment.*

shirk EG *We won't shirk our responsibility.*

> **WORD POWER**
> Synonyms
> circumvent
> give a wide berth to

❷ avoid VERB
to keep away from someone or something
EG *She thought he was trying to avoid her.*

dodge EG *He refuses to dodge his critics.*

elude EG *an attempt to elude photographers*

eschew FORMAL EG *He eschewed publicity and avoided nightclubs.*

evade EG *He managed to evade the police.*

shun EG *Everybody shunned him.*

sidestep EG *Rarely does he sidestep a question.*

steer clear of EG *It would be best to steer clear of her.*

◗ **aware**
 aware of ADJECTIVE
 conscious of something
 EG *She was acutely aware of the noise of the city.*
 acquainted with EG *He was well acquainted with American literature.*
 conscious of EG *She was very conscious of Max studying her.*
 familiar with EG *I am not familiar with your work.*
 mindful of EG *Everyone should be mindful of the dangers.*

> **WORD POWER**
> Antonym
> unaware

◗ **aware** ADJECTIVE
 knowing about something
 EG *Keep me aware of any developments.*
 informed EG *the importance of keeping the public properly informed*
 in the picture EG *He's always kept me in the picture.*
 knowledgeable EG *He's very knowledgeable about new technology.*

> **WORD POWER**
> Synonyms
> au courant
> in the loop

awful ADJECTIVE
 very unpleasant or very bad
 EG *the same awful jokes*
 appalling EG *living under the most appalling conditions*
 dreadful EG *They told us the dreadful news.*
 frightful EG *a frightful ordeal*
 ghastly EG *a mother accompanied by her ghastly unruly child*
 horrendous EG *The violence used was horrendous.*
 terrible EG *Her French is terrible.*

> **WORD POWER**
> Synonyms
> abysmal
> deplorable

Bb Bb

babble VERB
to talk in an excited way
EG *He babbled on and on.*
burble EG *He burbles on about the goals he has scored.*
chatter EG *Jane chattered about the children.*
gabble EG *I started to gabble in the interview.*
prattle EG *Alan is prattling on again.*

❶ back NOUN
the part that is behind the front
EG *the back of a postcard*
end EG *the end of the corridor*
rear EG *the rear of the building*
reverse EG *the reverse of the sheet*
stern EG *the stern of a boat*

> **WORD POWER**
> Antonym
> front

❷ back VERB
to support a person or organization
EG *His friends are backing him.*
advocate EG *Mr Jones advocates longer school days.*
encourage EG *The government is encouraging better child care.*
endorse EG *Do you endorse his opinion?*
favour EG *I favour a different approach.*
promote EG *Ann is promoting Alan's ideas.*
support EG *We supported his political campaign.*

> **WORD POWER**
> Synonyms
> champion
> espouse
> second
> Antonym
> oppose

background NOUN

where you come from
EG *a rich background*
culture EG *people from different cultures*
environment EG *the environment I grew up in*
history EG *She has an interesting history.*
upbringing EG *a strict upbringing*

❶ bad ADJECTIVE
harmful, unpleasant, or upsetting
EG *I have some bad news.*
damaging EG *the damaging effects of smoking*
distressing EG *It must have been a distressing experience.*
harmful EG *harmful rays from the sun*
painful EG *a painful injury*
terrible EG *terrible back pain*
unpleasant EG *The fish has an unpleasant smell.*

> **WORD POWER**
> Antonym
> good

❷ bad ADJECTIVE
of poor quality
EG *bad roads*
faulty EG *a car with faulty brakes*
imperfect EG *imperfect eyesight*
inadequate EG *His education is inadequate.*
inferior EG *tapes of inferior quality*
poor EG *a poor performance*
unsatisfactory EG *unsatisfactory answers*

> **WORD POWER**
> Synonyms
> defective
> deficient
> substandard
> Antonym
> satisfactory

❸ bad ADJECTIVE

evil in character
EG *a bad person*
corrupt EG *corrupt practices*
criminal EG *a criminal offence*
evil EG *evil influences*
immoral EG *His behaviour is immoral.*
wicked EG *a wicked thing to do*
wrong EG *I didn't do anything wrong.*

> *WORD POWER*
> Synonyms
> iniquitous
> nefarious
> villainous
> **Antonym**
> good

bait NOUN
something used to tempt someone
EG *Charles isn't taking the bait.*
bribe EG *a politician who took bribes*
decoy EG *He acted as a decoy to trap the murderer.*
inducement EG *financial inducements to talk to the newspapers*
lure EG *the lure of a huge salary*
temptation EG *the temptation of easy money*

● **balance** VERB
to make or remain steady
EG *Balancing on one leg is difficult.*
level EG *House prices have levelled.*
stabilize EG *attempts to stabilize the economy*
steady EG *He steadied himself and shot at goal.*

● **balance** NOUN
a stable relationship between things
EG *the chemical balance of the brain*
equilibrium EG *the political equilibrium of Europe*
equity EG *plans for greater equity of incomes*
equivalence EG *the lack of*

equivalence between film and radio
parity EG *She won pay parity with male colleagues.*

ball NOUN
a round object
EG *a ball of wool*
drop EG *a drop of blood*
globe EG *the globe of the eyeball*
pellet EG *an airgun pellet*
sphere EG *a sphere the size of the Earth*

> *WORD POWER*
> Synonyms
> globule
> orb
> spheroid

❶ **ban** VERB
to disallow something
EG *I am banned from taking part.*
bar EG *The press will be barred from the talks.*
disqualify EG *He was disqualified from driving.*
exclude EG *They were excluded from the maths class.*
forbid EG *The rules forbid the use of force.*
outlaw EG *regulations outlawing child labour*
prohibit EG *a law that prohibits alcohol*

> *WORD POWER*
> Synonyms
> banish
> proscribe
> suppress
> **Antonym**
> permit

❷ **ban** NOUN
a rule disallowing something
EG *a ban on smoking*
disqualification EG *a four-year disqualification from athletics*
embargo EG *an embargo on trade with the country*
prohibition EG *a prohibition on tobacco*
suppression EG *the suppression of*

A
B
C
D
E
F
G
H
I
J
K
L
M
N
O
P
Q
R
S
T
U
V
W
X
Y
Z

A
B
C
D
E
F
G
H
I
J
K
L
M
N
O
P
Q
R
S
T
U
V
W
X
Y
Z

anti-government protests

> **WORD POWER**
> Antonym
> permit

❶ banish VERB
to exile someone
EG *She banished him from the house.*
deport EG *Many fans are being deported from Italy.*
eject EG *He was ejected from the club.*
evict EG *Police evicted ten families from the building.*
exile EG *He was exiled from Russia.*
expel EG *patients expelled from hospitals*
transport EG *He was transported to a prison camp.*

❷ banish VERB
to get rid of something or someone
EG *to banish illness*
discard EG *Read the instructions before discarding the box.*
dismiss EG *I dismissed the idea from my mind.*
dispel EG *The myths are being dispelled.*
eliminate EG *They eliminated him from their enquiries.*
eradicate EG *projects to eradicate certain diseases*
remove EG *talks to remove the last obstacles to the deal*

❶ bank NOUN
a store of something
EG *a blood bank*
fund EG *a pension fund*
hoard EG *a hoard of treasure*
reserve EG *the world's oil reserves*
stock EG *stocks of paper and ink*
store EG *a secret store of sweets*

> **WORD POWER**
> Synonyms
> reservoir
> stockpile

❷ bank NOUN

the edge of a river or lake
EG *He sat fishing on the bank.*
brink EG *orchards near the brink of the sea cliffs*
edge EG *She stood too close to the edge and fell in.*
shore EG *He swam towards the shore.*
side EG *a picnic by the side of the river*

❶ bar NOUN
a piece of metal
EG *bars across the windows*
pole EG *He was tied to a pole.*
rail EG *a curtain rail*
rod EG *a fishing rod*
shaft EG *the shaft of a spear*

❷ bar VERB
to stop someone
EG *His bodyguards barred the way.*
obstruct EG *Vehicles have obstructed the entrance.*
prevent EG *A fence prevents people from entering.*

❶ bare ADJECTIVE
not covered
EG *bare legs*
exposed EG *His whole back is exposed.*
naked EG *a naked body*
nude EG *a nude model*
stripped EG *I got stripped to have a shower.*
uncovered EG *His arms were uncovered.*
undressed EG *She got undressed in the bathroom.*

> **WORD POWER**
> Antonym
> covered

❷ bare ADJECTIVE
with nothing on top or inside
EG *a small bare office*
empty EG *an empty room*
open EG *open country*
spartan EG *spartan accommodation*
vacant EG *a vacant chair*

barely ADVERB
only just
EG *She is barely sixteen.*
almost EG *I almost didn't make it.*
hardly EG *I could hardly believe it.*
just EG *They only just won.*
scarcely EG *I can scarcely hear her.*

barren ADJECTIVE
with nothing growing on it
EG *a barren desert*
arid EG *the arid lands of Botswana*
desert EG *desert regions*
desolate EG *a desolate place*
dry EG *poor, dry countries*
empty EG *the empty desert*
waste EG *waste land*

> **WORD POWER**
> Synonyms
> unfruitful
> unproductive
> Antonym
> fertile

barren ADJECTIVE
unable to produce babies
EG *women who are barren*
childless EG *childless couples*
infertile EG *infertile women*
sterile EG *sterile females*

> **WORD POWER**
> Antonym
> fertile

barrier NOUN
something preventing entry
EG *Demonstrators broke through the barriers.*
barricade EG *a barricade of vehicles*
fence EG *a garden fence*
obstruction EG *Check the exhaust pipe is clear of obstructions.*
wall EG *the huge city walls*

> **WORD POWER**
> Synonyms
> fortification
> obstacle
> rampart

❷ barrier NOUN
something that prevents progress
EG *plans to reduce the barriers to trade*
handicap EG *It is a handicap not knowing a foreign language.*
hindrance EG *a potential hindrance to the peace process*
hurdle EG *the first hurdle in a job search*
impediment EG *a serious impediment to free trade*
obstacle EG *the main obstacle to the takeover*

❶ base NOUN
the lowest part of something
EG *the base of the cliffs*
bed EG *the river bed*
bottom EG *the bottom of the lake*
foot EG *the foot of the mountain*
foundation EG *They have laid the foundations for the new building.*
pedestal EG *The statue is back on its pedestal.*
stand EG *a microphone stand*

> **WORD POWER**
> Antonym
> top

❷ base NOUN
the place you work from
EG *a military base*
camp EG *refugee camps*
centre EG *a health centre*
headquarters EG *army headquarters in Colombo*
post EG *a military post in the capital*
station EG *the police station*

❸ base VERB
to use as a foundation
EG *The film is based on a true story.*
build EG *a reputation built on lies*
derive EG *The name is derived from a Greek word.*
found EG *My hopes were founded on a mistake.*
ground EG *I like a film to be*

A
B
C
D
E
F
G
H
I
J
K
L
M
N
O
P
Q
R
S
T
U
V
W
X
Y
Z

grounded in reality.

hinge EG *The whole play hinges on one character.*

basic ADJECTIVE
most necessary
EG *the basic requirements for the job*

elementary EG *elementary computer training*

essential EG *essential reading and writing skills*

fundamental EG *fundamental rights*

key EG *key skills such as communication and teamwork*

necessary EG *They lack the necessary resources.*

vital EG *vital supplies*

> **WORD POWER**
> Synonyms
> central
> indispensable
> primary

basis NOUN
the main principle of something
EG *The same theme is the basis of several poems.*

core EG *the core of Asia's problems*

fundamental EG *the fundamentals of road safety*

heart EG *the heart of the matter*

premise EG *the premise of his argument*

principle EG *the principles of Buddhism*

❶ bay NOUN
a curve in a coastline
EG *the Bay of Biscay*

cove EG *a sandy cove with white cliffs*

gulf EG *the Gulf of Mexico*

inlet EG *a deep inlet on the west coast*

sound EG *streams that run into the sound*

❷ bay VERB
to make a howling noise
EG *wolves baying in the moonlight*

bark EG *a small dog barking at a seagull*

cry EG *I heard animals cry in the forest.*

howl EG *distant coyotes howling in the night*

yelp EG *A dog snapped and yelped at them.*

beach NOUN
an area beside the sea
EG *making sandcastles on the beach*

coast EG *a day at the coast*

sands EG *the long white sands of Goa*

seashore EG *walks along the seashore*

seaside EG *trips to the seaside*

shore EG *He swam out from the shore.*

strand EG *collecting shells on the strand*

❶ bear VERB
to carry something
EG *The ice wasn't thick enough to bear their weight.*

carry EG *He always carried a gun.*

convey EG *The taxi conveyed us to the centre.*

shoulder EG *He had to shoulder the blame for the mistake.*

support EG *Thick wooden posts support the ceiling.*

take EG *You'd better take an umbrella.*

❷ bear VERB
to have or show something
EG *The room bore the signs of a violent struggle.*

exhibit EG *He began to exhibit symptoms of the disease.*

harbour EG *She still harbours feelings of resentment.*

have EG *I have a grudge against her*

❸ bear VERB
to accept something
EG *He can't bear to talk about it.*

abide EG *I can't abide arrogant people.*

endure EG *The pain was hard to*

endure.

stomach EG *He could not stomach violence.*

suffer EG *I had to suffer his company all day.*

tolerate EG *Women tolerate pain better than men.*

beat VERB
to hit someone or something hard
EG *He threatened to beat her.*

batter EG *The waves kept battering the life raft.*

buffet EG *Their plane was buffeted by storms.*

hit EG *He hit me on the head.*

pound EG *Someone was pounding on the door.*

strike EG *She struck him across the mouth.*

thrash EG *He was thrashed by his father.*

beat VERB
to defeat
EG *She was easily beaten in the race.*

defeat EG *The team hasn't been defeated all year.*

outdo EG *One man was trying to outdo the other.*

outstrip EG *The company is outstripping its rivals.*

overcome EG *Molly had overcome her fear of flying.*

overwhelm EG *One attack could overwhelm the enemy.*

vanquish EG *the man who helped vanquish Napoleon*

> **WORD POWER**
> Synonyms
> conquer
> master
> surpass

beat NOUN
a rhythm
EG *the thumping beat of rock music*

cadence EG *the pulsing cadences of his music*

metre EG *the strict metre of the poem*

rhythm EG *His foot tapped a rhythm on the floor.*

stress EG *differences of stress in speech*

time EG *a song written in waltz time*

beautiful ADJECTIVE
attractive or pleasing
EG *beautiful music*

attractive EG *an attractive woman*

delightful EG *The perfume is delightful.*

fine EG *a fine summer's day*

gorgeous EG *a gorgeous man*

lovely EG *You look lovely.*

pleasing EG *a pleasing appearance*

> **WORD POWER**
> Synonyms
> exquisite
> fair
> Antonym
> ugly

❶ beauty NOUN
the quality of being beautiful
EG *an area of outstanding beauty*

attractiveness EG *the attractiveness of the region*

charm EG *a woman of great charm*

elegance EG *the elegance of the overall design*

loveliness EG *the loveliness of the scene*

> **WORD POWER**
> Antonym
> ugliness

❷ beauty NOUN
a good-looking person
EG *a dark-haired beauty*

hunk INFORMAL EG *The Swedish hunk is back again.*

stunner INFORMAL EG *the 23-year-old stunner*

❸ beauty NOUN
an attractive feature
EG *The beauty of the fund is its simplicity.*

A
B
C
D
E
F
G
H
I
J
K
L
M
N
O
P
Q
R
S
T
U
V
W
X
Y
Z

33

A
B
C
D
E
F
G
H
I
J
K
L
M
N
O
P
Q
R
S
T
U
V
W
X
Y
Z

advantage EG *the advantages of the new system over the old one*

asset EG *The one asset the job provided was contacts.*

attraction EG *The main attraction of the place is the monument.*

benefit EG *Every age has its benefits.*

because CONJUNCTION
for the reason that
EG *I went home because I was tired.*

as EG *Don't cook for me as I'll be home late.*

since EG *Since you didn't listen, I'll repeat that.*

> **WORD POWER**
> Synonyms
> in that
> on account of
> owing to

before ADVERB
at a previous time
EG *Have you been to Greece before?*

earlier EG *Here is a cake I made earlier.*

formerly EG *He had formerly been in the army.*

in advance EG *We booked the room well in advance.*

previously EG *Previously she had little time to work.*

sooner EG *I wish I'd arrived sooner.*

> **WORD POWER**
> Antonym
> after

beg VERB
to ask anxiously for something
EG *I begged him to leave me alone.*

beseech EG *Her eyes beseeched him to show mercy.*

implore EG *I implore you not to say anything.*

petition EG *He petitioned the Court to let him go free.*

plead EG *She was pleading with me to stay.*

> **WORD POWER**

> Synonyms
> entreat
> importune
> solicit

begin VERB
to start or cause to start
EG *She began to move around the room.*

commence FORMAL EG *He commenced his journey.*

inaugurate EG *The committee was inaugurated ten days ago.*

initiate EG *They wanted to initiate a discussion.*

originate EG *Mankind may have originated in Africa.*

set about EG *He set about tackling his problems.*

start EG *The meeting starts at 10 o'clock.*

> **WORD POWER**
> Synonyms
> instigate
> institute
> Antonym
> end

beginner NOUN
someone learning to do something
EG *a beginner's course*

apprentice EG *an apprentice in a law firm*

learner EG *young learners of French*

novice EG *Many of us are novices on the computer.*

starter EG *new starters at school*

trainee EG *a trainee in a newspaper office*

> **WORD POWER**
> Antonym
> expert

beginning NOUN
where something starts
EG *the beginning of the city*

birth EG *the birth of modern art*

commencement FORMAL EG *a date for the commencement of talks*

opening EG *the opening of the trial*
origin EG *the origins of civilization*
outset EG *There were lots of problems from the outset.*
start EG *the start of all the trouble*

> **WORD POWER**
> Synonyms
> inauguration
> initiation
> onset
> Antonym
> end

behave VERB
to act in a certain way
EG *They were behaving like animals.*
act EG *He is acting like a spoilt child.*
function EG *They are functioning as a team.*
operate EG *I know how Graham operates.*
work EG *My mind is working well today.*

belief NOUN
the certainty something is true
EG *belief in reincarnation*
confidence EG *I have every confidence that you'll do well.*
conviction EG *She speaks with conviction.*
judgment EG *My judgment is that he should leave.*
opinion EG *Robert has strong opinions.*
trust EG *She has complete trust that you'll help her.*
view EG *In my view, he is wrong.*

belief NOUN
a principle of a religion or system
EG *the culture and beliefs of ancient times*
creed EG *people of every race and creed*
doctrine EG *Christian doctrine*
dogma EG *religious dogma*
faith EG *Do you practise any faith?*
ideology EG *different political ideologies*
principle EG *the principles of Jewish faith*
tenet EG *the fundamental tenets of Islam*

believable ADJECTIVE
possible or likely to be the case
EG *The book is full of believable characters.*
credible EG *credible witnesses*
imaginable EG *It is scarcely imaginable that it happened here.*
likely EG *It's more likely that she forgot.*
plausible EG *a plausible explanation*
possible EG *It's quite possible that I'm wrong.*
probable EG *the most probable outcome*

> **WORD POWER**
> Antonym
> unbelievable

believe VERB
to accept something is true
EG *Don't believe everything you read in the papers.*
accept EG *He can't accept that he is wrong.*
assume EG *I assume these eggs are fresh.*
presume EG *The missing person is presumed to be dead.*
swallow INFORMAL EG *I found their story hard to swallow.*
trust EG *I trust that you will manage.*

> **WORD POWER**
> Antonym
> doubt

belittle VERB
to make someone or something seem less important
EG *He belittles my opinions.*
deride EG *He is derided as weak and incompetent.*
detract from EG *Her sour comments detracted from Meg's*

A
B
C
D
E
F
G
H
I
J
K
L
M
N
O
P
Q
R
S
T
U
V
W
X
Y
Z

happiness.

downgrade EG *I fear failure, but I downgrade my successes.*

scorn EG *Eleanor scorns the work of others.*

undervalue EG *We must never undervalue freedom.*

> **WORD POWER**
> Synonyms
> denigrate
> minimize
> Antonym
> praise

beloved ADJECTIVE
dearly loved
EG *He lost his beloved wife last year.*

adored EG *an adored father*

cherished EG *his most cherished possession*

darling EG *our darling child*

dearest EG *my dearest Maria*

precious EG *I love my precious cat.*

treasured EG *treasured memories*

> **WORD POWER**
> Antonym
> despised

below PREPOSITION OR ADVERB
lower down
EG *six centimetres below soil level*

beneath EG *She hid the letter beneath her mattress.*

down EG *I fell down to the bottom.*

lower EG *The price will fall lower than this.*

under EG *tunnels under the ground*

underneath EG *He crawled underneath the table.*

> **WORD POWER**
> Antonym
> above

❶ bend VERB
to make or become curved
EG *Bend the bar into a horseshoe.*

buckle EG *A wave buckled the ship's deck.*

curve EG *The wall curves to the left.*

turn EG *The road turns right at the end.*

twist EG *glass twisted into elaborate patterns*

warp EG *The wood had started to warp.*

❷ bend VERB
to move forwards and downwards
EG *I bent over and kissed her cheek.*

arch EG *Don't arch your back!*

bow EG *He turned and bowed to her.*

crouch EG *We were crouching in the bushes.*

incline EG *The woman inclined her head to one side.*

lean EG *She leant out of the window.*

stoop EG *Stooping down, he picked up a stone.*

❸ bend NOUN
a curve in something
EG *a bend in the road*

arc EG *the full arc of a rainbow*

corner EG *He drove round the corner.*

curve EG *the curve of the stream*

loop EG *The river curves in a loop.*

turn EG *a turn in the path*

> **WORD POWER**
> Synonyms
> angle
> arch
> twist

❶ benefit NOUN
an advantage
EG *the benefits of relaxation*

advantage EG *The advantages of the new system far outweigh its disadvantages.*

asset EG *A second language is an asset in this job.*

boon EG *a great boon for busy housewives*

gain EG *He used the knowledge for his personal gain.*

good EG *Study for your own good!*

help EG *It's no help to know I was*

right.

profit EG *the profits of working hard*

use EG *His training was of no use to him.*

> **WORD POWER**
> Antonym
> disadvantage

● **benefit** VERB
to help in something
EG *The experience will benefit you.*

aid EG *measures to aid working mothers*

assist EG *The extra money will assist you.*

enhance EG *His injury does not enhance our chances.*

further EG *His support will further our cause.*

help EG *The new laws won't help the environment.*

profit EG *It won't profit us to complain.*

> **WORD POWER**
> Antonym
> harm

benevolent ADJECTIVE
kind and helpful
EG *a benevolent ruler*

benign EG *a benign and loveable man*

charitable EG *charitable organizations*

compassionate EG *my compassionate friends*

humane EG *humane treatment of prisoners*

kind EG *You have been kind and helpful to us.*

> **WORD POWER**
> Synonyms
> altruistic
> beneficent
> philanthropic

beside PREPOSITION
next to
EG *I stood beside my father and my*

uncle.

adjacent to EG *a hotel adjacent to the beach*

alongside EG *a house alongside the river*

close to EG *The restaurant is close to their home.*

near EG *He stood very near the front door.*

next to EG *She sat down next to him.*

● **best** ADJECTIVE
of the highest standard
EG *the best film I have seen in a long time.*

finest EG *the finest foods*

foremost EG *the world's foremost scientists*

leading EG *He is ranked among the world's leading basketball players.*

outstanding EG *the outstanding athlete of his time*

pre-eminent EG *pre-eminent writers in America*

supreme EG *the supreme achievement of the human race*

> **WORD POWER**
> Synonyms
> first-rate
> principal
> superlative
> Antonym
> worst

❷ **best** NOUN
the preferred thing
EG *This team is the best I've ever seen.*

cream EG *the cream of society*

elite EG *the international elite of athletics*

favourite EG *Of all sports, soccer is my favourite.*

finest EG *Landlord, wine! And make it the finest!*

pick EG *the pick of this year's books*

> **WORD POWER**
> Antonym
> worst

A
B
C
D
E
F
G
H
I
J
K
L
M
N
O
P
Q
R
S
T
U
V
W
X
Y
Z

❶ betray VERB
to do someone harm
EG *I was betrayed by someone I had thought a friend.*
be unfaithful EG *He's been unfaithful to his wife.*
break your promise EG *I broke my promise to help her.*
double-cross INFORMAL EG *I was angry that he double-crossed me.*
inform on EG *people who inform on their colleagues*

❷ betray VERB
to show feelings
EG *Jeremy's voice betrayed little emotion.*
expose EG *She never exposed her hostile feelings.*
manifest EG *Fear can manifest itself in many ways.*
reveal EG *Her expression revealed nothing.*
show EG *His eyes showed his unhappiness.*

❶ better ADJECTIVE
of more worth than another
EG *Today was much better than yesterday.*
finer EG *I could have no finer teacher.*
greater EG *I now have greater ability in English.*
preferable EG *Grilling foods is preferable to frying.*
superior EG *superior intelligence*
surpassing EG *a day of surpassing beauty*
worthier EG *a worthier man than yourself*

> **WORD POWER**
> Antonym
> inferior

❷ better ADJECTIVE
well after being ill
EG *I hope you fell better soon.*
cured EG *I am cured now.*
healthier EG *She certainly looks healthier.*

improving EG *His condition was described as 'improving'.*
recovering EG *She is recovering after a bout of flu.*
stronger EG *John is feeling much stronger.*
well EG *Get well soon.*

> **WORD POWER**
> Antonym
> worse

beware VERB
to be cautious
EG *Beware of the dog.*
be careful EG *Be careful what you say to him.*
be cautious EG *Doctors are cautious about using the treatment.*
be wary EG *Michelle is wary of marriage.*
guard against EG *We have to guard against thieves.*
look out EG *Look out, there's a train coming.*
watch out EG *Watch out for fog and ice.*

bias NOUN
prejudice for or against a person or group
EG *bias against women*
bigotry EG *religious bigotry*
favouritism EG *His promotion was due to favouritism.*
prejudice EG *racial prejudice*

biased ADJECTIVE
showing prejudice
EG *biased attitudes*
one-eyed AUSTRALIAN AND NEW ZEALAND EG *I may be a bit one-eyed because of the family connection.*
one-sided EG *a one-sided argument*
partial EG *a very partial view of the situation*
prejudiced EG *Don't be prejudiced by what you read.*
slanted EG *a slanted newspaper article*
weighted EG *a scheme weighted towards those in need*

A
B
C
D
E
F
G
H
I
J
K
L
M
N
O
P
Q
R
S
T
U
V
W
X
Y
Z

WORD POWER
Antonym
neutral

big ADJECTIVE
of a large size
EG *a big house*
colossal EG *a colossal fortune*
enormous EG *enormous success*
gigantic EG *gigantic prehistoric animals*
great EG *a great crowd*
huge EG *A huge crowd gathered.*
immense EG *an immense cloud of smoke*
large EG *a large amount of cash*
massive EG *a massive iceberg*
vast EG *the vast majority of people*

WORD POWER
Antonym
small

big ADJECTIVE
of great importance
EG *a big name*
eminent EG *an eminent scientist*
important EG *the most important man in the country*
influential EG *I have influential friends in the company.*
leading EG *leading medical experts*
powerful EG *powerful countries*
principal EG *the principal question*
prominent EG *France's most prominent newspaper*
significant EG *a significant difference*

WORD POWER
Antonym
unimportant

bill NOUN
a statement of how much is owed
EG *a huge restaurant bill*
account EG *Please charge it to my account.*
charges EG *charges for eye tests*
invoice EG *They sent an invoice for the damage.*

statement EG *a credit card statement*

bit NOUN
a small amount
EG *a bit of coal*
crumb EG *a crumb of comfort*
fragment EG *glittering fragments of broken glass*
grain EG *His story contains a grain of truth.*
part EG *part of the problem*
piece EG *The vase was smashed to pieces.*
scrap EG *a scrap of evidence*

WORD POWER
Synonyms
iota
jot
speck

❶ bitter ADJECTIVE
angry and resentful
EG *a bitter row*
acrimonious EG *an acrimonious discussion*
begrudging EG *He gave me begrudging thanks.*
embittered EG *an embittered old lady*
rancorous EG *the issue that has led to rancorous disputes*
resentful EG *She is resentful of others' success.*
sour EG *a sour expression*

❷ bitter ADJECTIVE
tasting or smelling sharp
EG *bitter lemons*
acid EG *the acid smell of sweat*
acrid EG *clouds of acrid smoke*
astringent EG *astringent disinfectant*
sharp EG *a clean, sharp taste*
sour EG *a rich, sour stew*
tart EG *the tart qualities of citrus fruit*

WORD POWER
Antonym
sweet

black NOUN OR ADJECTIVE

> Shades of black:
> coal-black
> ebony
> inky
> jet
> jet-black
> pitch-black
> raven
> sable
> sooty

❶ blame VERB

to believe someone caused something

EG *Don't blame me for this trouble.*

accuse EG *She accused him of causing the fire.*

charge EG *He will be charged for murder.*

hold responsible EG *I hold you responsible for this mess.*

❷ blame NOUN

the responsibility for something bad

EG *I'm not going to take the blame for that!*

accountability EG *He escaped accountability for his crimes.*

fault EG *The fault was all yours.*

guilt EG *the sole guilt for the outbreak of war*

liability EG *He admitted liability for the crash.*

rap SLANG EG *A maid took the rap for stealing the letters.*

responsibility EG *responsibility for the murder*

> **WORD POWER**
> Synonyms
> culpability
> incrimination

❶ blank ADJECTIVE

with nothing on it

EG *a blank sheet of paper*

bare EG *bare walls*

clean EG *a clean sheet of paper*

clear EG *a clear patch of floor*

empty EG *an empty page*

plain EG *a plain envelope*

unmarked EG *an unmarked board*

❷ blank ADJECTIVE

showing no feeling

EG *John just looked blank.*

deadpan EG *a deadpan expression*

dull EG *a dull stare*

empty EG *She saw the empty look in his eyes.*

impassive EG *her impassive smile*

vacant EG *the vacant expression on his face*

bless VERB

to ask God's protection

EG *The bishop blessed the congregation.*

anoint EG *The priest anointed the child with oil.*

consecrate EG *ground that has been consecrated*

dedicate EG *The well was dedicated to saints.*

hallow EG *A building could be hallowed by prayer.*

> **WORD POWER**
> Antonym
> curse

❶ blessing NOUN

something good

EG *Good health is a blessing.*

benefit EG *the benefits of technology*

boon EG *This service is a boon to the elderly.*

gift EG *A cheerful nature is a gift.*

godsend EG *The extra twenty dollars was a godsend.*

help EG *My computer is a real help in my work.*

> **WORD POWER**
> Antonym
> disadvantage

❷ blessing NOUN

approval or permission to do something

EG *She got married with her parents' blessing.*

A
B
C
D
E
F
G
H
I
J
K
L
M
N
O
P
Q
R
S
T
U
V
W
X
Y
Z

approval EG *Does this plan have your approval?*
backing EG *We can't do anything without his backing.*
consent EG *He gave his consent to the article.*
leave EG *She gave us leave to start.*
permission EG *You have my permission to go.*
support EG *My manager has given his full support to my project.*

> *WORD POWER*
> Synonyms
> approbation
> sanction
> Antonym
> disapproval

block NOUN
a large piece
EG *a block of wood*
bar EG *a bar of soap*
brick EG *concrete bricks*
chunk EG *chunks of meat*
ingot EG *a gold ingot*
lump EG *lumps of metal*
piece EG *a big piece of cake*

block VERB
to close by putting something across
EG *Mud blocked the river.*
choke EG *The town was choked with cars.*
clog EG *Dishes clogged the sink.*
obstruct EG *The crash obstructed the road.*
plug EG *Have you plugged the leaks?*

> *WORD POWER*
> Antonym
> unblock

block VERB
to prevent something happening
EG *The council blocked his plans.*
bar EG *He was barred from entering.*
check EG *a policy to check population growth*
halt EG *attempts to halt the spread*

of disease
obstruct EG *Lack of funds obstructed our progress.*
stop EG *measures to stop the rising crime rate*
thwart EG *My plans were thwarted by Taylor.*

blockage NOUN
a thing that clogs something
EG *a blockage in the pipe*
block EG *a block in the blood vessel*
obstruction EG *an obstruction on the track*
stoppage EG *We have to clear the stoppage.*

blot out VERB
to cover and prevent from being seen
EG *The smoke blotted out the sky.*
eclipse EG *The moon eclipsed the sun.*
obliterate EG *Our view was obliterated by mist.*
obscure EG *My way was obscured by fog.*
shadow EG *Her veil shadowed her face.*

blow VERB
to move or cause to move in the wind
EG *The wind blew his papers away.*
buffet EG *The ship was buffeted by gales.*
drive EG *The strong wind drove us forward.*
flutter EG *The flags are fluttering.*
sweep EG *A sudden blast swept away the cloth.*
waft EG *His hair wafted in the breeze.*
whirl EG *The fallen leaves whirled around.*

blow NOUN
a hit from something
EG *a blow to the head*
bang EG *He suffered some bangs and bumps.*
clout INFORMAL EG *a clout on the*

41

A
B
C
D
E
F
G
H
I
J
K
L
M
N
O
P
Q
R
S
T
U
V
W
X
Y
Z

head

knock EG *Knocks can cause damage to the spine.*

smack EG *She gave the child a smack.*

thump EG *Ralph got a thump on the chest.*

whack EG *The horse got a whack from its rider.*

❸ **blow** NOUN
something disappointing or upsetting
EG *Marc's death was a terrible blow.*

bombshell EG *His departure was a bombshell for the team.*

disappointment EG *My exam results were a real disappointment.*

misfortune EG *a series of misfortunes*

setback EG *We faced many setbacks before we got the house.*

shock EG *The news came as a shock.*

upset EG *The defeat caused an upset.*

WORD POWER
Synonyms
calamity
catastrophe
jolt

blue NOUN OR ADJECTIVE

Shades of blue:
aqua
aquamarine
azure
cerulean
cobalt
cyan
duck-egg blue
electric blue
gentian
indigo
lapis lazuli
midnight blue
navy
Nile blue
peacock blue
periwinkle
petrol blue
royal blue
sapphire
saxe blue
sky-blue
teal
turquoise
ultramarine

❶ **blunt** ADJECTIVE
having rounded edges
EG *blunt scissors*

dull EG *a dull knife*

rounded EG *rounded edges*

unsharpened EG *an unsharpened pencil*

WORD POWER
Antonym
sharp

❷ **blunt** ADJECTIVE
saying what you think
EG *a blunt speaker*

bluff EG *a bluff old man*

brusque EG *His response was brusque.*

forthright EG *a forthright reply*

frank EG *I'll be frank with you.*

outspoken EG *an outspoken critic*

straightforward EG *She has a straightforward manner.*

WORD POWER
Synonyms
explicit
trenchant
Antonym
tactful

❶ **blush** VERB
to go red in the face
EG *I felt myself blushing.*

colour EG *I found myself colouring as I spoke.*

crimson EG *He looked at her and she crimsoned.*

flush EG *I saw her face flush.*

go red EG *His face went red as a beetroot.*

turn red EG *He turned red with embarrassment.*

turn scarlet EG *She turned scarlet*

with humiliation.

blush NOUN
a red colour
EG *Ann took the gift with a blush.*
colour EG *The walk will bring colour to your cheeks.*
flush EG *A slow flush spread over the man's face.*
glow EG *a healthy glow*

boast VERB
to talk proudly
EG *Carol boasted about her costume.*
brag EG *I don't mind bragging about my talents.*
crow EG *Stop crowing about your success.*
skite AUSTRALIAN AND NEW ZEALAND INFORMAL EG *That's nothing to skite about.*

boastful ADJECTIVE
tending to brag about things
EG *a boastful liar*
bragging EG *bragging stories about his time in the navy*
cocky EG *The boxer is cocky and brash.*
conceited EG *Young men tend to be conceited.*
crowing EG *crowing remarks*
egotistical EG *egotistical fibs*
swaggering EG *He has a swaggering arrogance.*

> **WORD POWER**
> Antonym
> modest

body NOUN
all your physical parts
EG *My whole body hurt.*
build EG *He is of medium build.*
figure EG *Janet has a nice figure.*
form EG *clothes that flatter your form*
frame EG *their bony frames*
physique EG *a powerful physique*
shape EG *his trim shape*

❷ **body** NOUN
a dead body

EG *Police found a body hidden in the forest.*
carcass EG *a sheep's carcass*
corpse EG *the corpse of a young man*
dead body EG *He'd never seen a dead body.*
remains EG *human remains*

❸ **body** NOUN
an organized group of people
EG *local voluntary bodies*
association EG *the Football Association*
band EG *a band of rebels*
company EG *the Royal Shakespeare Company*
confederation EG *a confederation of workers*
organization EG *student organizations*
society EG *I joined the local opera society.*

> **WORD POWER**
> Synonyms
> bloc
> collection
> corporation

❶ **boil** VERB
to bubble
EG *The water is boiling.*
bubble EG *Potatoes bubbled in the pot.*
fizz EG *The liquid fizzed and bubbled.*
foam EG *When the butter foams, add the onions.*
froth EG *The milk frothed over in the pan.*

> **WORD POWER**
> Synonyms
> effervesce
> seethe

❷ **boil** NOUN
a swelling on the skin
EG *five boils on his face*
blister EG *a blister on my index finger*
swelling EG *a swelling under the*

A
B
C
D
E
F
G
H
I
J
K
L
M
N
O
P
Q
R
S
T
U
V
W
X
Y
Z

eye
tumour EG *The tumours had all disappeared.*

> **WORD POWER**
> Synonyms
> blain
> carbuncle
> pustule

❶ **bold** ADJECTIVE
confident and not shy
EG *a bold question*
brash EG *a brash young sergeant*
brazen EG *a brazen young woman*
cheeky EG *a cheeky grin*
confident EG *I felt confident confronting him.*
forward EG *It was forward of you to ask him.*
impudent EG *an impudent child*

> **WORD POWER**
> Synonyms
> barefaced
> pert
> saucy
> Antonym
> shy

❷ **bold** ADJECTIVE
unafraid of risk or danger
EG *a bold attempt*
adventurous EG *an adventurous spirit*
brave EG *a brave woman*
courageous EG *courageous firefighters*
daring EG *daring feats*
fearless EG *a fearless warrior*
intrepid EG *an intrepid explorer*

> **WORD POWER**
> Synonyms
> audacious
> heroic
> valiant
> Antonym
> cowardly

❸ **bold** ADJECTIVE
clear and noticeable
EG *bold colours*

bright EG *bright light*
flashy EG *flashy clothes*
loud EG *a loud tie*
striking EG *a striking tartan patter*
strong EG *dressed in strong reds and yellows*
vivid EG *vivid green and purple*

> **WORD POWER**
> Synonyms
> conspicuous
> prominent
> pronounced
> Antonym
> dull

❶ **bomb** NOUN
an explosive device
EG *The bomb exploded in the centre of the city.*
device EG *Experts defused the device.*
explosive EG *a block of plastic explosive*
missile EG *long-range missiles*
rocket EG *a rocket launcher*
shell EG *Shells began to fall.*
torpedo EG *The torpedo struck the ship.*

> **WORD POWER**
> Synonyms
> grenade
> mine
> projectile

❷ **bomb** VERB
to attack with bombs
EG *His house was bombed.*
attack EG *We are being attacked!*
blow up EG *He attempted to blow up the building.*
bombard EG *Warships began to bombard the coast.*
destroy EG *Helicopters destroyed his village.*
shell EG *They shelled the troops heavily.*
torpedo EG *His ship was torpedoed in the Channel.*

❶ **bond** NOUN
a close relationship

EG *a special bond between us*

attachment EG *Mother and child form a close attachment.*

connection EG *a family connection*

link EG *the links of friendship*

relation EG *the relation between husband and wife*

tie EG *the ties of blood*

union EG *the union of father and son*

> *WORD POWER*
> Synonyms
> affiliation
> affinity

bond NOUN

an obligation to do something
EG *the social bonds of community*

agreement EG *He has broken our agreement.*

contract EG *He signed a two-year contract.*

obligation EG *your obligation to your father*

pledge EG *a pledge of support*

promise EG *You must keep your promises.*

word EG *I give you my word.*

> *WORD POWER*
> Synonyms
> compact
> covenant
> guarantee

bond VERB

to attach separate things
EG *Strips of wood are bonded together.*

bind EG *Tape was used to bind the files.*

fasten EG *I fastened the picture to the wall.*

fuse EG *The pieces to be joined are melted and fused together.*

glue EG *Glue the pieces together.*

paste EG *He pasted posters to the wall.*

book NOUN

a number of pages in a cover
EG *I'm reading a great book just now.*

publication EG *publications about job hunting*

textbook EG *He wrote a textbook on law.*

title EG *We publish a range of titles.*

tome EG *a heavy tome*

volume EG *small volumes of poetry*

work EG *my favourite work by this author*

Types of book:
anthology
atlas
autobiography
biography
dictionary
directory
encyclopedia
gazetteer
glossary
guidebook
manual
novel
phrasebook
thesaurus

Parts of a book:
appendix
bibliography
blurb
caption
chapter
contents
cover
footnote
foreword
glossary
heading
illustration
index
introduction
jacket
layout
line
page
preface
title

Religious books:
Bible (*Christianity*)
Book of Mormon (*Mormonism*)
Diamond Scriptures (*Zen Buddhism*)

Guru Granth *or* Adi Granth
(*Sikhism*)
I Ching (*Confucianism and
Taoism*)
Mahabharata (*Hinduism*)
Quran *or* Koran (*Islam*)
Ramayana (*Hinduism*)
Sutras (*Buddhism and Hinduism*)
Talmud (*Judaism*)
Tao-te-Ching (*Taoism*)
Torah (*Judaism*)
Tripitaka (*Buddhism*)
Veda (*Hinduism*)

❷ **book** VERB
to arrange to have or use
EG *The tickets are booked.*
charter EG *A plane was chartered
for them.*
engage EG *We engaged the services
of a plumber.*
organize EG *I have organized our
flights.*
reserve EG *Hotel rooms have been
reserved.*
schedule EG *A meeting is
scheduled for Monday.*

❶ **border** NOUN
a dividing line between things or
places
EG *the border between two countries*
borderline EG *the borderline
between health and sickness*
boundary EG *national boundaries*
frontier EG *the American frontier*
line EG *the line between fact and
fiction*

❷ **border** NOUN
an edge of something
EG *plain tiles with a bright border*
bounds EG *the bounds of good taste*
edge EG *the edge of town*
limits EG *the city limits*
margin EG *the western margins of
the island*
rim EG *the rim of the lake*

❸ **border** VERB
to form an edge
EG *Tall trees bordered the fields.*

edge EG *the woods that edge the
lake*
fringe EG *Street lights fringe the
bay.*
hem EG *dresses hemmed with
feathers*
rim EG *the restaurants rimming the
harbour*
trim EG *coats trimmed with fur
collars*

bored ADJECTIVE
impatient and not interested in
something
EG *I am bored with this business.*
fed up EG *He is fed up with this
country.*
tired EG *I am tired of this music.*
uninterested EG *He seems
uninterested in politics.*
wearied EG *He spoke in a wearied
voice.*

WORD POWER
Antonym
interested

boredom NOUN
a lack of interest
EG *the boredom of long trips*
apathy EG *political apathy*
dullness EG *a period of dullness*
flatness EG *a feeling of flatness*
monotony EG *the monotony of
winter*
tedium EG *the tedium of
unemployment*
weariness EG *a sense of weariness*

WORD POWER
Antonym
interest

boring ADJECTIVE
dull and uninteresting
EG *a boring job*
dull EG *dull tasks*
flat EG *a flat performance*
humdrum EG *humdrum lives*
monotonous EG *the monotonous
prison routine*
tedious EG *The work is tedious.*

tiresome EG *a tiresome old man*

WORD POWER
Synonyms
insipid
repetitive
stale
Antonym
interesting

boss NOUN
a person in charge of something
EG *He can't stand his boss.*
chief EG *the police chief*
director EG *the directors of the bank*
employer EG *He was sent to Rome by his employer.*
head EG *Heads of government met in New York.*
leader EG *The party's leader has resigned.*
manager EG *the company's marketing manager*

bossy ADJECTIVE
telling people what to do
EG *a rather bossy little girl*
arrogant EG *arrogant behaviour*
authoritarian EG *He has an authoritarian approach to parenthood.*
dictatorial EG *a dictatorial management style*
domineering EG *She is domineering and ruthless.*
imperious EG *He has an imperious manner.*
overbearing EG *an overbearing mother*

botch VERB
to do something badly
EG *a botched operation*
bungle EG *inefficient people who bungled the job*
mar EG *She marred her exit by twisting her ankle.*
mess up EG *He manages to mess up his life.*

❶ bother VERB
to cause worry or concern
EG *His lack of money bothers him.*
annoy EG *the things that annoy me*
concern EG *The future concerns me.*
disturb EG *It disturbs me to see you unhappy.*
get on someone's nerves
INFORMAL EG *This place gets on my nerves.*
trouble EG *Are you troubled by nightmares?*
worry EG *I'm worried by the amount he is drinking.*

WORD POWER
Synonyms
harass
inconvenience

❷ bother NOUN
trouble and difficulty
EG *I hate the bother of shopping.*
annoyance EG *Snoring can be an annoyance.*
difficulty EG *The strikes are causing difficulties for commuters.*
inconvenience EG *a minor inconvenience*
irritation EG *Noise is an irritation.*
trouble EG *You've caused me a lot of trouble.*
worry EG *It was a time of worry for us.*

WORD POWER
Synonyms
nuisance
strain

❶ bottom NOUN
the lowest part of something
EG *the bottom of the stairs*
base EG *the base of the spine*
bed EG *the river bed*
depths EG *the depths of the earth*
floor EG *the ocean floor*
foot EG *the foot of the bed*

WORD POWER
Antonym
top

❷ bottom NOUN
the part of the body you sit on

EG *Sit on your bottom!*

backside INFORMAL EG *the muscles in your backside*

behind INFORMAL EG *He kicked me on the behind.*

buttocks EG *exercises for your buttocks*

posterior HUMOROUS EG *He fell on his posterior.*

rear EG *I was thrown out on my rear.*

❸ bottom ADJECTIVE
in the lowest place or position
EG *the bottom drawer*

base EG *the base edge of the curtain*

basement EG *a basement flat*

ground EG *ground level*

lowest EG *the lowest part of the brain*

> ### WORD POWER
> Antonym
> highest

bounce VERB
to spring back or move up and down
EG *I bounced a ball against the wall.*

bob EG *The raft bobbed along.*

bound EG *He bounded up the stairway.*

bump EG *My bicycle bumped along the rough ground.*

jump EG *They jumped up and down to keep warm.*

ricochet EG *The bullets ricocheted off the jeep.*

> ### WORD POWER
> Synonyms
> rebound
> recoil

boy NOUN
a male child
EG *I knew him when he was a boy.*

fellow EG *a fine little fellow*

lad EG *I remember being a lad his age.*

schoolboy EG *a group of schoolboys*

youngster EG *I was only a*

youngster in 1970.

youth EG *gangs of youths who cause trouble*

boycott VERB
to refuse to have anything to do with
EG *Some parties are boycotting the elections.*

blacklist EG *He has been blacklisted by various societies.*

embargo EG *Imports of fruit were embargoed.*

exclude EG *I exclude animal products from my diet.*

reject EG *She rejected her parents' religion.*

spurn EG *You spurned his last offer.*

> ### WORD POWER
> Synonyms
> proscribe
> refrain from

braggart NOUN
a person who boasts
EG *He was a braggart and a liar.*

bigmouth SLANG EG *He's nothing but a bigmouth.*

boaster EG *an idle boaster looking for the main chance*

bragger EG *He was quite a bragger.*

show-off EG *I've always been a show-off.*

skite or **skiter** AUSTRALIAN AND NEW ZEALAND INFORMAL EG *a bit of a skite*

❶ brave ADJECTIVE
willing to do dangerous things
EG *a brave attempt to stop the attack*

bold EG *Amrita became a bold rebel.*

courageous EG *a courageous decision*

fearless EG *his fearless campaigning for justice*

heroic EG *The heroic sergeant risked his life.*

plucky EG *The plucky schoolgirl amazed the doctors.*

valiant EG *a valiant attempt to*

keep going

WORD POWER
Synonyms
daring
intrepid
valorous
Antonym
cowardly

brave VERB
to face something without fear
EG *Fans braved the rain to hear him sing.*
face EG *I can't face another three years of this.*
stand up to EG *I have tried to stand up to the bullies.*

bravery NOUN
the quality of being courageous
EG *He deserves praise for his bravery.*
boldness EG *an outward display of boldness*
courage EG *They do not have the courage to apologize.*
fortitude EG *He suffered with tremendous fortitude.*
heroism EG *acts of heroism*
pluck EG *He has pluck and presence of mind.*
valour EG *He won a medal for valour.*

WORD POWER
Synonyms
fearlessness
mettle
Antonym
cowardice

❶ breach NOUN
a breaking of an agreement or law
EG *a breach of contract*
infringement EG *an infringement of the rules*
offence EG *criminal offences*
trespass EG *a campaign of trespasses and demonstrations*
violation EG *a violation of the peace agreement*

WORD POWER
Synonyms
contravention
transgression

❷ breach NOUN
a gap in something
EG *the breach in the Berlin Wall*
crack EG *a large crack in the ice*
gap EG *a narrow gap in the curtains*
hole EG *We cut holes in the fabric.*
opening EG *an opening in the fence*
rift EG *The earthquake caused a deep rift.*
split EG *There's a split in my mattress.*

WORD POWER
Synonyms
chasm
fissure
rupture

❶ break VERB
to separate into pieces
EG *The plate broke.*
crack EG *A gas main cracked.*
fracture EG *You've fractured a rib.*
shatter EG *safety glass that doesn't shatter*
smash EG *The youths started smashing windows.*
snap EG *The pedal just snapped off.*
splinter EG *The ruler splintered into pieces.*

❷ break VERB
to fail to keep a rule or promise
EG *He broke his promise to attend.*
breach EG *breaches of discipline*
contravene EG *His behaviour contravenes our code of conduct.*
infringe EG *The judge ruled that he had infringed no rules.*
violate EG *They violated the peace agreement.*

❸ break NOUN
a short period of rest or change
EG *I took a five-minute break from work.*
interlude EG *a happy interlude in my life*

A
B
C
D
E
F
G
H
I
J
K
L
M
N
O
P
Q
R
S
T
U
V
W
X
Y
Z

A
B
C
D
E
F
G
H
I
J
K
L
M
N
O
P
Q
R
S
T
U
V
W
X
Y
Z

interval EG *a long interval when no-one spoke*
pause EG *After a pause Alex spoke.*
recess EG *The court adjourned for a recess.*
respite EG *They have had no respite from bombing.*
rest EG *I'll start again after a rest.*

❶ **breed** NOUN
a type of animal
EG *rare breeds of cattle*
kind EG *What kind of horse is that?*
species EG *Pandas are an endangered species.*
stock EG *cattle of Highland stock*
strain EG *a special strain of rat*
type EG *What type of dog should we get?*
variety EG *many varieties of birds*

❷ **breed** VERB
to produce and look after
EG *He breeds dogs for the police.*
cultivate EG *She cultivates fruit and vegetables.*
develop EG *A new variety of potato is being developed.*
keep EG *He keeps guinea pigs.*
nurture EG *trimming and nurturing plants and saplings*
raise EG *He raises birds of prey as a hobby.*
rear EG *the difficulties of rearing children*

❸ **breed** VERB
to produce offspring
EG *Frogs can breed in most ponds.*
multiply EG *Rats multiply quickly.*
produce EG *She produced a son.*
propagate EG *This plant is difficult to propagate.*
reproduce EG *the natural desire to reproduce*

WORD POWER
Synonyms
engender
procreate

❶ **brief** ADJECTIVE
lasting for a short time

EG *a brief appearance on television*
fleeting EG *a fleeting glimpse*
momentary EG *There was a momentary silence.*
quick EG *a quick look at the newspaper*
short EG *a short holiday*
swift EG *a swift glance at John's face*

WORD POWER
Synonyms
ephemeral
temporary
transitory
Antonym
long

❷ **brief** VERB
to give necessary information
EG *A spokesman briefed reporters.*
advise EG *I must advise you of my decision to retire.*
fill in INFORMAL EG *Can you fill me in on Wilbur's visit?*
inform EG *They would inform him of their progress.*
instruct EG *He instructed us in first aid.*
prepare EG *I will prepare you for this exam.*
prime EG *Arnold primed him for his duties.*

❶ **bright** ADJECTIVE
strong and startling
EG *a bright light*
brilliant EG *brilliant green eyes*
dazzling EG *a dazzling white shirt*
glowing EG *the glowing windows of the Cathedral*
luminous EG *a luminous star*
radiant EG *eyes as radiant as sapphires*
vivid EG *strong, vivid colours*

WORD POWER
Synonyms
blazing
illuminated
resplendent
Antonym

| dull

bright ADJECTIVE
clever and alert
EG *my brightest student*
brainy EG *I don't consider myself brainy.*
brilliant EG *She has a brilliant mind.*
clever EG *a clever child*
ingenious EG *an ingenious idea*
intelligent EG *Dolphins are an intelligent species.*
smart EG *He thinks he's as smart as Sarah.*

WORD POWER
Synonyms
acute
astute
sharp
Antonym
dim

bright ADJECTIVE
cheerful and lively
EG *a bright smile*
cheerful EG *Jack sounded quite cheerful about the idea.*
happy EG *a confident, happy child*
jolly EG *a jolly nature*
light-hearted EG *They are light-hearted and enjoy life.*
lively EG *He has a lively personality.*
merry EG *bursts of merry laughter*

bring VERB
to take somewhere
EG *Bring a friend to the party.*
bear EG *They bore the box into the kitchen.*
carry EG *She carried her son to the car.*
convey EG *Emergency supplies were conveyed by truck.*
lead EG *She led him into the house.*
take EG *He took cakes to the party.*
transport EG *The troops were transported to Moscow.*

bring VERB
to cause to happen

EG *Bring the vegetables to the boil.*
cause EG *My mistake caused me some worry.*
create EG *The new factory will create more jobs.*
inflict EG *The attack inflicted heavy casualties.*
produce EG *The drug produces side effects.*
result in EG *Many accidents result in serious injuries.*
wreak EG *Violent storms wreaked havoc.*

WORD POWER
Synonyms
effect
occasion

broken ADJECTIVE
in pieces
EG *a broken window*
burst EG *a burst pipe*
demolished EG *a demolished house*
fractured EG *He suffered a fractured skull.*
fragmented EG *fragmented images*
shattered EG *shattered glass*
smashed EG *smashed windows*

broken ADJECTIVE
not kept
EG *a broken promise*
infringed EG *a case of infringed human rights*
violated EG *a series of violated agreements*

WORD POWER
Synonyms
disobeyed
traduced
transgressed

brown NOUN OR ADJECTIVE

Shades of brown:
auburn
bay
beige
bronze
brunette
buff

burnt sienna
burnt umber
café au lait
camel
chestnut
chocolate
cinnamon
coffee
dun
fawn
ginger
hazel
khaki
mahogany
mocha
oatmeal
ochre
putty
russet
rust
sandy
sepia
tan
taupe
tawny
terracotta
umber

❶ build VERB
to make something
EG *The house was built last year.*
assemble EG *Workers were assembling planes.*
construct EG *plans to construct a temple on the site*
erect EG *The building was erected in 1900.*
fabricate EG *All the tools are fabricated from steel.*
form EG *hotels formed from cheap cement*
make EG *a wall made of bricks*

> **WORD POWER**
> Antonym
> dismantle

❷ build VERB
to develop gradually
EG *I want to build a relationship with them.*
develop EG *These battles could develop into war.*
extend EG *Three new products extend the range.*
increase EG *The population continues to increase.*
intensify EG *The conflict is bound to intensify.*
strengthen EG *Cycling strengthens the muscles.*

> **WORD POWER**
> Synonyms
> augment
> enlarge
> escalate

❸ build NOUN
the size of a body
EG *He is of medium build.*
body EG *a body of average size*
figure EG *Janet has a nice figure.*
form EG *clothes that flatter your form*
frame EG *their bony frames*
physique EG *a powerful physique*
shape EG *his trim shape*

building NOUN
a structure with walls
EG *a glass building*
edifice EG *historic edifices in the area*
structure EG *The museum is an impressive structure.*

❶ bulge VERB
to swell out
EG *He bulges out of his black T-shirt*
expand EG *The pipes expanded in the heat.*
protrude EG *His blue eyes protruded from his head.*
stick out EG *His stomach stuck out under his jacket.*
swell EG *My ankles swelled.*

❷ bulge NOUN
a lump in something
EG *My purse made a bulge in my pocket.*
bump EG *a bump in the road*
hump EG *a camel's hump*
lump EG *itchy red lumps on the skin*

A

C

D

E

F

G

H

I

J

K

L

M

N

O

P

Q

R

S

T

U

V

W

X

Y

Z

protrusion EG *a strange protrusion on his forehead*
swelling EG *a swelling on my foot*

❶ bump VERB
to hit something
EG *He bumped his head on the wall.*
bang EG *I banged my shin on the edge of the table.*
collide EG *The car collided with a tree.*
hit EG *She hit the last barrier and fell.*
jolt EG *We hit the wall with a jolt.*
knock EG *He knocked on the door.*
strike EG *His head struck the windscreen.*

❷ bump NOUN
a dull noise
EG *He heard a bump outside.*
bang EG *I heard four or five loud bangs.*
knock EG *They heard a knock at the door.*
thud EG *She tripped and fell with a thud.*
thump EG *There was a loud thump against the house.*

❸ bump NOUN
a raised part of something
EG *a bump in the road*
bulge EG *My purse made a bulge in my pocket.*
hump EG *a camel's hump*
knob EG *a door with a brass knob*
lump EG *itchy red lumps on the skin*
swelling EG *a swelling on my foot*

> **WORD POWER**
> Synonyms
> contusion
> node
> protuberance

❶ burden NOUN
a load that is carried
EG *My wet clothes were an added burden.*
load EG *a big load of hay*
weight EG *straining to lift heavy weights*

❷ burden NOUN
something that worries you
EG *the burden of looking after a sick parent*
anxiety EG *He expressed his anxieties to me.*
care EG *Forget all the cares of the day.*
strain EG *I find the travelling a strain.*
stress EG *the stress of exams*
trouble EG *The Sullivans have money troubles.*
worry EG *My son is a worry to me.*

> **WORD POWER**
> Synonyms
> affliction
> millstone
> trial

bureaucracy NOUN
complex rules and procedures
EG *Is there too much bureaucracy in government?*
administration EG *high administration costs*
officialdom EG *Officialdom is against us.*
red tape EG *Our application was delayed by red tape.*
regulations EG *absurd regulations about opening hours*

❶ burn VERB
to be on fire
EG *a fire burning in the fireplace*
be ablaze EG *The houses were ablaze.*
be on fire EG *The ship was on fire.*
blaze EG *The wreckage blazed.*
flame EG *We watched as the house flamed.*
flare EG *The match flared in the dark.*
flicker EG *The fire flickered and crackled.*

❷ burn VERB
to destroy with fire
EG *They burned the house down.*
char EG *charred bodies*

incinerate EG *Hospitals incinerate waste.*

scorch EG *The bonfire scorched the grass.*

shrivel EG *The papers shrivelled in the flames.*

singe EG *Her hair was singed and her coat burnt.*

❶ burst VERB
to split apart
EG *The balloon burst.*

break EG *He broke the box open.*

crack EG *A water pipe had cracked.*

explode EG *The glass exploded.*

puncture EG *The glass punctured the tyre.*

rupture EG *His appendix ruptured.*

split EG *The seam of my dress split.*

❷ burst VERB
to happen or appear suddenly
EG *to burst into flames*

barge EG *He barged into the room.*

break EG *Her face broke into a smile.*

erupt EG *Violence could erupt soon.*

rush EG *Water rushed out of the hole.*

❸ burst NOUN
a short period of something
EG *a burst of energy*

fit EG *a fit of rage*

outbreak EG *an outbreak of violence*

rush EG *a sudden rush of excitement*

spate EG *a spate of attacks on horses*

surge EG *a surge of emotion*

torrent EG *a torrent of words*

❶ business NOUN
the buying and selling of goods
EG *a career in business*

commerce EG *commerce between Europe and South America*

dealings EG *All dealings with the company were suspended.*

industry EG *the American car industry*

trade EG *French trade with the West Indies*

trading EG *trading between the two countries*

transaction EG *We settled the transaction over lunch.*

❷ business NOUN
an organization selling goods or services
EG *a family business*

company EG *the Ford Motor Company*

corporation EG *international corporations*

enterprise EG *small industrial enterprises*

establishment EG *shops and other commercial establishments*

firm EG *a firm of engineers*

organization EG *a well-run organization*

> **WORD POWER**
> Synonyms
> concern
> venture

❸ business NOUN
any event or situation
EG *This business has upset me.*

affair EG *He handled the affair badly.*

issue EG *What is your view on this issue?*

matter EG *This is a matter for the police.*

problem EG *solutions to the drug problem*

question EG *the whole question of TV censorship*

subject EG *He raised the subject of money.*

❶ bustle VERB
to move hurriedly
EG *My mother bustled about the room.*

dash EG *We dashed about purposefully.*

fuss EG *Waiters were fussing round the table.*

hurry EG *Claire hurried along the*

road.
rush EG *I'm rushing to finish the cooking.*
scurry EG *rats scurrying around*
scuttle EG *Crabs scuttle along the bank.*

❷ **bustle** NOUN
busy and noisy activity
EG *the bustle of modern life*
activity EG *a burst of activity in the building*
commotion EG *He heard a commotion outside.*
excitement EG *The news created great excitement.*
flurry EG *a flurry of activity*
fuss EG *He works without any fuss.*
hurry EG *the hurry and excitement of the city*

> *WORD POWER*
> Antonym
> peace

❶ **busy** ADJECTIVE
doing something
EG *What is it? I'm busy.*
active EG *He is active in local politics.*
employed EG *He was employed helping me.*
engaged EG *He was engaged in conversation.*
engrossed EG *She is engrossed in her work.*
occupied EG *He is occupied with the packing.*
working EG *I am working on a novel.*

> *WORD POWER*
> Antonym
> idle

❷ **busy** ADJECTIVE
full of activity
EG *a busy tourist resort*
active EG *an active, independent country*
full EG *a full life*
hectic EG *my hectic work schedule*
lively EG *a lively restaurant*
restless EG *a restless mind*

❸ **busy** VERB
to occupy or keep busy
EG *Kathryn busied herself in the kitchen.*
absorb EG *Her career absorbed her completely.*
employ EG *You'd be better employed helping me.*
engage EG *He was engaged in a meeting when I called.*
immerse EG *She immersed herself in her book.*
occupy EG *Try to occupy yourself with something.*

buy VERB
to obtain with money
EG *I'd like to buy him lunch.*
acquire EG *I have acquired a new car.*
invest in EG *I invested in a house.*
obtain EG *She went to obtain a ticket.*
pay for EG *He let me pay for his drink.*
procure EG *attempts to procure more food*
purchase EG *He purchased a sandwich for lunch.*

> *WORD POWER*
> Antonym
> sell

A
B
C
D
E
F
G
H
I
J
K
L
M
N
O
P
Q
R
S
T
U
V
W
X
Y
Z

Cc Cc

A B **C** D E F G H I J K L M N O P Q R S T U V W X Y Z

calculate VERB
to work out a number or amount
EG *how to calculate the cost of setting up a business*

count EG *Shareholders are counting the cost of the slump.*

determine EG *calculations to determine the rate of tax*

reckon EG *an amount reckoned at 140 billion marks*

work out EG *Work out the distance of the journey.*

calculated ADJECTIVE
deliberately planned
EG *Everything they said was calculated to wound.*

aimed EG *The restructuring is aimed at reducing costs.*

designed EG *a scheme designed to help poorer families*

intended EG *the intended effect of the revised guidelines*

planned EG *a carefully planned campaign*

> **WORD POWER**
> Antonym
> unplanned

❶ call VERB
to give a name
EG *a man called Jeffrey*

christen EG *his car, which he had christened Lola*

dub EG *a task that has been dubbed "Mission Impossible"*

label EG *He had been labelled a traitor.*

name EG *My mother insisted on naming me Horace.*

term EG *prisoners termed as political*

> **WORD POWER**
> Synonyms
> denominate
> designate
> entitle

❷ call VERB
to telephone
EG *He called me at my office.*

phone EG *I just phoned to ask how you were.*

ring INFORMAL EG *Could you ring for a taxi?*

telephone EG *Telephone first to see if she's at home.*

❸ call VERB
to say loudly
EG *I heard someone calling my name.*

cry EG *"See you soon!" they cried.*

cry out EG *crying out for help*

shout EG *He shouted something to his brother.*

yell EG *"Come on, Eric!" yelled a voice in the crowd.*

❹ call NOUN
an instance of someone shouting out
EG *a call for help*

cry EG *the cry of a seagull*

shout EG *I heard a distant shout.*

yell EG *He let out a yell.*

callous ADJECTIVE
not concerned about other people
EG *his callous disregard for human life*

cold EG *What a cold, unfeeling woman she was.*

heartless EG *It was a heartless thing to do.*

indifferent EG *indifferent to the suffering of others*

insensitive EG *insensitive remarks*

> **WORD POWER**
> Synonyms
> hard-bitten
> hardhearted
> unsympathetic
> Antonym
> caring

● **calm** ADJECTIVE
not worried or excited
EG *Try to keep calm.*
collected EG *She was cool and collected during her interrogation.*
composed EG *a very composed, business-like woman*
cool EG *We have to keep a cool head in this situation.*
impassive EG *He remained impassive as his sentence was passed.*
relaxed EG *a relaxed manner*

> **WORD POWER**
> Synonyms
> imperturbable
> unemotional
> unruffled
> Antonym
> worried

❷ **calm** ADJECTIVE
still because there is no wind
EG *Tuesday was a fine, clear and calm day.*
balmy EG *balmy summer evenings*
mild EG *a mild winter climate*
still EG *The air was still.*
tranquil EG *a tranquil lake*

> **WORD POWER**
> Antonym
> rough

❸ **calm** NOUN
the state of being peaceful
EG *He liked the calm of the evening.*
calmness EG *an aura of calmness*
peace EG *a wonderful feeling of peace*
peacefulness EG *the peacefulness of the gardens*
quiet EG *a quiet, relaxing holiday*
serenity EG *the peace and serenity of a tropical sunset*
stillness EG *the stillness of the summer night*

❹ **calm** VERB
to make less upset or excited
EG *We were trying to calm him.*
quieten EG *trying to quieten the restless horses*
relax EG *This music is supposed to relax you.*
soothe EG *I think a bath may soothe me.*

> **WORD POWER**
> Synonyms
> mollify
> placate

campaign NOUN
actions planned to get a certain result
EG *a campaign to educate people*
crusade EG *the crusade for human rights*
movement EG *the human rights movement*
operation EG *a full-scale military operation*
push EG *an all-out push to promote the show*

● **cancel** VERB
to stop something from happening
EG *We're going to have to cancel our picnic.*
abandon EG *He had to abandon his holiday plans.*
call off EG *The union has called off the strike.*

❷ **cancel** VERB
to stop something from being valid
EG *They were forced to cancel their contract.*
annul EG *The marriage was annulled.*
quash EG *His jail sentence was quashed when new evidence came to light.*
repeal EG *The new law was repealed within the year.*
revoke EG *His licence was immediately revoked.*

> **WORD POWER**
> Synonyms
> abrogate
> countermand

A
B
C
D
E
F
G
H
I
J
K
L
M
N
O
P
Q
R
S
T
U
V
W
X
Y
Z

A
B
C
D
E
F
G
H
I
J
K
L
M
N
O
P
Q
R
S
T
U
V
W
X
Y
Z

rescind

candidate NOUN
a person being considered for a position
EG *a candidate for the presidency*
applicant EG *one of thirty applicants for the manager's post*
competitor EG *several competitors for the contract*
contender EG *a strong contender for the chairmanship*

> *WORD POWER*
> Synonyms
> nominee
> possibility
> runner

capable ADJECTIVE
able to do something well
EG *a capable leader*
able EG *a very able businessman*
accomplished EG *an accomplished painter*
adept EG *an adept diplomat*
competent EG *a competent and careful driver*
efficient EG *efficient administration*
proficient EG *proficient with computers*
skilful EG *the country's most skilful politician*

> *WORD POWER*
> Antonym
> incompetent

❶ capture VERB
to take prisoner
EG *He was captured by rebels.*
apprehend EG *Police have not yet apprehended the killer.*
arrest EG *Seven people were arrested.*
catch EG *The thief was caught and the money was returned.*
seize EG *seized by armed police*
take EG *An army unit took the town.*

> *WORD POWER*

Antonym
release

❷ capture NOUN
the act of capturing
EG *He evaded capture for eight years*
arrest EG *Police made two arrests.*
seizure EG *the seizure of territory*
taking EG *the taking of hostages*
trapping EG *The trapping of these animals is illegal.*

car NOUN
a vehicle for carrying a few people
EG *I finally left the car at the garage*
automobile AMERICAN OR FORMAL EG *the Japanese automobile manufacturer, Nissan*
motor EG *Patricia's new motor*
vehicle EG *She managed to scramble out of the vehicle.*

❶ care VERB
to be concerned about something
EG *a company that cares about the environment*
be bothered EG *I am not bothered what others think about me.*
be concerned EG *We are concerned about the problem.*
be interested EG *He's not interested in what anyone else says.*
mind EG *I do not mind who wins.*

❷ care NOUN
something that causes you to worry
EG *without a care in the world*
anxiety EG *anxieties about money*
concern EG *Their main concern is unemployment.*
stress EG *the stresses of modern life*
trouble EG *She has had her share of troubles.*
woe EG *They blame the government for all their woes.*
worry EG *My biggest worry is how I will cope on my own.*

> *WORD POWER*
> Synonyms

tribulation
vexation

sloppy INFORMAL EG *sloppy work*

> *WORD POWER*
> Synonyms
> cavalier
> lackadaisical
> slapdash
> slipshod
> Antonym
> careful

❸ care NOUN
close attention when doing
something
EG *We took great care in choosing a
location.*
attention EG *medical attention*
caution EG *Proceed with caution.*
pains EG *She takes great pains with
her appearance.*

> *WORD POWER*
> Synonyms
> circumspection
> forethought

❷ careless ADJECTIVE
relaxed and unconcerned
EG *careless laughter*
casual EG *a casual remark*
nonchalant EG *a nonchalant
attitude*
offhand EG *his usual offhand way*

❶ careful ADJECTIVE
acting with care
EG *Be careful what you say to him.*
cautious EG *a cautious approach*
prudent EG *prudent management*

> *WORD POWER*
> Synonyms
> chary
> circumspect
> punctilious
> Antonym
> careless

carry VERB
to hold and take something
somewhere
EG *He was carrying a briefcase.*
bear EG *He arrived bearing gifts.*
convey FORMAL EG *The minibus
conveyed us to the station.*
lug EG *lugging boxes of books
around*
take EG *Don't forget to take your
camera.*
transport EG *goods being
transported abroad*

❷ careful ADJECTIVE
complete and well done
EG *It needs careful planning.*
meticulous EG *meticulous
attention to detail*
painstaking EG *a painstaking
search*
precise EG *precise instructions*
thorough EG *a thorough
examination*

> *WORD POWER*
> Antonym
> careless

carry out VERB
to do and complete something
EG *the surgeon who carried out the
operation*
accomplish EG *the desire to
accomplish a task*
achieve EG *We have achieved our
objective.*
fulfil EG *to fulfil a promise*
perform EG *people who have
performed acts of bravery*

> *WORD POWER*
> Synonyms
> execute
> implement

❶ careless ADJECTIVE
not taking enough care
EG *careless driving*
irresponsible EG *an irresponsible
attitude*
neglectful EG *neglectful parents*

carve VERB
to make something by cutting
EG *He carves his figures from pine.*

A
B
C
D
E
F
G
H
I
J
K
L
M
N
O
P
Q
R
S
T
U
V
W
X
Y
Z

chisel EG *the mason chiselling his stone*

cut EG *a figure cut from marble*

engrave EG *an engraved crystal goblet*

inscribe EG *the words inscribed on his monument*

sculpt EG *a sculpted clay figure*

> **WORD POWER**
> Synonyms
> hew
> whittle

❶ case NOUN
a particular situation or example
EG *a case of mistaken identity*

example EG *an example of what can go wrong*

illustration EG *a clear illustration of this point*

instance EG *a serious instance of corruption*

occasion EG *the last occasion on which he appeared*

occurrence EG *a frequent occurrence*

❷ case NOUN
a container for holding something
EG *a spectacle case*

box EG *a chocolate box*

container EG *a huge plastic container*

> **WORD POWER**
> Synonyms
> holder
> receptacle

❸ case NOUN
a trial or inquiry
EG *a libel case*

action EG *a civil action for damages*

lawsuit EG *the rising cost of defending a lawsuit*

proceedings EG *criminal proceedings against the former leader*

trial EG *Police lied at the trial.*

❶ casual ADJECTIVE

happening by chance
EG *a casual remark*

accidental EG *a verdict of accidental death*

chance EG *a chance meeting*

incidental EG *an incidental effect*

> **WORD POWER**
> Synonyms
> fortuitous
> serendipitous
> unintentional
> unpremeditated
> Antonym
> deliberate

❷ casual ADJECTIVE
showing no concern or interest
EG *a casual look over his shoulder*

careless EG *careless remarks*

cursory EG *a cursory glance*

nonchalant EG *his nonchalant attitude to life*

offhand EG *a deceptively offhand style*

relaxed EG *a relaxed manner*

> **WORD POWER**
> Synonyms
> blasé
> insouciant
> lackadaisical
> perfunctory
> Antonym
> concerned

cat NOUN
a small animal kept as a pet
EG *sharing his flat with four cats*

feline EG *Even the most cuddly feline has claws.*

kitty EG *a kitty stuck up a tree*

moggy *or* **moggie** BRITISH AND NEW ZEALAND SLANG EG *a grey, long-haired moggy*

pussy, puss, *or* **pussycat** INFORMAL EG *a fluffy little pussycat*

❶ catch VERB
to capture something
EG *another technique for catching criminals*

apprehend EG *the force necessary*

to apprehend a suspect
arrest EG *Police arrested the gunman.*
capture EG *Poachers had captured a gorilla.*
snare EG *He'd snared a rabbit.*
trap EG *Their aim was to trap drug-dealers.*

❷ catch NOUN
a device that fastens something
EG *windows fitted with safety catches*
bolt EG *the sound of a bolt being slid open*
clasp EG *the clasp of her handbag*
clip EG *She took the clip out of her hair.*
latch EG *You left the latch off the gate.*

❸ catch NOUN
a hidden difficulty
EG *The catch is that you have to fly via Paris.*
disadvantage EG *The disadvantage is that this plant needs frequent watering.*
drawback EG *The flat's only drawback was its size.*
snag EG *The snag is that you have to pay in advance.*

> **WORD POWER**
> Synonyms
> fly in the ointment
> stumbling block

❶ cause NOUN
what makes something happen
EG *the most common cause of back pain*
origin EG *the origin of the present war*
root EG *We need to get to the root of the problem.*
source EG *the source of the leak*

❷ cause NOUN
an aim supported by a group
EG *dedication to the cause of peace*
aim EG *political aims*
ideal EG *socialist ideals*

movement EG *the women's movement*

❸ cause NOUN
the reason for something
EG *They gave us no cause to believe that.*
basis EG *There is no basis for this assumption.*
grounds EG *discrimination on the grounds of race or religion*
justification EG *There was no justification for what he was doing.*
motivation EG *the motivation for his actions*
motive EG *Police have ruled out robbery as a motive.*
reason EG *You have every reason to be upset.*

❹ cause VERB
to make something happen
EG *This may cause delays.*
bring about EG *We must try to bring about a better world.*
create EG *The scheme may create even more confusion.*
generate EG *the excitement generated by this film*
produce EG *His comments produced a furious response.*
provoke EG *a move that has provoked a storm of protest*

> **WORD POWER**
> Synonyms
> effect
> engender
> give rise to
> lead to
> result in

cautious ADJECTIVE
acting very carefully to avoid danger
EG *a cautious approach*
careful EG *Be extremely careful when on holiday abroad.*
guarded EG *a guarded response*
tentative EG *a tentative approach*
wary EG *small firms remain wary of committing themselves to debt*

A
B
C
D
E
F
G
H
I
J
K
L
M
N
O
P
Q
R
S
T
U
V
W
X
Y
Z

WORD POWER
Antonym
daring

celebration NOUN
an event in honour of a special occasion
EG *his eightieth birthday celebrations*
festival EG *a religious festival*
festivity EG *the wedding festivities*
gala EG *the Olympics' opening gala*
party EG *a housewarming party*

WORD POWER
Synonyms
merrymaking
revelry

❶ centre NOUN
the middle of something
EG *the centre of the room*
core EG *the earth's core*
focus EG *Her children are the main focus of her life.*
heart EG *the heart of the problem*
hub EG *The kitchen is the hub of most households.*
middle EG *in the middle of the back row*

WORD POWER
Antonym
edge

❷ centre VERB
to have as the main subject
EG *All his thoughts were centred around himself.*
concentrate EG *Scientists are concentrating their efforts on finding a cure.*
focus EG *Attention is likely to focus on sales growth.*
revolve EG *Since childhood, her life has revolved around tennis.*

❶ ceremony NOUN
formal actions done for a special occasion
EG *his recent coronation ceremony*
observance EG *a Memorial Day observance*
pomp EG *His departure was*

celebrated with suitable pomp.
rite EG *a fertility rite*
ritual EG *a Summer Solstice ritual*
service EG *The President attended the morning service.*

❷ ceremony NOUN
formal and polite behaviour
EG *He hung up without ceremony.*
decorum EG *a responsibility to behave with decorum*
etiquette EG *the rules of diplomatic etiquette*
formality EG *his lack of stuffy formality*
niceties EG *social niceties*
protocol EG *minor breaches of protocol*

❶ challenge NOUN
a suggestion to try something
EG *They issued a challenge to their rivals.*
dare EG *He'd do almost anything for a dare.*
invite EG *We were invited to have a try at the limbo.*

❷ challenge VERB
to give someone a challenge
EG *He challenged his rival to a duel.*
dare EG *I dare you to ask him.*
defy EG *He looked at me as if he was defying me to argue.*

❸ challenge VERB
to question the truth or value of something
EG *challenging the authority of the state*
dispute EG *He disputed the charge.*
question EG *questioning the jury's verdict*

❶ chance NOUN
a possibility of something happening
EG *a good chance of success*
likelihood EG *the likelihood of infection*
odds EG *What are the odds of that happening?*
possibility EG *the possibility of*

pay cuts
probability EG *a probability of victory*
prospect EG *There is little prospect of peace.*

② chance NOUN
an opportunity to do something
EG *He didn't give me a chance to explain.*
occasion EG *I had no occasion to speak to her that day.*
opening EG *an opening for finding a peaceful outcome to the conflict*
opportunity EG *an opportunity to go abroad to study*
time EG *There was no time to think.*

③ chance NOUN
the way things happen without being planned
EG *events which were merely the result of chance*
accident EG *a strange accident of fate*
coincidence EG *It was no coincidence that she arrived just then.*
fortune EG *a change of fortune*
luck EG *His injury was just bad luck.*

① change NOUN
an alteration in something
EG *a change in her attitude*
alteration EG *some alterations in your diet*
difference EG *a noticeable difference in his behaviour*
modification EG *Some minor modifications were required.*
transformation EG *the transformation of a wilderness into a garden*

WORD POWER
Synonyms
metamorphosis
mutation
transition
transmutation
---

② change VERB

to make or become different
EG *Her views have changed since her husband's death.*
alter EG *There is no prospect of the decision being altered.*
convert EG *a plan to convert his spare room into an office*
moderate EG *They persuaded him to moderate his views.*
modify EG *He refused to modify his behaviour.*
reform EG *his plans to reform the economy*
transform EG *The landscape has been transformed.*

WORD POWER
Synonyms
metamorphose
mutate
transmute
---

③ change VERB
to exchange one thing for another
EG *Can I change this sweater for one a size bigger?*
barter EG *bartering wheat for cotton and timber*
exchange EG *the chance to sell back or exchange goods*
interchange EG *Meat can be interchanged with pulses as a source of protein.*
replace EG *His smile was replaced by a frown.*
substitute EG *You can substitute honey for the sugar.*
swap EG *Let's swap places.*
trade EG *They traded land for goods and money.*

changeable ADJECTIVE
likely to change all the time
EG *changeable weather*
erratic EG *erratic driving*
fickle EG *Fashion is a fickle business.*
irregular EG *an irregular heartbeat*
unpredictable EG *unpredictable behaviour*
unstable EG *The political situation*

A B C D E F G H I J K L M N O P Q R S T U V W X Y Z

A
B
C
D
E
F
G
H
I
J
K
L
M
N
O
P
Q
R
S
T
U
V
W
X
Y
Z

is unstable.
variable EG *a variable rate of interest*
volatile EG *a volatile atmosphere*

> ### WORD POWER
> Synonyms
> mercurial
> mutable
> protean
> Antonym
> constant

❶ character NOUN
the qualities of a person
EG *He has a dark side to his character.*
make-up EG *Determination has always been a part of his make-up.*
nature EG *a sunny nature*
personality EG *an outgoing personality*
temperament EG *his impulsive temperament*

> ### WORD POWER
> Synonyms
> disposition
> quality
> temper

❷ character NOUN
an honourable nature
EG *She showed real character in her attempt to win over the crowd.*
honour EG *He has acted with honour.*
integrity EG *a man of integrity*
strength EG *He had the strength to turn down the offer.*

❶ characteristic NOUN
a typical quality
EG *His chief characteristic is honesty.*
attribute EG *a normal attribute of human behaviour*
feature EG *a feature of the local culture*
property EG *This liquid has many unique properties.*
quality EG *leadership qualities*
trait EG *personality traits*

> ### WORD POWER
> Synonyms
> idiosyncrasy
> peculiarity
> quirk

❷ characteristic ADJECTIVE
typical of a person or thing
EG *He responded with characteristic generosity.*
distinctive EG *a distinctive voice*
distinguishing EG *no distinguishing marks*
typical EG *his typical British modesty*

> ### WORD POWER
> Synonyms
> idiosyncratic
> peculiar
> singular
> symptomatic
> Antonym
> uncharacteristic

❶ charm NOUN
an attractive quality
EG *a man of great personal charm*
allure EG *the allure of Egypt*
appeal EG *confident of his appeal to women*
attraction EG *the attractions of living by the sea*
fascination EG *It is hard to explain the fascination of this place.*
magnetism EG *a man of enormous magnetism*

❷ charm VERB
to use charm to please someone
EG *He charmed his 2,000-strong audience.*
bewitch EG *bewitched by her beauty*
captivate EG *The crowd was captivated by her honesty.*
delight EG *a style of music that has delighted audiences*
entrance EG *entranced by her smile*

> ### WORD POWER
> Synonyms

beguile
enchant
enrapture

chase VERB
to try to catch someone or
something
EG *She chased the thief for a*
hundred yards.
hunt EG *He fled to Portugal after*
being hunted by police.
pursue EG *She pursued the man*
who had snatched her bag.

chase VERB
to force to go somewhere
EG *Angry demonstrators chased him*
away.
drive EG *The troops drove the rebels*
into the jungle.
hound EG *He was hounded out of*
his job.

chat NOUN
a friendly talk
EG *We sat around and had a chat.*
conversation EG *a telephone*
conversation
gossip EG *Don't you enjoy a good*
gossip?
natter INFORMAL EG *Let's get*
together for a natter some time.
talk EG *We will have a talk about*
it later.

chat VERB
to talk in a friendly way
EG *He was chatting to his father.*
gossip EG *We gossiped into the*
night.
natter INFORMAL EG *His mother*
would natter to anyone.
talk EG *She's very easy to talk to.*

cheap ADJECTIVE
costing very little
EG *Cheap flights are available.*
bargain EG *selling at bargain prices*

economical EG *These cars are very*
economical to run.
inexpensive EG *an inexpensive*
wine
reasonable EG *His fees were quite*
reasonable.

cheap ADJECTIVE
inexpensive but of poor quality
EG *a suit made of some cheap*
material
inferior EG *an inferior imitation*
second-rate EG *second-rate*
equipment
tawdry EG *tawdry souvenirs*

cheat VERB
to get something from someone
dishonestly
EG *the people he cheated out of their*
life savings
con INFORMAL EG *He conned his way*
into a job.
deceive EG *Investors were deceived*
by a scam.
defraud EG *charges of conspiracy*
to defraud the government
dupe EG *Stamp collectors were*
duped into buying fakes.
fleece EG *He fleeced her out of*
thousands of pounds.
rip off SLANG EG *ticket touts ripping*
off soccer fans
swindle EG *two executives who*
swindled their employer

check VERB
to examine something
EG *Check all the details first.*
check out INFORMAL EG *Check out*

A
B
C
D
E
F
G
H
I
J
K
L
M
N
O
P
Q
R
S
T
U
V
W
X
Y
Z

65

A
B
C
D
E
F
G
H
I
J
K
L
M
N
O
P
Q
R
S
T
U
V
W
X
Y
Z

the financial figures.
examine EG *He examined her passport and stamped it.*
inspect EG *the right to inspect company files*
test EG *The drug must be tested in clinical trials.*

> ### WORD POWER
> Synonyms
> inquire into
> look over
> scrutinize

❷ **check** VERB
to reduce or stop something
EG *a policy to check fast population growth*
control EG *a measure to control illegal mining*
curb EG *reforms which aim to curb spending*
halt EG *an attempt to halt the spread of the disease*
inhibit EG *factors which inhibit growth*
restrain EG *the need to restrain wage rises*
stop EG *measures to stop the trade in ivory*

❸ **check** NOUN
an examination
EG *a thorough check of the equipment*
examination EG *a medical examination*
inspection EG *a routine inspection of the premises*
test EG *a test for cancer*

cheeky ADJECTIVE
rude and disrespectful
EG *cheeky teenagers*
impertinent EG *an impertinent question*
impudent EG *his rude and impudent behaviour*
insolent EG *a defiant, almost insolent look*
rude EG *She was often rude to her mother.*

> ### WORD POWER
> Antonym
> polite

cheerful ADJECTIVE
in a happy mood
EG *She was very cheerful despite her illness.*
bright EG *"May I help you?" said a bright voice.*
buoyant EG *in a buoyant mood*
cheery EG *a cheery nature*
happy EG *a confident, happy child*
jaunty EG *a jaunty tune*
jolly EG *a jolly, easy-going man*
light-hearted EG *They were light-hearted and enjoyed life.*
merry EG *a burst of merry laughter*

> ### WORD POWER
> Antonym
> miserable

chew VERB
to break food up with the teeth
EG *Eat slowly and chew your food properly.*
crunch EG *She crunched the ice cube loudly.*
gnaw EG *He sat and gnawed at an apple.*
munch EG *Sheep were munching the leaves.*

> ### WORD POWER
> Synonyms
> champ
> chomp
> masticate

child NOUN
a young person
EG *I lived in France as a child.*
ankle-biter AUSTRALIAN AND NEW ZEALAND SLANG EG *I knew him when he was just an ankle-biter.*
baby EG *She took care of me when I was a baby.*
bairn SCOTTISH EG *a two-year-old bairn*
infant EG *young mums with infants in prams*

A
B
C
D
E
F
G
H
I
J
K
L
M
N
O
P
Q
R
S
T
U
V
W
X
Y
Z

juvenile EG *a prison for juveniles*
kid INFORMAL EG *They've got three kids.*
minor EG *charged with selling cigarettes to minors*
offspring EG *parents choosing shoes for their offspring*
toddler EG *a toddler in a pushchair*
tot EG *The tot was too young to know what was happening.*
youngster EG *I was only a youngster in 1965.*

> **WORD POWER**
> Antonym
> adult

childish ADJECTIVE
immature and foolish
EG *I don't have time for this childish behaviour.*
immature EG *She is emotionally immature.*
infantile EG *infantile jokes*
juvenile EG *juvenile behaviour*
puerile EG *a puerile sense of humour*

> **WORD POWER**
> Antonym
> mature

choice NOUN
a range of things to choose from
EG *available in a choice of colours*
range EG *a range of sun-care products*
selection EG *an interesting selection of recipes*
variety EG *a variety of candidates from which to choose*

choice NOUN
the power to choose
EG *They had little choice in the matter.*
alternative EG *He said he could not see any alternative.*
option EG *He was given the option of going to jail or paying a fine.*
say EG *We don't have a say in the company's decisions.*

choose VERB
to decide to have or do something
EG *a number of foods to choose from*
opt for EG *He opted for early retirement.*
pick EG *She was picked for the debating team.*
select EG *She paused to select another cookie from the box.*
take EG *She took the option he offered her.*

> **WORD POWER**
> Synonyms
> elect
> fix on
> settle on

chop VERB
to cut down or into pieces
EG *I heard him chopping wood in the yard.*
cut EG *Cut the vegetables up.*
fell EG *43,000 square miles of tropical forest are felled each year.*
hack EG *They hacked away at the undergrowth.*
lop EG *Somebody had lopped the heads off our tulips.*

> **WORD POWER**
> Synonyms
> cleave
> hew

circulate VERB
to pass around
EG *He circulated rumours about everyone.*
distribute EG *distributing leaflets*
propagate EG *They propagated their political ideas.*
spread EG *spreading malicious gossip*

> **WORD POWER**
> Synonyms
> disseminate
> promulgate

city NOUN
a large town

67

EG *the city of London*
metropolis EG *a busy metropolis*
town EG *the oldest town in Europe*

> ### WORD POWER
> Synonyms
> conurbation
> municipality

civilized ADJECTIVE
having an advanced society
EG *a highly civilized country*
cultured EG *a mature and cultured nation*
enlightened EG *this enlightened century*

❶ claim VERB
to say something is the case
EG *He claims to have lived here all his life.*
allege EG *He is alleged to have killed a man.*
assert EG *The defendants continued to assert their innocence.*
hold EG *She holds that these measures are unnecessary.*
insist EG *They insisted that they had no money.*
maintain EG *I still maintain that I am not guilty.*
profess EG *She professed to hate her nickname.*

❷ claim NOUN
a statement that something is the case
EG *He rejected claims that he had taken bribes.*
allegation EG *allegations of theft*
assertion EG *his assertion that he did not plan to remarry*

> ### WORD POWER
> Synonyms
> pretension
> protestation

❶ class NOUN
a group of a particular type
EG *a new class of vehicle*
category EG *different categories of taxpayer*

genre EG *films of the horror genre*
grade EG *the lowest grade of staff*
group EG *a plan to help people in this group*
kind EG *the biggest prize of its kind in the world*
set EG *The fashionable set all go to this club.*
sort EG *several articles of this sort*
type EG *various types of vegetable*

❷ class VERB
to regard as being in a particular group
EG *They are officially classed as visitors.*
categorize EG *His films are hard to categorize.*
classify EG *Carrots are also classified as a fruit.*
designate EG *The house is designated as a national monument.*
grade EG *This ski-run is graded as easy.*
rank EG *She is ranked in the world's top 50 players.*
rate EG *He rates the film highly.*

classify VERB
to arrange similar things in groups
EG *We can classify the differences into three groups.*
arrange EG *Arrange the books in neat piles.*
categorize EG *This film is hard to categorize.*
grade EG *musical pieces graded according to difficulty*
rank EG *He was ranked among Britain's best-known millionaires.*
sort EG *sorting the material into folders*

> ### WORD POWER
> Synonyms
> pigeonhole
> systematize
> tabulate

❶ clean ADJECTIVE
free from dirt or marks

EG *clean shoes*

immaculate EG *immaculate white flannels*

impeccable EG *dressed in an impeccable trouser suit*

laundered EG *freshly laundered shirts*

spotless EG *The kitchen was spotless.*

washed EG *newly washed hair*

> *WORD POWER*
> Antonym
> dirty

clean ADJECTIVE

free from germs or infection
EG *a lack of clean water and sanitation*

antiseptic EG *an antiseptic hospital room*

hygienic EG *a hygienic kitchen*

purified EG *Only purified water is used.*

sterilized EG *sterilized milk*

uncontaminated EG *uncontaminated air*

unpolluted EG *unpolluted beaches*

> *WORD POWER*
> Antonym
> contaminated

clean VERB

to remove dirt from
EG *She cleaned the house from top to bottom.*

cleanse EG *a lotion to cleanse the skin*

dust EG *I vacuumed, dusted and polished the living room.*

scour EG *He scoured the sink.*

scrub EG *I started to scrub off the dirt.*

sponge EG *Sponge your face and body.*

swab EG *an old man swabbing the floor*

wash EG *He got a job washing dishes in a restaurant.*

wipe EG *He wiped the sweat from his face.*

> *WORD POWER*
> Antonym
> soil

❶ **clear** ADJECTIVE

easy to see or understand
EG *He made it clear he did not want to talk.*

apparent EG *There is no apparent reason for the crime.*

blatant EG *a blatant piece of cheating*

conspicuous EG *one conspicuous difference*

definite EG *a definite advantage*

evident EG *He ate with evident enjoyment.*

explicit EG *He was very explicit about his intentions.*

obvious EG *There are obvious dangers.*

plain EG *The results are plain to see.*

> *WORD POWER*
> Synonyms
> incontrovertible
> manifest
> palpable
> patent
> unequivocal

❷ **clear** ADJECTIVE

easy to see through
EG *a clear liquid*

crystalline EG *crystalline green waters*

glassy EG *The water was a deep glassy blue.*

translucent EG *translucent stones*

transparent EG *transparent glass walls*

> *WORD POWER*
> Synonyms
> limpid
> pellucid
> see-through
> Antonym
> cloudy

❸ **clear** VERB

to prove someone is not guilty

69

A
B
C
D
E
F
G
H
I
J
K
L
M
N
O
P
Q
R
S
T
U
V
W
X
Y
Z

EG *She was cleared of murder.*
absolve EG *He was absolved of all charges.*
acquit EG *acquitted of disorderly conduct*

> **WORD POWER**
> Antonym
> convict

clever ADJECTIVE
very intelligent
EG *My sister was always a lot cleverer than I was.*
brainy INFORMAL EG *I don't consider myself to be especially brainy.*
bright EG *an exceptionally bright child*
intelligent EG *a lively and intelligent woman*
shrewd EG *a shrewd businessman*
smart EG *a very smart move*

> **WORD POWER**
> Synonyms
> astute
> quick-witted
> sagacious
> Antonym
> stupid

climb VERB
to move upwards over something
EG *Climbing the first hill took half an hour.*
ascend EG *He ascended the ladder into the loft.*
clamber EG *They clambered up the stone walls.*
mount EG *He mounted the steps.*
scale EG *the first British woman to scale Everest*

❶ **close** VERB
to shut something
EG *Close the gate behind you.*
secure EG *The shed was secured by a padlock.*
shut EG *Someone had forgotten to shut the door.*

> **WORD POWER**

> Antonym
> open

❷ **close** VERB
to block so that nothing can pass
EG *All the roads out are closed.*
bar EG *Protesters barred the way to his car.*
block EG *The road was blocked by debris.*
obstruct EG *buskers obstructing the pavement*
seal EG *Soldiers had sealed the border.*

❸ **close** ADJECTIVE
near to something
EG *a restaurant close to their home*
adjacent EG *offices adjacent to the museum*
adjoining EG *a field adjoining the house*
near EG *My office is quite near.*
nearby EG *a nearby village*
neighbouring EG *leaders of neighbouring countries*

> **WORD POWER**
> Synonyms
> at hand
> nigh
> Antonym
> distant

❹ **close** ADJECTIVE
friendly and loving
EG *We became close friends.*
attached EG *She's very attached to her family.*
dear EG *a dear friend of mine*
devoted EG *a devoted couple*
intimate EG *an intimate relationship*
loving EG *They have a loving marriage.*

cloth NOUN
woven or knitted fabric
EG *a piece of red cloth*
fabric EG *waterproof fabric*
material EG *This material shrinks badly.*

textiles EG *a trader in clothes and textiles*

clothes PLURAL NOUN
the things people wear
EG *She spends all her money on clothes.*
attire EG *formal attire*
clothing EG *men's clothing*
costume EG *national costume*
dress EG *traditional dress*
garments EG *winter garments*
gear INFORMAL EG *trendy gear*
outfit EG *a stunning scarlet outfit*
wardrobe EG *next summer's wardrobe*
wear EG *evening wear*

> *WORD POWER*
> Synonyms
> apparel
> garb
> raiment

cloud NOUN
a mass of vapour or smoke
EG *The sky was dark with clouds.*
billow EG *Smoke billowed from the engine.*
fog EG *a fog of cigar smoke*
haze EG *a haze of exhaust fumes*
mist EG *The valley was wrapped in thick mist.*
vapour EG *warm vapour rising from the ground*

cloud VERB
to make something confusing
EG *Anger has clouded his judgement.*
confuse EG *You're just confusing the matter by bringing politics into it.*
distort EG *a distorted memory*
muddle EG *The question muddles up two separate issues.*

cloudy ADJECTIVE
full of clouds
EG *a cloudy sky*
dull EG *It's always dull and wet here.*
gloomy EG *gloomy weather*
leaden EG *leaden skies*

overcast EG *a damp, overcast morning*

> *WORD POWER*
> Antonym
> clear

❷ cloudy ADJECTIVE
difficult to see through
EG *a glass of cloudy liquid*
muddy EG *a muddy duck pond*
murky EG *murky waters*
opaque EG *an opaque glass jar*

> *WORD POWER*
> Antonym
> clear

❶ club NOUN
an organization for people with a special interest
EG *a swimming club*
association EG *the Women's Tennis Association*
circle EG *a local painting circle*
group EG *an environmental group*
guild EG *the Screen Writers' Guild*
society EG *a historical society*
union EG *the International Astronomical Union*

❷ club NOUN
a heavy stick
EG *armed with knives and clubs*
bat EG *a baseball bat*
stick EG *a crowd carrying sticks and stones*
truncheon EG *a policeman's truncheon*

❸ club VERB
to hit with a heavy object
EG *Two thugs clubbed him with baseball bats.*
bash EG *They bashed his head with a spade.*
batter EG *battered to death*
beat EG *beaten with rifle butts*
bludgeon EG *bludgeoning his wife with a hammer*

clumsiness NOUN
awkwardness of movement
EG *The accident was entirely the*

result of his own clumsiness.

awkwardness EG *They moved with the awkwardness of mechanical dolls.*

ungainliness EG *his physical ungainliness*

clumsy ADJECTIVE
moving awkwardly
EG *He is big and clumsy in his movements.*

awkward EG *an awkward gesture*

gauche EG *He makes me feel stupid and gauche.*

lumbering EG *a big, lumbering man*

uncoordinated EG *an uncoordinated dancer*

ungainly EG *As a youth he was lanky and ungainly.*

> **WORD POWER**
> Synonyms
> accident-prone
> bumbling
> gawky
> maladroit
> Antonym
> graceful

coast NOUN
the land next to the sea
EG *a holiday by the coast*

beach EG *a beautiful sandy beach*

border EG *the border of the Black Sea*

coastline EG *the stunning Caribbean coastline*

seaside EG *a day at the seaside*

shore EG *a bleak and rocky shore*

strand EG *boats fishing from the strand*

coat NOUN
an animal's fur or hair
EG *She gave the dog's coat a brush.*

fleece EG *a blanket of lamb's fleece*

fur EG *a kitten with black fur*

hair EG *He's allergic to cat hair.*

hide EG *rhino hide*

pelt EG *a wolf pelt*

skin EG *convicted of attempting to sell the skin of a Siberian tiger*

wool EG *Lanolin comes from sheep's wool.*

coating NOUN
a layer of something
EG *a thin coating of ice*

coat EG *a coat of paint*

covering EG *a covering of dust*

layer EG *a layer of dead leaves*

coax VERB
to persuade gently
EG *We coaxed her into coming with us.*

cajole EG *Her sister cajoled her into playing.*

persuade EG *My husband persuaded me to come.*

talk into EG *They've talked him into getting a new car.*

> **WORD POWER**
> Synonyms
> inveigle
> prevail upon
> wheedle

coil VERB
to wind in loops
EG *a coiled spring*

curl EG *dark, curling hair*

loop EG *A rope was looped between his hands.*

spiral EG *vines spiralling up towards the roof*

twine EG *This lily produces twining stems.*

twist EG *She twisted her hair into a bun.*

wind EG *a rope wound round her waist*

❶ cold ADJECTIVE
having a low temperature
EG *the coldest winter for ten years*

arctic EG *arctic conditions*

biting EG *a biting wind*

bitter EG *driven inside by the bitter cold*

bleak EG *The weather can be bleak on the coast.*

chilly EG *It's chilly for June.*

freezing EG *This house is freezing.*
icy EG *the icy north wind*
raw EG *a raw December morning*
wintry EG *wintry showers*

> *WORD POWER*
> Antonym
> hot

cold ADJECTIVE
not showing affection
EG *a cold, unfeeling woman*
aloof EG *He seemed aloof and detached.*
distant EG *She was polite but distant.*
frigid EG *a frigid smile*
lukewarm EG *a lukewarm response*
reserved EG *emotionally reserved*
stony EG *He gave me a stony look.*

> *WORD POWER*
> Synonyms
> standoffish
> undemonstrative
> Antonym
> warm

collapse VERB
to fall down
EG *The whole building is about to collapse.*
fall down EG *The ceiling fell down.*
give way EG *The bridge gave way beneath him.*

collapse VERB
to fail
EG *50,000 small businesses collapsed last year.*
fail EG *His hotel business has failed.*
fold EG *We were laid off when the company folded.*
founder EG *a foundering radio station*

collapse NOUN
the failure of something
EG *the collapse of his marriage*
downfall EG *the downfall of the government*
failure EG *the failure of his business empire*

colleague NOUN
a person someone works with
EG *I'll have to consult my colleagues.*
associate EG *business associates*
fellow worker EG *She started going out with a fellow worker.*
partner EG *her business partner*
workmate EG *the nickname his workmates gave him*

collect VERB
to gather together
EG *collecting signatures for a petition*
accumulate EG *Most children enjoy accumulating knowledge.*
assemble EG *trying to assemble a team*
gather EG *gathering information*
raise EG *They've raised over £100 for charity.*

> *WORD POWER*
> Synonyms
> aggregate
> amass
> Antonym
> scatter

collection NOUN
a group of things collected together
EG *a collection of paintings*
assortment EG *an assortment of pets*
group EG *a group of songs*
store EG *a vast store of knowledge*

colloquial ADJECTIVE
used in conversation
EG *a colloquial expression*
conversational EG *a conversational style*
everyday EG *He used plain, everyday English.*
informal EG *an informal expression*

> *WORD POWER*
> Synonyms
> demotic
> idiomatic
> vernacular

A B C D E F G H I J K L M N O P Q R S T U V W X Y Z

73

A B C D E F G H I J K L M N O P Q R S T U V W X Y Z

❶ colony NOUN
a country controlled by another country
EG *an American colony*
dependency EG *the tiny British dependency of Montserrat*
dominion EG *The Republic is a dominion of Brazil.*
territory EG *territories under Israeli control*

❷ colony NOUN
a group of settlers in a place
EG *a colony of Scots*
community EG *the Sikh community in Britain*
outpost EG *a remote outpost*
settlement EG *a Muslim settlement*

❶ colour NOUN
a shade or hue
EG *Her favourite colour is blue.*
hue EG *delicate pastel hues*
pigmentation EG *skin pigmentation*
shade EG *walls painted in two shades of green*
tint EG *a distinct orange tint*

❷ colour NOUN
a substance used to give colour
EG *food colour*
dye EG *hair dye*
paint EG *a pot of red paint*
pigment EG *a layer of blue pigment*

❸ colour VERB
to give something a colour
EG *Many women colour their hair.*
dye EG *Only dye clean garments.*
paint EG *She paints her toenails red.*
stain EG *Some foods can stain the teeth.*
tint EG *tinted glass*

❹ colour VERB
to affect the way you think
EG *Her upbringing has coloured her opinion of marriage.*
bias EG *a biased opinion*
distort EG *The shock of the accident distorted my judgement.*

prejudice EG *Criticism will prejudice the Government's decision*
slant EG *deliberately slanted news coverage*

❶ colourful ADJECTIVE
full of colour
EG *colourful clothes*
bright EG *a bright green dress*
brilliant EG *The garden has burst into brilliant flower.*
intense EG *an intense shade of blu*
jazzy INFORMAL EG *a jazzy tie*
rich EG *a rich blue glass bowl*
vibrant EG *vibrant orange shades*
vivid EG *vivid hues*

> ***WORD POWER***
> Synonyms
> kaleidoscopic
> multicoloured
> psychedelic
> Antonym
> dull

❷ colourful ADJECTIVE
interesting or exciting
EG *a colourful character*
graphic EG *a graphic account of his career*
interesting EG *He has had an interesting life.*
lively EG *a lively imagination*
rich EG *the rich history of the islan*
vivid EG *a vivid description*

> ***WORD POWER***
> Antonym
> dull

combination NOUN
a mixture of things
EG *a combination of charm and skill*
amalgamation EG *an amalgamation of two organizations*
blend EG *a blend of wine and spring water*
mix EG *a mix of fantasy and reality*
mixture EG *a mixture of horror, envy and awe*

> ***WORD POWER***
> Synonyms

amalgam
coalescence
composite
meld

combine VERB
to join or mix together
EG *trying to combine motherhood with work*
amalgamate EG *a plan to amalgamate the two parties*
blend EG *The band blends jazz and folk music.*
fuse EG *a performer who fuses magic and dance*
integrate EG *integrating various styles of art*
merge EG *The two countries have merged into one.*
mix EG *mixing business with pleasure*
unite EG *people uniting to fight racism*

WORD POWER
Synonyms
meld
synthesize
Antonym
separate

come VERB
to move or arrive somewhere
EG *Two men came into the room.*
appear EG *He appeared at about 9 o'clock.*
arrive EG *My brother has just arrived.*
enter EG *The class fell silent as the teacher entered.*
materialize EG *The car just materialized from nowhere.*
show up INFORMAL EG *He showed up over an hour late.*
turn up INFORMAL EG *I'll call you when she turns up.*

come VERB
to happen or take place
EG *Christmas only comes once a year.*
happen EG *Nothing ever happens*

on a Sunday.
occur EG *How did the accident occur?*
take place EG *The meeting never took place.*

❶ comfort NOUN
a state of ease
EG *He settled back in comfort.*
ease EG *a life of ease*
luxury EG *brought up in an atmosphere of luxury*
wellbeing EG *a wonderful sense of wellbeing*

❷ comfort NOUN
relief from worry or unhappiness
EG *Her words gave him some comfort.*
consolation EG *He knew he was right, but it was no consolation.*
help EG *Just talking to you has been a great help.*
relief EG *temporary relief from the pain*
satisfaction EG *At least I have the satisfaction of knowing I tried.*
support EG *His family were a great support to him.*

❸ comfort VERB
to give someone comfort
EG *trying to comfort the screaming child*
cheer EG *The thought did nothing to cheer him.*
console EG *"Never mind," he consoled me.*
reassure EG *He did his best to reassure her.*
soothe EG *She took him in his arms and soothed him.*

❶ comfortable ADJECTIVE
physically relaxing
EG *a comfortable chair*
cosy EG *a cosy living room*
easy EG *You've had an easy time of it.*
homely EG *a homely atmosphere*
relaxing EG *a relaxing holiday*
restful EG *a restful scene*

A
B
C
D
E
F
G
H
I
J
K
L
M
N
O
P
Q
R
S
T
U
V
W
X
Y
Z

A
B
C
D
E
F
G
H
I
J
K
L
M
N
O
P
Q
R
S
T
U
V
W
X
Y
Z

> **WORD POWER**
> Antonym
> uncomfortable

❷ **comfortable** ADJECTIVE
feeling at ease
EG *I don't feel comfortable around him.*
at ease EG *He is not at ease in female company.*
at home EG *We soon felt quite at home.*
contented EG *a contented life*
happy EG *I'm not very happy with that idea.*
relaxed EG *a relaxed attitude*

> **WORD POWER**
> Antonym
> uneasy

❶ **command** VERB
to order someone to do something
EG *She commanded me to lie down.*
bid EG *The soldiers bade us turn and go back.*
demand EG *They demanded that he leave.*
direct EG *His doctor has directed him to rest.*
order EG *He ordered his men to cease fire.*

> **WORD POWER**
> Synonyms
> charge
> enjoin

❷ **command** VERB
to be in charge of
EG *the general who commanded the UN troops*
control EG *He now controls the whole company.*
head EG *Who heads the firm?*
lead EG *He led the country between 1949 and 1984.*
manage EG *I manage a small team of workers.*
supervise EG *He supervised more than 400 volunteers.*

❸ **command** NOUN
an order to do something
EG *The execution was carried out at his command.*
bidding EG *They refused to leave at his bidding.*
decree EG *a presidential decree*
directive EG *a government directive*
injunction EG *He left her with the injunction to go to sleep.*
instruction EG *They were just following instructions.*
order EG *I don't take orders from you.*

> **WORD POWER**
> Synonyms
> behest
> edict
> fiat

❹ **command** NOUN
knowledge and ability
EG *a good command of English*
grasp EG *a good grasp of foreign languages*
knowledge EG *He has no knowledge of law.*
mastery EG *a mastery of grammar*

commemorate VERB
to do something in memory of
EG *concerts to commemorate the anniversary of his death*
celebrate EG *celebrating their golden wedding*
honour EG *celebrations to honour his memory*

> **WORD POWER**
> Synonyms
> memorialize
> pay tribute to

❶ **comment** VERB
to make a remark
EG *He refused to comment on the rumours.*
mention EG *I mentioned that I didn't like jazz.*
note EG *He noted that some issues remained to be settled.*
observe EG *"You're very pale," he*

observed.
point out EG *I should point out that these figures are approximate.*
remark EG *Everyone had remarked on her new hairstyle.*
say EG *"Well done," he said.*

> WORD POWER
> Synonyms
> interpose
> opine

comment NOUN
something you say
EG *sarcastic comments*
observation EG *a few general observations*
remark EG *snide remarks*
statement EG *That statement puzzled me.*

commit VERB
to do something
EG *A crime has been committed.*
carry out EG *attacks carried out by terrorists*
do EG *They have done a lot of damage.*
perform EG *people who have performed acts of bravery*
perpetrate EG *A fraud has been perpetrated.*

common ADJECTIVE
of many people
EG *a common complaint*
general EG *the general opinion*
popular EG *a popular belief*
prevailing EG *the prevailing atmosphere*
prevalent EG *Smoking is becoming more prevalent among girls.*
universal EG *The desire to look attractive is universal.*
widespread EG *widespread support*

> WORD POWER
> Antonym
> rare

common ADJECTIVE
not special

EG *the common man*
average EG *the average teenager*
commonplace EG *a commonplace observation*
everyday EG *your everyday routine*
ordinary EG *an ordinary day*
plain EG *My parents were just plain ordinary folks.*
standard EG *standard practice*
usual EG *In a usual week I watch about 15 hours of television.*

> WORD POWER
> Synonyms
> run-of-the-mill
> workaday
> Antonym
> special

common ADJECTIVE
having bad taste or manners
EG *a common, rude woman*
coarse EG *coarse humour*
rude EG *It's rude to stare.*
vulgar EG *vulgar remarks*

> WORD POWER
> Antonym
> refined

common sense NOUN
the ability to make good judgments
EG *Use your common sense.*
good sense EG *He had the good sense to call me at once.*
judgment EG *I respect your judgment.*
level-headedness EG *He prides himself on his level-headedness.*
prudence EG *His lack of prudence led to financial problems.*
wit EG *They don't have the wit to realize what's happening.*

communicate VERB
to be in touch with someone
EG *We communicate mainly by email.*
be in contact EG *I'll be in contact with him next week.*
be in touch EG *He hasn't been in touch with me yet.*

A
B
C
D
E
F
G
H
I
J
K
L
M
N
O
P
Q
R
S
T
U
V
W
X
Y
Z

A
B
C
D
E
F
G
H
I
J
K
L
M
N
O
P
Q
R
S
T
U
V
W
X
Y
Z

correspond EG *We correspond regularly.*

❷ **communicate** VERB
to pass on information
EG *The results will be communicated by post.*
convey EG *They have conveyed their views to the government.*
impart EG *the ability to impart knowledge*
inform EG *Will you inform me of any changes?*
pass on EG *I'll pass on your good wishes.*
spread EG *She has spread the news to everyone.*
transmit EG *He transmitted his enjoyment to the audience.*

> **WORD POWER**
> Synonyms
> disseminate
> make known

❶ **company** NOUN
a business
EG *a publishing company*
business EG *a family business*
corporation EG *multi-national corporations*
establishment EG *a commercial establishment*
firm EG *a firm of engineers*
house EG *the world's top fashion houses*

❷ **company** NOUN
a group of people
EG *the Royal Shakespeare Company*
assembly EG *an assembly of citizens*
band EG *bands of rebels*
circle EG *a large circle of friends*
community EG *a community of believers*
crowd EG *I don't go around with that crowd.*
ensemble EG *an ensemble of young musicians*
group EG *an environmental group*
party EG *a party of sightseers*

troupe EG *a troupe of actors*

> **WORD POWER**
> Synonyms
> concourse
> coterie

❸ **company** NOUN
the act of spending time with someone
EG *I could do with some company.*
companionship EG *He keeps a dog for companionship.*
presence EG *Your presence is not welcome here.*

compare VERB
to look at things for similarities or differences
EG *Compare these two illustrations.*
contrast EG *In this section we contrast four possible approaches.*
juxtapose EG *art juxtaposed with reality*
weigh EG *She weighed her options.*

compatible ADJECTIVE
going together
EG *Lifelong partners should be compatible.*
congenial EG *congenial company*
consistent EG *injuries consistent with a car crash*
harmonious EG *a harmonious partnership*
in keeping EG *This behaviour was in keeping with his character.*

> **WORD POWER**
> Synonyms
> accordant
> congruent
> congruous
> consonant
> Antonym
> incompatible

❶ **compensate** VERB
to repay someone for loss or damage
EG *You will be properly compensated for your loss.*
atone EG *He felt he had atoned for what he had done.*

refund EG *The company will refund the full cost.*
repay EG *collateral with which to repay swindled investors*
reward EG *Their patience was finally rewarded.*

> *WORD POWER*
> Synonyms
> make amends
> make restitution
> recompense
> reimburse
> remunerate

compensate VERB
to cancel out
EG *His lack of skill was compensated for by his enthusiasm.*
balance EG *The pros balance the cons.*
cancel out EG *The two influences cancel each other out.*
counteract EG *pills to counteract high blood pressure*
make up for EG *I'll make up for what I've done.*
offset EG *The loss is being offset by a new tax.*

> *WORD POWER*
> Synonyms
> counterbalance
> countervail
> redress

compensation NOUN
something that makes up for loss or damage
EG *compensation for his injuries*
amends EG *an attempt to make amends for his crime*
atonement EG *an act of atonement for our sins*
damages EG *damages for libel*
payment EG *a redundancy payment*

> *WORD POWER*
> Synonyms
> recompense
> reimbursement
> remuneration

reparation
restitution

compete VERB
to try to win
EG *companies competing for business*
contend EG *two groups contending for power*
contest EG *the candidates contesting in the election*
fight EG *rivals fighting for supremacy*
vie EG *The contestants vied to finish first.*

❶ competition NOUN
an attempt to win
EG *There's a lot of competition for places.*
contention EG *contention for the gold medal*
contest EG *the contest between capitalism and socialism*
opposition EG *They are in direct opposition for the job.*
rivalry EG *the rivalry between the two leaders*
struggle EG *a power struggle*

❷ competition NOUN
a contest to find the winner in something
EG *a surfing competition*
championship EG *a swimming championship*
contest EG *a beauty contest*
event EG *major sporting events*
tournament EG *a judo tournament*

competitor NOUN
a person who competes for something
EG *one of the youngest competitors in the event*
adversary EG *his political adversaries*
challenger EG *20 seconds faster than the nearest challenger*
competition EG *staying ahead of the competition*
contestant EG *contestants in the Miss World pageant*

A
B
C
D
E
F
G
H
I
J
K
L
M
N
O
P
Q
R
S
T
U
V
W
X
Y
Z

opponent EG *the best opponent I've played all season*
opposition EG *They can outplay the opposition.*
rival EG *a business rival*

complain VERB
to express dissatisfaction
EG *He came round to complain about the noise.*
carp EG *She is constantly carping at him.*
find fault EG *He's always finding fault with my work.*
grouse EG *You're always grousing about something.*
grumble EG *It's not in her nature to grumble.*
kick up a fuss INFORMAL EG *He kicks up a fuss whenever she goes out.*
moan EG *moaning about the weather*
whine EG *whining children*
whinge INFORMAL EG *Stop whingeing and get on with it.*

> **WORD POWER**
> Synonyms
> bemoan
> bewail

❶ complete ADJECTIVE
to the greatest degree possible
EG *a complete transformation*
absolute EG *absolute nonsense*
consummate EG *a consummate professional*
outright EG *an outright victory*
perfect EG *a perfect stranger*
thorough EG *a thorough snob*
total EG *a total failure*
utter EG *an utter shambles*

❷ complete ADJECTIVE
with nothing missing
EG *a complete set of tools*
entire EG *the entire plot*
full EG *a full report*
intact EG *the few buildings which have survived intact*
undivided EG *I want your undivided attention.*
whole EG *I told him the whole story.*

> **WORD POWER**
> Antonym
> incomplete

❸ complete VERB
to finish
EG *He has just completed his first novel.*
conclude EG *The judge concluded his summing-up.*
end EG *The crowd was in tears as he ended his speech.*
finish EG *I'll finish my report this week.*

complicated ADJECTIVE
complex and difficult
EG *a complicated situation*
complex EG *a complex issue*
convoluted EG *a convoluted plot*
elaborate EG *an elaborate theory*
intricate EG *an intricate process*
involved EG *a long, involved explanation*

> **WORD POWER**
> Synonyms
> Byzantine
> labyrinthine
> perplexing
> Antonym
> simple

compose VERB
to create or write
EG *He has composed a symphony.*
create EG *He has created a new ballet.*
devise EG *a play devised by the drama company*
invent EG *the man who invented gangsta rap*
produce EG *He has produced a book about the city.*
write EG *I've never been able to write poetry.*

compulsory ADJECTIVE
required by law

mandatory EG *the mandatory retirement age*

obligatory EG *an obligatory medical examination*

required EG *the required reading for this course*

requisite EG *the requisite documents*

> **WORD POWER**
> Antonym
> voluntary

conceit NOUN
excessive pride
EG *his insufferable conceit*

egotism EG *typical showbiz egotism*

pride EG *a blow to his pride*

self-importance EG *his bad manners and self-importance*

vanity EG *her vanity about her long hair*

> **WORD POWER**
> Synonyms
> amour-propre
> narcissism
> vainglory

conceited ADJECTIVE
too proud
EG *a conceited young idiot*

bigheaded INFORMAL EG *an arrogant, bigheaded man*

cocky EG *I was very cocky as a youngster.*

egotistical EG *an egotistical show-off*

self-important EG *self-important pop stars*

vain EG *a shallow, vain woman*

> **WORD POWER**
> Synonyms
> narcissistic
> swollen-headed
> vainglorious
> Antonym
> modest

❶ concentrate VERB
to give something all your attention
EG *Concentrate on your studies.*

be engrossed in EG *He was engrossed in his work.*

focus your attention on EG *focussing his attention on the race*

give your attention to EG *I gave my attention to the question.*

put your mind to EG *You could do it if you put your mind to it.*

❷ concentrate VERB
to be found in one place
EG *They are mostly concentrated in the urban areas.*

accumulate EG *Cholesterol accumulates in the arteries.*

collect EG *dust collecting in the corners*

gather EG *residents gathered in huddles*

❶ concern NOUN
a feeling of worry
EG *public concern about violence*

anxiety EG *anxiety about the economy*

apprehension EG *apprehension about the future*

disquiet EG *a growing sense of disquiet*

worry EG *She has no worries about his health.*

❷ concern NOUN
someone's duty or responsibility
EG *His private life is not my concern.*

affair EG *If you want to go, that's your affair.*

business EG *This is none of my business.*

responsibility EG *He's not my responsibility.*

❸ concern VERB
to make someone worried
EG *It concerns me that he doesn't want to go.*

bother EG *Nothing bothers me.*

distress EG *They are distressed by the accusations.*

disturb EG *disturbed by the news*

A B C D E F G H I J K L M N O P Q R S T U V W X Y Z

concern – conclusion

trouble EG *Is anything troubling you?*

worry EG *an issue that had worried him for some time*

> **WORD POWER**
> Synonyms
> disquiet
> perturb

❹ concern VERB
to affect or involve
EG *This concerns both of us.*

affect EG *the ways in which computers affect our lives*

apply to EG *This rule does not apply to us.*

be relevant to EG *These documents are relevant to the case.*

involve EG *meetings which involve most of the staff*

> **WORD POWER**
> Synonyms
> bear on
> pertain to
> touch

concise ADJECTIVE
using no unnecessary words
EG *a concise guide*

brief EG *a brief description*

short EG *a short speech*

succinct EG *a succinct explanation*

terse EG *a terse statement*

> **WORD POWER**
> Synonyms
> epigrammatic
> laconic
> pithy
> Antonym
> long

❶ conclude VERB
to decide something
EG *He concluded that she had been right.*

decide EG *I decided he must be ill.*

deduce EG *She deduced that I had written the letter.*

infer EG *His feelings were easily inferred from his reply.*

judge EG *The doctor judged that he was not fit enough to play.*

reckon INFORMAL EG *I reckon we should wait a while.*

suppose EG *There's no reason to suppose he'll be there.*

surmise EG *It is surmised that he must have known.*

❷ conclude VERB
to finish something
EG *He concluded the letter with a postscript.*

close EG *They closed the show with a song.*

end EG *His speech ended with a prayer for peace.*

finish EG *We finished the evening with a walk on the beach.*

round off EG *This rounded the afternoon off perfectly.*

wind up EG *She quickly wound up her conversation.*

> **WORD POWER**
> Antonym
> begin

❶ conclusion NOUN
a decision made after thinking carefully about something
EG *I've come to the conclusion that she was lying.*

deduction EG *a shrewd deduction about what was going on*

inference EG *There were two inferences to be drawn from her letter.*

judgment EG *My judgment is that things are going to get worse.*

verdict EG *The doctor's verdict was that he was fine.*

❷ conclusion NOUN
the finish or ending of something
EG *the conclusion of the programme*

close EG *bringing the talks to a close*

end EG *The war is coming to an end.*

ending EG *a dramatic ending*

finish EG *the finish of the race*

termination EG *the termination of their marriage*

> **WORD POWER**
> Antonym
> beginning

condemn VERB
to say that something is bad or unacceptable
EG *He was condemned for his arrogance.*
blame EG *I blame television for the rise in violence.*
censure EG *a motion censuring the government*
criticize EG *He was criticized for his failure to act.*
damn EG *The report damns the government's handling of the affair.*
denounce EG *He was denounced as a traitor.*

condemn VERB
to give a punishment
EG *condemned to death*
damn EG *sinners damned to eternal torment*
doom EG *doomed to die for his crime*
sentence EG *sentenced to ten years in prison*

condition NOUN
the state of something
EG *The house is in good condition.*
form EG *The team are not in good form this season.*
shape EG *He's in great shape for his age.*
state EG *Look at the state of my car!*

condition NOUN
something required for something else to be possible
EG *terms and conditions of the contract*
prerequisite EG *A science background is a prerequisite for the job.*
provision EG *a provision in his will forbidding the sale of the house*
proviso EG *The answer is yes, with*

one proviso.
qualification EG *He agreed, but with some qualifications.*
requirement EG *The product meets all legal requirements.*
requisite EG *the main requisite for membership*
stipulation EG *The only dress stipulation was "no jeans".*
terms EG *the terms of the agreement*

conference NOUN
a meeting for discussion
EG *a conference on education*
congress EG *a congress of coal miners*
convention EG *the Geneva convention*
discussion EG *a round of formal discussions*
forum EG *a forum for trade negotiations*
meeting EG *a meeting of shareholders*

> **WORD POWER**
> Synonyms
> colloquium
> convocation
> symposium

confess VERB
to admit to something
EG *Your son has confessed to his crimes.*
acknowledge EG *He acknowledged that he was a drug addict.*
admit EG *I admit to feeling jealous.*
own up EG *The headmaster is waiting for someone to own up.*

> **WORD POWER**
> Antonym
> deny

confession NOUN
the act of confessing
EG *a confession of adultery*
acknowledgment EG *an acknowledgment of his mistakes*
admission EG *an admission of guilt*

❶ confidence NOUN
a feeling of trust
EG *I have complete confidence in you.*
belief EG *his belief in his partner*
faith EG *He has great faith in her judgment.*
reliance EG *I don't put much reliance on that idea.*
trust EG *He destroyed my trust in people.*

> **WORD POWER**
> Antonym
> distrust

❷ confidence NOUN
sureness of yourself
EG *I've never had much confidence.*
aplomb EG *She handled the interview with aplomb.*
assurance EG *He led the orchestra with great assurance.*
self-assurance EG *his supreme self-assurance*
self-possession EG *an air of self-possession*

> **WORD POWER**
> Antonym
> shyness

❶ confident ADJECTIVE
sure about something
EG *confident of success*
certain EG *certain of getting a place on the team*
convinced EG *He is convinced it's your fault.*
positive EG *I'm positive it will happen.*
satisfied EG *We must be satisfied that the treatment is safe.*
secure EG *secure about his job prospects*
sure EG *I'm not sure I understand.*

> **WORD POWER**
> Antonym
> uncertain

❷ confident ADJECTIVE
sure of yourself

EG *a confident attitude*
assured EG *His playing became more assured.*
self-assured EG *a self-assured young man*
self-possessed EG *a self-possessed career woman*

> **WORD POWER**
> Antonym
> shy

❶ confine VERB
to limit to something specified
EG *They confined themselves to talking about the weather.*
limit EG *Limit yourself to six units of alcohol a week.*
restrict EG *The patient was restricted to a meagre diet.*

❷ confine VERB
to prevent from leaving
EG *confined to bed for two days*
hem in EG *hemmed in by spectators*
imprison EG *imprisoned in a tiny cell*
restrict EG *We were restricted to the building.*
shut up EG *He can't stand being shut up in the house.*

> **WORD POWER**
> Synonyms
> immure
> incarcerate
> intern

❶ confirm VERB
to say or show that something is true
EG *Police confirmed that they had received a call.*
bear out EG *The figures bear out his words.*
endorse EG *This theory has been endorsed by research.*
prove EG *The results prove his point.*
substantiate EG *no evidence to substantiate the claims*
validate EG *It is difficult to validate this belief.*

verify EG *I was asked to verify this statement.*

WORD POWER
Synonyms
authenticate
corroborate

② confirm VERB
to make something definite
EG *Can we confirm the arrangements for tomorrow?*
fix EG *The date for the election was fixed.*
settle EG *I've settled a time to see him.*

① conflict NOUN
disagreement and argument
EG *conflict between workers and management*
antagonism EG *antagonism within the team*
disagreement EG *The meeting ended in disagreement.*
discord EG *public discord*
friction EG *friction between him and his father*
hostility EG *hostility between parents and teachers*
opposition EG *a wave of opposition*
strife EG *a cause of strife in many marriages*

② conflict NOUN
a war or battle
EG *the conflict in the Gulf*
battle EG *a battle between two gangs*
combat EG *men who died in combat*
fighting EG *Villagers have left their homes to avoid the fighting.*
strife EG *civil strife*
war EG *the war between Israel and Egypt*

③ conflict VERB
to differ or disagree
EG *conflicting ideas*
be at variance EG *His statements are at variance with the facts.*
be incompatible EG *These two*

principles are incompatible.
clash EG *a decision which clashes with official policy*
differ EG *The two leaders differ on several issues.*
disagree EG *Governments disagree over the need for action.*

① confuse VERB
to mix two things up
EG *confusing fact with fiction*
mistake EG *I mistook you for someone else.*
mix up EG *He sometimes mixes up his words.*
muddle up EG *I keep muddling him up with his brother.*

② confuse VERB
to puzzle or bewilder
EG *Politics confuse me.*
baffle EG *Police are baffled by the murder.*
bewilder EG *His silence bewildered her.*
mystify EG *I was mystified by his attitude.*
puzzle EG *One thing still puzzles me.*

WORD POWER
Synonyms
bemuse
faze
nonplus
perplex

① confused ADJECTIVE
puzzled or bewildered
EG *confused about health risks*
baffled EG *He stared in baffled amazement.*
bewildered EG *bewildered holidaymakers*
muddled EG *She was muddled about the date.*
perplexed EG *perplexed by recent events*
puzzled EG *a puzzled expression*

WORD POWER
Synonyms
at a loss

A B **C** D E F G H I J K L M N O P Q R S T U V W X Y Z

at sea
flummoxed
nonplussed

❷ confused ADJECTIVE
in an untidy mess
EG *They lay in a confused heap.*
chaotic EG *the chaotic mess on his desk*
disordered EG *a disordered pile of papers*
disorganized EG *a disorganized lifestyle*
untidy EG *an untidy room*

> *WORD POWER*
> Antonym
> tidy

confusing ADJECTIVE
puzzling or bewildering
EG *a confusing situation*
baffling EG *a baffling statement*
bewildering EG *a bewildering choice of products*
complicated EG *a complicated voting system*
puzzling EG *a puzzling problem*

confusion NOUN
an untidy mess
EG *My life is in confusion.*
chaos EG *economic chaos*
disarray EG *The nation is in disarray.*
disorder EG *The emergency room was in disorder.*
disorganization EG *scenes of chaos and disorganization*
mess EG *He always leaves the bathroom in a mess.*

> *WORD POWER*
> Antonym
> order

❶ connect VERB
to join together
EG *Connect the pipe to the tap.*
affix EG *His name was affixed to his cubicle.*
attach EG *Attach the curtains to the rods with hooks.*

couple EG *The engine is coupled to a gearbox.*
fasten EG *A hatchet was fastened to his belt.*
join EG *two springs joined together*
link EG *the Channel Tunnel linking Britain with France*

> *WORD POWER*
> Antonym
> separate

❷ connect VERB
to associate one thing with another
EG *evidence connecting him with the robberies*
ally EG *The new government is allied with the military.*
associate EG *symptoms associated with migraine headaches*
link EG *research which links smoking with cancer*
relate EG *the denial that unemployment is related to crime*

❶ connection NOUN
a link or relationship
EG *a connection between drinking and liver disease*
affiliation EG *He has no affiliation with any political party.*
association EG *the association between the two companies*
bond EG *the bond between a mother and child*
correlation EG *the correlation between unemployment and crime*
correspondence EG *the correspondence between Eastern and Western religions*
link EG *a link between smoking and lung cancer*
relation EG *This theory bears no relation to reality.*
relationship EG *the relationship between humans and their environment*

❷ connection NOUN
a point where things are joined
EG *The fault was just a loose*

connection.

coupling EG *The coupling between the railway carriages snapped.*

fastening EG *a zip fastening*

junction EG *the junction between nerve and muscle*

link EG *a link between the city and the motorway*

conscience NOUN
a sense of right and wrong
EG *He had a guilty conscience.*

principles EG *It's against my principles to eat meat.*

scruples EG *a man with no moral scruples*

sense of right and wrong EG *children with no sense of right and wrong*

conservative ADJECTIVE
unwilling to change
EG *People get more conservative as they grow older.*

conventional EG *conventional tastes*

traditional EG *a traditional school*

> *WORD POWER*
> Synonyms
> hidebound
> reactionary
> Antonym
> radical

❶ consider VERB
to think of someone or something as
EG *They do not consider him a suitable candidate.*

believe EG *I believe him to be innocent.*

judge EG *His work was judged unsatisfactory.*

rate EG *The film was rated excellent.*

regard as EG *They regard the tax as unfair.*

think EG *Many people think him arrogant.*

> *WORD POWER*
> Synonyms

deem
hold to be

❷ consider VERB
to think carefully
EG *I will consider your offer.*

contemplate EG *He contemplated his fate.*

deliberate EG *The jury deliberated for three days.*

meditate EG *He meditated on the problem.*

muse EG *She sat musing on how unfair life was.*

ponder EG *pondering how to improve the team*

reflect EG *I reflected on the child's future.*

think about EG *I've been thinking about what you said.*

> *WORD POWER*
> Synonyms
> cogitate
> mull over
> ruminate

❸ consider VERB
to take into account
EG *We should consider her feelings.*

bear in mind EG *There are a few points to bear in mind.*

make allowances for EG *Remember to make allowances for delays.*

respect EG *We will respect your wishes.*

take into account EG *another factor to be taken into account*

think about EG *more important things to think about*

❶ consideration NOUN
careful thought about something
EG *a decision requiring careful consideration*

attention EG *I gave the question all my attention.*

contemplation EG *The problem deserves serious contemplation.*

deliberation EG *After much*

A
C
B
C
D
E
F
G
H
I
J
K
L
M
N
O
P
Q
R
S
T
U
V
W
X
Y
Z

deliberation, he called the police.
study EG *The proposals need careful study.*
thought EG *I've given the matter a great deal of thought.*

❷ **consideration** NOUN
concern for someone
EG *Show some consideration for other passengers.*
concern EG *concern for the homeless*
kindness EG *We have been treated with great kindness.*
respect EG *no respect for wildlife*
tact EG *a master of tact and diplomacy*

❸ **consideration** NOUN
something to be taken into account
EG *Safety is a major consideration.*
factor EG *an important factor in buying a house*
issue EG *Price is not the only issue.*
point EG *There is another point to remember.*

consist
consist of VERB
to be made up of
EG *The brain consists of millions of nerve cells.*
be composed of EG *The committee is composed of ten people.*
be made up of EG *The bouquet was made up of roses and carnations.*
comprise EG *The show comprises 50 paintings and sketches.*

❶ **constant** ADJECTIVE
going on all the time
EG *a city under constant attack*
continual EG *continual pain*
continuous EG *continuous gunfire*
eternal EG *an eternal hum in the background*
nonstop EG *nonstop music*
perpetual EG *her perpetual complaints*
relentless EG *relentless pressure*

WORD POWER
Synonyms
incessant
interminable
sustained
unremitting
Antonym
periodic

---

❷ **constant** ADJECTIVE
staying the same
EG *a constant temperature*
even EG *an even level of sound*
fixed EG *a fixed salary*
regular EG *a regular beat*
stable EG *a stable condition*
steady EG *travelling at a steady 50 miles per hour*
uniform EG *a uniform thickness*

WORD POWER
Synonyms
immutable
invariable
Antonym
changeable

---

consult VERB
to go to for advice
EG *Consult your doctor before undertaking exercise.*
ask for advice EG *Ask your bank manager for advice on mortgages.*
confer with EG *He is conferring with his lawyers.*
refer to EG *I had to refer to the manual.*

❶ **contact** NOUN
the state of being in touch with someone
EG *We must keep in contact.*
communication EG *The leaders were in constant communication.*
touch EG *I've lost touch with her over the years.*

❷ **contact** NOUN
someone you know
EG *a contact in the music business*
acquaintance EG *We met through a mutual acquaintance.*
connection EG *She had a*

connection in England.

contact VERB
to get in touch with
EG *We contacted the company to complain.*
approach EG *A journalist has approached me for a story.*
communicate with EG *We communicate mostly by email.*
get hold of EG *I've been trying to get hold of you all week.*
get in touch with EG *I will get in touch with my solicitors.*
reach EG *Where can I reach you in an emergency?*

contain VERB
to include as a part of
EG *Alcohol contains sugar.*
comprise EG *The band comprises two singers and two guitarists.*
include EG *The price includes VAT.*

contain VERB
to keep under control
EG *efforts to contain the disease*
control EG *He could hardly control his rage.*
curb EG *measures to curb inflation*
repress EG *people who repress their emotions*
restrain EG *unable to restrain her anger*
stifle EG *stifling the urge to scream*

container NOUN
something which holds things
EG *a plastic container for food*
holder EG *a cigarette holder*
vessel EG *storage vessels*

WORD POWER
Synonyms
receptacle
repository

continue VERB
to keep doing something
EG *Will you continue working after you're married?*
carry on EG *The assistant carried on talking.*
go on EG *Unemployment is likely to go on rising.*
keep on EG *He kept on trying.*
persist EG *She persists in using his nickname.*

continue VERB
to go on existing
EG *The fighting continued after they'd left.*
carry on EG *My work will carry on after I'm gone.*
endure EG *Their friendship has endured for 30 years.*
last EG *Nothing lasts forever.*
persist EG *The problem persists.*
remain EG *The building remains to this day.*
survive EG *companies which survived after the recession*

continue VERB
to start doing again
EG *After a moment, she continued speaking.*
carry on EG *He took a deep breath, then carried on.*
recommence EG *He recommenced work on his novel.*
resume EG *Police will resume the search today.*

continuous ADJECTIVE
going on without stopping
EG *continuous growth*
constant EG *under constant pressure*
continued EG *a continued improvement*
extended EG *conflict over an extended period*
prolonged EG *a prolonged drought*
uninterrupted EG *uninterrupted rule*

WORD POWER
Antonym
periodic

control NOUN
power over something
EG *He was forced to give up control of the company.*
authority EG *You have no*

A B C D E F G H I J K L M N O P Q R S T U V W X Y Z

89

authority here.
command EG *He was in command of the ceremony.*
direction EG *The team worked well under his direction.*
government EG *The entire country is under the government of one man.*
management EG *the day-to-day management of the business*
power EG *a position of great power*
rule EG *15 years of Communist rule*
supremacy EG *The party has re-established its supremacy.*

> WORD POWER
> Synonyms
> jurisdiction
> mastery
> superintendence

❷ control VERB
to be in charge of
EG *companies fighting to control the Internet*
administer EG *the authorities who administer the island*
be in charge of EG *She is in charge of the project.*
command EG *the general who commanded the troops*
direct EG *He will direct day-to-day operations.*
govern EG *his ability to govern France*
have power over EG *Her husband has total power over her.*
manage EG *the government's ability to manage the economy*
rule EG *the dynasty which ruled China*

convenient ADJECTIVE
helpful or easy to use
EG *a convenient mode of transport*
handy EG *Credit cards can be handy.*
helpful EG *a helpful fact sheet*
useful EG *a useful invention*

> WORD POWER
> Synonyms

labour-saving
serviceable
Antonym
inconvenient

convince VERB
to persuade that something is true
EG *I convinced him of my innocence.*
assure EG *She assured me that there was nothing wrong.*
persuade EG *I had to persuade him of the advantages.*
satisfy EG *He had to satisfy the doctors that he was fit to play.*

convincing ADJECTIVE
persuasive
EG *a convincing argument*
conclusive EG *conclusive proof*
effective EG *an effective speaker*
persuasive EG *persuasive reasons*
plausible EG *a plausible explanation*
powerful EG *a powerful speech*
telling EG *a telling criticism*

> WORD POWER
> Synonyms
> cogent
> incontrovertible
> Antonym
> unconvincing

cook VERB
to prepare food for eating by heating it in some way
EG *I enjoy cooking for friends.*
bake EG *a machine for baking bread*
barbecue EG *a Korean method of barbecuing meat*
boil EG *Boil the fruit and syrup together for half an hour.*
fry EG *Garnish the rice with thinly sliced fried onion.*
grill EG *Grill the fish for five minutes.*
microwave EG *Microwaved vegetables have a fresher flavour.*
poach EG *I had ordered poached eggs on toast for breakfast.*
roast EG *Roast the aubergine in the*

oven for about one hour until soft.
steam EG *mussels on a bed of steamed cabbage*
stew EG *You can stew the vegetables in oil.*
toast EG *This currant loaf is delicious either fresh or toasted.*

❶ **cool** ADJECTIVE
having a low temperature
EG *a gust of cool air*
chilled EG *a chilled bottle of wine*
chilly EG *a chilly afternoon*
cold EG *Your dinner's getting cold.*
refreshing EG *a refreshing breeze*

> **WORD POWER**
> Antonym
> warm

❷ **cool** ADJECTIVE
staying calm
EG *He kept cool through the whole thing.*
calm EG *Try to stay calm.*
collected EG *She was cool and collected throughout the interview.*
composed EG *a composed player*
level-headed EG *Simon is level-headed and practical.*
relaxed EG *a relaxed manner*
serene EG *a serene smile*

> **WORD POWER**
> Synonyms
> dispassionate
> imperturbable
> unemotional
> unexcited
> unruffled
> Antonym
> nervous

❸ **cool** VERB
to make or become cool
EG *Put the cookies on a wire rack to cool.*
chill EG *a glass of chilled champagne*
cool off EG *Dip the carrots in water to cool them off.*
freeze EG *Make double the quantity and freeze half for later.*

refrigerate EG *Refrigerate the dough overnight.*

> **WORD POWER**
> Antonym
> heat

cooperate VERB
to work together
EG *The family cooperated with the author of the book.*
collaborate EG *They collaborated on an album.*
join forces EG *The two political parties are joining forces.*
pull together EG *The staff and management pull together.*
work together EG *industry and government working together*

❶ **copy** NOUN
something made to look like something else
EG *He had kept a copy of the letter.*
counterfeit EG *This credit card is a counterfeit.*
duplicate EG *I lost my key and had to get a duplicate made.*
fake EG *How do I know this painting isn't a fake?*
forgery EG *The letter was a forgery.*
imitation EG *Beware of cheap imitations.*
replica EG *a replica of the Statue of Liberty*
reproduction EG *a reproduction of a famous painting*

> **WORD POWER**
> Synonyms
> facsimile
> likeness
> replication

❷ **copy** VERB
to do the same thing as someone else
EG *My little brother copies everything I do.*
ape EG *Generations of women have aped her style and looks.*
emulate EG *Sons are expected to emulate their fathers.*

91

follow EG *Where America goes, Britain will surely follow.*

imitate EG *Children imitate what they see on TV.*

mimic EG *He mimicked her accent.*

> ### WORD POWER
> Synonyms
> follow suit
> parrot
> simulate

❸ **copy** VERB
to make a copy of
EG *documents copied by hand*

counterfeit EG *These banknotes are very easy to counterfeit.*

duplicate EG *Videos are being illicitly duplicated all over the country.*

reproduce EG *a new method of reproducing oil paintings*

corny ADJECTIVE
unoriginal or sentimental
EG *corny old love songs*

banal EG *banal dialogue*

hackneyed EG *a hackneyed plot*

maudlin EG *a maudlin film*

sentimental EG *a sentimental ballad*

stale EG *stale ideas*

stereotyped EG *a stereotyped image of Britain*

trite EG *a trite ending*

> ### WORD POWER
> Synonyms
> mawkish
> old hat
> unoriginal

❶ **correct** ADJECTIVE
without mistakes
EG *a correct diagnosis*

accurate EG *an accurate description*

exact EG *an exact copy*

faultless EG *Hans's English was faultless.*

flawless EG *a flawless performance*

precise EG *precise calculations*

right EG *That clock never shows the right time.*

true EG *a true account*

❷ **correct** ADJECTIVE
socially acceptable
EG *correct behaviour*

acceptable EG *It is becoming more acceptable for women to drink.*

appropriate EG *appropriate dress*

fitting EG *behaving in a manner not fitting for a lady*

okay or **OK** INFORMAL EG *Is it okay if I bring a friend with me?*

proper EG *In those days it was not proper for women to go on the stage.*

seemly EG *It is not seemly to joke about such things.*

> ### WORD POWER
> Antonym
> wrong

❸ **correct** VERB
to make right
EG *trying to correct his faults*

amend EG *They want to amend the current system.*

cure EG *an operation to cure his limp*

improve EG *We must improve the situation.*

rectify EG *attempts to rectify the problem*

reform EG *He promised to reform his wicked ways.*

remedy EG *What is needed to remedy these deficiencies?*

right EG *I intend to right these wrongs.*

> ### WORD POWER
> Synonyms
> emend
> redress

correction NOUN
the act of making something right
EG *the correction of obvious mistakes*

adjustment EG *My car needs a brake adjustment.*

amendment EG *He has made lots of amendments to the script.*

righting EG *the righting of the country's domestic troubles*

WORD POWER
Synonyms
emendation
rectification

❶ corrupt ADJECTIVE
acting dishonestly or illegally
EG *corrupt politicians*
crooked EG *a crooked cop*
dishonest EG *a dishonest scheme*
fraudulent EG *fraudulent trading*
shady INFORMAL EG *shady deals*
unscrupulous EG *unscrupulous landlords*

WORD POWER
Synonyms
unethical
unprincipled
venal
Antonym
honest

❷ corrupt VERB
to make dishonest
EG *Organized crime has corrupted local government.*
bribe EG *accused of bribing officials*
buy off EG *Police were bought off by drugs dealers.*
fix INFORMAL EG *He fixed the match by bribing the players.*

❸ corrupt VERB
to make immoral
EG *TV is corrupting our children.*
deprave EG *material likely to deprave those who watch it*
pervert EG *perverted by their contact with criminals*

corruption NOUN
dishonest and illegal behaviour
EG *charges of corruption*
bribery EG *on trial for bribery*
dishonesty EG *She accused the government of dishonesty and incompetence.*
fraud EG *jailed for fraud*

WORD POWER

Synonyms
extortion
profiteering
venality

❶ cost NOUN
the amount of money needed
EG *The cost of petrol has increased.*
charge EG *We can arrange this for a small charge.*
expense EG *household expenses*
outlay EG *Buying wine in bulk is well worth the outlay.*
payment EG *an initial payment of just $100*
price EG *House prices are expected to rise.*
rate EG *specially reduced rates*

❷ cost NOUN
loss or damage
EG *the total cost in human misery*
detriment EG *These changes are to the detriment of staff morale.*
expense EG *I supported my husband's career at the expense of my own.*
penalty EG *paying the penalty for someone else's mistakes*

❸ cost VERB
to involve a cost of
EG *The air fares were going to cost a lot.*
come to EG *Lunch came to nearly 15.*
sell at EG *The books are selling at £1 per copy.*
set someone back INFORMAL EG *This wedding will set us back thousands of pounds.*

council NOUN
a governing group of people
EG *the city council*
assembly EG *the National Assembly*
board EG *the Pakistan Cricket Board*
committee EG *the management committee*
panel EG *a panel of judges*

A
B
C
D
E
F
G
H
I
J
K
L
M
N
O
P
Q
R
S
T
U
V
W
X
Y
Z

A
B
C
D
E
F
G
H
I
J
K
L
M
N
O
P
Q
R
S
T
U
V
W
X
Y
Z

WORD POWER
Synonyms
conclave
convocation
quango
synod

❶ **count** VERB
to add up
EG *I counted the money.*
add up EG *Add up the sales figures.*
calculate EG *First, calculate your monthly living expenses.*
tally EG *Computers now tally the votes.*

WORD POWER
Synonyms
compute
enumerate
tot up

❷ **count** VERB
to be important
EG *Our opinions don't count.*
carry weight EG *a politician whose words carry weight*
matter EG *It doesn't matter what she thinks.*
rate EG *This does not rate as one of my main concerns.*
signify EG *His absence does not signify much.*
weigh EG *This evidence did not weigh with the jury.*

❸ **count** NOUN
a counting or number counted
EG *The count revealed that our party had the majority.*
calculation EG *I did a quick calculation in my head.*
reckoning EG *By my reckoning we were about two miles from camp.*
sum EG *I've never been good at sums.*
tally EG *They keep a tally of visitors to the castle.*

WORD POWER
Synonyms
computation
enumeration

counteract VERB
to reduce the effect of something
EG *pills to counteract high blood pressure*
act against EG *The immune system acts against infection.*
offset EG *The slump was offset by a surge in exports.*

WORD POWER
Synonyms
counterbalance
countervail
negate
neutralize

countless ADJECTIVE
too many to count
EG *the star of countless films*
infinite EG *an infinite number of atoms*
innumerable EG *innumerable problems*
myriad EG *pop music in all its myriad forms*
untold EG *untold wealth*

WORD POWER
Synonyms
incalculable
limitless
measureless
multitudinous

❶ **country** NOUN
a political area
EG *the boundary between the two countries*
kingdom EG *The kingdom's power declined.*
land EG *America, land of opportunity*
state EG *a communist state*

❷ **country** NOUN
land away from towns and cities
EG *He lives right out in the country.*
bush NEW ZEALAND AND SOUTH AFRICAN EG *a trip out to the bush*
countryside EG *surrounded by beautiful countryside*
outback AUSTRALIAN AND NEW ZEALAND EG *nostalgic paintings of the*

outback
outdoors EG *He loves the great outdoors.*

courage NOUN
lack of fear
EG *His courage impressed everyone.*
bravery EG *an act of bravery*
daring EG *tales of daring and adventure*
guts INFORMAL EG *He didn't have the guts to admit he was wrong.*
heroism EG *the young soldier's heroism*
nerve EG *I didn't have the nerve to complain.*
pluck EG *You have to admire her pluck.*
valour EG *He was decorated for valour in the war.*

> **WORD POWER**
> Synonyms
> dauntlessness
> fearlessness
> grit
> intrepidity
> Antonym
> fear

❶ **course** NOUN
a series of lessons
EG *a course in computing*
classes EG *I go to dance classes.*
curriculum EG *the history curriculum*

❷ **course** NOUN
a policy of action
EG *He took the only course left open to him.*
plan EG *Your best plan is to see your doctor.*
policy EG *She decided the best policy was to wait.*
procedure EG *He did not follow the correct procedure.*

❸ **course** NOUN
a way taken to get somewhere
EG *She sensed the plane had changed course.*
direction EG *He went off in the opposite direction.*
line EG *the birds' line of flight*
path EG *the path of an oncoming car*
route EG *the most direct route*
trajectory EG *the trajectory of the missile*
way EG *What way do you go home?*

❶ **court** NOUN
a place where legal matters are decided
EG *He ended up in court for theft.*
bench EG *He was brought before the bench.*
law court EG *prisoners tried by a law court*
tribunal EG *The claim was thrown out by a European tribunal.*

❷ **court** VERB; OLD-FASHIONED
to intend to marry
EG *I was courting Billy at 19 and married him at 21.*
go steady EG *They've been going steady for six months now.*
woo EG *He wooed and married his first love.*

courtesy NOUN
polite and considerate behaviour
EG *a lack of courtesy to other drivers*
civility EG *Handle customers with tact and civility.*
courteousness EG *his courteousness and kindness*
gallantry EG *He treated me with old-fashioned gallantry.*
good manners EG *the rules of good manners*
grace EG *He didn't even have the grace to apologize.*
graciousness EG *The team displayed graciousness in defeat.*
politeness EG *basic standards of politeness*

❶ **cover** VERB
to protect or hide
EG *He covered his face.*
cloak EG *a land cloaked in mist*
conceal EG *The hat concealed her*

hair.

cover up EG *I covered him up with a blanket.*

hide EG *His sunglasses hid his eyes.*

mask EG *A cloud masked the sun.*

obscure EG *One wall was obscured by a huge banner.*

screen EG *The road was screened by a block of flats.*

shade EG *shading his eyes from the glare*

> **WORD POWER**
> Antonym
> reveal

❷ cover VERB

to form a layer over
EG *Tears covered his face.*

coat EG *Coat the fish with batter.*

overlay EG *The floor was overlaid with rugs.*

❸ cover NOUN

something which protects or hides
EG *a duvet cover*

case EG *a spectacle case*

coating EG *steel covered with a coating of zinc*

covering EG *a plastic covering*

jacket EG *the jacket of a book*

mask EG *a surgical mask*

screen EG *They put a screen round me.*

wrapper EG *Take the product from its sealed wrapper.*

COW NOUN

a farm animal kept for milk or meat
EG *a herd of dairy cows*

bovine EG *a herd of deranged bovines*

cattle EG *fields where cattle graze*

coward NOUN

someone who is easily scared
EG *He's too much of a coward to fight.*

chicken SLANG EG *We called him a chicken.*

wimp INFORMAL EG *He seems like a wimp to me.*

cowardly ADJECTIVE

easily scared
EG *too cowardly to tell the truth*

chicken SLANG EG *I was too chicken to complain.*

faint-hearted EG *This is no time to be faint-hearted.*

gutless INFORMAL EG *a gutless coward*

sookie NEW ZEALAND EG *a sookie thing to do*

> **WORD POWER**
> Synonyms
> craven
> lily-livered
> pusillanimous
> spineless
> timorous
> Antonym
> brave

cower VERB

to bend down with fear
EG *The hostages cowered in their seats.*

cringe EG *I cringed in horror.*

quail EG *She quailed at the sight.*

shrink EG *He shrank back in terror.*

❶ crack VERB

to become damaged, with lines on the surface
EG *A gas main has cracked.*

break EG *She broke her leg playing rounders.*

fracture EG *You've fractured a rib.*

snap EG *The mast snapped like a dry twig.*

❷ crack VERB

to find the answer to something
EG *We've managed to crack the problem.*

decipher EG *trying to decipher the code*

solve EG *attempts to solve the mystery*

work out EG *I've worked out where I'm going wrong.*

❸ crack NOUN

a line or gap caused by damage
EG *a large crack in the wall*
break EG *a train crash caused by a break in the rails*
cleft EG *a cleft in the rocks*
crevice EG *a crevice in the cliff-face*
fracture EG *a hip fracture*

> *WORD POWER*
> **Synonyms**
> fissure
> interstice

cram VERB
to stuff something into a container or place
EG *She crammed her mouth with nuts.*
jam EG *The place was jammed with people.*
pack EG *The drawers were packed with clothes.*
squeeze EG *The two of us were squeezed into one seat.*
stuff EG *wallets stuffed with dollars*

crash NOUN
an accident involving a moving vehicle
EG *a plane crash*
accident EG *a serious car accident*
bump EG *I had a bump in the car park.*
collision EG *a head-on collision*
pile-up INFORMAL EG *a 54-car pile-up*
smash EG *He nearly died in a car smash.*

❷ crash NOUN
a loud noise
EG *There was a sudden crash outside.*
bang EG *The door slammed with a bang.*
clash EG *the clash of cymbals*
din EG *the din of battle*
smash EG *the smash of falling crockery*

❸ crash NOUN
the failure of a business
EG *a stock market crash*
bankruptcy EG *Many firms are now facing bankruptcy.*
collapse EG *The economy is on the edge of collapse.*
depression EG *the Great Depression of the 1930s*
failure EG *a major cause of business failure*
ruin EG *Inflation has driven them to the brink of ruin.*

❹ crash VERB
to have an accident
EG *His car crashed into the rear of a van.*
bump EG *I've just bumped my car.*
collide EG *Two trains collided in London today.*
drive into EG *He drove his car into a tree.*
have an accident EG *My brother's had an accident on his moped.*
hurtle into EG *The racing car hurtled into the spectator enclosure.*
plough into EG *The plane had ploughed into the mountainside.*
wreck EG *He's wrecked his van.*

crawl VERB
to be full of
EG *The place is crawling with drunks.*
be alive with EG *The river was alive with frogs.*
be full of EG *The place was full of insects.*
be overrun SLANG EG *The area is overrun with tourists.*
swarm EG *The wood was swarming with police officers.*
teem EG *ponds teeming with fish*

craze NOUN
a brief enthusiasm for something
EG *the latest fitness craze*
fad EG *a new-age fad*
fashion EG *the fashion for Seventies toys*
trend EG *the latest trend among film stars*
vogue EG *a vogue for so-called health drinks*

❶ create VERB
to make something happen
EG *His reaction created a bad atmosphere.*
bring about EG *helping to bring about peace*
cause EG *Sugar causes dental decay.*
lead to EG *The takeover led to widespread redundancies.*
occasion EG *the distress occasioned by her dismissal*

❷ create VERB
to invent something
EG *creating a new style of painting*
coin EG *the man who coined the term "virtual reality"*
compose EG *Vivaldi composed many concertos.*
devise EG *We devised a scheme to help him.*
formulate EG *He formulated his plan for escape.*
invent EG *He invented the first electric clock.*
originate EG *the designer who originated platform shoes*

creative ADJECTIVE
able to invent
EG *her creative talents*
fertile EG *a fertile imagination*
imaginative EG *an imaginative writer*
inspired EG *his inspired use of colour*
inventive EG *an inventive storyline*

credit NOUN
praise for something
EG *He took all the credit for my idea.*
commendation EG *Both teams deserve commendation.*
glory EG *basking in reflected glory*
praise EG *Praise is due to all concerned.*
recognition EG *She got no recognition for her work.*
thanks EG *He received no thanks for his efforts.*

WORD POWER

Synonyms
acclaim
Brownie points
kudos
Antonym
disgrace

crime NOUN
an act that breaks the law
EG *the problem of organized crime*
misdemeanour EG *a financial misdemeanour*
offence EG *a serious offence*
violation EG *tax law violations*
wrong EG *I intend to right that wrong.*

WORD POWER
Synonyms
felony
malfeasance
misdeed
transgression

❶ criminal NOUN
someone who has committed a crime
EG *the country's most dangerous criminals*
crook INFORMAL EG *The man is a crook and a liar.*
culprit EG *the true culprit's identity*
delinquent EG *juvenile delinquents*
offender EG *a first-time offender*
skelm SOUTH AFRICAN EG *a skelm from the city*
villain EG *He tackled an armed villain single-handed.*

WORD POWER
Synonyms
evildoer
felon
lawbreaker
malefactor

❷ criminal ADJECTIVE
involving crime
EG *criminal activities*
corrupt EG *corrupt practices*
crooked EG *crooked business deals*
illegal EG *an illegal action*

illicit EG *illicit dealings*
unlawful EG *unlawful entry*

WORD POWER
Synonyms
culpable
felonious
indictable
iniquitous
nefarious
Antonym
legal

cripple VERB
to injure severely
EG *crippled in a car accident*
disable EG *disabled by polio*
lame EG *He was lamed for life.*
maim EG *mines maiming and killing civilians*
paralyse EG *paralysed in a riding accident*

cripple VERB
to prevent from working
EG *The crisis may cripple the Irish economy.*
bring to a standstill EG *The strike brought France to a standstill.*
impair EG *Their actions will impair France's national interests.*
put out of action EG *The port has been put out of action.*

critical ADJECTIVE
very important
EG *a critical point in history*
crucial EG *a crucial election campaign*
deciding EG *Price was a deciding factor.*
decisive EG *a decisive moment in my life*
momentous EG *a momentous decision*
pivotal EG *He played a pivotal role in the match.*
vital EG *vital information*

WORD POWER
Antonym
unimportant

critical ADJECTIVE
very serious
EG *a critical illness*
grave EG *grave danger*
precarious EG *a precarious financial situation*
serious EG *His condition is said to be serious.*

critical ADJECTIVE
finding fault with something or someone
EG *critical remarks*
carping EG *carping comments*
derogatory EG *derogatory references to women*
disapproving EG *a disapproving look*
disparaging EG *He spoke in disparaging tones.*
scathing EG *a scathing attack*

WORD POWER
Synonyms
captious
cavilling
censorious
fault-finding
Antonym
complimentary

criticism NOUN
expression of disapproval
EG *public criticism of his actions*
censure EG *They deserve praise rather than censure.*
disapproval EG *a chorus of disapproval*
disparagement EG *their disparagement of this book*
fault-finding EG *her husband's constant fault-finding*
flak INFORMAL EG *I got a lot of flak for that idea.*
panning INFORMAL EG *a panning from the critics*

WORD POWER
Synonyms
animadversion
denigration
stricture

99

A
B
C
D
E
F
G
H
I
J
K
L
M
N
O
P
Q
R
S
T
U
V
W
X
Y
Z

Antonym
praise

criticize VERB
to find fault
EG *The regime has been harshly criticized.*
censure EG *a decision for which she was censured*
condemn EG *He refused to condemn their behaviour.*
find fault with EG *She keeps finding fault with my work.*
knock INFORMAL EG *Don't knock it till you've tried it.*
pan INFORMAL EG *Critics panned the show.*
put down EG *She's always putting him down in front of the kids.*

> *WORD POWER*
> Synonyms
> disparage
> excoriate
> lambast *or* lambaste
> Antonym
> praise

❶ crooked ADJECTIVE
bent or twisted
EG *a crooked tree*
bent EG *a bent back*
deformed EG *born with a deformed right leg*
distorted EG *a distorted image*
irregular EG *irregular and discoloured teeth*
out of shape EG *The wires were bent out of shape.*
twisted EG *bits of twisted metal*
warped EG *warped wooden shutters*

> *WORD POWER*
> Antonym
> straight

❷ crooked ADJECTIVE
dishonest or illegal
EG *crooked business practices*
corrupt EG *corrupt police officers*
criminal EG *criminal activities*

dishonest EG *dishonest salespeople*
fraudulent EG *a fraudulent claim*
illegal EG *illegal trading*
shady INFORMAL EG *shady deals*

> *WORD POWER*
> Synonyms
> dishonourable
> nefarious
> unprincipled
> Antonym
> honest

❶ cross VERB
to go across
EG *the bridge which crosses the river*
ford EG *trying to find a safe place to ford the stream*
go across EG *going across the road*
span EG *the iron bridge spanning the railway*
traverse EG *a valley traversed by streams*

❷ cross VERB
to meet and go across
EG *the intersection where the roads cross*
crisscross EG *Phone wires criss-cross the street.*
intersect EG *The circles intersect in two places.*

❸ cross NOUN
a mixture of two things
EG *a cross between a collie and a retriever*
blend EG *a blend of the old and the new*
combination EG *a combination of fear and anger*
mixture EG *a mixture of two factors*

❹ cross ADJECTIVE
rather angry
EG *I'm very cross with him.*
angry EG *Are you angry with me?*
annoyed EG *I'm annoyed with myself for being so stupid.*
fractious EG *The children were getting fractious.*
fretful EG *the fretful expression on her face*

grumpy EG *a grumpy old man*
in a bad mood EG *He's in a bad mood about something.*
irritable EG *She had been restless and irritable all day.*

> *WORD POWER*
> Synonyms
> irascible
> peevish
> splenetic
> testy
> tetchy

crouch VERB
to squat down
EG *A man was crouching behind the car.*
bend down EG *I bent down and touched the grass.*
squat EG *He squatted on his heels to talk to the children.*

crowd NOUN
a large group of people
EG *A huge crowd gathered in the square.*
horde EG *hordes of tourists*
host EG *a host of fans*
mass EG *a heaving mass of people*
mob EG *a mob of demonstrators*
multitude EG *surrounded by a noisy multitude*
swarm EG *swarms of visitors*
throng EG *An official pushed through the throng.*

crowd VERB
to gather close together
EG *Hundreds of fans crowded into the hall.*
congregate EG *A large crowd congregated outside the stadium.*
gather EG *Dozens of people gathered to watch.*
swarm EG *Police swarmed into the area.*
throng EG *The crowds thronged into the mall.*

crowded ADJECTIVE
full of people
EG *a crowded room*

congested EG *congested cities*
full EG *The train was full.*
overflowing EG *buildings overflowing with students*
packed EG *By 10.30 the shop was packed.*

crucial ADJECTIVE
very important
EG *a crucial moment in his career*
central EG *central to the whole process*
critical EG *a critical point in the campaign*
decisive EG *ready to strike at the decisive moment*
momentous EG *a momentous event*
pivotal EG *He played a pivotal role in the match.*
vital EG *vital information*

crude ADJECTIVE
rough and simple
EG *a crude weapon*
primitive EG *They managed to make a primitive harness.*
rough EG *a rough sketch*
rudimentary EG *some form of rudimentary heating*
simple EG *a simple stringed instrument*

crude ADJECTIVE
rude and offensive
EG *a crude sense of humour*
coarse EG *coarse speech*
dirty EG *a dirty joke*
indecent EG *indecent lyrics*
obscene EG *obscene language*
tasteless EG *a tasteless remark*
vulgar EG *a vulgar phrase*

> *WORD POWER*
> Synonyms
> boorish
> crass
> smutty
> Antonym
> refined

cruel ADJECTIVE
deliberately causing hurt

A
B
C
D
E
F
G
H
I
J
K
L
M
N
O
P
Q
R
S
T
U
V
W
X
Y
Z

EG *I hate people who are cruel to animals.*

barbarous EG *a barbarous attack*

brutal EG *a brutal murder*

callous EG *callous treatment*

cold-blooded EG *a cold-blooded killer*

heartless EG *It was a heartless thing to do.*

inhumane EG *He was kept under inhumane conditions.*

sadistic EG *mistreated by sadistic guards*

vicious EG *a vicious blow*

> **WORD POWER**
> Antonym
> kind

cruelty NOUN
cruel behaviour
EG *an act of unbelievable cruelty*

barbarity EG *the barbarity of war*

brutality EG *police brutality*

callousness EG *the callousness of his murder*

inhumanity EG *man's inhumanity to man*

savagery EG *scenes of unimaginable savagery*

viciousness EG *the viciousness of the attacks*

> **WORD POWER**
> Antonym
> kindness

crumple VERB
to squash and wrinkle
EG *She crumpled the paper in her hand.*

crease EG *Don't crease the material.*

crush EG *Andrew crushed his empty can.*

screw up EG *He screwed the letter up in anger.*

wrinkle EG *trying not to wrinkle her silk skirt*

❶ crush VERB
to destroy the shape of by squeezing

EG *Their car was crushed by an army tank.*

crumble EG *Crumble the stock cubes into a jar.*

crumple EG *She crumpled the note up and threw it away.*

mash EG *Mash the bananas with a fork.*

squash EG *She squashed the wasp under her heel.*

❷ crush VERB
to defeat completely
EG *his bid to crush the uprising*

overcome EG *working to overcome the enemy forces*

put down EG *Soldiers moved in to put down the rebellion.*

quell EG *Troops eventually quelled the unrest.*

stamp out EG *steps to stamp out bullying in schools*

vanquish EG *his vanquished foe*

❶ cry VERB
to have tears coming from your eyes
EG *Stop crying and tell me what's wrong.*

bawl EG *One of the toddlers was bawling.*

blubber EG *He started to blubber like a child.*

sob EG *She was sobbing hysterically*

weep EG *She wept tears of joy.*

❷ cry VERB
to call out loudly
EG *"See you soon!" they cried.*

call EG *She called to me across the square.*

exclaim EG *'You must be mad!" she exclaimed.*

shout EG *"Over here!" they shouted*

yell EG *He yelled out of the window.*

❸ cry NOUN
a loud or high shout
EG *a cry of pain*

call EG *the call of a seagull*

exclamation EG *an exclamation of surprise*

shout EG *I heard a distant shout.*
yell EG *Bob let out a yell.*

cunning ADJECTIVE
clever and deceitful
EG *a cunning and ruthless businessman*
artful EG *an artful old woman*
crafty EG *a crafty plan*
devious EG *a devious mind*
sly EG *a sly trick*
wily EG *a wily politician*

> **WORD POWER**
> Synonyms
> foxy
> Machiavellian
> Antonym
> open

cunning NOUN
cleverness and deceit
EG *the cunning of today's criminals*
deviousness EG *the deviousness of drug traffickers*
guile EG *She was without guile or pretence.*

cure VERB
to make well
EG *a treatment which cures eczema*
heal EG *plants used to heal wounds*
remedy EG *an operation to remedy a blood clot on his brain*

cure NOUN
something that makes an illness better
EG *a cure for cancer*
medicine EG *herbal medicines*
remedy EG *a remedy for colds and flu*
treatment EG *the most effective treatment for malaria*

curiosity NOUN
the desire to know
EG *a curiosity about the past*
inquisitiveness EG *the inquisitiveness of children*
interest EG *a lively interest in current affairs*

curiosity NOUN

something unusual
EG *a museum displaying relics and curiosities*
freak EG *a freak of nature*
marvel EG *a marvel of science*
novelty EG *in the days when a motor car was a novelty*
oddity EG *Tourists are still something of an oddity here.*
rarity EG *Mexican restaurants are a rarity here.*

curious ADJECTIVE
wanting to know
EG *He was curious about my family.*
inquiring EG *He gave me an inquiring look.*
inquisitive EG *Cats are very inquisitive.*
interested EG *A crowd of interested villagers gathered.*
nosy INFORMAL EG *nosy neighbours*

> **WORD POWER**
> Antonym
> incurious

curious ADJECTIVE
strange and unusual
EG *a curious mixture of the old and the new*
bizarre EG *his bizarre behaviour*
extraordinary EG *an extraordinary story*
odd EG *an odd coincidence*
peculiar EG *a peculiar smell*
singular EG *singular talent*
strange EG *a strange taste*
unusual EG *an unusual name*

> **WORD POWER**
> Antonym
> ordinary

curve NOUN
a bending line
EG *a curve in the road*
arc EG *The ball rose in an arc.*
bend EG *a bend in the river*
trajectory EG *the trajectory of an artillery shell*
turn EG *every turn in the road*

A
B
C
D
E
F
G
H
I
J
K
L
M
N
O
P
Q
R
S
T
U
V
W
X
Y
Z

❷ curve VERB
to move in a curve
EG *The road curved sharply to the left.*
arc EG *A rainbow arced over the town.*
arch EG *a domed ceiling arching overhead*
bend EG *The path bent to the right.*
swerve EG *His car swerved off the road.*

❶ custom NOUN
a traditional activity
EG *an ancient Chinese custom*
convention EG *the conventions of Western art*
practice EG *an old Jewish practice*
ritual EG *an ancient Shintoist ritual*
tradition EG *different cultural traditions*

❷ custom NOUN
something a person always does
EG *It was a custom to start work at 8.30.*
habit EG *his habit of making tactless remarks*
practice EG *her usual practice of attending church*
routine EG *his daily routine*
wont EG *Paul woke early, as was his wont.*

customer NOUN
someone who buys something
EG *The shop was filled with customers.*
buyer EG *show homes to tempt potential buyers*
client EG *a solicitor and his client*
consumer EG *the increasing demands of consumers*
patron EG *the restaurant's patrons*
purchaser EG *a prospective purchaser*
shopper EG *late-night shoppers on their way home*

❶ cut VERB
to mark or injure with something sharp
EG *The thieves cut a hole in the fence.*
gash EG *She fell and gashed her hand.*
penetrate EG *The blade penetrated the skin.*
pierce EG *Pierce the potato with a fork.*
slash EG *vandals who slashed a priceless painting*
slice EG *Slice the tomato very thinly*
slit EG *He slit open the envelope.*

> **WORD POWER**
> Synonyms
> incise
> lacerate

❷ cut VERB
to reduce something
EG *The department's first priority is to cut costs.*
cut back EG *The Government has decided to cut back on defence spending.*
decrease EG *calls to decrease income tax*
lower EG *The Central Bank has lowered interest rates.*
reduce EG *Gradually reduce the dosage.*
slash EG *Holiday prices have been slashed.*

> **WORD POWER**
> Synonyms
> abridge
> downsize
> rationalize
> Antonym
> increase

❸ cut NOUN
a mark or injury made by cutting
EG *a cut on his left eyebrow*
gash EG *There was a deep gash across his forehead.*
incision EG *a tiny incision in the skin*
slash EG *jeans with slashes in the knees*
slit EG *Make a slit along the stem.*

cut NOUN
a reduction in something
EG *another cut in interest rates*
cutback EG *cutbacks in funding*
decrease EG *a decrease in foreign investment*
lowering EG *the lowering of taxes*
reduction EG *reductions in staff*
saving EG *household savings on energy use*

| WORD POWER

Antonym
increase

cynical ADJECTIVE
always thinking the worst of people
EG *a cynical attitude*

distrustful EG *distrustful of all politicians*

sceptical EG *a sceptical response*

A
B
C
D
E
F
G
H
I
J
K
L
M
N
O
P
Q
R
S
T
U
V
W
X
Y
Z

Dd Dd

❶ damage VERB
to cause harm to something
EG *A fire had severely damaged the school.*
harm EG *a warning that the product may harm the environment*
hurt EG *He had hurt his back in an accident.*
injure EG *Several policemen were injured in the clashes.*

❷ damage NOUN
harm that is done to something
EG *The bomb caused extensive damage to the restaurant.*
harm EG *All dogs are capable of doing harm to human beings.*
injury EG *He escaped without injury.*

❶ damp ADJECTIVE
slightly wet
EG *a damp towel*
clammy EG *clammy hands*
dank EG *The kitchen was dank and cheerless.*
humid EG *Visitors can expect hot and humid conditions.*
moist EG *The soil is reasonably moist after the September rain.*
sodden EG *We stripped off our sodden clothes.*
soggy EG *soggy cheese sandwiches*
wet EG *My hair was still wet.*

❷ damp NOUN
slight wetness
EG *There was damp all over the walls.*
dampness EG *I could see big circles of dampness under each arm.*
humidity EG *The heat and humidity were intolerable.*
moisture EG *Compost helps the soil retain moisture.*

> **WORD POWER**
> Synonyms
> clamminess
> dankness

danger NOUN
the possibility of harm
EG *Your life is in danger.*
hazard EG *a health hazard*
jeopardy EG *A series of setbacks have put the whole project in jeopardy.*
menace EG *In my view you are a menace to the public.*
peril EG *the perils of the sea*
risk EG *There is a small risk of brain damage.*
threat EG *Some couples see single women as a threat to their relationship.*

> **WORD POWER**
> Antonym
> safety

dangerous ADJECTIVE
likely to cause harm
EG *It's dangerous to drive when you're tired.*
hazardous EG *They have no way to dispose of the hazardous waste they produce.*
perilous EG *a perilous journey across the war-zone*
risky EG *Investing is risky.*
treacherous EG *Blizzards had made the roads treacherous.*

> **WORD POWER**
> Antonym
> safe

❶ dare VERB
to challenge someone to do something
EG *I dare you to ask him his name.*
challenge EG *He left a note at the scene of the crime, challenging detectives to catch him.*
defy EG *I defy you to watch it on your own.*
throw down the gauntlet EG *Jaguar has thrown down the gauntlet to competitors by giving the*

best guarantee on the market.

dare VERB
to have the courage to do something
EG *Nobody dared to complain.*
risk EG *The skipper was not willing to risk taking his ship through the straits.*
venture EG *the few Europeans who had ventured beyond the Himalayas*

daring ADJECTIVE
willing to take risks
EG *a daring escape by helicopter*
adventurous EG *an adventurous skier*
audacious EG *an audacious plan to win the presidency*
bold EG *bold economic reforms*
brave EG *He was not brave enough to report the loss of the documents.*
fearless EG *They were young and strong and fearless.*

> **WORD POWER**
> Synonyms
> intrepid
> valiant
> Antonym
> cautious

daring NOUN
the courage to take risks
EG *His daring may have cost him his life.*
audacity EG *He had the audacity to make a 200-1 bet on himself to win.*
boldness EG *the boldness of his economic programme*
bravery EG *He deserves the highest praise for his bravery.*
courage EG *He impressed everyone with his personal courage.*
guts INFORMAL EG *I haven't got the guts to tell him.*
nerve INFORMAL EG *He didn't have the nerve to meet me.*

> **WORD POWER**
> Synonyms
> fearlessness

intrepidity
temerity
Antonym
caution

❶ dark ADJECTIVE
lacking light
EG *It was too dark to see what was happening.*
cloudy EG *a cloudy sky*
dim EG *the dim outline of a small boat*
dingy EG *a dingy bedsit*
murky EG *the murky waters of the loch*
overcast EG *a cold, windy, overcast afternoon*
shadowy EG *a shadowy corner*

> **WORD POWER**
> Antonym
> light

❷ dark ADJECTIVE
dull in colour
EG *a dark suit*
black EG *a black leather coat*
swarthy EG *a broad swarthy face*

❸ dark NOUN
lack of light
EG *I've always been afraid of the dark.*
darkness EG *The room was plunged into darkness.*
dimness EG *I squinted to adjust my eyes to the dimness.*
dusk EG *She disappeared into the dusk.*
gloom EG *the gloom of a foggy November morning*

> **WORD POWER**
> Synonyms
> murk
> murkiness
> Antonym
> light

❶ daydream NOUN
a series of pleasant thoughts
EG *He learnt to escape into daydreams.*

A
B
C
D
E
F
G
H
I
J
K
L
M
N
O
P
Q
R
S
T
U
V
W
X
Y
Z

dream EG *My dream is to have a house in the country.*

fantasy EG *fantasies of romance and true love*

WORD POWER
Synonyms
castle in Spain
castle in the air
pipe dream
reverie

❷ **daydream** VERB
to think about pleasant things
EG *He daydreams of being a famous journalist.*

dream EG *She used to dream of becoming an actress.*

fantasize EG *I fantasized about writing music.*

dazed ADJECTIVE
unable to think clearly
EG *At the end of the interview I was dazed and exhausted.*

bewildered EG *Some shoppers looked bewildered by the sheer variety.*

confused EG *Things were happening too quickly and Brian was confused.*

dizzy EG *Her head hurt and she felt dizzy.*

light-headed EG *If you miss breakfast, you may feel light-headed.*

numbed EG *I'm so numbed with shock that I can hardly think.*

stunned EG *a stunned silence*

WORD POWER
Synonyms
disorientated
punch-drunk
stupefied

❶ **dead** ADJECTIVE
no longer alive
EG *My husband's been dead a year now.*

deceased EG *his recently deceased mother*

departed EG *my dear departed father*

extinct EG *the bones of extinct animals*

late EG *my late husband*

WORD POWER
Antonym
alive

❷ **dead** ADJECTIVE
no longer functioning
EG *a dead language*

defunct EG *the now defunct Social Democratic Party*

not working EG *The radio is not working.*

deadly ADJECTIVE
causing death
EG *a deadly disease*

destructive EG *the destructive power of nuclear weapons*

fatal EG *a fatal heart attack*

lethal EG *a lethal dose of sleeping pills*

mortal EG *Our lives were in mortal danger.*

deal VERB
to cope successfully with something
EG *He must learn to deal with stress.*

attend to EG *We have business to attend to first.*

cope with EG *She has had to cope with losing all her money.*

handle EG *I have learned how to handle pressure.*

manage EG *As time passed I learned to manage my grief.*

see to EG *Sarah saw to the packing while Jim fetched the car.*

take care of EG *Malcolm took care of all the arrangements.*

❶ **dear** NOUN
a person for whom you have affection
EG *What's the matter, dear?*

angel EG *Be an angel and fetch my bag.*

beloved OLD-FASHIONED EG *He took his beloved into his arms.*

darling EG *Thank you, darling.*

treasure INFORMAL EG *Charlie? Oh, he's a treasure.*

② dear ADJECTIVE
much loved
EG *a dear friend of mine*
beloved EG *He lost his beloved wife last year.*
cherished EG *his most cherished possession*
darling EG *his darling daughter*
esteemed EG *my esteemed colleagues*
precious EG *Her family's support is very precious to her.*
prized EG *one of the gallery's most prized possessions*
treasured EG *one of my most treasured memories*

③ dear ADJECTIVE
costing a lot
EG *They're too dear.*
costly EG *Having curtains professionally made can be costly.*
expensive EG *Wine's so expensive in this country.*
pricey INFORMAL EG *Medical insurance is very pricey.*

deceive VERB
to make someone believe something untrue
EG *I was really hurt that he had deceived me.*
con INFORMAL EG *The British motorist has been conned by the government.*
double-cross EG *They were frightened of being double-crossed.*
dupe EG *a plot to dupe stamp collectors into buying fake rarities*
fool EG *They tried to fool you into coming after us.*
mislead EG *He was furious with his doctors for having misled him.*
take in EG *I wasn't taken in for one moment.*
trick EG *His family tricked him into going to Pakistan.*

WORD POWER
Synonyms

bamboozle
beguile
hoodwink

① decent ADJECTIVE
of an acceptable standard
EG *He gets a decent pension.*
adequate EG *an adequate diet*
passable EG *She speaks passable French.*
reasonable EG *He couldn't make a reasonable living from his writing.*
respectable EG *investments that offer respectable rates of return*
satisfactory EG *I never got a satisfactory answer.*
tolerable EG *to make life more tolerable*

② decent ADJECTIVE
correct and respectable
EG *the decent thing to do*
proper EG *It is right and proper to do this.*
respectable EG *He came from a perfectly respectable middle-class family.*

WORD POWER
Antonym
improper

deceptive ADJECTIVE
likely to make people believe something untrue
EG *First impressions can be deceptive.*
false EG *'Thank you,' she said with false enthusiasm.*
fraudulent EG *fraudulent claims about being a nurse*
illusory EG *They argue that freedom is illusory.*
misleading EG *It would be misleading to say that we were friends.*
unreliable EG *His account is quite unreliable.*

WORD POWER
Synonyms
delusive
specious

A
B
C
D
E
F
G
H
I
J
K
L
M
N
O
P
Q
R
S
T
U
V
W
X
Y
Z

decide – decorate

decide VERB
to choose to do something
EG *She decided to do a secretarial course.*

choose EG *The council chose to inform the public about the risks.*

come to a decision EG *Have you come to a decision about where you're going tonight?*

determine FORMAL EG *He determined to rescue his two countrymen.*

elect FORMAL EG *I have elected to stay.*

make up your mind EG *He simply can't make his mind up whether he should stay.*

reach a decision EG *He demanded to know all the facts before reaching any decision.*

resolve FORMAL EG *She resolved to report the matter to the authorities.*

decision NOUN
a judgment about something
EG *The editor's decision is final.*

conclusion EG *I've come to the conclusion that she's a great musician.*

finding EG *It is the finding of this court that you are guilty.*

judgment EG *a landmark judgment by the Court of Appeal*

resolution EG *a resolution condemning violence*

ruling EG *He tried to have the court ruling overturned.*

verdict EG *The judges will deliver their verdict in October.*

declaration NOUN
a forceful or official announcement
EG *a declaration of war*

affirmation EG *her first public affirmation of her decision*

protestation FORMAL EG *his protestations of innocence*

statement EG *He made a formal statement to the police.*

testimony EG *His testimony was*

an important element in the case.

WORD POWER
Synonyms
assertion
avowal

declare VERB
to state something forcefully or officially
EG *He declared that he was going to be famous.*

affirm EG *a speech in which he affirmed a commitment to lower taxes*

announce EG *She was planning to announce her engagement.*

assert EG *He asserted his innocence*

certify EG *The president certified that the project would receive $650m.*

proclaim EG *He still proclaims himself a believer in the Revolution.*

profess FORMAL EG *Why do organisations profess that they care?*

pronounce EG *The authorities took time to pronounce their verdict.*

state EG *Please state your name.*

WORD POWER
Synonyms
attest
aver
avow

❶ **decorate** VERB
to make more attractive
EG *He decorated his room with pictures.*

adorn EG *Several oil paintings adorn the walls.*

deck EG *The house was decked with flowers.*

ornament EG *a high ceiling, ornamented with plaster fruits and flowers*

WORD POWER
Synonyms
beautify
bedeck
embellish
festoon

decorate VERB
to put paint or wallpaper on
EG *when they came to decorate the bedroom*
do up INFORMAL EG *He spent the summer doing up the barn.*
renovate EG *The couple spent thousands renovating the house.*

decrease VERB
to become or make less
EG *Population growth is decreasing by 1.4% each year.*
cut down EG *He cut down his coffee intake.*
decline EG *The number of staff has declined.*
diminish EG *The threat of nuclear war has diminished.*
drop EG *Temperatures can drop to freezing at night.*
dwindle EG *his dwindling authority*
lessen EG *changes to their diet that would lessen the risk of disease*
lower EG *The Central Bank has lowered interest rates.*
reduce EG *It reduces the risk of heart disease.*
shrink EG *The forests have shrunk to half their size.*

> **WORD POWER**
> **Synonyms**
> abate
> curtail
> subside
> wane
> **Antonym**
> increase

decrease NOUN
a lessening in the amount of something
EG *a decrease in the number of unemployed*
cutback EG *cutbacks in defence spending*
decline EG *the rate of decline in tobacco consumption*
drop EG *a drop in temperature*
lessening EG *a lessening of tension*
reduction EG *dramatic reductions*

in staff

> **WORD POWER**
> **Synonyms**
> abatement
> curtailment
> diminution
> **Antonym**
> increase

deep ADJECTIVE
having a long way to the bottom
EG *a deep hole*
bottomless EG *a bottomless pit*
yawning EG *a yawning chasm*

> **WORD POWER**
> **Antonym**
> shallow

deep ADJECTIVE
great or intense
EG *his deep love of Israel*
extreme EG *extreme poverty*
grave EG *a grave crisis*
great EG *the great gulf between the two teams*
intense EG *The pain was intense.*
profound EG *discoveries which had a profound effect on medicine*
serious EG *a serious problem*

deep ADJECTIVE
low in sound
EG *a deep voice*
bass EG *a beautiful bass voice*
low EG *Her voice was so low she was sometimes mistaken for a man.*

> **WORD POWER**
> **Synonyms**
> resonant
> sonorous
> **Antonym**
> high

defeat VERB
to win a victory over someone
EG *His guerrillas defeated the colonial army in 1954.*
beat EG *the team that beat us in the final*
conquer EG *During 1936, Mussolini conquered Abyssinia.*

crush EG *in his bid to crush the rebels*

rout EG *the battle at which the Norman army routed the English*

trounce EG *Australia trounced France by 60 points to 4.*

vanquish FORMAL EG *after the hero had vanquished the dragon*

❷ **defeat** NOUN
a failure to win
EG *a 2-1 defeat by Sweden*

conquest EG *He had led the conquest of southern Poland.*

debacle FORMAL EG *It will be hard for them to recover from this debacle.*

rout EG *The retreat turned into a rout.*

trouncing EG *after a 6-2 trouncing on Sunday*

WORD POWER
Antonym
victory

---

❶ **defence** NOUN
action to protect something
EG *The flat land offered no scope for defence.*

cover EG *They could not provide adequate air cover for ground operations.*

protection EG *Such a diet is believed to offer protection against cancer.*

resistance EG *Most people have a natural resistance to the disease.*

safeguard EG *legislation that offers safeguards against discrimination*

security EG *Airport security was tightened.*

❷ **defence** NOUN
an argument in support of something
EG *Chomsky's defence of his approach*

argument EG *There's a strong argument for lowering the price.*

excuse EG *There's no excuse for*

behaviour like that.

explanation EG *The authorities have given no explanation for his arrest.*

justification EG *The only justification for a zoo is educational*

plea EG *a plea of insanity*

❶ **defend** VERB
to protect from harm
EG *They would have killed him if he hadn't defended himself.*

cover EG *travel insurance covering you against theft*

guard EG *A few men were left outside to guard her.*

protect EG *What can women do to protect themselves from heart disease?*

safeguard EG *action to safeguard the ozone layer*

shelter EG *a wooden house, sheltered by a low roof*

shield EG *He shielded his head from the sun with an old sack.*

❷ **defend** VERB
to argue in support of
EG *I can't defend what he did.*

endorse EG *I can endorse their opinion wholeheartedly.*

justify EG *No argument can justify a war.*

stick up for INFORMAL EG *Why do you always stick up for her?*

support EG *Would you support such a move?*

uphold EG *upholding the artist's right to creative freedom*

defender NOUN
a person who argues in support of something
EG *a committed defender of human rights*

advocate EG *a strong advocate of free market policies*

champion EG *a champion of women's causes*

supporter EG *a major supporter of the tax reform*

❶ **definite** ADJECTIVE

unlikely to be changed
EG *It's too soon to give a definite answer.*

assured EG *Victory was still not assured.*

certain EG *Very little in life is certain.*

decided EG *Is anything decided yet?*

fixed EG *a world without fixed laws*

guaranteed EG *Success is not guaranteed.*

settled EG *Nothing is settled yet.*

❷ definite ADJECTIVE
certainly true
EG *The police had nothing definite against her.*

clear EG *It was a clear case of homicide.*

positive EG *We have positive proof that he was a blackmailer.*

> **WORD POWER**
> Synonyms
> black-and-white
> clear-cut
> cut-and-dried

deformed ADJECTIVE
abnormally shaped
EG *a deformed right leg*

disfigured EG *the scarred, disfigured face*

distorted EG *the distorted image caused by the projector*

degrade VERB
to humiliate someone
EG *the notion that pornography degrades women*

demean EG *I wasn't going to demean myself by acting like a suspicious wife.*

humiliate EG *He enjoyed humiliating me.*

❶ delay VERB
to put something off until later
EG *the decision to delay the launch until tomorrow*

defer EG *Customers often defer payment for as long as possible.*

postpone EG *The visit has been*

definite – delete

postponed indefinitely.

put off EG *women who put off having a baby*

shelve EG *The project has now been shelved.*

suspend EG *Relief convoys will be suspended until the fighting stops.*

❷ delay VERB
to slow or hinder something
EG *Various setbacks delayed production.*

check EG *a policy to check fast population growth*

hinder EG *Further investigation was hindered by the loss of all documentation.*

impede EG *Fallen rocks are impeding the progress of rescue workers.*

obstruct EG *The authorities are obstructing a UN investigation.*

set back EG *public protests that could set back reforms*

> **WORD POWER**
> Synonyms
> hold up
> retard
> Antonym
> hurry

❸ delay NOUN
a time when something is delayed
EG *a 7-hour stoppage that caused delays on most flights*

interruption EG *interruptions in the supply of food*

obstruction EG *Obstruction of justice is a criminal offence.*

setback EG *a setback for the peace process*

delete VERB
to remove something written
EG *The word 'exploded' had been deleted.*

cross out EG *He crossed out the first sentence and wrote it again.*

erase EG *It was unfortunate that she had erased the message.*

A B C D E F G H I J K L M N O P Q R S T U V W X Y Z

113

rub out EG *She rubbed out the marks in the margin.*

> ### WORD POWER
> Synonyms
> blue-pencil
> cancel
> edit out
> strike out

❶ deliberate ADJECTIVE
done on purpose
EG *a deliberate act of sabotage*

calculated EG *a calculated attempt to cover up her crime*

conscious EG *I made a conscious decision not to hide.*

intentional EG *The kick was intentional.*

premeditated EG *a premeditated attack*

studied EG *'It's an interesting match,' he said with studied understatement.*

> ### WORD POWER
> Antonym
> accidental

❷ deliberate ADJECTIVE
careful and not hurried
EG *His movements were gentle and deliberate.*

careful EG *The trip needs careful planning.*

cautious EG *a cautious approach*

measured EG *walking at the same measured pace*

methodical EG *Da Vinci was methodical in his research.*

> ### WORD POWER
> Antonym
> casual

❸ deliberate VERB
to think carefully about something
EG *The jury deliberated for five days before reaching a verdict.*

debate EG *He was debating whether or not he should tell her.*

meditate EG *She meditated on the uncertainties of his future.*

mull over EG *McLaren had been mulling over an idea to make a movie.*

ponder EG *He was pondering the problem when Phillipson drove up.*

reflect EG *I reflected on the child's future.*

delicious ADJECTIVE
tasting very nice
EG *a wide selection of delicious meal.*

appetizing EG *the appetizing smell of freshly baked bread*

delectable EG *delectable wine*

luscious EG *luscious fruit*

tasty EG *The food was very tasty.*

> ### WORD POWER
> Synonyms
> mouthwatering
> scrumptious

demand VERB
to need or require something
EG *This situation demands hard work.*

involve EG *Running a kitchen involves a great deal of discipline.*

need EG *a problem that needs careful handling*

require EG *Then he'll know what's required of him.*

take EG *Walking across the room took all her strength.*

want EG *The windows wanted cleaning.*

> ### WORD POWER
> Synonyms
> call for
> entail
> necessitate

❶ deny VERB
to say that something is untrue
EG *She denied both accusations.*

contradict EG *Her version contradicted the Government's claim.*

refute EG *He angrily refutes the charge.*

A B C D E F G H I J K L M N O P Q R S T U V W X Y Z

WORD POWER
Synonyms
abjure
disavow
disclaim
gainsay
rebut
repudiate
Antonym
admit

deny VERB
to refuse to believe something
EG *He denied the existence of God.*
reject EG *children who rejected their parents' religious beliefs*
renounce EG *after she renounced terrorism*

deny VERB
to refuse to give something
EG *His ex-partner denies him access to the children.*
refuse EG *The council had refused permission for the march.*
withhold EG *Financial aid for Russia has been withheld.*

department NOUN
a section of an organization
EG *the marketing department*
division EG *the bank's Latin American division*
office EG *Contact your local tax office.*
section EG *a top-secret section of the Foreign Office*
unit EG *the health services research unit*

depend VERB
to rely on
EG *You can depend on me.*
bank on EG *The government is banking on the Olympics to save the city money.*
count on EG *I can always count on you to cheer me up.*
rely on EG *They can always be relied on to turn up.*
trust EG *I knew I could trust him to meet a tight deadline.*

depend VERB
to be affected by
EG *Success depends on the quality of the workforce.*
be determined by EG *Social status is largely determined by occupation.*
hinge on EG *Victory or defeat hinged on her final putt.*

WORD POWER
Synonyms
be subject to
hang on
rest on

derelict ADJECTIVE
abandoned and in poor condition
EG *a derelict warehouse*
abandoned EG *a network of abandoned mines*
dilapidated EG *a dilapidated castle*
neglected EG *a neglected garden*
ruined EG *a ruined church*

descend VERB
to move downwards
EG *as we descend to the cellar*
dip EG *The sun dipped below the horizon.*
dive EG *The shark dived down and under the boat.*
fall EG *Bombs fell in the town.*
go down EG *after the sun has gone down*
plummet EG *as the plane plummeted through the air*
sink EG *A fresh egg will sink and an old egg will float.*

WORD POWER
Antonym
ascend

describe VERB
to give an account of something
EG *We asked her to describe what she did in her spare time.*
define EG *Culture can be defined in many ways.*
depict EG *a novel depicting a gloomy, futuristic America*

A
B
C
D
E
F
G
H
I
J
K
L
M
N
O
P
Q
R
S
T
U
V
W
X
Y
Z

portray EG *a writer who accurately portrays provincial life*

> **WORD POWER**
> Synonyms
> characterize
> detail

deserve VERB
to have a right to something
EG *He deserves a rest.*
be entitled to EG *She is entitled to feel proud.*
be worthy of EG *The bank might think you're worthy of a loan.*
earn EG *You've earned this holiday.*
justify EG *The decision was fully justified by economic conditions.*
merit EG *Such ideas merit careful consideration.*
warrant EG *no evidence to warrant a murder investigation*

❶ design VERB
to make a plan of something
EG *They wanted to design a machine that was both attractive and practical.*
draft EG *The legislation was drafted by Democrats.*
draw up EG *a working party to draw up a formal agreement*
plan EG *when we plan road construction*

❷ design NOUN
a plan or drawing
EG *his design for a new office*
model EG *an architect's model of a wooden house*
plan EG *when you have drawn a plan of the garden*

> **WORD POWER**
> Synonyms
> blueprint
> schema

❸ design NOUN
the shape or style of something
EG *a new design of clock*
form EG *the form of the human body*

pattern EG *a pattern of coloured dots*
shape EG *a kidney shape*
style EG *Several styles of hat were available.*

❶ desire VERB
to want something
EG *We can stay longer if you desire.*
crave EG *I crave her approval.*
fancy EG *She fancied living in Canada.*
long for EG *He longed for the winter to be over.*
want EG *I want a drink.*
wish EG *We wished to return.*
yearn EG *He yearned to sleep.*

> **WORD POWER**
> Synonyms
> ache for
> covet

❷ desire NOUN
a feeling of wanting something
EG *I had a strong desire to help people.*
appetite EG *She had lost her appetite for air travel.*
craving EG *a craving for sugar*
hankering EG *a hankering to be an actress*
longing EG *her longing to return home*
wish EG *Her wish is to be in films.*
yearning EG *a yearning for a child of my own*
yen INFORMAL EG *Mike had a yen to try cycling.*

❶ despair NOUN
a loss of hope
EG *feelings of despair*
dejection EG *There was an air of dejection about her.*
despondency EG *There's a mood of despondency in the country.*
gloom EG *the deepening gloom over the economy*
hopelessness EG *She had a feeling of hopelessness about the future.*

❷ despair VERB

to lose hope
EG *I despair at the attitude with which their work is received.*
feel dejected EG *Everyone has days when they feel dejected.*
feel despondent EG *John often felt despondent after visiting the job centre.*
lose heart EG *He appealed to his countrymen not to lose heart.*
lose hope EG *You mustn't lose hope.*

despite PREPOSITION
in spite of
EG *He fell asleep despite all the coffee he'd drunk.*
in spite of EG *In spite of all the gossip, Virginia stayed behind.*
notwithstanding FORMAL EG *Notwithstanding his age, Sikorski had an important job.*
regardless of EG *He led from the front, regardless of the danger.*

destroy VERB
to ruin something completely
EG *The building was completely destroyed.*
annihilate EG *The lava annihilates everything in its path.*
demolish EG *A storm moved over the island, demolishing buildings.*
devastate EG *A fire had devastated large parts of Windsor castle.*
obliterate EG *Whole villages were obliterated by fire.*
raze EG *The town was razed to the ground during the occupation.*
ruin EG *My wife was ruining her health through worry.*
wreck EG *the injuries which nearly wrecked his career*

destruction NOUN
the act of destroying something
EG *the destruction of the ozone layer*
annihilation EG *Leaders fear the annihilation of their people.*
demolition EG *the demolition of an old bridge*
devastation EG *A l.uge bomb*

blast brought chaos and devastation.
obliteration EG *the obliteration of three rainforests*

detail NOUN
an individual feature of something
EG *We discussed every detail of the performance.*
aspect EG *Climate affects every aspect of our lives.*
element EG *one of the key elements of the peace plan*
particular EG *You will find all the particulars in Chapter 9.*
point EG *Many of the points in the report are correct.*
respect EG *At least in this respect we are equals.*

> **WORD POWER**
> Synonyms
> fine point
> nicety

determination NOUN
a firm decision to do something
EG *the government's determination to beat inflation*
perseverance EG *Adam's perseverance proved worthwhile.*
persistence EG *She was determined to be a doctor and her persistence paid off.*
resolution EG *She acted with resolution and courage.*
resolve FORMAL EG *the American public's resolve to go to war if necessary*
tenacity EG *Hard work and sheer tenacity are crucial to career success.*

> **WORD POWER**
> Synonyms
> doggedness
> single-mindedness
> steadfastness
> willpower

determined ADJECTIVE
firmly decided
EG *She was determined not to repeat*

A
B
C
D
E
F
G
H
I
J
K
L
M
N
O
P
Q
R
S
T
U
V
W
X
Y
Z

her error.

bent on EG *They seem bent on destroying the city.*

dogged EG *dogged persistence*

intent on EG *He is intent on repeating his victory.*

persistent EG *He phoned again this morning. He's very persistent.*

purposeful EG *She had a purposeful air.*

resolute FORMAL EG *a decisive and resolute leader*

single-minded EG *a single-minded determination to win*

tenacious EG *a tenacious and persistent interviewer*

> *WORD POWER*
> Synonyms
> steadfast
> unflinching
> unwavering

devious ADJECTIVE
getting what you want by sly methods
EG *a devious politician*

calculating EG *a calculating businessman*

scheming EG *He was branded a "scheming liar".*

underhand EG *He used underhand tactics to win the election.*

wily EG *a wily old statesman*

dictionary NOUN

> Parts of a dictionary or thesaurus:
> antonym
> definition
> entry
> example
> homonym
> homophone
> pronunciation
> root word
> synonym
> word derivation

❶ die VERB
to stop living
EG *My mother died of cancer.*

cark it AUSTRALIAN AND NEW ZEALAND INFORMAL EG *You think you're about to cark it.*

expire FORMAL EG *before he finally expired*

pass away EG *He passed away last year.*

pass on EG *My mother passed on four years ago.*

perish FORMAL EG *the ferry disaster in which 193 passengers perished*

❷ die VERB
to fade away
EG *My love for you will never die.*

fade away EG *With time, they said, the pain will fade away.*

fade out EG *Thanks to supermarkets, the corner shop is gradually fading out.*

peter out EG *The six-month strike seemed to be petering out.*

die out VERB
to cease to exist
EG *That custom has died out now.*

disappear EG *Huge areas of the countryside are disappearing.*

fade EG *Prospects for peace had already started to fade.*

vanish EG *those species which have vanished*

❶ difference NOUN
a lack of similarity between things
EG *the vast difference in size*

contrast EG *the real contrast between the two poems*

discrepancy EG *discrepancies between their statements*

disparity EG *disparities between poor and wealthy districts*

distinction EG *a distinction between the body and the soul*

divergence EG *There's a substantial divergence of opinion within the party.*

variation EG *a wide variation in the prices charged*

> *WORD POWER*
> Antonym

similarity

difference NOUN
the amount by which two quantities differ
EG *The difference is 8532.*
balance EG *They were due to pay the balance on delivery.*
remainder EG *They own a 75% stake. The remainder is owned by the bank.*

different ADJECTIVE
unlike something else
EG *We have totally different views.*
contrasting EG *painted in contrasting colours*
disparate FORMAL EG *The republics are very disparate in size and wealth.*
dissimilar EG *His methods were not dissimilar to those used by Freud.*
divergent FORMAL EG *divergent opinions*
opposed EG *two opposed ideologies*
unlike EG *This was a foreign country, so unlike San Jose.*

WORD POWER
Synonyms
at odds
at variance
Antonym
similar

different ADJECTIVE
unusual and out of the ordinary
EG *The result is interesting and different.*
special EG *a special variety of strawberry*
unique EG *Each person's signature is unique.*

different ADJECTIVE
distinct and separate
EG *The lunch supports a different charity each year.*
another EG *Her doctor referred her to another therapist.*
discrete FORMAL EG *two discrete sets of nerves*

difference – difficulty

distinct EG *A word may have two quite distinct meanings.*
individual EG *Each family needs individual attention.*
separate EG *The word 'quarter' has two completely separate meanings.*

difficult ADJECTIVE
not easy to do or solve
EG *a difficult decision to make*
arduous EG *a long, arduous journey*
demanding EG *a demanding job*
hard EG *He found it hard to get work.*
intractable FORMAL EG *an intractable problem*
laborious EG *a laborious task*
uphill EG *an uphill battle*

WORD POWER
Synonyms
knotty
problematic
thorny
Antonym
easy

difficult ADJECTIVE
not easy to deal with
EG *I hope she isn't going to be difficult.*
demanding EG *a demanding child*
troublesome EG *a troublesome teenager*
trying EG *The whole business has been very trying.*

WORD POWER
Synonyms
obstreperous
refractory
unmanageable

difficulty NOUN
a problem
EG *The central difficulty is his drinking.*
complication EG *An added complication is the growing concern for the environment.*
hassle INFORMAL EG *all the usual hassles at the airport*

A B C D E F G H I J K L M N O P Q R S T U V W X Y Z

119

difficulty – dim

A B C **D** E F G H I J K L M N O P Q R S T U V W X Y Z

hurdle EG *preparing a CV, the first hurdle in a job search*
obstacle EG *To succeed, you must learn to overcome obstacles.*
pitfall EG *the pitfalls of working abroad*
problem EG *He left home because of family problems.*
snag EG *The only snag was that he had no transport.*
trouble EG *What seems to be the trouble?*

> **WORD POWER**
> Synonyms
> impediment
> stumbling block

❷ difficulty NOUN
the quality of being difficult
EG *the difficulty of the problem*
hardship EG *economic hardship*
strain EG *the stresses and strains of a busy career*
tribulation FORMAL EG *the trials and tribulations of everyday life*

> **WORD POWER**
> Synonyms
> arduousness
> laboriousness

❶ dig VERB
to break up soil or sand
EG *He dug a hole in the ground.*
burrow EG *The larvae burrow into cracks in the floor.*
excavate EG *A contractor was hired to excavate soil from the area.*
gouge EG *quarries which have gouged great holes in the hills*
hollow out EG *They hollowed out crude dwellings from the soft rock.*
quarry EG *The caves are quarried for cement.*
till EG *freshly tilled fields*
tunnel EG *The rebels tunnelled out of jail.*

❷ dig VERB
to push something in
EG *He could feel the beads digging into his palm.*

120

jab EG *A needle was jabbed into the baby's arm.*
poke EG *She poked a fork into the turkey skin.*
thrust EG *She thrust her hand into the sticky mess.*

❸ dig NOUN
a push or poke
EG *She silenced him with a dig in the ribs.*
jab EG *a swift jab in the stomach*
poke EG *a playful poke in the arm*
prod EG *He gave the donkey a prod in the backside.*
thrust EG *knife thrusts*

❶ dim ADJECTIVE
not bright or well-lit
EG *a dim outline of a small boat*
dark EG *a dark corridor*
dull EG *The stamp was a dark, dull blue.*
grey EG *a grey, wet, April Sunday*
murky EG *one murky November afternoon*
poorly lit EG *a poorly lit road*
shadowy EG *a shadowy corner*

❷ dim ADJECTIVE
vague or unclear
EG *a dim memory*
faint EG *a faint recollection*
hazy EG *Many details remain hazy.*
indistinct EG *the indistinct murmur of voices*
obscure EG *The origin of the custom is obscure.*
shadowy EG *the shadowy world of spies*
vague EG *I have a vague memory of shots being fired.*

> **WORD POWER**
> Synonyms
> fuzzy
> ill-defined
> Antonym
> clear

❸ dim ADJECTIVE; INFORMAL
slow to understand
EG *He is rather dim.*

dumb INFORMAL EG *I've met a lot of dumb people.*

obtuse EG *I've really been very obtuse.*

slow EG *He got hit on the head and he's been a bit slow since.*

stupid EG *How could I have been so stupid?*

thick INFORMAL EG *I must have seemed incredibly thick.*

> **WORD POWER**
> Antonym
> bright

❶ direct ADJECTIVE
in a straight line or with nothing in between
EG *the direct route*

first-hand EG *She has little first-hand knowledge of Quebec.*

immediate EG *his immediate superior*

personal EG *I have no personal experience of this.*

straight EG *Keep the boat in a straight line.*

uninterrupted EG *an uninterrupted view*

> **WORD POWER**
> Antonym
> indirect

❷ direct ADJECTIVE
open and honest
EG *He can be very direct sometimes.*

blunt EG *She is blunt about her personal life.*

candid EG *I haven't been completely candid with you.*

forthright EG *forthright language*

frank EG *She is always very frank.*

straight EG *He never gives you a straight answer.*

straightforward EG *his straightforward manner*

> **WORD POWER**
> Antonym
> devious

❸ direct VERB

to control and guide something
EG *Christopher will direct day-to-day operations.*

control EG *He now controls the entire company.*

guide EG *He should have let his instinct guide him.*

lead EG *He led the country between 1949 and 1984.*

manage EG *Within two years he was managing the store.*

oversee EG *an architect to oversee the work*

run EG *Is this any way to run a country?*

supervise EG *I supervise the packing of all mail orders.*

❶ direction NOUN
the line in which something is moving
EG *ten miles in the opposite direction*

course EG *The captain altered course.*

path EG *He stepped into the path of a reversing car.*

route EG *We took the wrong route.*

way EG *Does anybody know the way to the bathroom?*

❷ direction NOUN
control and guidance of something
EG *He was chopping vegetables under the chef's direction.*

charge EG *A few years ago he took charge of the company.*

command EG *In 1942 he took command of 108 Squadron.*

control EG *The restructuring involves Ronson giving up control of the company.*

guidance EG *the reports which were produced under his guidance*

leadership EG *The agency doubled in size under her leadership.*

management EG *The zoo needed better management.*

❶ dirt NOUN
dust or mud
EG *I started to scrub off the dirt.*

A
B
C
D
E
F
G
H
I
J
K
L
M
N
O
P
Q
R
S
T
U
V
W
X
Y
Z

dust EG *The furniture was covered in dust.*

filth EG *tons of filth and sewage*

grime EG *Kelly got the grime off his hands.*

muck EG *This congealed muck was interfering with the filter.*

mud EG *Their lorry got stuck in the mud.*

❷ **dirt** NOUN
earth or soil
EG *He drew a circle in the dirt with the stick.*

earth EG *a huge pile of earth*

soil EG *an area with very good soil*

❶ **dirty** ADJECTIVE
marked with dirt
EG *The kids have got their clothes dirty.*

filthy EG *a pair of filthy jeans*

grimy EG *a grimy industrial city*

grubby EG *kids with grubby faces*

mucky EG *a mucky floor*

muddy EG *his muddy boots*

soiled EG *a soiled white apron*

unclean EG *unclean water*

> **WORD POWER**
> Antonym
> clean

❷ **dirty** ADJECTIVE
unfair or dishonest
EG *a dirty fight*

corrupt EG *corrupt practices*

crooked EG *crooked business deals*

> **WORD POWER**
> Antonym
> honest

❸ **dirty** ADJECTIVE
sexually explicit
EG *a dirty joke*

blue EG *a blue movie*

filthy EG *a filthy book*

pornographic EG *pornographic videos*

rude EG *a rude joke*

> **WORD POWER**
> Synonyms

risqué
salacious
smutty

disadvantage NOUN
an unfavourable circumstance
EG *the advantages and disadvantages of allowing their soldiers to marry*

drawback EG *The apartment's only drawback was that it was too small.*

handicap EG *The tax issue was undoubtedly a handicap to Labour.*

minus EG *The plusses and minuses were about equal.*

weakness EG *the strengths and weaknesses of the argument*

> **WORD POWER**
> Synonyms
> downside
> hindrance
> Antonym
> advantage

❶ **disagree** VERB
to have a different opinion
EG *They can communicate even when they disagree.*

differ EG *They differ on lots of issues.*

dispute EG *Nobody disputed that Davey was clever.*

dissent EG *dissenting views*

> **WORD POWER**
> Antonym
> agree

❷ **disagree** VERB
to think that something is wrong
EG *I disagree with drug laws in general.*

object EG *We objected strongly but were outvoted.*

oppose EG *protesters opposing nuclear tests*

take issue with EG *I take issue with much of what he said.*

❶ **disagreement** NOUN

a dispute about something
EG *My driving instructor and I had a brief disagreement.*

altercation FORMAL EG *an altercation with the referee*

argument EG *an argument about money*

difference EG *We have our differences but we get along.*

dispute EG *a pay dispute*

quarrel EG *I had a terrible quarrel with my brother.*

row EG *a major diplomatic row*

squabble EG *minor squabbles about phone bills*

tiff EG *a lovers' tiff*

> **WORD POWER**
> Antonym
> agreement

❷ disagreement NOUN
an objection to something
EG *Britain and France have expressed some disagreement with the proposal.*

dissent EG *voices of dissent*

objection EG *I have no objection to banks making money.*

opposition EG *their opposition to the scheme*

❶ disappear VERB
to go out of sight
EG *The aircraft disappeared off the radar.*

be lost to view EG *They observed the comet for 70 days before it was lost to view.*

drop out of sight EG *After his first film he dropped out of sight.*

fade EG *We watched the harbour fade into the mist.*

recede EG *Luke receded into the distance.*

vanish EG *Anne vanished from outside her home the Wednesday before last.*

> **WORD POWER**
> Antonym
> appear

❷ disappear VERB
to stop existing
EG *The pain has finally disappeared.*

cease FORMAL EG *At 1 o'clock the rain ceased.*

die out EG *How did the dinosaurs die out?*

go away EG *All she wanted was for the pain to go away.*

melt away EG *His anger melted away.*

pass EG *He told her the fear would pass.*

vanish EG *species which have vanished*

disappointed ADJECTIVE
sad because something has not happened
EG *I was disappointed that Kluge was not there.*

dejected EG *Her refusal left him feeling dejected.*

despondent EG *After the interview John was despondent.*

disenchanted EG *She has become very disenchanted with the marriage.*

disillusioned EG *I've become very disillusioned with politics.*

downcast EG *After his defeat Mr Rabin looked downcast.*

saddened EG *He is saddened that they did not win anything.*

> **WORD POWER**
> Synonyms
> disheartened
> let down
> Antonym
> satisfied

❶ disappointment NOUN
a feeling of being disappointed
EG *Book early to avoid disappointment.*

dejection EG *There was an air of dejection about her.*

despondency EG *a mood of gloom and despondency*

regret EG *my one great regret in life*

123

A
B
C
D
E
F
G
H
I
J
K
L
M
N
O
P
Q
R
S
T
U
V
W
X
Y
Z

WORD POWER
Synonyms
disenchantment
disillusionment

❷ disappointment NOUN
something that disappoints you
EG *The reunion was a bitter disappointment.*
blow EG *It was a terrible blow when he was made redundant.*
setback EG *a setback for the peace process*

disapproval NOUN
the belief that something is wrong
EG *his mother's disapproval of his marriage*
censure EG *He deserves support, not censure.*
condemnation EG *the universal condemnation of French nuclear tests*
criticism EG *actions which have attracted fierce criticism*

WORD POWER
Antonym
approval

disapprove VERB
to think that something is wrong
EG *Everyone disapproved of their marrying so young.*
condemn EG *Political leaders condemned the speech.*
deplore FORMAL EG *He deplores violence.*
dislike EG *Her father seemed to dislike all her boyfriends.*
find unacceptable EG *I find such behaviour totally unacceptable.*
take a dim view of EG *They took a dim view of local trade unionists.*

WORD POWER
Synonyms
frown on
take exception to
Antonym
approve

disaster NOUN
a very bad accident
EG *another air disaster*
calamity FORMAL EG *It could only end in calamity.*
catastrophe EG *War would be a catastrophe.*
misfortune EG *She seemed to enjoy the misfortunes of others.*
tragedy EG *They have suffered an enormous personal tragedy.*

discard VERB
to get rid of something
EG *Read the instructions before discarding the box.*
cast aside EG *In America we seem to cast aside our elderly people.*
dispose of EG *how he disposed of the murder weapon*
dump INFORMAL EG *The getaway car was dumped near the motorway.*
jettison EG *The crew jettisoned excess fuel.*
shed EG *a snake that has shed its skin*
throw away EG *I never throw anything away.*
throw out EG *Why don't you throw out all those old magazines?*

discourage VERB
to make someone lose enthusiasm
EG *Don't let these problems discourage you.*
daunt EG *He was not the type of man to be daunted by adversity.*
deter EG *Tougher sentences would do nothing to deter crime.*
dissuade EG *He considered emigrating, but his family managed to dissuade him.*
put off EG *I wouldn't let it put you off applying.*

WORD POWER
Synonyms
demoralize
dishearten
Antonym
encourage

discuss VERB
to talk about something
EG *I will be discussing the situation with colleagues tomorrow.*
debate EG *The UN Security Council will debate the issue today.*
exchange views on EG *They exchanged views on a wide range of subjects.*
go into EG *We didn't go into that.*
talk about EG *What did you talk about?*

discussion NOUN
a talk about something
EG *informal discussions*
consultation EG *consultations between lawyers*
conversation EG *I struck up a conversation with him.*
debate EG *There has been a lot of debate among scholars about this.*
dialogue EG *a direct dialogue between the two nations*
discourse EG *a long tradition of political discourse*
talk EG *We had a long talk about it.*

disgrace NOUN
lack of respect
EG *She has brought disgrace upon the whole team.*
scandal EG *They often abandoned their children because of fear of scandal.*
shame EG *I don't want to bring shame on the family name.*

> **WORD POWER**
> Synonyms
> discredit
> dishonour
> Antonym
> credit

disgrace VERB
to bring shame upon
EG *I have disgraced my family's name.*
discredit EG *He said such methods discredited the communist fight worldwide.*

shame EG *I wouldn't shame my father by doing that.*

disgraceful ADJECTIVE
deserving of shame
EG *disgraceful behaviour*
scandalous EG *a scandalous waste of money*
shameful EG *the most shameful episode in US naval history*
shocking EG *a shocking invasion of privacy*

> **WORD POWER**
> Synonyms
> discreditable
> dishonourable

❶ disgust NOUN
a strong feeling of dislike
EG *his disgust at the incident*
nausea EG *I was overcome with a feeling of nausea.*
repulsion EG *a shudder of repulsion*
revulsion EG *They expressed their shock and revulsion at his death.*

❷ disgust VERB
to cause someone to feel disgust
EG *He disgusted many with his behaviour.*
repel EG *a violent excitement that frightened and repelled her*
revolt EG *The smell revolted him.*
sicken EG *What he saw there sickened him.*

> **WORD POWER**
> Synonyms
> nauseate
> turn your stomach

disgusting ADJECTIVE
very unpleasant or unacceptable
EG *one of the most disgusting sights I had ever seen*
foul EG *a foul stench*
gross EG *Don't be so gross!*
obnoxious EG *a most obnoxious character*
repellent EG *a very large, repellent toad*
revolting EG *The smell was*

A
B
C
D
E
F
G
H
I
J
K
L
M
N
O
P
Q
R
S
T
U
V
W
X
Y
Z

revolting.
sickening EG *a sickening attack on a pregnant woman*
vile EG *a vile odour*

> **WORD POWER**
> Synonyms
> nauseating
> repugnant

dishonest ADJECTIVE
not truthful
EG *It would be dishonest to mislead people.*
corrupt EG *corrupt police officers*
crooked EG *crooked business deals*
deceitful EG *The ambassador called the report deceitful and misleading.*
fraudulent EG *fraudulent claims about being a nurse*
lying EG *He called her 'a lying little twit'.*

> **WORD POWER**
> Synonyms
> mendacious
> untruthful
> Antonym
> honest

dishonesty NOUN
dishonest behaviour
EG *She accused the government of dishonesty.*
cheating EG *He was accused of cheating.*
corruption EG *The President faces 54 charges of corruption.*
deceit EG *the deceit and lies of the past*
trickery EG *They resorted to trickery in order to impress their clients.*

> **WORD POWER**
> Synonyms
> duplicity
> fraudulence
> mendacity
> Antonym
> honesty

disintegrate VERB
to break into many pieces
EG *At 420 mph the windscreen disintegrated.*
break up EG *There was a danger of the ship breaking up completely.*
crumble EG *The flint crumbled into fragments.*
fall apart EG *Bit by bit the building fell apart.*
fall to pieces EG *The radio handset fell to pieces.*
fragment EG *The clouds fragmented and out came the sun.*

❶ **dislike** VERB
to consider something unpleasant
EG *We don't serve it often because many people dislike it.*
abhor FORMAL EG *a man who abhorred violence*
be averse to EG *He's not averse to a little publicity.*
detest EG *Jean detested being photographed.*
hate EG *Most people hate him.*
loathe EG *a play loathed by the critics*
not be able to abide EG *I can't abide liars.*
not be able to bear EG *I can't bear people who speak like that.*
not be able to stand EG *He can't stand the sound of her voice.*

> **WORD POWER**
> Antonym
> like

❷ **dislike** NOUN
a feeling of not liking something
EG *She looked at him with dislike.*
animosity EG *The animosity between the two men grew.*
antipathy EG *their antipathy to my smoking*
aversion EG *I've always had an aversion to being part of a group.*
distaste EG *Roger looked at her with distaste.*
hatred EG *her hatred of authority*

hostility EG *hostility to ethnic groups*
loathing EG *He made no secret of his loathing of her.*

WORD POWER
Antonym
liking

disorder NOUN
a state of untidiness
EG *Inside, all was disorder.*
clutter EG *She prefers the worktop to be free of clutter.*
disarray EG *Her clothes were in disarray.*
muddle EG *a general muddle of pencils and boxes*

WORD POWER
Antonym
order

disorder NOUN
a lack of organization
EG *The men fled in disorder.*
chaos EG *Their concerts often ended in chaos.*
confusion EG *There was confusion when a man fired shots.*
disarray EG *The nation is in disarray following rioting.*
turmoil EG *the political turmoil of 1989*

disorder NOUN
a disease or illness
EG *a rare nerve disorder*
affliction EG *an affliction which can ruin a young man's life*
complaint EG *a common skin complaint*
condition EG *a heart condition*
disease EG *heart disease*
illness EG *mental illness*

disprove VERB
to show that something is not true
EG *the statistics that will prove or disprove the hypothesis*
discredit EG *There would be difficulties in discrediting the*

evidence.
give the lie to EG *This survey gives the lie to the idea that the economy is recovering.*
invalidate EG *Some of the other criticisms were invalidated years ago.*
prove false EG *It is hard to prove such claims false.*
refute EG *the kind of rumour that is impossible to refute*

WORD POWER
Antonym
prove

distant ADJECTIVE
far away in space or time
EG *a distant land*
far EG *Is it very far?*
outlying EG *outlying districts*
out-of-the-way EG *an out-of-the-way spot*
remote EG *a remote village*

WORD POWER
Synonyms
faraway
far-flung
far-off
Antonym
close

distant ADJECTIVE
cold and unfriendly
EG *He is polite but distant.*
aloof EG *He seemed aloof and detached.*
detached EG *He observed me with a detached curiosity.*
reserved EG *She's quite a reserved person.*
withdrawn EG *Her husband had become withdrawn and moody.*

WORD POWER
Synonyms
standoffish
unapproachable
Antonym
friendly

distinguish VERB

127

A B C D E F G H I J K L M N O P Q R S T U V W X Y Z

to see the difference between things
EG *Could he distinguish right from wrong?*

differentiate EG *At this age your baby cannot differentiate one person from another.*

discriminate EG *He is unable to discriminate a good idea from a terrible one.*

tell EG *How do you tell one from another?*

tell apart EG *I can only tell them apart by the colour of their shoes.*

tell the difference EG *I can't tell the difference between their policies and ours.*

❷ distinguish VERB
to recognize something
EG *I heard shouting but was unable to distinguish the words.*

discern EG *We could just discern a narrow ditch.*

make out EG *He couldn't make out what she was saying.*

pick out EG *Through my binoculars I picked out a group of figures.*

recognize EG *He did not think she could recognize his car in the snow.*

distract VERB
to stop someone from concentrating
EG *Playing video games distracts him from his homework.*

divert EG *They want to divert our attention from the real issues.*

draw away EG *to draw attention away from the crime*

> **WORD POWER**
> Synonyms
> sidetrack
> turn aside

❶ distress NOUN
great suffering
EG *Jealousy causes distress and painful emotions.*

heartache EG *the heartache of her divorce*

pain EG *eyes that seemed filled with pain*

sorrow EG *a time of great sorrow*

suffering EG *to put an end to his suffering*

❷ distress NOUN
the state of needing help
EG *The ship might be in distress.*

difficulty EG *rumours about banks being in difficulty*

need EG *When you were in need, I loaned you money.*

straits EG *The company's closure left them in desperate financial straits.*

trouble EG *a charity that helps women in trouble*

❸ distress VERB
to cause someone unhappiness
EG *Her death had profoundly distressed me.*

bother EG *It bothered me that boys weren't interested in me.*

disturb EG *dreams so vivid that they disturb me for days*

grieve EG *It grieved her to be separated from her son.*

pain EG *It pains me to think of you struggling all alone.*

sadden EG *The cruelty in the world saddens me deeply.*

trouble EG *He was troubled by the lifestyle of his son.*

upset EG *I'm sorry if I've upset you.*

worry EG *I didn't want to worry you.*

❶ distribute VERB
to hand something out
EG *They publish and distribute brochures.*

circulate EG *He has circulated a discussion document.*

hand out EG *One of my jobs was to hand out the prizes.*

pass around EG *Sweets were being passed around.*

pass round EG *She passed her holiday photos round.*

A B C **D** E F G H I J K L M N O P Q R S T U V W X Y Z

distribute VERB
to spread something through an area
EG *Distribute the topping evenly over the fruit.*

diffuse EG *Interest in books is more widely diffused than ever.*
disperse EG *The leaflets were dispersed throughout the country.*
scatter EG *She scattered the petals over the grave.*
spread EG *A thick layer of wax was spread over the surface.*

distribute VERB
to divide and share something
EG *Distribute chores evenly among all family members.*

allocate EG *funds allocated for nursery education*
allot EG *The seats are allotted to the candidates who have won the most votes.*
dispense FORMAL EG *The Union had already dispensed £400 in grants.*
divide EG *Paul divides his spare time between the bedroom and the study.*
dole out EG *I got out my wallet and began to dole out the money.*
share out EG *You could share out the money a bit more equally.*

WORD POWER
Synonyms
apportion
mete out

disturb VERB
to intrude on someone's peace
EG *She slept in a separate room so as not to disturb him.*

bother EG *I'm sorry to bother you.*
disrupt EG *Protesters disrupted the debate.*
intrude on EG *I don't want to intrude on your parents.*

disturb VERB
to upset or worry someone
EG *Some scenes may disturb you.*

agitate EG *The thought agitated her.*
distress EG *Her death had profoundly distressed me.*
shake EG *Well, it shook me quite a bit.*
trouble EG *He was troubled by the lifestyle of his son.*
unsettle EG *The presence of the two policemen unsettled her.*
upset EG *I'm sorry if I've upset you.*
worry EG *I didn't want to worry you.*

dive VERB
to jump or fall into water
EG *She was standing by the pool, about to dive in.*

jump EG *He ran along the board and jumped in.*
leap EG *as she leapt into the water*
submerge EG *Hippos are unable to submerge in the few remaining water holes.*

divide VERB
to split something up
EG *The idea is to divide the country into four sectors.*

cut up EG *Halve the tomatoes, then cut them up.*
partition EG *a plan to partition the country*
segregate EG *Police were used to segregate the two rival camps.*
separate EG *Fluff the rice with a fork to separate the grains.*
split EG *Split the chicken in half.*
split up EG *He split up the company.*

WORD POWER
Antonym
join

divide VERB
to form a barrier between things
EG *the frontier dividing Mexico from the USA*

bisect EG *The main street bisects the town.*
separate EG *the fence that separated the yard from the paddock*

A B C **D** E F G H I J K L M N O P Q R S T U V W X Y Z

❸ **divide** VERB
to cause people to disagree
EG *the enormous differences that still divide them*
come between EG *It's difficult to imagine anything coming between them.*
set against one another EG *The case has set neighbours against one another in the village.*
split EG *Women priests are accused of splitting the church.*

❶ **division** NOUN
separation into parts
EG *the unification of Germany after its division into two states*
partition EG *fighting which followed the partition of India*
separation EG *the separation of church and state*

❷ **division** NOUN
a disagreement
EG *There were divisions in the Party on economic policy.*
breach EG *a serious breach in relations between the two countries*
difference of opinion EG *Was there a difference of opinion over what to do with the money?*
rupture EG *a rupture of the family unit*
split EG *They accused both sides of trying to provoke a split in the party.*

❸ **division** NOUN
a section of something
EG *the Research Division*
department EG *the company's chemicals department*
section EG *a top-secret section of the Foreign Office*
sector EG *the nation's manufacturing sector*

dizzy ADJECTIVE
about to lose your balance
EG *He kept getting dizzy spells.*
giddy EG *She felt slightly giddy.*
light-headed EG *If you skip breakfast, you may feel light-headed.*

❶ **do** VERB
to carry out a task
EG *He just didn't want to do any work.*
carry out EG *Police believe the attacks were carried out by nationalists.*
execute FORMAL EG *The landing was skillfully executed.*
perform EG *people who have performed outstanding acts of bravery*
undertake EG *She undertook the arduous task of monitoring the elections.*

❷ **do** VERB
to be sufficient
EG *Home-made stock is best, but cubes will do.*
be adequate EG *The western diet should be perfectly adequate for most people.*
be sufficient EG *One teaspoon of sugar should be sufficient.*
suffice FORMAL EG *Often a far shorter letter will suffice.*

❸ **do** VERB
to perform well or badly
EG *Connie did well at school.*
fare EG *Some later expeditions fared better.*
get on EG *I asked him how he had got on.*
manage EG *How did your mother manage after your father died?*

❶ **dodge** VERB
to move out of the way
EG *We dodged behind a pillar out of sight of the tourists.*
duck EG *I wanted to duck down and slip past but they saw me.*
swerve EG *He swerved to avoid a truck.*

❷ **dodge** VERB
to avoid doing something
EG *dodging military service by feigning illness*
avoid EG *They managed to avoid paying their fares.*

elude EG *He eluded the police for 13 years.*

evade EG *by evading taxes*

get out of EG *He'll do almost anything to get out of paying his share.*

shirk EG *We can't shirk our responsibility.*

sidestep EG *Rarely, if ever, does he sidestep a question.*

dog NOUN
an animal often kept as a pet
EG *a children's book about dogs*

brak SOUTH AFRICAN EG *a rabid brak*

canine EG *a new canine was needed*

mongrel EG *a rescued mongrel called Chips*

mutt SLANG EG *the most famous mutts in the western world*

pooch SLANG EG *Julian's pet pooch*

doomed ADJECTIVE
certain to fail
EG *a doomed attempt to rescue the children*

condemned EG *Many women are condemned to poverty.*

hopeless EG *I don't believe your situation is as hopeless as you think.*

ill-fated EG *his ill-fated attempt on the world record*

double ADJECTIVE
twice the usual size
EG *a double whisky*

twice EG *Unemployment in Northern Ireland is twice the national average.*

twofold EG *a twofold risk*

double ADJECTIVE
consisting of two parts
EG *a double album*

dual EG *dual nationality*

twin EG *twin beds*

twofold EG *Their concern was twofold: personal and political.*

doubt NOUN
a feeling of uncertainty
EG *This raises doubts about the point of advertising.*

misgiving EG *I had misgivings about his methods.*

qualm EG *I have no qualms about recommending this approach.*

scepticism EG *The report has been greeted with scepticism.*

uncertainty EG *the uncertainties regarding the future funding of the company*

> **WORD POWER**
> Antonym
> certainty

doubt VERB
to feel uncertain about something
EG *No one doubted his ability.*

be dubious EG *I was dubious about the entire proposition.*

be sceptical EG *Other archaeologists are sceptical about his findings.*

query EG *No one queried my decision.*

question EG *It never occurs to them to question the doctor's decisions.*

> **WORD POWER**
> Antonym
> believe

doubtful ADJECTIVE
unlikely or uncertain
EG *It is doubtful whether he will appear again.*

debatable EG *Whether the Bank of England would do any better is highly debatable.*

dubious EG *This claim seems to us rather dubious.*

questionable EG *It is questionable whether the expenditure is justified.*

uncertain EG *It's uncertain whether they will accept the plan.*

> **WORD POWER**
> Antonym
> certain

downfall NOUN
the failure of a person or thing

A
B
C
D
E
F
G
H
I
J
K
L
M
N
O
P
Q
R
S
T
U
V
W
X
Y
Z

EG *His lack of experience had led to his downfall.*

collapse EG *The medical system is facing collapse.*

fall EG *the fall of the military dictator*

ruin EG *Inflation has driven them to the brink of ruin.*

drab ADJECTIVE
dull and unattractive
EG *the same drab grey dress*

dingy EG *his rather dingy office*

dismal EG *a dark dismal day*

dreary EG *a dreary little town*

gloomy EG *the gloomy days of winter*

grey EG *a New Year that will be grey and cheerless*

sombre EG *a worried official in sombre black*

> **WORD POWER**
> Synonyms
> cheerless
> lacklustre
> Antonym
> bright

drag VERB
to pull something along the ground
EG *He dragged his chair towards the table.*

draw EG *He drew his chair nearer the fire.*

haul EG *A crane was used to haul the car out of the stream.*

lug EG *Nobody wants to lug around huge suitcases.*

tow EG *They threatened to tow away my car.*

trail EG *She came down the stairs slowly, trailing the coat behind her.*

❶ drain VERB
to cause a liquid to flow somewhere
EG *Miners built the tunnel to drain water out of the lakes.*

draw off EG *The fluid can be drawn off with a syringe.*

pump EG *to get rid of raw sewage by pumping it out to sea*

❷ drain VERB
to flow somewhere
EG *rivers that drain into lakes*

discharge EG *Blood was discharging from its nostrils.*

empty EG *The Washougal empties into the Columbia River.*

flow EG *The waters of Lake Erie now flow into the Niagara River.*

seep EG *Radioactive water has seeped into underground reservoirs.*

❸ drain VERB
to use something up
EG *The prolonged boardroom battle drained him of energy and money.*

consume EG *plans which will consume hours of time*

exhaust EG *People are now living longer and exhausting natural resources.*

sap EG *The illness sapped his strength.*

tax EG *Overcrowding has taxed the city's ability to deal with waste.*

use up EG *They aren't the ones who use up the world's resources.*

drastic ADJECTIVE
severe and urgent
EG *It's time for drastic action.*

extreme EG *I would rather die than do anything so extreme.*

harsh EG *harsh new measures to combat drink-driving*

radical EG *radical economic reform*

severe EG *a severe shortage of drinking water*

❶ draw VERB
to make a picture
EG *He starts a drawing by painting simplified shapes.*

paint EG *He is painting a huge volcano.*

sketch EG *He sketched a map on the back of a menu.*

trace EG *She learned to draw by tracing pictures out of old storybooks.*

❷ draw VERB
to move somewhere
EG *as the car drew away*
move EG *She moved away from the window.*
pull EG *He pulled into the driveway.*

❸ draw VERB
to pull something
EG *He drew his chair nearer the fire.*
drag EG *He dragged his chair towards the table.*
haul EG *A crane was used to haul the car out of the stream.*
pull EG *a freight train pulling waggons*

❶ dream NOUN
mental pictures while sleeping
EG *He had a dream about Claire.*
hallucination EG *The drug induces hallucinations at high doses.*
trance EG *She seemed to be in a trance.*
vision EG *seeing the Virgin Mary in a vision*

> **WORD POWER**
> Synonyms
> delusion
> reverie

❷ dream NOUN
something that you want very much
EG *his dream of winning the lottery*
ambition EG *His ambition is to sail round the world.*
aspiration EG *one of his greatest aspirations*
daydream EG *He learned to escape into daydreams of becoming a writer.*
fantasy EG *fantasies of romance and true love*

> **WORD POWER**
> Synonyms
> Holy Grail
> pipe dream

dreary ADJECTIVE
dull or boring

EG *the dreary winter months*
boring EG *a boring job*
drab EG *The rest of the day's activities often seem drab.*
dull EG *There was scarcely a dull moment.*
humdrum EG *The new government seemed rather humdrum.*
monotonous EG *It's monotonous work, like most factory jobs.*
tedious EG *Such lists are tedious to read.*
uneventful EG *her dull, uneventful life*

> **WORD POWER**
> Antonym
> exciting

❶ dress NOUN
a piece of clothing
EG *a black dress*
frock EG *a party frock*
gown EG *wedding gowns*
robe EG *a fur-lined robe*

❷ dress NOUN
clothing in general
EG *evening dress*
attire FORMAL EG *women dressed in their finest attire*
clothes EG *casual clothes*
clothing EG *protective clothing*
costume EG *women in traditional costume*
garb FORMAL EG *his usual garb of a dark suit*

> **WORD POWER**
> Synonyms
> apparel
> raiment

❸ dress VERB
to put on clothes
EG *a tall woman dressed in black*
attire EG *He was attired in a smart blue suit.*
clothe EG *He lay down on the bed fully clothed.*
garb FORMAL EG *He was garbed in sweater, jacket and boots.*

A B C D E F G H I J K L M N O P Q R S T U V W X Y Z

A
B
C
D
E
F
G
H
I
J
K
L
M
N
O
P
Q
R
S
T
U
V
W
X
Y
Z

> **WORD POWER**
> Antonym
> undress

❶ drink VERB
to swallow liquid
EG *He drank some tea.*
gulp EG *She quickly gulped her coffee.*
guzzle EG *She guzzled gin and tonics like they were lemonade.*
sip EG *She sipped from her coffee mug.*
swig INFORMAL EG *I swigged down two white wines.*

> **WORD POWER**
> Synonyms
> imbibe
> quaff
> sup

❷ drink VERB
to drink alcohol
EG *He drinks little and eats carefully.*
booze INFORMAL EG *drunken businessmen who had been boozing all afternoon*
tipple EG *We saw a woman tippling from the sherry bottle.*

❶ drip VERB
to fall in small drops
EG *Rain dripped from the brim of his cap.*
dribble EG *Sweat dribbled down his face.*
splash EG *Tears splashed into her hands.*
trickle EG *A tear trickled down the old man's cheek.*

❷ drip NOUN
a small amount of a liquid
EG *drips of water*
bead EG *beads of sweat*
drop EG *a drop of blue ink*
droplet EG *water droplets*

> **WORD POWER**
> Synonyms
> dribble
> globule

❶ drop VERB
to fall downwards
EG *She let her head drop.*
descend EG *as the aircraft descended*
fall EG *Bombs fell in the town.*
plummet EG *His parachute failed to open and he plummeted to the ground.*
sink EG *She sank to her knees.*
tumble EG *The gun tumbled out of his hand.*

❷ drop VERB
to become less
EG *Temperatures can drop to freezing at night.*
decline EG *The number of staff has declined.*
decrease EG *Population growth is decreasing by 1.4% each year.*
diminish EG *diminishing resources*
fall EG *Her weight fell to under seven stone.*
plummet EG *Share prices have plummeted.*
sink EG *Pay increases have sunk to around 7%.*
slump EG *Net profits slumped by 41%.*
tumble EG *House prices have tumbled by almost 30%.*

> **WORD POWER**
> Antonym
> rise

❸ drop NOUN
a small amount of a liquid
EG *a drop of blue ink*
bead EG *beads of sweat*
drip EG *drips of water*
droplet EG *water droplets*

> **WORD POWER**
> Synonyms
> dribble
> globule

❶ drug NOUN
a treatment for disease
EG *a new drug in the fight against AIDS*

medication EG *She is not on any medication.*
medicine EG *herbal medicines*

❷ drug NOUN
an illegal substance
EG *She was sure Leo was taking drugs.*
narcotic EG *He was indicted for dealing in narcotics.*
stimulant EG *the use of stimulants in sport*

❶ drunk ADJECTIVE
having consumed too much alcohol
EG *I got drunk.*
babalas SOUTH AFRICAN EG *He was babalas again last night.*
intoxicated FORMAL EG *He appeared intoxicated.*
tipsy EG *I'm feeling a bit tipsy.*

> **WORD POWER**
> Synonyms
> bacchic
> inebriated
> Antonym
> sober

❷ drunk NOUN
someone who consumes too much alcohol
EG *A drunk lay in the alley.*
alcoholic EG *after admitting that he was an alcoholic*
boozer INFORMAL EG *He's a bit of a boozer.*

❶ dry ADJECTIVE
without any liquid
EG *The path was dry after the sunshine.*
arid EG *arid conditions*
dried-up EG *a dried-up river bed*
parched EG *parched brown grass*

> **WORD POWER**
> Antonym
> wet

❷ dry VERB
to remove liquid from something

EG *Wash and dry the lettuce.*
dehydrate EG *Avoid alcohol, which dehydrates the body.*
drain EG *The authorities have mobilized vast numbers of people to drain flooded land.*

> **WORD POWER**
> Synonyms
> dehumidify
> desiccate
> Antonym
> moisten

❶ dull ADJECTIVE
not interesting
EG *I found him rather dull.*
boring EG *a boring job*
drab EG *The rest of the day's activities often seem drab.*
humdrum EG *The new government seemed rather humdrum.*
monotonous EG *It's monotonous work, like most factory jobs.*
tedious EG *Such lists are tedious to read.*
uninteresting EG *Their media has a reputation for being dull and uninteresting.*

> **WORD POWER**
> Antonym
> interesting

❷ dull ADJECTIVE
not bright or clear
EG *a dark, dull blue colour*
drab EG *the same drab grey dress*
gloomy EG *Inside it's gloomy after all that sunshine.*
muted EG *He likes sombre, muted colours.*
sombre EG *an official in sombre black*
subdued EG *subdued lighting*

> **WORD POWER**
> Antonym
> bright

❸ dull ADJECTIVE
covered with clouds
EG *It's always dull and raining.*

cloudy EG *In the morning it was cloudy.*

leaden EG *a leaden sky*

murky EG *one murky November afternoon*

overcast EG *For three days it was overcast.*

> *WORD POWER*
> Antonym
> bright

❶ dumb ADJECTIVE
unable to speak
EG *We were all struck dumb for a minute.*

mute EG *a mute look of appeal*

silent EG *Suddenly they both fell silent.*

speechless EG *Alex was almost speechless with rage.*

❷ dumb ADJECTIVE; INFORMAL
slow to understand
EG *I've met a lot of pretty dumb people.*

dim EG *He is rather dim.*

obtuse FORMAL EG *I've really been very obtuse.*

stupid EG *How could I have been so stupid?*

thick INFORMAL EG *I must have seemed incredibly thick.*

> *WORD POWER*
> Antonym
> smart

❶ dump VERB
to get rid of something
EG *The getaway car was dumped near the motorway.*

discharge EG *The resulting salty water will eventually be discharged at sea.*

dispose of EG *how he disposed of the murder weapon*

get rid of EG *The cat had kittens, which they got rid of.*

jettison EG *The crew jettisoned their excess fuel.*

throw away EG *You should have thrown the letter away.*

throw out EG *You ought to throw out those empty bottles.*

❷ dump VERB
to put something down
EG *We dumped our bags at the hotel and went for a walk.*

deposit EG *Imagine if you were suddenly deposited on a desert island.*

drop EG *Many children had been dropped outside the stadium by their parents.*

❶ duty NOUN
something that you ought to do
EG *We have a duty as adults to listen to children.*

obligation EG *He had not felt an obligation to help save his old friend.*

responsibility EG *work and family responsibilities*

❷ duty NOUN
a task associated with a job
EG *He carried out his duties conscientiously and with considerable skill.*

assignment EG *dangerous assignments*

job EG *One of my jobs was to make the tea.*

responsibility EG *He handled his responsibilities as a counsellor very well.*

role EG *Both sides had important roles to play.*

❸ duty NOUN
tax paid to the government
EG *customs duties*

excise EG *These products are excused VAT and excise.*

levy FORMAL EG *An annual motorway levy is imposed on all drivers.*

tariff EG *America wants to eliminate tariffs on such items as electronics.*

tax EG *the tax on new cars and motorcycles*

dying

be dying for VERB
to want something very much
EG *I'm dying for a breath of fresh air.*
ache for EG *She still ached for the lost intimacy of marriage.*
hunger for EG *Jules hungered for adventure.*

long for EG *He longed for the winter to be over.*

pine for EG *I pine for the countryside.*

yearn for EG *He yearned for freedom.*

A
B
C
D
E
F
G
H
I
J
K
L
M
N
O
P
Q
R
S
T
U
V
W
X
Y
Z

Ee Ee

eager ADJECTIVE
wanting very much to do or
have something
EG *Robert is eager to earn some extra
money.*
anxious EG *She was anxious to
leave early.*
ardent EG *one of the government's
most ardent supporters*
avid EG *He's always been an avid
reader.*
enthusiastic EG *Tom usually
seems very enthusiastic.*
keen EG *Kirsty has always been a
keen swimmer.*
raring to go INFORMAL EG *They're
all ready and raring to go.*

> **_WORD POWER_**
> Synonyms
> fervent
> hungry
> zealous

❶ **early** ADJECTIVE
before the arranged or expected
time
EG *You're not late - I'm early!*
advance EG *We got an advance
copy of her new book.*
premature EG *The injury put a
premature end to his sporting career.*
untimely EG *her untimely death in
a car crash at the age of 21*

> **_WORD POWER_**
> Antonym
> late

❷ **early** ADJECTIVE
near the beginning of a period of
time
EG *the early 1970's*
primeval EG *These insects first
appeared in the primeval forests of
Europe.*
primitive EG *We found a fossil of
a primitive bird-like creature.*

❸ **early** ADVERB

before the arranged or expected
time
EG *We left early so we wouldn't
have to queue.*
ahead of time EG *The bus always
arrives ahead of time.*
beforehand EG *If you'd let me
know beforehand, you could have
come with us.*
in advance EG *You need to book in
advance to get a good seat.*
in good time EG *We arrived at the
airport in good time.*
prematurely EG *men who go
prematurely bald*

❶ **earn** VERB
to get money in return for doing
work
EG *He earns a lot more than I do.*
bring in EG *My job brings in just
enough to pay the bills.*
draw EG *I draw a salary, so I can
afford to run a car.*
get EG *How much do you get if
you're a lorry driver?*
make EG *She makes a lot of money.*
obtain EG *the profits obtained from
buying and selling shares*

> **_WORD POWER_**
> Synonyms
> net
> reap

❷ **earn** VERB
to receive something that you
deserve
EG *He earned the respect of his
troops.*
acquire EG *She has acquired a
reputation as a liar and a cheat.*
attain FORMAL EG *He finally
attained his pilot's licence.*
win EG *She won the admiration of
all her colleagues.*

❶ **earth** NOUN
the planet on which we live
EG *the tallest mountain on earth*

138

globe EG *from every corner of the globe*

planet EG *the effects of pollution on the atmosphere of our planet*

world EG *the first person to cycle round the world*

❷ **earth** NOUN
soil from the ground
EG *He filled a pot with earth and popped the seeds in it.*

clay EG *lumps of clay that stuck to his boots*

dirt EG *kneeling in the dirt*

ground EG *digging potatoes out of the ground*

soil EG *We planted some bulbs in the soil around the pond.*

> **WORD POWER**
> Synonyms
> loam
> topsoil
> turf

❶ **ease** NOUN
lack of difficulty or worry
EG *He passed his driving test with ease.*

leisure EG *living a life of leisure*

relaxation EG *The town has a feeling of relaxation and tranquillity about it.*

simplicity EG *The simplicity of the new scheme has made it popular with motorists.*

❷ **ease** VERB
to make or become less severe or intense
EG *The doctor gave him another injection to ease the pain.*

abate EG *By morning the storms had abated.*

calm EG *The government is taking steps to calm the situation.*

relax EG *He relaxed his grip on the axe and smiled.*

relieve EG *The pills will help relieve the pain for a while.*

slacken EG *Her grip on the rope slackened and she fell back.*

> **WORD POWER**
> Synonyms
> allay
> alleviate
> assuage

❸ **ease** VERB
to move slowly or carefully
EG *He eased the door open and peered outside.*

creep EG *The car crept down the ramp.*

edge EG *I edged the van slowly back into the garage.*

guide EG *Bob guided the plane out onto the tarmac.*

inch EG *The ambulance inched its way through the crowds of shoppers.*

lower EG *He lowered himself into the armchair.*

manoeuvre EG *We attempted to manoeuvre his canoe towards the shore.*

squeeze EG *They squeezed him into his seat and strapped him in.*

❶ **easy** ADJECTIVE
able to be done without difficulty
EG *The software is very easy to install.*

light EG *a few light exercises to warm up*

painless EG *Finding somewhere to stay was pretty painless in the end.*

simple EG *All you have to do is answer a few simple questions.*

smooth EG *a smooth changeover to the new system*

straightforward EG *The route is fairly straightforward so you shouldn't need a map.*

> **WORD POWER**
> Antonym
> hard

❷ **easy** ADJECTIVE
comfortable and without worries
EG *He has not had an easy life.*

carefree EG *a carefree summer spent on the beach*

A
B
C
D
E
F
G
H
I
J
K
L
M
N
O
P
Q
R
S
T
U
V
W
X
Y
Z

comfortable EG *a comfortable teaching job at a small private school*

leisurely EG *a leisurely weekend spent with a few close friends*

quiet EG *a quiet weekend in the sun*

relaxed EG *It's very relaxed here, you can do what you like.*

❶ eat VERB
to chew and swallow food
EG *For lunch he ate a cheese sandwich.*

chew EG *She sat in her chair chewing a piece of toffee.*

consume EG *We consumed a whole salmon between us.*

devour EG *She had devoured half a pizza in five minutes.*

gobble EG *He was so hungry he gobbled the lot.*

munch EG *munching an apple*

scoff SLANG EG *We had scoffed everything before anyone else sat down.*

swallow EG *Their baby would swallow a carton of yoghurt in seconds.*

❷ eat VERB
to have a meal
EG *We like to eat early.*

breakfast FORMAL EG *The ladies like to breakfast in their rooms.*

dine EG *We usually dine at about six.*

feed EG *Leopards only feed when they are hungry.*

have a meal EG *We could have a meal at Pizza Palace after the film.*

lunch FORMAL EG *We lunched at El Greco's.*

picnic EG *After our walk, we picnicked by the river.*

eat away VERB
to destroy something slowly
EG *The front of the car had been eaten away by rust.*

corrode EG *buildings corroded by acid rain*

destroy EG *Areas of the coast are being destroyed by the sea.*

dissolve EG *Chemicals in the water are dissolving the bridge.*

erode EG *the floods that erode the dry, loose soil*

rot EG *Too many sweets will rot your teeth.*

wear away EG *The weather soon wears away the paintwork.*

❶ eccentric ADJECTIVE
regarded as odd or peculiar
EG *His maths teacher was considered a bit eccentric.*

bizarre EG *He's quite a bizarre character.*

outlandish EG *his outlandish behaviour sometimes put people off*

quirky EG *a quirky, delightful film that is full of surprises*

strange EG *his strange views about UFOs*

weird EG *His taste in music is a bit weird.*

whimsical EG *a whimsical old gentleman*

❷ eccentric NOUN
someone who is regarded as odd or peculiar
EG *He's always been regarded as a bit of an eccentric.*

character INFORMAL EG *a well-known character who lived in Johnson Street*

crank EG *People regarded vegetarians as cranks in those days.*

❶ economic ADJECTIVE
concerning the way money is managed
EG *the need for economic reforms*

budgetary EG *a summit meeting to discuss various budgetary matters*

commercial EG *a purely commercial decision*

financial EG *The financial pressures on the government are mounting.*

WORD POWER
Synonyms
fiscal

monetary

❷ economic ADJECTIVE
making a profit
EG *goods that happen to be economic to produce*
productive EG *the need to make these industries more productive*
profitable EG *a new venture that has proved highly profitable*
viable EG *businesses that are no longer viable*

> *WORD POWER*
> Synonyms
> money-making
> profit-making
> remunerative

❶ economical ADJECTIVE
cheap to use and saving you money
EG *Our car may not be fast, but it's very economical.*
cheap EG *This isn't a very cheap way of buying stationery.*
cost-effective EG *the most cost-effective way of shopping*
economic EG *the most economic way to see the museum*
inexpensive EG *There are several good inexpensive restaurants in town.*

❷ economical ADJECTIVE
careful and sensible with money or materials
EG *He's never been very economical about housekeeping.*
careful EG *She's very careful with her pocket money.*
frugal EG *his frugal lifestyle*
prudent EG *the prudent use of precious natural resources*
thrifty EG *My mother was very thrifty because she had so little spare cash.*

economy NOUN
the careful use of things to save money
EG *improvements in the fuel economy of new cars*

frugality FORMAL EG *We must live with strict frugality if we are to survive.*
prudence EG *A lack of prudence could seriously affect his finances.*
restraint EG *We need to exercise some restraint in our spending.*
thrift EG *He was widely praised for his thrift and imagination.*

ecstasy NOUN
extreme happiness
EG *his feeling of ecstasy after winning the medal*
bliss EG *husband and wife living together in bliss and harmony*
delight EG *He squealed with delight when we told him.*
elation EG *His supporters reacted to the news with elation.*
euphoria EG *There was a sense of euphoria after our election victory.*
exaltation EG *the mood of exaltation that affected everyone*
joy EG *her joy at finding him after so long*
rapture EG *His speech was received with rapture by a huge crowd.*

❶ edge NOUN
the place where something ends or meets something else
EG *on the edge of the forest*
border EG *a pillowcase with a lace border*
boundary EG *The area beyond the western boundary belongs to Denmark.*
brim EG *He kept climbing until he reached the brim of the crater.*
fringe EG *the rundown areas on the fringes of the city*
lip EG *The lip of the jug was badly cracked.*
margin EG *standing on the margin of the land where it met the water*
rim EG *a large round mirror with a gold rim*

> *WORD POWER*
> Synonyms
> perimeter

A B C D E F G H I J K L M N O P Q R S T U V W X Y Z

periphery
Antonym
centre

❷ edge VERB
to move somewhere slowly
EG *He edged towards the phone, ready to grab it if it rang.*
creep EG *The car crept forward a few feet, then stopped.*
inch EG *The ambulance inched its way through the crowds.*
sidle EG *A man sidled up to him and tried to sell him a ticket.*

educated ADJECTIVE
having a high standard of learning
EG *He is an educated, tolerant and reasonable man.*
cultivated EG *His mother was an elegant, cultivated woman.*
cultured EG *a cultured man with a wide circle of friends*
intellectual EG *He is the intellectual type.*
learned EG *He was a scholar, a very learned man.*

> *WORD POWER*
> **Synonyms**
> erudite
> well-educated

education NOUN
the process of learning or teaching
EG *the importance of a good education*
coaching EG *extra coaching to help him pass his exams*
instruction EG *All instruction is provided by qualified experts.*
schooling EG *He began to wish he'd paid more attention to his schooling.*
training EG *His military training was no use to him here.*
tuition EG *personal tuition in the basics of photography*

effect NOUN
a direct result of something

EG *the effect that divorce has on children*
consequence EG *aware of the consequences of their actions*
end result EG *The end result of this process is still unclear.*
fruit EG *The new software is the fruit of three years' hard work.*
result EG *The result of all this uncertainty is that no-one is happy.*
upshot EG *The upshot is that we have a very unhappy workforce.*

efficient ADJECTIVE
able to work well without wasting time or energy
EG *The new hatchback has a much more efficient engine.*
businesslike EG *a highly businesslike approach that impressed everyone*
competent EG *an extremely competent piece of work*
economic EG *The new system is much more economic, and will save millions.*
effective EG *effective use of the time we have left*
organized EG *Tony seemed very organized, and completely in control of the situation.*
productive EG *the need to make farmers much more productive*

> *WORD POWER*
> **Antonym**
> inefficient

❶ effort NOUN
physical or mental energy
EG *It took a lot of effort, but we managed in the end.*
application EG *His talent, application and energy are a credit to the school.*
energy EG *He decided to devote his energy to writing another book.*
exertion EG *Is it really worth all the exertion?*
trouble EG *It's not worth the trouble.*
work EG *All the work I put in has*

now been wasted!

❷ effort NOUN
an attempt or struggle
EG *an unsuccessful effort to ban Sunday shopping*
attempt EG *an attempt to obtain an interview with the President*
bid EG *a last-minute bid to stop the trial going ahead*
stab INFORMAL EG *his latest stab at acting*
struggle EG *his struggle to clear his name*

❶ elaborate ADJECTIVE
having many different parts
EG *an elaborate research project*
complex EG *a complex explanation*
complicated EG *a complicated plan of the building's security system*
detailed EG *the detailed plans that have been drawn up*
intricate EG *an intricate system of levers and pulleys*
involved EG *a very involved operation, lasting many hours*

> **WORD POWER**
> Antonym
> simple

❷ elaborate ADJECTIVE
highly decorated
EG *elaborate wooden carvings*
fancy EG *the fancy plasterwork on the ceiling*
fussy EG *a rather fussy design*
ornate EG *an ornate wrought-iron staircase*

❸ elaborate VERB
to add more information about something
EG *He promised to elaborate on what had been said last night.*
develop EG *Maybe we should develop this idea.*
enlarge EG *He was enlarging on proposals made earlier.*
expand EG *a view that I will expand on later*

❶ eliminate VERB
to get rid of someone or something
EG *We've eliminated two of the four options so far.*
cut out EG *His guilty plea cut out the need for a long, costly trial.*
do away with EG *the attempt to do away with nuclear weapons altogether*
eradicate EG *Efforts to eradicate malaria seem to be failing.*
get rid of EG *Why don't we just get rid of the middlemen altogether?*
remove EG *You should try and remove these fatty foods from your diet.*
stamp out EG *We need to stamp out this disgusting practice.*

❷ eliminate VERB
to beat someone in a competition
EG *His team was eliminated in the first round.*
knock out EG *We were knocked out by the Dutch champions.*
put out EG *Decker finally put her fellow American out in the quarter final.*

embarrass VERB
to make someone feel ashamed or awkward
EG *You always embarrass me in front of my friends!*
disconcert EG *The way Anderson was smirking disconcerted her.*
fluster EG *Nothing could fluster him.*
humiliate EG *How dare you humiliate me like that!*
shame EG *Her son's behaviour had upset and shamed her.*

> **WORD POWER**
> Synonyms
> discomfit
> faze
> mortify

embarrassed ADJECTIVE
ashamed and awkward

A
B
C
D
E
F
G
H
I
J
K
L
M
N
O
P
Q
R
S
T
U
V
W
X
Y
Z

143

EG *I'm not embarrassed about taking my clothes off.*

ashamed EG *I felt so ashamed I wanted to die.*

awkward EG *It was a very awkward occasion.*

humiliated EG *A humiliated Mr Stevens admitted that the concert had been cancelled.*

red-faced EG *Red-faced executives had to explain this fact.*

self-conscious EG *I always feel self-conscious when I'm having my picture taken.*

sheepish EG *He looked very sheepish when he finally appeared.*

> ### WORD POWER
> Synonyms
> abashed
> bashful
> discomfited
> mortified

embarrassment NOUN
shame and awkwardness
EG *I laughed loudly to cover my embarrassment.*

awkwardness EG *the awkwardness of our first meeting*

bashfulness EG *Overcome with bashfulness, he lowered his voice.*

humiliation EG *the humiliation of having to ask for money*

self-consciousness EG *her painful self-consciousness*

shame EG *the shame he felt at having let her down*

> ### WORD POWER
> Synonyms
> chagrin
> discomfiture
> mortification

emergency NOUN
an unexpected and difficult situation
EG *This is an emergency!*

crisis EG *the economic crisis affecting parts of Africa*

pinch EG *I don't mind working late in a pinch.*

emit VERB
to give out or release something
EG *Polly blinked and emitted a long sigh.*

exude EG *a plant that exudes an extremely unpleasant smell*

give off EG *The fumes it gives off are poisonous, so watch out.*

give out EG *The alarm gave out a series of bleeps, then stopped.*

release EG *The factory is still releasing toxic fumes.*

send out EG *The volcano has been sending out smoke for weeks.*

utter EG *He uttered a loud snort and continued eating.*

> ### WORD POWER
> Synonyms
> produce
> radiate
> send forth

emphasis NOUN
special or extra importance
EG *too much emphasis on commercialism*

accent EG *In the new government the accent will be on co-operation.*

importance EG *There's not enough importance being given to environmental issues.*

prominence EG *Crime prevention has to be given more prominence.*

weight EG *This adds more weight to the government's case.*

emphasize VERB
to make something seem specially important or obvious
EG *He emphasized the need for everyone to remain calm.*

accent EG *a white dress accented by a coloured scarf*

accentuate EG *His shaven head accentuates his round face.*

highlight EG *This disaster has highlighted the difficulty faced by the government.*

play up EG *He played up his*

bad-boy image.

stress EG *I would like to stress that we are in complete agreement.*

underline EG *This underlines how important the new trade deal really is.*

WORD POWER
Synonyms
foreground
underscore

---

❶ **employ** VERB
to pay someone to work for you
EG *Mollison was employed by Mr Darnley as a bodyguard.*

appoint EG *We need to appoint a successor to Mr Stevens.*

commission EG *He has been commissioned to design a new bridge.*

engage FORMAL EG *They have finally engaged a suitable nanny.*

hire EG *I was hired as a gardener on the estate.*

take on EG *the need to take on more workers for the summer*

❷ **employ** VERB
to use something
EG *the tactics employed by the police*

bring to bear EG *We can bring two very different techniques to bear on this.*

make use of EG *He makes use of several highly offensive terms to describe them.*

use EG *the methods used in the investigation*

utilize EG *Engineers will utilize a range of techniques to improve the signal.*

employee NOUN
someone who is paid to work for someone else
EG *the way they look after their employees*

hand EG *He's been working as a farm hand down south.*

worker EG *Workers at the plant have been laid off.*

workman EG *A council workman finally arrived to fix the door.*

employer NOUN
someone that other people work for
EG *a meeting with her employer to discuss the issue*

boss EG *My boss has always been very fair.*

gaffer INFORMAL EG *You'll need to speak to the gaffer about that.*

employment NOUN
the fact of employing people
EG *the employment of children to work in shops*

engagement EG *the engagement of suitable staff*

enlistment EG *Enlistment in the armed forces is falling.*

hiring EG *The hiring of new staff is our top priority.*

recruitment EG *new policies on recruitment and training*

taking on EG *Taking on extra staff would make life a lot easier.*

❶ **empty** ADJECTIVE
having no people or things in it
EG *The roads were empty.*

bare EG *When she got there, the cupboard was bare.*

blank EG *all the blank pages in his diary*

clear EG *The runway must be kept clear at all times.*

deserted EG *By nightfall, the square was deserted.*

unfurnished EG *The flat was unfurnished when we moved in.*

uninhabited EG *The house has remained uninhabited since she moved out.*

vacant EG *two vacant lots on the industrial estate*

WORD POWER
Antonym
full

---

❷ **empty** ADJECTIVE
boring or without value or

A B C D E F G H I J K L M N O P Q R S T U V W X Y Z

145

meaning
EG *My life is empty without him.*
inane EG *a series of inane remarks*
meaningless EG *the feeling that his existence was meaningless*
worthless EG *a worthless film with nothing to say about anything*

❸ **empty** VERB
to remove people or things
EG *He emptied all the cupboards before Tony arrived.*
clear EG *The police cleared the building just in time.*
drain EG *She drained the bottles and washed them out.*
evacuate EG *Fortunately the building had been evacuated.*
unload EG *It only took twenty minutes to unload the van.*

> **WORD POWER**
> Antonym
> fill

enclose VERB
to surround a thing or place completely
EG *The book arrived enclosed in a red plastic bag.*
encircle EG *The area had been encircled by barbed wire.*
fence off EG *We decided to fence off the land.*
hem in EG *We were hemmed in by walls and hedges.*
surround EG *the low wall that surrounded the rose garden*
wrap EG *Wrap the chicken in foil and bake it in a medium oven.*

❶ **encourage** VERB
to give someone confidence
EG *We were very encouraged by the response.*
cheer EG *This news cheered us all and helped us keep going.*
hearten EG *I am heartened to hear that.*
reassure EG *He always reassures me when I'm feeling down.*

> **WORD POWER**

> Antonym
> discourage

❷ **encourage** VERB
to support a person or activity
EG *the need to encourage people to be sensible*
aid EG *I tried to aid his creative efforts.*
boost EG *Efforts to boost investment seem to be succeeding.*
favour EG *conditions which favour growth in the economy*
help EG *policies aimed at helping small businesses*
incite EG *He incited his followers to attack the police station.*
support EG *Rowe will support me in this campaign.*

> **WORD POWER**
> Synonyms
> foster
> further
> promote
> strengthen

❶ **end** NOUN
the last part of a period or event
EG *the end of the 20th century*
close EG *a fitting close to an illustrious career*
ending EG *a story with a happy ending*
finish EG *a race whose finish was nothing short of remarkable*

> **WORD POWER**
> Antonym
> beginning

❷ **end** NOUN
the furthest point of something
EG *the room at the end of the corridor*
extremity EG *a small port at the northern extremity of the peninsula*
point EG *the southernmost point of the island*
tip EG *He stuck the tip of the knife in the fire.*

❸ **end** NOUN
the purpose for which

something is done
EG *The army is being used for political ends.*
objective EG *His main objective was the recovery of the gold.*
purpose EG *whatever is necessary to achieve this purpose*
reason EG *My parents came to Germany for business reasons.*

❹ end VERB
to come or bring to a finish
EG *talks being held to end the fighting*
bring to an end EG *The treaty brought to an end fifty years of conflict.*
cease EG *By one o'clock the storm had ceased.*
conclude EG *The evening concluded with the usual speeches.*
finish EG *waiting for the film to finish*
stop EG *When is it all going to stop?*
terminate EG *the decision to terminate their contract*

WORD POWER
Antonym
begin

endanger VERB
to put someone or something in danger
EG *a dispute that could endanger the peace talks*
compromise EG *We will not allow safety to be compromised.*
jeopardize EG *a scandal that could jeopardize his government*
put at risk EG *those who were put at risk by her stupidity*
risk EG *He is risking the lives of others.*
threaten EG *A breakdown in this system could threaten the whole project.*

❶ endure VERB
to experience something difficult
EG *He had to endure hours of*

discomfort.
cope with EG *We've had a lot to cope with in the last few weeks.*
experience EG *The company has experienced heavy financial losses.*
go through EG *having to go through the public humiliation of a court case*
stand EG *I don't know how he stood it for so long.*
suffer EG *Steven has suffered years of pain from arthritis.*

❷ endure VERB
to continue to exist
EG *Our friendship has endured through everything.*
last EG *a car that is built to last*
live on EG *His name will live on as an inspiration to others.*
remain EG *When all the rest is forgotten, this fact will remain.*
survive EG *the few traces of their civilization that have survived*

enemy NOUN
someone who is against you
EG *She has many enemies in the government.*
adversary EG *face to face with his old adversary*
antagonist EG *He killed his antagonist in a duel.*
foe EG *He plays Dracula's foe, Dr. Van Helsing.*
opponent EG *Her political opponents will be delighted at this news.*

WORD POWER
Antonym
friend

energetic ADJECTIVE
full of energy
EG *an able, energetic and very determined politician*
animated EG *an animated conversation about politics and sport*
dynamic EG *a dynamic and ambitious businessman*
indefatigable EG *trying to keep up*

with their indefatigable boss

spirited EG *a spirited defence of his new tax proposals*

tireless EG *a tireless campaigner for the homeless*

vigorous EG *a vigorous campaign*

energy NOUN
the ability and strength to do things
EG *I'm saving my energy for tomorrow.*

drive EG *a man with immense drive and enthusiasm*

life EG *At 96, she's still as full of life as ever.*

spirit EG *Despite trailing 6-2, they played with a lot of spirit.*

strength EG *She put all her strength into finding a new job.*

vigour EG *They returned to their work with renewed vigour.*

vitality EG *a woman with considerable charm and endless vitality*

> **WORD POWER**
> Synonyms
> élan
> verve
> zeal
> zest

enjoy VERB
to find pleasure in something
EG *I haven't enjoyed a film as much as that in ages!*

appreciate EG *people who don't appreciate Satie's music*

delight in EG *He delights in playing practical jokes.*

like EG *Kirsty likes shopping.*

love EG *He loves skiing.*

relish EG *She relished the opportunity to get back at him.*

revel in EG *Stevens was revelling in the attention.*

take pleasure from EG *He took no pleasure from the knowledge that he had won.*

take pleasure in EG *She seemed to take pleasure in my discomfort.*

enlarge VERB
to make something larger
EG *plans to enlarge the 30,000 seat stadium*

add to EG *We've decided to add to this house rather than move again.*

expand EG *If we want to stay in business, we need to expand.*

extend EG *They extended the house by adding a conservatory.*

increase EG *They have increased the peace-keeping force to 2000.*

magnify EG *A more powerful lens will magnify the image.*

> **WORD POWER**
> Synonyms
> augment
> broaden
> distend
> elongate
> lengthen
> widen

enlarge on VERB
to give more information about something
EG *I'd like you to enlarge on that last point.*

develop EG *Maybe I should develop this idea a little bit further.*

elaborate on EG *He refused to elaborate on what he had said earlier.*

expand on EG *an idea that I will expand on later*

ensure VERB
to make sure about something
EG *We must ensure that this never happens again.*

guarantee EG *Further investment should guarantee that profits will rise.*

make certain EG *to make certain that he'll get there*

make sure EG *I will personally make sure that the job gets done.*

❶ enterprise NOUN
a business or company
EG *a small enterprise with a high turnover*

business EG *a medium-sized business*

company EG *a company that was doing very well*

concern EG *It's not a large concern, but it makes a profit.*

establishment EG *a modest establishment dedicated to sailing*

firm EG *a clothing firm*

operation EG *a one-man operation*

enterprise NOUN
a project or task
EG *a risky enterprise such as horse breeding*

effort EG *her latest fund-raising effort for cancer research*

endeavour EG *an endeavour that was bound to end in failure*

operation EG *He'd set up a small mining operation.*

project EG *a project that will attract a lot of media attention*

undertaking EG *This undertaking will rely on the hard work of our volunteers.*

venture EG *a venture that few were willing to invest in*

entertain VERB
to keep people amused or interested
EG *things that might entertain children in the school holidays*

amuse EG *He amused us all evening, singing and telling jokes.*

charm EG *He charmed Mrs Nisbet with his tales of life on the road.*

delight EG *a routine that will delight audiences*

enthral EG *He enthralled audiences all over Europe.*

please EG *He certainly knows how to please a crowd.*

entertainment NOUN
enjoyable activities
EG *Their main form of entertainment is the TV.*

amusement EG *looking for some amusement on a Saturday night*

enjoyment EG *We need a bit of*

enjoyment to cheer us up.

fun EG *It's not really my idea of family fun.*

pleasure EG *Hours of pleasure can be had with a pack of cards.*

recreation EG *a healthy and enjoyable form of recreation*

enthusiasm NOUN
eagerness and enjoyment in something
EG *We were disappointed by their lack of enthusiasm.*

eagerness EG *He could barely contain his eagerness.*

excitement EG *Her excitement got the better of her.*

interest EG *He doesn't show much interest in football.*

keenness EG *I don't doubt his keenness, it's his ability that worries me.*

warmth EG *He greeted us with his usual warmth and affection.*

> **WORD POWER**
> Synonyms
> ardour
> fervour
> relish
> zeal

enthusiastic ADJECTIVE
showing great excitement and eagerness for something
EG *He was very enthusiastic about the new scheme.*

ardent EG *one of the government's most ardent supporters*

avid EG *an avid reader*

devoted EG *a devoted Star Trek fan*

eager EG *He is eager to learn more about computers.*

excited EG *We are very excited about getting a new dog.*

keen EG *Dave is an keen angler.*

passionate EG *a passionate opponent of the government*

> **WORD POWER**
> Synonyms
> fervent

A
B
C
D
E
F
G
H
I
J
K
L
M
N
O
P
Q
R
S
T
U
V
W
X
Y
Z

wholehearted
zealous
Antonym
apathetic

❶ entrance NOUN
the way into a particular place
EG *I met Barry at the entrance to the station.*

door EG *She was waiting by the front door.*

doorway EG *the mass of people blocking the doorway*

entry EG *Kevin had been hanging round the back entry for hours.*

gate EG *the security guard at the main gate*

way in EG *Is this the way in?*

❷ entrance NOUN
a person's arrival somewhere
EG *She had failed to notice her father's entrance.*

appearance EG *She had timed her appearance at the dinner to perfection.*

arrival EG *journalists awaiting the arrival of the team*

entry EG *He was arrested on his entry into Mexico.*

❸ entrance NOUN
the right to enter somewhere
EG *He gained entrance to the hotel where the band were staying.*

access EG *We were denied access to the stadium.*

admission EG *no admission without a ticket*

entry EG *I was unable to gain entry to the meeting.*

❹ entrance VERB
to amaze and delight someone
EG *The audience was entranced by her voice.*

bewitch EG *Young Gordon's smile bewitched everyone.*

captivate EG *I was captivated by her piercing blue eyes.*

charm EG *He charmed Mr Darnley and made him feel young again.*

delight EG *a CD that will delight her many fans*

enthral EG *Audiences were enthralled by his spectacular stage act.*

fascinate EG *She never failed to fascinate him.*

WORD POWER
Synonyms
enchant
enrapture
spellbind

---

❶ entry NOUN
a person's arrival somewhere
EG *her dramatic entry*

appearance EG *She made her appearance to tumultuous applause*

arrival EG *He apologized for his late arrival.*

entrance EG *My entrance was spoiled when I tripped over the carpet.*

❷ entry NOUN
the way into a particular place
EG *He was hanging around at the entry to the station.*

door EG *I'll meet you at the front door.*

doorway EG *A bicycle was blocking the doorway.*

entrance EG *The bomb had been left outside the entrance to the building.*

gate EG *Guards were posted at the main gate.*

way in EG *I can't find the way in.*

❸ entry NOUN
something that has been written down
EG *the final entry in his journal*

item EG *A number of interesting items appear in his diary.*

note EG *He grunted and made a note in his pocket book.*

record EG *There is no record for 13 October in the log book.*

❶ envy NOUN
a feeling of resentment about

what someone else has
EG *his feelings of envy towards Kevin*
jealousy EG *the jealousy people felt towards him because of his money*
resentment EG *All the anger, bitterness and resentment suddenly melted away.*

envy VERB
to want something that someone else has
EG *I don't envy you one bit.*
be envious EG *people who were envious of her good fortune*
begrudge EG *Surely you don't begrudge me one night out.*
be jealous EG *I couldn't help being jealous when I knew he had won.*
covet EG *She coveted his job.*
resent EG *Anyone with money was resented and ignored.*

equal ADJECTIVE
the same in size, amount, or value
EG *equal numbers of men and women*
equivalent EG *A kilogram is equivalent to 2.2 pounds.*
identical EG *glasses containing identical amounts of water*
the same EG *different areas of research that have the same importance*

equal
equal to ADJECTIVE
having the necessary ability for something
EG *She was equal to any task they gave her.*
capable of EG *I'm no longer capable of this kind of work.*
up to EG *He said he wasn't up to a long walk.*

equal VERB
to be as good as something else
EG *a time that equalled the European record*
be equal to EG *The final score is equal to his personal best.*
match EG *able to match her*

previous time for the 100m

equip VERB
to supply someone with something
EG *The boat was equipped with an outboard motor.*
arm EG *The children arrived armed with a range of gardening tools.*
endow EG *The male bird is endowed with a vicious-looking beak.*
fit out EG *the amount spent on fitting out their offices*
provide EG *We provided them with waterproofs and sandwiches.*
supply EG *They supplied us with camping gear and a stove.*

equipment NOUN
the things you need for a particular job
EG *a shed full of gardening equipment*
apparatus EG *All the firemen were wearing breathing apparatus.*
gear EG *Police in riot gear have sealed off the area.*
paraphernalia EG *ashtrays, lighters and other paraphernalia associated with smoking*
stuff EG *The builders had left all their stuff in the garden.*
tackle EG *Martin kept all his fishing tackle in the spare room.*

WORD POWER
Synonyms
accoutrements
appurtenances

erode VERB
to wear something away and destroy it.
EG *The cliffs were being eroded by the constant pounding of the sea.*
corrode EG *buildings corroded by acid rain*
destroy EG *ancient monuments destroyed by pollution*
deteriorate EG *The tapestry had deteriorated badly where the roof was leaking.*

A B C D E F G H I J K L M N O P Q R S T U V W X Y Z

disintegrate EG *Once they were exposed to light the documents rapidly disintegrated.*

eat away EG *The chemicals in the water had eaten away the cables.*

wear away EG *rocks worn away by the action of the wind*

wear down EG *Some of her teeth were worn down with gnawing on the bars.*

err VERB
to make a mistake
EG *The builders had erred considerably in their original estimate.*

blunder EG *Fletcher had obviously blundered.*

go wrong EG *We must have gone wrong somewhere in our calculations.*

make a mistake EG *Okay, I made a mistake, I'm only human.*

miscalculate EG *They miscalculated, and now they're in deep trouble.*

❶ escape VERB
to manage to get away
EG *Three prisoners who escaped have given themselves up.*

break free EG *He was handcuffed to his bed, but somehow managed to break free.*

break out EG *two prisoners who broke out of the maximum security wing*

get away EG *She got away from her guards.*

make your escape EG *We made our escape down a drainpipe using knotted sheets.*

run away EG *I called him but he just ran away.*

run off EG *The children ran off when they spotted me.*

> **WORD POWER**
> Synonyms
> abscond
> bolt

❷ escape VERB

to manage to avoid something
EG *He was lucky to escape injury.*

avoid EG *She has managed to avoid arrest so far.*

dodge EG *He dodged his military service by pretending to be ill.*

duck EG *a pathetic attempt to duck her responsibilities*

elude EG *He managed to elude the police for 13 years.*

evade EG *He has now been charged with evading tax.*

❸ escape NOUN
something that distracts you from something unpleasant
EG *Cycling gives me an escape from the routine of work.*

distraction EG *a distraction from his troubles*

diversion EG *a pleasant diversion from my studies*

relief EG *The piano provides relief from all the stress.*

❶ essence NOUN
the most basic and important part of something
EG *The essence of good management is the ability to listen.*

core EG *the need to get to the core of the problem*

heart EG *a problem that reaches to the very heart of the party*

nature EG *the nature of what it is to be European*

soul EG *a song that captures the soul of this proud nation*

spirit EG *the spirit of modern manhood*

> **WORD POWER**
> Synonyms
> crux
> kernel
> quintessence
> substance

❷ essence NOUN
a concentrated liquid
EG *vanilla essence*

concentrate EG *orange concentrate*

A B C D E F G H I J K L M N O P Q R S T U V W X Y Z

extract EG *lemon extract*

❶ **essential** ADJECTIVE
extremely important
EG *Good ventilation is essential in a greenhouse.*
crucial EG *Her speech was a crucial part of the campaign.*
indispensable EG *She has become indispensable to the department.*
vital EG *a vital aspect of the plans that everyone has overlooked*

❷ **essential** ADJECTIVE
basic and important
EG *an essential part of any child's development*
basic EG *the basic laws of physics*
cardinal EG *He had broken one of the cardinal rules of business.*
fundamental EG *the fundamental principles of democracy*
key EG *Mollison had a key role to play in the negotiations.*
main EG *an attempt to analyse the main points of his theory*
principal EG *the principal idea that underpins their argument*

essentials PLURAL NOUN
the things that are most important
EG *We only had enough food money for the essentials.*
basics EG *We need to get back to basics.*
fundamentals EG *the fundamentals of road safety*
necessities EG *Water, food, and shelter are the necessities of life.*
prerequisites EG *Self-confidence is one of the prerequisites for a happy life.*
rudiments EG *teaching him the rudiments of car maintenance*

eternal ADJECTIVE
lasting forever
EG *the secret of eternal life*
everlasting EG *everlasting love*
immortal EG *your immortal soul*
unchanging EG *the unchanging laws of the cosmos*

❶ **even** ADJECTIVE
flat and level
EG *I need an even surface to write on.*
flat EG *a small hut with a flat roof*
horizontal EG *He drew a series of horizontal lines on the paper.*
level EG *checking the floor to make sure it was level*
smooth EG *the smooth marble floor tiles*

> **WORD POWER**
> Antonym
> uneven

❷ **even** ADJECTIVE
without changing or varying
EG *an even flow of liquid*
constant EG *The temperature remained more or less constant.*
regular EG *her quiet, regular breathing*
smooth EG *He caught the ball and passed it in one smooth motion.*
steady EG *a steady stream of people*
uniform EG *The prices rises are not uniform across the country.*

❸ **even** ADJECTIVE
the same
EG *At halftime the scores were still even.*
equal EG *The two teams shared equal points into the second round.*
identical EG *At the end of the contest, our scores were identical.*
level EG *The scores were level at halftime.*
neck and neck EG *They're still neck and neck with two minutes to go.*

❶ **event** NOUN
something that happens
EG *still amazed at the events of last week*
affair EG *He preferred to forget the whole affair.*
business EG *Do you remember that business with Jim?*
circumstance EG *due to circumstances beyond our control*

153

A
B
C
D
E
F
G
H
I
J
K
L
M
N
O
P
Q
R
S
T
U
V
W
X
Y
Z

episode EG *a rather embarrassing episode at Yvonne's wedding*
experience EG *an experience that changed his mind about going to university*
incident EG *the incident in the restaurant*
matter EG *She doesn't seem to be taking this matter seriously.*

❷ **event** NOUN
a competition
EG *The next event is the long jump.*
bout EG *This is his fifth heavyweight bout in three months.*
competition EG *the first competition of the afternoon*
contest EG *She's out of the contest for good.*

❶ **evil** NOUN
the force that causes bad things to happen
EG *the conflict between good and evil*
badness EG *behaving that way out of sheer badness*
immorality EG *the immorality that is typical of the arms trade*
sin EG *The whole town is a den of sin and corruption.*
vice EG *a place long associated with vice and immorality*
wickedness EG *the wickedness of his behaviour*

> **WORD POWER**
> Synonyms
> baseness
> depravity
> sinfulness
> Antonym
> good

❷ **evil** NOUN
something unpleasant or harmful
EG *a lecture on the evils of alcohol*
affliction EG *Hay fever is an affliction that affects thousands.*
ill EG *Many of the nation's ills are his responsibility.*
misery EG *the misery of drug*

addiction
sorrow EG *the joys and sorrows of family life*

❸ **evil** ADJECTIVE
morally wrong or bad
EG *an utterly evil man*
bad EG *He's not a bad man, he's just very unhappy.*
depraved EG *a throughly depraved film*
malevolent EG *a malevolent influence on the whole school*
sinful EG *He is a good person in a sinful world.*
vile EG *vile acts of brutality*
wicked EG *a wicked attack on a helpless child*

> **WORD POWER**
> Antonym
> good

❶ **exact** ADJECTIVE
correct in every detail
EG *It's an exact reproduction of the first steam engine.*
accurate EG *an accurate description of the man*
authentic EG *authentic Elizabethan costumes*
faithful EG *faithful copies of ancient stone tools*
faultless EG *She spoke with a faultless French accent.*
precise EG *It's difficult to give a precise date for the painting.*
true EG *Is this a true picture of life in the Middle Ages?*

> **WORD POWER**
> Antonym
> approximate

❷ **exact** VERB; FORMAL
to demand and obtain something
EG *They are certain to exact a high price for their cooperation.*
command EG *an excellent surgeon who commanded the respect of all his colleagues*
extract EG *to extract the maximum*

political advantage from this situation

impose EG *the first council to impose a fine for dropping litter*

insist on EG *She insisted on conducting all the interviews herself.*

insist upon EG *He insists upon good service.*

wring EG *attempts to wring concessions from the government*

exaggerate VERB
to make things seem worse than they are
EG *He thinks I'm exaggerating, but I'm not!*

overdo EG *I think he's overdoing it a bit when he complains like that.*

overestimate EG *I think we're overestimating their desire to cooperate.*

overstate EG *It's impossible to overstate the seriousness of this situation.*

exam NOUN
a test to find out how much you know
EG *a maths exam*

examination EG *a three-hour written examination*

oral EG *I got good marks for my French oral.*

test EG *I failed my history test again.*

❶ examination NOUN
a careful inspection of something
EG *The Navy is carrying out an examination of the wreck.*

analysis EG *An analysis of the ash revealed traces of lead oxide.*

inspection EG *The police inspection of the vehicle found no fingerprints.*

study EG *A study of the wreckage has thrown new light on the crash.*

❷ examination NOUN
a check carried out on someone by a doctor
EG *The doctor suggested an*

immediate examination of his ear.

check EG *a quick check just to make sure everything's working properly*

checkup EG *my annual checkup at the clinic*

medical EG *He had a medical before leaving England.*

❶ examine VERB
to look at something very carefully
EG *Police scientists are examining the scene of the crash.*

analyse EG *We haven't had time to analyse all the samples yet.*

go over EG *I'll go over your report tomorrow.*

go through EG *We went through his belongings and found a notebook.*

inspect EG *Customs officials inspected the vehicle.*

look over EG *Once we've looked the house over we should know what caused the fire.*

study EG *Experts are studying the frozen remains of a mammoth.*

> **WORD POWER**
> Synonyms
> peruse
> scrutinize

❷ examine NOUN
to give someone a medical examination
EG *I was examined by several specialists.*

check EG *Dr Mollison checked my nose and throat.*

inspect EG *I was inspected twice by Dr Stevens.*

look at EG *He said he wanted to look at my chest again just to make sure.*

test EG *They tested my eyes but my vision was fine.*

❶ example NOUN
something that represents a group of things
EG *some examples of medieval wood*

A B C D E F G H I J K L M N O P Q R S T U V W X Y Z

carving

illustration EG *Lo's success is an illustration of how well China is doing.*

sample EG *This drawing is a sample of his early work.*

specimen EG *I had to submit a specimen of my handwriting for analysis.*

❷ **example** NOUN
something that people can imitate
EG *His dedication is an example to us all.*

ideal EG *a woman who was the American ideal of beauty*

model EG *His conduct at the talks was a model of dignity.*

paragon EG *She is a paragon of neatness and efficiency.*

prototype EG *He was the prototype of the English gentleman.*

> WORD POWER
> Synonyms
> archetype
> exemplar
> paradigm

excellent ADJECTIVE
extremely good
EG *It's an excellent book, one of my favourites.*

beaut AUSTRALIAN AND NEW ZEALAND INFORMAL EG *a beaut spot to live*

brilliant EG *What a brilliant film!*

cracking BRITISH, AUSTRALIAN, AND NEW ZEALAND INFORMAL EG *You've done a cracking job in the garden!*

fine EG *There's a fine view from the bedroom window.*

first-class EG *a first-class effort*

great EG *He's a great player and we'll be sorry to lose him.*

outstanding EG *an outstanding performance*

superb EG *a superb craftsman*

> WORD POWER
> Antonym
> terrible

❶ **excess** NOUN
behaviour that goes beyond what is acceptable
EG *a life of excess*

extravagance EG *Examples of her extravagance were everywhere.*

indulgence EG *a moment of sheer indulgence*

> WORD POWER
> Synonyms
> debauchery
> dissipation
> intemperance
> overindulgence

❷ **excess** NOUN
a larger amount than necessary
EG *An excess of houseplants made the room look like a jungle.*

glut EG *the current glut of dairy products in Europe*

overdose EG *An overdose of sun can lead to skin problems later.*

surfeit EG *A surfeit of rich food did not help his digestive problems.*

surplus EG *Germany suffers from a surplus of teachers at the moment.*

> WORD POWER
> Synonyms
> overabundance
> plethora
> superabundance
> superfluity
> Antonym
> shortage

❸ **excess** ADJECTIVE
more than is needed
EG *problems associated with excess weight*

extra EG *Pour any extra liquid into a bowl and set aside.*

superfluous EG *all our superfluous belongings, things we don't need*

surplus EG *Farmers have to sell off their surplus stock cheap.*

excessive ADJECTIVE
too great
EG *an excessive reliance on government funding*

enormous EG *She spent an enormous amount on clothes.*

exaggerated EG *the exaggerated claims made by their supporters*

needless EG *a film that is full of needless violence*

undue EG *the need to avoid undue expense*

unreasonable EG *unreasonable increases in the price of petrol*

WORD POWER
Synonyms
disproportionate
exorbitant
immoderate
inordinate
profligate

❶ exchange VERB
to give something in return for something else
EG *We exchanged phone numbers.*

barter EG *Traders came from everywhere to barter in the markets.*

change EG *Can you change pesetas for pounds?*

swap EG *I wouldn't swap places with her for anything!*

switch EG *They switched cars and were away before the alarm was raised.*

trade EG *a secret deal to trade arms for hostages*

❷ exchange NOUN
the act of giving something for something else
EG *a ceasefire to allow the exchange of prisoners*

interchange EG *a meeting at which the interchange of ideas was encouraged*

swap EG *They agreed to a swap and made the necessary arrangements.*

switch EG *The switch went ahead as planned.*

trade EG *I am willing to make a trade with you.*

❶ excite VERB
to make someone feel enthusiastic or nervous
EG *The idea of visiting America really excited the kids.*

agitate EG *I've no idea what has agitated him.*

animate EG *There was plenty about this match to animate the capacity crowd.*

thrill EG *The reception he got at the meeting thrilled him.*

titillate EG *a meal that will titillate the taste buds of every gourmet*

❷ excite VERB
to cause a particular feeling or reaction
EG *The meeting failed to excite strong feelings in anyone.*

arouse EG *a move that has aroused deep public anger*

elicit EG *His proposal elicited a storm of protest.*

evoke EG *The film has evoked a sense of nostalgia in many older people.*

incite EG *a crude attempt to incite racial hatred*

inspire EG *The handling of the new car quickly inspires confidence.*

provoke EG *The suggestion has provoked anger.*

stir up EG *He's just trying to stir up trouble.*

WORD POWER
Synonyms
fire
foment
inflame
kindle
rouse

excited ADJECTIVE
happy and unable to relax
EG *We are very excited about getting a new dog.*

agitated EG *in an excited and agitated state*

enthusiastic EG *Tom usually seems very enthusiastic.*

feverish EG *a state of feverish anticipation*

157

high INFORMAL EG *I was feeling really high after Lorraine's party.*
thrilled EG *The children were thrilled when the snow came.*

> **WORD POWER**
> Antonym
> bored

excitement NOUN
interest and enthusiasm
EG *The release of his latest film has caused great excitement.*
activity EG *a scene of frenzied activity*
adventure EG *setting off in search of adventure*
agitation EG *He reacted to the news with considerable agitation.*
commotion EG *We decided to find out what all the commotion was about.*
enthusiasm EG *They greeted our arrival with enthusiasm.*
thrill EG *the thrill of scuba diving*

> **WORD POWER**
> Synonyms
> animation
> elation
> furore
> tumult

exciting ADJECTIVE
making you feel happy and enthusiastic
EG *the most exciting race I've ever seen*
dramatic EG *Their arrival was dramatic and exciting.*
electrifying EG *It was an electrifying performance.*
exhilarating EG *an exhilarating walk along the cliff tops*
rousing EG *a rousing speech*
stimulating EG *It's a stimulating book, full of ideas.*
thrilling EG *a thrilling opportunity to watch the lions as they feed*

> **WORD POWER**
> Synonyms
> intoxicating

sensational
stirring
Antonym
boring

❶ exclude VERB
to decide not to include something
EG *We cannot exclude this possibility altogether.*
eliminate EG *We can eliminate Mr Darnley from our list of suspects.*
ignore EG *We cannot afford to ignore this option.*
leave out EG *We can narrow it down by leaving out everywhere that's too expensive.*
omit EG *His name seems to have been omitted from the list.*
rule out EG *The police have already ruled out a retrial.*

> **WORD POWER**
> Antonym
> include

❷ exclude VERB
to stop someone going somewhere or doing something
EG *The university used to exclude women from all lectures.*
ban EG *Tony was banned from driving for three years.*
bar EG *She was barred from the tennis club.*
forbid EG *Carver was forbidden to attend any of the society's meetings.*
keep out EG *We need to keep out troublemakers.*

> **WORD POWER**
> Synonyms
> blackball
> debar

exclusive ADJECTIVE
available only to a few rich people
EG *one of Britain's most exclusive golf clubs*
chic EG *a chic nightclub in Monaco*
classy EG *a very classy restaurant*
posh INFORMAL EG *She took me to a*

posh hotel to celebrate.
select EG *a very lavish and very select party*
up-market EG *The area is much more up-market than it used to be.*

❶ excuse NOUN
a reason or explanation
EG *Stop making excuses and get on with it!*
explanation EG *You'd better have a good explanation for your conduct.*
justification EG *What possible justification can there be for this?*
pretext EG *His pretext for leaving early was an upset stomach.*
reason EG *This gave me the perfect reason for visiting London.*

❷ excuse VERB
to forgive someone or someone's behaviour
EG *Please excuse my late arrival.*
forgive EG *Forgive me, I'm so sorry.*
overlook EG *the need to overlook each other's failings*
pardon EG *Pardon my ignorance, but who is Cliff Hanley?*
turn a blind eye to EG *We can't be expected to turn a blind eye to this behaviour.*

exempt ADJECTIVE
excused from a duty or rule
EG *Teachers were exempt from military service.*
excused EG *Some MPs will have been officially excused attendance.*
immune EG *Members of the parliament are immune from prosecution.*
not liable EG *They are not liable to pay income tax.*

exercise NOUN
activity that keeps you fit
EG *I need to get more exercise.*
activity EG *a bit of physical activity to get the heart going*
exertion EG *I'm tired out by all this exertion.*
training EG *He needs to do a bit more training before the match.*

work EG *I'm doing a lot more work at the gym now I'm feeling better.*

❶ exhaust VERB
to make very tired
EG *I mustn't exhaust myself as I did last time.*
drain EG *My emotional turmoil had drained me.*
fatigue EG *He is easily fatigued.*
tire out EG *a great new job that tires me out*
wear out EG *Living out of a suitcase wears you out.*

❷ exhaust VERB
to use something up completely
EG *She has exhausted all my patience.*
consume EG *plans which will consume hours of time*
deplete EG *chemicals that deplete the earth's protective ozone shield*
run through EG *The project ran through its funds in months.*
use up EG *The gas has all been used up.*

expand VERB
to make or become larger
EG *The rails expanded and buckled in the fierce heat.*
develop EG *We need to develop the company's engineering division.*
enlarge EG *Plans to enlarge the stadium have been approved.*
extend EG *We're trying to extend our range of sports wear.*
fill out EG *The balloon had filled out and was already almost airborne.*
grow EG *The Japanese share of the market has grown dramatically.*
increase EG *We will need to increase our overseas operations.*
swell EG *The river had swollen rapidly.*

> **WORD POWER**
> Antonym
> decrease

expand on VERB

A
B
C
D
E
F
G
H
I
J
K
L
M
N
O
P
Q
R
S
T
U
V
W
X
Y
Z

expect – experience

to give more information about
something
EG *an idea that I will expand on
later*

develop EG *You should develop
this theme a little bit further.*

elaborate on EG *He refused to
elaborate on what he had said
earlier.*

enlarge on EG *I'd like you to
enlarge on that last point.*

❶ expect VERB
to believe that something is
going to happen
EG *The trial is expected to last
several weeks.*

anticipate EG *We do not
anticipate any problems.*

assume EG *He assumed that they
would wait for him.*

believe EG *Experts believe the
comet will pass close to the earth.*

imagine EG *The meal cost more
than we had imagined.*

presume EG *I presume they'll be
along shortly.*

reckon EG *We reckon it'll be a
fairly quick journey.*

think EG *I thought the concert
would be cancelled.*

> **WORD POWER**
> Synonyms
> envisage
> forecast
> foresee
> predict

❷ expect VERB
to believe that something is your
right
EG *I was expecting to have a bit of
time to myself.*

demand EG *a job that demands a
lot of time and money*

rely on EG *I'm relying on you to
help me.*

require EG *They require a lot of
her, maybe too much.*

expensive ADJECTIVE
costing a lot of money

EG *a very expensive Italian suit*

costly EG *a costly court case*

dear EG *Those trainers are far too
dear.*

pricey EG *Medical insurance can be
very pricey.*

> **WORD POWER**
> Synonyms
> exorbitant
> overpriced
> Antonym
> cheap

❶ experience NOUN
knowledge or skill in a particular
activity
EG *We're looking for someone with
engineering experience.*

expertise EG *They lack the
expertise to deal with such a
complex case.*

know-how EG *Her technical
know-how was invaluable.*

knowledge EG *We need someone
with knowledge of computing.*

training EG *His military training
made the difference between life
and death.*

understanding EG *someone with
considerable understanding of the
law*

❷ experience NOUN
something that happens to you
EG *a terrifying experience that she
still talks about*

adventure EG *a series of
hair-raising adventures during the
war*

affair EG *He seemed keen to forget
the affair and never discussed it.*

encounter EG *his first encounter
with alcohol*

episode EG *The episode has proved
deeply embarrassing for her.*

incident EG *an incident he would
rather forget*

ordeal EG *a painful ordeal that is
now over*

❸ experience VERB

to have something happen to you
EG *We are experiencing a few technical problems.*
encounter EG *The storms were the worst they had ever encountered.*
have EG *We're having a few difficulties with the computer.*
meet EG *The next time you meet a situation like this, be careful.*
undergo EG *The market is now undergoing a severe recession.*

experienced ADJECTIVE
very skilful as a result of practice
EG *an experienced diver*
expert EG *an expert pilot*
knowledgeable EG *He's very knowledgeable in this field.*
practised EG *a practised and accomplished surgeon*
seasoned EG *a seasoned climber*
well-versed EG *He is well-versed in many styles of jazz.*

❶ expert NOUN
a skilled or knowledgeable person
EG *A team of experts will be on hand to offer advice.*
ace INFORMAL EG *former motor-racing ace Stirling Moss*
authority EG *an authority on ancient Egypt*
buff INFORMAL EG *Cliff is a bit of a film buff.*
guru EG *fashion gurus who predicted a 70's revival*
master EG *He is a master in the art of office politics.*
professional EG *He's widely respected in the theatre as a true professional.*
specialist EG *a specialist in tropical diseases*
wizard EG *a financial wizard who made millions in the early 80's*

❷ expert ADJECTIVE
skilled and knowledgeable
EG *Mollison's expert approach impressed everyone.*
able EG *an able and dedicated surgeon*
adept EG *He's an adept guitar player.*
experienced EG *He was an experienced traveller and knew the area well.*
knowledgeable EG *He's very knowledgeable about Chinese pottery.*
proficient EG *Jackson is proficient in several European languages.*
skilful EG *the skilful use of light in his early paintings*
skilled EG *Ian is a highly skilled photographer.*

explain VERB
to give extra information about something
EG *He explained to us how the system worked.*
define EG *Can you define what you mean by 'excessive'?*
describe EG *an attempt to describe the whole process*
illustrate EG *Let me illustrate this point with an example.*

explanation NOUN
a helpful or clear description
EG *his lucid explanation of Einstein's theories*

A B C D E F G H I J K L M N O P Q R S T U V W X Y Z

A
B
C
D
E
F
G
H
I
J
K
L
M
N
O
P
Q
R
S
T
U
V
W
X
Y
Z

clarification EG *Her clarification has done little to help matters.*

definition EG *a definition of what we actually mean by 'symbolism'*

description EG *a fascinating description of how the pyramids were built*

exposition EG *the fullest available exposition of Coleridge's ideas*

❶ explode VERB
to burst or cause to burst loudly
EG *the sound of a bomb exploding nearby*

blow up EG *Their boat blew up as they slept.*

burst EG *Joey blew up the balloon until it burst.*

detonate EG *Troops managed to detonate the mine safely.*

go off EG *The bomb went off without any warning.*

set off EG *No-one knows who planted the bomb, or how it was set off.*

❷ explode VERB
to become angry suddenly
EG *I asked him if he'd finished and he just exploded.*

blow up EG *When she finally told him, he blew up and walked out.*

go berserk EG *He'll go berserk if he ever finds out.*

go mad EG *He went mad when I mentioned the kids.*

❸ explode VERB
to increase suddenly and rapidly
EG *Sales of computer games have exploded in recent years.*

rocket EG *Inflation has rocketed in the last few months.*

shoot up EG *Prices shot up and the shelves were soon empty.*

soar EG *Demand for shares in his new company has soared.*

explosion NOUN
a violent burst of energy
EG *The explosion shattered windows all along the street.*

bang EG *A loud bang made me run for cover.*

blast EG *Three people were killed in the blast.*

❶ expose VERB
to make something visible
EG *The wreck was exposed by the action of the tide.*

reveal EG *His shirt was open, revealing his tattooed chest.*

show EG *a short skirt which showed too much of her legs*

uncover EG *She removed her scarf and uncovered her head.*

❷ expose VERB
to tell the truth about someone or something
EG *He has been exposed as a liar and a cheat.*

bring to light EG *The truth will be brought to light eventually.*

reveal EG *an investigation that revealed widespread corruption*

show up EG *She was finally shown up as a hypocrite.*

uncover EG *We uncovered evidence of fraud.*

unearth EG *Investigators have unearthed new evidence.*

❶ express VERB
to say what you think
EG *She expressed interest in the plans for the new dam.*

communicate EG *People must learn to communicate their feelings.*

couch EG *Their demands, though extreme, are couched in moderate language.*

phrase EG *It sounds fine, but I would have phrased it differently.*

put EG *Absolutely - I couldn't have put it better.*

put across EG *the need to put across your message without offending anyone*

voice EG *Local people have voiced their concern over plans for a bypass.*

WORD POWER
Synonyms

articulate
enunciate
utter
verbalize

❷ express ADJECTIVE
very fast
EG *a special express delivery service*
direct EG *There's also a direct train.*
fast EG *delays due to an accident in the fast lane*
high-speed EG *the high-speed rail link between London and Paris*
nonstop EG *the new nonstop service to New York*

❶ expression NOUN
the look on your face that shows your feelings
EG *an aggrieved expression*
countenance EG *the beaming countenance of the prime minister*
face EG *Why are you all wearing such long faces?*

WORD POWER
Synonyms
aspect
mien

❷ expression NOUN
a word or phrase used to communicate
EG *a good old American expression*
idiom EG *talking in the idiom of the Home Counties*
phrase EG *What is the origin of the phrase?*
remark EG *her passing remark to the camera*
term EG *a derogatory term for an Arab*

❶ extend VERB
to have a particular size or position
EG *The region will extend way beyond the capital.*
continue EG *The caves continue for miles beneath the hills.*
hang EG *The branches hang down to the ground.*
reach EG *a long shirt that reached*

to her knees
stretch EG *an area of forest stretching as far as the eye could see*

❷ extend VERB
to stick out
EG *a brass peg that extended from the end of the mast*
jut out EG *The tip of the island juts out like a finger into the sea.*
project EG *the ruins of a fort which projected from the mud*
protrude FORMAL EG *a huge rock protruding from the surface of the lake*
stick out EG *pieces of rough metal that stuck out like spikes*

❸ extend VERB
to make something larger
EG *We'd like to extend the house and build a conservatory.*
add to EG *They will be adding to their range of children's wear.*
develop EG *He developed the US arm of the company.*
enlarge EG *plans to enlarge the conference centre*
expand EG *an unsuccessful attempt to expand the store's range of footwear*
widen EG *the need to widen the appeal of the scheme*

WORD POWER
Synonyms
augment
broaden
supplement

❶ extra ADJECTIVE
more than is usual or expected
EG *The company is taking on extra staff for the summer.*
added EG *The Tandoori Cottage has the added advantage of being cheap.*
additional EG *the need for additional funding*
excess EG *If there's any excess sauce, you can freeze it.*
further EG *the introduction of*

A
B
C
D
E
F
G
H
I
J
K
L
M
N
O
P
Q
R
S
T
U
V
W
X
Y
Z

further restrictions
more EG *We need three more places at the table.*

new EG *the burden of new legislation on top of all the recent changes*

spare EG *There are spare blankets in the cupboard.*

> WORD POWER
> Synonyms
> ancillary
> auxiliary
> supplementary

❷ **extra** NOUN
something that is not included with other things
EG *Air conditioning is an optional extra.*

accessory EG *the accessories you have to buy to make the place look good*

addition EG *the latest addition to the team*

bonus EG *The view from the hotel was an added bonus.*

extraordinary ADJECTIVE
unusual or surprising
EG *He really is an extraordinary man.*

amazing EG *What an amazing coincidence!*

bizarre EG *It's such a bizarre thing to happen.*

odd EG *It's an odd combination of colours.*

singular EG *Cathy gave me a smile of singular sweetness.*

strange EG *It's a strange piece of music.*

surprising EG *A surprising number of women prefer to wear trousers to work.*

unusual EG *It's a most unusual way to spend your holiday.*

> WORD POWER
> Antonym
> ordinary

❶ **extreme** ADJECTIVE

very great in degree or intensity
EG *those people living in extreme poverty*

acute EG *a mistake that caused acute embarrassment for everyone concerned*

deep EG *a decision that caused deep resentment*

dire EG *He is in dire need of hospital treatment.*

great EG *a change in the law that could cause many people great hardship*

intense EG *A number of people collapsed in the intense heat that day.*

profound EG *feelings of profound shock and anger*

severe EG *a business with severe financial problems*

❷ **extreme** ADJECTIVE
unusual or unreasonable
EG *I think that's rather an extreme reaction.*

drastic EG *Let's not do anything too drastic.*

exceptional EG *I think this is an exceptional case.*

excessive EG *a newspaper feature about the use of excessive force by the police*

extravagant EG *All that money being spent on hospitality seemed a bit extravagant.*

radical EG *The government is introducing a series of radical economic reforms.*

unreasonable EG *I don't think she's being the least bit unreasonable.*

❸ **extreme** NOUN
the highest or furthest degree or point
EG *We're just going from one extreme to the other.*

boundary EG *the boundaries of artistic freedom*

depth EG *the beauty of the countryside in the depths of winter*

end EG *There are extremist groups at both ends of the political spectrum.*
height EG *His behaviour was the height of bad manners.*
limit EG *The ordeal tested the limits of their endurance.*
ultimate EG *A Rolls-Royce is the ultimate in luxury.*

WORD POWER

Synonyms
acme
apex
nadir
pinnacle
zenith

A B C D E F G H I J K L M N O P Q R S T U V W X Y Z

165

Ff Ff

❶ face NOUN

the front part of the head
EG *A strong wind was blowing in my face.*

countenance EG *He met each enquiry with an impassive countenance.*

features EG *Her features were strongly defined.*

mug SLANG EG *He managed to get his ugly mug on the telly.*

> **WORD POWER**
> Synonyms
> lineaments
> physiognomy

❷ face NOUN

a surface or side of something
EG *the north face of Everest*

aspect EG *The house had a south-west aspect.*

exterior EG *The exterior of the building was made of brick.*

front EG *There was a large veranda at the front of the house.*

side EG *narrow valleys with steep sides*

surface EG *tiny waves on the surface of the water*

❸ face VERB

to look towards something or someone
EG *a room that faces on to the street*

be opposite EG *I was opposite her at the breakfast table.*

look at EG *She turned to look at the person who was speaking.*

overlook EG *The pretty room overlooks a beautiful garden.*

fact NOUN

a piece of information that is true
EG *a statement of verifiable fact*

certainty EG *A general election became a certainty three weeks ago.*

reality EG *Fiction and reality became increasingly blurred.*

truth EG *In the town, very few know the whole truth.*

> **WORD POWER**
> Antonym
> lie

factor NOUN

something that helps to cause a result
EG *Physical activity is an important factor in maintaining fitness.*

aspect EG *Exam results illustrate only one aspect of a school's success.*

cause EG *Smoking is the biggest preventable cause of death and disease.*

consideration EG *Money was also a consideration.*

element EG *Fitness has now become an important element in our lives.*

influence EG *Van Gogh was a major influence on the development of modern painting.*

part EG *Respect is a very important part of any relationship.*

> **WORD POWER**
> Synonyms
> circumstance
> determinant

factory NOUN

a building where goods are made
EG *He owned furniture factories in several areas.*

mill EG *a textile mill*

plant EG *The plant produces most of the company's output.*

works EG *the steel works*

fade VERB

to make or become less intense
EG *The fabric had faded in the bright sunlight.*

die away EG *The sound died away gradually.*

dim EG *The house lights dimmed.*

discolour EG *Exposure to bright*

light can cause wallpaper to discolour.
dull EG *Repeated washing had dulled the bright finish.*
wash out EG *This dye won't wash out.*

❶ fail VERB
to be unsuccessful
EG *He failed in his attempt to take over the company.*
be defeated EG *The vote to change the law was defeated.*
be in vain EG *It became clear that his efforts had been in vain.*
be unsuccessful EG *My job application was unsuccessful.*
come to grief EG *Many marriages have come to grief over lack of money.*
fall through EG *Negotiations with business leaders fell through last night.*

> *WORD POWER*
> Antonym
> succeed

❷ fail VERB
to omit to do something
EG *They failed to phone her.*
neglect EG *They never neglect their duties.*
omit EG *He had omitted to tell her of the change in his plans.*

❸ fail VERB
to become less effective
EG *His eyesight began to fail.*
cease EG *The secrecy about his condition had ceased to matter.*
decline EG *His power declined as he grew older.*
give out EG *All machines give out eventually.*
sink EG *Her spirits sank lower and lower.*
stop working EG *The boat came to a halt when the engine stopped working.*
wane EG *her mother's waning strength*

❶ failure NOUN
a lack of success
EG *to end in failure*
breakdown EG *a breakdown of the talks between the parties*
defeat EG *It is important not to admit defeat.*
downfall EG *people wishing to see the downfall of the government*
fiasco EG *The evening was a total fiasco.*
miscarriage EG *a miscarriage of justice*

> *WORD POWER*
> Antonym
> success

❷ failure NOUN
an unsuccessful person or thing
EG *The venture was a complete failure.*
disappointment EG *a disappointment to his family*
flop INFORMAL EG *The play turned out to be a flop.*
loser EG *He had always been a loser.*
no-hoper AUSTRALIAN AND NEW ZEALAND EG *hanging around a group of no-hopers*

> *WORD POWER*
> Synonyms
> incompetent
> ne'er-do-well

❸ failure NOUN
a weakness in something
EG *a failure in the insurance system*
deficiency EG *a serious deficiency in their defence system*
shortcoming EG *The book has many shortcomings.*

❶ faint ADJECTIVE
lacking in intensity
EG *a faint smell of tobacco*
dim EG *dim lighting*
faded EG *a faded sign on the side of the building*
indistinct EG *The lettering was worn and indistinct.*

A
B
C
D
E
F
G
H
I
J
K
L
M
N
O
P
Q
R
S
T
U
V
W
X
Y
Z

low EG *She spoke in a low voice.*
muted EG *some muted cheers from the gallery*
vague EG *a vague memory*

> **WORD POWER**
> Antonym
> strong

❷ faint ADJECTIVE
feeling dizzy and unsteady
EG *Feeling faint is one of the symptoms.*
dizzy EG *suffering from dizzy spells*
giddy EG *He felt giddy after the ride.*
light-headed EG *She felt light-headed because she hadn't eaten.*

> **WORD POWER**
> Synonyms
> enervated
> vertiginous

❸ faint VERB
to lose consciousness temporarily
EG *to faint from shock*
black out EG *The blood drained from his head and he blacked out.*
collapse EG *I collapsed when I heard the news.*
pass out EG *to pass out with pain*
swoon LITERARY EG *Women in the '20s swooned over Valentino.*

❶ fair ADJECTIVE
reasonable and just
EG *a fair trial*
equal EG *the commitment to equal opportunities*
equitable EG *an equitable allocation of resources*
impartial EG *an impartial observer*
legitimate EG *a legitimate claim to the money*
proper EG *It's right and proper that he should be here.*
upright EG *an upright and trustworthy man*

> **WORD POWER**
> Synonyms

disinterested
dispassionate
unbiased
> Antonym
> unfair

❷ fair ADJECTIVE
having light-coloured hair or pale skin
EG *long fair hair*
blonde or **blond** EG *a darker shade of blonde*
light EG *He had a light complexion and blue eyes.*

> **WORD POWER**
> Antonym
> dark

❸ fair NOUN
an outdoor entertainment
EG *a country fair*
bazaar EG *a fundraising bazaar*
carnival EG *the annual Antigua Carnival*
exhibition EG *an international trade exhibition*
festival EG *a rock festival*
fete EG *The church fete was a popular attraction.*
show EG *an agricultural show*

❶ faith NOUN
trust in a thing or a person
EG *to have great faith in something*
confidence EG *They had no confidence in the police.*
trust EG *His trust in them was misplaced.*

❷ faith NOUN
a person's or community's religion
EG *They believed in the old faith.*
belief EG *united by belief*
creed EG *open to all, regardless of creed*
persuasion EG *people of all religious persuasions*
religion EG *the Christian religion*

❶ faithful ADJECTIVE
loyal to someone or something

EG *a faithful dog*

devoted EG *They are devoted to each other.*

loyal EG *a sign of true and loyal friendship*

staunch EG *a staunch member of the party*

true EG *a true believer*

> **WORD POWER**
> **Synonyms**
> steadfast
> unwavering
> **Antonym**
> unfaithful

❷ **faithful** ADJECTIVE
accurate and truthful
EG *The film was faithful to the novel.*

accurate EG *an accurate description of the event*

exact EG *an exact copy of the original*

strict EG *We demand strict adherence to the rules.*

true EG *The film was quite true to life.*

❶ **fake** NOUN
a deceitful imitation of a thing or person
EG *These paintings are fakes.*

copy EG *It wasn't real, just a copy.*

forgery EG *The signature was a forgery.*

fraud EG *Many psychics are frauds.*

imitation EG *The "antique" chair is in fact a clever imitation.*

reproduction EG *a reproduction of a famous painting*

sham EG *The election was denounced as a sham.*

❷ **fake** ADJECTIVE
imitation and not genuine
EG *fake fur*

artificial EG *It's made with artificial sweeteners.*

counterfeit EG *a large number of counterfeit documents*

false EG *a false passport*

imitation EG *bound in imitation leather*

phoney or **phony** INFORMAL EG *He used a phoney accent.*

> **WORD POWER**
> **Synonyms**
> assumed
> pseudo-
> **Antonym**
> real

❸ **fake** VERB
to pretend to experience something
EG *He faked his own death.*

feign EG *to feign illness*

pretend EG *Todd shrugged with pretended indifference.*

simulate EG *writhing around in simulated agony*

❶ **fall** VERB
to descend towards the ground
EG *The tile fell from the roof.*

collapse EG *The bridge collapsed on to the road.*

drop EG *bombs dropping from the sky*

plunge EG *A bus plunged into the river.*

topple EG *He toppled slowly backwards.*

trip EG *She tripped and broke her leg.*

> **WORD POWER**
> **Antonym**
> rise

❷ **fall** VERB
to become lower or less
EG *Output fell by more than half.*

decline EG *a declining birth rate*

decrease EG *The number of bankruptcies decreased last year.*

diminish EG *Resources are diminishing steadily.*

dwindle EG *his dwindling authority*

plummet EG *plummeting share prices*

subside EG *The flood waters have subsided.*

> **WORD POWER**
> Synonyms
> abate
> depreciate
> ebb
> Antonym
> increase

❸ fall NOUN
a reduction in amount
EG *a fall in the exchange rate*
decline EG *signs of economic decline*
decrease EG *an overall decrease of 10%*
drop EG *the sharp drop in export sales*
reduction EG *The bank announced a reduction in interest rates.*
slump EG *a slump in property prices*

> **WORD POWER**
> Antonym
> rise

❶ false ADJECTIVE
not true or correct
EG *He gave a false name and address.*
erroneous EG *to arrive at an erroneous conclusion*
fictitious EG *the source of the fictitious rumours*
incorrect EG *a decision based on incorrect information*
mistaken EG *I had a mistaken view of what had happened.*
untrue EG *The remarks were completely untrue.*

> **WORD POWER**
> Antonym
> true

❷ false ADJECTIVE
not genuine but intended to seem so
EG *false hair*
artificial EG *an artificial limb*
bogus EG *their bogus insurance claim*

fake EG *a fake tan*
forged EG *They crossed the frontier using forged documents.*
simulated EG *a simulated display of affection*

> **WORD POWER**
> Synonyms
> ersatz
> pseudo-
> spurious
> Antonym
> genuine

❸ false ADJECTIVE
unfaithful and deceitful
EG *They turned out to be false friends.*
deceitful EG *deceitful and misleading remarks*
disloyal EG *He was accused of being disloyal to the company.*
insincere EG *A lot of actors are insincere.*
unfaithful EG *left alone by her unfaithful husband*

> **WORD POWER**
> Synonyms
> duplicitous
> perfidious

fame NOUN
the state of being very well-known
EG *The film brought him international fame.*
eminence EG *to achieve eminence as a politician*
glory EG *my moment of glory*
prominence EG *He came to prominence with his bestselling novel.*
renown EG *a singer of great renown*
reputation EG *the city's reputation as a place of romance*

familiar ADJECTIVE
knowing something well
EG *Most children are familiar with stories.*
acquainted with EG *Peter was well acquainted with Wordsworth.*

aware of EG *aware of the dangers of smoking*
knowledgeable about EG *They were very knowledgeable about gardening.*
versed in EG *She was well versed in company law.*

WORD POWER
Antonym
unfamiliar

① family NOUN
a group of relatives
EG *My family are always supportive of me.*
descendants EG *Their descendants lived there for centuries.*
relations EG *friends and relations*
relatives EG *She had relatives in many countries.*

② family NOUN
a group of related species
EG *Tigers are members of the cat family.*
class EG *several classes of butterflies*
classification EG *The classification includes conifers.*
kind EG *different kinds of roses*

famous ADJECTIVE
very well-known
EG *the most famous woman of her time*
celebrated EG *his most celebrated film*
distinguished EG *a distinguished academic family*
illustrious EG *the most illustrious scientists of the century*
legendary EG *His skills are legendary.*
noted EG *He is noted for his generosity.*
renowned EG *The area is renowned for its cuisine.*

WORD POWER
Synonyms
lionized
signal
Antonym

family – fanatical

unknown

fan NOUN
an enthusiast about something or someone
EG *a fan of the new band*
adherent EG *The movement was gaining adherents everywhere.*
admirer EG *one of her many admirers*
devotee EG *a devotee of chamber music*
lover EG *an art lover*
supporter EG *rival football supporters*
zealot EG *a religious zealot*

WORD POWER
Synonyms
aficionado
buff
enthusiast

fanatic NOUN
someone who is extremely enthusiastic about something
EG *a football fanatic*
activist EG *political activists*
devotee EG *a devotee of the movement*
extremist EG *groups of religious extremists*
militant EG *The militants took over the organization.*
zealot EG *He was a supporter but not a zealot.*

fanatical ADJECTIVE
showing extreme support for something
EG *a fanatical patriot*
fervent EG *a fervent supporter*
obsessive EG *obsessive about motor racing*
passionate EG *a passionate interest*
rabid EG *a rabid racist group*
wild EG *I am wild about this band.*

WORD POWER
Synonyms
immoderate
zealous

171

A
B
C
D
E
F
G
H
I
J
K
L
M
N
O
P
Q
R
S
T
U
V
W
X
Y
Z

❶ fancy VERB
to want to have or do something
EG *He fancied a drink.*
be attracted to EG *I am attracted to the idea of emigrating.*
hanker after EG *to hanker after a bigger car*
have a yen for EG *She had a yen for some new clothes.*
would like EG *I would really like some ice cream.*

❷ fancy ADJECTIVE
special and elaborate
EG *dressed up in fancy clothes*
decorated EG *She preferred decorated surfaces to plain ones.*
elaborate EG *his elaborate costume ideas*
extravagant EG *the extravagant frescoes in the upper church*
intricate EG *covered with intricate patterns*
ornate EG *an ornate picture frame*

> **WORD POWER**
> Synonyms
> baroque
> embellished
> ornamented
> Antonym
> plain

❶ far ADVERB
at a great distance from something
EG *The sea was far below us.*
afar EG *seen from afar*
a great distance EG *They travelled a great distance.*
a long way EG *The guy's lonely and a long way from home.*
deep EG *deep into the jungle*
miles EG *He lived miles away.*

❷ far ADVERB
to a great extent or degree
EG *far better than the others*
considerably EG *The dinners were considerably less formal than before.*
incomparably EG *South Africa seems incomparably richer than the rest of Africa.*
much EG *I feel much better now.*
very much EG *Things got very much worse.*

❸ far ADJECTIVE
very distant
EG *in the far south of the country*
distant EG *the distant horizon*
long EG *a long distance from here*
outlying EG *The outlying areas are accessible only by air.*
remote EG *a cottage in a remote village*

> **WORD POWER**
> Antonym
> near

fascinate VERB
to be of intense interest to someone
EG *He was fascinated by the new discovery.*
absorb EG *totally absorbed by her career*
bewitch EG *Bill was bewitched by her charm.*
captivate EG *Her looks captivated the whole world.*
enthral EG *She sat enthralled by the actors.*
intrigue EG *Her story intrigued them.*

> **WORD POWER**
> Synonyms
> beguile
> enchant
> spellbind
> transfix

❶ fashion NOUN
a popular style of dress or behaviour
EG *changing fashions in clothing*
craze EG *the latest health craze*
fad EG *just a passing fad*
style EG *a revival of an old style*
trend EG *the current trend in footwear*
vogue EG *a vogue for fitness training*

②fashion NOUN
a manner or way of doing
something
EG *It works in a similar fashion.*
manner EG *in a friendly manner*
method EG *He did it by his usual
method.*
mode EG *a different mode of life*
way EG *in her usual resourceful way*

③fashion VERB
to make and shape something
EG *fashioned from rough wood*
construct EG *an inner frame
constructed from timber*
create EG *It was created from odds
and ends.*
make EG *a doll made from fabric*
mould EG *They moulded the cups
from clay.*
shape EG *Shape the dough into a
loaf.*
work EG *a machine for working the
stone*

fashionable ADJECTIVE
very popular
EG *a fashionable restaurant*
current EG *the current thinking on
the subject*
in INFORMAL EG *Jogging was the in
thing.*
latest EG *all the latest hairstyles*
popular EG *the most popular movie*
prevailing EG *contrary to
prevailing attitudes*

> **WORD POWER**
> Synonyms
> chic
> in vogue
> trendsetting
> Antonym
> old-fashioned

①fast ADJECTIVE
moving at great speed
EG *a fast train*
accelerated EG *at an accelerated
pace*
hurried EG *He ate a hurried
breakfast.*

quick EG *a quick learner*
rapid EG *a rapid rise through the
company*
speedy EG *best wishes for a speedy
recovery*
swift EG *as swift as an arrow*

> **WORD POWER**
> Synonyms
> fleet
> mercurial
> winged
> Antonym
> slow

②fast ADVERB
quickly and without delay
EG *You'll have to move fast.*
hastily EG *sheltering in hastily
erected tents*
hurriedly EG *students hurriedly
taking notes*
quickly EG *She worked quickly and
methodically.*
rapidly EG *moving rapidly across
the field*
swiftly EG *They had to act swiftly
to save him.*

> **WORD POWER**
> Antonym
> slowly

③fast ADVERB
firmly and strongly
EG *She held fast to the rail.*
firmly EG *with windows firmly shut*
securely EG *The door was securely
locked and bolted.*
tightly EG *held tightly in his arms*

fasten VERB
to close or attach something
EG *Fasten your seat belts.*
attach EG *He attached a label to
the plant.*
fix EG *It was fixed on the wall.*
join EG *joined together by string*
lock EG *a locked door*
secure EG *The chest was secured
with a lock and chain.*
tie EG *Tie your shoelaces.*

A
B
C
D
E
F
G
H
I
J
K
L
M
N
O
P
Q
R
S
T
U
V
W
X
Y
Z

A
B
C
D
E
F
G
H
I
J
K
L
M
N
O
P
Q
R
S
T
U
V
W
X
Y
Z

fat ADJECTIVE
weighing too much
EG *a fat man*
obese EG *dangerously obese*
overweight EG *He was overweight for his height.*
plump EG *a plump little woman*
stout EG *a stout, middle-aged man*

> *WORD POWER*
> Synonyms
> corpulent
> elephantine
> portly
> Antonym
> thin

❶ **fatal** ADJECTIVE
causing death
EG *fatal injuries*
deadly EG *a deadly disease*
incurable EG *It was regarded as an incurable illness.*
lethal EG *a lethal dose of sleeping pills*
mortal EG *They were in mortal danger.*
terminal EG *terminal cancer*

❷ **fatal** ADJECTIVE
having an undesirable effect
EG *The mistake was fatal to my plans.*
calamitous EG *a calamitous air crash*
catastrophic EG *The water shortage is potentially catastrophic.*
disastrous EG *This could have disastrous consequences for industry.*
lethal EG *a lethal left hook*

fate NOUN
a power believed to control events
EG *the fickleness of fate*
chance EG *a victim of chance*
destiny EG *We are masters of our own destiny.*
fortune EG *Remember, fortune favours the brave.*
providence EG *His death was an act of providence.*

> *WORD POWER*
> Synonyms
> kismet
> nemesis
> predestination

❶ **fault** NOUN
something for which someone is responsible
EG *It was all my fault.*
blame EG *They put the blame on her.*
liability EG *The company was forced to admit liability.*
responsibility EG *He accepted full responsibility for the error.*

❷ **fault** NOUN
a defective quality in something
EG *a minor technical fault*
blemish EG *a blemish on an otherwise outstanding career*
defect EG *a manufacturing defect*
deficiency EG *serious deficiencies in the system*
drawback EG *The plan had one major drawback.*
failing EG *the country's many failings*
flaw EG *serious character flaws*
imperfection EG *small imperfections on the surface*
weakness EG *his one weakness*

> *WORD POWER*
> Antonym
> strength

❸ **fault** VERB
to find reasons to be critical of someone
EG *Her conduct cannot be faulted.*
blame EG *I don't blame him.*
censure EG *He was censured by the committee.*
criticize EG *The minister criticized the police.*

faulty ADJECTIVE
containing flaws or errors
EG *Faulty goods should be sent back.*
defective EG *a lorry with defective brakes*

flawed EG *The test results were seriously flawed.*
imperfect EG *an imperfect specimen*
invalid EG *That's an invalid argument.*
unsound EG *a building that is structurally unsound*

> **WORD POWER**
> Synonyms
> fallacious
> imprecise
> malfunctioning

❶ favour NOUN
a liking or approval of something
EG *The proposals met with favour.*
approval EG *to gain his father's approval*
esteem EG *in high esteem*
grace EG *to fall from grace*
support EG *They gave us their full support.*

> **WORD POWER**
> Antonym
> disapproval

❷ favour NOUN
a kind and helpful action
EG *Can you do me a favour?*
courtesy EG *the courtesy of a personal response*
good turn EG *to do someone a good turn*
kindness EG *She did me the kindness of calling.*
service EG *a service to your country*

> **WORD POWER**
> Antonym
> wrong

❸ favour VERB
to prefer something or someone
EG *They favoured the eldest child.*
prefer EG *the preferred candidate*
single out EG *He is always being singled out for special treatment.*

❶ favourable ADJECTIVE
of advantage and benefit to someone
EG *favourable conditions*
advantageous EG *the most advantageous course of action*
beneficial EG *a beneficial effect on our health*
good EG *He got a very good deal.*
opportune EG *an opportune moment to attack*
suitable EG *Conditions were not suitable for life to flourish.*

> **WORD POWER**
> Synonyms
> auspicious
> propitious
> timely
> Antonym
> unfavourable

❷ favourable ADJECTIVE
positive and expressing approval
EG *a positive response*
affirmative EG *to give an affirmative answer*
amicable EG *amicable discussions*
approving EG *a warm, approving glance*
friendly EG *The proposal was given a friendly reception.*
positive EG *a positive effect on the situation*
sympathetic EG *He got a sympathetic hearing.*
welcoming EG *a welcoming atmosphere*

> **WORD POWER**
> Antonym
> unfavourable

❶ favourite ADJECTIVE
being someone's best-liked person or thing
EG *my favourite hotel*
best-loved EG *our best-loved music*
dearest EG *Her dearest wish was fulfilled.*
favoured EG *the favoured child of elderly parents*
preferred EG *his preferred method of exercise*

A B C D E F G H I J K L M N O P Q R S T U V W X Y Z

175

❷ favourite NOUN
the thing or person someone likes best
EG *The youngest was always her favourite.*
darling EG *the spoilt darling of the family*
idol EG *the idol of his fans*
pet EG *the teacher's pet*
pick EG *the pick of the bunch*

favouritism NOUN
unfair favour shown to a person or group
EG *There was never a hint of favouritism.*
bias EG *political bias in broadcasting*
one-sidedness EG *The committee must show no one-sidedness.*

> *WORD POWER*
> Synonyms
> nepotism
> partiality
> partisanship
> Antonym
> impartiality

❶ fear NOUN
an unpleasant feeling of danger
EG *shivering with fear*
alarm EG *I looked at him with growing alarm.*
awe EG *in awe of his great powers*
dread EG *She thought with dread of the coming storm.*
fright EG *He jumped with fright at the noise.*
panic EG *a moment of panic*
terror EG *to shake with terror*

> *WORD POWER*
> Synonyms
> apprehensiveness
> cravenness
> trepidation

❷ fear VERB
to feel frightened of something
EG *There is nothing to fear.*
be afraid EG *The dog was afraid of him.*

be frightened EG *I am frightened of thunder.*
be scared EG *Are you scared of snakes?*
dread EG *He dreaded angry scenes.*
take fright EG *The horse took fright at the sudden noise.*

❶ feature NOUN
a particular characteristic of something
EG *an unusual feature of the room*
aspect EG *every aspect of our lives*
attribute EG *a normal attribute of human behaviour*
characteristic EG *their physical characteristics*
mark EG *distinguishing marks*
property EG *the magnetic properties of iron*
quality EG *skills and personal qualities*

❷ feature NOUN
a special article or programme
EG *a news feature*
article EG *a travel article*
column EG *the advice column*
item EG *an item about chemical waste*
piece EG *a specially-written piece*
report EG *a film report on the scandal*
story EG *front-page news stories*

❸ feature VERB
to include and draw attention to something
EG *featuring an interview with the president*
emphasize EG *to emphasize their differences*
give prominence to EG *The Times is alone in giving prominence to the visit.*
spotlight EG *a book spotlighting female singers*
star EG *starring a major Australian actor*

❶ feel VERB
to experience emotionally

EG *I felt enormous happiness.*
experience EG *They seem to experience more distress than the others.*
suffer EG *suffering from pangs of conscience*
undergo EG *to undergo a change of heart*

❷ feel VERB
to believe that something is the case
EG *She feels she is in control of her life.*
believe EG *I believe they are right.*
consider EG *We consider them to be our friends.*
deem EG *I deemed it best to cancel the party.*
judge EG *She was judged to be capable of anything.*
think EG *I think I am very lucky.*

❸ feel VERB
to touch something physically
EG *Feel this lovely material!*
finger EG *He was fingering the coins in his pocket.*
fondle EG *She fondled the dog's ears.*
stroke EG *I stroked the smooth wooden surface.*
touch EG *He touched my face.*

❶ feeling NOUN
the experiencing of an emotion
EG *feelings of envy*
emotion EG *trembling with emotion*
fervour EG *religious fervour*
heat EG *He spoke with some heat about his experiences.*
passion EG *She argued with great passion.*
sentiment EG *I'm afraid I don't share your sentiments.*

❷ feeling NOUN
a physical sensation
EG *a feeling of pain*
sensation EG *a very pleasant sensation*

sense EG *a slight sense of heat at the back of my throat*

❸ feeling NOUN
an opinion on something
EG *strong feelings on politics*
inclination EG *neither the time nor the inclination*
opinion EG *a consensus of opinion*
point of view EG *an unusual point of view on the subject*
view EG *Make your views known.*

❶ fellowship NOUN
a feeling of friendliness within a group
EG *a sense of community and fellowship*
brotherhood EG *a symbolic act of brotherhood*
camaraderie EG *the camaraderie among soldiers*
companionship EG *the companionship between old friends*

❷ fellowship NOUN
a group of people with a common interest
EG *a fellowship of writers*
association EG *a trade association*
brotherhood EG *a secret international brotherhood*
club EG *a youth club*
league EG *the League of Nations*
society EG *the historical society*

❶ female NOUN
a person or animal which can have babies
EG *Hay fever affects males more than females.*
girl EG *a girls' school*
lady EG *a nice young lady*
sheila AUSTRALIAN AND NEW ZEALAND INFORMAL EG *his role as a sheila in his own play*
woman EG *the number of women in the police force*

> **WORD POWER**
> Antonym
> male

❷ female ADJECTIVE

relating to females
EG *the world's greatest female distance runner*

feminine EG *the traditional feminine role*

girlish EG *She gave a girlish giggle.*

womanly EG *a womanly shape*

WORD POWER
Antonym
male
---

fertile ADJECTIVE
capable of producing plants or offspring
EG *fertile soil*

fruitful EG *The fruitful earth gave forth its treasures.*

productive EG *the most productive vineyards*

prolific EG *Chinchillas are prolific breeders.*

rich EG *This plant grows in moist rich ground.*

WORD POWER
Synonyms
fecund
generative
Antonym
barren
---

❶ festival NOUN
an organized series of events
EG *an arts festival*

carnival EG *The carnival lasted for three days.*

entertainment EG *theatrical entertainments*

fair EG *The book fair attracted many visitors.*

fete EG *a church fete*

gala EG *the May Day gala*

❷ festival NOUN
a day or period of religious celebration
EG *open except on days of religious festivals*

anniversary EG *The anniversary is celebrated each spring.*

holiday EG *the Easter holiday*

Christian festivals:
Advent
Ascension Day
Ash Wednesday
Candlemas
Christmas
Corpus Christi
Easter
Epiphany
Good Friday
Lent
Maundy Thursday
Michaelmas
Palm Sunday
Pentecost
Quadragesima
Shrove Tuesday
Trinity
Whitsun

Jewish festivals:
Feast of Tabernacles
Hanukkah, Hanukah *or* Chanukah
Passover *or* Pesach
Purim
Rosh Hashanah
Shavuot, Shabuoth *or* Pentecost
Sukkoth *or* Succoth
Yom Kippur *or* Day of Atonement

Hindu festivals:
Diwali
Durga-puja
Dussehra
Ganesh Chaturthi
Holi
Janmashtami
Navaratri
Raksha Bandhan
Ramanavami
Sarasvati-puja

Muslim festivals:
Al Hijrah
Ashura
Eid-ul-Adha *or* Id-ul-Adha
Eid-ul-Fitr *or* Id-ul-Fitr
Lailat-ul-Isra' wa'l Mi'raj
Lailat-ul-Qadr
Mawlid al-Nabi
Ramadan

Sikh festivals:
Baisakhi Mela
Diwali Mela
Hola Mohalla Mela
the Gurpurabs

Buddhist festivals:
Wesak

few ADJECTIVE
small in number
EG *a few moments ago*
infrequent EG *at infrequent intervals*
meagre EG *a society with meagre resources*
not many EG *Not many people attended the meeting.*
scanty EG *scanty memories of his childhood*
scarce EG *Resources are scarce.*
sparse EG *a bare landscape with sparse trees*

> **WORD POWER**
> Antonym
> many

fidget VERB
to move and change position restlessly
EG *fidgeting in his seat*
fiddle INFORMAL EG *She fiddled with her pencil.*
jiggle EG *He's jiggling his keys.*
squirm EG *He squirmed and wriggled with impatience.*
twitch EG *Everybody twitched in their seats.*

❶ field NOUN
an area of farm land
EG *a field full of sheep*
green EG *on the village green*
meadow EG *a grassy meadow*
pasture EG *cows grazing in the pasture*

❷ field NOUN
a particular subject or interest
EG *a breakthrough in the field of physics*
area EG *a politically-sensitive area*

department EG *Health care isn't my department.*
domain EG *in the domain of art*
province EG *This is the province of a different section.*
speciality EG *His speciality was mythology.*
territory EG *an expert in his own territory of history*

> **WORD POWER**
> Synonyms
> bailiwick
> discipline
> metier

❶ fierce ADJECTIVE
wild and aggressive
EG *a fierce lion*
aggressive EG *encouraging aggressive behaviour in later life*
dangerous EG *These birds are dangerous.*
ferocious EG *two and a half days of ferocious violence*
murderous EG *a murderous attack*

> **WORD POWER**
> Synonyms
> barbarous
> fell
> feral
> Antonym
> gentle

❷ fierce ADJECTIVE
very intense
EG *a fierce contest*
intense EG *We found ourselves standing in intense heat.*
keen EG *a keen interest in cars*
relentless EG *The pressure was relentless.*
strong EG *a strong dislike*

❶ fight VERB
to take part in a battle or contest
EG *He fought the world champion.*
battle EG *The gang battled with the police.*
brawl EG *men brawling drunkenly in the street*
grapple EG *grappling with an*

A B C D E
F
G H I J K L M N O P Q R S T U V W X Y Z

alligator
struggle EG *He was struggling with police outside the club.*

❷ fight NOUN
an aggressive struggle
EG *a fight to the death*
action EG *wounded in action*
battle EG *a gun battle*
bout EG *a wrestling bout*
combat EG *the end of a long combat*
duel EG *He was killed in a duel.*
skirmish EG *a minor border skirmish*

❸ fight NOUN
an angry disagreement
EG *a fight with my mother*
argument EG *an argument over a boyfriend*
blue AUSTRALIAN SLANG EG *a bloke I'd had a blue with years ago*
dispute EG *a dispute over ticket allocation*
row EG *Maxine and I had a terrible row.*
squabble EG *a family squabble over Sunday lunch*

fighter NOUN
someone who physically fights another person
EG *a tough street fighter*
soldier EG *well-equipped soldiers*
warrior EG *a brave warrior*

fill VERB
to make something full
EG *Fill it up with water.*
cram EG *Mourners crammed the small church.*
gorge EG *gorged with food*
pack EG *a lorry packed with explosives*
stock EG *a lake stocked with carp*
stuff EG *Stuff the pillow with feathers.*

> **_WORD POWER_**
> Antonym
> empty

❶ final ADJECTIVE
being the last one in a series
EG *the fifth and final day*
closing EG *in the closing stages of the race*
concluding EG *the concluding part of the serial*
eventual EG *the eventual aim of their policies*
last EG *his last chance*
ultimate EG *The ultimate outcome will be different.*

> **_WORD POWER_**
> Antonym
> first

❷ final ADJECTIVE
unable to be changed or questioned
EG *The judges' decision is final.*
absolute EG *absolute authority*
conclusive EG *conclusive proof*
definite EG *too soon to give a definite answer*
definitive EG *the definitive account of the war*

❶ finally ADVERB
happening after a long time
EG *It finally arrived.*
at last EG *He came at last.*
at the last moment EG *They changed their minds at the last moment.*
eventually EG *The flight eventually left.*
in the end EG *It all turned out right in the end.*
in the long run EG *a success in the long run*

❷ finally ADVERB
in conclusion of something
EG *Finally, I'd like to talk about safety measures.*
in conclusion EG *In conclusion, we have to agree.*
in summary EG *It was, in summary, a satisfactory outcome.*
lastly EG *Lastly, I would like to thank my agent.*

❶ finance VERB

to provide the money for something

EG *financed by the government*

back EG *a fund backed by local businesses*

fund EG *The scheme is funded by the banks.*

pay for EG *He paid for his trip out of his savings.*

support EG *She supported herself through university.*

❷ finance NOUN

the managing of money and investments

EG *the world of high finance*

banking EG *the international banking system*

budgeting EG *We must exercise caution in our budgeting this year.*

commerce EG *industry and commerce*

economics EG *the economics of the third world*

investment EG *tax incentives to encourage investment*

financial ADJECTIVE

relating to money

EG *financial difficulties*

economic EG *an economic crisis*

fiscal EG *the long-term fiscal policy of this country*

money EG *on the money markets*

> **WORD POWER**
> Synonyms
> budgetary
> monetary
> pecuniary

❶ find VERB

to discover something

EG *I can't find my notes.*

come across EG *He came across the book by chance.*

discover EG *They discovered the body in the bushes.*

locate EG *locating the position of the gene*

track down EG *to track down her parents*

turn up EG *They failed to turn up any evidence.*

unearth EG *to unearth the missing copy*

> **WORD POWER**
> Synonyms
> descry
> espy
> ferret out
> Antonym
> lose

❷ find VERB

to realize or learn something

EG *We found that we got on well.*

become aware EG *I became aware of his work last year.*

detect EG *I detected a note of envy in her voice.*

discover EG *It was discovered that the goods were missing.*

learn EG *I flew from New York on learning of his death.*

realize EG *They realized too late that it was wrong.*

❶ fine ADJECTIVE

very good and admirable

EG *fine clothes*

admirable EG *with many admirable qualities*

beautiful EG *a beautiful view of the river*

excellent EG *inns with excellent cuisine*

magnificent EG *his magnificent country house*

outstanding EG *an area of outstanding natural beauty*

splendid EG *a splendid collection of cartoons*

❷ fine ADJECTIVE

small in size or thickness

EG *powder with very fine particles*

delicate EG *delicate curtains to let in the light*

lightweight EG *certain lightweight fabrics*

powdery EG *soft powdery dust*

sheer EG *a sheer chiffon shirt*
small EG *netting with a small mesh*

❸ **fine** ADJECTIVE
subtle and precise
EG *the fine details*
fastidious EG *fastidious attention to detail*
keen EG *a keen eye for a bargain*
precise EG *a gauge with precise adjustment*
refined EG *a woman of refined tastes*
sensitive EG *The radio had very sensitive tuning.*
subtle EG *a very subtle distinction*

❶ **finish** VERB
to complete something
EG *to finish a report*
close EG *They have closed the deal.*
complete EG *She completed her first novel.*
conclude EG *He concluded his speech.*
end EG *That ended our discussion.*
finalize EG *to finalize an agreement*

❷ **finish** NOUN
the last part of something
EG *to see it through to the finish*
close EG *to bring to a close*
completion EG *The project is nearing completion.*
conclusion EG *at the conclusion of the programme*
end EG *the end of the race*
ending EG *The film had an unexpected ending.*
finale EG *the grand finale of the evening*

❸ **finish** NOUN
the surface appearance of something
EG *a glossy finish*
grain EG *the smooth grain of the wood*
lustre EG *a similar lustre to silk*
polish EG *The bodywork had a high polish.*
shine EG *It gives a beautiful shine to the hair.*
surface EG *a polished surface*
texture EG *paper with a linen-like texture*

❶ **fire** NOUN
the flames produced when something burns
EG *a ball of fire*
blaze EG *The firemen were hurt in the blaze.*
combustion EG *Energy is released by combustion.*
flames EG *rescued from the flames*
inferno EG *The building was an inferno.*

❷ **fire** VERB
to shoot or detonate something
EG *to fire a cannon*
detonate EG *to detonate an explosive device*
explode EG *They exploded a bomb.*
launch EG *The protesters launched the missile from a boat.*
set off EG *the largest nuclear explosion ever set off on Earth*
shoot EG *people shooting guns in all directions*

❸ **fire** VERB; INFORMAL
to dismiss someone from a job
EG *She was fired yesterday.*
discharge EG *A trooper has been*

discharged from the army.
dismiss EG *He was dismissed by the bank.*
make redundant EG *Many people were made redundant.*
sack INFORMAL EG *Jones was sacked for disciplinary reasons.*

❶ firm ADJECTIVE
solid and not soft
EG *Leave the ice cream until it is firm.*
compressed EG *compressed wood pulp made into cardboard*
congealed EG *a bowl of congealed grease*
hard EG *The snow was hard and slippery.*
rigid EG *Pour the mixture into a rigid plastic container.*
set EG *The glue wasn't completely set.*
solid EG *a block of solid wax*
stiff EG *egg whites beaten until stiff*

> **WORD POWER**
> Antonym
> soft

❷ firm ADJECTIVE
resolute and determined
EG *The department needs a firm manager.*
adamant EG *He was adamant that he would not resign.*
determined EG *She was determined to finish the game.*
inflexible EG *his inflexible routine*
resolute EG *a willingness to take resolute action*
staunch EG *many staunch supporters*
unshakable EG *an unshakable belief in democracy*

> **WORD POWER**
> Synonyms
> obdurate
> steadfast
> unwavering

❸ firm NOUN
a commercial organization

EG *a firm of builders*
business EG *a stockbroking business*
company EG *his software development company*
corporation EG *one of the leading banking corporations*
enterprise EG *small business enterprises*
organization EG *a multinational organization*

❶ first ADJECTIVE
done or in existence before anything else
EG *the first moon landing*
earliest EG *The earliest settlers lived there.*
initial EG *our initial meeting*
opening EG *There was a standing ovation on opening night.*
original EG *She was one of the original cast.*
primeval EG *the primeval forests of Europe*

> **WORD POWER**
> Antonym
> last

❷ first ADVERB
done or occurring before anything else
EG *You must do that first.*
beforehand EG *Bill had prepared beforehand.*
earlier EG *I did that one earlier.*
firstly EG *Firstly, I'd like to thank you all for coming.*
initially EG *not as bad as they initially predicted*
to begin with EG *To begin with, we must prepare the soil.*

❸ first ADJECTIVE
more important than anything else
EG *our first responsibility*
chief EG *the chief pilot*
foremost EG *one of our foremost thinkers*
leading EG *the team's leading scorer*

A
B
C
D
E
F
G
H
I
J
K
L
M
N
O
P
Q
R
S
T
U
V
W
X
Y
Z

A
B
C
D
E
F
G
H
I
J
K
L
M
N
O
P
Q
R
S
T
U
V
W
X
Y
Z

prime EG *He was the prime suspect.*
principal EG *the principal reason*

❶ fit VERB
to be the right shape or size
EG *made to fit a child*
belong EG *I just didn't belong there.*
correspond EG *The two angles didn't correspond exactly.*
dovetail EG *The movement's interests dovetailed with her own.*
go EG *small enough to go in your pocket*
match EG *Match the pegs with the holes.*

❷ fit VERB
to place something in position
EG *a fitted carpet*
adapt EG *shelves adapted to suit the smaller books*
arrange EG *Arrange the pieces to form a picture.*
place EG *Place the card in the slots.*
position EG *plants which are carefully positioned in the alcove*

❸ fit ADJECTIVE
in good physical condition
EG *a reasonably fit person*
healthy EG *a healthy mind in a healthy body*
in good condition EG *in good condition for his age*
robust EG *a strong, robust man*
trim EG *a trim figure*
well EG *Alison was looking well.*

> **WORD POWER**
> Antonym
> unfit

❶ fitting ADJECTIVE
appropriate and suitable for something
EG *a fitting end*
appropriate EG *an appropriate outfit for the occasion*
correct EG *the correct thing to say*
proper EG *It isn't proper that she should be here.*
right EG *He always said just the right thing.*

suitable EG *some hymns suitable for a wedding*

> **WORD POWER**
> Synonyms
> apposite
> decorous
> seemly

❷ fitting NOUN
a part attached to something else
EG *fixtures and fittings*
accessory EG *bathroom accessories*
attachment EG *a wide range of attachments*
component EG *special components*
part EG *Extra parts can be added later.*
unit EG *The unit plugs into any TV set.*

❶ fix VERB
to attach or secure something
EG *fixed to the wall*
attach EG *The label was attached with glue.*
bind EG *sticks bound together with string*
fasten EG *Fasten the two parts securely.*
secure EG *firmly secured by strong nails*
stick EG *She stuck the pictures into the book.*

❷ fix VERB
to repair something broken
EG *The bike is fixed now.*
correct EG *to correct our mistakes*
mend EG *They finally got round to mending the roof.*
patch up EG *Patch up those holes.*
repair EG *I had my shoes repaired.*

❸ fix NOUN; INFORMAL
a difficult situation
EG *in a bit of a fix*
difficulty EG *He was in real difficulties with money.*
mess EG *Their economy was in a mess.*
predicament EG *a tricky predicament*

quandary EG *in a quandary about what to do*

flabby ADJECTIVE
fat and with loose flesh
EG *a flabby stomach*
floppy EG *the floppy bodies in tracksuits*
sagging EG *a sagging double chin*
slack EG *The skin around her eyelids is now slack and baggy.*

> **WORD POWER**
> Synonyms
> flaccid
> pendulous
> Antonym
> taut

flash NOUN
a sudden short burst of light
EG *a flash of lightning*
burst EG *a burst of fire*
flare EG *the sudden flare of a match*
sparkle EG *sparkles from her sequinned dress*

❷ flash VERB
to shine briefly and often repeatedly
EG *They signalled by flashing a light.*
flare EG *matches flaring in the darkness*
glint EG *the low sun glinting off the windscreens*
glitter EG *the glittering crown on his head*
sparkle EG *Diamonds sparkled on her wrists.*
twinkle EG *stars twinkling in the night sky*

flashy ADJECTIVE
showy in a vulgar way
EG *flashy clothes*
flamboyant EG *an unsuitably flamboyant outfit*
garish EG *curtains in garish colours*
showy EG *an expensive and showy watch*
tacky INFORMAL EG *tacky red sunglasses*
tasteless EG *a house with tasteless decor*

> **WORD POWER**
> Synonyms
> meretricious
> ostentatious
> Antonym
> modest

❶ flat NOUN
a set of rooms for living in
EG *a two-bedroomed flat*
apartment EG *a huge apartment overlooking the park*
rooms EG *We shared rooms while we were students.*

❷ flat ADJECTIVE
level and smooth
EG *a flat surface*
horizontal EG *horizontal with the ground*
level EG *a completely level base*
levelled EG *The floor must be levelled before you start.*
smooth EG *a smooth marble top*
unbroken EG *the unbroken surface of the sea*

> **WORD POWER**
> Antonym
> uneven

❸ flat ADJECTIVE
without emotion or interest
EG *a dreadfully flat speech*
boring EG *a boring menu*
dull EG *He told some really dull stories.*
insipid EG *an insipid performance*
monotonous EG *an interesting story expressed in a monotonous voice*
weak EG *A weak ending spoiled the story.*

❶ flatter VERB
to praise someone insincerely
EG *flattering remarks*
compliment EG *She was often complimented for her looks.*
fawn EG *surrounded by fawning attendants*

A B C D E F G H I J K L M N O P Q R S T U V W X Y Z

A B C D E F G H I J K L M N O P Q R S T U V W X Y Z

❷ flatter VERB
to make more attractive
EG *clothes that flatter your figure*
enhance EG *an enhancing neckline*
set off EG *Blue sets off the colour of your eyes.*
suit EG *That shade really suits your skin tone.*

flattery NOUN
flattering words and behaviour
EG *susceptible to flattery*
adulation EG *received with adulation by the critics*
fawning EG *the constant fawning of her courtiers*

> **WORD POWER**
> Synonyms
> blandishment
> obsequiousness
> sycophancy

flaw NOUN
an imperfection in something
EG *The program contained serious flaws.*
blemish EG *A small blemish spoiled the surface.*
defect EG *a manufacturing defect*
fault EG *a fault in the engine*
imperfection EG *slight imperfections in the weave*

flee VERB
to run away from something
EG *to flee the country*
bolt EG *He bolted for the exit.*
escape EG *They escaped across the frontier.*
fly EG *to fly from war*
leave EG *to leave the scene of the crime*
run away EG *to run away from the police*
take flight EG *250,000 took flight from the floods.*

❶ flexible ADJECTIVE
able to bend or be bent easily
EG *long flexible bristles*
elastic EG *an elastic rope*
lithe EG *lithe and graceful*

movements
pliable EG *baskets made from pliable cane*
supple EG *exercises to keep you supple*

> **WORD POWER**
> Synonyms
> ductile
> lissom *or* lissome
> pliant

❷ flexible ADJECTIVE
able to adapt or change
EG *flexible working hours*
adaptable EG *an adaptable attitude to work*
discretionary EG *the discretionary powers of the courts*
open EG *an open mind*

flinch VERB
to move suddenly with fear or pain
EG *The sharp pain made her flinch.*
cringe EG *to cringe in terror*
shrink EG *She shrank from the flames.*
start EG *They started at the sudden noise.*
wince EG *I could see him wincing with pain.*

❶ float VERB
to be supported by water
EG *leaves floating on the river*
be on the surface EG *The oil is on the surface of the sea.*
bob EG *toys bobbing in the bath*
drift EG *to drift in on the tide*
lie on the surface EG *The boat lay on the surface of the lake.*
stay afloat EG *They could stay afloat without swimming.*

> **WORD POWER**
> Antonym
> sink

❷ float VERB
to be carried on the air
EG *floating on the breeze*
drift EG *The music drifted in*

through the window.

glide EG *eagles gliding above us*

hang EG *A haze of perfume hung in the room.*

hover EG *Butterflies hovered above the flowers.*

❶ flood NOUN

a large amount of water coming suddenly

EG *Many people were drowned in the floods.*

deluge EG *houses overwhelmed by the deluge*

downpour EG *a downpour of torrential rain*

spate EG *The river was in spate.*

torrent EG *Torrents of water gushed into the reservoir.*

❷ flood NOUN

a sudden large amount of something

EG *a flood of angry letters*

rush EG *a sudden rush of panic*

stream EG *a stream of bad language*

torrent EG *He replied with a torrent of abuse.*

❸ flood VERB

to overflow with water

EG *The river flooded its banks.*

deluge EG *Heavy rain deluged the capital.*

drown EG *a drowned village*

overflow EG *an overflowing bath*

submerge EG *to prevent water submerging the cobbled streets*

swamp EG *His small boat was swamped by the waves.*

❶ flow VERB

to move or happen in a continuous stream

EG *a river flowing gently down into the valley*

circulate EG *to circulate round the entire house*

glide EG *models gliding down the catwalk*

roll EG *rolling gently to the sea*

run EG *A stream ran beside the road.*

slide EG *Tears slid down her cheeks.*

❷ flow NOUN

a continuous movement of something

EG *traffic flow*

current EG *currents of air*

drift EG *the drift towards the cities*

flood EG *a flood of complaints*

stream EG *a constant stream of visitors*

tide EG *to slow the tide of change*

fluent ADJECTIVE

expressing yourself easily and without hesitation

EG *a fluent speaker of French*

articulate EG *an articulate young woman*

easy EG *the easy flow of his argument*

effortless EG *He spoke with effortless ease.*

flowing EG *a smooth, flowing presentation*

ready EG *a ready answer*

> **WORD POWER**
> Antonym
> hesitant

❶ fly VERB

to move through the air

EG *to fly to Paris*

flit EG *butterflies flitting among the flowers*

flutter EG *The birds fluttered on to the feeder.*

sail EG *a kite sailing above the trees*

soar EG *eagles soaring in the sky*

❷ fly VERB

to move very quickly

EG *She flew down the stairs.*

dart EG *She darted to the window.*

dash EG *We had to dash.*

hurry EG *They hurried to catch the train.*

race EG *I had to race round the shops.*

rush EG *rushing off to work*

speed EG *The car sped off.*

A B C D E F G H I J K L M N O P Q R S T U V W X Y Z

tear EG *He tore off down the road.*

❶ foam NOUN

a mass of tiny bubbles

EG *waves tipped with foam*

bubbles EG *She liked to have bubbles in the bath.*

froth EG *Yeast swells up to form a froth.*

head EG *the foamy head on beer*

lather EG *It took a lot of shampoo to get a good lather.*

❷ foam VERB

to swell and form bubbles

EG *a foaming river*

bubble EG *The boiling liquid bubbled up.*

fizz EG *a drink fizzing in the glass*

froth EG *It frothed up over the top.*

❶ focus VERB

to concentrate your vision on something

EG *His eyes began to focus.*

aim EG *Astronomers aimed optical telescopes in their direction.*

concentrate EG *concentrating his gaze on a line of ants*

direct EG *He directed the light on to the roof.*

fix EG *Their radar was fixed on the enemy ship.*

❷ focus NOUN

the centre of attention

EG *the focus of the conversation*

centre EG *She was the centre of an admiring crowd.*

focal point EG *the focal point of the whole room*

hub EG *the hub of the financial world*

target EG *a target group*

❶ foil VERB

to prevent something from happening

EG *The police foiled an armed robbery.*

check EG *to check the rise in crime*

counter EG *countering the threat of strike action*

defeat EG *an important role in defeating the rebellion*

frustrate EG *a frustrated attempt*

thwart EG *to thwart someone's plans*

> **WORD POWER**
> Synonyms
> circumvent
> nullify

❷ foil NOUN

a contrast to something

EG *a perfect foil for his temperament*

antithesis EG *the antithesis of his crooked brother*

background EG *a fitting background for her beauty*

complement EG *the perfect complement to the antique furniture*

contrast EG *The green woodwork is a stunning contrast to the black walls.*

❶ fold VERB

to bend something

EG *He folded the paper carefully.*

bend EG *Bend the top towards you.*

crease EG *Crease along the dotted line.*

crumple EG *He crumpled the note and put it in his pocket.*

tuck EG *Tuck in the top and bottom*

turn under EG *The bottom was turned under.*

❷ fold NOUN

a crease in something

EG *hanging in folds*

bend EG *There was a bend in the photograph.*

crease EG *sharp creases in his shirt*

pleat EG *a skirt with pleats*

wrinkle EG *all the little wrinkles on Paul's face*

❶ follow VERB

to pursue someone

EG *We were being followed.*

hound EG *constantly hounded by photographers*

pursue EG *He was pursued across several countries.*

stalk EG *Her former husband was stalking her.*
track EG *They tracked him to his home.*

❷ **follow** VERB
to come after someone or something
EG *Night follows day.*
come after EG *Summer comes after spring.*
succeed EG *He was succeeded by his son.*
supersede EG *Horses were superseded by cars.*

> *WORD POWER*
> Antonym
> precede

❸ **follow** VERB
to act in accordance with something
EG *Follow the instructions carefully.*
comply EG *in order to comply with EC regulations*
conform EG *conforming to the new safety requirements*
obey EG *You must obey the law.*
observe EG *The army was observing a ceasefire.*

follower NOUN
a supporter of a person or belief
EG *a loyal follower of the movement*
believer EG *many devout believers in the faith*
disciple EG *one of his disciples*
fan EG *football fans*
henchman EG *always surrounded by his henchmen*
supporter EG *He was a major supporter of the plan.*

> *WORD POWER*
> Synonyms
> adherent
> protagonist
> Antonym
> leader

❶ **fond** ADJECTIVE
feeling affection or liking
EG *a fond father*
adoring EG *an adoring husband*
affectionate EG *an affectionate smile*
devoted EG *a devoted couple*
doting EG *doting grandparents*
having a liking for EG *She had a great liking for chocolate.*
loving EG *a loving son*

❷ **fond** ADJECTIVE
unlikely to happen or be fulfilled
EG *fond wishes for a better life*
deluded EG *a deluded belief in future improvement*
empty EG *empty promises of full employment*
foolish EG *What foolish dreams we have!*
naive EG *her naive belief in others' goodness*
vain EG *the vain hope that he might lose weight*

> *WORD POWER*
> Synonyms
> delusory
> overoptimistic

food NOUN
things eaten to provide nourishment
EG *our favourite food*
diet EG *a healthy balanced diet*
fare EG *traditional regional fare*
foodstuffs EG *basic foodstuffs*
kai AUSTRALIAN AND NEW ZEALAND INFORMAL EG *There's no kai in the house.*
nourishment EG *unable to take nourishment*
provisions EG *provisions for two weeks*
refreshment EG *Refreshments will be provided.*
tucker AUSTRALIAN AND NEW ZEALAND INFORMAL EG *some of the cheapest pub tucker in town*

> *WORD POWER*
> Synonyms
> provender

A
B
C
D
E
F
G
H
I
J
K
L
M
N
O
P
Q
R
S
T
U
V
W
X
Y
Z

subsistence
victuals

❶ **fool** NOUN
an unintelligent person
EG *What a stupid fool he is!*
dope INFORMAL EG *He felt such a dope.*
dunce EG *I was a complete dunce at chemistry.*
idiot EG *acting like an idiot*
ignoramus EG *the ignoramus of the group*
moron EG *They treated him like a moron.*

❷ **fool** VERB
to trick someone
EG *Don't let him fool you.*
con INFORMAL EG *conned out of all his money*
deceive EG *deceiving the audience*
dupe EG *in order to dupe the medical staff*
mislead EG *a deliberately misleading statement*
trick EG *They tricked him into believing it.*

> **WORD POWER**
> Synonyms
> bamboozle
> hoodwink

foolish ADJECTIVE
silly and unwise
EG *feeling foolish*
inane EG *an inane remark*
nonsensical EG *a nonsensical thing to say*
senseless EG *It would be senseless to stop her.*
silly EG *a silly thing to say*
unintelligent EG *a weak and unintelligent man*
unwise EG *He had made some unwise investments.*

> **WORD POWER**
> Antonym
> wise

forbid VERB

to order someone not to do something
EG *forbidden to go out*
ban EG *banned from driving*
exclude EG *Women were excluded from the classes.*
outlaw EG *the outlawed political parties*
prohibit EG *Fishing is prohibited.*
veto EG *Their application was vetoed.*

> **WORD POWER**
> Antonym
> allow

❶ **force** VERB
to compel someone to do something
EG *We were forced to turn right.*
compel EG *I felt compelled to act.*
drive EG *They are driving the company into bankruptcy.*
make EG *They made me do it.*
oblige EG *We were obliged to abandon the car.*
pressurize EG *trying to pressurize them*

> **WORD POWER**
> Synonyms
> coerce
> obligate

❷ **force** NOUN
a pressure to do something
EG *They made him agree by force.*
compulsion EG *a compulsion to write*
duress EG *carried out under duress*
pressure EG *under pressure to resign*

❸ **force** NOUN
the strength of something
EG *the force of the explosion*
impact EG *the impact of the blast*
might EG *the full might of the army*
power EG *massive computing power*
pressure EG *the pressure of work*
strength EG *The storm was gaining strength.*

foreign ADJECTIVE
relating to other countries
EG *foreign travel*
distant EG *in that distant land*
exotic EG *filmed in an exotic location*
overseas EG *a long overseas trip*

forest NOUN

> Types of forest:
> bush
> coppice
> copse
> grove
> jungle
> spinney
> thicket
> wood
> woodland

forget VERB
to fail to remember something
EG *I forgot to lock the door.*
fail to remember EG *He failed to remember my name.*
omit EG *omitting to mention the details*
overlook EG *to overlook an important fact*

> *WORD POWER*
> Antonym
> remember

forgive VERB
to stop blaming someone for something
EG *Can you ever forgive me?*
absolve EG *The verdict absolved him from blame.*
condone EG *We cannot condone violence.*
excuse EG *Please excuse our bad behaviour.*
pardon EG *Relatives had begged authorities to pardon him.*

> *WORD POWER*
> Antonym
> blame

forgiveness NOUN
the act of forgiving

EG *I ask for your forgiveness.*
acquittal EG *The jury voted for acquittal.*
mercy EG *to beg for mercy*
pardon EG *a presidential pardon*
remission EG *with remission for good behaviour*

> *WORD POWER*
> Synonyms
> absolution
> exoneration

❶ formal ADJECTIVE
in accordance with convention
EG *a formal dinner*
conventional EG *a conventional style of dress*
correct EG *polite and correct behaviour*
precise EG *They spoke very precise English.*
stiff EG *his stiff manner and lack of humour*

> *WORD POWER*
> Antonym
> informal

❷ formal ADJECTIVE
official and publicly recognized
EG *No formal announcement has been made.*
approved EG *a legally approved method of dealing with these*
legal EG *They have a legal responsibility.*
official EG *according to the official figures*
prescribed EG *There is a prescribed procedure for situations like this.*
regular EG *through the regular channels*

former ADJECTIVE
existing in the past
EG *a former tennis champion*
ancient EG *the ancient civilizations*
bygone EG *memories of a bygone age*
old EG *our old school*
past EG *a long list of past winners*

A B C D E F G H I J K L M N O P Q R S T U V W X Y Z

formidable ADJECTIVE
difficult to overcome
EG *They faced formidable obstacles.*
challenging EG *a more challenging job*
daunting EG *a daunting prospect*
difficult EG *A difficult task lay ahead.*
intimidating EG *She was an intimidating opponent.*
mammoth EG *a mammoth undertaking*
onerous EG *onerous responsibilities*

fort NOUN
a building for defence and shelter
EG *They had to abandon the fort.*
castle EG *a heavily-guarded castle*
citadel EG *The citadel towered above the river.*
fortification EG *fortifications along the border*
fortress EG *an ancient fortress*

fragile ADJECTIVE
easily broken or damaged
EG *fragile china*
breakable EG *Anything breakable or sharp had to be removed.*
dainty EG *a dainty Japanese tea service*
delicate EG *a delicate instrument*
flimsy EG *packed in a flimsy box*
frail EG *a frail shell*

> **WORD POWER**
> Synonyms
> frangible
> infirm
> Antonym
> tough

fragrance NOUN
a pleasant smell
EG *the fragrance of the roses*
aroma EG *the aroma of fresh bread*
bouquet EG *a wine with a lively fruit bouquet*
perfume EG *enjoying the perfume of the lemon trees*
scent EG *flowers chosen for their scent*
smell EG *a sweet smell of pine*

fragrant ADJECTIVE
having a pleasant smell
EG *fragrant oils*
aromatic EG *a plant with aromatic leaves*
perfumed EG *perfumed body cream*
sweet-smelling EG *posies of sweet-smelling flowers*

> **WORD POWER**
> Antonym
> smelly

frank ADJECTIVE
open and straightforward
EG *a frank discussion*
blunt EG *his blunt approach*
candid EG *She was completely candid with me.*
honest EG *my honest opinion*
open EG *an open, trusting nature*
plain EG *plain talking*
straightforward EG *spoken in a straightforward manner*

❶ **fraud** NOUN
the act of deceiving someone
EG *electoral fraud*
deceit EG *deliberate deceit*
deception EG *obtaining money by deception*
guile EG *children's lack of guile*
hoax EG *a bomb hoax*
trickery EG *They had to resort to trickery.*

> **WORD POWER**
> Synonyms
> chicanery
> duplicity
> spuriousness

❷ **fraud** NOUN
someone or something that deceives you
EG *Many psychics are frauds.*
charlatan EG *exposed as a charlatan*
cheat EG *Cheats will be disqualified.*

fake EG *The painting was a fake.*
forgery EG *just a clever forgery*
imposter EG *an imposter with false documents*
quack EG *He tried all sorts of quacks.*

❶ free ADJECTIVE
not being held prisoner
EG *a free man*
at large EG *Three prisoners are at large.*
at liberty EG *the last top Nazi still at liberty*
liberated EG *newly liberated slaves*
loose EG *He broke loose from his bonds.*

> **WORD POWER**
> Antonym
> captive

❷ free ADJECTIVE
available without payment
EG *a free brochure*
complimentary EG *complimentary tickets*
gratis EG *The meal was gratis.*
unpaid EG *unpaid voluntary work*
without charge EG *They mended it without charge.*

❸ free VERB
to release from captivity
EG *to free the slaves*
discharge EG *discharged from prison*
liberate EG *liberated under the terms of the amnesty*
release EG *The hostages were soon released.*
set at liberty EG *He was set at liberty after ten years.*
set loose EG *The animals were set loose after treatment.*

> **WORD POWER**
> Synonyms
> emancipate
> unfetter
> Antonym
> imprison

❶ freedom NOUN
the ability to choose
EG *freedom of action*
discretion EG *Use your own discretion.*
latitude EG *There is more latitude for personal opinions.*
leeway EG *granted more leeway to pass reforms*
licence EG *a licence to kill*
scope EG *plenty of scope for improvement*

❷ freedom NOUN
the state of being free or being set free
EG *gaining their freedom after months of captivity*
emancipation EG *the emancipation of the slaves*
liberty EG *three months' loss of liberty*
release EG *the immediate release of the captives*

> **WORD POWER**
> Synonyms
> deliverance
> manumission
> Antonym
> captivity

❸ freedom NOUN
the absence of something unpleasant
EG *freedom from pain*
exemption EG *granted exemption from all taxes*
immunity EG *information in exchange for immunity from prosecution*

frenzy NOUN
wild and uncontrolled behaviour
EG *gripped by a frenzy of nationalism*
agitation EG *in a state of intense agitation*
fury EG *She stalked out in a fury.*
hysteria EG *mass hysteria*
madness EG *a moment of madness*
rage EG *She flew into a rage.*

A B C D E F G H I J K L M N O P Q R S T U V W X Y Z

A
B
C
D
E
F
G
H
I
J
K
L
M
N
O
P
Q
R
S
T
U
V
W
X
Y
Z

WORD POWER
Synonyms
delirium
paroxysm

❶ frequent ADJECTIVE
happening often
EG *his frequent visits*
common EG *a common occurrence*
continual EG *continual demands
for money*
everyday EG *an everyday event*
habitual EG *a habitual daydreamer*
recurrent EG *a recurrent theme in
her work*
repeated EG *His parents made
repeated attempts to visit.*

WORD POWER
Antonym
rare

❷ frequent VERB
to go somewhere often
EG *a restaurant which he frequents*
attend EG *He often attends their
meetings.*
haunt EG *She haunted their house.*
patronize EG *to patronize a hotel*
visit EG *a place we often visit*

WORD POWER
Antonym
avoid

friend NOUN
a person you know and like
EG *lifelong friends*
china SOUTH AFRICAN INFORMAL EG *a
drinking session with his chinas*
companion EG *my constant
companion*
confidant or **confidante** EG *her
only confidant*
crony EG *surrounded by her cronies*
mate INFORMAL EG *going out with
his mates*
pal EG *We are great pals.*

WORD POWER
Synonyms
alter ego
soul mate

Antonym
enemy

friendly ADJECTIVE
kind and pleasant
EG *a very friendly crowd*
affectionate EG *on affectionate
terms*
amiable EG *He was very amiable
company.*
close EG *The two were very close.*
cordial EG *a most cordial welcome*
genial EG *a genial host*
welcoming EG *a welcoming house*

WORD POWER
Synonyms
companionable
comradely
convivial
Antonym
unfriendly

friendship NOUN
a state of being friendly with
someone
EG *I value our friendship.*
affection EG *to win their affection*
attachment EG *the deep
attachment between them*
closeness EG *her closeness to her
sister*
goodwill EG *as a gesture of
goodwill*

WORD POWER
Antonym
hostility

frighten VERB
to make someone afraid
EG *trying to frighten us*
alarm EG *alarmed by the noise*
intimidate EG *She is intimidated
by her boss.*
scare EG *You aren't scared of mice,
are you?*
startle EG *I didn't mean to startle
you.*
terrify EG *Heights terrified her.*
terrorize EG *The gunmen
terrorized the villagers.*

unnerve EG *an unnerving silence*

frightened ADJECTIVE
having feelings of fear about
something
EG *frightened of thunder*
afraid EG *Jane was afraid of the
other children.*
alarmed EG *Don't be alarmed.*
petrified EG *petrified of wasps*
scared EG *scared of being alone in
the house*
startled EG *a startled animal*
terrified EG *a terrified look*

> *WORD POWER*
> Synonyms
> cowed
> panicky
> terror-stricken

frightening ADJECTIVE
causing someone to feel fear
EG *a frightening experience*
alarming EG *an alarming increase*
hair-raising EG *at hair-raising
speed*
intimidating EG *threatening and
intimidating behaviour*
menacing EG *a menacing glance*
terrifying EG *one of the most
terrifying diseases*

frivolous ADJECTIVE
not serious or sensible
EG *a frivolous new dress*
flippant EG *a flippant comment*
foolish EG *saying foolish and
inappropriate things*
juvenile EG *juvenile behaviour*
puerile EG *your puerile schoolboy
humour*
silly EG *making silly jokes*

> *WORD POWER*
> Antonym
> serious

❶ front NOUN
the part that faces forward
EG *the front wall of the house*
face EG *the face of the building*
frontage EG *a restaurant with a*

river frontage

> *WORD POWER*
> Antonym
> back

❷ front NOUN
the outward appearance of
something
EG *a respectable front*
appearance EG *the appearance of
fair treatment*
exterior EG *his tough exterior*
face EG *a brave face*
show EG *a convincing show of
affection*

❸ front
in front PREPOSITION
further forward
EG *too close to the car in front*
ahead EG *ahead of the rest of the
field*
before EG *I'm before you.*
leading EG *the leading rider*

frown VERB
to draw the eyebrows together
EG *She frowned in concentration.*
glare EG *The woman glared angrily
at him.*
glower EG *She glowered but said
nothing.*
knit your brows EG *He knitted
his brows in concentration.*
scowl EG *He scowled at the waiter.*

frozen ADJECTIVE
extremely cold
EG *frozen to the bone*
arctic EG *arctic weather conditions*
chilled EG *chilled to the marrow*
frigid EG *frigid temperatures*
icy EG *an icy wind*
numb EG *numb with cold*

frustrate VERB
to prevent something from
happening
EG *His efforts were frustrated.*
block EG *They are blocking the
peace process.*
check EG *to check the spread of the*

A
B
C
D
E
F
G
H
I
J
K
L
M
N
O
P
Q
R
S
T
U
V
W
X
Y
Z

A
B
C
D
E
F
G
H
I
J
K
L
M
N
O
P
Q
R
S
T
U
V
W
X
Y
Z

virus
foil EG *They foiled all my plans.*
thwart EG *his way to thwart your club's ambitions*

> **WORD POWER**
> Synonyms
> forestall
> nullify

❶ **full** ADJECTIVE
filled with something
EG *full of books*
filled EG *filled up to the top*
loaded EG *The van was loaded with furniture.*
packed EG *The train was packed.*
saturated EG *completely saturated with liquid*

> **WORD POWER**
> Antonym
> empty

❷ **full** ADJECTIVE
missing nothing out
EG *I want a full account of what happened.*
comprehensive EG *a comprehensive guide to the area*
detailed EG *a detailed descriptions*
exhaustive EG *an exhaustive treatment of the subject*
extensive EG *extensive coverage of the earthquake*
maximum EG *the way to take maximum advantage of pay TV*
thorough EG *a thorough search*

❸ **full** ADJECTIVE
loose-fitting
EG *a full skirt*
baggy EG *a baggy sweater*
loose EG *hidden under his loose shirt*
voluminous EG *voluminous sleeves*

❶ **fun** NOUN
an enjoyable activity
EG *It was great fun.*
amusement EG *There is no amusement for teenagers in this village.*

enjoyment EG *It gave us much enjoyment.*
entertainment EG *little opportunity for entertainment*
pleasure EG *to mix business and pleasure*
recreation EG *time for recreation*

❷ **fun**
make fun of VERB
to tease someone
EG *Don't make fun of him.*
deride EG *This theory is widely derided.*
laugh at EG *They laughed at his hat.*
mock EG *He was often mocked by his classmates.*
ridicule EG *She allowed them to ridicule her.*
taunt EG *a fellow pupil who had taunted him about his height*

> **WORD POWER**
> Synonyms
> lampoon
> rib
> satirize

❶ **fund** NOUN
an amount of money
EG *the pension fund*
capital EG *difficulty in raising capital*
foundation EG *money from a research foundation*
pool EG *a reserve pool of cash*
reserve EG *a drain on the cash reserves*
supply EG *to curb money supply and inflation*

❷ **fund** NOUN
a large amount of something
EG *an extraordinary fund of energy*
hoard EG *his hoard of supplies*
mine EG *a mine of information*
reserve EG *oil reserves*
reservoir EG *the body's short-term reservoir of energy*
store EG *a store of fuel*

❸ **fund** VERB

to provide the money for
something
EG *to raise money to fund research
into breast cancer*
finance EG *big projects financed by
foreign aid*
pay for EG *His parents paid for his
holiday.*
subsidize EG *heavily subsidized by
the government*
support EG *He is supporting
himself through college.*

❶ **funny** ADJECTIVE
being strange or odd
EG *They heard a funny noise.*
mysterious EG *in mysterious
circumstances*
odd EG *There was something odd
about her.*
peculiar EG *It tasted very peculiar.*
puzzling EG *a puzzling
development*
strange EG *A strange thing
happened.*
unusual EG *a most unusual man*

❷ **funny** ADJECTIVE
causing amusement
EG *a funny story*
amusing EG *a most amusing
lecturer*
comic EG *comic moments*
comical EG *the comical expression
on his face*
hilarious EG *We thought it was
hilarious.*
humorous EG *a humorous
magazine*
witty EG *a very witty speech*

WORD POWER
Synonyms
droll
jocular
risible
Antonym
serious

❶ **fuss** NOUN
anxious or excited behaviour
EG *What's all the fuss about?*

agitation EG *in a state of intense
agitation*
bother EG *I don't want any bother.*
commotion EG *a commotion in
the market*
confusion EG *in the confusion
after an ammunition dump blew up*
stir EG *The play caused a stir here.*
to-do EG *a big to-do*

WORD POWER
Synonyms
ado
fluster
palaver

❷ **fuss** VERB
to behave in a nervous or restless
way
EG *Waiters fussed around the table.*
bustle EG *shoppers bustling around
the store*
fidget EG *He was fidgeting with his
tie.*
fret EG *Stop fretting about the
details.*

fussy ADJECTIVE
difficult to please
EG *fussy about his food*
choosy INFORMAL EG *Cats can be
choosy about what they eat.*
discriminating EG *a
discriminating visitor*
exacting EG *She failed to meet his
exacting standards.*
fastidious EG *Disney was also
fastidious about cleanliness.*
particular EG *very particular about
the colours he used*

WORD POWER
Synonyms
faddish
finicky
pernickety

futile ADJECTIVE
having no chance of success
EG *a futile effort to run away*
abortive EG *the abortive coup
attempt*
forlorn EG *forlorn hopes of future*

197

improvement
unsuccessful EG *an unsuccessful bid for independence*
useless EG *It was useless to even try.*
vain EG *in the vain hope of success*

future ADJECTIVE
relating to a time after the present
EG *to predict future growth*
approaching EG *concerned about the approaching winter*
coming EG *in the coming months*
forthcoming EG *candidates for the forthcoming elections*
impending EG *her impending marriage*
later EG *We'll discuss it at a later date.*
prospective EG *my prospective employers*

Gg Gg

gadget NOUN
a small machine or tool
EG *kitchen gadgets such as toasters and kettles*

appliance EG *Switch off all electrical appliances when they're not in use.*

device EG *a device that warns you when the batteries need changing*

machine EG *a machine for slicing vegetables*

tool EG *a tool for cutting wood, metal or plastic*

> **WORD POWER**
> Synonyms
> implement
> instrument
> utensil

❶ gain VERB
to get something gradually
EG *Students can gain valuable experience by working.*

achieve EG *Achieving our goals makes us feel good.*

acquire EG *Companies should reward workers for acquiring more skills.*

earn EG *She has earned the respect of the world's top women cyclists.*

obtain EG *You would need to obtain permission to copy the design.*

secure EG *He failed to secure enough votes for outright victory.*

win EG *The long-term aim is to win promotion.*

> **WORD POWER**
> Synonyms
> attain
> capture
> reap

❷ gain VERB
to get an advantage
EG *Areas of the world would actually gain from global warming.*

benefit EG *Both sides have benefited from the talks.*

profit EG *Frankie is now profiting from his crimes.*

❸ gain NOUN
an increase or improvement in something
EG *The Party has made substantial gains in local elections.*

advance EG *advances in computer technology*

growth EG *The area has seen a rapid population growth.*

improvement EG *a major improvement in standards*

increase EG *an increase of 7% in visitors to the UK*

rise EG *a 3% rise in electricity prices*

❶ gamble VERB
to bet money on something
EG *John gambled heavily on the horses.*

back EG *I backed Germany to win 1-0.*

bet EG *He bet them 500 pounds they would lose.*

❷ gamble VERB
to take a risk
EG *Few firms will be willing to gamble on new products.*

chance EG *Armstrong chanced a gallop to the water.*

risk EG *One of his daughters risked everything to join him in exile.*

stake EG *He has staked his reputation on the outcome.*

> **WORD POWER**
> Synonyms
> hazard
> take a chance
> venture

❸ gamble NOUN
a risk that someone takes
EG *We are taking a gamble on a young player.*

chance EG *You take a chance on*

the weather when you holiday in the UK.

lottery EG *Robinson described the final as a bit of a lottery.*

risk EG *How much risk are you prepared to take?*

game NOUN
an occasion on which people compete
EG *South Africa's first game of the season*

clash EG *the clash between Australia and the West Indies*

contest EG *The rain spoiled a good contest.*

match EG *a football match*

❶ gap NOUN
a space or a hole in something
EG *They squeezed through a gap in the fence.*

break EG *stars twinkling between the breaks in the clouds*

chink EG *All the walls have wide chinks in them.*

crack EG *a crack in the curtains*

hole EG *a hole in the wall*

opening EG *an opening in the trees*

space EG *the space between their car and the one in front*

> **WORD POWER**
> Synonyms
> cleft
> cranny
> crevice

❷ gap NOUN
a period of time
EG *After a gap of nearly a decade, Manley was back.*

hiatus FORMAL EG *The shop is open again after a two year hiatus.*

interlude EG *a happy interlude in the Kents' life*

interval EG *There was a long interval of silence.*

lull EG *a lull in the conversation*

pause EG *Then, after a pause, he goes on.*

❸ gap NOUN

a difference between people or things
EG *the gap between rich and poor*

difference EG *He denied there were any major differences between them.*

disparity FORMAL EG *disparities between poor and wealthy school districts*

inconsistency EG *There were major inconsistencies in his evidence.*

❶ garbage NOUN
things that people do not want
EG *piles of garbage*

debris EG *screws, bolts and other debris from a scrapyard*

junk INFORMAL EG *What are you going to do with all that junk?*

litter EG *If you see litter in the corridor, pick it up.*

refuse FORMAL EG *refuse collection and street cleaning*

rubbish EG *household rubbish*

trash EG *I forgot to take out the trash.*

waste EG *industrial waste*

❷ garbage NOUN; INFORMAL
ideas and opinions that are untrue or unimportant
EG *I personally think this is complete garbage.*

drivel EG *What absolute drivel!*

gibberish EG *a politician talking gibberish*

nonsense EG *all that poetic nonsense about love*

rubbish EG *He's talking rubbish.*

garbled ADJECTIVE
confused or incorrect
EG *A garbled message awaited us at the desk.*

confused EG *the latest twist in a murky and confused story*

distorted EG *a distorted version of what was said*

incomprehensible EG *Her speech was incomprehensible.*

jumbled EG *his jumbled account of how Jack had been hired*

unintelligible EG *He muttered something unintelligible.*

❶ gasp VERB
to breathe in quickly through your mouth
EG *She gasped for air.*
choke EG *People began to choke as smoke filled the air.*
gulp EG *She gulped air into her lungs.*
pant EG *Amy climbed rapidly until she was panting with the effort.*
puff EG *I could see he was unfit because he was puffing.*

> **WORD POWER**
> Synonyms
> catch your breath
> fight for breath

❷ gasp NOUN
a short quick breath of air
EG *An audible gasp went round the court.*
gulp EG *I took in a large gulp of air.*
pant EG *Her breath came in pants.*
puff EG *He blew out a little puff of air.*

❶ gather VERB
to come together in a group
EG *We gathered around the fireplace.*
assemble EG *a place for students to assemble between classes*
congregate EG *Youngsters love to congregate here in the evenings.*
flock EG *The criticisms will not stop people flocking to see the film.*
mass EG *The General was massing his troops for a counterattack.*
round up EG *The police rounded up a number of suspects.*

> **WORD POWER**
> Synonyms
> convene
> marshal
> muster
> Antonym
> scatter

❷ gather VERB
to bring things together
EG *I suggest we gather enough firewood to last the night.*
accumulate EG *In five years it has accumulated a huge debt.*
amass EG *She has amassed a personal fortune of $38 million.*
collect EG *1.5 million signatures have been collected.*
hoard EG *They've begun to hoard food and gasoline.*
stockpile EG *People are stockpiling food for the coming winter.*

❸ gather VERB
to learn or believe something
EG *"He speaks English." "I gathered that."*
assume EG *I assume the eggs are fresh.*
conclude EG *He concluded that Oswald was somewhat abnormal.*
hear EG *I heard that he was forced to resign.*
learn EG *She wasn't surprised to learn that he was involved.*
understand EG *I understand that he's just taken early retirement.*

gathering NOUN
a meeting with a purpose
EG *polite social gatherings*
assembly EG *an assembly of party members*
congregation EG *The congregation sang hymns and said prayers.*
get-together INFORMAL EG *family get-togethers*
meeting EG *Can we have a meeting to discuss that?*
rally EG *a pre-election rally*

> **WORD POWER**
> Synonyms
> conference
> congress
> convention

gaudy ADJECTIVE
colourful in a vulgar way
EG *gaudy fake jewellery*

bright EG *fake fur, dyed in bright colours*

flashy EG *women in flashy satin suits*

garish EG *They climbed the garish purple-carpeted stairs.*

loud EG *a loud checked shirt*

showy EG *He favoured large showy flowers.*

tacky INFORMAL EG *tacky red sunglasses*

vulgar EG *I think it's a very vulgar house.*

> **WORD POWER**
> Synonyms
> jazzy
> ostentatious
> tasteless
> tawdry

❶ general ADJECTIVE
relating to the whole of something
EG *a general decline in employment*

broad EG *a broad outline of the Society's development*

comprehensive EG *a comprehensive guide to the region*

overall EG *The overall quality of pupils' work had shown a marked improvement.*

> **WORD POWER**
> Synonyms
> generic
> indiscriminate
> panoramic
> sweeping
> Antonym
> specific

❷ general ADJECTIVE
widely true, suitable or relevant
EG *The project should raise general awareness about bullying.*

accepted EG *the accepted version of events*

broad EG *a film with broad appeal*

common EG *Such behaviour is common to all young people.*

universal EG *Music and sports*

programmes have a universal appeal.

widespread EG *The proposals have attracted widespread support.*

> **WORD POWER**
> Antonym
> special

generosity NOUN
willingness to give money, time or help
EG *She is well known for her generosity.*

benevolence EG *Banks are not known for their benevolence.*

charity EG *private acts of charity*

kindness EG *We have been treated with such kindness by everybody.*

> **WORD POWER**
> Synonyms
> bounty
> liberality
> munificence
> open-handedness
> Antonym
> meanness

❶ generous ADJECTIVE
willing to give money, time or help
EG *The gift is generous by any standards.*

charitable EG *Individuals can be charitable and help their neighbours.*

hospitable EG *He was very hospitable to me when I came to New York.*

kind EG *She is warm-hearted and kind to everyone.*

lavish EG *The Princess received a number of lavish gifts from her hosts.*

liberal EG *Don't be too liberal with your spending.*

> **WORD POWER**
> Synonyms
> munificent
> open-handed
> prodigal
> unstinting

A B C D E F G H I J K L M N O P Q R S T U V W X Y Z

Antonym
mean

❷ generous ADJECTIVE
very large
EG *a generous portion of spaghetti*
abundant EG *an abundant supply of hot food*
ample EG *There is ample space for a good-sized kitchen.*
plentiful EG *a plentiful supply of beer*

WORD POWER
Antonym
meagre

❶ genius NOUN
a very clever or talented person
EG *a mathematical genius*
brain EG *the financial brain behind the company*
master EG *Spiro Rosakis is a master of his craft.*
mastermind EG *the mastermind of the plot to kill the ex-prime minister*
virtuoso EG *The man is a virtuoso of pop music.*

❷ genius NOUN
extraordinary ability or talent
EG *a poet of genius*
brains EG *She has brains as well as beauty.*
brilliance EG *his brilliance as a director*
intellect EG *people of great intellect*

gentle ADJECTIVE
not violent or rough
EG *a quiet and gentle man*
benign EG *a good-looking chap with a benign expression*
kind EG *I fell in love with him because of his kind nature.*
kindly EG *a kindly old gentleman*
meek EG *He was a meek, mild-mannered fellow.*
mild EG *Alexis was quiet, mild and happy-go-lucky.*
placid EG *a look of impatience on her normally placid face*

soft EG *She had a very soft heart.*
tender EG *Her voice was tender.*

WORD POWER
Synonyms
compassionate
humane
lenient
sweet-tempered
Antonym
cruel

genuine ADJECTIVE
not false or pretend
EG *They're convinced the picture is genuine.*
authentic EG *an authentic French recipe*
bona fide EG *We are happy to donate to bona fide charities.*
dinkum AUSTRALIAN AND NEW ZEALAND INFORMAL EG *They are all dinkum stolen bank notes.*
real EG *a real Rembrandt*

WORD POWER
Antonym
fake

❶ get VERB
to fetch or receive something
EG *I'll get us all a cup of coffee.*
acquire EG *I have recently acquired a new camera.*
fetch EG *Sylvia fetched a towel from the bathroom.*
obtain EG *Evans was trying to obtain a false passport.*
procure FORMAL EG *It remained very difficult to procure food.*
receive EG *I received your letter of November 7.*
secure FORMAL EG *He failed to secure enough votes for outright victory.*

❷ get VERB
to change from one state to another
EG *People draw the curtains once it gets dark.*
become EG *The wind became stronger.*

A B C D E F G H I J K L M N O P Q R S T U V W X Y Z

grow EG *He grew to love his work.*
turn EG *The leaves have turned golden-brown.*

get on VERB
to enjoy someone's company
EG *I get on very well with his wife.*
be compatible EG *Mary and I are very compatible.*
hit it off INFORMAL EG *They hit it off straight away.*

ghost NOUN
the spirit of a dead person
EG *the ghost of the drowned girl*
apparition EG *She felt as if she were seeing a ghostly apparition.*
phantom EG *She was relentlessly pursued by a grossly disfigured phantom.*
spectre EG *The Tower is said to be haunted by the spectre of Anne Boleyn.*
spirit EG *the spirits of our dead ancestors*

❶ gift NOUN
something you give someone
EG *He showered her with gifts.*
bequest FORMAL EG *They received a bequest of $310,000.*
bonsela SOUTH AFRICAN EG *a generous bonsela*
contribution EG *companies that make charitable contributions*
donation EG *donations of food and clothing for victims of the hurricane*
legacy EG *What about the legacy from your uncle?*
present EG *This book would make a great Christmas present.*

❷ gift NOUN
a natural skill or ability
EG *a gift for comedy*
ability EG *It's obvious he has an exceptional ability.*
aptitude EG *She realised she had an aptitude for writing.*
flair EG *Tony found he had a real flair for design.*
talent EG *Both her children have a talent for music.*

❶ give VERB
to provide someone with something
EG *I gave her a CD.*
award EG *The Mayor awarded him a medal.*
deliver EG *The Canadians plan to deliver more food to southern Somalia.*
donate EG *Others donated second-hand clothes.*
grant EG *Permission was granted a few weeks ago.*
hand EG *Isabel handed me a glass of orange juice.*
present EG *The Queen presented the prizes.*
provide EG *The government was not in a position to provide them with food.*
supply EG *a contract to supply radar equipment to the Philippines*

> **WORD POWER**
> Synonyms
> accord
> administer
> bestow
> confer
> Antonym
> take

❷ give VERB
to collapse or break under pressure
EG *My knees gave under me.*
buckle EG *His left wrist buckled under the strain.*
cave in EG *Half the ceiling caved in.*
collapse EG *The roof supports had collapsed.*
give way EG *He fell when a ledge gave way beneath him.*
yield EG *The handle yielded to her grasp.*

give in VERB
to admit that you are defeated
EG *Juppe should not give in to the strikers.*

capitulate EG *Cohen capitulated to virtually every demand.*
concede EG *Mr Pyke is not prepared to concede defeat.*
submit EG *Mrs Jones submitted to an operation on her right knee.*
succumb EG *The Minister said his country would never succumb to pressure.*
surrender EG *He surrendered to American troops.*
yield EG *an enemy who had shown no desire to yield*

glad ADJECTIVE
happy about something
EG *They'll be glad to get away from it all.*
delighted EG *Frank will be delighted to see you.*
happy EG *Jacques is very happy that you are here.*
joyful EG *a joyful reunion with his mother*
overjoyed EG *Shelley was overjoyed to see me.*
pleased EG *They're pleased to be going home.*

> **WORD POWER**
> Antonym
> sorry

❶ glance NOUN
a brief look at something
EG *The boys exchanged glances.*
glimpse EG *They caught a glimpse of their hero.*
look EG *Lucille took a last look in the mirror.*
peek EG *Could I just have another quick peek at the bedroom?*
peep EG *Would you take a peep out of the window?*

❷ glance VERB
to look at something quickly
EG *He glanced at his watch.*
glimpse EG *I soon glimpsed the doctor in his garden.*
look EG *Bethan looked quickly at the elegant people around her.*

peek EG *She had peeked at him through a crack in the wall.*
peep EG *Now and then she peeped to see if he was noticing her.*
scan EG *She scanned the advertisement pages of the newspaper.*

❸ glance VERB
to hit something quickly and bounce away
EG *My fist glanced off his jaw.*
bounce EG *The ball bounced off the opposite post.*
brush EG *She brushed her lips across Michael's cheek.*
skim EG *pebbles skimming across the water*

> **WORD POWER**
> Synonyms
> rebound
> ricochet

❶ glare VERB
to look angrily at someone
EG *Joe glared at his brother.*
frown EG *She looked up to see Vic frowning at her.*
glower EG *He glowered at me but said nothing.*
scowl EG *Robert scowled, and slammed the door behind him.*

❷ glare NOUN
an angry look
EG *The waiter lowered his eyes to avoid Harold's furious glare.*
frown EG *There was a deep frown on the boy's face.*
scowl EG *Chris met the remark with a scowl.*

❸ glare NOUN
very bright light
EG *the glare of the headlights*
blaze EG *There was a sudden blaze of light.*
glow EG *the glow of the fire*

❶ gloomy ADJECTIVE
feeling very sad
EG *They are gloomy about their chances of success.*

A B C D E F **G** H I J K L M N O P Q R S T U V W X Y Z

dejected EG *Everyone has days when they feel dejected.*

down EG *The old man sounded really down.*

glum EG *What on earth are you looking so glum about?*

miserable EG *She went to bed, miserable and depressed.*

sad EG *You must feel sad about what's happened.*

> ### WORD POWER
> Synonyms
> blue
> despondent
> downhearted
> Antonym
> cheerful

❷ **gloomy** ADJECTIVE
dark and depressing
EG *a gloomy house on the edge of Phoenix Park*

dark EG *The house looked dark and gloomy.*

dismal EG *damp and dismal weather*

dreary EG *the dreary, industrial city of Ludwigshafen*

dull EG *It's always dull and raining.*

> ### WORD POWER
> Antonym
> sunny

❶ **glory** NOUN
fame and admiration that someone gets
EG *It was her moment of glory.*

fame EG *The film earned him international fame.*

honour EG *the honour of captaining one's country*

immortality EG *Some people want to achieve immortality through their work.*

praise EG *Holbrooke deserves full praise for his efforts.*

prestige EG *I'm not in this job for the prestige.*

> ### WORD POWER

> Synonyms
> acclaim
> renown
> Antonym
> disgrace

❷ **glory** NOUN
something impressive or beautiful
EG *Spring arrived in all its glory.*

grandeur EG *the grandeur of the country mansion*

magnificence EG *the magnificence of the sunset*

majesty EG *the majesty of Niagara Falls*

splendour EG *the splendour of the palace of Versailles*

❸ **glory** VERB
to enjoy something very much
EG *The workers were glorying in their new-found freedom.*

gloat EG *Their rivals were gloating over their triumph.*

relish EG *He relished the idea of getting some cash.*

revel EG *a ruthless killer who revels in his job*

gloss NOUN
a bright shine on a surface
EG *aluminium foil with a high gloss surface*

brilliance EG *ceramic tiles of great brilliance*

gleam EG *the gleam of brass*

polish EG *His boots had a high polish.*

sheen EG *The carpet had a silvery sheen to it.*

shine EG *This gel gives a beautiful shine to the hair.*

glossy ADJECTIVE
smooth and shiny
EG *The leaves were dark and glossy.*

bright EG *Her eyes were bright with excitement.*

brilliant EG *The woman had brilliant green eyes.*

polished EG *a highly polished floor*

shiny EG *a shiny new sports car*

sleek EG *sleek black hair*

❶ glow NOUN
a dull steady light
EG *the glow of the fire*

gleam EG *the first gleam of dawn*

glimmer EG *In the east there was the slightest glimmer of light.*

light EG *the light of the evening sun*

❷ glow VERB
to shine with a dull steady light
EG *A light glowed behind the curtains.*

gleam EG *Lights gleamed in the deepening mist.*

glimmer EG *A few stars still glimmered.*

shine EG *Scattered lights shone on the horizon.*

smoulder EG *A very small fire was smouldering in the grate.*

glue VERB
to stick things together
EG *Glue the two halves together.*

fix EG *Fix the fabric to the roller.*

paste EG *The children were busy pasting gold stars on a chart.*

seal EG *He sealed the envelope and put on a stamp.*

stick EG *I stuck the notice on the board.*

❶ go VERB
to move or travel somewhere
EG *I went home at the weekend.*

advance EG *Rebel forces are advancing on the capital.*

drive EG *My husband and I drove to Liverpool to see my mum.*

fly EG *He flew to Los Angeles.*

journey FORMAL EG *They intended to journey up the Amazon.*

leave EG *What time are you leaving?*

proceed FORMAL EG *The taxi proceeded along a lonely road.*

set off EG *He set off for the station.*

travel EG *Students often travel hundreds of miles to get here.*

❷ go VERB
to work properly
EG *stuck on the motorway with a car that won't go*

function EG *All the instruments functioned properly.*

work EG *The pump doesn't work and we have no running water.*

❸ go NOUN
an attempt to do something
EG *I always wanted to have a go at waterskiing.*

attempt EG *one of his rare attempts at humour*

shot INFORMAL EG *a shot at winning a brand new car*

stab INFORMAL EG *Several sports stars have had a stab at acting and singing.*

try EG *After a few tries, Patrick had given up.*

gobble VERB
to eat food very quickly
EG *Pete gobbled all the beef stew.*

bolt EG *Being under stress can cause you to bolt your food.*

devour EG *She devoured two bars of chocolate.*

wolf EG *Pitt wolfed down a peanut butter sandwich.*

❶ good ADJECTIVE
pleasant, acceptable or satisfactory
EG *We had a really good time.*

acceptable EG *The school was failing to provide an acceptable standard of education.*

excellent EG *The recording quality is excellent.*

fine EG *one of Britain's finest restaurants*

great EG *I thought it was a great idea.*

satisfactory EG *It seemed a very satisfactory arrangement.*

splendid EG *I had a splendid view from my window.*

superb EG *a superb 18-hole golf course*

A
B
C
D
E
F
G
H
I
J
K
L
M
N
O
P
Q
R
S
T
U
V
W
X
Y
Z

good – grab

A
B
C
D
E
F
G
H
I
J
K
L
M
N
O
P
Q
R
S
T
U
V
W
X
Y
Z

WORD POWER
Synonyms
agreeable
commendable
first-rate
Antonym
bad

❷ good ADJECTIVE
skilful or successful
EG *I'm not very good at art.*
able EG *one of the ablest members of the government*
accomplished EG *an accomplished linguist*
capable EG *She's a very capable speaker.*
clever EG *Rory was just so clever at writing.*
expert EG *an expert gardener*
first-rate EG *a first-rate scientist*
skilled EG *a skilled editor*
talented EG *Howard is a talented pianist.*

WORD POWER
Synonyms
adept
competent
proficient
Antonym
incompetent

❸ good ADJECTIVE
kind, thoughtful and loving
EG *You are so good to me.*
benevolent EG *He smiled at them like a benevolent uncle.*
charitable EG *Mr Wray is a very charitable man.*
gracious EG *a lovely and gracious woman*
kind EG *She is warm-hearted and kind to everyone.*
obliging EG *Piggott was the kindest and most obliging of men.*

WORD POWER
Synonyms
altruistic
humane
kind-hearted
kindly
Antonym
unkind

goodwill NOUN
kindness and helpfulness towards other people
EG *I invited them to dinner as a gesture of goodwill.*
benevolence EG *He chuckles often and radiates benevolence.*
favour EG *in order to gain the favour of whoever is in power*
friendliness EG *Visitors remarked on the friendliness of the people.*
friendship EG *The two countries signed treaties of friendship.*

gossip NOUN
informal conversation about other people
EG *Don't you like a good gossip?*
dirt EG *the latest dirt on the other candidates*
hearsay EG *They have had only hearsay and rumour to go on.*

WORD POWER
Synonyms
chitchat
prattle
scandal
tittle-tattle

go through VERB
to experience an unpleasant event
EG *I was going through a very difficult time.*
endure EG *He'd endured years of pain and sleepless nights.*
experience EG *British business was experiencing a severe recession.*
undergo EG *Magee underwent emergency surgery.*

grab VERB
to take hold of something roughly
EG *I grabbed him by the neck.*
clutch EG *Michelle clutched my arm.*
grasp EG *He grasped both my*

208

hands.

seize EG *She seized a carving fork and advanced in my direction.*

snatch EG *Mick snatched the cards from Archie's hand.*

grace NOUN
an elegant way of moving
EG *He moved with the grace of a trained boxer.*

elegance EG *She is elegance personified.*

poise EG *Ballet classes are important for poise and grace.*

> *WORD POWER*
> Antonym
> clumsiness

grade VERB
to arrange things according to quality
EG *The oil is tasted and graded according to quality.*

class EG *They are officially classed as visitors.*

classify EG *Rocks can be classified according to their origin.*

group EG *The fact sheets are grouped into seven sections.*

rate EG *He was rated as one of the country's top young players.*

sort EG *The students are sorted into three ability groups.*

> *WORD POWER*
> Synonyms
> evaluate
> sequence

gradual ADJECTIVE
happening or changing slowly
EG *the gradual improvement in communications*

continuous EG *Our policy is one of continuous improvement.*

progressive EG *One symptom of the disease is progressive loss of memory.*

slow EG *The distribution of passports has been a slow process.*

steady EG *a steady rise in sales*

> *WORD POWER*
> Antonym
> sudden

grammar NOUN

Grammar words:
active
aspect
comparative
passive
person
plural
possessive
singular
superlative
tense
voice

❶ grand ADJECTIVE
very impressive in size or appearance
EG *a grand building in the centre of town*

imposing EG *the imposing gates at the entrance to the estate*

impressive EG *The old boat presented an impressive sight.*

magnificent EG *magnificent views over the San Fernando valley*

majestic EG *a stupendous vista of majestic peaks*

monumental EG *a monumental sculpture of a human face*

splendid EG *a splendid Victorian mansion*

> *WORD POWER*
> Synonyms
> glorious
> grandiose
> palatial

❷ grand ADJECTIVE; INFORMAL
pleasant or enjoyable
EG *It was a grand day.*

brilliant INFORMAL EG *I've had a brilliant time.*

great INFORMAL EG *I had a great time at university.*

marvellous INFORMAL EG *It was a marvellous day and we were all so happy.*

A B C D E F **G** H I J K L M N O P Q R S T U V W X Y Z

terrific INFORMAL EG *Everybody there was having a terrific time.*
wonderful EG *It was a wonderful experience.*

grateful ADJECTIVE
pleased and wanting to thank someone
EG *I am grateful to you for your help.*
appreciative EG *We have been very appreciative of their support.*
indebted EG *I am deeply indebted to him for his help.*
thankful EG *I'm just thankful that I've got a job.*

> **WORD POWER**
> Antonym
> ungrateful

gratitude NOUN
the feeling of being grateful
EG *I wish to express my gratitude to Kathy Davis for her help.*
appreciation EG *their appreciation of his efforts*
recognition EG *an honour given in recognition of his help to the college*
thanks EG *They accepted their certificates with words of thanks.*

> **WORD POWER**
> Antonym
> ingratitude

❶ graze VERB
to slightly injure your skin
EG *He fell heavily and grazed his left arm.*
scrape EG *She stumbled and fell, scraping her palms and knees.*
scratch EG *The branches scratched my hands and face.*
skin EG *He fell and skinned both his knees.*

❷ graze NOUN
a slight injury to your skin
EG *He just has a slight graze.*
abrasion FORMAL EG *He had severe abrasions to his right cheek.*
scratch EG *She had scratches to her face.*

❶ great ADJECTIVE
very large in size
EG *great columns of ice*
colossal EG *a colossal bronze statue of King George V*
enormous EG *His writings cover an enormous range of subjects.*
gigantic EG *a gigantic oak tree*
huge EG *huge tracts of forest*
immense EG *an immense cloud of smoke*
vast EG *vast stretches of land*

> **WORD POWER**
> Antonym
> little

❷ great ADJECTIVE
important or famous
EG *the great novels of the nineteenth century*
celebrated EG *Rebel Without Cause is his most celebrated film.*
distinguished EG *a distinguished scholar*
famed EG *the famed Brazilian photographer Sebastiao Salgado*
famous EG *England's most famous landscape artist*
outstanding EG *an outstanding athlete*

> **WORD POWER**
> Synonyms
> eminent
> illustrious
> prominent
> renowned

❸ great ADJECTIVE; INFORMAL
very good
EG *I thought it was a great idea.*
excellent EG *Sue does an excellent job as Fred's personal assistant.*
fantastic INFORMAL EG *I have a fantastic social life.*
marvellous INFORMAL EG *This is a marvellous book.*
superb EG *a superb staircase made from oak*
terrific INFORMAL EG *You look terrific, Ann.*

tremendous INFORMAL EG *I thought the film was absolutely tremendous.*
wonderful EG *It's wonderful to see you.*

greedy ADJECTIVE
wanting more than you need
EG *greedy bosses who award themselves huge pay rises*
materialistic EG *During the 1980s Britain became a very materialistic society.*
snoep SOUTH AFRICAN INFORMAL EG *a bunch of snoep businessmen*

> ### WORD POWER
> Synonyms
> acquisitive
> avaricious
> grasping
> voracious

green ADJECTIVE
concerned with environmental issues
EG *Children and adolescents are now aware of green issues.*
conservationist EG *a chorus of protest from conservationist groups*
ecological EG *shared interest in ecological issues*

> ### WORD POWER
> Synonyms
> eco-friendly
> environmentally friendly
> non-polluting
> ozone-friendly

> Shades of green:
> apple green
> avocado
> bottle-green
> chartreuse
> eau de nil
> emerald
> grass-green
> jade
> khaki
> lime
> Lincoln green
> olive
> pea green
> pistachio

> sage
> sea green
> turquoise

greet VERB
to say hello to someone when they arrive
EG *The president was greeted by local political leaders.*
meet EG *A nurse met me at the entrance.*
receive FORMAL EG *250 guests were received by the bride and bridegroom.*
welcome EG *She was there to welcome him home.*

> ### WORD POWER
> Synonyms
> hail
> salute

grey NOUN OR ADJECTIVE

> Shades of grey:
> ash
> charcoal
> gunmetal
> hoary
> leaden
> pewter
> platinum
> silver
> silvery
> slate
> steel grey
> stone
> taupe
> whitish

grief NOUN
a feeling of extreme sadness
EG *a huge outpouring of national grief*
distress EG *the intense distress they were causing my family*
heartache EG *She has suffered more heartache than anyone deserves.*
misery EG *All that money brought nothing but misery.*
sadness EG *It is with a mixture of sadness and joy that I say farewell.*

A
B
C
D
E
F
G
H
I
J
K
L
M
N
O
P
Q
R
S
T
U
V
W
X
Y
Z

sorrow EG *a time of great sorrow*
unhappiness EG *There was a lot of unhappiness in my adolescence.*

WORD POWER
Synonyms
anguish
dejection
heartbreak
woe
Antonym
happiness

❶ grieve VERB
to feel extremely sad
EG *He still grieves for his wife.*
lament EG *All who knew Spender will lament his death.*
mourn EG *The whole nation mourns the death of their great leader.*

❷ grieve VERB
to make someone feel extremely sad
EG *It grieved Elaine to be separated from her son.*
distress EG *It distresses me that the President has not tackled crime.*
pain EG *It pains me to think of you struggling all alone.*
sadden EG *The cruelty in the world saddens me.*
upset EG *The news upset me.*

WORD POWER
Antonym
cheer

grim ADJECTIVE
looking very serious
EG *Her face was grim.*
grave EG *Mrs Williams was looking very grave.*
severe EG *He leaned towards me, a severe expression on his face.*
solemn EG *What a solemn-faced kid he had been.*
stern EG *Michael gave the dog a stern look.*

❶ grip NOUN
a firm hold on something
EG *His strong hand eased the bag from her grip.*
clasp EG *With one last clasp of his hand, she left him.*
grasp EG *The spade slipped from her grasp and fell to the ground.*
hold EG *He released his hold on the camera.*

❷ grip NOUN
someone's control over something
EG *The president maintains an iron grip on his country.*
clutches EG *She fell into the clutches of the wrong sort of person.*
control EG *The port area is under the control of rebel forces.*
influence EG *Alexandra fell under the influence of Grigori Rasputin.*
power EG *I was really in the power of my mother.*

❸ grip VERB
to hold something firmly
EG *Alison gripped the steering wheel and stared straight ahead.*
clutch EG *Michelle clutched my arm.*
grasp EG *He grasped both my hands.*
hold EG *He was struggling to hold on to the rope.*

ground NOUN
the surface of the earth
EG *We slid down the roof and dropped to the ground.*
dirt EG *They sat on the dirt in the shade of a tree.*
earth EG *The road winds for miles through parched earth.*
land EG *800 acres of agricultural land*
soil EG *In Southern India the soil is fertile.*
terrain EG *Farms give way to hilly terrain.*

❶ grounds PLURAL NOUN
the land surrounding a building
EG *the grounds of the university*
estate EG *Lord Wyville's estate in Yorkshire*

gardens EG *an elegant Regency house set in beautiful gardens*
land EG *Their home is on his father's land.*

❷ grounds PLURAL NOUN
the reason for doing or thinking something
EG *Owen was against it on the grounds of expense.*
basis EG *Could you tell me on what basis the fee is calculated?*
cause EG *No one had cause to get angry or unpleasant.*
excuse EG *There's no excuse for behaviour like that.*
justification EG *There was no justification for what I was doing.*
reason EG *Who would have a reason to want to kill her?*

WORD POWER
Synonyms
foundation
pretext
rationale

❶ group NOUN
a number of people or things
EG *a group of football supporters*
band EG *a band of rebels*
bunch EG *They're a nice bunch of lads.*
collection EG *a collection of essays from foreign affairs experts*
crowd EG *A small crowd of onlookers has gathered.*
gang EG *Gangs of teenagers hang out in shop doorways.*
pack EG *a pack of journalists eager to question him*
party EG *a party of sightseers*
set EG *Different sets of people often use the same buildings.*

WORD POWER
Synonyms
aggregation
assemblage
coterie

❷ group VERB
to link people or things together

EG *Their responses are grouped into 11 categories.*
arrange EG *He started to arrange the books in piles.*
class EG *They are officially classed as visitors.*
classify EG *Rocks can be classified according to their origin.*
organize EG *I was organizing the vast array of junk we had collected.*
sort EG *The students are sorted into three ability groups.*

WORD POWER
Synonyms
assort
marshal

❶ grow VERB
to increase in size or amount
EG *Bacteria grow more quickly once food is contaminated.*
develop EG *These clashes could develop into open warfare.*
expand EG *Will the universe continue to expand forever?*
increase EG *Industrial output increased by 2%.*
multiply EG *Her husband multiplied his demands on her time.*

WORD POWER
Antonym
shrink

❷ grow VERB
to be alive or exist
EG *Trees and bushes grew down to the water's edge.*
flourish EG *The plant flourishes in slightly harsher climates.*
germinate EG *Heat will encourage seeds to germinate.*
sprout EG *It only takes a few days for beans to sprout.*

WORD POWER
Synonyms
shoot
spring up

❸ grow VERB
to change gradually

EG *I grew a little afraid of the guy next door.*

become EG *The wind became stronger.*

get EG *The boys were getting bored.*

turn EG *In October it turned cold.*

growth NOUN
the act of getting bigger
EG *the growth of the fishing industry*

development EG *What are your plans for the development of your company?*

enlargement EG *the enlargement of the European Union*

expansion EG *a new period of economic expansion*

increase EG *a sharp increase in the number of homeless people*

grumpy ADJECTIVE
bad-tempered and annoyed
EG *a grumpy old man*

irritable EG *He had missed his dinner and grew irritable.*

sulky EG *She still looked like a sulky teenager.*

sullen EG *Several leading players have maintained a sullen silence.*

surly EG *They were surly, sometimes downright rude to me.*

> **WORD POWER**
> Synonyms
> bad-tempered
> cantankerous
> ill-tempered

❶ **guarantee** NOUN
something that makes another thing certain
EG *The package offered a guarantee of job security.*

assurance EG *a written assurance that he would start work at once*

pledge EG *a pledge of support from the Ministry of Culture*

promise EG *I'd made him a promise that I'd write a book for him.*

undertaking EG *She gave an undertaking not to repeat the*

allegations.

word EG *He simply cannot be trusted to keep his word.*

❷ **guarantee** VERB
to make it certain that something will happen
EG *Reports of this kind are guaranteed to cause anxiety.*

ensure EG *We need to ensure that every student has basic literacy skills.*

pledge EG *Both sides pledged that a nuclear war would never be fought.*

promise EG *He promised that the rich would not get preferential treatment.*

❶ **guard** VERB
to protect someone
EG *Police were guarding his home yesterday.*

defend EG *He and his friends defended themselves against racist thugs.*

protect EG *What can women do to protect themselves from heart disease?*

safeguard EG *measures to safeguard their forces from chemical weapons*

shelter EG *A neighbour sheltered the boy for seven days.*

shield EG *She had shielded him from the terrible truth.*

watch over EG *two policewomen to watch over him*

❷ **guard** VERB
to stop someone making trouble or escaping
EG *The soldiers had been guarding paramilitary prisoners.*

patrol EG *Prison officers continued to patrol the grounds.*

police EG *It is extremely difficult to police the border.*

supervise EG *Only two staff were supervising over 100 prisoners.*

❸ **guard** NOUN
someone who guards people or places

EG *The prisoners overpowered their guards and locked them in a cell.*

sentry EG *We can sneak past the sentries.*

warden EG *The siege began when the prisoners seized three wardens.*

> **WORD POWER**
> Synonyms
> sentinel
> warder
> watchman

❶ guess VERB
to form an idea or opinion about something
EG *Wood guessed that he was a very successful banker.*

estimate EG *It's difficult to estimate how much money is involved.*

imagine EG *'Was he meeting someone?' 'I imagine so.'*

reckon EG *Toni reckoned that it must be about three o'clock.*

speculate EG *The reader can speculate what will happen next.*

suppose EG *I supposed you would have a meal somewhere.*

suspect EG *I suspect they were right.*

think EG *Nora thought he was seventeen years old.*

> **WORD POWER**
> Synonyms
> conjecture
> hazard
> surmise

❷ guess NOUN
an attempt to give the right answer
EG *My guess is that the answer will be negative.*

feeling EG *My feeling is that everything will come right for us.*

reckoning EG *By my reckoning, 50% of the team will be available.*

speculation EG *speculations about the future of the universe*

> **WORD POWER**
> Synonyms

conjecture
hypothesis

❶ guide VERB
to lead someone somewhere
EG *He took Elliott by the arm and guided him out.*

accompany EG *We accompanied Joe to the magazine's midtown offices.*

direct EG *Officials directed him to the wrong airport.*

escort EG *I escorted him to the door.*

lead EG *The nurse led me to a large room.*

> **WORD POWER**
> Synonyms
> conduct
> convoy
> shepherd
> usher

❷ guide VERB
to influence someone
EG *He should have let his instinct guide him.*

counsel FORMAL EG *Green was counselled not to talk to reporters.*

govern EG *Our thinking is as much governed by habit as by behaviour.*

influence EG *My dad influenced me to do electronics.*

❶ guilty ADJECTIVE
having done something wrong
EG *They were found guilty of murder.*

convicted EG *a convicted drug dealer*

criminal EG *He had a criminal record for petty theft.*

> **WORD POWER**
> Synonyms
> blameworthy
> culpable
> felonious
> Antonym
> innocent

❷ guilty ADJECTIVE
unhappy because you have done something bad

A B C D E F G H I J K L M N O P Q R S T U V W X Y Z

EG *When she saw me she looked guilty.*

ashamed EG *Zumel said he was not ashamed of what he had done.*

regretful EG *Surprisingly, she didn't feel regretful about her actions.*

remorseful FORMAL EG *He felt remorseful for what he had done.*

sorry EG *She was very sorry about all the trouble she'd caused.*

gullible ADJECTIVE
easily tricked
EG *I'm so gullible I would have believed him.*

naive EG *It would be naive to believe Mr Gonzalez's statement.*

trusting EG *She has an open, trusting nature.*

gush VERB
to flow in large quantities
EG *Piping-hot water gushed out.*

flow EG *Tears flowed down his cheeks.*

pour EG *Blood was pouring from his broken nose.*

spurt EG *a fountain that spurts water nine stories high*

stream EG *water streaming from the pipes*

❶ habit NOUN
something that is done regularly
EG *his habit of smiling at everyone he saw*
convention EG *It's just a social convention that men don't wear skirts.*
custom EG *an ancient Japanese custom*
practice EG *the practice of clocking in at work*
routine EG *my daily routine*
tradition EG *a family tradition at Christmas*

❷ habit NOUN
an addiction to something
EG *her cocaine habit*
addiction EG *his addiction to gambling*
dependence EG *the effects of drug dependence*

habitat NOUN
the natural home of a plant or animal
EG *the habitat of the spotted owl*
environment EG *a safe environment for marine mammals*
territory EG *a bird's territory*

hackneyed ADJECTIVE
used too often to be meaningful
EG *hackneyed postcard snaps of lochs and glens*
banal EG *banal lyrics*
clichéd EG *clichéd slogans*
stale EG *Her relationship with Mark has become stale.*
tired EG *a tired excuse*
trite EG *The film is teeming with trite ideas.*

WORD POWER
Synonyms
run-of-the-mill
threadbare
timeworn
Antonym
original

---

❶ hail NOUN
a lot of things falling together
EG *a hail of bullets*
barrage EG *a barrage of angry questions*
bombardment EG *the sound of heavy aerial bombardment*
shower EG *a shower of rose petals*
storm EG *The announcement provoked a storm of protest.*
volley EG *A volley of shots rang out.*

❷ hail VERB
to attract someone's attention
EG *He hailed me from across the street.*
call EG *He called me over the Tannoy.*
signal to EG *The lollipop lady signalled to me to stop.*
wave down EG *I ran on to the road and waved down a taxi.*

❶ halt VERB
to come or bring to a stop
EG *She held her hand out to halt him.*
draw up EG *The car drew up outside the house.*
pull up EG *The cab pulled up, and the driver jumped out.*
stop EG *The event literally stopped the traffic.*

❷ halt VERB
to bring something to an end
EG *Production was halted.*
cease EG *A small number of firms have ceased trading.*
check EG *We have managed to check the spread of terrorism.*
curb EG *efforts to curb the spread of nuclear weapons*
cut short EG *They had to cut short a holiday abroad.*
end EG *They decided to end the ceasefire.*
terminate EG *His contract has been terminated.*

A
B
C
D
E
F
G
H
I
J
K
L
M
N
O
P
Q
R
S
T
U
V
W
X
Y
Z

WORD POWER
Antonym
begin

❸ **halt** NOUN
an interruption or end to
something
EG *He brought the car to a halt.*
close EG *Their 18-month marriage
was brought to a close.*
end EG *The war came to an end.*
pause EG *There was a pause before
he replied.*
standstill EG *The country was
brought to a standstill by strikes.*
stop EG *He slowed the car almost
to a stop.*
stoppage EG *Air and ground crew
are staging a 24-hour stoppage
today.*

WORD POWER
Synonyms
impasse
termination

hamper VERB
to make movement or progress
difficult for someone
EG *I was hampered by a lack of
information.*
frustrate EG *His attempt was
frustrated by the weather.*
hinder EG *A thigh injury hindered
her mobility.*
impede EG *Their work was being
impeded by shortages of supplies.*
obstruct EG *charged with
obstructing the course of justice*
restrict EG *Her life is restricted by
asthma.*

WORD POWER
Synonyms
encumber
fetter

hand down VERB
to pass from one generation to
another
EG *Recipes are handed down from
mother to daughter.*
bequeath EG *He bequeathed all*

his silver to his children.
give EG *a typewriter given to me by
my father*
pass down EG *an heirloom passed
down from generation to generation*
pass on EG *My parents passed on
their love of classical music to me.*

WORD POWER
Synonyms
bestow
will

❶ **handicap** NOUN
a physical or mental disability
EG *He learnt to overcome his
handicap.*
defect EG *a rare birth defect*
disability EG *children with
learning disabilities*

❷ **handicap** NOUN
something that makes progress
difficult
EG *Being a foreigner was not a
handicap.*
barrier EG *Taxes are the most
obvious barrier to free trade.*
disadvantage EG *the
disadvantage of unemployment*
drawback EG *The flat's only
drawback was that it was too small.*
hindrance EG *She was a help
rather than a hindrance to my work.*
impediment EG *an impediment to
economic development*
obstacle EG *the main obstacle to
the deal*

❸ **handicap** VERB
to make something difficult for
someone
EG *Greater levels of stress may
seriously handicap some students.*
burden EG *We decided not to
burden him with the news.*
hamper EG *I was hampered by a
lack of information.*
hinder EG *A thigh injury hindered
her mobility.*
impede EG *Fallen rocks impeded
the progress of the rescue workers.*

restrict EG *laws to restrict foreign imports*

❶ handle NOUN
the part of an object by which it is held
EG *a broom handle*
grip EG *He fitted new grips to his golf clubs.*
hilt EG *the hilt of the small, sharp knife*

❷ handle VERB
to hold or move with the hands
EG *Wear rubber gloves when handling cat litter.*
feel EG *The doctor felt his arm.*
finger EG *He fingered the few coins in his pocket.*
grasp EG *Grasp the end firmly.*
hold EG *Hold it by the edge.*
touch EG *She touched his hand reassuringly.*

❸ handle VERB
to deal or control with something
EG *She handled the travel arrangements.*
administer EG *The project is administered by the World Bank.*
conduct EG *This is no way to conduct a business.*
deal with EG *The matter has been dealt with by the school.*
manage EG *Within two years he was managing the store.*
supervise EG *I supervise the packing of all mail orders.*
take care of EG *He took care of the catering arrangements.*

❶ handsome ADJECTIVE
very attractive in appearance
EG *a handsome man*
attractive EG *an attractive young woman*
good-looking EG *good-looking actors*

> **WORD POWER**
> Antonym
> ugly

❷ handsome ADJECTIVE
large and generous
EG *a handsome profit*
ample EG *ample space for a good-sized kitchen*
considerable EG *his considerable wealth*
generous EG *a generous gift*
liberal EG *a liberal donation*
plentiful EG *a plentiful supply of vegetables*
sizable or **sizeable** EG *He inherited the house and a sizeable chunk of land.*

> **WORD POWER**
> Antonym
> small

❶ handy ADJECTIVE
conveniently near
EG *Keep a pencil and paper handy.*
at hand EG *Having the right equipment at hand will be enormously useful.*
at your fingertips EG *Firms need information at their fingertips.*
close EG *a secluded area close to her home*
convenient EG *Martin drove along until he found a convenient parking space.*
nearby EG *He tossed the match into a nearby wastepaper bin.*
on hand EG *Experts are on hand to offer advice.*

❷ handy ADJECTIVE
easy to handle or use
EG *handy hints on looking after indoor plants*
convenient EG *a convenient way of paying*
easy to use EG *This ice cream maker is cheap and easy to use.*
helpful EG *helpful instructions*
neat EG *It had been such a neat, clever plan.*
practical EG *the most practical way of preventing crime*
useful EG *useful information*

A B C D E F G H I J K L M N O P Q R S T U V W X Y Z

❶ hang VERB
to be attached at the top with
the lower part free
EG *His jacket hung from a hook
behind the door.*
dangle EG *A gold bracelet dangled
from his left wrist.*
droop EG *Pale wilting roses
drooped from a vase.*

❷ hang VERB
to fasten something to another
thing by its top
EG *She came out of the house to
hang clothes on the line.*
attach EG *He attached the picture
to the wall with a nail.*
drape EG *He draped the coat round
his shoulders.*
fasten EG *stirrups fastened to the
saddle*
fix EG *He fixed a pirate flag to the
mast.*
suspend EG *The TV is suspended
from the ceiling on brackets.*

happen VERB
to take place
EG *The accident happened on
Wednesday.*
come about EG *It came about
almost by accident.*
follow EG *He was arrested in the
confusion which followed.*
occur EG *The crash occurred on a
sharp bend.*
result EG *Ignore the early warnings
and illness could result.*
take place EG *The festival took
place last September.*

> **WORD POWER**
> Synonyms
> ensue
> materialize

happiness NOUN
a feeling of great pleasure
EG *Money can't buy happiness.*
delight EG *To my delight, it
worked perfectly.*
ecstasy EG *a state of almost

religious ecstasy
elation EG *His supporters reacted to
the news with elation.*
joy EG *tears of joy*
pleasure EG *Everybody takes
pleasure in eating.*
satisfaction EG *job satisfaction*

> **WORD POWER**
> Synonyms
> exuberance
> felicity
> merriment
> Antonym
> sadness

❶ happy ADJECTIVE
feeling or causing joy
EG *a happy atmosphere*
cheerful EG *They are both cheerful
in spite of their colds.*
delighted EG *He was delighted
with the public response.*
glad EG *The people seem genuinely
glad to see you.*
joyful EG *A wedding is a joyful
celebration.*
pleased EG *They're pleased to be
going home.*
thrilled EG *The children were
thrilled when the snow came.*

> **WORD POWER**
> Antonym
> sad

❷ happy ADJECTIVE
fortunate or lucky
EG *a happy coincidence*
auspicious EG *His career had an
auspicious start.*
favourable EG *favourable weather
conditions*
fortunate EG *a fortunate accident*
lucky EG *He had a lucky escape.*
opportune EG *The timing of the
meeting was opportune.*

> **WORD POWER**
> Synonyms
> felicitous
> propitious
> seasonable

Antonym
unlucky

❶ **hard** ADJECTIVE
firm, solid, or rigid
EG *a hard piece of cheese*
firm EG *a firm mattress*
rigid EG *rigid plastic containers*
solid EG *solid rock*
stiff EG *stiff metal wires*
strong EG *It has a strong casing which won't crack or chip.*
tough EG *dark brown beans with a rather tough outer skin*

> **WORD POWER**
> Antonym
> soft

❷ **hard** ADJECTIVE
requiring a lot of effort
EG *hard work*
arduous EG *a long, arduous journey*
exhausting EG *It's a pretty exhausting job.*
laborious EG *Keeping the garden tidy can be a laborious task.*
rigorous EG *rigorous military training*
strenuous EG *Avoid strenuous exercise in the evening.*
tough EG *Change is often tough to deal with.*

> **WORD POWER**
> Antonym
> easy

❸ **hard** ADJECTIVE
difficult to understand
EG *That's a very hard question.*
baffling EG *a baffling remark*
complex EG *a complex problem*
complicated EG *a complicated system of voting*
difficult EG *It was a very difficult decision to make.*
puzzling EG *Some of this book is rather puzzling.*

> **WORD POWER**
> Antonym
> simple

harden VERB
to make or become stiff or firm
EG *Give the cardboard two coats of varnish to harden it.*
bake EG *The soil had been baked solid by the heatwave.*
cake EG *The blood had begun to cake and turn brown.*
freeze EG *The lake freezes in winter.*
set EG *Lower the heat and allow the omelette to set.*
stiffen EG *paper that had been stiffened with paste*

> **WORD POWER**
> Synonyms
> anneal
> solidify
> Antonym
> soften

hardly ADVERB
almost not or not quite
EG *I could hardly believe what I was seeing.*
barely EG *His voice was barely audible.*
just EG *Her hand was just visible under her coat.*
only just EG *For centuries farmers there have only just managed to survive.*
scarcely EG *He could scarcely breathe.*

hardship NOUN
difficult circumstances
EG *Many people are suffering economic hardship.*
adversity EG *They manage to enjoy life despite adversity.*
destitution EG *a life of poverty and destitution*
difficulty EG *Many new golf clubs are in serious financial difficulty.*
misfortune EG *She seemed to enjoy the misfortunes of others.*
want EG *They were fighting for freedom of speech and freedom from want.*

A B C D E F G H I J K L M N O P Q R S T U V W X Y Z

A B C D E F G H I J K L M N O P Q R S T U V W X Y Z

❶ harm VERB
to injure someone or damage
something
EG *The hijackers seemed anxious
not to harm anyone.*
abuse EG *Animals are still being
exploited and abused.*
damage EG *He damaged his knee
during training.*
hurt EG *He fell and hurt his back.*
ill-treat EG *They thought he had
been ill-treating is wife.*
ruin EG *My wife was ruining her
health through worry.*
wound EG *The bomb killed six
people and wounded another five.*

❷ harm NOUN
injury or damage
EG *All dogs are capable of doing
harm to human beings.*
abuse EG *The abuse of animals is
inexcusable.*
damage EG *The bomb caused
extensive damage.*
hurt EG *an evil desire to cause hurt
and damage*
injury EG *The two other passengers
escaped serious injury.*

harmful ADJECTIVE
having a bad effect on
something
EG *Whilst most stress is harmful,
some is beneficial.*
damaging EG *damaging
allegations about his personal life*
destructive EG *the awesome
destructive power of nuclear
weapons*
detrimental EG *levels of
radioactivity which are detrimental
to public health*
hurtful EG *Her comments can only
be hurtful to the family.*
pernicious EG *The pernicious
influence of secret societies.*

WORD POWER
Synonyms
baleful
baneful
deleterious
injurious
Antonym
harmless

harmless ADJECTIVE
safe to use or be near
EG *This experiment was harmless to
the animals.*
innocuous EG *Both mushrooms
look innocuous but are in fact
deadly.*
nontoxic EG *a cheap and nontoxic
method of cleaning up our water*
not dangerous EG *The tests are
not dangerous to the environment.*
safe EG *The doll is safe for children.*

WORD POWER
Antonym
harmful

harsh ADJECTIVE
severe, difficult, and unpleasant
EG *harsh weather conditions*
austere EG *The life of the troops
was still comparatively austere.*
cruel EG *an unusually cruel winter*
hard EG *He had a hard life.*
ruthless EG *the ruthless treatment
of staff*
severe EG *My boss gave me a severe
reprimand.*
stern EG *a stern warning*

WORD POWER
Synonyms
Draconian
Spartan
Antonym
mild

hasty ADJECTIVE
done or happening suddenly
and quickly
EG *The signs of their hasty departure
could be seen everywhere.*
brisk EG *a brisk walk*
hurried EG *a hurried breakfast*

prompt EG *It is not too late, but prompt action is needed.*
rapid EG *a rapid retreat*
swift EG *my swift departure*

❶ **hate** VERB
to have a strong dislike for something or someone
EG *Most people hate him, but they don't care to say so.*
abhor EG *He abhorred violence.*
be sick of EG *We're sick of being ripped off.*
despise EG *A lot of people despise and loathe what I do.*
detest EG *Jean detested being photographed.*
dislike EG *those who dislike change*
loathe EG *a play universally loathed by the critics*

> **WORD POWER**
> Antonym
> love

❷ **hate** NOUN
a strong dislike
EG *a violent bully, destructive and full of hate*
animosity EG *The animosity between the two men grew.*
aversion EG *I've always had an aversion to being part of a group.*
dislike EG *Consider what your likes and dislikes are about your job.*
hatred EG *her hatred of authority*
hostility EG *He looked at her with open hostility.*
loathing EG *Critics are united in their unmitigated loathing of the band.*

> **WORD POWER**
> Synonyms
> animus
> detestation
> enmity
> odium
> Antonym
> love

hateful ADJECTIVE
extremely unpleasant
EG *It was a hateful thing to say.*
abhorrent EG *Discrimination is abhorrent to my council and our staff.*
despicable EG *a despicable crime*
horrible EG *a horrible little boy*
loathsome EG *the loathsome spectacle we were obliged to witness*
obnoxious EG *He was a most obnoxious character. No-one liked him.*
offensive EG *an offensive remark*

hatred NOUN
an extremely strong feeling of dislike
EG *He has been accused of inciting racial hatred.*
animosity EG *The animosity between the two men grew.*
antipathy EG *public antipathy towards scientists*
aversion EG *my aversion to housework*
dislike EG *his dislike of modern buildings*
hate EG *These people are so full of hate.*
revulsion EG *They expressed their revulsion at his violent death.*

> **WORD POWER**
> Antonym
> love

haughty ADJECTIVE
showing excessive pride
EG *He spoke in a haughty tone.*
arrogant EG *an air of arrogant indifference*
conceited EG *They had grown too conceited and pleased with themselves.*
disdainful EG *She cast a disdainful glance at me.*
proud EG *She was said to be proud and arrogant.*
snobbish EG *They had a snobbish dislike for their intellectual inferiors.*
stuck-up INFORMAL EG *She was a famous actress, but she wasn't a bit stuck-up.*

A
B
C
D
E
F
G
H
I
J
K
L
M
N
O
P
Q
R
S
T
U
V
W
X
Y
Z

WORD POWER
Antonym
humble

❶ have VERB
to own something
EG *We have two tickets for the concert.*
hold EG *He does not hold a firearm certificate.*
keep EG *We keep chickens.*
own EG *His father owns a local pub.*
possess EG *He is said to possess a fortune.*

❷ have VERB
to experience something
EG *He had a marvellous time.*
endure EG *The company endured heavy losses.*
enjoy EG *The average German will enjoy 40 days' paid holiday this year.*
experience EG *Widows seem to experience more distress than do widowers.*
feel EG *I felt a sharp pain in my shoulder.*
sustain EG *He had sustained a cut on his left eyebrow.*
undergo EG *He recently underwent brain surgery.*

❶ health NOUN
the condition of your body
EG *Smoking is bad for your health.*
condition EG *He remains in a critical condition in hospital.*
constitution EG *He must have an extremely strong constitution.*
shape EG *He was still in better shape than many younger men.*

❷ health NOUN
a state in which a person is feeling well.
EG *In hospital they nursed me back to health.*
fitness EG *He has fitness problems.*
good condition EG *He is in great condition for a man of 56.*
wellbeing EG *Singing can create a*

sense of wellbeing.

WORD POWER
Antonym
illness

❶ healthy ADJECTIVE
having good health
EG *She was a very healthy child.*
active EG *an active lifestyle*
fit EG *A short, physically fit man of 61.*
in good shape INFORMAL EG *I kept myself in good shape by swimming.*
robust EG *a robust and vibrant young man*
strong EG *a strong constitution*
well EG *I'm not very well today.*

WORD POWER
Antonym
ill

❷ healthy ADJECTIVE
producing good health
EG *a healthy diet*
beneficial EG *Wine in moderation is beneficial to health.*
bracing EG *a bracing walk*
good for you EG *Regular, moderate exercise is good for you.*
nourishing EG *sensible, nourishing food*
nutritious EG *a hot, nutritious meal*
wholesome EG *fresh, wholesome ingredients*

WORD POWER
Synonyms
invigorating
salubrious
salutary
Antonym
unhealthy

❶ heap NOUN
a pile of things
EG *a heap of rubble*
hoard EG *a hoard of silver and jewels*
mass EG *a mass of flowers*
mound EG *The bulldozers piled up*

huge mounds of dirt.

pile EG *a pile of betting slips*

stack EG *stacks of books on the bedside table*

❷ **heap** VERB
to pile things up
EG *She heaped vegetables onto his plate.*

pile EG *He was piling clothes into the suitcase.*

stack EG *They stacked up pillows behind his back.*

heaps PLURAL NOUN; INFORMAL
plenty of something
EG *heaps of cash*

loads INFORMAL EG *I've got loads of money.*

lots INFORMAL EG *lots of fun*

plenty EG *We've got plenty of time for a drink.*

stacks EG *stacks of magazines*

tons INFORMAL EG *I've got tons of work to do.*

❶ **hear** VERB
to listen to something
EG *I heard the sound of gunfire.*

catch EG *I don't believe I caught your name.*

eavesdrop EG *The government illegally eavesdropped on his phone conversations.*

heed EG *Few at the conference heeded his warning.*

listen in EG *Secret agents listened in on his phone calls.*

listen to EG *He spent his time listening to the radio.*

overhear EG *I overheard two doctors discussing my case.*

❷ **hear** VERB
to learn about something
EG *I heard that he was forced to resign.*

ascertain EG *They had ascertained that he was not a spy.*

discover EG *She discovered that they'd escaped.*

find out EG *As soon as we found*

this out, we closed the ward.

gather EG *I gather the report is critical of the judge.*

learn EG *She wasn't surprised to learn that he was involved.*

understand EG *I understand that she's just taken early retirement.*

❶ **heat** NOUN
the quality of being warm or hot
EG *the heat of the sun*

high temperature EG *The suffering caused by the high temperature has been great.*

warmth EG *the warmth of the sand between her toes*

> **WORD POWER**
> Antonym
> cold

❷ **heat** NOUN
a state of strong emotion
EG *in the heat of the election campaign*

excitement EG *in a state of great excitement*

fervour EG *religious fervour*

intensity EG *the intensity of feeling about this issue*

passion EG *He spoke with great passion.*

vehemence EG *I was surprised by the vehemence of his criticism.*

❸ **heat** VERB
to raise the temperature of something
EG *Heat the oil in a frying pan.*

reheat EG *Reheat the soup to a gentle simmer.*

warm up EG *Just before serving, warm up the tomato sauce.*

> **WORD POWER**
> Antonym
> cool

heathen NOUN; OLD-FASHIONED
someone who does not believe in an established religion
EG *She called us all heathens and hypocrites.*

A B C D E F G **H** I J K L M N O P Q R S T U V W X Y Z

pagan EG *the sky-god of the ancient pagans*
unbeliever EG *punishing unbelievers and traitors*

> ### WORD POWER
> Synonyms
> idolater
> infidel
> Antonym
> believer

❶ heaven NOUN
the place where good people are believed to go when they die
EG *She told them their mother was now in heaven.*
next world EG *He said, "We will see each other again in the next world."*
paradise EG *They believed they would go to paradise if they died in battle.*

> ### WORD POWER
> Synonyms
> Elysium (*Greek myth*)
> happy hunting ground (*Native American legend*)
> nirvana (*Buddhism, Hinduism*)
> Valhalla (*Norse myth*)
> Zion (*Christianity*)
> Antonym
> hell

❷ heaven NOUN
a place or situation liked very much
EG *I was in cinematic heaven.*
bliss EG *a scene of domestic bliss*
ecstasy EG *the ecstasy of being in love*
paradise EG *The Algarve is a golfer's paradise.*
rapture EG *the sheer rapture of listening to Bach's music*

❶ heavy ADJECTIVE
great in weight or force
EG *a heavy frying pan*
bulky EG *a bulky grey sweater*
massive EG *a massive blue whale*

> ### WORD POWER

Antonym
light

❷ heavy ADJECTIVE
serious or important
EG *a heavy speech*
deep EG *a period of deep personal crisis*
grave EG *the grave crisis facing the country*
profound EG *Anna's patriotism was profound.*
serious EG *It was a question which deserved serious consideration.*
solemn EG *a simple, solemn ceremony*
weighty EG *Surely such weighty matters merit a higher level of debate.*

> ### WORD POWER
> Antonym
> trivial

❶ heed VERB
to pay attention to someone's advice
EG *Few at the conference heeded his warning.*
follow EG *If you are not going to follow my advice, we are both wasting our time.*
listen to EG *They won't listen to my advice.*
pay attention to EG *The food industry is now paying attention to young consumers.*
take notice of EG *We want the government to take notice of what we think.*

❷ heed NOUN
careful attention
EG *He pays too much heed to her.*
attention EG *He never paid much attention to his audience.*
notice EG *So do they take any notice of public opinion?*

❶ hell NOUN
the place where souls of evil people are believed to go after death

EG *Milton's Satan would rather "reign in Hell, than serve in Heaven".*

abyss EG *Satan rules over the dark abyss.*

inferno EG *an inferno described in loving detail by Dante*

> **WORD POWER**
> Synonyms
> fire and brimstone
> Gehenna (*New Testament, Judaism*)
> Hades (*Greek myth*)
> hellfire
> Tartarus (*Greek myth*)
> underworld
> Antonym
> heaven

❷ **hell** NOUN; INFORMAL
an unpleasant situation or place
EG *Bullies can make your life hell.*

agony EG *the agony of divorce*

anguish EG *the anguish of families unable to trace relatives who've disappeared*

misery EG *All that money brought nothing but sadness and misery.*

nightmare EG *The years in prison were a nightmare.*

ordeal EG *the painful ordeal of the last year*

❶ **help** VERB
to make something easier or better for someone
EG *He began to help with the chores.*

aid EG *a software system to aid managers*

assist EG *information to assist you*

lend a hand EG *I'd be glad to lend a hand.*

support EG *He thanked everyone who had supported the strike.*

❷ **help** NOUN
assistance or support
EG *The books were not much help.*

advice EG *He has given me lots of good advice in my time here.*

aid EG *millions of dollars of aid*

assistance EG *I would be grateful for any assistance.*

guidance EG *the reports which were produced under his guidance*

helping hand EG *Most mums would be grateful for a helping hand.*

support EG *Only 60 clubs pledged their support for the scheme.*

helper NOUN
a person who gives assistance
EG *There is an adult helper for every two children.*

aide EG *a presidential aide*

assistant EG *a research assistant*

deputy EG *I can't make it so I'll send my deputy.*

henchman EG *Adolf Eichmann, Hitler's notorious henchman*

right-hand man EG *He was the perfect right-hand man for the president.*

supporter EG *He is a strong supporter of the plan.*

❶ **helpful** ADJECTIVE
giving assistance or advice
EG *The staff in the office are very helpful.*

accommodating EG *Lindi seemed a nice, accomodating girl.*

cooperative EG *I made every effort to be cooperative.*

kind EG *I must thank you for being so kind to me.*

supportive EG *Her boss was very supportive.*

> **WORD POWER**
> Antonym
> unhelpful

❷ **helpful** ADJECTIVE
making a situation better
EG *Having the right equipment will be enormously helpful.*

advantageous EG *an advantageous arrangement*

beneficial EG *beneficial changes in the tax system*

constructive EG *constructive*

227

A
B
C
D
E
F
G
H
I
J
K
L
M
N
O
P
Q
R
S
T
U
V
W
X
Y
Z

criticism
profitable EG *a profitable exchange of ideas*
useful EG *useful information*

helpless ADJECTIVE
weak or unable to cope
EG *a helpless baby*
defenceless EG *a savage attack on a defenceless girl*
powerless EG *He was powerless to help.*
unprotected EG *She felt unprotected and defenseless.*
vulnerable EG *the most vulnerable members of society*
weak EG *taking ruthless advantage of a weak old man*

hesitant ADJECTIVE
uncertain about something
EG *At first he was hesitant to accept the role.*
diffident EG *John was as outgoing as Helen was diffident.*
doubtful EG *I was very doubtful about the chances for success.*
reluctant EG *She was reluctant to get involved.*
unsure EG *He made her feel awkward and unsure of herself.*
wavering EG *wavering voters*

> **WORD POWER**
> Synonyms
> irresolute
> vacillating

hesitate VERB
to pause or show uncertainty
EG *She hesitated before replying.*
dither EG *We're still dithering over whether to marry.*
pause EG *The crowd paused for a minute, wondering what to do next.*
waver EG *Louise never wavered in her determination to take up the post.*

❶ **hide** VERB
to put something where it cannot be seen
EG *She hid her face in her hands.*

cache EG *He has £289 million cached away.*
conceal EG *The hat concealed her hair.*
secrete EG *She secreted the gun in the kitchen cabinet.*
stash INFORMAL EG *He had stashed money away in a secret offshore account.*

❷ **hide** NOUN
the skin of a large animal
EG *the process of tanning hides*
pelt EG *a bed covered with beaver pelts*
skin EG *a leopard skin coat*

❶ **high** ADJECTIVE
tall or a long way above the ground
EG *a high tower*
elevated EG *an elevated platform on the stage*
lofty EG *lofty ceilings hung with chandeliers*
soaring EG *the soaring spires of churches like St Peter's*
steep EG *steep cliffs*
tall EG *a tall building*
towering EG *towering volcanic peaks*

> **WORD POWER**
> Antonym
> low

❷ **high** ADJECTIVE
great in degree, quantity, or intensity
EG *There is a high risk of heart disease.*
excessive EG *use of excessive force by the army*
extraordinary EG *He has shown an extraordinary level of maturity in the way he has handled the situation.*
extreme EG *the wretched conditions of people living in extreme poverty*
great EG *He did not live to a great age.*

hill NOUN

Types of hill:
brae (*Scottish*)
down
dune
elevation
fell
foothill
height
hillock
hummock
knoll
kopje (*South African*)
mound
prominence
tor

hinder VERB
to get in the way of someone or something
EG *A thigh injury hindered her mobility.*
block EG *The President is blocking the release of the two men.*
check EG *We have managed to check the spread of terrorism.*
delay EG *Various problems have delayed producton.*
frustrate EG *They have frustrated his efforts to gain a work permit.*
hamper EG *I was hampered by a lack of information.*
impede EG *Fallen rocks are impeding the progress of rescue workers.*

WORD POWER
Synonyms
encumber
stymie

❶ hint NOUN
an indirect suggestion
EG *He gave a strong hint that there would be a referendum sooner rather than later.*
clue EG *How a man shaves may be a telling clue to his age.*
indication EG *He gave no indication that he was ready to compromise.*
intimation EG *I did not have any intimation that he was going to resign.*
suggestion EG *We reject any suggestion that the law needs amending.*

❷ hint NOUN
a helpful piece of advice
EG *I hope to get some fashion hints.*
advice EG *Don't be afraid to ask for advice.*
pointer EG *Here are a few pointers to help you make your choice.*
suggestion EG *Can I give you a few suggestions?*
tip EG *tips for busy managers*

❸ hint VERB
to suggest something indirectly
EG *Criticism is hinted at but never made explicit.*
imply EG *The report implied that his death was inevitable.*
indicate EG *She has indicated that she may resign.*
insinuate EG *an article which insinuated that he was lying*
intimate EG *He intimated that he was contemplating a shake-up of the company.*
suggest EG *Are you suggesting that I need to lose some weight?*

❶ hire VERB
to pay money to use something
EG *She hired the car for three days.*
charter EG *They chartered a jet to fly her home.*
lease EG *He went to Toronto, where he leased an apartment.*
rent EG *She rents a house with three other girls.*

❷ hire VERB
to employ the services of someone
EG *The staff have been hired on short-term contracts.*
appoint EG *The Prime Minister has appointed a civilian as defence minister.*
commission EG *You can commission her to paint something*

229

especially for you.

employ EG *They employed me as a nanny.*

engage EG *We engaged the services of a recognized engineer.*

sign up EG *He persuaded the company to sign her up.*

❶ hit VERB
to strike someone or something forcefully
EG *Both men had been hit with baseball bats.*

bang EG *He banged the table with his shoe.*

beat EG *The rain was beating on the windowpanes.*

knock EG *She knocked on the door.*

slap EG *I slapped him hard across the face.*

smack EG *She smacked me on the side of the head.*

thump EG *I wanted to thump him.*

❷ hit VERB
to collide with something
EG *The car had apparently hit a traffic sign.*

bang into EG *She fell after another skier banged into her.*

bump EG *The boat bumped against something.*

collide with EG *He almost collided with Daisy.*

meet head-on EG *Their cars met head-on down a narrow alleyway.*

run into EG *The mail train ran into a derailed goods train at 75mph.*

smash into EG *The car plunged down a cliff and smashed into a tree.*

❸ hit NOUN
the action of hitting something
EG *Give it a good hard hit with the hammer.*

blow EG *He went to hospital after a blow to the face.*

knock EG *a painful knock on the knee*

rap EG *There was a rap on the door.*

slap EG *She reached forward and gave him a slap.*

smack EG *a smack with a ruler*

stroke EG *six strokes of the cane*

❶ hoard VERB
to store for future use
EG *People have begun to hoard food and petrol.*

save EG *Save some fuel in case of emergencies.*

stockpile EG *People are stockpiling food for the coming winter.*

store EG *It's perfect for storing eggs or vegetables.*

❷ hoard NOUN
a store of things
EG *a hoard of silver and jewels*

cache EG *a cache of weapons and explosives*

fund EG *a scholarship fund for engineering students*

reserve EG *the world's oil reserves*

stockpile EG *stockpiles of nuclear warheads*

store EG *I have a store of food and water here.*

supply EG *food supplies*

hoarse ADJECTIVE
rough and unclear
EG *Nick's voice was hoarse with screaming.*

croaky EG *He sounds a bit croaky today.*

gruff EG *his gruff Scottish growl*

husky EG *Her deep husky voice was her trademark.*

rasping EG *Both men sang in a deep rasping tone.*

> **WORD POWER**
> Antonym
> clear

hobby NOUN
an enjoyable activity pursued in your spare time
EG *My hobbies are music and photography.*

diversion EG *Finger painting is very messy but an excellent* diversion.

leisure activity EG *America's top leisure activity is watching television.*

leisure pursuit EG *His main leisure pursuit is hill walking.*

pastime EG *His favourite pastime is golf.*

❶ hold VERB

to carry or support something
EG *Hold the baby while I load the car.*

carry EG *He was carrying a briefcase.*

clasp EG *She clasped the children to her.*

clutch EG *He was clutching a photograph.*

embrace EG *The couple in the corridor were embracing each other.*

grasp EG *He grasped both my hands.*

grip EG *They gripped the rope tightly.*

❷ hold NOUN

power or control over someone or something
EG *The party has a considerable hold over its own leader.*

control EG *He will have to give up his control of the company.*

dominance EG *the gang's dominance of the London underworld*

sway EG *ideas that held sway for centuries*

❸ hold NOUN

the act or a way of holding something
EG *He grabbed the rope and got a hold on it.*

grasp EG *His hand was taken in a warm, firm grasp.*

grip EG *His strong hand eased the bag from her grip.*

❶ hole NOUN

an opening or hollow in something
EG *The builders had cut holes into the stone.*

gap EG *The wind was tearing through gaps in the window frames.*

hollow EG *Water gathers in a hollow and forms a pond.*

opening EG *He squeezed through a narrow opening in the fence.*

pit EG *He lost his footing and began to slide into his pit.*

split EG *The seat has a few small splits around the corners.*

tear EG *I peered through a tear in the van's curtains.*

❷ hole NOUN

a weakness in a theory or argument
EG *There are some holes in that theory.*

defect EG *A defect in the aircraft caused the crash.*

error EG *NASA discovered a mathematical error in its calculations.*

fault EG *There is a fault in the computer program.*

flaw EG *Almost all of these studies have serious flaws.*

loophole EG *They exploited a loophole in the law to avoid prosecution.*

❸ hole NOUN; INFORMAL

a difficult situation
EG *He admitted that the government was in a hole.*

fix INFORMAL EG *This will put homeowners in a fix.*

hot water INFORMAL EG *They have already been in hot water over high prices this year.*

mess EG *the many reasons why the economy is in such a mess*

predicament EG *the once great club's current predicament*

tight spot EG *This was one tight spot he couldn't get out of.*

holiday NOUN

break
EG *They are currently taking a short break in Spain.*

leave EG *Why don't you take a few days' leave?*

recess EG *Parliament returns today after its summer recess.*

time off EG *He took time off to go sailing with wife.*

vacation EG *We went on vacation to Puerto Rico.*

❶ holy ADJECTIVE
relating to God or a particular religion
EG *All Christian holy places were closed for a day in protest.*

blessed EG *Blessed are the peacemakers, for they shall be called the children of God.*

consecrated EG *the consecrated bread from the Eucharist*

hallowed EG *hallowed ground*

sacred EG *sacred music*

sacrosanct EG *For him the Sabbath was sacrosanct.*

venerated EG *Jerusalem is Christianity's most venerated place.*

❷ holy ADJECTIVE
religious and leading a good life
EG *In the East, holy men have always had long hair.*

devout EG *She is a devout Catholic.*

pious EG *He was brought up by pious female relatives.*

religious EG *They are both very religious.*

saintly EG *his saintly mother*

virtuous EG *a virtuous family man*

> **WORD POWER**
> Synonyms
> god-fearing
> godly
> Antonym
> wicked

❶ home NOUN
the building in which someone lives
EG *They stayed at home and watched TV.*

abode EG *a luxurious abode*

dwelling EG *One thousand new dwellings are planned for the area.*

house EG *our new house*

residence EG *the Royal Family's private residence*

❷ home ADJECTIVE
involving your own country
EG *the home news pages of this newspaper*

domestic EG *over 100 domestic flights a day to 15 UK destinations*

internal EG *The government stepped up internal security.*

national EG *major national and international issues*

native EG *He was glad to be back on his native soil.*

> **WORD POWER**
> Antonym
> foreign

homely ADJECTIVE
simple, ordinary and comfortable
EG *The room was small and homely.*

comfortable EG *A home should be warm and comfortable.*

cosy EG *Guests can relax in the cosy bar.*

modest EG *the modest home of a family who lived off the land*

simple EG *They celebrated mass in a simple chapel.*

welcoming EG *The restaurant is small and very welcoming.*

> **WORD POWER**
> Antonym
> grand

honest ADJECTIVE
truthful and trustworthy
EG *He is a very honest, decent man.*

law-abiding EG *law-abiding citizens*

reputable EG *a reputable car dealer*

trustworthy EG *He is a trustworthy and level-headed leader.*

truthful EG *She could not give him a truthful answer.*

virtuous EG *a virtuous family man*

❶ honour NOUN
personal integrity
EG *I can no longer serve with honour in your government.*
decency EG *No-one had the decency to tell me to my face.*
goodness EG *He retains a faith in human goodness.*
honesty EG *His reputation for honesty and integrity is second to none.*
integrity EG *He was praised for his fairness and high integrity.*

❷ honour NOUN
an award or mark of respect
EG *He was showered with honours - among them an Oscar.*
accolade EG *the ultimate international accolade, the Nobel Peace prize*
commendation EG *The officer received a commendation for brave conduct.*
homage EG *films that pay homage to our literary heritage*
praise EG *He had won consistently high praise for his theatre work.*
recognition EG *At last, her father's work has received popular recognition.*
tribute EG *He paid tribute to the organizing committee.*

❸ honour VERB
to give someone special praise
EG *He was honoured by the French government with the Legion d'Honneur.*
commemorate EG *a plaque commemorating the servicemen who died*
commend EG *I commended her for that action.*
decorate EG *He was decorated for his gallantry by the General.*
glorify EG *My philosophy of life is to glorify God in all I do.*
praise EG *He praised their excellent work.*

hooligan NOUN
a destructive and violent young person
EG *English football hooligans*
delinquent EG *a nine-year-old delinquent*
hoon AUSTRALIAN AND NEW ZEALAND INFORMAL EG *the rocks hurled by hoons*
lout EG *He was attacked by stone-throwing louts.*
tough EG *Residents may be too terrified of local toughs to protest.*
vandal EG *The Scout hut was burnt down by vandals.*
yob BRITISH AND AUSTRALIAN SLANG EG *drunken yobs chanting football songs*

hope NOUN
a wish or feeling of desire and expectation
EG *There was little hope of recovery.*
ambition EG *His ambition is to sail around the world.*
dream EG *his dream of becoming a pilot*
expectation EG *The hotel was being renovated in expectation of a tourist boom.*

❶ hopeless ADJECTIVE
certain to fail or be unsuccessful
EG *Our situation is hopeless.*
forlorn EG *the forlorn hope of finding a better life*
futile EG *their futile attempts to avoid publicity*
impossible EG *The tax is impossible to administer.*
pointless EG *a pointless exercise*

that would only waste more time
useless EG *She knew it was useless to protest.*
vain EG *a vain attempt to sign a goalkeeper*

❷ hopeless ADJECTIVE
bad or inadequate
EG *I don't drive and the buses are hopeless.*
inadequate EG *The problem lies with inadequate staffing.*
pathetic EG *the pathetic state of the rail network*
poor EG *The flat was in a poor state of repair.*
useless INFORMAL EG *My husband is useless around the house.*

❶ horrible ADJECTIVE
disagreeable or unpleasant
EG *a horrible little boy*
awful EG *I had an awful time.*
disagreeable EG *a disagreeable odour*
horrid EG *My parents are horrid to each other.*
mean EG *Why are you always so mean to me?*
nasty EG *This divorce could turn nasty.*
unpleasant EG *He's a very unpleasant little man.*

❷ horrible ADJECTIVE
causing shock, fear, or disgust
EG *horrible crimes*
appalling EG *They have been living under the most appalling conditions.*
dreadful EG *She told me the dreadful news.*
grim EG *a grim discovery*
gruesome EG *gruesome murders*
terrifying EG *a terrifying experience*

horrify VERB
to cause to feel horror or shock
EG *a crime trend that will horrify parents*
appal EG *I was appalled by her behaviour.*

disgust EG *He disgusted everyone with his boorish behaviour.*
dismay EG *He was deeply dismayed by the decision.*
outrage EG *Human rights campaigners were outraged by the execution.*
shock EG *Pictures of emaciated prisoners shocked the world.*
sicken EG *What he saw at the accident sickened him.*

❶ horror NOUN
a strong feeling of alarm or disgust
EG *He gazed in horror at the knife.*
alarm EG *She sat up in alarm.*
dread EG *She thought with dread of the cold winter to come.*
fear EG *I stood there crying and shaking with fear.*
fright EG *He uttered a shriek and jumped with fright.*
panic EG *He felt a sudden rush of panic at the thought.*
terror EG *She shook with terror.*

❷ horror NOUN
a strong fear of something
EG *his horror of death*
abhorrence EG *their abhorrence of racism*
aversion EG *Many people have a natural aversion to insects.*
disgust EG *I threw the book aside in disgust.*
hatred EG *My hatred for him is intense.*
loathing EG *She looked at him with loathing.*
revulsion EG *They expressed their revulsion at his violent death.*

WORD POWER
Synonyms
abomination
odium
repugnance

horse NOUN
an animal kept for riding
EG *a fall from a horse*

brumby AUSTRALIAN AND NEW ZEALAND EG *There's a mob of about 30 brumbies up there.*

equine EG *the history and uses of equines*

moke AUSTRALIAN AND NEW ZEALAND SLANG EG *a tired old moke*

nag INFORMAL EG *He unhitched his sorry-looking nag from a nearby post.*

pony EG *Peter trotted about on the fat pony he had been given.*

> **WORD POWER**
> Synonyms
> mount
> steed

hostile ADJECTIVE
unfriendly, aggressive, and unpleasant
EG *The Governor faced hostile crowds.*

antagonistic EG *They were nearly all antagonistic to the idea.*

belligerent EG *a belligerent war of words between India and Pakistan*

malevolent EG *He fixed our photographer with a malevolent stare.*

unkind EG *All last summer he'd been unkind to her.*

> **WORD POWER**
> Antonym
> friendly

hostility NOUN
aggressive or unfriendly behaviour towards someone or something
EG *hostility to Black and ethnic groups*

animosity EG *The animosity between the two men grew.*

antagonism EG *a history of antagonism between the two sides*

hatred EG *her lifelong hatred of authority*

ill will EG *He didn't bear anyone any ill will.*

malice EG *There was no malice in her voice.*

resentment EG *There is growing resentment against newcomers.*

> **WORD POWER**
> Synonyms
> animus
> detestation
> enmity
> Antonym
> friendship

❶ hot ADJECTIVE
having a high temperature
EG *a hot climate*

boiling EG *It's boiling in here.*

heated EG *a heated swimming pool*

scalding EG *Her son was burned by scalding tea.*

scorching EG *It was a scorching hot day.*

warm EG *a warm, dry summer*

> **WORD POWER**
> Antonym
> cold

❷ hot ADJECTIVE
very spicy
EG *a hot, aromatic Thai red curry*

peppery EG *a rich, peppery extra virgin olive oil*

spicy EG *a spicy Cajun sauce*

> **WORD POWER**
> Antonym
> bland

house NOUN
a building where a person or family lives
EG *They live in a large house with eight rooms.*

abode EG *I went round the streets and found his new abode.*

building EG *Their flat was on the first floor of the building.*

dwelling EG *One thousand new dwellings are planned for the area.*

home EG *One in four people are without adequate homes.*

residence EG *the Royal Family's private residence*

❶ hug VERB
to hold someone close to you
EG *Lynn and I hugged each other.*
clasp EG *She clasped the children to her.*
cuddle EG *They used to kiss and cuddle in front of everyone.*
embrace EG *The couple in the corridor were embracing each other.*
squeeze EG *He kissed her on the cheek and squeezed her tight.*

❷ hug NOUN
the act of holding someone close to you
EG *She gave him a hug.*
clinch SLANG EG *They were caught in a clinch when her parents returned home.*
embrace EG *a young couple locked in an embrace*

huge ADJECTIVE
extremely large in amount, size, or degree
EG *a huge crowd*
colossal EG *a colossal waste of money*
enormous EG *The main bedroom is enormous.*
giant EG *a giant statue*
immense EG *He wielded immense power.*
massive EG *a massive surge in popularity*
vast EG *this vast area of northern Canada*

> **WORD POWER**
> Synonyms
> gargantuan
> prodigious
> Antonym
> tiny

❶ humble ADJECTIVE
not vain or boastful
EG *He gave a great performance, but he was very humble.*
meek EG *He was a meek, mild-mannered fellow.*
modest EG *He's modest, as well as*

being a great player.
unassuming EG *She has a gentle, unassuming manner.*

> **WORD POWER**
> Antonym
> haughty

❷ humble ADJECTIVE
ordinary or unimportant
EG *A splash of wine will transform a humble casserole.*
lowly EG *He was irked by his lowly status.*
modest EG *his modest beginnings*
ordinary EG *It was just an ordinary weekend.*
simple EG *a simple dinner of rice and beans*

❸ humble VERB
to make someone feel humiliated
EG *the little car company that humbled the industry giants*
disgrace EG *I have disgraced the family's name.*
humiliate EG *His teacher continually humiliates him in maths lessons.*

humid ADJECTIVE
damp and hot
EG *a hot, humid Italian summer*
clammy EG *My shirt was clammy with sweat.*
muggy EG *The weather was muggy and overcast.*
steamy EG *The air was hot and steamy from the heat of a hundred bodies.*
sticky EG *four hot, sticky days in the middle of August*

humiliate VERB
to hurt someone's pride
EG *He enjoyed humiliating me.*
disgrace EG *I have disgraced my family.*
embarrass EG *It embarrassed him that he had no idea of what was going on.*
humble EG *The champion was*

humbled by the unseeded qualifier.
put down EG *I know that I do put people down occasionally.*
shame EG *Her son's affair had shamed her.*

❶ humour NOUN
something which is thought to be funny
EG *The film's humour contains a serious message.*
comedy EG *his career in comedy*
wit EG *She was known for her biting wit.*

> **WORD POWER**
> Synonyms
> drollery
> jocularity

❷ humour NOUN
the mood someone is in
EG *He hasn't been in a good humour lately.*
frame of mind EG *Clearly, she was not in the right frame of mind to continue.*
mood EG *Lily was in one of her aggressive moods.*
spirits EG *He was in very low spirits.*
temper EG *Lee stormed off the field in a furious temper.*

❸ humour VERB
to please someone so that they will not become upset
EG *I nodded, partly to humour him.*
flatter EG *I knew she was just flattering me.*
indulge EG *He did not agree with indulging children.*
mollify EG *The investigation was undertaken primarily to mollify pressure groups.*
pander to EG *politicians who pander to big business*

hungry ADJECTIVE
wanting to eat
EG *I didn't have any lunch, so I'm really hungry.*
famished EG *Isn't dinner ready?*

I'm famished.
ravenous EG *a pack of ravenous animals*
starving EG *starving refugees*

❶ hurry VERB
to move or do something as quickly as possible
EG *She hurried through the empty streets.*
dash EG *He dashed upstairs.*
fly EG *I must fly or I'll miss my train.*
get a move on INFORMAL EG *Get a move on because my car's on a double yellow line.*
rush EG *I've got to rush. I've got a meeting in a few minutes.*
scurry EG *Reporters scurried to find telephones.*

❷ hurry VERB
to make something happen more quickly
EG *his attempt to hurry the process of independence*
accelerate EG *They must now accelerate the development of their new car.*
hasten EG *This will hasten the closure of small pubs.*
quicken EG *He quickened his pace a little.*
speed up EG *an effort to speed up the negotiations*

> **WORD POWER**
> Antonym
> slow down

❶ hurt VERB
to cause someone to feel pain
EG *I didn't mean to hurt her.*
harm EG *The hijackers seemed anxious not to harm anyone.*
injure EG *motorists who kill, maim, and injure*
wound EG *The bomb killed six people and wounded another five.*

❷ hurt VERB
to upset someone or something
EG *What you said really hurt me.*

A B C D E F G H I J K L M N O P Q R S T U V W X Y Z

distress EG *I did not want to frighten or distress the horse.*
sadden EG *He is saddened that they did not win anything.*
upset EG *I'm sorry if I've upset you.*
wound EG *My relatives have wounded me in the past.*

❸ **hurt** ADJECTIVE
upset or offended
EG *He felt hurt by all the lies.*
aggrieved EG *He is still aggrieved at the size of the fine.*
offended EG *He was offended at being left out.*
upset EG *I'm upset by your attitude.*
wounded EG *I think she feels desperately wounded and unloved.*

> **WORD POWER**
> Synonyms
> piqued
> rueful

hygiene NOUN
the principles and practice of health and cleanliness
EG *Be extra careful about personal hygiene.*
cleanliness EG *Many of the beaches fail to meet minimum standards of cleanliness.*
sanitation EG *the hazards of contaminated water and poor sanitation*

hypnotize VERB

to put someone into a state in which they seem to be asleep but can respond to suggestions
EG *She will hypnotize you and will stop you from smoking.*
put in a trance EG *A stage hypnotist put her in a trance.*
put to sleep EG *First the hypnotist will put you to sleep.*

> **WORD POWER**
> Synonyms
> entrance
> mesmerize

❶ **hysterical** ADJECTIVE
in a state of uncontrolled excitement or panic
EG *Calm down. Don't get hysterical.*
frantic EG *A bird had been locked in and was by now quite frantic.*
frenzied EG *her frenzied attempts to get free*
overwrought EG *One overwrought man had to be restrained by friends.*
raving EG *He looked at her as if she were a raving lunatic.*

❷ **hysterical** ADJECTIVE INFORMAL
extremely funny
EG *His stand-up routine was hysterical.*
comical EG *Her expression is almost comical.*
hilarious EG *He had a fund of hilarious jokes on the subject.*

❶ idea NOUN

a plan or suggestion for something

EG *She said she'd had a brilliant idea.*

plan EG *I have a cunning plan.*

recommendation EG *a range of recommendations for change*

scheme EG *a proposed scheme*

solution EG *He came up with a solution to the problem.*

suggestion EG *Do you have a better suggestion?*

> **WORD POWER**
> Synonyms
> hypothesis
> theory

❷ idea NOUN

an opinion or belief about something

EG *old-fashioned ideas about women*

belief EG *my religious beliefs*

conviction EG *a firm conviction that things have improved*

impression EG *your first impressions of college*

notion EG *I have a notion of what he is like.*

opinion EG *a favourable opinion of our neighbours*

view EG *Make your views known to local politicians.*

❸ idea NOUN

what you know about something

EG *They had no idea where they were.*

clue EG *I don't have a clue what you mean.*

guess EG *My guess is he went east.*

hint EG *He gave no hint about where he was.*

inkling EG *We had an inkling that something was happening.*

notion EG *I have a notion how it is done.*

suspicion EG *I have a strong suspicion they are lying.*

❶ ideal NOUN

a principle or idea you try to achieve

EG *I don't live up to my ideal of myself.*

principle EG *acts that go against your principles*

standard EG *My father has high moral standards.*

value EG *the values of liberty and equality*

❷ ideal NOUN

the best example of something

EG *She remains his feminine ideal.*

epitome EG *The hotel was the epitome of luxury.*

example EG *He was held up as an example of courage.*

model EG *a model of good manners*

paragon EG *You are not a paragon of virtue.*

prototype EG *He was the prototype of a strong leader.*

standard EG *the standard by which we are compared*

> **WORD POWER**
> Synonyms
> archetype
> criterion
> paradigm

❸ ideal ADJECTIVE

being the best example of something

EG *the ideal person for the job*

classic EG *a classic example of hypocrisy*

complete EG *She is the complete athlete.*

consummate EG *a consummate politician*

model EG *She is a model pupil.*

perfect EG *He is the perfect husband for her.*

supreme EG *a supreme method of cooking vegetables*

❶ identify VERB
to recognize or name someone or something
EG *I tried to identify her perfume.*

diagnose EG *This illness is easily diagnosed.*

label EG *Poisonous substances should be labelled as such.*

name EG *The victims of the fire have been named.*

pinpoint EG *They could not pinpoint the cause of death.*

place EG *The man was familiar, but I couldn't place him.*

recognize EG *a man I recognized as Luke's father*

❷ identify
identify with VERB
to understand someone's feelings
EG *I can't identify with the characters.*

associate with EG *I associate myself with the green movement.*

empathize with EG *I empathize with the people who live here.*

feel for EG *I pitied and felt for him.*

relate to EG *We have difficulty relating to each other.*

respond to EG *She responded to his pain.*

idiot NOUN
a stupid person
EG *You're an idiot!*

fool EG *He'd been a fool to get involved.*

galah AUSTRALIAN INFORMAL EG *sounding like an illiterate galah*

imbecile EG *I don't want to deal with these imbeciles.*

moron EG *I think that Gordon is a moron.*

oaf EG *You clumsy oaf!*

twit INFORMAL EG *I feel such a twit.*

idiotic ADJECTIVE
extremely foolish or silly
EG *an idiotic thing to do*

crazy EG *You were crazy to leave then.*

daft INFORMAL EG *He's not so daft as to listen to them.*

dumb INFORMAL EG *I've met a lot of dumb people.*

foolish EG *It is foolish to risk injury.*

senseless EG *acts of senseless violence*

stupid EG *stupid ideas*

WORD POWER
Synonyms
foolhardy
insane
moronic

idle ADJECTIVE
doing nothing
EG *a popular occupation for idle, wealthy young women*

jobless EG *One in four people are now jobless.*

redundant EG *redundant workers*

unemployed EG *jobs for the unemployed*

WORD POWER
Synonyms
inactive
stationary
Antonym
busy

❶ ignorant ADJECTIVE
not knowing about something
EG *He was completely ignorant of the rules.*

inexperienced EG *I am inexperienced at decorating.*

innocent EG *He is innocent about the harm he is doing.*

oblivious EG *John appeared oblivious to his surroundings.*

unaware EG *She was unaware that she was being filmed.*

unconscious EG *He was unconscious of his failure.*

❷ ignorant ADJECTIVE
not knowledgeable about things
EG *People are afraid to appear ignorant.*

green EG *The new boy is very green and immature.*
naive EG *a shy, naive man*
unaware EG *Young children are fairly unaware.*

> **WORD POWER**
> Synonyms
> uneducated
> unlearned
> untutored

ignore VERB
to take no notice of someone or something
EG *Her husband ignored her.*
blank SLANG EG *The crowd blanked her for the first four numbers.*
discount EG *They simply discounted his feelings.*
disregard EG *He disregarded his father's advice.*
neglect EG *They never neglect their duties.*
overlook EG *a fact that we all tend to overlook*

ill ADJECTIVE
unhealthy or sick
EG *Payne was seriously ill with pneumonia.*
ailing EG *The President is said to be ailing.*
poorly BRITISH INFORMAL EG *Julie is still poorly.*
queasy EG *I feel queasy on boats.*
sick EG *He's very sick and he needs treatment.*
unhealthy EG *an unhealthy-looking fellow*
unwell EG *She felt unwell back at the office.*

> **WORD POWER**
> Synonyms
> indisposed
> infirm
> under the weather
> Antonym
> healthy

illegal ADJECTIVE
forbidden by the law

EG *an illegal organization*
banned EG *banned substances*
criminal EG *a criminal offence*
illicit EG *illicit drugs*
outlawed EG *a place where hunting is outlawed*
prohibited EG *a country where alcohol is prohibited*
unlawful EG *unlawful acts*

> **WORD POWER**
> Synonyms
> proscribed
> unauthorized
> wrongful
> Antonym
> legal

illness NOUN
a particular disease
EG *a mystery illness*
affliction EG *a severe mental affliction*
ailment EG *common ailments*
complaint EG *a skin complaint*
disease EG *He has been cured of the disease.*
disorder EG *a rare nervous disorder*
lurgy BRITISH, AUSTRALIAN, AND NEW ZEALAND INFORMAL EG *It's only a matter of days before Joan gets the lurgy as well.*
sickness EG *radiation sickness*

❶ illusion NOUN
a thing that you think you can see
EG *Painters create the illusion of space.*
hallucination EG *Perhaps the footprint was a hallucination.*
mirage EG *I began to see mirages.*
semblance EG *A semblance of normality has been restored.*

> **WORD POWER**
> Synonyms
> chimera
> phantasm

❷ illusion NOUN
a false belief
EG *Their hopes proved to be an*

A
B
C
D
E
F
G
H
I
J
K
L
M
N
O
P
Q
R
S
T
U
V
W
X
Y
Z

imaginary – immediate

illusion.

delusion EG *I was under the delusion that I could win.*

fallacy EG *It's a fallacy that the rich are generous.*

fancy EG *childhood fancies*

misconception EG *There are many misconceptions about school.*

imaginary ADJECTIVE
existing in your mind but not in real life
EG *an imaginary friend*

fictional EG *a fictional character*

fictitious EG *a fictitious illness*

hypothetical EG *a hypothetical situation*

ideal EG *in an ideal world*

illusory EG *Freedom is illusory.*

invented EG *distorted or invented stories*

mythological EG *mythological creatures*

> **WORD POWER**
> Antonym
> real

imagination NOUN
the ability to form new ideas
EG *a girl who lacks imagination*

creativity EG *She paints with great creativity.*

ingenuity EG *the ingenuity of engineers*

inventiveness EG *the artistic inventiveness of Mozart*

originality EG *a composer of great originality*

vision EG *a leader with vision*

❶ imagine VERB
to have an idea of something
EG *He could not imagine a more peaceful scene.*

conceive EG *I can't even conceive that much money.*

envisage EG *I envisage them staying together.*

fantasize EG *I fantasized about writing music.*

picture EG *I tried to picture the*

place.

visualize EG *He could not visualize her as old.*

❷ imagine VERB
to believe that something is the case
EG *I imagine you're talking about my brother.*

assume EG *Don't assume we are similar.*

believe EG *I believe you have my pen.*

gather EG *I gather that his mother was Scottish.*

guess INFORMAL EG *I guess he's right.*

suppose EG *He supposed I would be back at school.*

suspect EG *Susan suspected that things would get worse.*

> **WORD POWER**
> Synonyms
> fancy
> surmise

imitate VERB
to copy someone or something
EG *She imitated her parents.*

ape EG *She is aping her sister's style.*

copy EG *I used to copy everything my big brother did.*

emulate EG *Sons are expected to emulate their fathers.*

impersonate EG *He could impersonate all the other students.*

mimic EG *He mimicked her accent.*

simulate EG *a machine which simulates natural sounds*

> **WORD POWER**
> Synonyms
> mirror
> mock
> parody

❶ immediate ADJECTIVE
happening or done without delay
EG *My immediate reaction was fear.*

instant EG *He took an instant dislike to Mark.*

instantaneous EG *The applause*

242

was instantaneous.

❷ immediate ADJECTIVE
most closely connected to you
EG *my immediate family*
close EG *I have a few close friends.*
direct EG *your direct descendants*
near EG *near relatives*

❶ immediately ADVERB
right away
EG *Ingrid answered Peter's letter immediately.*
at once EG *You must come at once.*
directly EG *He will be there directly.*
instantly EG *She'd been knocked down in the street and died almost instantly.*
now EG *Get out, now!*
promptly EG *The telephone was answered promptly.*
right away EG *You'd better tell them right away.*
straightaway EG *I'd like to see you straightaway.*

❷ immediately ADVERB
very near in time or position
EG *immediately behind the house*
closely EG *He rushed out, closely followed by Kemp.*
directly EG *James stopped directly under the window.*
right EG *He stood right behind me.*

imminent ADJECTIVE
going to happen very soon
EG *my sister's imminent arrival*
close EG *My birthday is quite close.*
coming EG *the coming dawn*
forthcoming EG *their forthcoming marriage*
impending EG *impending doom*
looming EG *My exams are looming.*
near EG *in the near future*

immune ADJECTIVE
not subject to or affected by

something
EG *He seems immune to pressure.*
exempt EG *She is exempt from blame.*
free EG *He was not completely free of guilt.*
protected EG *He is protected from the law.*
resistant EG *crops that are resistant to disease*
safe EG *I was safe from punishment.*
unaffected EG *She is unaffected by the sight of blood.*

❶ impatient ADJECTIVE
easily annoyed
EG *You are too impatient with others.*
brusque EG *a brusque manner*
curt EG *He had spoken in a very curt tone of voice.*
irritable EG *Brian was nervous and irritable with her.*

❷ impatient ADJECTIVE
eager to do something
EG *He was impatient to leave.*
eager EG *Children are eager to learn.*
restless EG *The kids were bored and restless.*

imperfect ADJECTIVE
having faults or problems
EG *We live in an imperfect world.*
broken EG *broken toys*
damaged EG *damaged goods*
defective EG *defective eyesight*
faulty EG *a car with faulty brakes*
flawed EG *a flawed character*

A B C D E F G H I J K L M N O P Q R S T U V W X Y Z

243

A B C D E F G H I J K L M N O P Q R S T U V W X Y Z

WORD POWER
Synonyms
deficient
impaired
Antonym
perfect

impersonal ADJECTIVE
not concerned with people and their feelings
EG *I found him strangely distant and impersonal.*
aloof EG *His manner was aloof.*
cold EG *Sharon was very cold with me.*
detached EG *He felt emotionally detached from the victims.*
formal EG *Business relationships are usually formal.*
neutral EG *He told me the news in a neutral manner.*
remote EG *She was beautiful but remote.*

WORD POWER
Synonyms
bureaucratic
businesslike
dispassionate

❶ **important** ADJECTIVE
necessary or significant
EG *Her sons are the most important thing to her.*
momentous EG *the momentous decision to go to war*
serious EG *a serious matter*
significant EG *a significant discovery*
weighty EG *We discussed weighty matters.*

WORD POWER
Synonyms
salient
seminal
Antonym
unimportant

❷ **important** ADJECTIVE
having great influence or power
EG *the most important person in the country*

eminent EG *an eminent scientist*
foremost EG *a foremost expert in American history*
influential EG *one of the most influential books ever written*
leading EG *a leading nation in world politics*
notable EG *notable celebrities*
powerful EG *large, powerful countries*

WORD POWER
Synonyms
pre-eminent
prominent

❶ **impose** VERB
to force something on someone
EG *Fines were imposed on the culprits.*
dictate EG *The policy is dictated from the top.*
enforce EG *It is a difficult law to enforce.*
inflict EG *Inflicting punishment to stop crime is not the answer.*
levy EG *a tax levied on imported goods*
ordain EG *the task of trying to ordain parliamentary behaviour*

❷ **impose**
impose on VERB
to take advantage of someone
EG *I should stop imposing on your hospitality.*
abuse EG *They abused my hospitality by eating everything.*
take advantage of EG *He took advantage of her generosity.*
use EG *She's just using you.*

impossible ADJECTIVE
unable to happen or be believed
EG *You shouldn't promise impossible things.*
absurd EG *absurd claims to have met big stars*
hopeless EG *a hopeless task*
inconceivable EG *It's inconceivable that people can still be living in those conditions.*

ludicrous EG *his ludicrous plan to build a house*
out of the question EG *Is a pay increase out of the question?*
unthinkable EG *The idea of splitting up is unthinkable.*

> **WORD POWER**
> Synonyms
> outrageous
> unattainable
> unworkable
> Antonym
> possible

❶ **impression** NOUN
the way someone or something seems to you
EG *your first impressions of college*
feeling EG *the feeling that she was wasting her life*
hunch EG *Was your hunch right or wrong?*
idea EG *I had my own ideas about what had happened.*
notion EG *I have a notion of what he is like.*
sense EG *She has the sense that she was in trouble.*

❷ **impression**
make an impression VERB
to have a strong effect on people
EG *He certainly made an impression on his teachers.*
cause a stir EG *News of her death caused a stir.*
influence EG *You can't do anything to influence him.*
make an impact EG *Events can make an impact on our lives.*

impressionable ADJECTIVE
easy to influence
EG *impressionable teenagers*
gullible EG *I'm so gullible I'd have believed him.*
open EG *an open, trusting nature*
receptive EG *moulding their young, receptive minds*
sensitive EG *Ouija boards can be dangerous, especially to sensitive*

people.
susceptible EG *Children can be susceptible to advertisements.*
vulnerable EG *vulnerable old people*

> **WORD POWER**
> Synonyms
> ingenuous
> suggestible

impressive ADJECTIVE
tending to impress
EG *an impressive achievement*
awesome EG *awesome mountains, deserts and lakes*
exciting EG *He tells the most exciting stories.*
grand EG *a grand old building*
powerful EG *a powerful image*
stirring EG *stirring music*
striking EG *her striking personality*

> **WORD POWER**
> Synonyms
> dramatic
> moving

imprison VERB
to lock someone up
EG *He was imprisoned for murder.*
confine EG *Keep your dog confined to the house.*
detain EG *They'll be detained and charged.*
incarcerate EG *Prisoners were incarcerated in terrible conditions.*
jail EG *An innocent man was jailed.*
lock up EG *You people should be locked up!*
send to prison EG *The judge sent him to prison for life.*

> **WORD POWER**
> Synonyms
> constrain
> immure
> intern
> Antonym
> free

improbable ADJECTIVE
unlikely or unbelievable

245

A B C D E F G H I J K L M N O P Q R S T U V W X Y Z

EG *improbable stories*

doubtful EG *It was doubtful if they would arrive on time.*

dubious EG *dubious evidence*

far-fetched EG *This all sounds a bit far-fetched.*

implausible EG *a film with an implausible ending*

unbelievable EG *an unbelievable storyline*

unlikely EG *It is unlikely that he is alive.*

> **WORD POWER**
> Antonym
> probable

improve VERB
to get or make better
EG *He improved their house.*

advance EG *Medical technology has advanced.*

better EG *They tried to better their working conditions.*

enhance EG *Good jewellery enhances your outfits.*

look up INFORMAL EG *Things are looking up for me now.*

progress EG *Jack's condition is progressing well.*

upgrade EG *You'll have to upgrade your image.*

> **WORD POWER**
> Synonyms
> ameliorate
> develop
> reform
> Antonym
> worsen

impudence NOUN
disrespectful talk or behaviour towards someone
EG *Have you ever heard such impudence?*

audacity EG *He had the audacity to speak up.*

boldness EG *I was amazed at her boldness towards him.*

cheek INFORMAL EG *I can't believe he had the cheek to complain.*

chutzpah AMERICAN INFORMAL EG *He had the chutzpah to ask us to leave.*

gall EG *the most presumptuous question any interviewer has ever had the gall to ask*

impertinence EG *His words sounded like impertinence.*

insolence EG *I got punished for insolence.*

nerve EG *You've got a nerve coming round here after what you've done.*

inability NOUN
a lack of ability to do something
EG *an inability to concentrate*

impotence EG *a sense of impotence in the situation*

inadequacy EG *my inadequacy as a gardener*

incompetence EG *the incompetence of government officials*

ineptitude EG *political ineptitude*

> **WORD POWER**
> Antonym
> ability

inappropriate NOUN
not suitable for a purpose or occasion
EG *This behaviour is inappropriate.*

improper EG *the improper use of resources*

incongruous EG *an incongruous assortment of clothes*

unfit EG *houses that are unfit for living in*

unseemly EG *He thought crying was unseemly.*

unsuitable EG *food that is unsuitable for children*

untimely EG *their unjustified and untimely interference*

> **WORD POWER**
> Antonym
> appropriate

incentive NOUN
something that encourages you to do something
EG *the incentive to work*

bait EG *He added some bait to*

make the agreement sweeter.
encouragement EG *She didn't get much encouragement to do anything.*
inducement EG *Are gangster films an inducement to crime?*
motivation EG *Money is my motivation.*
stimulus EG *He needed all the stimulus he could get.*

> **WORD POWER**
> Synonyms
> lure
> motive
> spur

incident NOUN
an event
EG *Little incidents can shape our lives.*
circumstance EG *This is a fortunate circumstance.*
episode EG *I'm glad this episode is over.*
event EG *recent events in Europe*
happening EG *the latest happenings in sport*
occasion EG *I remember that occasion fondly.*
occurrence EG *Nancy wondered about the strange occurrence.*

incite VERB
to excite someone into doing something
EG *The campaigners incited a riot.*
agitate for EG *Workers agitated for better conditions.*
goad EG *He tried to goad me into a response.*
instigate EG *The violence was instigated by a few people.*
provoke EG *I provoked him into doing something stupid.*
whip up EG *an attempt to whip up public hostility to the president*

include VERB
to have as a part
EG *A British breakfast always includes sausages.*

contain EG *This sheet contains a list of names.*
cover EG *The books covers many topics.*
embrace EG *a small county embracing two cities*
encompass EG *classes which encompass a wide range of activities*
incorporate EG *The new cars incorporate many improvements.*
involve EG *a high-energy workout which involves nearly every muscle*

> **WORD POWER**
> Antonym
> exclude

income NOUN
the money someone or something earns
EG *families on low incomes*
earnings EG *his earnings as an accountant*
pay EG *We complained about our pay.*
profits EG *The bank made profits of millions of dollars.*
salary EG *The lawyer was paid a good salary.*
takings EG *The shop had huge takings that week.*
wages EG *His wages have gone up.*

> **WORD POWER**
> Synonyms
> proceeds
> receipts
> revenue

incomparable ADJECTIVE
too good to be compared with anything else
EG *an area of incomparable beauty*
inimitable EG *his inimitable style*
peerless LITERARY EG *He gave a peerless performance.*
superlative EG *The hotel has superlative views.*
supreme EG *the supreme piece of writing about the war*
unparalleled EG *unparalleled happiness*

A
B
C
D
E
F
G
H
I
J
K
L
M
N
O
P
Q
R
S
T
U
V
W
X
Y
Z

unrivalled EG *an unrivalled knowledge of music*

> **WORD POWER**
> Synonyms
> matchless
> unequalled

incompetent ADJECTIVE
lacking the ability to do something properly
EG *You are incompetent, and you know it.*

bungling EG *a bungling amateur*
cowboy BRITISH INFORMAL EG *cowboy builders*
incapable EG *an incapable leader*
inept EG *an inept performance*
unable EG *He felt unable to handle the situation.*
useless EG *I felt useless and a failure.*

> **WORD POWER**
> Synonyms
> ineffectual
> inexpert
> unskilful
> Antonym
> competent

incomplete ADJECTIVE
not finished or whole
EG *an incomplete book*

deficient EG *a deficient diet*
half-pie NEW ZEALAND INFORMAL EG *His report was half-pie.*
insufficient EG *insufficient information*
partial EG *The concert was a partial success.*

> **WORD POWER**
> Synonyms
> imperfect
> undeveloped
> unfinished
> Antonym
> complete

❶ increase VERB
to make or become larger in amount

EG *The population continues to increase.*
enlarge EG *They are trying to enlarge their customer base.*
expand EG *We will expand the size of the picture.*
extend EG *She plans to extend her stay.*
grow EG *The sound grew in volume.*
multiply EG *viruses which can multiply rapidly in the human body*
swell EG *His anger swelled within him.*

> **WORD POWER**
> Synonyms
> augment
> escalate
> Antonym
> decrease

❷ increase NOUN
a rise in the amount of something
EG *a pay increase*
gain EG *a gain in speed*
growth EG *the growth of unemployment*
increment EG *tiny increments of movement*
rise EG *a rise in prices*
upsurge EG *an upsurge of interest in books*

> **WORD POWER**
> Antonym
> decrease

❶ incredible ADJECTIVE
totally amazing
EG *a champion with incredible skill*
amazing EG *an amazing success*
astonishing EG *an astonishing piece of good luck*
astounding EG *an astounding discovery*
extraordinary EG *extraordinary beauty*
marvellous EG *a marvellous thing to do*
sensational INFORMAL EG *a sensational performance*

❷ incredible ADJECTIVE
impossible to believe
EG *the incredible stories of some children*
absurd EG *absurd ideas*
far-fetched EG *This all sounds very far-fetched to me.*
improbable EG *highly improbable claims*
unbelievable EG *The film has an unbelievable plot.*
unimaginable EG *unimaginable wealth*
unthinkable EG *It's unthinkable that Tom forgot your birthday.*

> **WORD POWER**
> Synonyms
> implausible
> inconceivable
> preposterous

indecent ADJECTIVE
shocking or rude
EG *indecent lyrics*
crude EG *crude pictures*
dirty EG *dirty jokes*
improper EG *improper behaviour*
lewd EG *lewd comments*
rude EG *a rude gesture*
vulgar EG *vulgar language*

❶ independent ADJECTIVE
separate from other people or things
EG *an independent political party*
autonomous EG *an autonomous country*
free EG *Do we have a free press?*
liberated EG *liberated countries*
separate EG *We live separate lives.*
unrelated EG *two unrelated incidents*

❷ independent ADJECTIVE
not needing other people's help
EG *a fiercely independent woman*
individualistic EG *individualistic behaviour*
liberated EG *a genuinely liberated woman*
self-sufficient EG *I am quite*

self-sufficient.
unaided EG *She raised her children unaided.*

indicate VERB
to show that something is true
EG *a gesture which indicates his relief*
denote EG *Messy writing denotes a messy mind.*
reveal EG *His diary revealed his disturbed state of mind.*
show EG *I would like to show my appreciation.*
signal EG *Ted signalled that everything was all right.*
signify EG *A white flag signifies surrender.*

> **WORD POWER**
> Synonyms
> imply
> manifest
> point to

indirect ADJECTIVE
not done or going directly but by another way
EG *the indirect effects of smoking*
meandering EG *the meandering course of the river*
oblique EG *oblique threats*
rambling EG *In a rambling answer, he denied the charge.*
roundabout EG *a roundabout way of getting information*
tortuous EG *a tortuous path*
wandering EG *a wandering route through the woods*

> **WORD POWER**
> Antonym
> direct

industrious ADJECTIVE
tending to work hard
EG *industrious groups of students*
busy EG *an exceptionally busy man*
conscientious EG *Sherry was slow but conscientious.*
diligent EG *Williams was diligent in the writing of letters.*
hard-working EG *an exceptionally*

A
B
C
D
E
F
G
H
I
J
K
L
M
N
O
P
Q
R
S
T
U
V
W
X
Y
Z

disciplined and hard-working young man
tireless EG *a tireless and willing worker*

> **WORD POWER**
> Antonym
> lazy

inefficient ADJECTIVE
badly organized and slow
EG *an inefficient government*
disorganized EG *My boss is completely disorganized.*
incapable EG *If he fails he will be considered incapable.*
incompetent EG *an incompetent officer*
inept EG *an inept use of power*
sloppy EG *sloppy management*

> **WORD POWER**
> Synonyms
> ineffectual
> inexpert
> slipshod
> Antonym
> efficient

inexperienced ADJECTIVE
lacking experience of a situation or activity
EG *inexperienced drivers*
green INFORMAL EG *He was a young lad, and very green.*
new EG *a new mother*
raw EG *raw talent*
unaccustomed EG *Kate is unaccustomed to being on TV.*

> **WORD POWER**
> Antonym
> experienced

infect VERB
to cause disease in something
EG *One mosquito can infect many people.*
affect EG *Neil has been affected by the virus.*
blight EG *trees blighted by pollution*
contaminate EG *These substances can contaminate fish.*

taint EG *blood that had been tainted with HIV*

infectious ADJECTIVE
spreading from one person to another
EG *infectious diseases*
catching EG *There is no suggestion that multiple sclerosis is catching.*
contagious EG *a highly contagious disease of the lungs*
spreading EG *The spreading virus is threatening the population.*

> **WORD POWER**
> Synonyms
> communicable
> virulent

❶ inferior ADJECTIVE
having a lower position than something or someone else
EG *Women were given inferior status.*
lesser EG *the work of lesser writers*
lower EG *lower animals*
minor EG *a minor celebrity*
secondary EG *He was relegated to a secondary position.*
second-class EG *second-class citizens*
subordinate EG *His subordinate officers followed his example.*

> **WORD POWER**
> Antonym
> superior

❷ inferior ADJECTIVE
of low quality
EG *inferior quality cassette tapes*
mediocre EG *mediocre music*
poor EG *a poor standard of service*
second-class EG *a second-class education*
second-rate EG *second-rate restaurants*
shoddy EG *Customers no longer tolerate shoddy goods.*

> **WORD POWER**
> Antonym
> superior

❸ inferior NOUN

a person in a lower position than another

EG *You must still be polite to your inferiors.*

junior EG *the office junior*

menial EG *menials in poorly paid jobs*

subordinate EG *All her subordinates adored her.*

underling EG *Every underling feared him.*

> **WORD POWER**
> Antonym
> superior

infinite ADJECTIVE

without any limit or end

EG *an infinite number of possibilities*

boundless EG *boundless energy*

eternal EG *the secret of eternal youth*

everlasting EG *our everlasting friendship*

inexhaustible EG *an inexhaustible supply of ideas*

perpetual EG *a perpetual source of worry*

untold EG *untold wealth*

> **WORD POWER**
> Synonyms
> bottomless
> interminable
> limitless

❶ influence NOUN

power over other people

EG *He has quite a lot of influence.*

authority EG *You have no authority over me.*

control EG *Teachers have a lot of control over students.*

importance EG *a politician of great importance*

power EG *a position of power*

sway EG *My mother holds sway at home.*

> **WORD POWER**
> Synonyms
> ascendancy

domination

❷ influence NOUN

an effect that someone or something has

EG *under the influence of alcohol*

effect EG *Your age has an effect on your views.*

hold EG *He is losing his hold on the public.*

magnetism EG *a man of great personal magnetism*

spell EG *under the spell of one of his teachers*

weight EG *the weight of the law*

❸ influence VERB

to have an effect on someone or something

EG *I never try to influence my children.*

affect EG *He will not let personal preference affect his choice.*

control EG *I can't control him.*

direct EG *I don't need you directing my life.*

guide EG *Let your instinct guide you.*

manipulate EG *I hate the way he manipulates people.*

sway EG *efforts to sway voters*

inform VERB

to tell someone about something

EG *Please inform me of your progress.*

advise FORMAL EG *I can advise you of his whereabouts.*

enlighten EG *a history lesson which enlightens you*

notify EG *Ann was notified of her sister's illness.*

tell EG *Tell me what is going on.*

> **WORD POWER**
> Synonyms
> apprise
> communicate

inform on VERB

to tell the police about someone who has committed a crime

EG *Somebody must have informed on the thieves.*

251

betray EG *They betrayed their associates to the police.*

denounce EG *He was denounced as a dangerous rebel.*

grass on BRITISH SLANG EG *He grassed on the members of his own gang.*

tell on INFORMAL EG *It's all right, I won't tell on you.*

informal ADJECTIVE
relaxed and casual
EG *His manner was informal and relaxed.*

casual EG *a casual attitude towards money*

colloquial EG *colloquial language*

easy EG *easy conversation*

familiar EG *John was too familiar towards his teacher.*

natural EG *Beth was friendly and natural with us.*

relaxed EG *a relaxed atmosphere in class*

> **WORD POWER**
> Antonym
> formal

information NOUN
the details you know about something
EG *Pat would not give any information about Sarah.*

data EG *The survey provided valuable data.*

drum AUSTRALIAN INFORMAL EG *I don't have the drum on this yet.*

facts EG *Pass on all the facts to the police.*

material EG *highly secret material*

news EG *We have news of your brother.*

notice EG *advance notice of the event*

word EG *I received word that the guests had arrived.*

ingredient NOUN
a thing that something is made from
EG *Place all the ingredients in a pan.*

component EG *the components of hamburgers*

constituent EG *the main constituent of fish oil*

element EG *the various elements in a picture*

inhabit VERB
to live in a place
EG *the people who inhabit these islands*

dwell EG *the people who dwell in the forest*

live EG *She has lived here for ten years.*

lodge EG *Some people lodged permanently in the hallway.*

occupy EG *Forty tenants occupy the block.*

populate EG *a swamp populated by huge birds*

reside FORMAL EG *He resides in the country.*

inhabitant NOUN
someone who lives in a place
EG *an inhabitant of Norway*

citizen EG *American citizens*

inmate EG *prison inmates*

native EG *Dr Brown is a native of New Zealand.*

occupant EG *the previous occupant of the house*

resident EG *the residents of the retirement home*

inheritance NOUN
something that is passed on
EG *The house would be his son's inheritance.*

bequest EG *His aunt left a bequest for him in her will.*

heritage EG *This building is part of our heritage.*

legacy EG *His politeness was the legacy of his upbringing.*

injury NOUN
damage to part of the body
EG *He sustained serious injuries in the accident.*

damage EG *brain damage*

harm EG *Dogs can do harm to human beings.*
wound EG *a head wound*

injustice NOUN
unfairness and lack of justice
EG *the injustice of the system*
bias EG *He shows bias against women.*
discrimination EG *racial discrimination*
inequality EG *people concerned about social inequality*
prejudice EG *prejudice against workers over 45*
unfairness EG *the unfairness of the decision*
wrong EG *I intend to right past wrongs.*

> **WORD POWER**
> Antonym
> justice

innocence NOUN
inexperience of evil or unpleasant things
EG *the innocence of babies*
gullibility EG *I'm paying for my gullibility back then.*
inexperience EG *their inexperience of the real world*
naivety EG *There was a youthful naivety to his honesty.*
simplicity EG *She prayed with childlike simplicity.*

> **WORD POWER**
> Synonyms
> artlessness
> ingenuousness
> unworldliness

❶ innocent ADJECTIVE
not guilty of a crime
EG *the arrest of innocent suspects*
blameless EG *I have led a blameless life.*
clear EG *He was clear of blame for the accident.*
not guilty EG *Both men were found not guilty.*

> **WORD POWER**
> Antonym
> guilty

❷ innocent ADJECTIVE
without experience of evil or unpleasant things
EG *They seem so young and innocent.*
childlike EG *childlike trust*
guileless EG *Her eyes were as guileless as a doll's.*
naive EG *I was young and naive when I left home.*
pure EG *She had led a pure life.*
spotless EG *a spotless, pure child*
virginal EG *a shy, virginal princess*

> **WORD POWER**
> Synonyms
> artless
> ingenuous
> unworldly

insert VERB
to put something into something else
EG *He inserted the key into the lock.*
enter EG *Enter your name in the box.*
implant EG *a device implanted in the arm*
introduce EG *Scientists introduced new genes into mice.*
place EG *Cover the casserole tightly and place in the oven.*
put EG *She put a coin in the slot.*
set EG *diamonds set in gold*

inside ADJECTIVE
surrounded by the main part and often hidden
EG *We booked an inside cabin.*
inner EG *the inner ear*
innermost EG *the innermost parts of the galaxy*
interior EG *a car with plenty of interior space*
internal EG *your internal organs*

> **WORD POWER**
> Antonym
> outside

A B C D E F G H I J K L M N O P Q R S T U V W X Y Z

insides PLURAL NOUN INFORMAL
the parts inside your body
EG *My insides ached from eating too much.*
entrails EG *chicken entrails*
guts EG *fish guts*
innards EG *the innards of a human body*
internal organs EG *damage to internal organs*

> **WORD POWER**
> Synonyms
> viscera
> vitals

insincere ADJECTIVE
saying things you do not mean
EG *A lot of actors are insincere.*
deceitful EG *deceitful and misleading remarks*
dishonest EG *dishonest salespeople*
false EG *a false confession*
two-faced EG *the most two-faced politicians in the world*

> **WORD POWER**
> Antonym
> sincere

insist VERB
to demand something forcefully
EG *My family insisted I should not give in.*
demand EG *The teacher demanded an explanation.*
press EG *She is pressing for improvements to education.*
urge EG *We urge vigorous action be taken immediately.*

inspect VERB
to examine something carefully
EG *the right to inspect company files*
check EG *Check each item for obvious flaws.*
examine EG *He examined her passport and stamped it.*
eye EG *We eyed each other thoughtfully.*
investigate EG *Police are investigating the scene of the crime.*
scan EG *The officer scanned the room.*
survey EG *He surveyed the ruins of the building.*

> **WORD POWER**
> Synonyms
> audit
> scrutinize
> vet

instinct NOUN
a natural tendency to do something
EG *My first instinct was to protect myself.*
feeling EG *You seem to have a feeling for drawing.*
impulse EG *Peter resisted an impulse to smile.*
intuition EG *You should trust your intuition.*
sixth sense EG *Some sixth sense told him to keep going.*
urge EG *He fought the urge to panic.*

insufficient ADJECTIVE
not enough for a particular purpose
EG *insufficient information*
deficient EG *a deficient diet*
inadequate EG *The problem lies with inadequate staffing.*
lacking EG *My confidence is lacking.*
scant EG *Gareth paid scant attention to what was going on.*
short EG *She was short of breath.*

> **WORD POWER**
> Antonym
> sufficient

❶ insult VERB
to offend someone by being rude to them
EG *I did not mean to insult you.*
abuse EG *footballers abusing referees*
affront EG *He pretended to be affronted by what I said.*
offend EG *I had no intention of offending the community.*
put down EG *They seemed to*

delight in putting me down.
slag BRITISH INFORMAL EG *He's always slagging me in front of his mates.*
slight EG *They felt slighted by not being consulted.*
snub EG *He snubbed her in public and made her feel foolish.*

> **WORD POWER**
> Antonym
> compliment

❷ **insult** NOUN
a rude remark that offends someone
EG *The two men exchanged insults.*
abuse EG *Raft hurled verbal abuse at his co-star.*
affront EG *She took my words as a personal affront.*
offence EG *I meant no offence to Mr Hardy.*
slight EG *She is very sensitive to slights.*
snub EG *This was a deliberate snub to me.*

> **WORD POWER**
> Antonym
> compliment

intelligence NOUN
the ability to understand and learn things
EG *students of high intelligence*
cleverness EG *Her cleverness gets in the way of her emotions.*
comprehension EG *an idea beyond human comprehension*
intellect EG *Lucy's lack of intellect disappointed her father.*
perception EG *You have brilliant perception and insight.*
sense EG *They have the sense to seek help.*
understanding EG *I've got no sense, no understanding.*
wit EG *He had the wit to see this was a good idea.*

> **WORD POWER**
> Synonyms
> acumen

nous

intelligent ADJECTIVE
able to understand and learn things
EG *Dolphins are an intelligent species.*
acute EG *His relaxed exterior hides a very acute mind.*
brainy INFORMAL EG *I don't consider myself brainy.*
bright EG *an exceptionally bright child*
clever EG *a clever girl*
quick EG *His quick mind soon grasped the situation.*
sharp EG *a very sharp intellect*
smart EG *He thinks he's as smart as Sarah.*

> **WORD POWER**
> Antonym
> stupid

❶ **intend** VERB
to decide or plan to do something
EG *She intended to move back to Cape Town.*
aim EG *We aim to raise funds for charity.*
be determined EG *Kate was determined to enjoy the day.*
mean EG *I didn't mean any harm.*
plan EG *He planned to leave Adelaide on Monday.*
propose EG *Where do you propose building such a huge thing?*
resolve EG *She resolved to report the matter.*

❷ **intend** VERB
to mean for a certain use
EG *a book intended for serious students*
aim EG *children's games aimed at developing quickness*
design EG *The house had been designed for a large family.*
earmark EG *That money was earmarked for house repairs.*
mean EG *I was not meant for*

A
B
C
D
E
F
G
H
I
J
K
L
M
N
O
P
Q
R
S
T
U
V
W
X
Y
Z

domestic life.

❶ intense ADJECTIVE
very great in strength or amount
EG *intense heat*

acute EG *an acute shortage of accommodation*

deep EG *He felt a deep sense of relief.*

extreme EG *Proceed with extreme caution.*

fierce EG *There was fierce competition for the job.*

great EG *Dawes felt a great pain and weakness.*

powerful EG *I had a powerful urge to scream at him.*

profound EG *The book had a profound effect in the USA.*

severe EG *I had severe problems.*

❷ intense ADJECTIVE
tending to have strong feelings
EG *He was dark-haired and intense.*

ardent EG *one of his most ardent supporters*

earnest EG *Ella was a pious, earnest woman.*

fervent EG *a fervent admirer of Beethoven's music*

fierce EG *fierce loyalty to his friends*

impassioned EG *He made an impassioned appeal for peace.*

passionate EG *He is very passionate about the project.*

vehement EG *a vehement critic of the plan*

intention NOUN
a plan to do something
EG *He announced his intention of retiring.*

aim EG *The aim of this book is to inform you.*

goal EG *The goal is to raise a lot of money.*

idea EG *I bought books with the idea of reading them.*

object EG *It was his object in life to find the island.*

objective EG *His objective was to play golf and win.*

purpose EG *He did not know the purpose of Vincent's visit.*

interesting ADJECTIVE
making you want to know, learn or hear more
EG *an interesting hobby*

absorbing EG *an absorbing conversation*

compelling EG *compelling drama*

entertaining EG *a cheerful and entertaining companion*

gripping EG *a gripping story*

intriguing EG *the intriguing character of the author*

stimulating EG *My trip to India had been stimulating.*

WORD POWER
Antonym
boring

❶ interfere VERB
to try to influence a situation
EG *Stop interfering and leave me alone.*

butt in EG *I butted in where I didn't belong.*

intervene EG *Soldiers don't like civilians intervening in their affairs.*

intrude EG *I don't want to intrude on your meeting.*

meddle EG *Scientists should not meddle in such matters.*

tamper EG *the price we pay for tampering with the environment*

❷ interfere VERB
to have a damaging effect on a situation
EG *His problems interfered with his work.*

conflict EG *an evening that conflicted with my work schedule*

disrupt EG *Strikes disrupted air traffic in Italy.*

hinder EG *A thigh injury hindered her movement.*

impede EG *Fallen rocks impeded the progress of the rescue workers.*

inhibit EG *factors which inhibit growth*

obstruct EG *Lack of funds obstructed our progress.*

interrogate VERB
to question someone thoroughly
EG *I interrogated everyone even slightly involved.*

examine EG *Lawyers examined the witnesses.*

grill INFORMAL EG *Jenkins kept telling police who grilled him: "I didn't kill her."*

question EG *He was questioned by police.*

quiz EG *She quizzed me quite closely for a while.*

> *WORD POWER*
> Synonyms
> cross-examine
> cross-question

❶ interrupt VERB
to start talking when someone else is talking
EG *He tried to speak, but she interrupted him.*

butt in EG *Mirella butted in without a greeting.*

heckle EG *It is easy to heckle from the safety of the audience.*

❷ interrupt VERB
to stop a process or activity for a time
EG *The match was interrupted by rain.*

break EG *allowing passengers to break their journey with a stay in Fiji*

discontinue EG *Do not discontinue the treatment without seeing your doctor.*

suspend EG *Relief convoys will be suspended until the fighting stops.*

interval NOUN
a period of time between two moments or dates
EG *There was a long interval of silence.*

break EG *a short break from work*

gap EG *the gap between school terms*

hiatus EG *There was a momentary hiatus in the sounds.*

interlude EG *It was a happy interlude in the Kents' life.*

intermission EG *There will be a short intermission between acts.*

pause EG *a pause between two periods of intense activity*

intervene VERB
to step in to prevent conflict
EG *I relied on them to intervene if anything happened.*

arbitrate EG *A committee was set up to arbitrate in the dispute.*

mediate EG *efforts to mediate between the two communities*

❶ introduction NOUN
the act of presenting someone or something new
EG *the introduction of a single European currency*

establishment EG *the establishment of a democratic system*

inauguration EG *the inauguration of the President*

initiation EG *your initiation into adulthood*

institution EG *the institution of new laws*

launch EG *the launch of this popular author's new book*

❷ introduction NOUN
a piece of writing at the beginning of a book
EG *The book contains a new introduction by the author.*

foreword EG *I am happy to write the foreword to this collection.*

preface EG *I read through the preface quickly.*

prologue EG *the General Prologue to The Canterbury Tales*

intrude VERB
to disturb someone or something
EG *I don't want to intrude on your parents.*

A B C D E F G H I J K L M N O P Q R S T U V W X Y Z

257

butt in EG *I butted in where I didn't belong.*

encroach EG *Does your work encroach on your private life?*

infringe EG *She promised not to infringe on his space.*

interrupt EG *Georgina interrupted his thoughts.*

trespass EG *I don't like to trespass on your time.*

violate EG *These men were violating her family's privacy.*

invade VERB
to enter a country by force
EG *The allies invaded the Italian mainland at Anzio.*

attack EG *Government planes attacked the town.*

enter EG *The Taleban entered western Kabul.*

occupy EG *Soldiers occupied the town within a few minutes.*

violate EG *A helicopter violated Greek territory yesterday.*

❶ invent VERB
to be the first person to think of a device
EG *He invented the first electric clock.*

coin EG *Lanier coined the term 'virtual reality'.*

come up with INFORMAL EG *He came up with a gadget to relieve hayfever.*

conceive EG *He conceived the first portable computer.*

create EG *The company decided to create a new perfume.*

formulate EG *He formulated his plan for escape.*

originate EG *the designer who originated platform shoes*

> **WORD POWER**
> Synonyms
> design
> devise
> improvise

❷ invent VERB
to make up a story or excuse

EG *I tried to invent a plausible excuse.*

concoct EG *A newspaper concocted an imaginary interview.*

fabricate EG *The evidence against them was fabricated.*

make up EG *Donna was known for making up stories about herself.*

manufacture EG *The children manufactured an elaborate tale.*

investigate VERB
to find out all the facts about something
EG *Police are still investigating the incidents.*

examine EG *I have examined all the possible alternatives.*

explore EG *a book which explores the history of technology*

probe EG *He probed into her private life.*

research EG *I'm researching for an article on New England.*

sift EG *I sifted the evidence for conclusions.*

study EG *Experts are studying the security in the building.*

invincible ADJECTIVE
unable to be defeated
EG *When Woods is on form he is invincible.*

impregnable EG *an impregnable fortress*

indomitable EG *the indomitable spirit of the Polish people*

unbeatable EG *a performance record that is unbeatable*

> **WORD POWER**
> Synonyms
> indestructible
> insurmountable
> unassailable

invisible ADJECTIVE
unable to be seen
EG *His face was invisible beneath his hat.*

concealed EG *a concealed weapon*

disguised EG *a disguised panel in*

the wall
hidden EG *a hidden camera*
inconspicuous EG *She tried to make herself inconspicuous.*
unseen EG *His work was guided by an unseen hand.*

> **WORD POWER**
> Synonyms
> imperceptible
> indiscernible
> Antonym
> visible

involve VERB
to have as a necessary part
EG *Running a kitchen involves a great deal of discipline.*
incorporate EG *The program incorporates a range of activities.*
require EG *Caring for a baby requires special skills.*
take in EG *This study takes in a number of areas.*

> **WORD POWER**
> Synonyms
> entail
> necessitate

irrational ADJECTIVE
not based on logical reasons
EG *irrational fears*
absurd EG *It was an absurd over-reaction.*
crazy EG *crazy ideas*
illogical EG *his completely illogical arguments*
nonsensical EG *Such an idea sounds paradoxical, if not downright nonsensical.*
unsound EG *The thinking is good-hearted, but muddled and unsound.*

> **WORD POWER**
> Synonyms
> injudicious
> silly
> unreasoning

❶ **irregular** ADJECTIVE
not smooth or even

EG *an irregular surface*
asymmetrical EG *She has asymmetrical features.*
bumpy EG *bumpy roads*
jagged EG *jagged fragments of stained glass*
lopsided EG *his lopsided smile*
ragged EG *the ragged edges of a tear*
uneven EG *uneven teeth*

> **WORD POWER**
> Antonym
> regular

❷ **irregular** ADJECTIVE
not forming a regular pattern
EG *He worked irregular hours.*
erratic EG *a planet with an erratic orbit*
haphazard EG *a haphazard system*
occasional EG *occasional rain showers*
patchy EG *Her career has been patchy.*
random EG *The stock market is random and unpredictable.*
variable EG *a variable rate of interest*

> **WORD POWER**
> Synonyms
> fitful
> sporadic
> Antonym
> regular

irresponsible ADJECTIVE
not concerned with the consequences of your actions
EG *an irresponsible attitude*
careless EG *a careless driver*
reckless EG *reckless spending*
thoughtless EG *a thoughtless remark*
wild EG *a night of wild abandon*

> **WORD POWER**
> Antonym
> responsible

irritable ADJECTIVE
easily annoyed

A B C D E F G H I J K L M N O P Q R S T U V W X Y Z

A
B
C
D
E
F
G
H
I
J
K
L
M
N
O
P
Q
R
S
T
U
V
W
X
Y
Z

EG *Nicol was unusually tense and irritable.*
bad-tempered EG *You're very bad-tempered today.*
cantankerous EG *a cantankerous old man*
petulant EG *He was like a petulant child.*
ratty BRITISH AND NEW ZEALAND INFORMAL EG *There's no need to get ratty.*

WORD POWER
Synonyms
irascible
tetchy

irritate VERB
to annoy someone
EG *Their attitude irritates me.*
anger EG *This article angered me.*
annoy EG *It just annoyed me to hear him going on.*
bother EG *Nothing bothers me.*
exasperate EG *Bertha was exasperated by the delay.*
needle INFORMAL EG *If her remark needled him, he didn't show it.*
ruffle EG *He doesn't get ruffled by anything.*

WORD POWER

Synonyms
gall
provoke

❶ **item** NOUN
one of a collection or list of things
EG *an item on the agenda*
article EG *articles of clothing*
matter EG *He dealt with a variety of matters.*
point EG *Many of the points in the report are correct.*
thing EG *Big things are paid for by the government.*

❷ **item** NOUN
a newspaper or magazine article
EG *There was an item in the paper about him.*
article EG *a short article in one of the papers*
feature EG *The magazine contained a special feature on the project.*
notice EG *notices in today's national newspapers*
piece EG *I disagree with your recent piece about Australia.*
report EG *a film report on the scandal*

Jj Jj

jagged ADJECTIVE
sharp and spiky
EG *jagged black cliffs*
barbed EG *barbed wire*
craggy EG *craggy mountains*
rough EG *the rough surface of the rock*
serrated EG *a serrated knife*

> **WORD POWER**
> Antonym
> smooth

❶ jail NOUN
a place where prisoners are held
EG *sentenced to 18 months in jail*
nick BRITISH, AUSTRALIAN, AND NEW ZEALAND SLANG EG *He spent seven years in the nick.*
prison EG *his release from prison*

> **WORD POWER**
> Synonyms
> lockup
> penitentiary

❷ jail VERB
to put in prison
EG *He was jailed for twenty years.*
detain EG *Police can detain a suspect for 48 hours.*
imprison EG *imprisoned for 18 months on charges of theft*
incarcerate EG *They have been incarcerated as political prisoners.*

❶ jam NOUN
a crowded mass of people or things
EG *stuck in a jam on the motorway*
crowd EG *elbowing his way through the crowd*
crush EG *We got separated in the crush.*
mass EG *a mass of excited fans*
mob EG *a growing mob of demonstrators*
multitude EG *surrounded by a noisy multitude*
throng EG *An official pushed through the throng.*

❷ jam NOUN
a difficult situation
EG *We're in a real jam now.*
dilemma EG *faced with a dilemma*
fix INFORMAL EG *a difficult economic fix*
hole SLANG EG *He admitted that the government was in a hole.*
plight EG *the plight of the Third World countries*
predicament EG *a way out of our predicament*
quandary EG *We're in a quandary over our holiday plans.*
trouble EG *You are in serious trouble.*

❸ jam VERB
to push something somewhere roughly
EG *He jammed his hat on to his head.*
cram EG *He crammed the bank notes into his pocket.*
force EG *I forced the key into the ignition.*
ram EG *He rammed the muzzle of the gun against my forehead.*
stuff EG *She stuffed the newspaper into a litter bin.*

❹ jam VERB
to become stuck
EG *The second time he fired, his gun jammed.*
stall EG *The engine stalled.*
stick EG *She tried to open the window but it was stuck.*

jealous ADJECTIVE
wanting to have something which someone else has
EG *She was jealous of his success.*
envious EG *envious of the attention his brother was getting*
resentful EG *resentful of her husband's hobby*

261

A B C D E F G H I J K L M N O P Q R S T U V W X Y Z

WORD POWER
Synonyms
covetous
emulous

❶ job NOUN
the work someone does to earn money
EG *I'm still looking for a job.*
employment EG *unable to find employment*
occupation EG *his occupation as a carpenter*
position EG *He's leaving to take up a position abroad.*
post EG *She has resigned her post as his assistant.*
profession EG *She chose nursing as her profession.*
trade EG *her trade as a jeweller*

❷ job NOUN
a duty or responsibility
EG *It's your job to find out what's going on.*
concern EG *The technical aspects are the concern of the engineers.*
duty EG *I consider it my duty to write and thank you.*
function EG *an important function to fill*
responsibility EG *It's not my responsibility to look after your mother.*
role EG *Our role is to keep the peace.*
task EG *She had the task of breaking the bad news.*

❶ join VERB
to become a member of something
EG *He joined the Army five years ago.*
enlist EG *He was 18 when he enlisted in the US Navy.*
enrol EG *She has enrolled in an acting class.*
sign up EG *I've signed up as a member.*

WORD POWER
Antonym
resign

❷ join VERB
to fasten two things together
EG *two sticks joined together by a chain*
attach EG *The gadget can be attached to any surface.*
connect EG *two rooms connected by a passage*
couple EG *an engine coupled to a gearbox*
fasten EG *a wooden bench fastened to the floor*
link EG *tree houses linked by ropes*
tie EG *He tied the dog to a post by its leash.*

WORD POWER
Synonyms
append
knit
splice
Antonym
separate

❶ joke NOUN
something that makes people laugh
EG *I heard a great joke today.*
gag INFORMAL EG *a gag about unscrupulous lawyers*
jest EG *It was only intended as a jest.*
lark EG *They just did it for a lark.*
prank EG *an end-of-term prank*
quip EG *a famous quip by Groucho Marx*
wisecrack INFORMAL EG *She was tempted to make a wisecrack.*
witticism EG *laughing at each other's witticisms*

WORD POWER
Synonyms
jape
sally

❷ joke VERB
to say something funny
EG *She was always joking about her appearance.*
banter EG *He played trick shots and bantered with the crowd.*

chaff EG *They chaffed us about our chances of winning.*

jest EG *drinking and jesting with his cronies*

kid INFORMAL EG *Don't worry, I'm only kidding.*

quip EG *"You'll have to go on a diet," he quipped.*

tease EG *"You must be in love," she teased.*

❶ **journey** NOUN
the act of travelling from one place to another
EG *the journey from Paris to Bordeaux*

excursion EG *The trip includes an excursion to Zermatt.*

expedition EG *an expedition to the South Pole*

passage EG *a 10-hour passage from Swansea*

tour EG *a two-month tour of Europe*

trek EG *a trek through the Gobi desert*

trip EG *a business trip*

voyage EG *the first space shuttle voyage*

❷ **journey** VERB
to travel from one place to another
EG *In 1935, she journeyed through Turkey and Africa.*

go EG *We went from Glasgow to London in six hours.*

proceed EG *proceeding along the road in the wrong direction*

tour EG *He toured China in 1993.*

travel EG *Gran travelled down by train.*

trek EG *trekking through the jungle*

voyage EG *They voyaged as far as Spain.*

joy NOUN
great happiness
EG *Her face shone with joy.*

bliss EG *an expression of pure bliss*

delight EG *He let out a yell of delight.*

ecstasy EG *Her eyes closed in ecstasy.*

elation EG *He felt a surge of elation at the news.*

rapture EG *His speech was received with rapture.*

WORD POWER
Synonyms
exaltation
exultation
felicity
Antonym
misery

---

joyful ADJECTIVE
extremely happy
EG *a joyful smile*

delighted EG *I'm delighted to be here.*

elated EG *the elated faces of the freed hostages*

jubilant EG *the jubilant crowds*

over the moon INFORMAL EG *I was over the moon to hear about your promotion.*

WORD POWER
Synonyms
cock-a-hoop
enraptured

---

❶ **judge** NOUN
the person in charge of a law court
EG *The judge awarded him £2000 in damages.*

beak BRITISH SLANG EG *a third appearance before the beak*

justice EG *his appointment as a Justice of the High Court*

magistrate EG *defendants appearing before a magistrate*

❷ **judge** NOUN
someone who picks the winner or keeps control of a competition
EG *A panel of judges are selecting the finalists.*

referee EG *The referee awarded a free kick against Rourke.*

umpire EG *The umpire's decision is final.*

A B C D E F G H I **J** K L M N O P Q R S T U V W X Y Z

❸ **judge** VERB
to form an opinion about
someone or something
EG *Don't judge people by their looks.*
appraise EG *The teachers are
appraised by an official.*
assess EG *It is too early to assess
the impact of the change.*
consider EG *We consider him to be
dangerous.*
estimate EG *The cost of the
damage is estimated at over a
million dollars.*
evaluate EG *a test to evaluate a
candidate's potential*
rate EG *The film was rated a hit.*

❹ **judge** VERB
to pick the winner or keep
control in a competition
EG *Entrants will be judged in two
age categories.*
referee EG *He has refereed in two
World Cups.*
umpire EG *He umpired baseball
games.*

> **WORD POWER**
> Synonyms
> adjudge
> adjudicate

❶ **jump** VERB
to leap up or over something
EG *I jumped over the fence.*
bound EG *He bounded up the steps.*
clear EG *The horse cleared the gate
by inches.*
hurdle EG *He crossed the lawn and
hurdled the fence.*
leap EG *He had leapt from a
window and escaped.*
spring EG *The lion roared once and
sprang.*
vault EG *Ned vaulted over a fallen
tree.*

❷ **jump** VERB
to increase suddenly
EG *Sales jumped by 25% last year.*
escalate EG *Costs escalated
dramatically.*

increase EG *Trading has increased
by 20% this month.*
rise EG *Unemployment is rising
rapidly.*
surge EG *The party's share of the
vote surged from 10% to 17%.*

❸ **jump** NOUN
a leap into the air
EG *the longest ever jump by a man*
bound EG *With one bound Jack
was free.*
leap EG *Smith took the gold medal
with a leap of 2.37 metres.*
vault EG *She regained the record
with a vault of 3.80 metres.*

❶ **justice** NOUN
fairness in the way that people
are treated
EG *He wants freedom, justice and
equality.*
equity EG *Income should be
distributed with some sense of
equity.*
fairness EG *concern about the
fairness of the election campaign*
impartiality EG *a system lacking
impartiality*

> **WORD POWER**
> Antonym
> injustice

❷ **justice** NOUN
the person in charge of a law
court
EG *his appointment as a Justice of
the High Court*
judge EG *The judge awarded him
£2000 in damages.*
magistrate EG *defendants
appearing before a magistrate*

justify VERB
to show that something is
reasonable or necessary
EG *How can you justify what you've
done?*
defend EG *Her conduct is hard to
defend.*
excuse EG *That still doesn't excuse
his behaviour.*

explain EG *She left a note explaining her actions.*
vindicate EG *Ministers are confident their decision will be vindicated.*

warrant EG *These allegations warrant an investigation.*

Kk Kk

① keen ADJECTIVE
showing eagerness and
enthusiasm for something
EG *a keen amateur photographer*
ardent EG *one of his most ardent
supporters*
avid EG *an avid reader*
eager EG *We're eager to have
another baby.*
enthusiastic EG *Tom was very
enthusiastic about the place.*
fond of EG *Are you fond of Chinese
cuisine?*
into INFORMAL EG *I'm really into
football.*

② keen ADJECTIVE
quick to notice or understand
things
EG *a keen intellect*
astute EG *an astute judge of
character*
brilliant EG *She had a brilliant
mind.*
perceptive EG *a perceptive gaze*
quick EG *His quick mind soon
grasped the situation.*
shrewd EG *Her questions showed a
shrewd perception.*

① keep VERB
to have and look after
something
EG *His father keeps a small shop.*
care for EG *vintage cars lovingly
cared for by their owners*
maintain EG *The house costs a
fortune to maintain.*
preserve EG *the need to preserve
the rainforests*

② keep VERB
to store something
EG *She kept her money under the
mattress.*
deposit EG *You are advised to
deposit your valuables in the hotel
safe.*
hold EG *Our stock is held in a*

warehouse.
store EG *Store the cookies in an
airtight tin.*

③ keep VERB
to do what you said you would
do
EG *I always keep my promises.*
carry out EG *He carried out his
threat.*
fulfil EG *He fulfilled all his
responsibilities.*
honour EG *The two sides have
agreed to honour a new ceasefire.*

kidnap VERB
to take someone away by force
EG *Four tourists have been
kidnapped by rebels.*
abduct EG *people claiming to have
been abducted by aliens*
capture EG *The guerrillas shot
down one plane and captured the
pilot.*
seize EG *hostages seized by terrorists*

kill VERB
to make someone or something
die
EG *The earthquake killed 62 people.*
assassinate EG *the plot to
assassinate Martin Luther King*
butcher EG *The guards butchered
hundreds of prisoners.*
destroy EG *The jockey was unhurt
but his horse had to be destroyed.*
execute EG *He was executed for
treason.*
exterminate EG *an effort to
exterminate all the rats*
massacre EG *300 civilians have
been massacred by the rebels.*
murder EG *the widow of the
murdered leader*
slaughter EG *Whales are being
slaughtered for commercial gain.*
slay EG *a painting of Saint George
slaying the dragon*

| *WORD POWER*

Synonyms
annihilate
dispatch

kin NOUN
the people who are related to
you
EG *She has gone to live with her
husband's kin.*
family EG *There's a history of heart
disease in our family.*
kindred EG *his loyalty to his
friends and kindred*
people EG *She was reunited with
her people.*
relations EG *I was staying with
relations in Atlanta.*
relatives EG *On Sundays his
relatives come to visit.*

❶ kind NOUN
a particular type of person or
thing
EG *I don't like that kind of film.*
brand EG *his favourite brand of
whisky*
breed EG *a rare breed of cattle*
class EG *a better class of restaurant*
sort EG *a dozen trees of various sorts*
species EG *a rare species of moth*
type EG *What type of guns were
they?*
variety EG *a new variety of rose*

❷ kind ADJECTIVE
considerate towards other
people
EG *Thank you for being so kind to
me.*
benevolent EG *a very benevolent
employer*
benign EG *a benign ruler*
charitable EG *a charitable nature*
compassionate EG *My father was
a deeply compassionate man.*
considerate EG *a caring and
considerate husband*
humane EG *the humane treatment
of prisoners*
kindly EG *a kindly old man*
thoughtful EG *a thoughtful*

gesture

> **WORD POWER**
> Antonym
> cruel

kindness NOUN
the quality of being considerate
towards other people
EG *Everyone has treated me with
great kindness.*
benevolence EG *an act of selfless
benevolence*
charity EG *Ms Rubens writes with
warmth and charity.*
compassion EG *He showed no
compassion to his victim.*
gentleness EG *the gentleness with
which she treated her mother*
humanity EG *Her speech showed
great maturity and humanity.*

> **WORD POWER**
> Synonyms
> kindliness
> magnanimity
> philanthropy
> tenderness
> Antonym
> cruelty

king NOUN
a man who is the head of a royal
family
EG *the king and queen of Spain*
monarch EG *the coronation of the
new monarch*
sovereign EG *the first British
sovereign to visit the country*

❶ know VERB
to understand or be aware of
something
EG *I don't know anything about cars.*
apprehend EG *It is impossible to
apprehend the whole painting at
once.*
be aware of EG *Smokers are aware
of the risks they run.*
comprehend EG *They do not
comprehend the nature of the
problem.*
perceive EG *the world as we*

A
B
C
D
E
F
G
H
I
J
K
L
M
N
O
P
Q
R
S
T
U
V
W
X
Y
Z

perceive it
see EG *Don't you see what he's up to?*
understand EG *too young to understand what was happening*

❷ know VERB
to be familiar with a person or thing
EG *I believe you two already know each other.*
be acquainted with EG *Are you acquainted with my husband?*
be familiar with EG *I am familiar with his work.*

recognize EG *She recognized him at once.*

knowledge NOUN
all you know about something
EG *She had no knowledge of French.*

education EG *a man with little education*

learning EG *people of great learning*

scholarship EG *a lifetime of scholarship*

wisdom EG *a source of wisdom and knowledge*

❶ label NOUN
a piece of paper or plastic attached to something for information
EG *He peered at the label on the bottle.*

sticker EG *She's got a disabled sticker on her car.*
tag EG *a name tag*
ticket EG *a price ticket*

❷ label VERB
to put a label on something
EG *The produce was labelled "Made in China".*

flag EG *Flag the pages which need corrections.*
sticker EG *products stickered at a special price*
tag EG *The pigeon was tagged with a numbered band.*

❶ labour NOUN
very hard work
EG *the labour of weeding and digging*

effort EG *legs aching with the effort of the climb*
exertion EG *She felt dizzy with the exertion of walking.*
industry EG *At last his industry was rewarded.*
toil EG *their day's toil in the fields*
work EG *All our work is starting to pay off.*

❷ labour NOUN
the workforce of a country or industry
EG *unskilled labour*

employees EG *Only a third of all employees are union members.*
workers EG *Thousands of workers have been laid off.*
workforce EG *a country where half the workforce is unemployed*

❸ labour VERB
to work very hard
EG *peasants labouring in the fields*
slave EG *We've been slaving half*

the night to finish this.
toil EG *workers toiling in wretched conditions*
work EG *He works twelve hours a day.*

> **WORD POWER**
> Antonym
> relax

❶ lack NOUN
the shortage or absence of something which is needed
EG *a lack of funds*

absence EG *an absence of evidence*
deficiency EG *tests for vitamin deficiency*
scarcity EG *a scarcity of water*
shortage EG *a food shortage*
want EG *becoming weak from want of rest*

> **WORD POWER**
> Synonyms
> dearth
> insufficiency
> scantiness
> Antonym
> abundance

❷ lack VERB
to be without something that is needed
EG *She lacks confidence.*

be deficient in EG *Your diet is deficient in vitamins.*
be short of EG *I'm short of cash.*
miss EG *Your jacket is missing a button.*

lag VERB
to make slower progress than other people or things
EG *He is now lagging 10 points behind the champion.*

fall behind EG *The city is falling behind in attracting tourists.*
trail EG *The Communist party is trailing badly in the opinion polls.*

lake NOUN

Types of lake:
lagoon
loch (*Scottish*)
lough (*Irish*)
mere
reservoir
tarn

❶ lame ADJECTIVE

unable to walk properly because
of an injured leg
EG *She was lame in one leg.*

crippled EG *a woman crippled by
arthritis*

hobbling EG *a hobbling old man*

limping EG *limping from a
hamstring injury*

❷ lame ADJECTIVE

weak or unconvincing
EG *a lame excuse*

feeble EG *his feeble attempt at
humour*

flimsy EG *MPs condemned his
evidence as flimsy.*

pathetic EG *a pathetic attempt at
humour*

poor EG *a poor effort*

unconvincing EG *an unconvincing
argument*

weak EG *a weak performance*

❶ lament VERB

to express sorrow or regret over
something
EG *She lamented the death of her
brother.*

grieve EG *grieving over his dead
wife and son*

mourn EG *We mourned the loss of
our home.*

wail EG *a mother wailing for her
lost child*

weep EG *She wept for her lost love.*

> **WORD POWER**
> Synonyms
> bemoan
> bewail

❷ lament NOUN

something you say to express
sorrow or regret
EG *a lament for a vanished age*

moan EG *a moan of sorrow*

wail EG *wails of grief*

> **WORD POWER**
> Synonyms
> lamentation
> plaint

❶ land NOUN

an area of ground which
someone owns
EG *a dispute over land*

estate EG *a shooting party on his
estate in Yorkshire*

grounds EG *the palace grounds*

property EG *travellers who camped
on his property*

❷ land NOUN

a region or country
EG *America is the land of
opportunity.*

country EG *the boundary between
the two countries*

nation EG *the nation's financial
crisis*

province EG *The Algarve is
Portugal's southernmost province.*

region EG *the region of Tuscany*

territory EG *the disputed territory
of Kashmir*

❸ land VERB

to arrive on the ground after
flying or sailing
EG *We landed in New York around
noon.*

alight EG *A thrush alighted on a
nearby branch.*

dock EG *The ship docked in Le
Havre.*

touch down EG *The plane touched
down in Barbados.*

❶ language NOUN

the system of words people use
to communicate
EG *She speaks four languages.*

dialect EG *the Cantonese dialect*

idiom EG *the Gaelic folk idiom*

jargon EG *scientific jargon*
lingo INFORMAL EG *I don't speak the lingo.*
tongue EG *The French feel passionately about their native tongue.*
vernacular EG *an Indian vernacular derived from Sanskrit*
vocabulary EG *a new word in the German vocabulary*

WORD POWER
Synonyms
argot
cant
lingua franca
patois

❷ language NOUN
the style in which you speak or write
EG *He explained the process in plain language.*
phrasing EG *The phrasing of this report is confusing.*
style EG *a simple writing style*
wording EG *The wording of the contract was ambiguous.*

WORD POWER
Synonyms
phraseology
terminology

large ADJECTIVE
of a greater size or amount than usual
EG *a large room*
big EG *Her husband was a big man.*
colossal EG *a colossal task*
enormous EG *an enormous house*
giant EG *a giant bird*
gigantic EG *a gigantic spider*
great EG *a great hall as long as a church*
huge EG *huge profits*
immense EG *an immense chamber*
massive EG *a massive ship*
vast EG *a vast desert*

WORD POWER
Synonyms
gargantuan

sizable *or* sizeable
Antonym
small

❶ last ADJECTIVE
the most recent
EG *last year*
most recent EG *her most recent film*
previous EG *his previous marriage*

WORD POWER
Antonym
first

❷ last ADJECTIVE
happening or remaining after all the others of its kind
EG *the last three chapters of the book*
closing EG *the closing years of this century*
concluding EG *the concluding scene of the film*
final EG *This is your final chance.*

WORD POWER
Antonym
first

❸ last VERB
to continue to exist or happen
EG *The film lasted for two and a half hours.*
carry on EG *Our marriage can't carry on like this.*
continue EG *The exhibition continues till 25 November.*
endure EG *Somehow their friendship endures.*
persist EG *The problem persists.*
remain EG *The building remains to this day.*
survive EG *companies which survived after the recession*

❶ late ADJECTIVE
after the expected time
EG *The train was late.*
behind EG *I've got behind with my payments.*
belated EG *a belated birthday card*
delayed EG *The kick-off was delayed by 10 minutes.*

A
B
C
D
E
F
G
H
I
J
K
L
M
N
O
P
Q
R
S
T
U
V
W
X
Y
Z

overdue EG *The birth is two weeks overdue.*

> #### WORD POWER
> **Synonyms**
> behindhand
> tardy
> unpunctual
> **Antonym**
> early

❷ **late** ADJECTIVE
dead, especially recently
EG *my late husband*
dead EG *He has been dead for a year now.*
deceased EG *his recently deceased mother*
departed EG *memories of departed friends*

❶ **laugh** VERB
to make a noise which shows you are amused or happy
EG *You never laugh at my jokes.*
chortle EG *He began chortling to himself.*
chuckle EG *He chuckled with pleasure.*
giggle EG *Both girls began to giggle.*
guffaw EG *Everyone guffawed loudly.*
snigger EG *People were sniggering behind my back.*
titter EG *The audience tittered nervously.*

❷ **laugh** NOUN
the noise you make when amused or happy
EG *She has a very infectious laugh.*
chortle EG *"That's what you think," he said with a chortle.*
chuckle EG *We had a quiet chuckle at his mistake.*
giggle EG *She gave a nervous giggle.*
guffaw EG *He let out a huge guffaw of amusement.*
snigger EG *barely able to stifle a snigger*
titter EG *A titter went round the room.*

❶ **law** NOUN
a country's system of rules
EG *The use of this drug is against the law.*
charter EG *a citizen's charter for France*
code EG *a code of conduct*
constitution EG *proposed changes to the constitution*

❷ **law** NOUN
one of the rules of a country
EG *The anti-stalking law was introduced in 1990.*
act EG *A new act has been passed by Parliament.*
code EG *a code designed to protect the rights of children*
decree EG *a decree lifting sanctions against China*
regulation EG *regulations outlawing child labour*
rule EG *a rule that was imposed in 1962*
statute EG *a practice regulated by statute*

> #### WORD POWER
> **Synonyms**
> edict
> ordinance

lawyer NOUN
someone who advises people about the law
EG *I'm discussing the matter with my lawyers.*
advocate EG *A public advocate will be appointed to represent you.*
attorney EG *a prosecuting attorney*
barrister EG *The author is a practising barrister.*
counsel EG *His counsel advised him to appeal against the verdict.*
solicitor EG *She took advice from a solicitor.*

❶ **lay** VERB
to put something somewhere
EG *Lay a sheet of newspaper on the floor.*
place EG *She placed a mug of coffee*

in front of him.
put EG *He put the photograph on the desk.*
set EG *He set his briefcase on the floor.*
set down EG *I set the glasses down on the table.*
settle EG *He settled his coat over my shoulders.*
spread EG *She spread a towel over the sand and lay down.*

❷ **lay** VERB
to arrange or set something out
EG *A man came to lay the carpet.*
arrange EG *He started to arrange the books in piles.*
set out EG *The flower garden was set out with large beds of roses.*

layer NOUN
something that covers a surface or comes between two other things
EG *A fresh layer of snow covered the street.*
blanket EG *a blanket of fog*
coat EG *a coat of paint*
coating EG *a crisp chocolate coating*
covering EG *a thin covering of dust*
film EG *a film of plastic*
sheet EG *a sheet of ice*
stratum EG *the correct geological stratum*

layout NOUN
the way in which something is arranged
EG *the layout of the garden*
arrangement EG *the arrangement of a room*
design EG *the design of the museum*
format EG *the format of the book*
plan EG *a detailed plan of the house*

laze VERB
to relax and do no work
EG *We spent a few days lazing around by the pool.*
idle EG *We spent hours idling in one of the cafés.*
loaf EG *loafing around the house all day*
lounge EG *They lounged in the shade.*

> **WORD POWER**
> Antonym
> work

lazy ADJECTIVE
not willing to work
EG *a lazy and incompetent employee*
idle EG *an idle young layabout*
slack EG *Many workers have simply become too slack.*

> **WORD POWER**
> Synonyms
> good-for-nothing
> indolent
> shiftless
> slothful
> workshy
> Antonym
> industrious

❶ **lead** VERB
to guide or take someone somewhere
EG *She led him into the house.*
conduct EG *He asked if he might conduct us to the ball.*
escort EG *They were escorted by police to their plane.*
guide EG *He took me by the arm and guided me out.*
steer EG *Nick steered them towards the door.*
usher EG *I ushered him into the office.*

❷ **lead** VERB
to be in charge of
EG *He led the country between 1949 and 1984.*
command EG *the general who commanded the troops*
direct EG *He will direct day-to-day operations.*
govern EG *his ability to govern the country*
head EG *Who heads the firm?*
manage EG *I manage a small team of workers.*

supervise EG *He supervised more than 400 volunteers.*

❸ lead NOUN
a clue which may help solve a crime
EG *The police are following up several leads.*

clue EG *a vital clue to the killer's identity*
indication EG *All the indications suggest that he is the murderer.*
trace EG *No traces of violence were found on the body.*

leader NOUN
the person in charge of something
EG *the leader of the Republican Party*
boss INFORMAL EG *Who's the boss around here?*
captain EG *the captain of the team*
chief EG *the chief of police*
commander EG *a commander in the Royal Navy*
director EG *the director of the film*
head EG *Heads of government met in New York.*
principal EG *the principal of the school*
ringleader EG *the ringleader of the gang*

> **WORD POWER**
> Antonym
> follower

lead to VERB
to cause something to happen
EG *Smoking leads to heart disease and cancer.*
cause EG *Knocks can cause damage to the spine.*
contribute to EG *injuries which contributed to his death*
produce EG *The drug produces side effects.*

> **WORD POWER**
> Synonyms
> bring on
> conduce to
> result in

leaflet NOUN
a piece of paper with information about a subject
EG *Protesters were handing out leaflets in the street.*
booklet EG *a booklet about mortgage rates*
brochure EG *a travel brochure*
circular EG *A circular was sent out to shareholders.*
pamphlet EG *an anti-vivisection pamphlet*

> **WORD POWER**
> Synonyms
> handbill
> mailshot

❶ leak VERB
to escape from a container or other object
EG *The gas had leaked from a cylinder.*
escape EG *A vent was opened to let some air escape.*
ooze EG *Blood was oozing from the wound.*
seep EG *Radioactive water has seeped into underground reservoirs.*
spill EG *70,000 tonnes of oil spilled from the tanker.*

❷ leak NOUN
a hole which lets gas or liquid escape
EG *Have you plugged the leaks?*
chink EG *A mist rose from the chinks in the pavement.*
crack EG *The lava oozed through cracks in the rock.*
fissure EG *Water trickled out of fissures in the limestone.*
hole EG *The sea was flowing in through the hole in the ship's hull.*
puncture EG *My tyre has a slow puncture.*

❶ learn VERB
to gain knowledge by studying or training
EG *I am trying to learn French.*
grasp EG *The basics of the*

language are easy to grasp.
master EG *He's having trouble mastering the piano.*
pick up EG *You'll soon pick up enough German to get by.*

❷ learn VERB
to find out about something
EG *On learning who she was, I asked to meet her.*
ascertain EG *They had ascertained that he was not a spy.*
determine EG *calculations to determine the rate of tax*
discover EG *She discovered that they'd escaped.*
find out EG *As soon as we found this out, we closed the ward.*
gather EG *I gather the report is critical of the judge.*
hear EG *I heard he had moved away.*
understand EG *I understand that she's just taken early retirement.*

learned ADJECTIVE
having gained a lot of knowledge by studying
EG *a very learned man*
academic EG *I feel intimidated by academic people.*
erudite EG *a witty and erudite leader*
intellectual EG *an artistic and intellectual couple*
literate EG *a literate and educated readership*
scholarly EG *a scholarly researcher*

> **WORD POWER**
> Synonyms
> lettered
> well-read

least ADJECTIVE
as small or few as possible
EG *Stick to foods with the least fat.*
fewest EG *Which product has the fewest calories?*
lowest EG *the lowest temperatures on record for this time of year*
minimum EG *the minimum height*

for a policeman
slightest EG *He showed only the slightest hint of emotion.*
smallest EG *the smallest measurable unit of light*

> **WORD POWER**
> Antonym
> most

❶ leave VERB
to go away from a person or place
EG *He is not allowed to leave the country.*
abandon EG *He claimed that his parents had abandoned him.*
depart EG *A number of staff departed during his time as director.*
desert EG *Medical staff have deserted the city's main hospital.*
forsake EG *I would never forsake my children.*
go EG *Let me know when you're ready to go.*
quit EG *He quit his job as an office boy.*
withdraw EG *Troops withdrew from the country last month.*

> **WORD POWER**
> Synonyms
> abscond
> decamp

❷ leave NOUN
a period of time off work
EG *Why don't you take a few days' leave?*
holiday EG *I still have several days' holiday to take.*
time off EG *He took time off to go sailing with his wife.*
vacation EG *We went on vacation to Puerto Rico.*

> **WORD POWER**
> Synonyms
> furlough
> sabbatical

left-wing ADJECTIVE
believing in socialist policies

A B C D E F G H I J K L M N O P Q R S T U V W X Y Z

275

EG *a left-wing demonstration*
leftist EG *three leftist guerrilla groups*
liberal EG *a politician with liberal views*
radical EG *a radical feminist*
socialist EG *Europe's last socialist state*

legacy NOUN
property someone leaves you when they die
EG *He left his sons a generous legacy.*
bequest EG *He made a bequest to his favourite charity.*
estate EG *documents concerning the estate*
heirloom EG *a family heirloom*
inheritance EG *She was worried she'd lose her inheritance to her stepmother.*

❶ legal ADJECTIVE
relating to the law
EG *the Dutch legal system*
forensic EG *the forensic skill of a good barrister*
judicial EG *a judicial review*
judiciary EG *various levels of the judiciary system*

❷ legal ADJECTIVE
allowed by the law
EG *The strike was perfectly legal.*
authorized EG *an authorized procedure*
lawful EG *What I did was lawful and proper.*
legitimate EG *a legitimate business*
permissible EG *the current permissible levels of pesticide in food*
rightful EG *the rightful owner of the property*
valid EG *a valid passport*

> **WORD POWER**
> Synonyms
> constitutional
> licit
> sanctioned
> Antonym
> illegal

leisure NOUN
time when you can relax
EG *There wasn't a lot of time for leisure.*
free time EG *He played piano in his free time.*
recreation EG *Saturday afternoons are for recreation.*
relaxation EG *Make time for a bit of relaxation.*
time off EG *I haven't had any time off all day.*

> **WORD POWER**
> Antonym
> work

leisurely ADJECTIVE
unhurried or calm
EG *a leisurely walk along the beach*
comfortable EG *going at a comfortable speed*
easy EG *an easy pace*
gentle EG *His movements were gentle and deliberate.*
relaxed EG *a relaxed meal*
unhurried EG *an unhurried way of life*

> **WORD POWER**
> Antonym
> hasty

❶ length NOUN
the distance from one end of something to the other
EG *The fish was about a metre in length.*
distance EG *Work out the distance of the journey.*
extent EG *the extent of the rain forest*
span EG *a butterfly with a two-inch wing span*

❷ length NOUN
the amount of time something lasts for
EG *The film is over two hours in length.*
duration EG *The duration of the course is one year.*
period EG *for a limited period only*

space EG *A dramatic change takes place in the space of a few minutes.*
span EG *The batteries have a life span of six hours.*
term EG *a 12-month term of service*

lengthen VERB
to make something longer
EG *The runway had to be lengthened.*
extend EG *They have extended the deadline.*
make longer EG *You can make your hair longer by using extensions.*
prolong EG *a move which will prolong the strike*
stretch EG *Take care not to stretch the fabric.*

> **WORD POWER**
> Synonyms
> elongate
> protract
> Antonym
> shorten

lessen VERB
to decrease in size or amount
EG *changes to their diet that would lessen the risk of disease*
abate EG *The storm gradually abated.*
decrease EG *Population growth is decreasing by 1.4% each year.*
diminish EG *The threat of war has diminished.*
dwindle EG *his dwindling authority*
lower EG *The Central Bank has lowered interest rates.*
minimize EG *attempts to minimize the risk of developing cancer*
reduce EG *Gradually reduce the dosage.*
shrink EG *The forests have shrunk to half their size.*

> **WORD POWER**
> Synonyms
> de-escalate
> downsize
> Antonym
> increase

lesson NOUN

a period of time for being taught
EG *Johanna took piano lessons.*
class EG *I go to dance classes.*
coaching EG *He needs extra coaching in maths.*
lecture EG *a series of lectures on art*
period EG *We get six periods of French a week.*
tutoring EG *a growing demand for private tutoring*

❶ let VERB
to allow someone to do something
EG *The authorities won't let her leave the country.*
allow EG *I pleaded to be allowed to go.*
give permission EG *Who gave you permission to come here?*
permit EG *Permit me to express my opinion.*
sanction EG *He may now be ready to sanction the use of force.*

> **WORD POWER**
> Antonym
> forbid

❷ let VERB
to let someone use your property for money
EG *She always lets her house for the summer.*
hire out EG *The machines are hired out to farmers.*
lease EG *She plans to lease the building to students.*
rent EG *He rents rooms to backpackers.*

❶ level ADJECTIVE
completely flat
EG *a plateau of level ground*
flat EG *Cricket should be played on a totally flat field.*
horizontal EG *Every horizontal surface was covered with plants.*

> **WORD POWER**
> Antonym
> uneven

A B C D E F G H I J K L M N O P Q R S T U V W X Y Z

❷ level VERB

to make something flat
EG *We levelled the ground.*
flatten EG *Flatten the dough and cut it into four pieces.*
plane EG *planing the surface of the wood*
smooth EG *He smoothed his hair.*

❸ level NOUN

a point on a scale which measures something
EG *Crime levels have started to decline.*
grade EG *the lowest grade of staff*
rank EG *He rose to the rank of captain.*
stage EG *an early stage of development*
standard EG *a decent standard of living*
status EG *We were reduced to the status of animals.*

❶ lie VERB

to rest somewhere horizontally
EG *The injured man was lying on his back.*
loll EG *He was lolling on the sofa.*
lounge EG *We lounged on the beach all day.*
recline EG *She reclined on the couch.*
sprawl EG *They sprawled in a lawn chair, snoozing.*

> **WORD POWER**
> Synonyms
> be prostrate
> be recumbent
> be supine
> repose

❷ lie VERB

to say something that is not true
EG *She always lies about her age.*
fib EG *He fibbed when she asked him where he'd been.*
perjure oneself EG *All of the witnesses perjured themselves.*
tell a lie EG *He could never tell a lie or do anything devious.*

> **WORD POWER**
> Synonyms
> dissimulate
> equivocate
> forswear oneself
> prevaricate

❸ lie NOUN

something you say which is not true
EG *His whole story was a lie.*
deceit EG *the deceits of political leaders*
fabrication EG *She described the magazine interview as "a complete fabrication".*
falsehood EG *He accused them of spreading falsehoods about him.*
fib EG *I caught him out in another fib.*
fiction EG *His account of events is a complete fiction.*

life NOUN

the time during which you are alive
EG *a long and active life*
existence EG *a very miserable existence*
life span EG *This species of snake has a life span of up to 25 years.*
lifetime EG *a lifetime devoted to service for others*
time EG *If I had my time again, I would do things differently.*

❶ lift VERB

to move something to a higher position
EG *straining to lift heavy weights*
elevate EG *a mechanism to elevate the platform*
hoist EG *I hoisted my rucksack on to my shoulder.*
pick up EG *Anthony picked up his case from the floor.*
raise EG *He raised his hand to wave.*

> **WORD POWER**
> Antonym
> lower

❷ **lift** VERB
to remove something such as a ban or law
EG *the decision to lift sanctions against Iran*
cancel EG *The government has cancelled the state of emergency.*
end EG *pressure to end the embargo*
relax EG *an attempt to persuade the US Congress to relax the law*
remove EG *an amendment to remove the ban on divorce*

> **WORD POWER**
> Synonyms
> rescind
> revoke

❶ **light** NOUN
brightness that enables you to see things
EG *Cracks of light filtered through the shutters.*
brightness EG *the brightness of the full moon*
brilliance EG *the brilliance of the noonday sun*
glare EG *shading his eyes from the glare*
glow EG *the red glow of the dying fire*
illumination EG *The only illumination came from a small window.*
radiance EG *The bedside lamp cast a soft radiance over her face.*

> **WORD POWER**
> Synonyms
> incandescence
> luminescence
> luminosity
> phosphorescence
> Antonym
> dark

❷ **light** ADJECTIVE
pale in colour
EG *a light blue shirt*
bleached EG *bleached pine tables*
blonde or **blond** EG *blonde hair*
fair EG *to protect my fair skin*

pale EG *dressed in pale pink*
pastel EG *delicate pastel shades*

> **WORD POWER**
> Antonym
> dark

❸ **light** ADJECTIVE
not weighing much
EG *working out with light weights*
flimsy EG *a flimsy cardboard box*
lightweight EG *They will carry lightweight skis on their backs.*
portable EG *a portable television*
slight EG *She is small and slight.*

> **WORD POWER**
> Antonym
> heavy

❹ **light** VERB
to make a place bright
EG *The room was lit by a single candle.*
brighten EG *The late afternoon sun brightened the room.*
illuminate EG *No streetlights illuminated the road.*
light up EG *Fireworks lit up the sky.*

> **WORD POWER**
> Antonym
> darken

❺ **light** VERB
to make a fire start burning
EG *It's time to light the barbecue.*
ignite EG *A stray spark ignited the fireworks.*
kindle EG *I kindled a fire in the stove.*

> **WORD POWER**
> Antonym
> extinguish

❶ **like** ADJECTIVE
similar to another thing
EG *He looks just like my father.*
akin EG *She looked at me with something akin to hatred.*
alike EG *They are very alike in temperament.*

analogous EG *a process analogous to the curing of tobacco*
identical EG *Nearly all the houses were identical.*
parallel EG *Our situation is parallel to yours.*
same EG *His uniform was exactly the same colour as the car.*
similar EG *a taste similar to that of celery*

> *WORD POWER*
> Antonym
> unlike

❷ like VERB
to find someone or something pleasant
EG *I really like this music.*
adore INFORMAL EG *All her employees adored her.*
be fond of EG *Are you fond of Chinese cuisine?*
be keen on EG *I'm not very keen on sport.*
be partial to EG *I'm partial to men with dark hair.*
enjoy EG *Most children enjoy cartoons.*
love EG *She loves reading.*

> *WORD POWER*
> Antonym
> dislike

likely ADJECTIVE
having a good chance of happening
EG *It seems likely that he will come back.*
anticipated EG *the anticipated result*
expected EG *the expected response*
liable EG *He is liable to be a nuisance.*
possible EG *It's quite possible that I'm wrong.*
probable EG *the probable outcome*

> *WORD POWER*
> Antonym
> unlikely

❶ limit NOUN
a point beyond which something cannot go
EG *the speed limit*
bounds EG *the bounds of good taste*
deadline EG *We finished the job within the deadline.*
maximum EG *He was given two years in prison, the maximum allowed for the charges.*
ultimate EG *This hotel is the ultimate in luxury.*
utmost EG *His skills were tested to the utmost.*

❷ limit VERB
to prevent something from going any further
EG *Limit yourself to six units of alcohol a week.*
confine EG *Damage was confined to a small portion of the building.*
curb EG *measures to curb inflation*
fix EG *The mortgage rate is fixed at 8.5%.*
ration EG *I'm rationing myself to ten cigarettes a day.*
restrict EG *The patient was restricted to a meagre diet.*

> *WORD POWER*
> Synonyms
> circumscribe
> delimit
> demarcate
> straiten

limp ADJECTIVE
not stiff or firm
EG *a limp lettuce leaf*
drooping EG *the drooping branches of a birch*
flabby EG *a flabby stomach*
floppy EG *She fondled the dog's floppy ears.*
slack EG *his slack belly*
soft EG *a soft dough*

> *WORD POWER*
> Synonyms
> flaccid
> pliable

Antonym
stiff

❶ line NOUN
a long thin mark on something
EG *Draw a line down the centre of the page.*
rule EG *He drew a rule under the last name.*
score EG *There was a long score on the car's bonnet.*
streak EG *dark streaks on the surface of the moon*
stripe EG *a green jogging suit with white stripes down the sides*

❷ line NOUN
a row of people or things
EG *a line of spectators*
column EG *a column of figures*
file EG *A file of mourners walked behind the coffin.*
queue EG *a long queue of angry motorists*
rank EG *ranks of police in riot gear*
row EG *a row of pretty little cottages*

❸ line NOUN
the route along which something moves
EG *the line of flight*
course EG *the course of the river*
path EG *The lava annihilates everything in its path.*
route EG *the most direct route*
track EG *a railway track*
trajectory EG *the trajectory of the missile*

❶ link NOUN
a connection between two things
EG *the link between sunbathing and skin cancer*
affiliation EG *He has no affiliation with any political party.*
association EG *the association between the two companies*
attachment EG *Mother and child form a close attachment.*
bond EG *The experience created a bond between us.*

connection EG *He has denied any connection to the bombing.*
relationship EG *the relationship between humans and their environment*
tie EG *She has ties with this town.*

WORD POWER
Synonyms
affinity
liaison

❷ link VERB
to connect two things
EG *tree houses linked by ropes*
attach EG *Attach the curtains to the rods with hooks.*
connect EG *two rooms connected by a passage*
couple EG *The engine is coupled to a gearbox.*
fasten EG *a wooden bench fastened to the floor*
join EG *the skin which joins the eye to the eyelid*
tie EG *He tied the dog to the tree by its lead.*

WORD POWER
Antonym
separate

❶ liquid NOUN
a substance which is not solid and can be poured
EG *Drink plenty of liquids for the next few days.*
fluid EG *The fluid can be removed with a syringe.*
liquor EG *Pour the liquor off into the pan.*
solution EG *a solution of honey and vinegar*

❷ liquid ADJECTIVE
in the form of a liquid
EG *wash in warm water with liquid detergent*
fluid EG *a fluid fertiliser*
molten EG *molten metal*
runny EG *a dessertspoon of runny honey*

A
B
C
D
E
F
G
H
I
J
K
L
M
N
O
P
Q
R
S
T
U
V
W
X
Y
Z

❶ list NOUN
a set of things written down one
below the other
EG *There were six names on the list.*
catalogue EG *a chronological
catalogue of the Beatles' songs*
directory EG *a telephone directory*
index EG *The book includes a
comprehensive subject index.*
inventory EG *an inventory of
stolen goods*
listing EG *a listing of all the
schools in the area*
record EG *Keep a record of
everything you eat and drink.*
register EG *a register of births,
deaths and marriages*

❷ list VERB
to set things down in a list
EG *All the ingredients are listed on
the label.*
catalogue EG *I was cataloguing
my video collection.*
index EG *Most of the archive has
been indexed.*
record EG *400 species of fungi
have been recorded.*
register EG *a registered charity*

> **WORD POWER**
> Synonyms
> enumerate
> itemize
> tabulate

listen VERB
to hear and pay attention to
something
EG *I'll repeat that for those of you
who weren't listening.*
attend EG *Close your books and
attend to me.*
hark EG *Hark! I hear the sound of
footsteps.*
hear EG *Will you hear me saying
my lines?*
pay attention EG *Pay attention or
you won't know what to do.*

❶ little ADJECTIVE
small in size or amount

EG *a little old lady*
diminutive EG *a joke about his
diminutive stature*
miniature EG *He looked like a
miniature version of his brother.*
minute EG *Only a minute amount
is needed.*
petite EG *a petite blonde*
small EG *We can arrange this for a
small fee.*
tiny EG *a tiny kitten*
wee EG *You need to calm down a
wee bit.*

> **WORD POWER**
> Synonyms
> infinitesimal
> Lilliputian
> Antonym
> large

❷ little NOUN
a small amount or degree
EG *Would you like a little fruit juice?*
bit EG *He just wants a bit of
attention.*
dash EG *an all-action film with a
dash of romance*
hint EG *She added a hint of
vermouth to the gin.*
spot EG *How about a spot of lunch?*
touch EG *I've got a touch of flu.*
trace EG *There was a trace of irony
in his reply.*

> **WORD POWER**
> Synonyms
> modicum
> trifle

❶ live VERB
to have your home somewhere
EG *She has lived here for 20 years.*
dwell EG *the people who dwell in
the forest*
inhabit EG *the fish that inhabit the
coral reefs*
reside EG *He used to reside in
England.*
stay SCOTTISH AND SOUTH AFRICAN EG
*We've stayed in this house since we
got married.*

❷ live VERB
to be alive
EG *He will not live much longer.*
be alive EG *You are lucky to be alive.*
exist EG *the chances of finding life existing on Mars*

❸ live ADJECTIVE
not dead or artificial
EG *a live spider*
alive EG *It is unlikely that he is still alive.*
animate EG *an animate object*
living EG *living tissue*

lively ADJECTIVE
full of life and enthusiasm
EG *a lively personality*
active EG *an active youngster*
animated EG *an animated discussion*
energetic EG *She gave an energetic performance.*
perky EG *He wasn't quite as perky as usual.*
sparkling EG *I was enjoying a sparkling conversation.*
sprightly EG *a sprightly old man*
vivacious EG *She is vivacious and charming.*

> *WORD POWER*
> Antonym
> dull

❶ load NOUN
something being carried
EG *This truck can carry a load of up to 10 tons.*
cargo EG *The boat was carrying its usual cargo of bananas.*
consignment EG *The first consignment of food has been sent.*
freight EG *Most of the freight was carried by rail.*
shipment EG *a shipment of weapons*

❷ load VERB
to put a lot of things on or into
EG *The trucks were loaded with blankets and supplies.*

fill EG *The van was filled with crates.*
pack EG *helicopters packed with medical supplies*
pile EG *Her trolley was piled with groceries.*
stack EG *stalls stacked with wares*

❶ loan NOUN
a sum of money that you borrow
EG *a small business loan*
advance EG *She was paid a $100,000 advance on her next novel.*
credit EG *He can't get credit to buy the equipment.*
mortgage EG *I took out a second mortgage on the house.*

❷ loan VERB
to lend something to someone
EG *He loaned us the painting for our exhibition.*
advance EG *I advanced him some money till we got home.*
lend EG *Will you lend me your jacket?*

❶ local ADJECTIVE
belonging to the area where you live
EG *This is a local shop for local people.*
community EG *the revival of family and community life*
district EG *the district council*
neighbourhood EG *a neighbourhood watch scheme*
parish EG *the parish priest*
regional EG *the regional elections*

❷ local NOUN
a person who lives in a particular area
EG *That's what the locals call the place.*
inhabitant EG *the inhabitants of Glasgow*
native EG *She is proud to be a native of Sydney.*
resident EG *a protest by residents of the village*

A B C D E F G H I J K **L** M N O P Q R S T U V W X Y Z

location NOUN
a place or position
EG *a house with a beautiful location*
place EG *the place where the temple used to stand*
point EG *a popular meeting point for tourists*
position EG *The ship radioed its position to the coastguard.*
site EG *the site of the murder*
situation EG *The hotel has a superb isolated location.*
spot EG *Can you show me the spot where it happened?*
whereabouts EG *His exact whereabouts are still not known.*

> **WORD POWER**
> Synonyms
> locale
> locus

❶ lock VERB
to close and fasten something with a key
EG *Are you sure you locked the door?*
latch EG *He latched the gate.*
padlock EG *The box has been padlocked shut.*

> **WORD POWER**
> Antonym
> unlock

❷ lock NOUN
a device used to fasten something
EG *The lock had been burst open.*
latch EG *A key clicked in the latch of the front door.*
padlock EG *He put a padlock on the door of his flat.*

❶ logical ADJECTIVE
using logic to work something out
EG *a logical argument*
consistent EG *a consistent and well-presented theory*
rational EG *a rational analysis*
reasoned EG *a reasoned discussion*
sound EG *His reasoning is sound, but he has missed the point.*

valid EG *Both sides put forward valid points.*

> **WORD POWER**
> Synonyms
> cogent
> coherent
> Antonym
> illogical

❷ logical ADJECTIVE
sensible in the circumstances
EG *a logical deduction*
judicious EG *the judicious use of military force*
obvious EG *I jumped to the obvious conclusion.*
plausible EG *a plausible explanation*
reasonable EG *a reasonable course of action*
sensible EG *the sensible thing to do*
wise EG *a wise decision*

> **WORD POWER**
> Antonym
> illogical

❶ lonely ADJECTIVE
unhappy because of being alone
EG *She's lonely and just wants to talk.*
alone EG *scared of being alone in the house*
forlorn EG *He looked a forlorn figure as he left the pitch.*
forsaken EG *a forsaken and bitter man*
lonesome EG *I'm lonesome without you.*

❷ lonely ADJECTIVE
isolated and not visited by many people
EG *a lonely hillside*
deserted EG *a deserted farmhouse*
desolate EG *a desolate place*
isolated EG *Many of the villages are in isolated areas.*
remote EG *a remote outpost*
secluded EG *a secluded area close to her home*
uninhabited EG *an uninhabited*

island

WORD POWER
Synonyms
godforsaken
out-of-the-way
unfrequented

❶ long ADJECTIVE
continuing for a great amount of time
EG *a long interval when no-one spoke*
interminable EG *an interminable meeting*
lengthy EG *a lengthy process*
lingering EG *a lingering death*
prolonged EG *a prolonged drought*
protracted EG *a protracted civil war*
sustained EG *a sustained period of full employment*

WORD POWER
Antonym
short

❷ long ADJECTIVE
great in length or distance
EG *a long line of people*
elongated EG *an elongated shadow on the wall*
extensive EG *the extensive grounds of his estate*
lengthy EG *a lengthy tailback*

WORD POWER
Antonym
short

❸ long VERB
to want something very much
EG *He longed for a cigarette.*
ache EG *She still ached for her dead husband.*
covet EG *She coveted his job.*
crave EG *I crave her approval.*
hunger EG *Jules hungered for adventure.*
lust EG *She lusted after a designer kitchen.*
pine EG *I pine for the countryside.*
yearn EG *He yearned for freedom.*

longing NOUN

a strong wish for something
EG *her longing to return home*
craving EG *a craving for sugar*
desire EG *her desire for a child of her own*
hankering EG *a hankering to be an actress*
hunger EG *a hunger for success*
thirst EG *a thirst for adventure*
yearning EG *a yearning to be part of a normal family*

❶ look VERB
to turn your eyes towards something and see it
EG *She looked at me with something like hatred.*
eye EG *She eyed him with suspicion.*
gaze EG *He gazed round the room.*
glance EG *He glanced at his watch.*
observe EG *He observed me with a detached curiosity.*
peek EG *She peeked into the pram.*
regard EG *The assistant regarded him with amusement.*
survey EG *The driver surveyed the wreckage.*
view EG *I viewed the mountains from my hotel room.*

WORD POWER
Synonyms
contemplate
scrutinize

❷ look VERB
to appear or seem to be
EG *the desire to look attractive*
appear EG *He appeared intoxicated.*
look like EG *You look like you need a good night's sleep.*
seem EG *She seemed tense.*
seem to be EG *They seem to be lacking in enthusiasm.*

❸ look NOUN
the action of turning your eyes towards something
EG *Lucy took a last look in the mirror.*
gaze EG *her concentrated gaze*
glance EG *a cursory glance*

A B C D E F G H I J K **L** M N O P Q R S T U V W X Y Z

285

glimpse EG *a fleeting glimpse*
peek EG *Give me a peek at his letter.*

❹ **look** NOUN
the way someone or something appears
EG *He had the look of a desperate man.*

air EG *a nonchalant air*
appearance EG *He was fastidious about his appearance.*
bearing EG *a man of military bearing*
expression EG *I saw his puzzled expression.*
face EG *Why are you all wearing such long faces?*
semblance EG *a semblance of normality*

look after VERB
to take care of someone or something
EG *Will you look after my cats when I go on holiday?*

care for EG *vintage cars lovingly cared for by their owners*
mind EG *Jim will mind the shop while I'm away.*
nurse EG *My mother nursed him while he was ill.*
take care of EG *I'll take care of the house for you.*
tend EG *He tended his flower beds.*
watch EG *My mother will watch the kids while we're out.*

lookalike NOUN
a person who looks like someone else
EG *an Elvis lookalike*

dead ringer INFORMAL EG *a dead ringer for his brother*
double EG *He's the exact double of his father at that age.*
spitting image INFORMAL EG *She is the spitting image of me.*

look for VERB
to try to find a person or thing
EG *I'm looking for my son.*

forage EG *foraging for food*

hunt EG *Police are hunting for clues.*
search EG *Rescue teams are searching for the missing crew members.*
seek EG *They have had to seek work as labourers.*

❶ **loose** ADJECTIVE
not firmly held or fixed
EG *a loose tooth*

free EG *She broke her fall with her free hand.*
unsecured EG *corridors blocked by unsecured objects*
wobbly EG *a wobbly bridge*

> **WORD POWER**
> Antonym
> secure

❷ **loose** ADJECTIVE
not fitting closely
EG *Wear loose clothes for comfort.*

baggy EG *a baggy black jumper*
slack EG *Those trousers are very slack on you.*
sloppy EG *wearing a sloppy t-shirt, jeans and trainers*

> **WORD POWER**
> Antonym
> tight

loosen VERB
to make something looser
EG *He loosened his tie.*

slacken EG *We slackened the guy-ropes.*
undo EG *She began to undo the tiny buttons.*
untie EG *He untied his shoes and slipped them off.*

> **WORD POWER**
> Antonym
> tighten

❶ **loot** VERB
to steal from a place during a riot or battle
EG *Gangs began breaking windows and looting shops.*

pillage EG *The bandits pillaged the church.*

plunder EG *They plundered and burned the town.*
raid EG *Rustlers have raided a village in the region.*
ransack EG *The three raiders ransacked the house.*

❷ loot NOUN
stolen or illegal money or goods
EG *The loot was never recovered.*
booty EG *They divided the booty between them.*
haul EG *the biggest haul of cannabis ever seized*
plunder EG *pirates in search of easy plunder*
spoils EG *the spoils of war*
swag SLANG EG *The thieves carried the swag off in a stolen car.*

❶ lose VERB
to be unable to find
EG *I've lost my keys.*
drop EG *She's dropped a contact lens.*
mislay EG *I seem to have mislaid my glasses.*
misplace EG *Somehow my suitcase was misplaced.*

> **WORD POWER**
> Antonym
> find

❷ lose VERB
to be beaten
EG *We lost the match.*
be beaten EG *He was soundly beaten in the election.*
be defeated EG *They were defeated in the final.*

> **WORD POWER**
> Antonym
> win

lost ADJECTIVE
unable to be found
EG *a mother wailing for her lost child*
mislaid EG *searching for his mislaid keys*
misplaced EG *I've found your misplaced glasses.*

missing EG *a missing person*
vanished EG *unable to contact the vanished convoy*

❶ lot
a lot or **lots** NOUN
a large amount of something
EG *Remember to drink lots of water.*
abundance EG *an abundance of food*
a great deal EG *I've spent a great deal of time on this project.*
masses INFORMAL EG *There were masses of flowers at her funeral.*
piles INFORMAL EG *He's got piles of money.*
plenty EG *We've got plenty of time.*
quantities EG *She drank quantities of hot, sweet tea.*
scores EG *There were scores of witnesses.*

❷ lot NOUN
an amount or number
EG *We've just sacked one lot of builders.*
batch EG *a batch of cookies*
bunch INFORMAL EG *My neighbours are a noisy bunch.*
crowd EG *They're a real crowd of villains.*
group EG *a small group of football supporters*
quantity EG *a small quantity of water*
set EG *a set of photographs*

❶ loud ADJECTIVE
having a high level of sound
EG *a loud explosion*
blaring EG *a blaring television*
deafening EG *a deafening roar*
noisy EG *a noisy old car*
resounding EG *a resounding slap*
strident EG *her strident voice*
thunderous EG *thunderous applause from the crowd*

> **WORD POWER**
> Synonyms
> clamorous
> sonorous

A
B
C
D
E
F
G
H
I
J
K
L
M
N
O
P
Q
R
S
T
U
V
W
X
Y
Z

stentorian
Antonym
quiet

❷ **loud** ADJECTIVE
too brightly coloured
EG *a loud tie*
flamboyant EG *a flamboyant outfit*
flashy EG *flashy clothes*
garish EG *a garish three-piece suite*
gaudy EG *a gaudy purple-and-orange hat*
lurid EG *She painted her toenails a lurid pink.*

> *WORD POWER*
> **Antonym**
> dull

lovable ADJECTIVE
easy to love
EG *His vulnerability makes him very lovable.*
adorable EG *an adorable black kitten*
charming EG *a charming young Frenchman*
enchanting EG *He was an enchanting baby.*
endearing EG *one of his most endearing qualities*
sweet EG *a sweet little girl*

> *WORD POWER*
> **Synonyms**
> engaging
> winsome
> **Antonym**
> hateful

❶ **love** VERB
to feel strong affection for someone
EG *I loved my husband very much.*
adore EG *She adored her parents.*
cherish EG *He genuinely loved and cherished her.*
worship EG *She had worshipped him from afar for years.*

> *WORD POWER*
> **Synonyms**

be in love with
dote on
hold dear
idolize
Antonym
hate

❷ **love** VERB
to like something very much
EG *We both love fishing.*
appreciate EG *I know you appreciate good food.*
enjoy EG *Do you enjoy opera?*
like EG *I've always liked horror films.*
relish EG *I relish the challenge of dangerous sports.*

> *WORD POWER*
> **Synonyms**
> delight in
> have a weakness for
> take pleasure in
> **Antonym**
> hate

❸ **love** NOUN
a strong feeling of affection
EG *a mother's love for her children*
adoration EG *He had been used to female adoration all his life.*
affection EG *She thought of him with great affection.*
ardour EG *an attempt to rekindle their lost ardour*
devotion EG *At first she was flattered by his devotion.*
infatuation EG *consumed with infatuation for her*
passion EG *the object of her passion*

> *WORD POWER*
> **Antonym**
> hatred

❹ **love** NOUN
a strong liking for something
EG *her love of animals*
devotion EG *his devotion to literature*
fondness EG *a fondness for good wine*

liking EG *my liking for classical music*

weakness EG *He had a weakness for cats.*

> **WORD POWER**
> Synonyms
> partiality
> penchant
> Antonym
> hatred

lovely ADJECTIVE
very attractive and pleasant
EG *You look lovely.*

attractive EG *Polperro is an attractive harbour village.*

beautiful EG *She's a very beautiful woman.*

delightful EG *a delightful garden*

enjoyable EG *I've had a very enjoyable time.*

pleasant EG *a pleasant little apartment*

pretty EG *a pretty room overlooking a beautiful garden*

> **WORD POWER**
> Antonym
> horrible

loving ADJECTIVE
feeling or showing love
EG *a loving husband and father*

affectionate EG *openly affectionate with each other*

devoted EG *a devoted couple*

doting EG *a doting father*

fond EG *She gave him a fond smile.*

tender EG *Her voice was tender.*

warm EG *a warm and loving mother*

> **WORD POWER**
> Synonyms
> demonstrative
> solicitous
> warm-hearted
> Antonym
> cold

❶ **lower** VERB
to move something downwards

EG *They lowered the coffin into the grave.*

drop EG *He dropped his plate into the sink.*

let down EG *They let the barrier down.*

take down EG *The pilot took the helicopter down.*

> **WORD POWER**
> Antonym
> raise

❷ **lower** VERB
to make something less in amount
EG *a commitment to lower taxes*

cut EG *The first priority is to cut costs.*

decrease EG *The government plans to decrease interest rates.*

diminish EG *to diminish the prestige of the monarchy*

lessen EG *a diet that would lessen the risk of disease*

minimize EG *attempts to minimize the risk of cancer*

reduce EG *Gradually reduce the dosage.*

slash EG *We're slashing our prices.*

> **WORD POWER**
> Antonym
> increase

loyal ADJECTIVE
firm in your friendship or support
EG *a loyal friend*

constant EG *I've lost my best friend and constant companion.*

dependable EG *a cheerful, dependable mate*

faithful EG *She remained faithful to her husband.*

staunch EG *a staunch supporter*

true EG *a true friend*

trusty EG *a trusty ally*

> **WORD POWER**
> Synonyms
> steadfast
> true-hearted

A B C D E F G H I J K L M N O P Q R S T U V W X Y Z

A
B
C
D
E
F
G
H
I
J
K
L
M
N
O
P
Q
R
S
T
U
V
W
X
Y
Z

unswerving
unwavering
Antonym
treacherous

luck NOUN
something that happens by
chance
EG *It was just luck that we
happened to meet.*
accident EG *It came about almost
by accident.*
chance EG *We only met by chance.*
destiny EG *Is it destiny that brings
people together?*
fate EG *a simple twist of fate*
fortune EG *smiled on by fortune*

> **WORD POWER**
> Synonyms
> fortuity
> predestination

❶ lucky ADJECTIVE
having a lot of good luck
EG *He had always been lucky at
cards.*
blessed EG *being blessed with good
looks*
charmed EG *She seems to have a
charmed life.*
fortunate EG *He was extremely
fortunate to survive.*

> **WORD POWER**
> Antonym
> unlucky

❷ lucky ADJECTIVE
happening by chance with good
consequences
EG *a lucky break*
fortuitous EG *a fortuitous
combination of circumstances*
fortunate EG *a fortunate accident*
opportune EG *I had arrived at an
opportune moment.*
timely EG *his timely intervention*

> **WORD POWER**
> Synonyms
> adventitious
> propitious

providential
Antonym
unlucky

❶ lump NOUN
a solid piece of something
EG *a big lump of dough*
ball EG *a ball of clay*
cake EG *a cake of soap*
chunk EG *a chunk of bread*
hunk EG *a hunk of beef*
piece EG *a piece of cake*
wedge EG *a wedge of cheese*

❷ lump NOUN
a bump on the surface of
something
EG *I've got a big lump on my head.*
bulge EG *My purse made a bulge in
my pocket.*
bump EG *a bump in the road*
hump EG *a hump on his back*
swelling EG *a swelling over one eye*

> **WORD POWER**
> Synonyms
> protrusion
> protuberance
> tumescence

lustful ADJECTIVE
feeling or showing strong sexual
desire
EG *lustful thoughts*
carnal EG *carnal desires*
lecherous EG *a lecherous old man*
lewd EG *his arrest for lewd
behaviour*

> **WORD POWER**
> Synonyms
> lascivious
> libidinous
> wanton

luxurious ADJECTIVE
expensive and full of luxury
EG *a luxurious lifestyle*
de luxe EG *de luxe cars*
lavish EG *a lavish party*
opulent EG *an opulent office*
plush INFORMAL EG *a plush hotel*
sumptuous EG *a sumptuous feast*

WORD POWER
Antonym
plain

❶ luxury NOUN
comfort in expensive
surroundings
EG *a life of luxury*
affluence EG *the trappings of
affluence*
opulence EG *the sheer opulence of
her new life*
sumptuousness EG *The hotel
lobby was sumptuousness itself.*

❷ luxury NOUN
something enjoyable which you
do not have often
EG *Telephones are still a luxury in
poor countries.*
extra EG *The car is a basic model
with no extras.*
extravagance EG *Eating out is an
extravagance.*
indulgence EG *This car is one of
my few indulgences.*
treat EG *I only eat cakes as a treat.*

❶ lying NOUN
the action of telling lies
EG *I've had enough of your lying.*
deceit EG *the deceits of political
leaders*

dishonesty EG *deliberate
dishonesty*
fabrication EG *His story is pure
fabrication.*
fibbing EG *Her fibbing eventually
got her into trouble.*
perjury EG *This witness has
committed perjury.*

WORD POWER
Synonyms
dissimulation
duplicity
mendacity

❷ lying ADJECTIVE
telling lies
EG *The man is just a lying cheat.*
deceitful EG *deceitful and
misleading remarks*
dishonest EG *a dishonest account
of events*
false EG *a false confession*
untruthful EG *She unwittingly
gave untruthful answers.*

WORD POWER
Synonyms
dissembling
mendacious
Antonym
honest

A
B
C
D
E
F
G
H
I
J
K
L
M
N
O
P
Q
R
S
T
U
V
W
X
Y
Z

Mm Mm

machine NOUN
a piece of equipment
EG *a machine to pump water out of mines*
apparatus EG *an apparatus for use in fires*
appliance EG *electrical appliances*
contraption EG *a strange contraption called the General Gordon Gas Bath*
device EG *a timer device for a bomb*
instrument EG *navigation instruments*
mechanism EG *the locking mechanism*

❶ mad ADJECTIVE
mentally ill
EG *She was afraid of going mad.*
barmy SLANG EG *Bill used to say I was barmy.*
batty SLANG EG *some batty uncle of theirs*
crazy INFORMAL EG *If I worried about all this stuff, I'd go crazy.*
deranged EG *after a deranged man shot 14 people*
insane EG *Some people can't take it and go insane.*
loony SLANG EG *She's as loony as her brother!*

> **WORD POWER**
> Antonym
> sane

❷ mad ADJECTIVE
very foolish or unwise
EG *He'd be mad to refuse.*
barmy SLANG EG *a barmy idea*
crazy INFORMAL EG *People thought they were crazy to try it.*
daft INFORMAL EG *That's a daft question.*
foolhardy EG *Some described the act as foolhardy.*
foolish EG *It would be foolish to raise hopes unnecessarily.*
stupid EG *It would be stupid to*

pretend otherwise.

❸ mad ADJECTIVE; INFORMAL
angry about something
EG *They both got mad at me for interfering.*
angry EG *She was angry at her husband.*
crazy INFORMAL EG *This sitting around is driving me crazy.*
enraged EG *I got more and more enraged at my father.*
fuming EG *Mrs Vine was still fuming.*
furious EG *He is furious at the way his wife has been treated.*
incensed EG *Mum was incensed at his lack of compassion.*
infuriated EG *He knew how infuriated this would make me.*
irate EG *Bob was very irate, shouting and screaming about the flight delay.*
livid INFORMAL EG *I am absolutely livid about it.*

magic NOUN
a special power
EG *They believe in magic.*
sorcery EG *the use of sorcery to combat evil influences*
witchcraft EG *people who practise witchcraft*

> **WORD POWER**
> Synonyms
> necromancy
> occultism

magical ADJECTIVE
wonderful and exciting
EG *Paris is a magical city.*
bewitching EG *bewitching brown eyes*
enchanting EG *an enchanting child*

> **WORD POWER**
> Synonyms
> entrancing

| spellbinding |

main ADJECTIVE
most important
EG *the main reason*
cardinal EG *one of the cardinal rules of movie reviewing*
chief EG *one of his chief rivals*
foremost EG *one of the foremost scholars on ancient Indian culture*
leading EG *a leading industrial nation*
major EG *one of the major causes of cancer*
predominant EG *Her predominant emotion was confusion.*
primary EG *the primary source of water in the region*
prime EG *the prime suspect*
principal EG *the principal source of sodium in our diets*

mainly ADVERB
true in most cases
EG *The staff were mainly Russian.*
chiefly EG *He painted chiefly portraits.*
generally EG *It is generally true that the darker the fruit the higher its iron content.*
largely EG *The early studies were done on men, largely by male researchers.*
mostly EG *Cars are mostly metal.*
predominantly EG *Business is conducted predominantly by phone.*
primarily EG *The body is made up primarily of bone, muscle, and fat.*
principally EG *This is principally because the market is weak.*

> **WORD POWER**
> Synonyms
> for the most part
> in general
> on the whole

major ADJECTIVE
very important or serious
EG *a major problem*
critical EG *a critical factor*
crucial EG *He took the crucial*

decisions himself.
leading EG *a leading industrial nation*
outstanding EG *an outstanding contribution*
significant EG *Her upbringing had a significant effect on her relationships.*

> **WORD POWER**
> Antonym
> minor

majority NOUN
more than half
EG *The majority of our cheeses are made with pasteurized milk.*
best part EG *for the best part of 24 hours*
better part EG *I spent the better part of £100 on her.*
bulk EG *the bulk of the world's great poetry*
mass EG *the mass of the population*
most EG *Most of the book is completely true.*

> **WORD POWER**
> Synonyms
> lion's share
> preponderance

❶ **make** VERB
to construct something
EG *Sheila makes all her own clothes.*
assemble EG *Workers were assembling planes.*
build EG *Workers at the site build the F-16 jet fighter.*
construct EG *the campaign to construct a temple on the site*
create EG *It's great for a radio producer to create a show like this.*
fabricate EG *All the tools are fabricated from high quality steel.*
fashion EG *Stone Age settlers fashioned necklaces from sheep's teeth.*
form EG *a figure formed from clay*
manufacture EG *They manufacture plastics.*
produce EG *We try to produce*

items that are the basics of a stylish wardrobe.

❷ make VERB
to force someone to do something
EG *Mary made him clean up the plate.*

compel EG *legislation to compel cyclists to wear a helmet*
drive EG *Jealousy drives people to murder.*
force EG *A back injury forced her to withdraw from the competition.*
oblige EG *Finally I was obliged to abandon the car.*

> **WORD POWER**
> Synonyms
> coerce
> impel

❸ make NOUN
a particular type
EG *a certain make of wristwatch*

brand EG *a brand of cigarette*
model EG *To keep the cost down, opt for a basic model.*

❶ make up VERB
to form the parts of something
EG *Women police officers make up 13% of the police force.*

compose EG *The force would be composed of troops from NATO countries.*
comprise EG *a crowd comprised of the wives and children of scientists*
constitute EG *Hindus constitute 83% of India's population.*
form EG *Cereals form the staple diet.*

❷ make up VERB
to invent a story
EG *It's very unkind of you to make up stories about him.*

concoct EG *The prisoner concocted the story to get a lighter sentence.*
fabricate EG *Officers fabricated evidence against them.*
invent EG *I must invent something I can tell my mother.*

> **WORD POWER**
> Synonyms
> formulate
> manufacture

❶ making NOUN
the act of creating something
EG *the making of this movie*

assembly EG *the assembly of an explosive device*
building EG *The building of the airport continues.*
construction EG *boat construction*
creation EG *the creation of large parks and forests*
fabrication EG *the design and fabrication of the space shuttle*
manufacture EG *the manufacture of nuclear weapons*
production EG *These proteins stimulate the production of blood cells.*

❷ making
in the making ADJECTIVE
about to become something
EG *a captain in the making*

budding EG *a budding author*
emergent EG *an emergent state*
potential EG *a potential champion*
up-and-coming EG *an up-and-coming golfer*

male ADJECTIVE
relating to men
EG *a deep male voice*

manly EG *He was the ideal of manly beauty.*
masculine EG *masculine characteristics like facial hair*

> **WORD POWER**
> Antonym
> female

❶ man NOUN
an adult male human being
EG *a young man*

bloke BRITISH, AUSTRALIAN, AND NEW ZEALAND INFORMAL EG *a really nice bloke*
chap INFORMAL EG *I am a very lucky chap.*

gentleman EG *It seems this gentleman was waiting for the doctor.*

guy INFORMAL EG *a guy from Manchester*

male EG *A high proportion of crime is perpetrated by young males.*

> **WORD POWER**
> Antonym
> woman

❷ man NOUN
people in general
EG *All men are equal.*

humanity EG *He has rendered a great service to humanity.*

human race EG *Can the human race carry on expanding?*

mankind EG *the evolution of mankind*

> **WORD POWER**
> Synonyms
> Homo sapiens
> humankind

❶ manage VERB
to succeed in doing something
EG *We managed to find somewhere to sit.*

cope with EG *how my mother coped with bringing up three children*

succeed in EG *We have succeeded in persuading cinemas to show the video.*

❷ manage VERB
to be in charge of something
EG *Within two years he was managing the store.*

be in charge of EG *Who's in charge of the canteen?*

command EG *Who would command the troops in the event of war?*

control EG *He now controls the largest retail development empire in southern California.*

direct EG *Christopher will direct day-to-day operations.*

run EG *Is this any way to run a country?*

❶ management NOUN
the act of running an organization
EG *The zoo needed better management.*

control EG *The restructuring involves Mr Ronson giving up control of the company.*

direction EG *Organizations need clear direction.*

running EG *the day-to-day running of the clinic*

❷ management NOUN
the people who run an organization
EG *The management is doing its best.*

administration EG *They would like the college administration to exert more control.*

board EG *a recommendation which he wants to put before the board*

bosses INFORMAL EG *a dispute between workers and bosses*

directors EG *the board of directors of a local bank*

employers EG *Employers are said to be considering the demand.*

manager NOUN
a person in charge of running an organization
EG *the manager of Daiwa's New York branch*

boss INFORMAL EG *He cannot stand his boss.*

director EG *the financial director of Braun UK*

executive EG *an advertising executive*

❶ manner NOUN
the way that you do something
EG *She smiled again in a friendly manner.*

fashion EG *another drug that works in a similar fashion*

mode EG *He switched automatically into interview mode.*

style EG *Kenny's writing style*

A
B
C
D
E
F
G
H
I
J
K
L
M
N
O
P
Q
R
S
T
U
V
W
X
Y
Z

A
B
C
D
E
F
G
H
I
J
K
L
M
N
O
P
Q
R
S
T
U
V
W
X
Y
Z

way EG *He had a strange way of talking.*

❷ manner NOUN
the way that someone behaves
EG *his kind manner*

bearing EG *his military bearing*

behaviour EG *her anti-social behaviour*

conduct EG *principles of civilized conduct*

demeanour EG *a cheerful demeanour*

> **WORD POWER**
> Synonyms
> comportment
> deportment

❶ manoeuvre VERB
to move something skilfully
EG *It took expertise to manoeuvre the boat so close to the shore.*

guide EG *He took Elliott by the arm and guided him out.*

navigate EG *He attempted to navigate his way through the crowds.*

negotiate EG *I negotiated my way out of the airport.*

steer EG *I steered him towards the door.*

❷ manoeuvre NOUN
a clever action
EG *manoeuvres to block the electoral process*

dodge EG *a tax dodge*

ploy EG *a cynical marketing ploy*

ruse EG *This was a ruse to divide them.*

tactic EG *The tactic paid off.*

> **WORD POWER**
> Synonyms
> machination
> stratagem

❶ many ADJECTIVE
a large number
EG *Among his many hobbies was the breeding of fine horses.*

countless EG *She brought joy to*

countless people.

innumerable EG *He has invented innumerable excuses.*

myriad EG *the myriad other tasks we are trying to perform*

numerous EG *Sex crimes were just as numerous as they are today.*

umpteen INFORMAL EG *He has produced umpteen books.*

> **WORD POWER**
> Synonyms
> multifarious
> multitudinous
> Antonym
> few

❷ many NOUN
a large number of people or things
EG *in many of these neighbourhoods*

a lot EG *A lot of people would agree with you.*

a mass EG *a mass of books and papers*

a multitude EG *for a multitude of reasons*

large numbers EG *Large numbers of people stayed away.*

lots INFORMAL EG *lots of strange new animals*

plenty EG *plenty of vegetables*

scores EG *Scores of people were injured.*

> **WORD POWER**
> Antonym
> few

❶ mark NOUN
a small stain
EG *I can't get this mark off the curtain.*

blemish EG *If there is the slightest blemish it is rejected.*

blot EG *an ink blot*

blotch EG *His face was covered in red blotches.*

smudge EG *There was a dark smudge on his forehead.*

stain EG *grass stains*

streak EG *dark streaks on the*

surface of the moon

❷ mark VERB
to stain something
EG *to stop the horses' hooves from marking the turf*
smudge EG *Her face was smudged with dirt.*
stain EG *His clothing was stained with mud.*
streak EG *Rain had begun to streak the window-panes.*

market NOUN
a place to buy or sell things
EG *the fish market at Billingsgate*
bazaar EG *an Eastern bazaar*
fair EG *a craft fair*

marriage NOUN
the relationship between a husband and wife
EG *six years of marriage*
matrimony FORMAL EG *the bonds of matrimony*
wedlock FORMAL EG *a child conceived out of wedlock*

marsh NOUN

Types of marsh:
bog
fen
mire
morass
mudflats
quagmire
quicksands
saltmarsh
slough
swamp
wetland

❶ master NOUN
a male schoolteacher
EG *a retired maths master*
instructor EG *a college instructor*
teacher EG *her chemistry teacher*
tutor EG *an adult education tutor in German*

❷ master VERB
to learn how to do something
EG *She found it easy to master the typewriter.*

become proficient in EG *He quickly became proficient in the language.*
get the hang of INFORMAL EG *It's a bit tricky till you get the hang of it.*
grasp EG *It took him a while to grasp the basics of the process.*
learn EG *He enjoyed learning new skills.*

❶ match NOUN
an organized game
EG *a football match*
competition EG *a surfing competition*
contest EG *one of the best contests in recent boxing history*
game EG *England's first game of the new season*

❷ match VERB
to be similar to
EG *The shoes matched her dress.*
agree EG *Their statements do not agree.*
correspond EG *The two maps correspond closely.*
fit EG *The punishment must always fit the crime.*
go with EG *The curtains didn't go with the carpet.*
suit EG *the best package to suit your needs*
tally EG *The figures didn't seem to tally.*

WORD POWER
Synonyms
accord
harmonize

❶ material NOUN
any type of cloth
EG *the thick material of her skirt*
cloth EG *a piece of cloth*
fabric EG *silk and other delicate fabrics*

❷ material NOUN
a solid substance
EG *the materials to make red dye*
matter EG *waste matter from industries*

A
B
C
D
E
F
G
H
I
J
K
L
M
N
O
P
Q
R
S
T
U
V
W
X
Y
Z

stuff EG *the stuff from which the universe is made*
substance EG *a crumbly black substance*

❶ matter NOUN
something that you have to deal with
EG *business matters*
affair EG *The funeral was a sad affair.*
business EG *This whole business has upset me.*
issue EG *a major political issue*
question EG *the difficult question of unemployment*
situation EG *The situation is now under control.*
subject EG *a difficult subject on which to reach a compromise*

❷ matter NOUN
any substance
EG *The atom is the smallest divisible particle of matter.*
material EG *a conducting material such as metal*
stuff EG *a dress made from some flimsy stuff*
substance EG *a poisonous substance*

❸ matter VERB
to be important
EG *It does not matter how long their hair is.*
be of consequence EG *Their choice of partner is of no consequence to anyone but themselves.*
count EG *It's as if my opinions just don't count.*
make a difference EG *Exercise makes all the difference.*

❶ mature VERB
to become fully developed
EG *Children mature earlier these days.*
come of age EG *The money was held in trust until he came of age.*
grow up EG *She grew up in Tokyo.*
reach adulthood EG *She died before reaching adulthood.*

❷ mature ADJECTIVE
fully developed
EG *He's very mature for his age.*
adult EG *a pair of adult birds*
full-grown EG *a full-grown male orang-utan*
fully-fledged EG *He has developed into a fully-fledged adult.*
grown EG *a grown man*
grown-up EG *They have two grown-up children.*

❶ maximum NOUN
the most that is possible
EG *a maximum of fifty men*
ceiling EG *an agreement to put a ceiling on salaries*
height EG *when emigration was at its height*
most EG *The most he'll make is a hundred pounds.*
upper limit EG *the need to put an upper limit on spending*
utmost EG *He did his utmost to make her agree.*

WORD POWER
Antonym
minimum

❷ maximum ADJECTIVE
being the most that is possible
EG *the maximum recommended intake*
top EG *a top speed of 200 mph*
utmost EG *a question of the utmost importance*

WORD POWER
Antonym
minimum

maybe ADVERB
it is possible that
EG *Maybe I should have done a bit more.*
conceivably EG *The mission could conceivably be accomplished within a week.*
it could be EG *It could be that's why he refused.*

298

perhaps EG *Perhaps, in time, she'll understand.*

possibly EG *Television is possibly to blame for this.*

> *WORD POWER*
> Synonyms
> mayhap
> peradventure
> perchance

meagre ADJECTIVE
very small and inadequate
EG *his meagre pension*

inadequate EG *inadequate portions*

measly INFORMAL EG *The average British bathroom measures a measly 3.5 square metres.*

paltry EG *a paltry fine of £150*

scant EG *She berated the police for paying scant attention to the theft.*

sparse EG *sparse vegetation*

> *WORD POWER*
> Synonyms
> exiguous
> insubstantial
> scanty
> skimpy

meal NOUN
an occasion when people eat
EG *She sat next to him throughout the meal.*

banquet EG *a state banquet at Buckingham Palace*

dinner EG *a series of official dinners*

feast EG *the wedding feast*

kai AUSTRALIAN AND NEW ZEALAND INFORMAL EG *a cheap kai in a local restaurant*

> *WORD POWER*
> Synonyms
> repast
> spread

❶ **mean** VERB
to convey a message
EG *The red signal means that you can shoot.*

denote EG *Red eyes denote strain and fatigue.*

indicate EG *Today's vote indicates a change in policy.*

signify EG *Becoming a father signified that he was now an adult.*

❷ **mean** VERB
to intend to do something
EG *I meant to phone you, but didn't have time.*

aim EG *I aim to arrive early.*

intend EG *She intended to move back to France.*

plan EG *They plan to marry in the summer.*

❸ **mean** ADJECTIVE
unwilling to spend money
EG *Don't be mean with the tip.*

miserly EG *He is miserly with both his time and his money.*

snoep SOUTH AFRICAN INFORMAL EG *Have you ever met anyone as snoep as him?*

tight INFORMAL EG *He was so tight that he wouldn't even spend three roubles.*

> *WORD POWER*
> Synonyms
> parsimonious
> penny-pinching
> stingy
> tight-fisted
> Antonym
> generous

meaning NOUN
the idea expressed by something
EG *the meaning of this dream*

drift EG *Grace was beginning to get his drift.*

gist EG *I could not get the gist of their conversation.*

message EG *the message of the film*

sense EG *The word has two main senses.*

significance EG *The President's visit is loaded with symbolic significance.*

> *WORD POWER*
> Synonyms
> connotation

A
B
C
D
E
F
G
H
I
J
K
L
M
N
O
P
Q
R
S
T
U
V
W
X
Y
Z

import

❶ measure VERB
to check the size of something
EG *We measured how tall he was.*
gauge EG *He gauged the wind at over 30 knots.*
survey EG *geological experts who surveyed the cliffs*

> **WORD POWER**
> Synonyms
> calibrate
> quantify

❷ measure NOUN
an amount of something
EG *There has been a measure of agreement.*
amount EG *a certain amount of disappointment*
degree EG *a degree of success*
portion EG *I have spent a considerable portion of my life here.*
proportion EG *A large proportion of my time was spent abroad.*

❸ measure NOUN
an action in order to achieve something
EG *Tough measures are needed to maintain order.*
expedient EG *I reduced my spending by the simple expedient of destroying my credit card.*
manoeuvre EG *manoeuvres to block the electoral process*
means EG *The move is a means to fight crime.*
procedure EG *safety procedures*
step EG *steps to discourage drink-driving*

medicine NOUN
something you take to make you better
EG *They prevent the food and medicine from reaching Iraq.*
drug EG *Three new drugs recently became available.*
medication EG *some medication for her ulcers*
muti SOUTH AFRICAN INFORMAL EG

muti for treating a fever
remedy EG *At the moment we are trying a herbal remedy.*

❶ medium ADJECTIVE
average in size
EG *He was of medium height.*
average EG *a ginger tomcat of average size*
medium-sized EG *a medium-sized saucepan*
middling EG *Small and middling flats have increased in price much more than luxury ones.*

❷ medium NOUN
a means of communication
EG *the medium of television*
channel EG *through diplomatic channels*
vehicle EG *The play seemed an ideal vehicle for his music.*

> **WORD POWER**
> Synonyms
> agency
> instrument

meek ADJECTIVE
quiet and timid
EG *a meek, mild-mannered fellow*
deferential EG *the traditional requirement for Asian women to be deferential to men*
docile EG *docile, obedient children*
mild EG *a mild man*
submissive EG *Most doctors want their patients to be submissive.*
timid EG *a timid child*
unassuming EG *He's very polite and unassuming.*

> **WORD POWER**
> Synonyms
> acquiescent
> compliant
> mild-mannered
> Antonym
> bold

❶ meet VERB
to be in the same place as someone

EG *I met her quite by chance.*
bump into INFORMAL EG *I bumped into a friend of yours today.*
come across EG *where I came across a group of noisy children*
come upon EG *We turned the corner and came upon a group of hikers.*
encounter EG *the most gifted child he had ever encountered*
run across EG *We ran across some old friends.*
run into EG *You'll never guess who I ran into the other day.*

❷ **meet** VERB
to gather in a group
EG *We meet for lunch once a week.*
assemble EG *a convenient place for students to assemble between classes*
congregate EG *Youngsters love to congregate here in the evening.*
convene EG *Senior officials convened in October.*
gather EG *We all gathered in the boardroom.*
get together EG *the last time we all got together*

❸ **meet** VERB
to fulfil a need
EG *services intended to meet the needs of the elderly*
answer EG *Would communism answer their needs?*
fulfil EG *All the requirements were fulfilled.*
satisfy EG *Candidates must satisfy the general conditions for admission.*

❶ **meeting** NOUN
an event at which people come together for a purpose
EG *a business meeting*
audience EG *an audience with the Pope*
conference EG *a conference on education*
congress EG *a medical congress*
convention EG *the annual convention of the World Boxing Council*

gathering EG *a social gathering*
get-together INFORMAL EG *a get-together I had at my home*
reunion EG *a family reunion*

WORD POWER
Synonyms
conclave
convocation

❷ **meeting** NOUN
an occasion when you meet someone
EG *a chance meeting*
assignation LITERARY EG *She had an assignation with her boyfriend.*
encounter EG *a remarkable encounter with a group of soldiers*
rendezvous EG *Baxter arranged a six o'clock rendezvous.*
tryst EG *a lovers' tryst*

melodramatic ADJECTIVE
behaving in an exaggerated way
EG *Don't you think you're being rather melodramatic?*
histrionic EG *She let out a histrionic groan.*
sensational EG *sensational tabloid newspaper reports*
theatrical EG *In a theatrical gesture Glass clamped his hand over his eyes.*

❶ **melt** VERB
to become liquid
EG *The snow had melted.*
dissolve EG *Heat gently until the sugar dissolves.*
thaw EG *It's so cold the snow doesn't get a chance to thaw.*

WORD POWER
Synonyms
deliquesce
liquefy

❷ **melt** VERB
to disappear
EG *Her inhibitions melted.*
disappear EG *The immediate threat has disappeared.*
disperse EG *The crowd dispersed*

peacefully.
dissolve EG *His new-found optimism dissolved.*
evaporate EG *My anger evaporated.*
vanish EG *All her fears suddenly vanished.*

memorable ADJECTIVE
likely to be remembered
EG *a memorable victory*
catchy EG *a catchy tune*
historic EG *a historic meeting*
notable EG *with a few notable exceptions*
striking EG *the most striking feature of those statistics*
unforgettable EG *an unforgettable experience*

memory NOUN
the ability to remember
EG *Every detail is fresh in my memory.*
recall EG *a man blessed with total recall*
remembrance FORMAL EG *My remembrance of the incident is somewhat hazy.*

> ### WORD POWER
> Synonyms
> recollection
> retention

mend VERB
to repair something broken
EG *I should have had the catch mended.*
darn EG *a woman darning socks*
fix EG *If something is broken, we get it fixed.*
patch EG *They patched the barn roof.*
renovate EG *The couple spent thousands renovating the house.*
repair EG *to get her car repaired*
restore EG *experts who specialize in restoring ancient parchments*

❶ mention VERB
to talk about something briefly
EG *I may not have mentioned it to her.*

allude to EG *She alluded to his absence in vague terms.*
bring up EG *Why are you bringing it up now?*
broach EG *I broached the subject of her early life.*
hint EG *The President hinted that he might make some changes.*
intimate EG *He did intimate that he is seeking legal action.*
refer to EG *In his speech, he referred to a recent trip to Canada.*
touch on EG *The film touches on these issues, but only superficially.*
touch upon EG *I'd like to touch upon a more serious question now.*

❷ mention NOUN
a brief comment about something
EG *There was no mention of elections.*
allusion EG *She made an allusion to the events in Los Angeles.*
reference EG *He made no reference to any agreement.*

❶ merciful ADJECTIVE
showing kindness
EG *He is merciful and sympathetic to others.*
compassionate EG *a deeply compassionate man*
humane EG *the desire for a more humane society*
kind EG *She is warm-hearted and kind to everyone.*

> ### WORD POWER
> Antonym
> merciless

❷ merciful ADJECTIVE
showing forgiveness
EG *We can only hope the court is merciful.*
forgiving EG *I don't think people are in a very forgiving mood.*
lenient EG *He believes the government is already lenient with drug traffickers.*

> ### WORD POWER

Antonym
merciless

merciless ADJECTIVE
showing no kindness or
forgiveness
EG *the merciless efficiency of a
modern police state*
callous EG *his callous disregard for
human life*
cruel EG *Children can be so cruel.*
heartless EG *I couldn't believe they
were so heartless.*
implacable EG *a powerful and
implacable enemy*
ruthless EG *his ruthless treatment
of employees*

WORD POWER
Synonyms
hard-hearted
pitiless
unforgiving
Antonym
merciful

❶ mercy NOUN
the quality of kindness
EG *He showed no mercy.*
compassion EG *his compassion for
a helpless woman*
kindness EG *He was treated with
kindness by numerous officials.*
pity EG *She saw no pity in their
faces.*

WORD POWER
Synonyms
benevolence
charity

❷ mercy NOUN
the quality of forgiveness
EG *He threw himself upon the mercy
of the court.*
forgiveness EG *He fell to his knees
begging for forgiveness.*
leniency EG *He said he would
show no leniency towards them.*

WORD POWER
Synonyms
clemency

forbearance

❶ merit NOUN
worth or value
EG *Box-office success mattered more
than artistic merit.*
excellence EG *the top US award
for excellence in journalism*
value EG *The value of this work
experience should not be
underestimated.*
virtue EG *There is little virtue in
such an approach.*
worth EG *people who had already
proved their worth to their
companies*

❷ merit NOUN
a good quality that something
has
EG *Whatever its merits, their work
would never be used.*
advantage EG *The great
advantage of home-grown oranges
is their flavour.*
asset EG *Her leadership qualities
were her greatest asset.*
strength EG *The book's strength
lay in its depiction of modern-day
Tokyo.*
strong point EG *Science was never
my strong point at school.*
virtue EG *Its other great virtue is its
hard-wearing quality.*

❸ merit VERB
to deserve something
EG *Such ideas merit careful
consideration.*
be entitled to EG *She is entitled to
feel proud.*
be worthy of EG *The bank might
think you're worthy of a loan.*
deserve EG *He deserves a rest.*
earn EG *Companies must earn a
reputation for honesty.*
warrant EG *no evidence to warrant
a murder investigation*

❶ mess NOUN
a state of untidiness
EG *I'll clear up the mess later.*

A B C D E F G H I J K L M N O P Q R S T U V W X Y Z

chaos EG *Their concerts often ended in chaos.*

disarray EG *He found the room in disarray.*

disorder EG *Inside all was disorder.*

❷ mess NOUN
a situation that is full of problems
EG *the reasons why the economy is in such a mess*

fix INFORMAL EG *The government has really got itself into a fix.*

jam INFORMAL EG *They were in a real jam.*

muddle EG *Our finances are in a muddle.*

turmoil EG *Her marriage was in turmoil.*

❸ mess VERB
to spoil something
EG *He had messed up his career.*

botch up EG *I hate having builders botch up repairs on my house.*

bungle EG *Two prisoners bungled an escape bid.*

make a hash of INFORMAL EG *The government made a total hash of things.*

muck up SLANG EG *He always seemed to muck everything up.*

❶ message NOUN
a piece of information for someone
EG *He left a message on her answerphone.*

bulletin EG *a news bulletin*

communication EG *The ambassador brought a communication from the President.*

despatch or **dispatch** EG *this despatch from our West Africa correspondent*

memo EG *office memos*

memorandum EG *a memorandum from the Ministry of Defence*

note EG *I'll have to leave a note for Karen.*

word EG *There is no word from the authorities on the reported attack.*

> **WORD POWER**
> Synonyms
> communiqué
> missive

❷ message NOUN
the idea conveyed by something
EG *the story's anti-drugs message*

meaning EG *while we discussed the meaning of the play*

moral EG *the moral of the story*

point EG *My point is that I'm not going to change.*

theme EG *The book's central theme is power.*

messenger NOUN
someone who carries a message
EG *There will be a messenger at the airport to collect the photographs.*

courier EG *a motorcycle courier*

envoy EG *an envoy to the King*

runner EG *a bookie's runner*

> **WORD POWER**
> Synonyms
> emissary
> go-between
> herald

method NOUN
a way of doing something
EG *the traditional method of making wine*

approach EG *different approaches to gathering information*

mode EG *the capitalist mode of production*

procedure EG *He did not follow the correct procedure.*

technique EG *the techniques of modern agriculture*

way EG *a way of making new friends*

❶ middle NOUN
the part furthest from the edges
EG *in the middle of the room*

centre EG *the centre of the table*

halfway point EG *Postle was third fastest at the halfway point.*

midst EG *a house in the midst of huge trees*

WORD POWER
Synonyms
midpoint
midsection

❷ **middle** ADJECTIVE
furthest from the edges
EG *the middle house*
central EG *central London*
halfway EG *a point halfway between the two posts*

❶ **mild** ADJECTIVE
not strong or powerful
EG *a mild shampoo*
insipid EG *It tasted bland and insipid.*
weak EG *weak beer*

WORD POWER
Antonym
strong

❷ **mild** ADJECTIVE
gentle and good-tempered
EG *a mild man*
gentle EG *her gentle nature*
meek EG *a meek, mild-mannered fellow*
placid EG *a placid child who rarely cried*

WORD POWER
Synonyms
easy-going
equable
pacific
peaceable

❸ **mild** ADJECTIVE
warmer than usual
EG *The area is famous for its mild winter climate.*
balmy EG *balmy summer evenings*
temperate EG *a temperate climate*

❶ **mind** NOUN
your ability to think
EG *You have a very suspicious mind.*
brain EG *Once you stop using your brain you soon go stale.*

head EG *I can't get that song out of my head.*
imagination EG *Africa was alive in my imagination.*
intellect EG *good health and a lively intellect*
psyche EG *disturbing elements of the human psyche*

❷ **mind** VERB
to be annoyed by something
EG *I don't mind what you do.*
be bothered EG *I'm not bothered if he has another child.*
care EG *young men who did not care whether they lived or died*
object EG *I don't object to his smoking.*

❸ **mind** VERB
to look after something
EG *My mother is minding the shop.*
keep an eye on EG *She asked me to keep an eye on the children.*
look after EG *I looked after the dogs while she was away.*
take care of EG *There was no one else to take care of the children.*
watch EG *She bought the tickets while I watched the cases.*

minimum ADJECTIVE
being the least possible
EG *the minimum height for a policeman*
least possible EG *I try to cause the least amount of trouble possible.*
minimal EG *The aim is to incur minimal expense.*

WORD POWER
Antonym
maximum

minor ADJECTIVE
less important
EG *a minor injury*
lesser EG *They pleaded guilty to lesser charges.*
petty EG *petty crime*
secondary EG *matters of secondary importance*
slight EG *We have a slight problem.*

A
B
C
D
E
F
G
H
I
J
K
L
M
N
O
P
Q
R
S
T
U
V
W
X
Y
Z

trifling EG *Outside California these difficulties may seem trifling.*
trivial EG *trivial details*

> **WORD POWER**
> Antonym
> major

miracle NOUN
a surprising and fortunate event
EG *the Italian economic miracle*
marvel EG *a marvel of high technology*
wonder EG *the wonders of science*

❶ **miserable** ADJECTIVE
very unhappy
EG *a job which made me miserable*
dejected EG *Everyone has days when they feel dejected.*
depressed EG *He seemed somewhat depressed.*
down EG *Try to support each other when one of you is feeling down.*
downcast EG *After his defeat Mr Rabin looked downcast.*
low EG *"I didn't ask for this job," he tells friends when he is low.*
melancholy EG *It was in these hours that he felt most melancholy.*
mournful EG *He looked mournful, even near to tears.*
sad EG *It left me feeling sad and empty.*
unhappy EG *She is desperately unhappy.*
wretched EG *I feel really confused and wretched.*

> **WORD POWER**
> Synonyms
> disconsolate
> sorrowful
> Antonym
> cheerful

❷ **miserable** ADJECTIVE
causing unhappiness
EG *a miserable little flat*
gloomy EG *Officials say the outlook for next year is gloomy.*
pathetic EG *a pathetic sight*
sorry EG *The fires have left the*

industry in a sorry state.
wretched EG *He died in wretched poverty.*

misery NOUN
great unhappiness
EG *All that money brought nothing but misery.*
depression EG *He's been suffering from depression.*
despair EG *feelings of despair*
grief EG *her grief at her husband's suicide*
melancholy EG *with an air of melancholy*
sadness EG *with a mixture of sadness and joy*
sorrow EG *a time of great sorrow*
unhappiness EG *There was a lot of unhappiness in my adolescence.*
woe EG *a tale of woe*

> **WORD POWER**
> Antonym
> joy

misfortune NOUN
an unfortunate event
EG *I had the misfortune to fall off my bike.*
adversity EG *times of adversity*
bad luck EG *He has had his share of bad luck.*

misrepresent VERB
to give a false account of something
EG *Keynes deliberately misrepresented the views of his opponents.*
distort EG *The minister said his remarks had been distorted by the press.*
falsify EG *falsifying personal details on his CV*
twist EG *You're twisting my words.*

❶ **miss** VERB
to fail to notice
EG *It's on the second floor. You can't miss it.*
fail to notice EG *He failed to notice that the lights had turned red.*

A B C D E F G H I J K L **M** N O P Q R S T U V W X Y Z

mistake EG *There's no mistaking her sincerity.*
overlook EG *a fact that we all tend to overlook*

❷ miss VERB
to feel the loss of
EG *The boys miss their father.*
long for EG *Steve longed for the good old days.*
pine for EG *Make sure your pet won't pine for you while you're away.*
yearn for EG *He yearned for his freedom.*

❶ mistake NOUN
something that is wrong
EG *spelling mistakes*
blunder EG *It had been a monumental blunder to give him the assignment.*
error EG *a mathematical error*
gaffe EG *a social gaffe*
oversight EG *By an unfortunate oversight, full instructions do not come with the product.*
slip EG *There must be no slips.*

> **WORD POWER**
> Synonyms
> inaccuracy
> miscalculation

❷ mistake VERB
to think one thing is another thing
EG *I mistook him for the owner of the house.*
confuse with EG *I can't see how anyone could confuse you with your brother!*
misinterpret as EG *She misinterpreted his remarks as a threat.*
mix up with EG *People often mix me up with other actors.*
take for EG *She had taken him for a journalist.*

mistreat VERB
to treat someone badly
EG *She had been mistreated by men*
in the past.
abuse EG *parents who abuse their children*
ill-treat EG *They thought Mr Smith had been ill-treating his wife.*

mix VERB
to combine things
EG *Mix the ingredients together slowly.*
amalgamate EG *a need to amalgamate the two companies*
blend EG *Blend the butter with the sugar.*
combine EG *Combine the flour with 3 tablespoons of water.*
merge EG *how to merge the graphic with text*
mingle EG *the mingled smell of flowers and cigar smoke*

> **WORD POWER**
> Synonyms
> intermingle
> interweave

mixture NOUN
a combination of things
EG *a sticky mixture of flour and water*
alloy EG *an alloy of copper and tin*
amalgamation EG *an amalgamation of two organizations*
blend EG *a blend of wine and sparkling water*
combination EG *a fantastic combination of colours*
compound EG *a compound of water, sugar, vitamins and enzymes*
fusion EG *fusions of jazz and pop*
medley EG *We communicated in a medley of foreign words and gestures.*

> **WORD POWER**
> Synonyms
> amalgam
> composite
> conglomeration
> mix

mix up VERB
to confuse two things

EG *People often mix us up.*

confuse EG *Great care is taken to avoid confusing the two projects.*

muddle EG *Critics have begun to muddle the two names.*

mix-up NOUN

a mistake in something planned

EG *a mix-up with the bookings*

mistake EG *There must be some mistake.*

misunderstanding EG *Ensure that there is no misunderstanding about the instructions.*

muddle EG *There's been a muddle about whose responsibility it is.*

❶ moan VERB

to make a low sound

EG *Laura moaned in her sleep.*

groan EG *He began to groan with pain.*

grunt EG *The driver grunted, convinced that Michael was crazy.*

❷ moan VERB

to complain about something

EG *Carol is always moaning about her husband.*

complain EG *People always complain that the big banks are unfriendly.*

groan EG *His parents were beginning to groan about the price of college tuition.*

grumble EG *A tourist grumbled that the waiter spoke too much Spanish.*

whine EG *They come to me to whine about their troubles.*

whinge INFORMAL EG *Stop whingeing and get on with it.*

> **WORD POWER**
> Synonyms
> bleat
> carp

❸ moan NOUN

a low sound

EG *She let out a faint moan.*

groan EG *a groan of disappointment*

grunt EG *grunts of disapproval*

❶ mock VERB

to make fun of someone

EG *Don't mock me.*

deride FORMAL EG *Other countries are derided for selling arms to the enemy.*

laugh at EG *I thought they were laughing at me because I was ugly.*

make fun of EG *Don't make fun of me.*

poke fun at EG *She poked fun at people's shortcomings.*

ridicule EG *Mr Goss ridiculed that suggestion.*

scoff at EG *Some people may scoff at the idea that animals communicate.*

❷ mock ADJECTIVE

not genuine

EG *mock surprise*

artificial EG *artificial limbs*

bogus EG *their bogus insurance claim*

counterfeit EG *counterfeit money*

dummy EG *dummy weapons*

fake EG *a fake fur*

false EG *false teeth*

feigned EG *with feigned indifference*

imitation EG *imitation leather*

phoney or **phony** INFORMAL EG *a phoney excuse*

pretended EG *with pretended zeal*

sham EG *sham marriages*

> **WORD POWER**
> Synonyms
> ersatz
> pseudo

mockery NOUN

the act of mocking someone

EG *Was there a glint of mockery in his eyes?*

derision EG *shouts of derision*

jeering EG *there was a chorus of jeering, whistles and laughter*

ridicule EG *Davis was subjected to public ridicule.*

❶ model NOUN

a copy of something
EG *an architect's model of a wooden house*
dummy EG *a tailor's dummy*
replica EG *a replica of the Statue of Liberty*
representation EG *a representation of a human figure*

> *WORD POWER*
> Synonyms
> facsimile
> mock-up

❷ model NOUN
a perfect example of something
EG *The essay is a model of clarity.*
epitome EG *the epitome of good taste*
example EG *He is an example to the younger lads.*
ideal EG *the Japanese ideal of beauty*
paragon EG *a paragon of virtue*

> *WORD POWER*
> Synonyms
> archetype
> exemplar

❸ model VERB
to make something into a shape
EG *clay modelled into the shape of a bear*
carve EG *One of the prisoners had carved a wooden chess set.*
fashion EG *Stone Age settlers fashioned necklaces from sheep's teeth.*
form EG *figures formed from modelling clay*
mould EG *We moulded a chair out of mud.*
sculpt EG *An artist sculpted a full-size replica of her head.*
shape EG *Shape each half into a loaf.*

❶ moderate ADJECTIVE
neither too much nor too little
EG *moderate exercise*
average EG *I was only average academically.*

fair EG *Reimar had a fair command of English.*
medium EG *a medium size*
middling EG *The Beatles enjoyed only middling success until 1963.*
reasonable EG *reasonable force*

❷ moderate VERB
to become or make less extreme
EG *They are hoping he can be persuaded to moderate his views.*
abate EG *The storm had abated.*
curb EG *You must curb your extravagant tastes.*
ease EG *Tensions had eased.*
relax EG *Rules have been relaxed recently.*
soften EG *to soften the blow of steep price rises*
temper EG *He had to learn to temper his enthusiasm.*
tone down EG *He toned down his statements after the meeting.*

❶ modern ADJECTIVE
relating to the present time
EG *modern society*
contemporary EG *contemporary music*
current EG *the current situation*
present EG *the government's present economic difficulties*
present-day EG *Even by present-day standards these were large aircraft.*
recent EG *in recent years*

❷ modern ADJECTIVE
new and involving the latest ideas
EG *modern technology*
latest EG *the latest fashions*
new EG *new methods of treating cancer*
up-to-date EG *Germany's most up-to-date electric power station*
up-to-the-minute EG *up-to-the-minute information*

> *WORD POWER*
> Antonym
> old-fashioned

❶ modest ADJECTIVE
small in size or amount
EG *a modest improvement*
limited EG *They may only have a limited amount of time.*
middling EG *The Beatles enjoyed only middling success until 1963.*
moderate EG *moderate exercise*
small EG *a relatively small problem*

❷ modest ADJECTIVE
not boastful
EG *Lord Carrington is modest about his achievements.*
humble EG *He gave a great performance, but he was very humble.*
unassuming EG *She has a gentle, unassuming manner.*

> **WORD POWER**
> Synonyms
> self-effacing
> unpretentious
> Antonym
> conceited

❶ moment NOUN
a short period of time
EG *He paused for a moment.*
instant EG *The pain disappeared in an instant.*
minute EG *See you in a minute.*
second EG *Seconds later, firemen reached the door.*
split second EG *Her gaze met Michael's for a split second.*

> **WORD POWER**
> Synonyms
> flash
> trice

❷ moment NOUN
a point in time
EG *At that moment, the doorbell rang.*
instant EG *At that instant the museum was plunged into darkness.*
point EG *At this point Diana arrived.*
time EG *It seemed like a good time to tell her.*

money NOUN
coins or banknotes
EG *I needed to earn some money.*
capital EG *Companies are having difficulty in raising capital.*
cash EG *We were desperately short of cash.*
dosh BRITISH, AUSTRALIAN, AND NEW ZEALAND EG *They'll have the dosh to pay for a new sign.*
dough INFORMAL EG *He worked hard for his dough.*
funds EG *The concert will raise funds for research into AIDS.*

mood NOUN
a state of mind
EG *She was in a really cheerful mood.*
frame of mind EG *Lewis was not in the right frame of mind to continue.*
humour EG *Could that have been the source of his good humour?*
spirits EG *A bit of exercise will help lift his spirits.*
state of mind EG *I want you to get into a whole new state of mind.*
temper EG *I was in a bad temper last night.*

❶ moody ADJECTIVE
depressed or unhappy
EG *Tony, despite his charm, could sulk and be moody.*
irritable EG *He had missed his dinner, and grew irritable.*
morose EG *She was morose and reticent.*
sulky EG *a sulky adolescent*
sullen EG *a sullen and resentful workforce*

> **WORD POWER**
> Synonyms
> huffy
> ill-tempered
> testy
> tetchy

❷ moody ADJECTIVE
liable to change your mood
EG *David's mother was unstable*

and moody.
temperamental EG *He is very temperamental.*
volatile EG *He has a volatile temper.*

more ADJECTIVE
greater than something else
EG *I've got more chips than you.*
added EG *For added protection choose lipsticks with a sun screen.*
additional EG *The US is sending additional troops to the region.*
extra EG *Extra staff have been taken on.*
further EG *There are likely to be further delays.*

motivate VERB
to cause a particular behaviour
EG *What motivates athletes to take drugs?*
drive EG *Jealousy drives people to murder.*
inspire EG *What inspired you to change your name?*
lead EG *His abhorrence of racism led him to write the book.*
move EG *It was punk that first moved him to join a band.*
prompt EG *Japan's recession has prompted consumers to cut back on buying cars.*
provoke EG *The destruction of the mosque has provoked much anger.*

mountain NOUN

Types of mountain:
alp
ben (*Scottish*)
elevation
height
mount

peak
precipice
range
ridge

❶ **move** VERB
to change position
EG *The train began to move.*
budge EG *Her mother refused to budge from London.*
go EG *It took us an hour to go three miles.*
proceed EG *He proceeded down the spiral stairway.*
shift EG *He shifted from foot to foot.*
stir EG *Ellen shook him, and he started to stir.*

❷ **move** VERB
to change residence
EG *She had often considered moving to London.*
migrate EG *Peasants have migrated to the cities.*
move house EG *They move house fairly frequently.*
relocate EG *if the company was to relocate*

❸ **move** VERB
to cause a deep emotion
EG *Her story moved us to tears.*
affect EG *Her loss still clearly affects him.*
touch EG *Her enthusiasm touched me.*

❶ **movement** NOUN
a change of position
EG *They monitor the movement of the fish going up river.*
flow EG *the frantic flow of cars and buses along the street*
motion EG *the wind from the car's motion*

❷ **movement** NOUN
a group of people with similar aims
EG *the peace movement*
campaign EG *the campaign against public smoking*
faction EG *the leaders of the*

country's warring factions

group EG *members of an environmental group*

organization EG *the International Labour Organization*

moving ADJECTIVE
causing deep emotion
EG *It was a moving moment.*

affecting EG *one of the most affecting scenes in the film*

emotional EG *an emotional reunion*

poignant EG *a poignant love story*

stirring EG *a stirring speech*

touching EG *the touching tale of a wife who stood by husband she loved*

❶ **muddle** NOUN
a state of disorder
EG *Our finances are in a muddle.*

chaos EG *Their concerts often ended in chaos.*

confusion EG *There was confusion when a man fired shots.*

disarray EG *He found the room in disarray.*

disorder EG *Inside all was disorder.*

disorganization EG *a state of complete disorganization*

jumble EG *a meaningless jumble of words*

mess EG *the reasons why the economy is in such a mess*

tangle EG *a tangle of wires*

❷ **muddle** VERB
to mix things up
EG *One or two critics have begun to muddle the two names.*

confuse EG *Great care is taken to avoid confusing the two projects.*

jumble EG *a number of animals whose remains were jumbled together*

mix up EG *People often mix us up.*

multiply VERB
to increase in number
EG *The trip wore on and the hazards multiplied.*

increase EG *The population continues to increase.*

proliferate EG *Computerized databases are proliferating fast.*

spread EG *Cholera is not spreading as quickly as it did in the past.*

mumble VERB
to speak quietly
EG *He mumbled a few words.*

murmur EG *He murmured something to the professor.*

mutter EG *He sat there muttering to himself.*

❶ **murder** NOUN
the act of killing someone
EG *after being found guilty of murder*

assassination EG *the assassination of John F. Kennedy*

homicide EG *the scene of the homicide*

killing EG *a brutal killing*

manslaughter EG *She was found guilty of manslaughter.*

slaughter EG *the imperial army's slaughter of Chinese civilians*

slaying LITERARY EG *a trail of motiveless slayings*

❷ **murder** VERB
to kill someone
EG *a thriller about two men who murder a third*

assassinate EG *Robert Kennedy was assassinated in 1968.*

kill EG *a man who killed his wife*

slaughter EG *Thirty four people were slaughtered while queueing up to cast their votes.*

slay LITERARY EG *the field where Saint George is reputed to have slain the dragon*

take the life of EG *He admitted to taking the lives of at least 35 more women.*

❶ **mysterious** ADJECTIVE
strange and not well understood
EG *He died in mysterious circumstances.*

arcane FORMAL EG *the arcane world of high finance*

baffling EG *a baffling array of wires*
cryptic EG *My father's notes are more cryptic here.*
enigmatic EG *one of Orson Welles's most enigmatic films*
mystifying EG *I find your attitude rather mystifying.*

> ### WORD POWER
> Synonyms
> abstruse
> recondite

❷ **mysterious** ADJECTIVE
secretive about something
EG *Stop being so mysterious.*
furtive EG *with a furtive glance*
over her shoulder
secretive EG *the secretive world of spying*

mystery NOUN
something that is not understood
EG *the mystery surrounding his death*
conundrum EG *this theological conundrum*
enigma EG *Iran remains an enigma for the outside world.*
puzzle EG *"Women are a puzzle,"* *he said.*
riddle EG *the answer to the riddle of why it was never finished*

A
B
C
D
E
F
G
H
I
J
K
L
M
N
O
P
Q
R
S
T
U
V
W
X
Y
Z

Nn Nn

❶ naked ADJECTIVE
not wearing any clothes
EG *a naked man diving into the sea*
bare EG *her bare feet*
nude EG *nude bathing*
stark-naked EG *She didn't seem to notice I was stark-naked.*
unclothed EG *an unclothed male body*
undressed EG *She couldn't remember getting undressed.*

WORD POWER
Antonym
clothed

❷ naked ADJECTIVE
openly displayed or shown
EG *naked aggression*
blatant EG *evidence of blatant discrimination*
evident EG *the party's evident dislike of the president*
manifest EG *his manifest enthusiasm*
open EG *open opposition to the government*
unmistakable EG *with unmistakable amusement in his eyes*

WORD POWER
Synonyms
overt
patent
stark
Antonym
secret

❶ name NOUN
a word that identifies a person or thing
EG *My name is Joe.*
designation EG *a level four alert, a designation reserved for very serious incidents*
epithet EG *the common epithet for the Buddha*
nickname EG *He's heard your*

nickname is Codfish.
term EG *I don't know the medical term for it.*
title EG *Your actual title would be business manager.*

WORD POWER
Synonyms
appellation
denomination
sobriquet

❷ name NOUN
the opinion people have about someone
EG *to protect Janet's good name*
character EG *a series of personal attacks on my character*
reputation EG *I know Chris has a bad reputation.*

❸ name VERB
to give a name to someone or something
EG *a little girl named Betsy*
baptize EG *She could be baptized Margaret.*
call EG *in a town called Fishingport*
christen EG *He wanted to christen his son Arthur Albert.*
dub EG *a girl cruelly dubbed "the Worm"*
style EG *a character who styled himself the Memory Man*
term EG *He had been termed a temporary employee.*

narrow ADJECTIVE
having a small distance from side to side
EG *a narrow stream*
fine EG *the fine hairs on her arms*
slender EG *long slender legs*
slim EG *a slim volume of Auden's poems*
thin EG *a thin layer of clay*

WORD POWER
Antonym
wide

A B C D E F G H I J K L M N O P Q R S T U V W X Y Z

narrow-minded ADJECTIVE
unwilling to consider new ideas
or other people's opinions
EG *their own narrow-minded view of
the world*
biased EG *a biased view*
bigoted EG *bigoted opinions*
insular EG *those insular British
travellers*
opinionated EG *the most
opinionated rubbish I have read*
prejudiced EG *a whole host of
prejudiced and xenophobic ideas*

> **WORD POWER**
> Synonyms
> parochial
> reactionary
> Antonym
> tolerant

nasty ADJECTIVE
very unpleasant
EG *a nasty taste*
disagreeable EG *a disagreeable
experience*
disgusting EG *the most disgusting
behaviour*
foul EG *They produce a foul smell
of rotten eggs.*
horrible EG *I've got a horrible
feeling about this one.*
repellent EG *the most repellent
human being I have ever met*
unpleasant EG *some unpleasant
surprises*
vile EG *All the food is vile.*

> **WORD POWER**
> Antonym
> pleasant

❶ natural ADJECTIVE
normal and to be expected
EG *the natural reaction to a failed
marriage*
common EG *It is a common
response.*
everyday EG *the everyday drudgery
of work*
normal EG *Biting is normal for
puppies when they are teething.*

ordinary EG *The cottage looks
quite ordinary from the road.*
typical EG *typical symptoms of
stress*
usual EG *It was not usual for the
women to accompany them.*

> **WORD POWER**
> Antonym
> unnatural

❷ natural ADJECTIVE
not trying to pretend
EG *He was so natural with the
children.*
candid EG *rather candid about her
marriage*
frank EG *an unusually frank
interview*
genuine EG *He always seems so
genuine.*
real EG *She came across as a real
person.*
unaffected EG *She sang with
unaffected simplicity.*

> **WORD POWER**
> Synonyms
> artless
> ingenuous
> Antonym
> false

❸ natural ADJECTIVE
existing from birth and not
learned
EG *I never had much natural rhythm.*
inborn EG *an inborn sense of
optimism*
inherent EG *the inherent goodness
of people*
innate EG *the innate conservatism
of his predecessor*
instinctive EG *an instinctive
distrust of authority*
intuitive EG *an intuitive
understanding of the market*
native EG *He relies on his native
wit to get him through.*

> **WORD POWER**
> Synonyms
> immanent

A B C D E F G H I J K L M N O P Q R S T U V W X Y Z

315

indigenous

nature NOUN
someone's character
EG *It's not in my nature to sit still.*
character EG *the funny side of his character*
make-up EG *Compromise was never part of his make-up.*
personality EG *his dominating personality*

❶ naughty ADJECTIVE
tending to behave badly
EG *a naughty little boy*
bad EG *the bad behaviour of their teenage children*
disobedient EG *Lucy was similarly disobedient.*
impish EG *an impish sense of humour*
mischievous EG *a mischievous child*
wayward EG *He tried to control his wayward son.*

> **WORD POWER**
> Antonym
> well-behaved

❷ naughty ADJECTIVE
rude or indecent
EG *a programme all about naughty words*
bawdy EG *a series of bawdy jokes*
lewd EG *his arrest for lewd behaviour*
obscene EG *making obscene gestures to the crowd*
vulgar EG *The lyrics were vulgar.*

> **WORD POWER**
> Synonyms
> ribald
> risqué
> smutty

near ADJECTIVE
not far away
EG *A beautiful woman is near.*
adjacent EG *an adjacent room*
adjoining EG *A phone rang in an adjoining office.*

close EG *a close neighbour*
nearby EG *the nearby village*

> **WORD POWER**
> Antonym
> far

nearly ADVERB
not completely but almost
EG *The beach was nearly empty.*
almost EG *Over the past decade their wages have almost doubled.*
as good as EG *The World Championship is as good as over.*
just about EG *We are just about finished with this section.*
practically EG *The house was practically a wreck.*
virtually EG *Their country is virtually bankrupt.*

❶ neat ADJECTIVE
having everything arranged in a tidy way
EG *The house was clean and neat.*
orderly EG *an orderly office*
smart EG *a smart navy blue suit*
spruce EG *Mundo was looking spruce in a suit.*
tidy EG *He always kept his bedroom tidy.*
trim EG *a street of trim little villas*

> **WORD POWER**
> Antonym
> untidy

❷ neat ADJECTIVE
not mixed with anything else
EG *a small glass of neat vodka*
pure EG *a carton of pure orange juice*
straight EG *calling for a straight whisky*

> **WORD POWER**
> Synonyms
> undiluted
> unmixed

❶ necessary ADJECTIVE
needed so that something can happen
EG *Make the necessary arrangements.*

essential EG *It is essential that you visit a dentist.*

imperative EG *It is imperative we end up with a win.*

indispensable EG *Jordan is an indispensable part of the peace process.*

required EG *That book is required reading.*

vital EG *Bone marrow is vital for producing blood cells.*

> **WORD POWER**
> Synonyms
> de rigueur
> requisite
> Antonym
> unnecessary

❷ necessary ADJECTIVE; FORMAL
certain to happen or exist
EG *a necessary consequence of war*

certain EG *one certain outcome of the conference*

inevitable EG *She now accepts that a divorce is inevitable.*

inexorable EG *The growth in travel has been inexorable.*

unavoidable EG *The union knows that job losses are unavoidable.*

need VERB
to believe you must have or do something
EG *You need some fresh air.*

demand EG *The children demand her attention.*

require EG *If you require further information, please telephone.*

want EG *I want a drink.*

❶ neglect VERB
to fail to look after someone or something
EG *unhappy and neglected children*

ignore EG *They see the government ignoring poor people.*

overlook EG *Pensioners feel they are being overlooked.*

turn your back on EG *Do not turn your back on the unemployed.*

❷ neglect VERB; FORMAL
to fail to do something
EG *He had neglected to give her his address.*

fail EG *I was shattered and I failed to tell her about the good bits.*

forget EG *She forgot to lock her door.*

omit EG *He omitted to mention his connection with the company.*

❸ neglect NOUN
lack of care
EG *Most of her plants died from neglect.*

disregard EG *a callous disregard for his victims*

indifference EG *Indifference to patients is rare in America.*

unconcern EG *the government's unconcern for the environment*

nervous ADJECTIVE
worried about something
EG *She had been nervous before the match.*

anxious EG *I was very anxious about her safety.*

apprehensive EG *Their families are apprehensive about the trip.*

edgy EG *I was edgy and tired.*

jittery INFORMAL EG *She still feels jittery when she visits her sister.*

jumpy EG *The Italians are getting jumpy after drawing against the Swiss.*

tense EG *too tense to sleep*

toey AUSTRALIAN SLANG EG *Dad's getting a bit toey.*

uptight INFORMAL EG *an uptight British couple*

worried EG *You had me worried for a moment.*

> **WORD POWER**
> Antonym
> calm

neutral ADJECTIVE
not supporting either side
EG *We stayed neutral during the war.*

disinterested EG *a disinterested*

A
B
C
D
E
F
G
H
I
J
K
L
M
N
O
P
Q
R
S
T
U
V
W
X
Y
Z

observer
dispassionate EG *a full and dispassionate account*
impartial EG *How can he give impartial advice?*
nonaligned EG *the Arab and nonaligned countries*

> **WORD POWER**
> Synonyms
> nonpartisan
> unbiased
> unprejudiced
> Antonym
> biased

never ADVERB
at no time at all
EG *I never said I was leaving.*
at no time EG *At no time did he see the helicopter.*
not ever EG *The problem won't ever go away.*

new ADJECTIVE
recently created or discovered
EG *a new hotel*
current EG *all the current gossip on the stars*
latest EG *We review all the latest films.*
recent EG *Lawson's most recent novel*
up-to-date EG *the most up-to-date computers*

> **WORD POWER**
> Synonyms
> state-of-the-art
> ultramodern
> Antonym
> old

news NOUN
information about things that have happened
EG *news about the civil war*
bulletin EG *the main evening bulletin*
disclosure EG *disclosures about his private life*
dispatch EG *the latest dispatches from the war zone*

information EG *up-to-date information on weather*
intelligence EG *military intelligence from behind Iraqi lines*
latest INFORMAL EG *the latest on the bomb explosion*
tidings FORMAL EG *the bearer of bad tidings*
word EG *There is no word about casualties.*

❶ **next** ADJECTIVE
coming immediately after something else
EG *Their next child was a girl.*
ensuing EG *the ensuing years of violence*
following EG *The following day I went to work as usual.*
subsequent EG *As subsequent events showed, he was wrong.*
succeeding EG *succeeding generations of students*

❷ **next** ADVERB
coming immediately after something else
EG *Steve arrived next.*
afterwards EG *I felt dizzy afterwards and had to sit down.*
subsequently EG *She was subsequently married to his cousin.*

❸ **next** ADJECTIVE
in a position nearest to something
EG *in the next room*
adjacent EG *I pulled into the adjacent driveway.*
adjoining EG *in adjoining streets*
closest EG *Britain's closest neighbours*
nearest EG *the nearest Italian restaurant*
neighbouring EG *Liberians fleeing to neighbouring countries*

nice ADJECTIVE
attractive or enjoyable
EG *Did you have a nice time, dear?*
agreeable EG *an agreeable place to live*
attractive EG *an attractive young*

woman
charming EG *a charming little shop*
delightful EG *Stephens was a delightful man.*
enjoyable EG *What an enjoyable day that was.*
good EG *a really good party*
pleasant EG *a pleasant way to spend the day*
pleasurable EG *Much of my job is pleasurable.*

❶ noble ADJECTIVE
deserving admiration because of honesty, bravery and unselfishness
EG *a good and noble thing to do*
generous EG *It reflects his generous nature.*
honourable EG *His colleagues were honourable people.*
magnanimous EG *Miss Balding is magnanimous in victory.*
upright EG *a very upright, trustworthy man*
virtuous EG *the virtuous Mrs Friendall*
worthy EG *less worthy members of our profession*

> **WORD POWER**
> Antonym
> ignoble

❷ noble NOUN
someone from the highest social rank
EG *The Scottish nobles were united.*
aristocrat EG *All his sisters had married German aristocrats.*
lord EG *They assumed that Amy was a snob because her father was a lord.*
nobleman EG *a Spanish nobleman*
peer EG *He was made a life peer in 1981.*

> **WORD POWER**
> Antonym
> peasant

noise NOUN
a loud or unpleasant sound

EG *He is making an awful noise.*
commotion EG *There was a commotion in the corridor.*
din EG *He'd never heard a din like it.*
hubbub EG *the hubbub of Paris in the 1880s*
pandemonium EG *There was pandemonium in the classroom.*
racket EG *There was a terrible racket going on.*
row EG *Whatever is that row?*
uproar EG *The courtroom was in an uproar.*

> **WORD POWER**
> Synonyms
> clamour
> rumpus
> tumult
> Antonym
> silence

noisy ADJECTIVE
making a lot of noise
EG *a noisy audience of schoolchildren*
deafening EG *a deafening roar*
loud EG *The disco music was a little too loud.*
piercing EG *her piercing laugh*
strident EG *the strident vocals of Joy Malcolm*
tumultuous EG *He took the field to tumultuous applause.*
vociferous EG *vociferous support from the Scottish fans*

> **WORD POWER**
> Synonyms
> clamorous
> riotous
> uproarious
> Antonym
> quiet

nominate VERB
to suggest someone for a position
EG *The party refused to nominate him as its candidate.*
name EG *He'll be naming a new captain.*
propose EG *Cliff was proposed as*

A
B
C
D
E
F
G
H
I
J
K
L
M
N
O
P
Q
R
S
T
U
V
W
X
Y
Z

chairman.

recommend EG *He recommended him as his successor at Boston.*

select EG *no prospect of being selected to stand for Parliament*

submit EG *Mr Heath submitted a list of 200 names.*

suggest EG *Some commentators have suggested Clark for the job.*

nonsense NOUN
foolish words or behaviour
EG *I say the allegations are complete nonsense.*

bull SLANG EG *They're teaching our kids a load of bull.*

drivel EG *mindless drivel aimed at Middle America*

garbage INFORMAL EG *One source claimed the rumours were complete garbage.*

inanity EG *the burbling inanities of the tabloids*

rot EG *She is talking complete rot.*

rubbish EG *complete and utter rubbish*

waffle BRITISH INFORMAL EG *He writes smug, sanctimonious waffle.*

normal ADJECTIVE
usual and ordinary
EG *my normal routine*

average EG *What's your average day like?*

conventional EG *conventional tastes*

habitual EG *their country of habitual residence*

ordinary EG *It was just an ordinary weekend.*

regular EG *It looks like a regular cigarette.*

routine EG *a routine medical check*

standard EG *standard practice*

typical EG *A typical day begins at 8.30.*

usual EG *She did not collect him at the usual time.*

> **WORD POWER**
> Antonym
> unusual

❶ notice VERB
to become aware of something
EG *Then I noticed Billy wasn't laughing.*

detect EG *He detects signs of growing support for his plan.*

discern EG *I did not discern any change in attitudes.*

note EG *I noted that the rain had stopped.*

observe EG *I've observed how hard he had to work.*

perceive EG *gradually perceiving the possibilities*

see EG *I saw that the lobby was swarming with police.*

spot EG *Allen spotted me on the other side of the dance floor.*

❷ notice NOUN
a written announcement
EG *a handwritten notice in the window*

advertisement EG *one advertisement in a local paper*

bill EG *students posting bills near the campus for a demo*

poster EG *a poster advertising a charity concert*

sign EG *a hand-written cardboard sign hung round his neck*

❸ notice NOUN
warning that something is going to happen
EG *She was transferred without notice.*

advance warning EG *advance warning of the attack*

intimation EG *He has given no intimation of an intention to resign.*

notification EG *Official notification is expected to arrive today.*

warning EG *I was sacked without warning.*

noticeable ADJECTIVE
obvious and easy to see
EG *a noticeable improvement*

conspicuous EG *a conspicuous lack of sympathy*

evident EG *He ate with evident enjoyment.*
obvious EG *There are obvious dangers.*
perceptible EG *Germany is showing a perceptible improvement.*
unmistakable EG *a growing but unmistakable impatience*

> **WORD POWER**
> Synonyms
> manifest
> salient

notorious ADJECTIVE
well-known for something bad
EG *The district was notorious for violent crime.*
disreputable EG *a low and disreputable character*
infamous EG *an industry infamous for late payment of debts*
scandalous EG *her scandalous affair with the president*

nuisance NOUN
someone or something that is annoying
EG *Sorry to be a nuisance.*
annoyance EG *Snoring can be an annoyance.*
bother EG *Most men hate the bother of shaving.*
hassle INFORMAL EG *Writing out a cheque is a hassle.*
inconvenience EG *the inconvenience of a rail strike*
irritation EG *He describes the tourists as "an irritation".*
pain INFORMAL EG *She found dressing up for the occasion a real pain.*
pest EG *I didn't want to be a cry baby or a pest.*

> **WORD POWER**
> Synonyms
> plague
> vexation

❶ numb ADJECTIVE
unable to feel anything
EG *Your right arm goes numb.*

dead EG *Hillier suffered a dead leg playing for the reserves.*
frozen EG *a frozen shoulder*
insensitive EG *The brain itself is insensitive to pain.*
paralysed EG *He has been left with a paralysed arm.*

> **WORD POWER**
> Synonyms
> benumbed
> insensible

❷ numb VERB
to make you unable to feel anything
EG *The cold numbed my fingers.*
dull EG *morphine to dull the pain*
freeze EG *an epidural to freeze the hip area*
paralyse EG *people paralysed by illness or injury*
stun EG *the gun used to stun the animals*

> **WORD POWER**
> Synonyms
> benumb
> deaden
> immobilize

❶ number NOUN
a word or symbol used for counting
EG *Pick a number between one and ten.*
digit EG *a six-digit password*
figure EG *a figure between a hundred and a thousand*
numeral EG *Roman numerals*

> **WORD POWER**
> Synonyms
> character
> integer

❷ number NOUN
a quantity of things or people
EG *Adrian has introduced me to a large number of people.*
collection EG *a huge collection of books about Keats*
crowd EG *a huge crowd of*

supporters

horde EG *a horde of drunken villagers*

multitude EG *Bands can play to multitudes of fans.*

numerous ADJECTIVE
existing or happening in large numbers

EG *on numerous occasions*

lots EG *I've got lots of photos of the kids.*

many EG *I have met Imran many times.*

several EG *He is fluent in several languages.*

oaf NOUN
a clumsy or aggressive person
EG *You drunken oaf!*
brute EG *Custer was an idiot and a brute.*
lout EG *a drunken lout*

oath NOUN
a formal promise
EG *He took an oath of loyalty to the government.*
pledge EG *The meeting ended with a pledge to step up cooperation.*
promise EG *If you make a promise, you should keep it.*
vow EG *I made a silent vow to be more careful.*

obedient ADJECTIVE
tending to do what you are told
EG *He was always very obedient to his parents.*
law-abiding EG *law-abiding citizens*
submissive EG *Most doctors want their patients to be submissive.*
subservient EG *her willingness to be subservient to her children*

WORD POWER
Synonyms
biddable
compliant
Antonym
disobedient

obey VERB
to do what you are told
EG *Most people obey the law.*
abide by EG *They have got to abide by the rules.*
adhere to EG *All members adhere to a strict code of practice.*
comply with EG *The army will comply with the ceasefire.*
follow EG *Take care to follow the instructions carefully.*
observe EG *forcing motorists to observe speed restrictions*

WORD POWER
Antonym
disobey

❶ object NOUN
anything solid and non-living
EG *everyday objects such as wooden spoons*
article EG *household articles*
thing EG *What's that thing in the middle of the fountain?*

❷ object NOUN
an aim or purpose
EG *The object of the exercise is to raise money for the charity.*
aim EG *The aim of the festival is to increase awareness of Hindu culture.*
goal EG *The goal is to raise as much money as possible.*
idea EG *The idea is to give children the freedom to explore.*
intention EG *It is my intention to remain in my position.*
objective EG *His objective was to win.*
purpose EG *What is the purpose of your visit?*

❸ object VERB
to express disapproval
EG *A lot of people will object to the book.*
oppose EG *Many parents oppose bilingual education in schools.*
protest EG *He picked up the cat before Rosa could protest.*

WORD POWER
Synonyms
demur
expostulate
Antonym
approve

objection NOUN
disapproval of something
EG *despite objections by the White House*
opposition EG *Opposition to this*

plan has come from the media.
protest EG *protests against the government*

> **WORD POWER**
> Antonym
> support

obscene ADJECTIVE
indecent and likely to upset people
EG *obscene pictures*
bawdy EG *a bawdy song*
blue EG *a blue movie*
dirty EG *a dirty book*
filthy EG *a filthy joke*
indecent EG *an indecent suggestion*
lewd EG *lewd comments*
pornographic EG *a pornographic magazine*

> **WORD POWER**
> Synonyms
> ribald
> salacious
> smutty

❶ obscure ADJECTIVE
known by only a few people
EG *an obscure Mongolian dialect*
little-known EG *a little-known Austrian composer*
unknown EG *an unknown writer*

> **WORD POWER**
> Antonym
> famous

❷ obscure ADJECTIVE
difficult to understand
EG *The news was shrouded in obscure language.*
arcane EG *the arcane world of contemporary classical music*
cryptic EG *cryptic comments*
opaque EG *the opaque language of the inspector's reports*

> **WORD POWER**
> Synonyms
> abstruse
> esoteric
> recondite
> Antonym

simple

❸ obscure VERB
to make something difficult to see
EG *His view was obscured by trees.*
cloak EG *a land permanently cloaked in mist*
cloud EG *Perhaps anger had clouded his vision.*
conceal EG *The hat concealed her hair.*
hide EG *The compound was hidden by trees and shrubs.*
mask EG *A thick grey cloud masked the sun.*
screen EG *Most of the road was screened by a block of flats.*
shroud EG *Mist shrouded the outline of Buckingham Palace.*

> **WORD POWER**
> Antonym
> expose

observant ADJECTIVE
good at noticing things
EG *Painting makes you really observant of things.*
attentive EG *the attentive audience*
perceptive EG *a perceptive remark*
vigilant EG *He warned the public to be vigilant.*
watchful EG *Keep a watchful eye on babies and toddlers.*

> **WORD POWER**
> Synonyms
> eagle-eyed
> sharp-eyed

obsession NOUN
a compulsion to think about something
EG *her obsession with Christopher*
complex EG *I have never had a complex about my height.*
fixation EG *the country's fixation on the war*
mania EG *a mania for horror films*
preoccupation EG *today's preoccupation with royal misdeeds*

thing INFORMAL EG *He's got this thing about ties.*

obstacle NOUN
something which makes it difficult to go forward
EG *a large obstacle to improving housing conditions*
barrier EG *Taxes are the most obvious barrier to free trade.*
difficulty EG *the difficulties ahead*
hindrance EG *The higher rates have been a hindrance to economic recovery.*
hurdle EG *the first hurdle for many women returning to work*
impediment EG *There was no legal impediment to the marriage.*
obstruction EG *an obstruction in the road*

> *WORD POWER*
> Synonyms
> bar
> stumbling block

obstinate ADJECTIVE
unwilling to change your mind
EG *He is obstinate and will not give up.*
dogged EG *his dogged insistence on their rights*
headstrong EG *He's young and very headstrong.*
inflexible EG *His opponents viewed him as dogmatic and inflexible.*
intractable EG *He protested but Wright was intractable.*
stubborn EG *a stubborn character who is used to getting his own way*
wilful EG *a wilful child*

> *WORD POWER*
> Synonyms
> intransigent
> recalcitrant
> refractory
> Antonym
> flexible

obvious ADJECTIVE
easy to see or understand
EG *an obvious injustice*

apparent EG *It was apparent that he had lost interest.*
blatant EG *a blatant foul*
clear EG *a clear breach of the rules*
evident EG *His love of nature is evident in his paintings.*
overt EG *parents who showed us no overt affection*
palpable EG *The tension between them is palpable.*
plain EG *It was plain to him that I was having a nervous breakdown.*
self-evident EG *The implications for this country are self-evident.*

> *WORD POWER*
> Synonyms
> conspicuous
> manifest
> patent

❶ occasion NOUN
an important event
EG *The launch of a ship was a big occasion.*
affair EG *The visit was to be a purely private affair.*
event EG *A new book by Grass is always an event.*

❷ occasion NOUN
an opportunity to do something
EG *an important occasion for setting out government policy*
chance EG *the chance to practise medicine in British hospitals*
opportunity EG *I had an opportunity to go to New York.*
time EG *This was no time to make a speech.*

❸ occasion VERB; FORMAL
to cause something
EG *damage occasioned by fire*
bring about EG *the only way to bring about peace*
give rise to EG *The judge's decision gave rise to practical problems.*
induce EG *an economic crisis induced by high oil prices*
produce EG *The drug is known to*

A
B
C
D
E
F
G
H
I
J
K
L
M
N
O
P
Q
R
S
T
U
V
W
X
Y
Z

A
B
C
D
E
F
G
H
I
J
K
L
M
N
O
P
Q
R
S
T
U
V
W
X
Y
Z

produce side-effects in women.
prompt EG *The demonstration prompted fears of more violence.*
provoke EG *The incident has provoked outrage in Okinawa.*

occasional ADJECTIVE
happening sometimes
EG *an occasional outing*
intermittent EG *after three hours of intermittent rain*
odd EG *at odd moments*
periodic EG *periodic bouts of illness*
sporadic EG *a year of sporadic fighting*

> **WORD POWER**
> Antonym
> frequent

odd ADJECTIVE
strange or unusual
EG *an odd coincidence*
bizarre EG *his bizarre behaviour*
curious EG *a curious mixture of the ancient and modern*
funny EG *There's something funny about him.*
peculiar EG *Rachel thought it tasted peculiar.*
queer OLD-FASHIONED EG *There's something a bit queer going on.*
singular FORMAL EG *Where he got that singular notion I just can't think.*
strange EG *Then a strange thing happened.*
weird EG *That first day was weird.*

> **WORD POWER**
> Antonym
> ordinary

offend VERB
to upset or embarrass someone
EG *He says he had no intention of offending the community.*
affront EG *He pretended to be affronted, but inwardly he was pleased.*
insult EG *Buchanan says he was insulted by the judge's remarks.*
outrage EG *Many people have been*

outraged by what was said.

> **WORD POWER**
> Antonym
> please

offensive ADJECTIVE
rude and upsetting
EG *offensive behaviour*
abusive EG *abusive language*
insulting EG *an insulting remark*
objectionable EG *I find your tone highly objectionable.*

❶ offer VERB
to ask if someone wants something
EG *Rhys offered him an apple.*
hold out EG *I held out my ticket for him to check.*
tender EG *She has tendered her resignation.*

> **WORD POWER**
> Synonyms
> extend
> proffer

❷ offer NOUN
something that someone offers you
EG *He had refused several excellent job offers.*
proposition EG *I made her a proposition.*
tender EG *a tender for a public contract*

❶ official ADJECTIVE
approved by someone in authority
EG *the official figures*
authorized EG *the authorized biography*
certified EG *a certified accountant*
formal EG *No formal announcement has been made.*
licensed EG *a licensed doctor*

> **WORD POWER**
> Antonym
> unofficial

❷ official NOUN

someone in authority
EG *a senior UN official*
executive EG *a senior bank executive*
officer EG *a local authority education officer*
representative EG *trade union representatives*

> *WORD POWER*
> Synonyms
> bureaucrat
> functionary

often ADVERB
happening many times
EG *They often spent Christmas at Prescott Hill.*
frequently EG *He was frequently depressed.*
repeatedly EG *Both men have repeatedly denied the allegations.*

okay or **OK** ADJECTIVE; INFORMAL
acceptable or satisfactory
EG *Is it okay if I come by myself?*
acceptable EG *It is becoming more acceptable for women to drink.*
all right EG *if it's all right with you*

❶ old ADJECTIVE
having lived for a long time
EG *an old lady*
aged EG *an aged parent*
ancient EG *her ancient grandparents*
elderly EG *an elderly man*

> *WORD POWER*
> Antonym
> young

❷ old ADJECTIVE
in the past
EG *my old art teacher*
ex- EG *his ex-wife*
former EG *a former lover*
previous EG *the previous tenants*

> *WORD POWER*
> Synonyms
> erstwhile
> one-time
> Antonym

new

old-fashioned ADJECTIVE
no longer fashionable
EG *old-fashioned shoes*
antiquated EG *an antiquated system*
archaic EG *archaic practices such as these*
dated EG *Some of the language sounds quite dated.*
obsolete EG *So much equipment becomes obsolete almost as soon as it's made.*
outdated EG *outdated attitudes*
outmoded EG *toiling in outmoded factories*
out of date EG *a make of car that is now out of date*
passé EG *Punk is passé.*

> *WORD POWER*
> Synonyms
> behind the times
> obsolescent
> old-time
> Antonym
> fashionable

omen NOUN
a sign of what will happen
EG *Her appearance at this moment is an omen of disaster.*
sign EG *people who look to the skies for signs*
warning EG *a warning of trouble to come*

> *WORD POWER*
> Synonyms
> augury
> portent

ominous ADJECTIVE
suggesting that something bad will happen
EG *an ominous silence*
sinister EG *a sinister message*
threatening EG *a threatening sky*

> *WORD POWER*
> Synonyms
> inauspicious

portentous
unpropitious

omit VERB
to not include something
EG *Omit the salt in this recipe.*
exclude EG *Women felt excluded form the workplace.*
leave out EG *The Spaniard has been left out of the team.*
miss out EG *What about Sally? You've missed her out!*
skip EG *It is all too easy to skip meals.*

❶ only ADVERB
involving one person or thing
EG *Only Keith knows whether he will continue.*
just EG *It's not just a financial matter.*
merely EG *Watson was far from being merely a furniture expert.*
purely EG *a racing machine, designed purely for speed*
simply EG *Most of the damage was simply because of fallen trees.*
solely EG *decisions based solely upon what we see in magazines*

❷ only ADJECTIVE
having no other examples
EG *their only hit single*
one EG *My one aim is to look after the horses well.*
sole EG *Our sole intention is to reunite her with her baby.*

❶ open VERB
to cause something not to be closed
EG *She opened the door.*
uncover EG *When the seedlings sprout, uncover the tray.*
undo EG *I managed secretly to undo a corner of the parcel.*
unlock EG *She unlocked the case.*

WORD POWER
Synonyms
unfasten
unseal
Antonym

shut

❷ open ADJECTIVE
not closed
EG *an open box of chocolates*
ajar EG *He left the door ajar.*
uncovered EG *The uncovered bucket in the corner stank.*
undone EG *pictures of him with his shirt undone*
unlocked EG *an unlocked room*

WORD POWER
Synonyms
unfastened
unsealed
Antonym
shut

❸ open ADJECTIVE
not trying to deceive someone
EG *He had always been open with her.*
candid EG *I haven't been completely candid with him.*
frank EG *My client has been less than frank with me.*
honest EG *He had been honest with her and she had tricked him!*

❶ opening ADJECTIVE
coming first
EG *the opening day of the season*
first EG *the first night of the play*
inaugural EG *his inaugural address*
initial EG *the aim of this initial meeting*
introductory EG *an introductory offer*

❷ opening NOUN
the first part of something
EG *the opening of the film*
beginning EG *the beginning of the book*
commencement FORMAL EG *at the commencement of the course*
start EG *four years after the start of the Great War*

WORD POWER
Antonym
conclusion

❸ opening NOUN
a hole or gap
EG *a narrow opening in the fence*
chink EG *a chink in the wall*
cleft EG *a narrow cleft in the rocks*
crack EG *Kathryn had seen him through a crack in the curtains.*
gap EG *the wind tearing through gaps in the window frames*
hole EG *a hole in the wall*
slot EG *a slot in which to insert a coin*
space EG *a half-inch space between the curtains*
vent EG *Steam escaped from the vent at the front of the machine.*

> **WORD POWER**
> Synonyms
> aperture
> fissure

opinion NOUN
a belief or view
EG *I wasn't asking for your opinion.*
assessment EG *What is your assessment of the situation?*
belief EG *his religious beliefs*
estimation EG *He has gone down considerably in my estimation.*
judgment EG *In your judgment, what has changed?*
point of view EG *Thanks for your point of view, John.*
view EG *Make your views known to your local MP.*
viewpoint EG *to include as many viewpoints as possible*

oppose VERB
to disagree with something
EG *protesters opposing planned nuclear tests*
fight against EG *a lifetime fighting against racism*
resist EG *They resisted our attempts to modernize.*
speak out against EG *He spoke out strongly against some of the radical ideas.*

> **WORD POWER**

Synonyms
take a stand against
take issue with
Antonym
support

❶ opposite ADJECTIVE
completely different to something
EG *I take the opposite view to you.*
conflicting EG *three powers with conflicting interests*
contrary EG *He has a contrary opinion to mine.*
contrasting EG *two men with completely contrasting backgrounds*
opposed EG *This was a straight conflict of directly opposed aims.*
reverse EG *The wrong attitude will have exactly the reverse effect.*

> **WORD POWER**
> Synonyms
> antithetical
> diametrically opposed

❷ opposite NOUN
a completely different person or thing
EG *He was the complete opposite of Raymond.*
antithesis FORMAL EG *The antithesis of the Middle Eastern buyer is the Japanese.*
contrary EG *I'm not a feminist, quite the contrary.*
converse EG *Don't you think that the converse might also be possible?*
reverse EG *This didn't upset him at all, in fact quite the reverse.*

> **WORD POWER**
> Synonyms
> inverse
> obverse

opposition NOUN
disagreement about something
EG *Much of the opposition to this plan has come from the media.*
disapproval EG *His action had been greeted with almost universal disapproval.*

A B C D E F G H I J K L M N O P Q R S T U V W X Y Z

A
B
C
D
E
F
G
H
I
J
K
L
M
N
O
P
Q
R
S
T
U
V
W
X
Y
Z

hostility EG *There is hostility to this method among traditionalists.*

resistance EG *Initially I met resistance from my own family.*

> **WORD POWER**
> Antonym
> support

oppressed ADJECTIVE
treated cruelly or unfairly
EG *a member of an oppressed minority*

abused EG *those who work with abused children*

downtrodden EG *the downtrodden, bored housewife*

> **WORD POWER**
> Synonyms
> enslaved
> tyrannized

oppression NOUN
cruel or unfair treatment
EG *the oppression of black people throughout history*

persecution EG *the persecution of minorities*

tyranny EG *The 1930s was a decade of tyranny in Europe.*

> **WORD POWER**
> Synonyms
> subjection
> subjugation

optimistic ADJECTIVE
hopeful about the future
EG *an optimistic mood*

buoyant EG *She was in a buoyant mood.*

confident EG *I am confident that everything will come out right in time.*

hopeful EG *I am hopeful this misunderstanding will be rectified.*

positive EG *a positive frame of mind*

sanguine EG *They have begun to take a more sanguine view.*

> **WORD POWER**
> Antonym
> pessimistic

oral ADJECTIVE
spoken rather than written
EG *oral history*

spoken EG *the spoken word*

verbal EG *a verbal agreement*

orange NOUN OR ADJECTIVE

> Shades of orange:
> amber
> apricot
> carrot
> ochre
> peach
> tangerine

ordeal NOUN
a difficult and unpleasant experience
EG *the ordeal of being arrested*

hardship EG *One of the worst hardships is having so little time.*

nightmare EG *Taking my son Peter to a restaurant was a nightmare.*

torture EG *Waiting for the result was torture.*

trial EG *the trials of adolescence*

tribulation FORMAL EG *the trials and tribulations of everyday life*

❶ order NOUN
a command by someone in authority
EG *I don't take orders from him any more.*

command EG *The tanker failed to respond to a command to stop.*

decree EG *He issued a decree ordering all armed groups to disband.*

dictate EG *to ensure that the dictates of the Party are followed*

directive EG *a new EU directive*

instruction EG *MPs defied a party instruction to vote against the Bill.*

❷ order NOUN
a well-organized situation
EG *the wish to impose order upon confusion*

harmony EG *the ordered harmony of the universe*
regularity EG *the chessboard regularity of their fields*
symmetry EG *the beauty and symmetry of a snowflake*

> **WORD POWER**
> Antonym
> disorder

❸ **order** VERB
to tell someone to do something
EG *He ordered his men to stop firing.*
command EG *He commanded his troops to attack.*
decree EG *the rule that decreed no alcohol on the premises*
direct EG *a court order directing the group to leave the land*
instruct EG *The family has instructed solicitors to sue Thomson.*
ordain EG *Nehru ordained that socialism should rule.*

> **WORD POWER**
> Antonym
> forbid

orderly ADJECTIVE
well-organized or well-arranged
EG *Their vehicles were parked in orderly rows.*
neat EG *She put her wet clothes in a neat pile in the corner.*
regular EG *regular rows of wooden huts*
tidy EG *a tidy desk*

> **WORD POWER**
> Antonym
> disorderly

ordinary ADJECTIVE
not special or different
EG *an ordinary day*
conventional EG *a respectable married woman with conventional opinions*
normal EG *He lives a normal life.*
regular EG *the regular barman*
routine EG *a routine procedure*
standard EG *It was standard*

practice.
usual EG *all the usual inner-city problems*

> **WORD POWER**
> Synonyms
> run-of-the-mill
> unexceptional
> unremarkable
> Antonym
> special

❶ **organization** NOUN
a group or business
EG *charitable organizations*
association EG *research associations*
body EG *the Chairman of the policemen's representative body*
company EG *the Ford Motor Company*
confederation EG *the Confederation of Indian Industry*
group EG *an environmental group*
institution EG *financial institutions*
outfit INFORMAL EG *We are a professional outfit.*

❷ **organization** NOUN
the planning and arranging of something
EG *He was involved in the organization of conferences and seminars.*
organizing EG *His duties involved the organizing of transport.*
planning EG *The trip needs careful planning.*
structuring EG *improvements in the structuring of courses*

organize VERB
to plan and arrange something
EG *Organizing a wedding takes time.*
arrange EG *The bank can arrange a loan for students.*
establish EG *How do you establish a workable system?*
jack up NEW ZEALAND INFORMAL EG *to jack up a demonstration*
plan EG *A team meeting was*

planned for last night.
set up EG *This tribunal was set up by the government.*

❶ origin NOUN
the beginning or cause of something
EG *the origins of the custom*
derivation EG *The derivation of its name is obscure.*
root EG *His sense of guilt had its roots in his childhood.*
source EG *the source of the problem*

> **WORD POWER**
> Synonyms
> genesis
> provenance

❷ origin NOUN
someone's family background
EG *She was of Swedish origin.*
ancestry EG *Noel can trace her ancestry to the 11th century.*
descent EG *All the contributors were of African descent.*
extraction EG *a Malaysian citizen of Australian extraction*
lineage EG *a respectable family of ancient lineage*
stock EG *people of Mediterranean stock*

❶ original ADJECTIVE
being the first example of something
EG *the original owner of the cottage*
first EG *Her first reaction was disgust.*
initial EG *His initial response was to disbelieve her.*

❷ original ADJECTIVE
imaginative and clever
EG *a stunningly original idea*
fresh EG *These designers are full of fresh ideas.*
new EG *These proposals aren't new.*
novel EG *a novel way of losing weight*

> **WORD POWER**
> Synonyms
> innovative

innovatory
Antonym
unoriginal

ornament NOUN
an object that you display
EG *a shelf containing ornaments*
adornment EG *a building without any adornments*
bauble EG *a Christmas tree decorated with coloured baubles.*
decoration EG *The only wall decorations are candles.*
knick-knack EG *Her flat is spilling over with knick-knacks.*
trinket EG *She sold trinkets to tourists.*

outbreak NOUN
a sudden occurrence of something
EG *the outbreak of war*
eruption EG *this sudden eruption of violence*
explosion EG *the global explosion of interest in rugby*

outdo VERB
to do something better than another person
EG *She would love to outdo her sister Manuela.*
go one better than EG *You always have to go one better than anyone else.*
outshine EG *Jesse has begun to outshine me in sports.*
surpass EG *determined to surpass the achievements of his older brothers*
top EG *How are you going to top that?*

> **WORD POWER**
> Synonyms
> best
> eclipse

❶ outline VERB
to describe something in a general way
EG *The mayor outlined his plan to clean up the town's image.*

sketch EG *Tudjman sketched his vision of a future Bosnia.*
summarize EG *The article can be summarized in three sentences.*

> **WORD POWER**
> Synonyms
> adumbrate
> delineate

❷ outline NOUN
a general description of something
EG *an outline of the survey's findings*
rundown INFORMAL EG *Here's a rundown of the options.*
summary EG *a summary of the report*
synopsis EG *a brief synopsis of the book*

> **WORD POWER**
> Synonyms
> résumé
> thumbnail sketch

❸ outline NOUN
the shape of something
EG *the hazy outline of the goalposts*
contours EG *the contours of her body*
figure EG *Alistair saw the dim figure of Rose in the chair.*
form EG *She'd never been so glad to see his bulky form.*
shape EG *dark shapes of herons silhouetted against the moon*
silhouette EG *the dark silhouette of the castle ruins*

❶ outlook NOUN
your general attitude towards life
EG *I adopted a positive outlook on life.*
attitude EG *Being unemployed produces negative attitudes to work.*
perspective EG *It gave him a new perspective on life.*
view EG *an optimistic view of the future*

❷ outlook NOUN
the future prospects of

something
EG *The economic outlook is one of rising unemployment.*
future EG *a conference on the country's political future*
prospects EG *a detailed review of the company's prospects*

out of date ADJECTIVE
no longer useful
EG *The information is already out of date.*
antiquated EG *an antiquated system*
archaic EG *archaic practices such as these*
obsolete EG *So much equipment becomes obsolete almost as soon as it's made.*
old-fashioned EG *old-fashioned shoes*
outdated EG *outdated attitudes*
outmoded EG *toiling in outmoded factories*

> **WORD POWER**
> Antonym
> modern

❶ outside NOUN
the outer part of something
EG *The moth was on the outside of the glass.*
exterior EG *the exterior of the building*
facade EG *the refurbishing of the cathedral's facade*
face EG *the face of the watch*
surface EG *the surface of the road*

> **WORD POWER**
> Antonym
> inside

❷ outside ADJECTIVE
not inside
EG *an outside toilet*
exterior EG *the oven's exterior surfaces*
external EG *the external walls*
outdoor EG *outdoor activities*
outer EG *the outer suburbs of the city*

A B C D E F G H I J K L M N O P Q R S T U V W X Y Z

outward EG *with no outward sign of injury*
surface EG *Its total surface area was seven thousand square feet.*

WORD POWER
Antonym
inside

outskirts PLURAL NOUN
the edges of an area
EG *the outskirts of New York*
edge EG *We were on a hill, right on the edge of town.*
perimeter EG *the perimeter of the airport*
periphery EG *countries on the periphery of Europe*

WORD POWER
Synonyms
environs
purlieus

❶ over PREPOSITION
more than a particular amount
EG *It cost over a million dollars.*
above EG *speeds above 50 mph*
exceeding EG *a budget exceeding $700 million a year*
in excess of EG *a fortune in excess of 150 million pounds*
more than EG *The airport had been closed for more than a year.*

❷ over ADJECTIVE
completely finished
EG *I am glad it's all over.*
at an end EG *The matter is now at an end.*
complete EG *The work of restoring the farmhouse is complete.*
done EG *When her deal is done, the client emerges with her purchase.*
finished EG *once the season's finished*
gone EG *Any chance of winning was now gone.*
past EG *The time for loyalty is past.*
up EG *when the six weeks were up*

overcome VERB
to manage to deal with something
EG *Molly had overcome her fear of flying.*
conquer EG *He has never conquered his addiction to smoking.*
get the better of EG *She didn't allow her emotions to get the better of her.*
master EG *His genius alone has mastered every crisis.*
surmount EG *I realized I had to surmount the language barrier.*
triumph over EG *a symbol of good triumphing over evil*
vanquish LITERARY EG *the man who helped vanquish Napoleon*

overrule VERB
to reject a decision offically
EG *The Court of Appeal overruled this decision.*
overturn EG *when the Russian parliament overturned his decision*
reverse EG *They will not reverse the decision to increase prices.*

WORD POWER
Synonyms
countermand
override

❶ overturn VERB
to knock something over
EG *Alex jumped up so violently that he overturned his glass.*
capsize EG *I didn't count on his capsizing the raft.*
knock down EG *Isabel rose so abruptly that she knocked down her chair.*
knock over EG *Emma knocked over the box of cornflakes.*
tip over EG *He tipped the table over in front of him.*
topple EG *Winds and rain toppled trees and electricity lines.*
upset EG *Don't upset the piles of sheets under the box.*

WORD POWER
Synonyms
upend

upturn

❷ overturn VERB
to reject a decision officially
EG *when the Russian parliament overturned his decision*
overrule EG *The Court of Appeal overruled this decision.*
reverse EG *They will not reverse the decision to increase prices.*

WORD POWER
Synonyms
countermand
override

❶ own ADJECTIVE
belonging to a particular person or thing
EG *She stayed in her own house.*
personal EG *That's my personal opinion.*
private EG *76 bedrooms, all with private bathrooms*

❷ own VERB
to have something that belongs to you
EG *His father owns a local pub.*

have EG *They have a house in France.*
keep EG *His father kept a village shop.*
possess EG *I would give her everything I possess.*

❸ own
on your own ADVERB
without other people
EG *I work best on my own.*
alone EG *She lives alone.*
by oneself EG *I didn't know if I could raise a child by myself.*
independently EG *several people working independently*
unaided EG *She brought us up completely unaided.*

owner NOUN
the person to whom something belongs
EG *the owner of the store*
possessor EG *the proud possessor of a truly incredible voice*
proprietor EG *the proprietor of a local restaurant*

A
B
C
D
E
F
G
H
I
J
K
L
M
N
O
P
Q
R
S
T
U
V
W
X
Y
Z

Pp Pp

pacify VERB
to calm down someone who is
angry
EG *She shrieked again, refusing to be
pacified.*
appease EG *The offer has not
appeased separatists.*
calm EG *A business lunch helped
calm her nerves.*
mollify EG *The investigation was
undertaken to mollify pressure
groups.*
placate EG *He went aboard to
placate the angry passengers.*
soothe EG *She took him in his
arms and soothed him.*

WORD POWER
Synonyms
assuage
propitiate

❶ **pain** NOUN
an unpleasant feeling of physical
hurt
EG *I felt a sharp pain in my lower
back.*
ache EG *Poor posture can cause
neck aches.*
discomfort EG *Steve had some
discomfort but no real pain.*
irritation EG *These oils may cause
irritation to sensitive skin.*
soreness EG *The soreness lasted for
about six weeks.*
trouble EG *back trouble*
twinge EG *He felt a slight twinge
in his hamstring.*

❷ **pain** NOUN
a feeling of deep unhappiness
EG *the pain of rejection*
agony EG *the agony of divorce*
anguish EG *Mark looked at him in
anguish.*
distress EG *Jealousy causes distress
and painful emotions.*
grief EG *The grief soon gave way to
anger.*

misery EG *All that money brought
nothing but sadness and misery.*

❶ **painful** ADJECTIVE
causing emotional pain
EG *painful memories*
distressing EG *one of the most
distressing episodes in his life*
grievous EG *Their loss would be a
grievous blow to our industry.*
saddening EG *a saddening
experience*
unpleasant EG *an unpleasant truth*

❷ **painful** ADJECTIVE
causing physical pain
EG *a painful knock on the knee*
aching EG *his aching joints*
excruciating EG *an excruciating
headache*
sore EG *a sore throat*
tender EG *My leg is very tender and
sore.*

pale ADJECTIVE
rather white or without much
colour
EG *Migrating birds filled the pale sky.*
ashen EG *He fell back, shocked, his
face ashen.*
colourless EG *a colourless liquid*
faded EG *a girl in faded jeans*
sallow EG *His face was sallow and
shiny with sweat.*
wan EG *He looked wan and tired.*
white EG *He turned white and
began to stammer.*

❶ **panic** NOUN
a very strong feeling of fear or
anxiety
EG *The earthquake caused panic
among the population.*
alarm EG *She sat up in alarm.*
dismay EG *She discovered to her
dismay that she was pregnant.*
fear EG *my fear of the dark*
fright EG *To hide my fright I asked
a question.*

hysteria EG *mass hysteria*
terror EG *She shook with terror.*

❷ **panic** VERB
to become afraid or anxious
EG *Guests panicked when the bomb exploded.*
become hysterical EG *Miss Brady became hysterical when he produced the gun.*
go to pieces EG *England went to pieces when they conceded a goal.*
lose your nerve EG *They lost their nerve and pulled out of the deal.*

paragraph NOUN

> Parts of a paragraph:
> clause
> phrase
> sentence
> word

paralyse VERB
to make someone lose feeling and movement
EG *Her sister had been paralysed in a road accident.*
cripple EG *He heaved his crippled leg into an easier position.*
disable EG *He was disabled by polio.*

parent NOUN
your father or your mother
EG *I told my parents I was moving out.*
father EG *Her father was furious.*
mother EG *the mother of two girls*
old AUSTRALIAN AND NEW ZEALAND INFORMAL EG *a visit to the olds*
patriarch EG *a domineering patriarch*

parody NOUN
an amusing imitation of someone else's style
EG *a parody of an American sitcom*
imitation EG *I can do a pretty good imitation of him.*
satire EG *a sharp satire on the American political process*
spoof INFORMAL EG *a spoof on Hollywood life*

takeoff INFORMAL EG *She did a brilliant takeoff of the Queen.*

> **WORD POWER**
> Synonyms
> lampoon
> skit

❶ **part** NOUN
a piece or section of something
EG *I like that part of Edinburgh.*
bit EG *a bit of paper*
fraction EG *a fraction of a second*
fragment EG *fragments of glass*
piece EG *a piece of cheese*
portion EG *Damage was confined to a small portion of the castle.*
section EG *a large orchestra, with a vast percussion section*

❷ **part** NOUN
a person's involvement in something
EG *He tried to conceal his part in the accident.*
capacity EG *He has served the club in many capacities.*
duty EG *My duty is to look after the animals.*
function EG *Their main function is to raise capital for industry.*
involvement EG *You have no proof of my involvement in anything.*
role EG *the drug's role in preventing infection*

❸ **part**
take part in VERB
to do an activity with other people
EG *Thousands took part in the demonstrations.*
be instrumental in EG *He was instrumental in tracking down the killers.*
be involved in EG *My grandparents were involved in the Methodist church.*
have a hand in EG *He had a hand in three of the goals.*
join in EG *I hope that everyone will*

be able to join in the fun.

participate in EG *They expected him to participate in the ceremony.*

play a part in EG *He continued to play a part in drug operations from prison.*

participate VERB
to take part in an activity
EG *Over half the population participate in sport.*

be involved in EG *HMS Cardiff was also involved in the exercise.*

engage in EG *They have refused to engage in all-party talks.*

enter into EG *We entered into discussions with them weeks ago.*

join in EG *Their rivals refused to join in any price war.*

take part EG *The oldest car taking part was built in 1907.*

❶ **particular** ADJECTIVE
relating to only one thing or person
EG *That particular place is dangerous.*

distinct EG *The book is divided into two distinct parts.*

exact EG *Do you think I could get the exact thing I want?*

express EG *I bought the camera for the express purpose of taking railway photographs.*

peculiar EG *This is not a problem peculiar to London.*

precise EG *the precise location of the ship*

specific EG *There are several specific problems to be dealt with.*

❷ **particular** ADJECTIVE
especially great or intense
EG *Pay particular attention to the forehead.*

exceptional EG *children with exceptional ability*

marked EG *a marked increase in crime in the area*

notable EG *Two other notable events took place last week.*

singular EG *It was a goal of singular brilliance.*

special EG *a special occasion*

uncommon EG *Both are blessed with an uncommon ability to fix things.*

WORD POWER
Synonyms
especial
noteworthy

❸ **particular** ADJECTIVE
not easily satisfied
EG *Ted was very particular about the colours he used.*

choosy INFORMAL EG *Skiers should be choosy about the insurance policy they buy.*

exacting EG *exacting standards of craftsmanship*

fastidious EG *He was fastidious about his appearance.*

fussy EG *She is very fussy about her food.*

meticulous EG *meticulous attention to detail*

❶ **partner** NOUN
either member of a couple in a relationship
EG *My partner moved in with me last year.*

husband or **wife** EG *Are husbands and wives included in the invitation?*

mate EG *She has found her ideal mate.*

spouse EG *Anything left to your spouse is free from inheritance tax.*

❷ **partner** NOUN
the person someone is doing something with
EG *my tennis partner*

companion EG *her travelling companion*

team-mate EG *his team-mate at Ferrari*

part of speech NOUN

Parts of speech:
adjective
adverb

conjunction
noun
plural noun
preposition
pronoun
reflexive verb
verb

❶ party NOUN
a social event where people
enjoy themselves
EG *Most teenagers like to go to
parties.*
celebration EG *a New Year's Eve
celebration*
function EG *a charity function at
the hotel*
gathering EG *a gathering of
friends and relatives*
get-together INFORMAL EG *a
family get-together*
hooley or **hoolie** NEW ZEALAND EG *a
hooley down on the beach*
reception EG *a wedding reception*

❷ party NOUN
an organization for people with
the same political beliefs
EG *his resignation as party leader*
alliance EG *The two parties have
agreed to form an electoral alliance.*
clique EG *the clique attached to
Prime Minister*
coalition EG *a coalition of
right-wing and religious factions*
faction EG *the party's small
pro-European faction*
grouping EG *two main political
groupings pressing for independence*

❸ party NOUN
a group who are doing
something together
EG *a research party of scientists*
band EG *a small but dedicated
band of supporters*
crew EG *a ship's crew*
gang EG *a gang of criminals*
squad EG *the West Indies squad to
tour Australia*
team EG *Each consultant has a
team of doctors under him.*

unit EG *the health services research
unit*

❶ pass VERB
to exceed or go past something
EG *He gave a triumphant wave as he
passed the winning post.*
exceed EG *The demand for places
at some schools exceeds the supply.*
go beyond EG *Did your
relationship go beyond a close
friendship?*
outdo EG *The Colombian fans
outdid the home supporters in
fervour.*
outstrip EG *Demand continues to
outstrip supply.*
overtake EG *Britain's lottery will
this year overtake Japan's as the
world's biggest.*
surpass EG *He was determined to
surpass the achievements of his
brothers.*

❷ pass VERB
to be successful in a test
EG *Wendy has just passed her
driving test.*
get through EG *I got through my
banking exams last year.*
graduate EG *He graduated in
engineering.*
qualify EG *I qualified as a doctor.*
succeed EG *the skills and qualities
needed to succeed*

> **WORD POWER**
> Antonym
> fail

❸ pass NOUN
a document that allows you to
go somewhere
EG *Don't let any cars onto the land
unless they've got a pass.*
identification EG *Passport control
asked me if I had any further
identification.*
passport EG *You should take your
passport with you when changing
money.*
ticket EG *I'm not going to renew
my season ticket.*

A
B
C
D
E
F
G
H
I
J
K
L
M
N
O
P
Q
R
S
T
U
V
W
X
Y
Z

❶ **passage** NOUN
a space that connects two places
EG *He cleared a passage for himself through the crammed streets.*
channel EG *a drainage channel*
course EG *the river's twisting course*
path EG *A group of reporters blocked the path.*
road EG *the road between Jerusalem and Bethlehem*
route EG *the most direct route to the town centre*
way EG *This is the way in.*

❷ **passage** NOUN
a narrow space that connects one place with another
EG *up some stairs and along a narrow passage towards a door*
aisle EG *the frozen food aisle*
corridor EG *They sat crowded together in the hospital corridor.*
hall EG *The lights were on in the hall and in the bedroom.*
lobby EG *the cramped pitch-dark lobby*

❸ **passage** NOUN
a section of a book or piece of music
EG *a passage from the Bible*
excerpt EG *an excerpt from her speech*
extract EG *an extract from his new book*
quotation EG *a favourite quotation from St Augustine*
section EG *a section from the first movement of Beethoven's Eroica symphony*

❶ **passion** NOUN
a strong feeling of physical attraction
EG *the passion had gone from their relationship*
desire EG *sexual desire*
infatuation EG *Daisy's infatuation for the doctor*
love EG *our love for each other*
lust EG *He is obsessed by his lust for her.*

❷ **passion** NOUN
any strong emotion
EG *He spoke with great passion.*
emotion EG *Her voice trembled with emotion.*
excitement EG *I was in a state of great excitement.*
fire EG *His speeches were full of fire.*
intensity EG *His intensity alarmed me.*
warmth EG *He greeted us both with warmth and affection.*
zeal EG *his zeal for teaching*

passionate ADJECTIVE
expressing very strong feelings about something
EG *I'm a passionate believer in public art.*
ardent EG *ardent supporters of capital punishment*
emotional EG *an emotional farewell*
heartfelt EG *My heartfelt sympathy goes out to all the relatives.*
impassioned EG *He made an impassioned appeal for peace.*
intense EG *intense hatred*
strong EG *Many viewers have strong opinions about violence on TV.*

passive ADJECTIVE
submissive or not playing an active part
EG *His passive attitude made things easier for me.*
docile EG *docile, obedient children*
receptive EG *The voters had seemed receptive to his ideas.*
resigned EG *She was already resigned to losing her home.*
submissive EG *Most doctors want their patients to be submissive.*

> **WORD POWER**
> Synonyms
> acquiescent
> compliant
> inactive
> quiescent

A B C D E F G H I J K L M N O P Q R S T U V W X Y Z

A B C D E F G H I J K L M N **O** **P** Q R S T U V W X Y Z

❶ past
the past NOUN
the period of time before the present
EG *We would like to put the past behind us.*
antiquity EG *famous monuments of classical antiquity*
days gone by EG *This brings back memories of days gone by.*
former times EG *In former times he would have been clapped in irons.*
long ago EG *The old men told stories of long ago.*

❷ past ADJECTIVE
happening or existing before the present
EG *details of his past activities*
ancient EG *ancient history*
bygone EG *a bygone era*
former EG *Remember him as he was in his former years.*
olden EG *We were talking about the olden days on his farm.*
previous EG *She has a teenage daughter from a previous marriage.*

> **WORD POWER**
> Synonyms
> erstwhile
> quondam
> Antonym
> future

❸ past PREPOSITION
situated on the other side of somewhere
EG *It's just past the church there.*
beyond EG *Beyond the garden was a small orchard.*
by EG *She was sitting in a chair by the window.*
over EG *He lived in the house over the road.*

pastime NOUN
a hobby or something done for pleasure
EG *His favourite pastime is snooker.*
activity EG *activities range from canoeing to birdwatching*

diversion EG *Finger painting is very messy but an excellent diversion.*
hobby EG *My hobbies are squash and swimming.*
recreation EG *Saturday afternoon is for recreation and outings.*

❶ path NOUN
a strip of ground for people to walk on
EG *We followed the paths along the clifftops.*
footpath EG *It is accessible only by footpath.*
pathway EG *a pathway leading towards the nearby river*
towpath EG *He took a cycle trip along a canal towpath.*
track EG *We set off over a rough mountain track.*
trail EG *He was following a broad trail through the trees.*
way EG *the Pennine Way*

❷ path NOUN
the space ahead of someone as they move along
EG *A group of reporters stood in his path.*
course EG *obstacles blocking our course*
direction EG *St Andrews was 10 miles in the opposite direction.*
passage EG *Two men elbowed a passage through the shoppers.*
route EG *All escape routes were blocked by armed police.*
way EG *Get out of my way!*

❶ pathetic ADJECTIVE
causing someone to feel pity
EG *She now looked small, shrunken, and pathetic.*
heartbreaking EG *a heartbreaking succession of miscarriages*
sad EG *He seemed a rather sad figure.*

> **WORD POWER**
> Synonyms
> pitiable

A B C D E F G H I J K L M N O P Q R S T U V W X Y Z

plaintive

❷ **pathetic** ADJECTIVE
very poor or unsuccessful
EG *pathetic excuses*
feeble EG *This is a particularly feeble argument.*
lamentable EG *a lamentable display by the league leaders*
pitiful EG *They are paid pitiful wages.*
poor EG *The flat was in a poor state of repair.*
sorry EG *Their oil industry is in a sorry state.*

patience NOUN
the ability to stay calm in a difficult situation
EG *It was exacting work and required all his patience.*
calmness EG *calmness under pressure*
composure EG *He regained his composure and went on to win the match.*
cool SLANG EG *The big Irishman was on the verge of losing his cool.*
restraint EG *They behaved with more restraint than I'd expected.*
tolerance EG *a low tolerance of errors*

> **WORD POWER**
> Synonyms
> equanimity
> forbearance
> imperturbability

❶ **patient** ADJECTIVE
staying calm in a difficult situation
EG *Please be patient - your cheque will arrive.*
calm EG *She is usually a calm and diplomatic woman.*
composed EG *a composed and charming manner*
long-suffering EG *long-suffering train commuters*
philosophical EG *He is philosophical about the defeat.*

serene EG *She looks dreamily into the distance, serene, calm and happy.*

> **WORD POWER**
> Antonym
> impatient

❷ **patient** NOUN
a person receiving medical treatment
EG *patients who wish to change their doctor*
case EG *He is a suitable case for treatment.*
invalid EG *elderly invalids*
sick person EG *a ward full of very sick people*
sufferer EG *asthma sufferers*

❶ **pattern** NOUN
a decorative design of repeated shapes
EG *red and purple thread stitched into a pattern of flames*
design EG *tableware decorated with a blackberry design*
motif EG *a rose motif*

❷ **pattern** NOUN
a diagram or shape used as a guide for making something
EG *sewing patterns*
design EG *They drew up the design for the house in a week.*
diagram EG *Follow the diagram on page 20.*
plan EG *a plan of the garden*
stencil EG *flower stencils*
template EG *Make a paper template of the seat of the chair.*

❶ **pause** VERB
to stop doing something for a short time
EG *On leaving, she paused for a moment at the door.*
break EG *They broke for lunch.*
delay EG *Various problems delayed the launch.*
halt EG *Striking workers halted production at the plant.*
rest EG *He rested briefly before*

pressing on.

take a break EG *He needs to take a break from work.*

wait EG *I waited to see how she responded.*

❷ pause NOUN

a short period when activity stops

EG *There was a pause while the barmaid set down two plates.*

break EG *Do you want to have a little break?*

halt EG *Agricultural production was brought to a halt.*

interruption EG *The sudden interruption stopped her in mid-flow.*

interval EG *I had a drink during the interval.*

rest EG *I think he's due for a rest now.*

stoppage EG *Miners have voted for a one-day stoppage next month.*

> **WORD POWER**
> Synonyms
> caesura
> entr'acte

❶ pay VERB

to give money to someone to settle a debt

EG *You can pay by credit card.*

compensate EG *Farmers could be compensated for their loss of subsidies.*

honour EG *The bank refused to honour the cheque.*

settle EG *I settled the bill for our drinks.*

> **WORD POWER**
> Synonyms
> recompense
> reimburse
> remunerate

❷ pay VERB

to give someone a benefit

EG *It pays to be honest.*

be advantageous EG *It is easy to imagine cases where cheating is advantageous.*

be worthwhile EG *He believed the operation had been worthwhile.*

❸ pay NOUN

money paid to someone for work done

EG *their complaints about pay and conditions*

earnings EG *his earnings as an accountant*

fee EG *solicitors' fees*

income EG *a modest income*

payment EG *a redundancy payment*

salary EG *The lawyer was paid a good salary.*

wages EG *His wages have gone up.*

> **WORD POWER**
> Synonyms
> emolument
> recompense
> reimbursement
> remuneration
> stipend

payment NOUN

an amount of money that is paid to someone

EG *mortgage payments*

advance EG *She was paid a £100,000 advance for her next two novels.*

deposit EG *A $50 deposit is required when ordering.*

instalment EG *The first instalment is payable on application.*

premium EG *higher insurance premiums*

remittance EG *Please make your remittance payable in sterling.*

❶ peace NOUN

a state of undisturbed calm and quiet

EG *They left me in peace to recover from the funeral.*

calm EG *the rural calm of Grand Rapids, Michigan*

quiet EG *He wants some peace and quiet before his match.*

silence EG *They stood in silence.*

A
B
C
D
E
F
G
H
I
J
K
L
M
N
O
P
Q
R
S
T
U
V
W
X
Y
Z

stillness EG *An explosion shattered the stillness of the night air.*
tranquillity EG *The hotel is a haven of tranquillity.*

WORD POWER
Synonyms
quietude
repose

❷ **peace** NOUN
freedom from war
EG *The people do not believe that the leaders want peace.*
armistice EG *the armistice between North Korea and the United Nations*
cessation of hostilities EG *a resolution calling for an immediate cessation of hostilities*
truce EG *an uneasy truce between the two sides*

WORD POWER
Antonym
war

peaceful ADJECTIVE
quiet and calm
EG *a peaceful house in the heart of the countryside*
calm EG *a calm spot amid the bustle of the city*
placid EG *the placid waters of Lake Erie*
quiet EG *The street was unnaturally quiet.*
serene EG *a beautiful, serene park*
still EG *In the room it was very still.*
tranquil EG *the tranquil paradise of his native Antigua*

❶ **peak** NOUN
the point at which something is at its greatest or best
EG *the peak of the morning rush hour*
climax EG *The tournament is building up to a dramatic climax.*
culmination EG *The marriage was the culmination of an eight-month romance.*
high point EG *The high point of this trip was a day at the races.*
zenith EG *His career is now at its*

zenith.

WORD POWER
Synonyms
acme
apogee
ne plus ultra

❷ **peak** NOUN
the pointed top of a mountain
EG *snow-covered peaks*
brow EG *He overtook a car as he approached the brow of a hill.*
crest EG *Burns was clear over the crest of the hill.*
pinnacle EG *He plunged 25 metres from a rocky pinnacle.*
summit EG *the first man to reach the summit of Mount Everest*
top EG *the top of Mount Sinai*

WORD POWER
Synonyms
aiguille
apex

❸ **peak** VERB
to reach the highest point or greatest level
EG *His career peaked during the 1970s.*
be at its height EG *when trade union power was at its height*
climax EG *a tour that climaxed with a three-night stint at Wembley Arena*
come to a head EG *The siege came to a head with the death of a marshal.*
culminate EG *The celebration of the centenary will culminate with a dinner.*
reach its highest point EG *The stockmarket reached its highest point since the 1987 crash.*

❶ **peek** VERB
to have a quick look at something
EG *She peeked at him through a crack in the wall.*
glance EG *He glanced at his watch.*
peep EG *Children came to peep at*

him round the doorway.

snatch a glimpse EG *Spectators lined the route to snatch a glimpse of the Queen.*

sneak a look EG *We sneaked a look at his diary.*

❷ **peek** NOUN
a quick look at something
EG *He took his first peek at the new course yesterday.*

glance EG *Trevor and I exchanged a glance.*

glimpse EG *Some people had waited all day to catch a glimpse of her.*

look EG *She took a last look in the mirror.*

peep EG *He took a peep at his watch.*

pent-up ADJECTIVE
held back for a long time without release
EG *She had a lot of pent-up anger to release.*

inhibited EG *inhibited sexuality*
repressed EG *repressed hostility*
suppressed EG *Deep sleep allowed suppressed anxieties to surface.*

❶ **people** PLURAL NOUN
men, women, and children
EG *Millions of people have lost their homes.*

human beings EG *The disease can be transmitted to human beings.*

humanity EG *crimes against humanity*

humans EG *millions of years before humans appeared on earth*

mankind EG *the evolution of mankind*

❷ **people** PLURAL NOUN
all the men, women, and children of a particular place
EG *It's a triumph for the American people.*

citizens EG *the citizens of New York City*

inhabitants EG *the inhabitants of Hong Kong*

population EG *Africa's rapidly rising population*

public EG *the British public*

perceptive ADJECTIVE
good at noticing or realizing things
EG *a perceptive account of the poet's life*

acute EG *His relaxed exterior hides an extremely acute mind.*

astute EG *He made a series of astute business decisions.*

aware EG *They are politically very aware.*

penetrating EG *He never stopped asking penetrating questions.*

sharp EG *He has a sharp eye and an excellent memory.*

WORD POWER
Synonyms
insightful
percipient
perspicacious

❶ **perfect** ADJECTIVE
of the highest standard and without fault
EG *His English was perfect.*

expert EG *There is a great deal to learn from his expert approach.*

faultless EG *faultless technique*
flawless EG *her flawless complexion*
masterly EG *a masterly performance*

polished EG *polished promotional skills*

skilled EG *a skilled repair job*

WORD POWER
Antonym
imperfect

❷ **perfect** ADJECTIVE
complete or absolute
EG *They have a perfect right to say so.*

absolute EG *absolute nonsense*
complete EG *The resignation came as a complete surprise.*

consummate EG *He acted the part with consummate skill.*

A
B
C
D
E
F
G
H
I
J
K
L
M
N
O
P
Q
R
S
T
U
V
W
X
Y
Z

sheer EG *an act of sheer desperation*
unmitigated EG *Last year's crop was an unmitigated disaster.*
utter EG *utter nonsense*

❸ **perfect** VERB
to make something as good as it can be
EG *The technique was perfected during the 1960s.*
hone EG *a chance to hone their skills*
improve EG *Their French has improved enormously.*
polish EG *He spent time polishing the script.*
refine EG *Surgical techniques are constantly being refined.*

period NOUN
a particular length of time
EG *a period of a few months*
interval EG *a long interval when no-one spoke*
spell EG *a long spell of dry weather*
stretch EG *an 18-month stretch in the army*
term EG *a 5-year prison term*
time EG *At 15 he left home for a short time.*
while EG *I haven't seen him for a long while.*

permanent ADJECTIVE
lasting for ever or present all the time
EG *a permanent solution to the problem*
abiding EG *one of his abiding interests*
constant EG *Inflation is a constant threat.*
enduring EG *an enduring friendship*
eternal EG *the quest for eternal youth*
lasting EG *We are well on our way to a lasting peace.*
perpetual EG *a perpetual source of worry*

WORD POWER

Synonyms
immutable
steadfast
Antonym
temporary

permission NOUN
authorization to do something
EG *He asked permission to leave the room.*
approval EG *The plan will require official approval.*
assent EG *He requires the assent of parliament.*
authorization EG *his request for authorization to use military force*
consent EG *Can she be examined without my consent?*
go-ahead EG *The government gave the go-ahead for five major road schemes.*
licence EG *He has given me licence to do the job as I see fit.*

WORD POWER
Antonym
ban

❶ **permit** VERB
to allow something or make it possible
EG *The guards permitted me to bring my camera.*
allow EG *Smoking will not be allowed.*
authorize EG *They are expected to authorize the use of military force.*
enable EG *The test should enable doctors to detect the disease early.*
give the green light to EG *He has been given the green light to resume training.*
grant EG *Permission was granted a few weeks ago.*
sanction EG *The chairman will not sanction a big-money signing.*

WORD POWER
Antonym
ban

❷ **permit** NOUN
an official document allowing

someone to do something
EG *a work permit*
authorization EG *We didn't have authorization to go.*
licence EG *a driving licence*
pass EG *a rail pass*
passport EG *My passport expires next year.*
permission EG *Permission for the march has not been granted.*
warrant EG *Police issued a warrant for his arrest.*

persecute VERB
to treat someone with continual cruelty and unfairness
EG *The Communists began by brutally persecuting the Church.*
hound EG *He has been hounded by the press.*
ill-treat EG *They thought Mr Smith had been ill-treating his wife.*
oppress EG *Minorities here have been oppressed for generations.*
pick on EG *She was repeatedly picked on by the manager.*
torment EG *They were tormented by other pupils.*
torture EG *He would not torture her further by trying to argue with her.*

person NOUN
a man, woman, or child
EG *The amount of sleep we need varies from person to person.*
human EG *the common ancestor of humans and the great apes*
human being EG *This protein occurs naturally in human beings.*
individual EG *the rights and responsibilities of the individual*
living soul EG *The nearest living soul was 20 miles away.*
soul EG *a tiny village of only 100 souls*

personal ADJECTIVE
belonging to a particular person or thing
EG *personal belongings*
individual EG *Divide the*

vegetables among four individual dishes.
own EG *My wife decided I should have my own shop.*
particular EG *his own particular style of preaching*
peculiar EG *her own peculiar talents*
private EG *my private life*
special EG *Every person will have his or her own special problems.*

❶ **personality** NOUN
a person's character and nature
EG *She has such a kind, friendly personality.*
character EG *a negative side to his character*
identity EG *our own sense of cultural identity*
individuality EG *People should be free to express their individuality.*
make-up EG *There was some fundamental flaw in his make-up.*
nature EG *She trusted people. That was her nature.*
psyche EG *disturbing elements of the human psyche*

❷ **personality** NOUN
a famous person in entertainment or sport
EG *television personalities*
big name EG *the big names in French cinema*
celebrity EG *Hollywood celebrities*
famous name EG *a famous name from Inter Milan's past*
household name EG *The TV series that made him a household name.*
star EG *film stars*

persuade VERB
to make someone do something by reason or charm
EG *He persuaded the company to sign her up.*
bring round INFORMAL EG *We will do what we can to bring them round to our point of view.*
coax EG *She coaxed Bobby into*

talking about himself.

induce EG *I would do anything to induce them to stay.*

sway EG *Don't ever be swayed by fashion.*

talk into EG *He talked me into marrying him.*

win over EG *By the end of the day he had won over the crowd.*

> *WORD POWER*
> Synonyms
> impel
> inveigle

perverted ADJECTIVE
practising abnormal and unacceptable behaviour
EG *She has been a victim of perverted phone calls and letters.*

depraved EG *the work of depraved and evil criminals*

deviant EG *Not all drug abusers produce deviant offspring.*

immoral EG *those who think that birth control is immoral*

unhealthy EG *His interest developed into an unhealthy obsession.*

> *WORD POWER*
> Synonyms
> debauched
> vitiated

pessimistic ADJECTIVE
believing that bad things will happen
EG *a pessimistic view of life*

despondent EG *despondent about their children's future*

gloomy EG *a gloomy view of the future*

glum EG *They are not entirely glum about the car industry's prospects.*

hopeless EG *Even able pupils feel hopeless about job prospects.*

> *WORD POWER*
> Antonym
> optimistic

❶ pest NOUN

an insect or animal that damages crops or livestock
EG *10% of the crop was lost to a pest called corn rootworm.*

bane EG *The bane of farmers across the country is the badger.*

blight EG *potato blight*

scourge EG *This parasitic mite is the scourge of honey bees.*

❷ pest NOUN
an annoying person
EG *I didn't want to be a cry baby or a pest.*

bane EG *Student journalists were the bane of my life.*

bore EG *I don't enjoy his company. He's a bore and a fool.*

nuisance EG *He could be a bit of a nuisance when he was drunk.*

pain INFORMAL EG *She's been a real pain recently.*

pain in the neck INFORMAL EG *I've always been a pain in the neck to publishers.*

pester VERB
to bother someone continually
EG *He gets fed up with people pestering him for money.*

annoy EG *She kept on annoying me.*

badger EG *She badgered her doctor time and again.*

bother EG *We are playing a trick on a man who keeps bothering me.*

bug INFORMAL EG *Stop bugging me.*

drive someone up the wall SLANG EG *I sang in the bath and drove my sister up the wall.*

get on someone's nerves INFORMAL EG *I was beginning to get on her nerves.*

> *WORD POWER*
> Synonyms
> bedevil
> chivvy

❶ petty ADJECTIVE
small and unimportant
EG *endless rules and petty regulations*

insignificant EG *In 1949, Bonn was a small, insignificant city.*
measly INFORMAL EG *The average bathroom measures a measly 3.5 square metres.*
trifling EG *The sums involved are trifling.*
trivial EG *trivial details*
unimportant EG *It was an unimportant job, and paid very little.*

❷ **petty** ADJECTIVE
selfish and small-minded
EG *I think that attitude is a bit petty.*
cheap EG *politicians making cheap political points*
mean EG *I'd feel mean saying no.*
small-minded EG *their small-minded preoccupation with making money*

❶ **pick** VERB
to choose something
EG *He picked ten people to interview for six sales jobs.*
choose EG *There are several options to choose from.*
decide upon EG *He decided upon a career in publishing.*
hand-pick EG *He was hand-picked for his job by the Admiral.*
opt for EG *I think we should opt for a more cautious approach.*
select EG *the party's policy of selecting candidates*
settle on EG *I finally settled on an Audi TT roadster.*

❷ **pick** VERB
to remove a flower or fruit with your fingers
EG *He helps his mother pick fruit.*
gather EG *We spent the afternoon gathering berries.*
harvest EG *Many farmers are refusing to harvest the cane.*
pluck EG *I plucked a lemon from the tree.*

❸ **pick** NOUN
the best
EG *the pick of the country's young athletes*
elite EG *the elite of women's tennis*
flower EG *the flower of Polish manhood*
pride EG *the hovercraft, once the pride of British maritime engineering*

pick on VERB
to criticize someone unfairly or treat them unkindly
EG *Bullies pick on younger children.*
bait EG *He delighted in baiting his mother.*
tease EG *He teased me mercilessly about going to Hollywood.*
torment EG *They were tormented by other pupils.*

❶ **picture** NOUN
a drawing, painting, or photograph
EG *It's got a picture of me on the cover.*
drawing EG *She did a drawing of me.*
illustration EG *Tolkien's illustrations for The Hobbit*
painting EG *his collection of Impressionist paintings*
photograph EG *He wants to take some photographs of the house.*
portrait EG *Velazquez's portrait of Pope Innocent X*
sketch EG *pencil sketches*

❷ **picture** VERB
to imagine something clearly
EG *He pictured her with long black hair.*
conceive of EG *I can't conceive of doing work that doesn't interest me.*
imagine EG *It's difficult to imagine anything coming between them.*
see EG *A good idea, but can you see Taylor trying it?*
visualize EG *He could not visualize her as old.*

WORD POWER
Synonyms
envision
see in the mind's eye

A B C D E F G H I J K L M N O P Q R S T U V W X Y Z

❶ piece NOUN
a portion or part of something
EG *a piece of cheese*
bit EG *a bit of paper*
chunk EG *He was accused of stealing a tin of pineapple chunks.*
fragment EG *There were fragments of cork in the wine.*
part EG *The engine has got only three moving parts.*
portion EG *Damage was confined to a small portion of the castle.*
slice EG *a slice of bread*

❷ piece NOUN
something that has been written, created, or composed
EG *his piece on fox hunting*
article EG *a newspaper article*
composition EG *Schubert's piano compositions*
creation EG *the fashion designer's latest creations*
study EG *Leonardo's studies of horsemen*
work EG *In my opinion, this is Rembrandt's greatest work.*

piece together VERB
to assemble things or parts to make something complete
EG *Doctors painstakingly pieced together the broken bones.*
assemble EG *He is assembling evidence concerning a murder.*
join EG *Join all the sections together.*
mend EG *I should have had it mended, but never got round to it.*
patch together EG *A hasty deal was patched together.*
repair EG *the cost of repairing earthquake damage*
restore EG *The trust is playing a leading part in restoring old cinemas.*

pierce VERB
to make a hole in something with a sharp instrument
EG *Pierce the potato with a fork.*
bore EG *tunnels bored into the foundations of the building*

drill EG *I drilled five holes at equal distance.*
lance EG *It's a painful experience having the boil lanced.*
penetrate EG *The Earth's atmosphere was penetrated by a meteor.*
puncture EG *The bullet punctured the skull.*

pig NOUN
a farm animal kept for meat
EG *the number of pigs at the trough*
hog EG *He's as fat as a hog.*
piggy INFORMAL EG *These two piggies are going to market!*
porker EG *a 30kg Vietnamese potbellied porker*
swine EG *herds of oxen, sheep and swine*

❶ pile NOUN
a quantity of things lying one on top of another
EG *a pile of books*
heap EG *a compost heap*
hoard EG *a hoard of jewels*
mound EG *The bulldozers piled up hug mounds of dirt.*
mountain EG *They have mountains of coffee to sell.*
stack EG *a stack of magazines on the table*

❷ pile NOUN
the raised fibres of a soft surface
EG *the carpet's thick pile*
down EG *The whole plant is covered with fine down.*
fur EG *This creature's fur is short and dense.*
hair EG *He has black hair.*
nap EG *The cotton is lightly brushed to heighten the nap.*

❸ pile VERB
to put things one on top of another
EG *A few newspapers were piled on the table.*
heap EG *She heaped more carrots onto his plate.*

hoard EG *They've begun to hoard petrol and food.*

stack EG *They are stacked neatly in piles of three.*

pink NOUN OR ADJECTIVE

Shades of pink:
coral
flesh
fuchsia
oyster pink
rose
salmon
shell pink
shocking pink

pit NOUN

a large hole in something
EG *He lost his footing and began to slide into the pit.*

chasm EG *The coach plunged down the chasm.*

hole EG *The builders had cut holes into the soft stone.*

pothole EG *She was seriously injured when she fell 90 feet down a pothole.*

❶ pity VERB

to feel sorry for someone
EG *I don't know whether to hate or pity him.*

feel for EG *She cried on the phone and I really felt for her.*

feel sorry for EG *This is my biggest win but I don't feel sorry for the bookies.*

sympathize with EG *I sympathize with you for your loss.*

❷ pity NOUN

sympathy for other people's suffering
EG *She saw no pity in their faces.*

charity EG *They showed a lack of charity and understanding to her.*

compassion EG *his compassion for a helpless woman*

kindness EG *He was treated with kindness by numerous officials.*

mercy EG *Neither side showed any mercy.*

sympathy EG *We expressed our sympathy for her loss.*

understanding EG *We would like to thank them for their patience and understanding.*

WORD POWER
Synonyms
clemency
forbearance

❸ pity NOUN

a regrettable fact
EG *It's a pity they can't all have the same opportunities.*

crime INFORMAL EG *It would be a crime to travel to Australia and not stop in Sydney.*

crying shame EG *It would be a crying shame to split up a winning partnership.*

shame EG *It's a shame it had to close.*

❶ place NOUN

any point or area
EG *The pain is always in the same place.*

area EG *a picnic area*

location EG *The first thing he looked at was his office's location.*

point EG *The pain originated from a point in his right thigh.*

position EG *the ship's position*

site EG *a bat sanctuary with special nesting sites*

spot EG *the island's top tourist spots*

❷ place

take place VERB
to happen
EG *The meeting took place on Thursday.*

come about EG *That came about when we went to Glastonbury last year.*

go on EG *This has been going on for around a year.*

happen EG *We cannot say for sure what will happen.*

occur EG *The crash occurred when the crew shut down the wrong*

A
B
C
D
E
F
G
H
I
J
K
L
M
N
O
P
Q
R
S
T
U
V
W
X
Y
Z

engine.

❸ place VERB
to put something somewhere
EG *Chairs were placed in rows for the parents.*
deposit EG *Imagine if you were suddenly deposited on a desert island.*
locate EG *the best city in which to locate a business*
plant EG *So far no one has admitted to planting the bomb.*
position EG *plants which are carefully positioned in the alcove*
put EG *She put the photograph on her desk.*
situate EG *The hotel is situated next to the railway station.*

❶ plain ADJECTIVE
very simple in style with no decoration
EG *It was a plain, grey stone house.*
austere EG *The church was austere and simple.*
bare EG *bare wooden floors*
spartan EG *her spartan home in a tiny village*
stark EG *a stark white, characterless fireplace*

> **WORD POWER**
> Antonym
> fancy

❷ plain ADJECTIVE
obvious and easy to recognize or understand
EG *It was plain to him that I was having a nervous breakdown.*
clear EG *The book is clear and readable.*
comprehensible EG *a comprehensible manual*
distinct EG *a distinct smell of burning coal*
evident EG *His footprints were clearly evident in the heavy dust.*
obvious EG *an obvious injustice*
unmistakable EG *His voice was unmistakable.*

❸ plain NOUN

Types of plain:
flat
flatland
grassland
llano
lowland
mesa
plateau
prairie
savannah
steppe
tableland

❶ plan NOUN
a way thought out to do something
EG *a plan to amalgamate the two parties*
method EG *He did it by his usual method.*
proposal EG *The proposals need careful study.*
scheme EG *The scheme was an abject failure.*
strategy EG *What should our marketing strategy achieve?*
system EG *the advantages of the new system over the old one*

❷ plan NOUN
a detailed diagram of something that is to be made
EG *a detailed plan of the prison*
blueprint EG *a blueprint for a new bathroom*
diagram EG *a circuit diagram*
layout EG *He tried to recall the layout of the farmhouse.*
scale drawing EG *scale drawings of locomotives*

❸ plan VERB
to decide in detail what is to be done
EG *when we plan road construction*
arrange EG *We arranged a social event once a year.*
design EG *He approached me to design the restaurant.*
devise EG *We devised a plan.*
draft EG *The legislation was*

drafted by the committee.
formulate EG *He formulated his plan for escape.*

❶ play VERB
to take part in games or use toys
EG *Polly was playing with her teddy bear.*
amuse oneself EG *He amused himself by rollerskating round the building.*
entertain oneself EG *I used to entertain myself by building model planes.*
frolic EG *Tourists sunbathe and frolic in the ocean.*
have fun EG *having fun with your friends*

❷ play VERB
to take part in a sport or game
EG *Alain was playing cards with his friends.*
compete EG *Eight entrants competed for the prize.*
participate EG *Sixteen teams participated in the tournament.*
take on EG *Scotland take on South Africa at Murrayfield.*
take part EG *The teams taking part are cricket's bitterest enemies.*
vie with EG *Arsenal are vying with Leeds for second spot in the league.*

❸ play NOUN
a piece of drama performed on stage, radio, or television
EG *Chekhov's best play*
comedy EG *a romantic comedy*
drama EG *He also wrote radio dramas and film scripts.*
pantomime EG *He regularly performs in Christmas pantomimes.*
show EG *a one-woman show*
tragedy EG *Shakespeare's tragedies*

❶ pleasant ADJECTIVE
enjoyable or attractive
EG *I've got a pleasant little flat.*
agreeable EG *workers in more agreeable and better paid occupations*
delightful EG *It was the most*

delightful garden I'd ever seen.
enjoyable EG *an enjoyable meal*
lekker SOUTH AFRICAN SLANG EG *a lekker little town*
lovely EG *He had a lovely voice.*
nice EG *It's nice to be here together again.*
pleasurable EG *He found sailing more pleasurable than skiing.*

> *WORD POWER*
> Antonym
> unpleasant

❷ pleasant ADJECTIVE
friendly or charming
EG *an extremely pleasant and obliging man*
affable EG *He is an affable and approachable man.*
amiable EG *She had been surprised at how amiable and polite he had seemed.*
charming EG *He can be charming to his friends.*
friendly EG *She has a friendly relationship with her customers.*
likable or **likeable** EG *He's an immensely likable man.*
nice EG *He's a nice fellow, very quiet and courteous.*

> *WORD POWER*
> Antonym
> unpleasant

please VERB
to give pleasure to
EG *I was tidying my bedroom to please mum.*
amuse EG *The thought seemed to amuse him.*
charm EG *He charmed all of us.*
delight EG *music that has delighted audiences all over the world*
entertain EG *Children's TV not only entertains but also teaches.*

pleased ADJECTIVE
happy or satisfied
EG *I'm pleased with the way things have been going.*

A B C D E F G H I J K L M N O P Q R S T U V W X Y Z

contented EG *She had a contented smile on her face.*

delighted EG *I know he will be delighted to see you.*

glad EG *I'm glad he changed his mind in the end.*

happy EG *She's a confident and happy child.*

satisfied EG *satisfied customers*

pleasure NOUN
a feeling of happiness and satisfaction
EG *Everybody takes pleasure in eating.*

amusement EG *Her impersonations provided great amusement.*

enjoyment EG *her enjoyment of the countryside*

happiness EG *My happiness helped to erase the bad memories.*

joy EG *tears of joy*

satisfaction EG *job satisfaction*

plenty NOUN
a lot of something
EG *There's plenty to go round.*

enough EG *Have you had enough?*

great deal EG *I've spent a great deal of time on this project.*

heaps INFORMAL EG *You have heaps of time.*

lots INFORMAL EG *He has made lots of amendments to the script.*

plethora EG *a plethora of new products*

❶ plot NOUN
a secret plan made by a group of people
EG *the plot to assassinate Martin Luther King*

conspiracy EG *a conspiracy to steal nuclear missiles*

intrigue EG *political intrigues*

plan EG *a secret government plan to build a nuclear waste dump*

scheme EG *an elaborate scheme to dupe the police*

WORD POWER

Synonyms
cabal
machination
stratagem

❷ plot NOUN
the story of a novel or play
EG *The film has a ludicrously complicated plot.*

narrative EG *a fast-moving narrative*

scenario EG *The movie's scenario is nonsensical.*

story EG *I doubt the appeal of cinematic sex without a story.*

story line EG *It sounds like a typical story line from a soap opera.*

❸ plot VERB
to plan something secretly with others
EG *Prosecutors allege the defendants plotted to overthrow the government.*

conspire EG *The countries had secretly conspired to acquire nuclear weapons.*

hatch EG *He hatched a plot to murder his wife.*

plan EG *I suspect they are secretly planning to raise taxes.*

scheme EG *He claimed that they were scheming against him.*

WORD POWER
Synonyms
cabal
collude
machinate

plump ADJECTIVE
rather fat
EG *a plump, fresh-faced young woman*

beefy INFORMAL EG *beefy bodyguards*

burly EG *burly shipyard workers*

chubby EG *I was quite chubby as a child.*

fat EG *I could eat what I liked without getting fat.*

stout EG *He was a tall, stout man of sixty.*

tubby EG *He's a bit on the tubby*

side.

❶ **point** NOUN
the purpose or meaning something has
EG *Cutting costs is not the point of the exercise.*
aim EG *The aim of this book is to inform you.*
goal EG *The goal is to raise a lot of money.*
intention EG *It was never my intention to injure anyone.*
object EG *It was his object in life to find the island.*
purpose EG *He did not know the purpose of Vincent's visit.*

❷ **point** NOUN
a quality or feature
EG *Tact was never her strong point.*
attribute EG *Cruelty is a regrettable attribute of human behaviour.*
characteristic EG *their physical characteristics*
feature EG *They're one of my best features.*
quality EG *mature people with leadership qualities*
side EG *the dark side of his character*
trait EG *Creativity is a human trait.*

❸ **point** NOUN
the thin sharp end of something
EG *the point of a needle*
nib EG *the nib of my pen*
prong EG *the prongs of a fork*
tip EG *the tip of my scissors*

poison NOUN
a substance that can kill people or animals
EG *Mercury is a known poison.*
toxin EG *the liver's ability to break down toxins*
venom EG *the cobra's deadly venom*

poisonous ADJECTIVE
containing something that causes death or illness
EG *a large cloud of poisonous gas*

noxious EG *Many household products give off noxious fumes.*
toxic EG *The cost of cleaning up toxic waste.*
venomous EG *The adder is Britain's only venomous snake.*

❶ **poke** VERB
to jab or prod someone or something
EG *She poked a fork into the turkey skin.*
dig EG *His companions were digging him in the ribs.*
elbow EG *As I tried to get past him he elbowed me in the face.*
jab EG *Somebody jabbed an umbrella into his leg.*
nudge EG *She nudged me awake after I dozed off.*
prod EG *He prodded Murray with the shotgun.*
stab EG *He stabbed at Frank with his forefinger.*

❷ **poke** NOUN
a jab or prod
EG *She gave Richard a playful poke.*
dig EG *She silenced him with a sharp dig in the small of the back.*
jab EG *a quick jab of the brakes*
nudge EG *She slipped her arm under his and gave him a nudge.*
prod EG *He gave the donkey a mighty prod in the backside.*

❶ **polish** VERB
to make smooth and shiny by rubbing
EG *He polished his shoes every morning.*
buff EG *He was already buffing the car's hubs.*
shine EG *Let him dust and shine the furniture.*
wax EG *a Sunday morning spent washing and waxing the car*

❷ **polish** VERB
to improve a skill or technique
EG *Polish up your writing skills.*
brush up EG *She spent the summer brushing up on her driving.*

A B C D E F G H I J K L M N O P Q R S T U V W X Y Z

A
B
C
D
E
F
G
H
I
J
K
L
M
N
O
P
Q
R
S
T
U
V
W
X
Y
Z

improve EG *I want to improve my golf game.*

perfect EG *We perfected a hand-signal system.*

refine EG *Surgical techniques are constantly being refined.*

❸ **polish** NOUN
elegance or refinement
EG *The opera lacks the polish of his later work.*

class INFORMAL EG *For sheer class, Mark Waugh is the best batsman of the World Cup.*

elegance EG *The furniture combined practicality with elegance.*

finesse EG *It's good but it lacks the finesse of vintage champagne.*

grace EG *Ballet classes are important for learning poise and grace.*

refinement EG *a girl who possessed both dignity and refinement*

style EG *Paris, you have to admit, has style.*

> *WORD POWER*
> Synonyms
> politesse
> suavity
> urbanity

❶ **polite** ADJECTIVE
having good manners
EG *It's not polite to point at people.*

civil EG *I have to force myself to be civil to him.*

courteous EG *Her reply was courteous but firm.*

respectful EG *Their children are always respectful to their elders.*

well-behaved EG *well-behaved little girls*

well-mannered EG *a very pleasant and well-mannered student*

> *WORD POWER*
> Antonym
> rude

❷ **polite** ADJECTIVE

cultivated or refined
EG *Certain words are not acceptable in polite society.*

cultured EG *He is immensely cultured and well-read.*

genteel EG *two ladies with genteel manners and voices*

refined EG *His speech and manner are very refined.*

sophisticated EG *Recently her tastes have become more sophisticated.*

urbane EG *She describes him as charming and urbane.*

politeness NOUN
the quality of being civil to someone
EG *She listened to him but only out of politeness.*

civility EG *Handle customers with tact and civility.*

courtesy EG *He did not even have the courtesy to reply to my fax.*

decency EG *He should have had the decency to inform me.*

etiquette EG *the rules of diplomatic etiquette*

pollute VERB
to contaminate with something harmful
EG *Heavy industry pollutes our rivers with noxious chemicals.*

contaminate EG *Have any fish been contaminated in the Arctic Ocean?*

infect EG *a virus which is spread mainly by infected blood*

poison EG *Drilling operations have poisoned the Nile delta.*

taint EG *blood tainted with the hepatitis viruses*

> *WORD POWER*
> Synonyms
> adulterate
> befoul
> smirch

pompous ADJECTIVE
behaving in a way that is too serious and self-important

EG *a pompous man with a high opinion of his own capabilities*
arrogant EG *an air of arrogant indifference*
grandiose EG *grandiose plans which never got off the ground*
ostentatious EG *an ostentatious wedding reception*
pretentious EG *His response was full of pretentious nonsense.*
puffed up EG *He is puffed up with own importance.*

WORD POWER
Synonyms
pontifical
portentous
vainglorious

ponder VERB
to think about something deeply
EG *I'm continually pondering how to improve the team.*
brood EG *I guess everyone broods over things once in a while.*
consider EG *You have to consider the feelings of those around you.*
contemplate EG *He lay in bed contemplating his future.*
mull over EG *I'll leave you alone here so you can mull it over.*
reflect EG *I reflected on the child's future.*
think EG *I have often thought about this problem.*

❶ **poor** ADJECTIVE
having little money
EG *They see the government ignoring poor people.*
broke INFORMAL EG *He was broke when I married him.*
destitute EG *destitute people living on the streets*
hard up INFORMAL EG *Her parents were very hard up.*
impoverished EG *one of the most impoverished suburbs of Rio de Janeiro*
penniless EG *a penniless refugee*
poverty-stricken EG *a teacher of poverty-stricken kids*

WORD POWER
Antonym
rich

❷ **poor** ADJECTIVE
of a low quality or standard
EG *He was a poor actor.*
feeble EG *a feeble attempt to save Figo's shot*
inferior EG *The cassettes were of inferior quality.*
mediocre EG *His school record was mediocre.*
second-rate EG *Passengers are fed up using a second-rate service.*
shoddy EG *shoddy goods*
unsatisfactory EG *questions to which he received unsatisfactory answers*

❶ **popular** ADJECTIVE
liked or approved of by a lot of people
EG *These delicious pastries will be very popular.*
fashionable EG *fashionable wine bars*
favourite EG *Britain's favourite soap opera*
in demand EG *He was much in demand as a lecturer.*
in favour EG *He is now back in favour with the manager.*
sought-after EG *one of the most sought-after new names in Hollywood*
well-liked EG *She was very sociable and well-liked by the other students.*

WORD POWER
Antonym
unpopular

❷ **popular** ADJECTIVE
involving or intended for ordinary people
EG *the popular press*
common EG *Much of the countryside has fallen out of common ownership and into private hands.*

A
B
C
D
E
F
G
H
I
J
K
L
M
N
O
P
Q
R
S
T
U
V
W
X
Y
Z

357

conventional EG *a respectable married woman with conventional opinions*
general EG *general awareness about bullying*
prevalent EG *Smoking is becoming increasingly prevalent among younger women.*
universal EG *universal health care*

❶ **pose** VERB
to ask a question
EG *When I finally posed the question, 'Why?' he merely shrugged.*
ask EG *I wasn't the only one asking questions.*
put EG *Some workers may be afraid to put questions publicly.*
submit EG *Passengers are invited to submit questions.*

> *WORD POWER*
> Synonyms
> posit
> propound

❷ **pose** VERB
to pretend to be someone else
EG *The team posed as drug dealers to trap the ringleaders.*
impersonate EG *He was once jailed for impersonating a policeman.*
masquerade as EG *He masqueraded as a doctor and fooled everyone.*
pass oneself off as EG *He frequently passed himself off as a lawyer.*
pretend to be EG *We spent the afternoon pretending to be foreign tourists.*

❶ **position** NOUN
the place where someone or something is
EG *The ship's name and position were reported to the coastguard.*
location EG *She knew the exact location of their headquarters.*
place EG *The pain is always in the same place.*

point EG *The pain originated from a point in his right thigh.*
whereabouts EG *Finding his whereabouts proved surprisingly easy.*

❷ **position** VERB
to put something somewhere
EG *Position trailing plants near the edges.*
arrange EG *Arrange the books in neat piles.*
lay out EG *Grace laid out the knives and forks at the table.*
locate EG *the best city in which to locate a business*
place EG *Chairs were placed in rows for the parents.*
put EG *She put the photograph on her desk.*

❶ **positive** ADJECTIVE
completely sure about something
EG *I was positive he'd known about that money.*
certain EG *It wasn't a balloon - I'm certain about that.*
confident EG *My Ryan is confident of success.*
convinced EG *He was convinced that I was part of the problem.*
sure EG *It is impossible to be sure about the value of the land.*

❷ **positive** ADJECTIVE
providing definite proof of the truth or identity of something
EG *positive evidence*
clear EG *a clear case of mistaken identity*
clear-cut EG *The issue is not so clear-cut.*
conclusive EG *Research on the matter is far from conclusive.*
concrete EG *He had no concrete evidence.*
firm EG *There is no firm evidence to prove this.*

> *WORD POWER*
> Synonyms
> incontrovertible

indisputable
unequivocal

❸ positive ADJECTIVE
tending to emphasize what is good
EG *I anticipate a positive response.*
constructive EG *We welcome constructive criticism.*
helpful EG *Camilla's helpful comments*

> *WORD POWER*
> Antonym
> negative

❶ possess VERB
to have something as a quality
EG *He possesses both stamina and great technique.*
be blessed with EG *She was blessed with a photographic memory.*
be born with EG *Mozart was born with perfect pitch.*
enjoy EG *I have always enjoyed good health.*
have EG *They have talent in abundance.*

❷ possess VERB
to own something
EG *He was said to possess a huge fortune.*
acquire EG *I have acquired a new car.*
control EG *He now controls the entire company.*
hold EG *He does not hold a firearm certificate.*
occupy EG *US forces now occupy part of the country.*
seize EG *Troops have seized the airport and railway terminals.*
take over EG *They plan to take over another airline.*

possession NOUN
ownership of something
EG *How did this picture come into your possession?*
control EG *The restructuring involves his giving up control of the firm.*
custody EG *She will have custody of their two children.*
ownership EG *the growth of home ownership*
tenure EG *his 28-year tenure of the house*

possessions PLURAL NOUN
the things owned by someone
EG *People had lost all their possessions.*
assets EG *The group had assets worth over 10 million dollars.*
belongings EG *He was identified only by his personal belongings.*
effects EG *His daughters were collecting his effects.*
estate EG *She left her entire estate to a charity.*
property EG *the rightful owner of the property*
things EG *She told him to take all his things and not to return.*

possibility NOUN
something that might be true or might happen
EG *the possibility of a ban*
chance EG *There's no chance of that happening.*
hope EG *We had absolutely no hope of raising the money.*
likelihood EG *the likelihood of infection*
odds EG *What are the odds of that happening?*
prospect EG *There is little prospect of peace.*
risk EG *It reduces the risk of heart disease.*

❶ possible ADJECTIVE
likely to happen or able to be done
EG *I am grateful to the staff for making this work possible.*
attainable EG *I always thought promotion was attainable.*
feasible EG *Whether such cooperation is feasible is a matter of doubt.*

A B C D E F G H I J K L M N O **P** Q R S T U V W X Y Z

A
B
C
D
E
F
G
H
I
J
K
L
M
N
O
P
Q
R
S
T
U
V
W
X
Y
Z

practicable EG *It was not reasonably practicable for Mr Tyler to attend.*

viable EG *commercially viable products*

workable EG *This isn't a workable solution in most cases.*

> **WORD POWER**
> Antonym
> impossible

❷ possible ADJECTIVE
likely or capable of being true or correct
EG *It's possible there's an explanation for all this.*

conceivable EG *It is just conceivable that a survivor might be found.*

imaginable EG *a place of no imaginable strategic value*

likely EG *Experts say a 'yes' vote is still the likely outcome.*

potential EG *the channel's potential audience*

postpone VERB
to put off to a later time
EG *The visit has been postponed until tomorrow.*

adjourn EG *The proceedings have been adjourned until next week.*

defer EG *Customers often defer payments for as long as possible.*

delay EG *I wanted to delay my departure until June.*

put back EG *The news conference has been put back a couple of hours.*

put off EG *The Association has put off the event until October.*

shelve EG *Sadly, the project has now been shelved.*

❶ potential ADJECTIVE
possible but not yet actual
EG *potential sources of finance*

likely EG *A draw is the likely outcome.*

possible EG *Her family is discussing a possible move to America.*

probable EG *A bomb was the accident's most probable cause.*

❷ potential NOUN
ability to achieve future success
EG *Denmark recognized the potential of wind energy early.*

ability EG *You have the ability to become a good pianist.*

aptitude EG *more aptitude for academic work than the others*

capability EG *We experience differences in mental capability depending on the time of day.*

capacity EG *people's creative capacities*

power EG *the power of speech*

wherewithal EG *She didn't have the financial wherewithal to do it.*

pour VERB
to flow quickly and in large quantities
EG *Blood was pouring from his broken nose.*

course EG *The tears coursed down her cheeks.*

flow EG *compressor stations that keep that gas flowing*

gush EG *Piping-hot water gushed out.*

run EG *Water was running down the walls.*

spout EG *a fountain that spouts water 40 feet into the air*

stream EG *She came in, rain streaming from her clothes and hair.*

poverty NOUN
the state of being very poor
EG *Garvey died in loneliness and poverty.*

destitution EG *refugees living in destitution*

hardship EG *Many people are suffering economic hardship.*

insolvency EG *Several companies are on the brink of insolvency.*

want EG *We are fighting for freedom from want.*

> **WORD POWER**
> Synonyms

beggary
indigence
penury
privation

❶ **power** NOUN
control over people and
activities
EG *a position of great power and
influence*
ascendancy EG *The extremists in
the party are gaining ascendancy.*
control EG *He has been forced to
give up control over the company.*
dominion EG *They truly believe
they have dominion over us.*
sovereignty EG *the resumption of
Chinese sovereignty over Hong Kong
in 1997*
supremacy EG *The party has
re-established its supremacy.*

❷ **power** NOUN
authority to do something
EG *The police have the power of
arrest.*
authority EG *The judge had no
authority to order a second trial.*
authorization EG *I don't have the
authorization to make such a
decision.*
licence EG *He has given me licence
to do the job as I see fit.*
privilege EG *the ancient powers
and privileges of parliament*
right EG *the right to vote*

❸ **power** NOUN
physical strength
EG *Power and bulk are vital to
success in rugby.*
brawn EG *He's got plenty of brains
as well as brawn.*
might EG *The might of the army
could prove a decisive factor.*
strength EG *He threw it forward
with all his strength.*
vigour EG *His body lacks the vigour
of a normal two-year-old.*

❶ **powerful** ADJECTIVE
able to control people and

events
EG *Russia and India, two large,
powerful countries*
commanding EG *We're in a more
commanding position than we've
been in for ages.*
dominant EG *He was a dominant
figure in the Italian film industry.*
influential EG *He had been
influential in shaping economic
policy.*

❷ **powerful** ADJECTIVE
physically strong
EG *It's such a big powerful dog.*
mighty EG *a mighty river*
strapping EG *He was a bricklayer -
a big, strapping fellow.*
strong EG *I'm not strong enough to
carry him.*
sturdy EG *The camera was
mounted on a sturdy tripod.*
vigorous EG *He was a vigorous,
handsome young man.*

> **WORD POWER**
> Antonym
> weak

❸ **powerful** ADJECTIVE
having a strong effect
EG *a powerful argument*
compelling EG *a compelling
reason to leave*
convincing EG *convincing evidence*
effective EG *Antibiotics are
effective against this organism.*
forceful EG *forceful action to stop
the suffering*
persuasive EG *Mr. Knight made a
persuasive case for removing the tax.*
telling EG *He spoke reasonably,
carefully, and with telling effect.*

powerless ADJECTIVE
unable to control or influence
events
EG *I was powerless to save her.*
helpless EG *Many people felt
helpless against the violence.*
impotent EG *The West is impotent
to influence the Balkan war.*

A
B
C
D
E
F
G
H
I
J
K
L
M
N
O
P
Q
R
S
T
U
V
W
X
Y
Z

A
B
C
D
E
F
G
H
I
J
K
L
M
N
O
P
Q
R
S
T
U
V
W
X
Y
Z

incapable EG *He is incapable as a manager.*

❶ **practical** ADJECTIVE
involving experience rather than theory
EG *practical suggestions for healthy eating*

applied EG *plans to put more money into applied research*

pragmatic EG *a pragmatic approach to the problems of Latin America*

❷ **practical** ADJECTIVE
likely to be effective
EG *The clothes are lightweight and practical for holidays.*

functional EG *The design is functional but stylish.*

sensible EG *sensible footwear*

WORD POWER
Antonym
impractical

❸ **practical** ADJECTIVE
able to deal effectively with problems
EG *the practical common sense essential in management*

accomplished EG *an accomplished cook*

experienced EG *a team packed with experienced professionals*

proficient EG *A great number of them are proficient in foreign languages.*

seasoned EG *The author is a seasoned academic.*

skilled EG *amateur but highly skilled observers of wildlife*

veteran EG *a veteran broadcaster*

❶ **practice** NOUN
something that people do regularly
EG *a public inquiry into bank practices*

custom EG *I have tried to adapt to local customs.*

habit EG *a survey on eating habits*

method EG *her usual method of getting through the traffic*

routine EG *We had to change our daily routine and lifestyle.*

way EG *a return to the old ways of doing things*

❷ **practice** NOUN
regular training or exercise
EG *I need more practice.*

drill EG *The teacher ran them through the drill again.*

exercise EG *Lack of exercise can lead to feelings of exhaustion.*

preparation EG *Behind any successful event lie months of preparation.*

rehearsal EG *rehearsals for a concert tour*

training EG *her busy training schedule*

❶ **practise** VERB
to do something repeatedly so as to gain skill
EG *Lauren practises the piano every day.*

polish EG *They just need to polish their technique.*

rehearse EG *She was in her room rehearsing her lines.*

train EG *He was training for the new season.*

❷ **practise** VERB
to take part in the activities of a religion, craft, or custom
EG *Acupuncture has been practised in China for thousands of years.*

do EG *I used to do karate.*

follow EG *Do you follow any particular religion?*

observe EG *American forces are observing Christmas quietly.*

❶ **praise** VERB
to express strong approval of someone
EG *Many others praised Sanford for taking a strong stand.*

admire EG *All those who knew him will admire him for his work.*

applaud EG *He should be applauded for his courage.*

approve EG *Not everyone approves of the festival.*

congratulate EG *I must congratulate the organizers for a well run event.*

pay tribute to EG *He paid tribute to his captain.*

> **WORD POWER**
> Synonyms
> acclaim
> eulogize
> extol
> laud
> Antonym
> criticize

❷ praise NOUN
something said or written to show approval
EG *She is full of praise for the range of services available.*

accolade EG *the ultimate international accolade, the Nobel Peace Prize*

approval EG *an obsessive drive to gain her mother's approval*

commendation EG *They received a commendation from the Royal Society of Arts.*

congratulation EG *I offered her my congratulations.*

tribute EG *We marched past in tribute to our fallen comrades.*

> **WORD POWER**
> Synonyms
> encomium
> eulogy
> panegyric
> Antonym
> criticism

precaution NOUN
an action intended to prevent something from happening
EG *It's still worth taking precautions against accidents.*

insurance EG *Farmers grew a mixture of crops as an insurance against crop failure.*

preventative measure EG *a preventative measure against heart disease*

protection EG *protection against damage to buildings*

provision EG *People need to make decent provision for their old age.*

safeguard EG *legislation that offers safeguards against discrimination*

precious ADJECTIVE
of great value and importance
EG *precious jewels*

expensive EG *an expensive new coat*

invaluable EG *I was to gain invaluable experience over that year.*

priceless EG *his priceless collection of Chinese art*

prized EG *These shells were very highly prized by the Indians.*

valuable EG *valuable books*

> **WORD POWER**
> Antonym
> worthless

predicament NOUN
a difficult situation
EG *The decision will leave her in a peculiar predicament.*

fix INFORMAL EG *The government has really got itself into a fix.*

hot water INFORMAL EG *His antics keep landing him in hot water with officials.*

jam INFORMAL EG *We are in a real jam now.*

scrape INFORMAL EG *He's had his fair share of scrapes with the law.*

tight spot EG *This was one tight spot he couldn't get out of.*

predict VERB
to say that something will happen in the future
EG *The opinion polls are predicting a very close contest.*

forecast EG *He forecasts that house prices will rise by 5% this year.*

foresee EG *He did not foresee any*

A B C D E F G H I J K L M N O P Q R S T U V W X Y Z

A
B
C
D
E
F
G
H
I
J
K
L
M
N
O
P
Q
R
S
T
U
V
W
X
Y
Z

problems.

foretell EG *prophets who have foretold the end of the world*

prophesy EG *She prophesied a bad ending for the expedition.*

> **WORD POWER**
> Synonyms
> forebode
> portend
> presage
> prognosticate
> soothsay

prediction NOUN
something that is forecast in advance
EG *He was unwilling to make a prediction for the coming year.*

forecast EG *a forecast of heavy weather to come*

prophecy EG *the interpreters of Biblical prophecy*

prefer VERB
to like one thing more than another thing
EG *Does he prefer a particular sort of music?*

be partial to EG *I'm quite partial to mussels.*

favour EG *Both sides favour a diplomatic solution.*

go for EG *They went for a more up-market approach.*

incline towards EG *The majority are inclined towards a forgiving attitude.*

like better EG *I like the flat shoes better.*

prefix NOUN

Prefixes:
ante-
anti-
auto-
bi-
centi-
co-
contra-
de-
demi-

dis-
ex-
extra-
hyper-
in-
inter-
intra-
mega-
micro-
mid-
milli-
mini-
mono-
multi-
neo-
non-
over-
poly-
post-
pre-
pro-
pseudo-
re-
self-
semi-
step-
sub-
super-
tele-
trans-
tri-
ultra-
un-
under-
vice-

❶ prejudice NOUN
an unreasonable or unfair dislike or preference
EG *prejudice against workers over 45*

bias EG *Bias against women permeates every level of the judicial system.*

partiality EG *She is criticized for her one-sidedness and partiality.*

preconception EG *preconceptions about the sort of people who did computing*

❷ prejudice NOUN
intolerance towards certain people or groups

EG *racial prejudice*
bigotry EG *religious bigotry*
chauvinism EG *the growth of Russian chauvinism*
discrimination EG *sex discrimination*
racism EG *the fight to rid sport of racism*
sexism EG *sexism in the workplace*

premonition NOUN
a feeling that something unpleasant is going to happen
EG *He had a premonition that he would die.*
foreboding EG *His triumph was overshadowed by an uneasy sense of foreboding.*
funny feeling INFORMAL EG *I have a funny feeling something unpleasant is about to happen.*
omen EG *Her appearance at this moment is an omen of disaster.*
sign EG *a sign of impending doom*

> **WORD POWER**
> Synonyms
> portent
> presage
> presentiment

preoccupied ADJECTIVE
totally involved with something or deep in thought
EG *I am preoccupied with my tennis career.*
absorbed EG *They were completely absorbed in each other.*
engrossed EG *Tom didn't notice because he was too engrossed in his work.*
immersed EG *He's becoming really immersed in his studies.*
oblivious EG *When he was in his car he was totally oblivious to everybody else.*
wrapped up EG *She's wrapped up in her new career.*

❶ present ADJECTIVE
being at a place or event
EG *He had been present at the birth*
of his son.
at hand EG *Having the right equipment at hand will be very useful.*
here EG *He was here a minute ago.*
in attendance EG *Police and several fire engines are in attendance.*
there EG *The group of old buildings is still there today.*
to hand EG *I haven't got the instructions to hand.*

> **WORD POWER**
> Antonym
> absent

❷ present NOUN
something given to someone
EG *a birthday present*
bonsela SOUTH AFRICAN EG *your kind bonsela to the hospital*
donation EG *Employees make regular donations to charity.*
gift EG *a Christmas gift*
offering EG *Hindus kill turtles ritually as an offering to their gods.*

❸ present VERB
to give something to someone
EG *The Mayor presented the prizes.*
award EG *For his dedication he was awarded a medal of merit.*
bestow EG *The Queen bestowed on him a knighthood.*
donate EG *He frequently donates large sums to charity.*
give EG *She gave me a pen for my birthday.*
grant EG *France has agreed to grant him political asylum.*
hand out EG *One of my jobs was to hand out the prizes.*

❶ press VERB
to apply force or weight to something
EG *Press the blue button.*
compress EG *Poor posture compresses the body's organs.*
crush EG *Peel and crush the garlic.*
mash EG *Mash the bananas with a*

fork.

push EG *She pushed the door open.*

squeeze EG *He squeezed her arm reassuringly.*

❷ press VERB

to try hard to persuade someone to do something

EG *Trade Unions are pressing him to stand firm.*

beg EG *I begged him to come back with me.*

implore EG *'Tell me what to do!' she implored him.*

petition EG *All the attempts to petition the government had failed.*

plead EG *I pleaded to be allowed to go.*

pressurize EG *He thought she was trying to pressurize him.*

urge EG *He had urged her to come to Ireland.*

> **WORD POWER**
> Synonyms
> entreat
> exhort
> importune

pretend VERB

to claim or give the appearance of something untrue

EG *Sometimes the boy pretended to be asleep.*

counterfeit EG *the coins he is alleged to have counterfeited*

fake EG *He faked his own death last year.*

falsify EG *He was charged with falsifying business records.*

feign EG *The striker was accused of feigning injury.*

pass oneself off as EG *She tried to pass herself off as an actress.*

pretentious ADJECTIVE

making unjustified claims to importance

EG *Many critics thought her work and ideas pretentious and empty.*

affected EG *She passed along with an affected air and a disdainful*

look.

conceited EG *I thought him conceited and arrogant.*

ostentatious EG *an ostentatious wedding reception*

pompous EG *He's pompous and has a high opinion of his own capabilities.*

snobbish EG *a snobbish dislike for their intellectual inferiors*

> **WORD POWER**
> Synonyms
> bombastic
> grandiloquent
> magniloquent
> vainglorious

❶ pretty ADJECTIVE

attractive in a delicate way

EG *She's a very charming and very pretty girl.*

attractive EG *She has a round attractive face.*

beautiful EG *a beautiful child*

cute EG *a cute little baby*

lovely EG *his lovely wife*

❷ pretty ADVERB; INFORMAL

quite or rather

EG *He spoke pretty good English.*

fairly EG *Both ships are fairly new.*

kind of INFORMAL EG *I was kind of embarrassed about it.*

quite EG *It was quite hard.*

rather EG *She's rather vain.*

prevent VERB

to stop something from happening

EG *the most practical way of preventing crime*

avert EG *A fresh tragedy was narrowly averted yesterday.*

foil EG *The plot was foiled by policemen.*

hinder EG *Research is hindered by lack of cash.*

impede EG *Fallen rocks are impeding the progress of the rescue workers.*

stop EG *a new diplomatic initiative*

to try to stop the war
thwart EG *Her ambition to become an artist was thwarted by failing eyesight.*

previous ADJECTIVE
happening or existing before something else
EG *the previous year*
earlier EG *His earlier works include impressive still lifes.*
former EG *a former president of Mexico*
one-time EG *the country's one-time military rulers*
past EG *a return to the turbulence of past centuries*
preceding EG *This is examined in detail in the preceding chapter.*
prior EG *I can't make it. I have a prior engagement.*

❶ price NOUN
the amount of money paid for something
EG *a sharp increase in the price of petrol*
amount EG *I was asked to pay the full amount.*
charge EG *an annual management charge of 1.25%*
cost EG *the cost of a loaf of bread*
fee EG *the annual membership fee*
figure EG *A figure of £2000 was mentioned.*
value EG *The company's market value rose to 5.5 billion dollars.*

❷ price VERB
to fix the price or value of something
EG *I just can't imagine why it has been priced at this level.*
cost EG *We hope it won't cost too much.*
estimate EG *His personal riches were estimated at $368 million.*
put a price on EG *The company has refused to put a price on its bid.*
value EG *I had my jewellery valued for insurance purposes.*

❶ pride NOUN

a feeling of satisfaction about your achievements
EG *We take pride in offering you the highest standards.*
delight EG *Haig took obvious delight in proving his critics wrong.*
pleasure EG *Our first win gave me great pleasure.*
satisfaction EG *His success was a great source of satisfaction to him.*

❷ pride NOUN
an excessively high opinion of yourself
EG *His pride may still be his downfall.*
arrogance EG *He has a swaggering arrogance.*
conceit EG *He knew, without conceit, that he was considered a genius.*
egotism EG *typical showbiz egotism*
smugness EG *a trace of smugness in his voice*
snobbery EG *intellectual snobbery*
vanity EG *her vanity about her long hair*

> **WORD POWER**
> Synonyms
> haughtiness
> hauteur
> hubris
> superciliousness
> Antonym
> humility

priest NOUN

> Types of priest:
> guru (*Hinduism or Sikhism*)
> high priest *or* high priestess
> imam (*Muslim*)
> lama (*Buddhism*)
> minister (*Christianity*)
> priest
> rabbi (*Judaism*)
> shaman *or* medicine man
> vicar (*Christianity*)

prim ADJECTIVE
behaving very correctly and easily shocked by anything rude

EG *We tend to assume the Victorians were very prim and proper.*

proper EG *He was very pompous and proper.*

prudish EG *I'm not prudish but I think those photos are obscene.*

puritanical EG *He has a puritanical attitude towards sex.*

strait-laced EG *He very strait-laced and narrow-minded.*

❶ prime ADJECTIVE
main or most important
EG *a prime cause of brain damage*

chief EG *The job went to one of his chief rivals.*

leading EG *a leading industrial nation*

main EG *the city's main tourist area*

principal EG *our principal source of foreign exchange earnings*

❷ prime ADJECTIVE
of the best quality
EG *prime beef*

best EG *He'll have the best care.*

choice EG *our choicest chocolates*

first-rate EG *He's a first-rate officer.*

select EG *With that historic win he now joins a select band of golfers.*

superior EG *superior coffee beans*

primitive ADJECTIVE
very simple or basic
EG *a very small primitive cottage*

crude EG *crude stone carvings*

rough EG *a rough wooden table*

rude EG *He constructed a rude cabin for himself.*

rudimentary EG *The bomb was rudimentary but lethal.*

simple EG *a simple shelter*

❶ principle NOUN
a set of moral rules guiding personal conduct
EG *a woman of principle*

conscience EG *the law on freedom of conscience and religious organizations*

integrity EG *He has always been a man of integrity.*

morals EG *public morals*

scruples EG *a man with no moral scruples*

sense of duty EG *He did it out of a sense of duty to his men.*

❷ principle NOUN
a general rule or scientific law
EG *the basic principles of Marxism*

axiom EG *the long-held axiom that education leads to higher income*

canon EG *the canons of political economy*

doctrine EG *Christian doctrine*

fundamental EG *the fundamentals of astronomy*

law EG *the laws of motion*

> **WORD POWER**
> Synonyms
> dictum
> precept
> verity

printing NOUN

> **Printing words:**
> bold print
> character
> fount *or* font
> italics
> lower case
> roman
> size
> typeface
> upper case

prison NOUN
a building where criminals are kept in captivity
EG *a high-security prison*

dungeon EG *The castle's dungeons haven't been used for years.*

jail EG *Three prisoners escaped from the jail.*

nick BRITISH, AUSTRALIAN, AND NEW ZEALAND SLANG EG *I was banged up in the nick for six months.*

penal institution EG *Thirty years in a penal institution is indeed a harsh penalty.*

prisoner NOUN
someone kept in prison or
captivity
EG *top-security prisoners*
captive EG *the difficulties of
spending four months as a captive*
convict EG *convicts serving life
sentences*
hostage EG *negotiations to release
the hostages*

❶ private ADJECTIVE
for few people rather than
people in general
EG *a private bathroom*
exclusive EG *Many of our cheeses
are exclusive to our shops in Britain.*
individual EG *Divide the
vegetables among four individual
dishes.*
personal EG *It's for my own
personal use.*
special EG *her own special problems*

❷ private ADJECTIVE
taking place among a small
number of people
EG *He was buried in a private
ceremony.*
clandestine EG *He had a
clandestine meeting with his lover.*
confidential EG *confidential
information about her private life*
secret EG *a secret love affair*

> *WORD POWER*
> Antonym
> public

❶ prize NOUN
a reward given to the winner of
something
EG *He won first prize at the Leeds
Piano Competition.*
accolade EG *the ultimate
international accolade, the Nobel
Peace Prize*
award EG *the Booker Prize,
Britain's top award for fiction*
honour EG *He was showered with
honours - among them an Oscar.*
trophy EG *They haven't won a*

trophy since 1991.

❷ prize ADJECTIVE
of the highest quality or
standard
EG *a prize bull*
award-winning EG *an
award-winning restaurant*
first-rate EG *a first-rate thriller
writer*
outstanding EG *an outstanding
horse*
top EG *Holland's top striker*

❸ prize VERB
to value highly
EG *These ornaments are prized by
collectors.*
cherish EG *We cherish our
independence.*
esteem EG *one of Europe's most
esteemed awards*
treasure EG *She treasures her
memories of those joyous days.*
value EG *I value the work he gives
me.*

probability NOUN
the likelihood of something
happening
EG *the probability of a serious
earthquake*
chances EG *The chances of success
for the product are good.*
likelihood EG *the likelihood of
infection*
odds EG *The odds are that you are
going to fail.*
prospect EG *the prospect for peace
in Rwanda*

probable ADJECTIVE
likely to be true or to happen
EG *a misunderstanding about the
probable cost*
apparent EG *There is no apparent
reason for the crime.*
feasible EG *Whether this is
feasible is a matter of doubt.*
likely EG *Further delays are likely.*
on the cards EG *A promotion is
definitely on the cards for you.*
plausible EG *a plausible*

A
B
C
D
E
F
G
H
I
J
K
L
M
N
O
P
Q
R
S
T
U
V
W
X
Y
Z

explanation

> **WORD POWER**
> Synonyms
> ostensible
> verisimilar
> Antonym
> improbable

probably ADVERB
in all likelihood
EG *The wedding's probably going to be in late August.*
doubtless EG *He will doubtless try to change my mind.*
in all probability EG *Victory will, in all probability, earn France the title.*
likely EG *The entire surplus will most likely be handed over.*
presumably EG *The spear is presumably the murder weapon.*

❶ problem NOUN
an unsatisfactory situation causing difficulties
EG *the economic problems of the inner city*
difficulty EG *This company is facing great difficulties.*
predicament EG *the once great club's current predicament*
quandary EG *We're in a quandary over our holiday plans.*
trouble EG *I had trouble parking this morning.*

❷ problem NOUN
a puzzle that needs to be solved
EG *a mathematical problem*
conundrum EG *an apparently insoluble conundrum*
puzzle EG *The data has presented astronomers with a puzzle.*
riddle EG *the riddle of the birth of the universe*

❶ process NOUN
a method of doing or producing something
EG *The building process was spread over three years.*
course of action EG *It is*

important that we take the right course of action.
means EG *The move is a means to fight crime.*
method EG *new teaching methods*
procedure EG *the correct procedure for applying for a visa*
system EG *an efficient filing system*

❷ process VERB
to deal with or treat something
EG *Your application is being processed.*
deal with EG *the way that banks deal with complaints*
dispose of EG *They disposed of the problem quickly.*
handle EG *She didn't know how to handle the problem.*
take care of EG *They left it to me to try and take care of the problem.*

❶ produce VERB
to make something
EG *a white wine produced mainly from black grapes*
construct EG *an inner frame constructed from timber*
create EG *It was created from odds and ends.*
invent EG *He invented the first electric clock.*
make EG *One of my jobs was to make the tea.*
manufacture EG *They manufacture plastics.*

❷ produce VERB
to bring out something so it can be seen or discussed
EG *To hire a car you must produce a driving licence.*
advance EG *Many new theories have been advanced recently.*
bring forward EG *We will bring forward new proposals for legislation.*
bring to light EG *new evidence brought to light by the police*
put forward EG *He has put forward new peace proposals.*

product NOUN

something that is made to be
sold
EG *Many household products give off
noxious fumes.*
commodity EG *basic commodities
such as bread and milk*
goods EG *imported goods*
merchandise EG *The club sells a
wide range of merchandise.*
produce EG *locally grown produce*

❶ **productive** ADJECTIVE
producing a large number of
things
EG *Training makes workers highly
productive.*
fertile EG *a product of his fertile
imagination*
fruitful EG *a landscape that was
fruitful and lush*
prolific EG *She is a prolific writer
of novels and short stories.*

WORD POWER
Synonyms
fecund
generative
Antonym
unproductive

❷ **productive** ADJECTIVE
bringing favourable results
EG *I'm hopeful the talks will be
productive.*
constructive EG *constructive
criticism*
useful EG *We made some progress
during a useful exchange.*
valuable EG *The experience was
very valuable.*
worthwhile EG *It had been a
worthwhile discussion.*

WORD POWER
Antonym
unproductive

profession NOUN
a job that requires advanced
education or training
EG *Harper was a teacher by
profession.*
business EG *May I ask you what*

business you're in?
career EG *a career in journalism*
occupation EG *her new occupation
as an author*

❶ **profit** NOUN
money gained in business or
trade
EG *The bank made pre-tax profits of
$3.5 million.*
earnings EG *his earnings as an
accountant*
proceeds EG *The proceeds from the
concert will go to charity.*
revenue EG *tax revenues*
surplus EG *Japan's trade surplus*
takings EG *the pub's weekly
takings*

WORD POWER
Antonym
loss

❷ **profit** VERB
to gain or benefit from
something
EG *They profited shamefully at the
expense of my family.*
capitalize on EG *The rebels are
trying to capitalize on the public's
discontent.*
exploit EG *They are trying to
exploit the troubles to their
advantage.*
make the most of EG *Happiness
is the ability to make the most of
what you have.*
take advantage of EG *She took
advantage of him even after their
divorce.*

❶ **programme** NOUN
a planned series of events
EG *a programme of official
engagements*
agenda EG *This is sure to be an
item on the agenda again next week.*
schedule EG *We both have such
hectic schedules.*
timetable EG *We've finally
managed to agree on a timetable for
formal talks.*

A
B
C
D
E
F
G
H
I
J
K
L
M
N
O
P
Q
R
S
T
U
V
W
X
Y
Z

programme – promote

② programme NOUN
a broadcast on radio or television
EG *local news programmes*
broadcast EG *a broadcast by the President*
show EG *my favourite TV show*

① progress NOUN
improvement or development
EG *progress in the fight against cancer*
advance EG *dramatic advances in road safety*
breakthrough EG *a breakthrough in their research*
headway EG *The police are making little headway in the investigation.*
improvement EG *considerable room for improvement in facilities for patients*

② progress VERB
to become more advanced or skilful
EG *His reading is progressing well.*
advance EG *Japan has advanced from a rural society to an industrial power.*
blossom EG *In just a few years it has blossomed into an international event.*
develop EG *workshops designed to develop acting skills*
improve EG *Their French has improved enormously.*

promiscuous ADJECTIVE
having many casual sexual relationships
EG *a promiscuous teenager*
loose EG *If you wear a short skirt in here you're considered a loose woman.*
wanton EG *A woman with many sexual partners is still considered wanton.*

> **WORD POWER**
> Synonyms
> libertine
> licentious
> of easy virtue

① promise VERB
to say that you will definitely do or not do something
EG *I promise not to be back too late.*
assure EG *She assured me that she would deal with the problem.*
give your word EG *He had given us his word he would join the club.*
guarantee EG *Most countries guarantee the right to free education.*
pledge EG *They have pledged to support the opposition.*
vow EG *I vowed that someday I would return to live in Europe.*

② promise VERB
to show signs of
EG *This promised to be a very long night.*
hint at EG *One finding hints at support for this theory.*
indicate EG *His early work indicates talent.*
show signs of EG *Already she shows signs of beauty.*

> **WORD POWER**
> Synonyms
> augur
> bespeak
> betoken
> bid fair

③ promise NOUN
an undertaking to do or not do something
EG *If you make a promise, you should keep it.*
assurance EG *He gave written assurance that he would start work at once.*
guarantee EG *They can give no guarantee that they will fulfil their obligations.*
pledge EG *a pledge to step up cooperation between the two countries*
undertaking EG *an undertaking that he would be a responsible parent*
vow EG *I kept my marriage vows.*

① promote VERB

to encourage the progress or
success of something
EG *All attempts to promote a
ceasefire have failed.*
back EG *She backed the new
initiative enthusiastically.*
support EG *He thanked everyone
who had supported the strike.*

❷ **promote** VERB
to encourage the sale of a
product by advertising
EG *She's in Europe promoting her
new film.*
advertise EG *She is contracted to
advertise their beauty products.*
plug INFORMAL EG *He was on the
show to plug his latest film.*
publicize EG *I was publicizing the
film in London.*

❸ **promote** VERB
to raise someone to a higher
rank or position
EG *He has been promoted twice in
two years.*
elevate EG *He was elevated to the
post of Prime Minister.*
upgrade EG *He was upgraded to
supervisor.*

❶ **prone** ADJECTIVE
having a tendency to be affected
by or do something
EG *She is prone to depression.*
disposed EG *I might have been
disposed to like him in other
circumstances.*
given EG *I am not very given to
emotional displays.*
inclined EG *Nobody felt inclined to
argue with Smith.*
liable EG *equipment that is liable
to break*
susceptible EG *She's very
susceptible to colds and flu.*

❷ **prone** ADJECTIVE
lying flat and face downwards
EG *We were lying prone on the grass.*
face down EG *He was lying face
down on his bed.*
prostrate EG *The injured jockey*

lay prostrate on the ground.

proof NOUN
evidence that confirms that
something is true or exists
EG *You have to have proof of
residence in the state of Texas.*
confirmation EG *further
confirmation that house prices are
no longer falling*
evidence EG *To date there is no
evidence to support this theory.*
testimony EG *His testimony was
an important element of the
prosecution case.*
verification EG *verification of her
story*

WORD POWER
Synonyms
authentication
certification
corroboration
substantiation

❶ **proper** ADJECTIVE
correct or most suitable
EG *the proper course of action*
appropriate EG *a smart outfit
appropriate to the job*
apt EG *an apt title for the book*
correct EG *the correct way to do
things*
fitting EG *His address was a fitting
end to a bitter campaign.*
right EG *He's the right man for the
job.*
suitable EG *She had no other dress
suitable for the occasion.*

WORD POWER
Antonym
improper

❷ **proper** ADJECTIVE
accepted or conventional
EG *She wanted a proper wedding.*
accepted EG *the accepted way of
doing things*
conventional EG *conventional
surgical methods*
orthodox EG *orthodox police
methods*

A B C D E F G H I J K L M N O P Q R S T U V W X Y Z

A
B
C
D
E
F
G
H
I
J
K
L
M
N
O
P
Q
R
S
T
U
V
W
X
Y
Z

❶ property NOUN
the things that belong to someone
EG *her personal property*

assets EG *The company has assets of 3.5 billion francs.*

belongings EG *I collected my belongings and left.*

effects EG *After the funeral he sorted his father's personal effects.*

estate EG *His estate was valued at $150,000.*

possessions EG *People had lost their homes and all their possessions.*

❷ property NOUN
a characteristic or quality
EG *Mint has powerful healing properties.*

attribute EG *a normal attribute of human behaviour*

characteristic EG *their physical characteristics*

feature EG *a feature of the local culture*

hallmark EG *The killing had the hallmarks of a professional assassination.*

quality EG *mature people with leadership qualities*

trait EG *Creativity is a human trait.*

proportion NOUN
part of an amount or group
EG *a tiny proportion of the population*

percentage EG *It has a high percentage of protein.*

quota EG *Britain's fishing quota has been cut.*

segment EG *a fast-growing segment of the market*

share EG *I pay a share of the phone and gas bills.*

prospect NOUN
expectation or something anticipated
EG *There was no prospect of going home.*

expectation EG *The hotel was being renovated in expectation of a tourist boom.*

hope EG *There is little hope of improvement now.*

outlook EG *Officials say the outlook for next year is gloomy.*

promise EG *New Year brought the promise of better things to come.*

protect VERB
to prevent someone or something from being harmed
EG *Cash dispensers are protected by thick steel and glass.*

defend EG *I had to defend myself against the attack.*

guard EG *Soldiers guarded homes near the airport.*

safeguard EG *action to safeguard the ozone layer*

shelter EG *a wooden house, sheltered by a low pointed roof*

shield EG *He shielded his head from the sun with a newspaper.*

protection NOUN
something that protects
EG *a diet believed to offer protection against some cancers*

barrier EG *a flood barrier*

buffer EG *Keep savings as a buffer against unexpected cash needs.*

cover EG *air cover for ground operations*

safeguard EG *a safeguard against weeds*

shelter EG *an air-raid shelter*

❶ protest VERB
to disagree with someone or object to something
EG *She protested that she was a patriot, not a traitor.*

complain EG *People always complain that the big banks are unhelpful.*

disagree EG *I disagree with the drug laws in general.*

disapprove EG *Her mother disapproved of her working in a pub.*

object EG *We objected strongly but were outvoted.*

oppose EG *Many parents oppose bilingual education in schools.*

WORD POWER
Synonyms
demur
expostulate
remonstrate
---

❷ **protest** NOUN
a strong objection
EG *The council has ignored their protests by backing the scheme.*
complaint EG *the way that banks deal with complaints*
objection EG *I questioned the logic of his objections.*
outcry EG *The incident caused an international outcry.*

proud ADJECTIVE
feeling pleasure or satisfaction
EG *I was proud of our players today.*
gratified EG *He was gratified by the audience's response.*
honoured EG *I am honoured to work with her.*
pleased EG *I was pleased to call him my friend.*

prove VERB
to provide evidence that something is definitely true
EG *History will prove him to have been right all along.*
ascertain EG *They had ascertained that he was not a spy.*
confirm EG *X-rays confirmed that he had not broken any bones.*
demonstrate EG *You have to demonstrate that you are reliable.*
establish EG *The autopsy established the cause of death.*
verify EG *I can verify that it takes about thirty seconds.*

WORD POWER
Synonyms
authenticate
corroborate
evince
substantiate
Antonym
---

disprove

provide VERB
to make something available to someone
EG *I'll be glad to provide a copy of this.*
contribute EG *NATO agreed to contribute troops and equipment.*
equip EG *proposals to equip all officers with body armour*
furnish EG *They'll be able to furnish you with the rest of the details.*
outfit EG *They outfitted him with artificial legs.*
supply EG *the blood vessels supplying oxygen to the brain*

pry VERB
to try to find out about someone else's private business
EG *We do not want people prying into our business.*
interfere EG *I wish everyone would stop interfering and just leave me alone.*
intrude EG *The press were intruding into my personal life.*
poke your nose in INFORMAL EG *Who asked you to poke your nose in?*
poke your nose into INFORMAL EG *strangers who poke their noses into our affairs*
snoop INFORMAL EG *He was snooping around Kim's hotel room.*

pub NOUN
a place where alcoholic drinks are served
EG *He goes to the pub most nights.*
bar BRITISH EG *He works in a bar.*
boozer BRITISH, AUSTRALIAN, AND NEW ZEALAND INFORMAL EG *the local boozer*
inn EG *a village inn*
lounge EG *the hotel lounge*
public house EG *a robbery at a public house in New Milton*
saloon EG *a Wild West saloon*
tavern EG *an old country tavern*

A B C D E F G H I J K L M N O P Q R S T U V W X Y Z

❶ public NOUN
people in general
EG *the public's confidence in the government*

masses EG *a quest to bring the Internet to the masses*
nation EG *The President spoke to the nation.*
people EG *the will of the people*
populace EG *a large proportion of the populace*
society EG *a menace to society*

❷ public ADJECTIVE
relating to people in general
EG *public support for the idea*

civic EG *a sense of civic pride*
general EG *The project should raise general awareness about bullying.*
popular EG *Popular anger has been expressed in demonstrations.*
universal EG *the universal outrage at the deaths*

❸ public ADJECTIVE
provided for everyone to use or open to anyone
EG *public transport*

communal EG *a communal dining room*
community EG *a village community centre*
open to the public EG *Part of the castle is now open to the public.*
universal EG *universal health care*

> **WORD POWER**
> Antonym
> private

publicity NOUN
information or advertisements about an item or event
EG *government publicity campaigns*

advertising EG *tobacco advertising in women's magazines*
plug INFORMAL EG *The whole interview was an unashamed plug for her new book.*
promotion EG *They've spent a lot of money on advertising and promotion.*

publish VERB
to make a piece of writing available for reading
EG *We publish a range of titles.*

bring out EG *The newspapers all brought out special editions.*
print EG *a letter printed in the Times yesterday*
put out EG *a statement put out by the Iraqi news agency*

❶ pull VERB
to draw an object towards you
EG *a wooden plough pulled by oxen*

drag EG *He dragged his chair towards the table.*
draw EG *He drew his chair nearer the fire.*
haul EG *A crane was used to haul the car out of the stream.*
tow EG *They threatened to tow away my van.*
tug EG *She kicked him, tugging his thick hair.*
yank EG *She yanked open the drawer.*

> **WORD POWER**
> Antonym
> push

❷ pull NOUN
the attraction or influence of something
EG *The pull of Mexico was too strong.*

attraction EG *The attraction of Hollywood began to pall.*
lure EG *The lure of rural life is as strong as ever.*
magnetism EG *the sheer magnetism of his presence*

punctual ADJECTIVE
arriving or leaving at the correct time
EG *The most punctual airline last year was Swissair.*

in good time EG *It is now 5am and we are in good time.*
on time EG *I'm generally early or on time for an appointment.*

prompt EG *We expect you to be prompt for all your classes.*

punctuation NOUN

> **Punctuation marks:**
> apostrophe
> asterisk
> bracket
> bullet point
> colon
> comma
> dash
> exclamation mark
> full stop
> hyphen
> question mark
> semicolon
> speech marks *or* quotation marks

punish VERB
to make someone suffer a penalty for some misbehaviour
EG *I got punished for insolence.*

discipline EG *He was disciplined by his company but not dismissed.*

penalize EG *Bad teaching is not penalized in a formal way.*

rap someone's knuckles EG *The company got its knuckles rapped for this advertisement.*

sentence EG *He has admitted the charge and will be sentenced later.*

throw the book at EG *The football authorities seem certain to throw the book at him.*

punishment NOUN
a penalty for a crime or offence
EG *The punishment must always fit the crime.*

penalty EG *One of those arrested could face the death penalty.*

retribution EG *He didn't want any further involvement for fear of retribution.*

> **WORD POWER**
> **Synonyms**
> chastening
> chastisement
> just deserts

pupil NOUN

a student taught at a school
EG *She is a model pupil.*

scholar SOUTH AFRICAN EG *a bunch of rowdy scholars*

schoolboy or **schoolgirl** EG *a group of ten-year-old schoolboys*

schoolchild EG *The bus was packed with schoolchildren.*

student EG *The students are sorted into three ability groups.*

❶ **pure** ADJECTIVE
clean and free from harmful substances
EG *The water is pure enough to drink.*

clean EG *Tiled kitchen floors are easy to keep clean.*

germ-free EG *chlorine gas used to keep water germ-free*

pasteurized EG *The milk is pasteurized to kill bacteria.*

spotless EG *She kept the kitchen spotless.*

sterilized EG *sterilized surgical equipment*

> **WORD POWER**
> **Synonyms**
> unadulterated
> unblemished
> uncontaminated
> unpolluted
> untainted
> **Antonym**
> impure

❷ **pure** ADJECTIVE
complete and total
EG *a matter of pure luck*

absolute EG *You're talking absolute nonsense.*

complete EG *complete and utter rubbish*

outright EG *an outright rejection of the deal*

sheer EG *acts of sheer desperation*

unmitigated EG *Last year's crop was an unmitigated disaster.*

utter EG *This, of course, is utter nonsense.*

A B C D E F G H I J K L M N O P Q R S T U V W X Y Z

purple NOUN OR ADJECTIVE

Shades of purple:
amethyst
aubergine
gentian
heather
heliotrope
indigo
lavender
lilac
magenta
mauve
mulberry
plum
puce
royal purple
violet

❶ purpose NOUN
the reason for something
EG *What is the purpose of this meeting?*
aim EG *the aim of the policy*
function EG *Their main function is to raise capital for industry.*
intention EG *The intention of the scheme is to encourage faster sales.*
object EG *the object of the exercise*
point EG *I don't see the point of it.*
reason EG *What is the real reason for the delay?*

❷ purpose
on purpose ADVERB
deliberately
EG *Did you do that on purpose?*
by design EG *The pair met often - at first by chance but later by design.*
deliberately EG *It looks as if the fire was started deliberately.*
intentionally EG *I've never hurt anyone intentionally.*
knowingly EG *He said that he'd never knowingly taken illegal drugs.*
purposely EG *They are purposely withholding information.*

❶ push VERB
to apply force to something in order to move it
EG *She pushed the door open.*
press EG *He pressed his back against the door.*
ram EG *He rammed the key into the lock.*
shove EG *He shoved her aside.*
thrust EG *They thrust him into the back of the jeep.*

| *WORD POWER* |
| Antonym |
| pull |

❷ push VERB
to persuade someone into doing something
EG *His mother pushed him into auditioning for a part.*
encourage EG *She encouraged me to stick to the diet.*
persuade EG *They persuaded him to moderate his views.*
press EG *Trade unions are pressing him to stand firm.*
urge EG *He had urged her to come to Ireland.*

❶ put VERB
to place something somewhere
EG *She put the photograph on the desk.*
deposit EG *On his way out he deposited a glass in front of me.*
lay EG *Lay a sheet of newspaper on the floor.*
place EG *He placed it in the inside pocket of his jacket.*
position EG *Plants were carefully positioned in the alcove.*
rest EG *He rested his arms on the back of the chair.*

❷ put VERB
to express something
EG *I think you put that very well.*
phrase EG *I would have phrased it quite differently.*
word EG *You misinterpreted his letter, or else he worded it poorly.*

put off VERB
to delay something
EG *Ministers have put off making a decision until next month.*
defer EG *Customers often defer*

payment for as long as possible.
delay EG *She wants to delay the wedding.*
postpone EG *The visit has been postponed indefinitely.*
put back EG *The news conference has been put back a couple of hours.*
put on ice EG *The decision has been put on ice until October.*
reschedule EG *Since I'll be away, I'd like to reschedule the meeting.*

put up with VERB
to tolerate something disagreeable
EG *They won't put up with a return to the bad old days.*
abide EG *I can't abide arrogant people.*
bear EG *He can't bear to talk about it.*
stand EG *She cannot stand her boss.*
stand for EG *We won't stand for it any more.*
stomach EG *He could not stomach violence.*
tolerate EG *She can no longer tolerate the position she is in.*

> **WORD POWER**
> Synonyms
> brook
> countenance

❶ puzzle VERB
to perplex and confuse
EG *There was something about her that puzzled me.*
baffle EG *An apple tree producing square fruit is baffling experts.*
bewilder EG *His silence bewildered her.*
confuse EG *German politics surprised and confused him.*
mystify EG *The audience were mystified by the plot.*
stump EG *I was stumped by an unexpected question.*

> **WORD POWER**
> Synonyms
> confound
> flummox
> nonplus
> perplex

❷ puzzle NOUN
a game or question that requires a lot of thought to solve
EG *a crossword puzzle*
brain-teaser INFORMAL EG *It took me ages to solve that brain-teaser.*
poser EG *Here is a little poser for you.*
problem EG *a mathematical problem*
riddle EG *See if you can answer this riddle.*

Qq Qq

❶ qualification NOUN
a skill or achievement
EG *His qualifications are impressive.*
ability EG *a man of considerable abilities*
accomplishment EG *Carl was proud of his son's accomplishments.*
achievement EG *the highest academic achievement*
capability EG *Her capabilities were not fully appreciated.*
quality EG *Colley's leadership qualities*
skill EG *a skill you can use*

> **WORD POWER**
> Synonyms
> attribute
> endowment

❷ qualification NOUN
something added to make a statement less strong
EG *The argument is not true without qualification.*
condition EG *You can make any conditions you like.*
exception EG *a major exception to this general argument*
modification EG *to consider modifications to his proposal*
reservation EG *men whose work I admire without reservation*

❶ quality NOUN
the measure of how good something is
EG *The quality of food is very poor.*
calibre EG *a man of your calibre*
distinction EG *a chef of great distinction*
grade EG *high grade meat and poultry*
merit EG *a work of real merit*
value EG *He set a high value upon their friendship.*
worth EG *a person's true worth*

❷ quality NOUN

a characteristic of something
EG *These qualities are essential for success.*
aspect EG *every aspect of our lives*
characteristic EG *their physical characteristics*
feature EG *the most striking feature of his work*
mark EG *the mark of a great composer*
property EG *the magnetic properties of iron*
trait EG *the young Ms Rankine's personality traits*

> **WORD POWER**
> Synonyms
> attribute
> peculiarity

❶ quantity NOUN
an amount you can measure or count
EG *a large quantity of alcohol*
amount EG *a small amount of mayonnaise*
number EG *There are a limited number of seats available.*
part EG *the greater part of his wealth*
sum EG *a large sum of money*

> **WORD POWER**
> Synonyms
> portion
> quota

❷ quantity NOUN
the amount of something that there is
EG *emphasis on quality rather than quantity*
extent EG *the extent of the damage*
measure EG *The government has had a fair measure of success.*
size EG *He gauged the size of the audience.*
volume EG *the sheer volume of traffic and accidents*

❶ quarrel NOUN
an angry argument
EG *I had a terrible quarrel with my brother.*

argument EG *an argument about money*

disagreement EG *My instructor and I had a brief disagreement.*

dispute EG *Brand eavesdropped on the petty dispute.*

feud EG *a two-year feud between neighbours*

fight EG *It was a silly fight about where we parked the car.*

row EG *Maxine and I had a terrible row.*

squabble EG *minor squabbles about phone bills*

❷ quarrel VERB
to have an angry argument
EG *My brother quarrelled with my father.*

argue EG *They were still arguing later.*

bicker EG *They bickered endlessly over procedure.*

clash EG *She had clashed with Doyle in the past.*

fall out INFORMAL EG *Mum and I used to fall out a lot.*

fight EG *The couple often fought with their son.*

row EG *He had rowed with his girlfriend.*

squabble EG *The children were squabbling over the remote control.*

❶ question NOUN
a problem that needs to be discussed
EG *Can we get back to the question of the car?*

issue EG *What is your view on this issue?*

motion EG *The conference is now debating the motion.*

point EG *There is another point to consider.*

subject EG *He raised the subject of money.*

topic EG *the topic of where to go on holiday*

❷ question VERB
to ask someone questions
EG *A man is being questioned by police.*

examine EG *Lawyers examined the witnesses.*

interrogate EG *I interrogated everyone even slightly involved.*

probe EG *tabloid journalists probing us for details*

quiz EG *She quizzed me quite closely for a while.*

❸ question VERB
to express doubts about something
EG *He never stopped questioning his own beliefs.*

challenge EG *Rose convincingly challenged the story.*

dispute EG *Nobody disputed that Davey was clever.*

distrust EG *I distrusted my ability to keep quiet.*

doubt EG *Nobody doubted his sincerity.*

query EG *No one queried my decision.*

suspect EG *Do we suspect the motives of our friends?*

A B C D E F G H I J K L M N O P Q R S T U V W X Y Z

❶ quick ADJECTIVE
moving with great speed
EG *You'll have to be quick to catch the flight.*
brisk EG *a brisk walk*
fast EG *a very fast driver*
hasty EG *He spoke in a hasty, nervous way.*
rapid EG *a rapid rise through the company*
speedy EG *a speedy recovery*
swift EG *She is as swift as an arrow.*

> **WORD POWER**
> Synonyms
> express
> headlong
> Antonym
> slow

❷ quick ADJECTIVE
lasting only a short time
EG *a quick chat*
brief EG *a brief meeting*
cursory EG *a cursory glance inside the van*
hasty EG *a hasty meal of bread and soup*
hurried EG *He ate a hurried breakfast.*
perfunctory EG *With a perfunctory smile, she walked past Jessica.*

> **WORD POWER**
> Antonym
> long

❸ quick ADJECTIVE
happening without any delay
EG *a quick response*
hasty EG *This is no hasty decision.*
prompt EG *Prompt action is needed.*
sudden EG *this week's sudden cold snap*

quickly ADVERB
with great speed
EG *Stop me if I'm speaking too quickly.*
fast EG *How fast were you driving?*

hastily EG *sheltering in hastily erected tents*
hurriedly EG *students hurriedly taking notes*
rapidly EG *moving rapidly across the field*
speedily EG *She speedily recovered herself.*
swiftly EG *They had to act swiftly to save him.*

> **WORD POWER**
> Antonym
> slowly

❶ quiet ADJECTIVE
making very little noise
EG *The children were quiet and contented.*
hushed EG *Tales were exchanged in hushed tones.*
inaudible EG *a tiny, almost inaudible squeak*
low EG *I spoke in a low voice to Sullivan.*
silent EG *He could speak no English and was silent.*
soft EG *There was some soft music playing.*

> **WORD POWER**
> Synonyms
> noiseless
> soundless
> Antonym
> noisy

❷ quiet ADJECTIVE
peaceful and calm
EG *a quiet evening at home*
calm EG *The city seems relatively calm today.*
mild EG *The night was mild.*
peaceful EG *a peaceful old house*
restful EG *a restful scene*
serene EG *the beautiful, serene park*
tranquil EG *a tranquil lake*

> **WORD POWER**
> Synonyms
> motionless
> placid
> untroubled

❸ quiet NOUN
silence or lack of noise
EG *The teacher called for quiet.*
calmness EG *the calmness of this area*
peace EG *I enjoy peace and quiet.*
serenity EG *the peace and serenity of a tropical sunset*
silence EG *There was a silence around the table.*
stillness EG *the stillness of the summer night*
tranquillity EG *the tranquillity of village life*

> **WORD POWER**
> Antonym
> noise

quit VERB
to leave a place or stop doing something
EG *Leigh quit his job as a salesman.*
discontinue EG *Do not discontinue the treatment without seeing your doctor.*
give up EG *She gave up smoking last year.*
leave EG *He left school with no qualifications.*
resign EG *Scott resigned from the firm.*
retire EG *Littlejohn was forced to retire from the race.*
stop EG *I stopped working last year to have a baby.*

> **WORD POWER**
> Synonyms
> abandon
> cease

❶ quite ADVERB
fairly but not very
EG *He is quite old.*

fairly EG *Both ships are fairly new.*
moderately EG *a moderately attractive man*
rather EG *I made some rather bad mistakes.*
reasonably EG *I can dance reasonably well.*
somewhat EG *He's somewhat deaf.*

❷ quite ADVERB
completely and totally
EG *Jane lay quite still.*
absolutely EG *I absolutely refuse to get married.*
completely EG *something completely different*
entirely EG *an entirely new approach*
fully EG *He has still not fully recovered.*
perfectly EG *They are perfectly safe to eat.*
totally EG *The fire totally destroyed the house.*

> **WORD POWER**
> Synonyms
> precisely
> wholly

quote VERB
to repeat the exact words someone has said
EG *She quoted a great line from Shakespeare.*
cite EG *She cites a favourite poem by George Herbert.*
extract EG *This material has been extracted from the handbook.*
recite EG *They recited poetry to one another.*
repeat EG *Could you repeat the whole interview word for word?*

A
B
C
D
E
F
G
H
I
J
K
L
M
N
O
P
Q
R
S
T
U
V
W
X
Y
Z

Rr Rr

❶ race NOUN
a group of human beings with similar physical characteristics
EG *Discrimination on the grounds of race is illegal.*

ethnic group EG *Ethnic group and nationality are often different.*

nation EG *a mature and cultured nation*

people EG *an address to the American people*

❷ race VERB
to move very quickly
EG *Her heart raced uncontrollably.*

dash EG *He dashed upstairs.*

fly EG *I must fly or I'll miss my train.*

hurry EG *They hurried down the street.*

run EG *The gunmen escaped by running into the woods.*

speed EG *speeding along as fast as I could*

tear EG *The door flew open and she tore into the room.*

❶ rage NOUN
a feeling of very strong anger
EG *trembling with rage*

anger EG *She felt deep anger at what he had said.*

frenzy EG *Their behaviour drove her into a frenzy.*

fury EG *Her face was distorted with fury and pain.*

wrath EG *He incurred the wrath of the referee.*

❷ rage VERB
to be angry or speak angrily about something
EG *He was raging at their lack of response.*

be furious EG *He is furious at the way his wife has been treated.*

fume EG *I was still fuming over her remark.*

lose your temper EG *They had*
never seen me lose my temper before.

rave EG *She cried and raved for weeks.*

storm EG *"It's a disaster", he stormed.*

❸ rage VERB
to continue with great force
EG *The fire raged out of control.*

be at its height EG *when the storm was at its height*

rampage EG *a mob rampaging through the town*

storm EG *armies storming across the continent*

surge EG *The flood surged through the village.*

❶ raid VERB
to attack something by force
EG *Soldiers raided the capital.*

assault EG *Their stronghold was assaulted by pirates.*

attack EG *We are being attacked!*

break into EG *No-one saw them break into the warehouse.*

invade EG *The invading army took all their food supplies.*

plunder EG *plundering the homes of the inhabitants*

> **WORD POWER**
> Synonyms
> pillage
> rifle
> sack

❷ raid NOUN
an attack on something
EG *a bank raid*

attack EG *a surprise attack on the house*

break-in EG *The break-in occurred last night.*

foray EG *Guerillas made forays into the territory.*

> **WORD POWER**
> Synonyms
> incursion

sortie

❶ rain NOUN
water falling from the clouds
EG *A spot of rain fell on her hand.*
deluge EG *homes damaged in the deluge*
downpour EG *A two-day downpour swelled water levels.*
drizzle EG *The drizzle had stopped and the sun was shining.*
rainfall EG *four years of below average rainfall*
showers EG *bright spells followed by scattered showers*

❷ rain VERB
to fall from the sky in drops
EG *It rained the whole weekend.*
drizzle EG *It was starting to drizzle when I left.*
pour EG *We drove all the way in pouring rain.*
teem EG *It teemed the entire day.*

❶ raise VERB
to make something higher
EG *a drive to raise standards of literacy*
elevate EG *Emotional stress can elevate blood pressure.*
heave EG *He heaved his crippled leg into an easier position.*
hoist EG *He climbed on the roof to hoist the flag.*
lift EG *She lifted the last of her drink to her lips.*

> **WORD POWER**
> Antonym
> lower

❷ raise VERB
to look after children until they are grown up
EG *the house where she was raised*
bring up EG *She brought up four children single-handed.*
nurture EG *the best way to nurture a child to adulthood*
rear EG *He reared his sister's family as well as his own.*

❸ raise VERB
to mention or suggest something
EG *He had raised no objections at the time.*
advance EG *Some important ideas were advanced at the conference.*
bring up EG *I hesitate to bring up this matter with you, but I have no choice.*
broach EG *Eventually I broached the subject of her early life.*
introduce EG *always willing to introduce a new topic*
moot EG *The project was first mooted last year.*
suggest EG *one possibility that might be suggested*

❶ ramble NOUN
a long walk in the countryside
EG *They went for a ramble through the woods.*
excursion EG *They organized an excursion into the hills.*
hike EG *a long hike along the valley floor*
stroll EG *The next day we took a stroll along the river bank.*
walk EG *We often go for walks in the country.*

❷ ramble VERB
to go for a long walk
EG *freedom to ramble across the moors*
amble EG *ambling along a country lane*
stray EG *You mustn't stray across the border.*
stroll EG *whistling as he strolled along the road*
walk EG *We finished the evening by walking along the beach.*
wander EG *He loved to wander in the woods.*

> **WORD POWER**
> Synonyms
> perambulate
> rove

A B C D E F G H I J K L M N O P Q R S T U V W X Y Z

385

❸ ramble VERB
to talk in a confused way
EG *He started rambling and repeating himself.*
babble EG *She babbled on and on about the visitors.*
chatter EG *I was so nervous that I chattered away like an idiot.*

❶ rampage VERB
to rush about angrily or violently
EG *children rampaging round the garden*
go berserk EG *The crowd went berserk at the sight of him.*
rage EG *His shop was stormed by a raging mob.*
run amok EG *He was arrested after running amok with a gun.*
run riot EG *The prisoners ran riot after the announcement.*

❷ rampage
on the rampage ADJECTIVE
rushing about in a wild and violent way
EG *a bull on the rampage*
amok EG *The gunman ran amok and killed several people.*
berserk EG *The fans went berserk and mobbed the stage.*
wild EG *They just went wild after he left.*

❶ random ADJECTIVE
not based on a definite plan
EG *random violence against innocent victims*
aimless EG *after several hours of aimless searching*
arbitrary EG *Arbitrary arrests and detention without trial were common.*
haphazard EG *He had never seen such a haphazard approach to writing.*
indiscriminate EG *the indiscriminate use of fertilisers*
spot EG *picked up in a spot check*

> **WORD POWER**
> Synonyms
> desultory
> fortuitous
> unpremeditated

❷ random
at random ADVERB
without any definite plan
EG *chosen at random*
aimlessly EG *wandering around aimlessly for hours*
arbitrarily EG *The questions were chosen quite arbitrarily.*
haphazardly EG *The books were stacked haphazardly on the shelves.*
indiscriminately EG *This disease strikes indiscriminately.*
randomly EG *a randomly selected sample*

> **WORD POWER**
> Synonyms
> adventitiously
> unsystematically
> willy-nilly

❶ range NOUN
the maximum limits of something
EG *Tactical nuclear weapons have shorter ranges.*
bounds EG *the bounds of good taste*
extent EG *the full extent of my knowledge*
field EG *The subject covers a very wide field.*
limits EG *outside the city limits*
province EG *This doesn't fall within our province.*
scope EG *He promised to widen the scope of their activities.*

❷ range NOUN
a number of different things of the same kind
EG *a wide range of colours*
assortment EG *There was a good assortment to choose from.*
class EG *Cars in this class are expensive.*
gamut EG *I experienced the whole gamut of emotions.*
selection EG *a wide selection of*

delicious meals

series EG *a completely new model series*

variety EG *The shop stocks a variety of local craft products.*

❸ **range** VERB

to vary between two extremes
EG *goods ranging between the everyday and the exotic*

extend EG *The reclaimed land extends from here to the river.*

go EG *Their sizes go from very small to enormous.*

run EG *Accommodation runs from log cabins to high-standard hotels.*

stretch EG *with interests that stretched from chemicals to sugar*

vary EG *The cycle of sunspots varies between 8 to 15 years.*

❶ **rank** NOUN

someone's level in a group
EG *He rose to the rank of captain.*

class EG *relationships between social classes*

echelon EG *the upper echelons of society*

grade EG *Staff turnover is high among the junior grades.*

level EG *various levels of the judiciary system*

standing EG *a woman of wealth and social standing*

station EG *a humble station in life*

status EG *promoted to the status of foreman*

❷ **rank** NOUN

a row of people or things
EG *ranks of police in riot gear*

column EG *a column of figures*

file EG *They walked in single file to the top.*

line EG *He waited in a line of slow-moving vehicles.*

row EG *She lived in the middle of a row of pretty cottages.*

❸ **rank** ADJECTIVE

complete and absolute
EG *It was rank stupidity to go there alone.*

absolute EG *not intended for absolute beginners*

complete EG *her complete ignorance*

downright EG *That was just downright rudeness.*

sheer EG *his sheer stupidity*

unmitigated EG *an unmitigated villain*

utter EG *his utter disregard for other people*

WORD POWER
Synonyms
arrant
egregious

---

rare ADJECTIVE

not common or frequent
EG *a rare species of bird*

exceptional EG *in exceptional circumstances*

few EG *Genuine friends are few.*

scarce EG *Jobs are becoming increasingly scarce.*

sparse EG *Information about the tests is sparse.*

sporadic EG *occurring at only sporadic intervals*

uncommon EG *The disease is uncommon in younger women.*

unusual EG *an unusual variety but a very attractive one*

WORD POWER
Antonym
common

---

❶ **rash** ADJECTIVE

acting in a hasty and foolish way
EG *It would be rash to act on such flimsy evidence.*

foolhardy EG *Some described his behaviour as foolhardy.*

hasty EG *This is no hasty decision.*

impetuous EG *As usual, he reacted in a heated and impetuous way.*

impulsive EG *He is too impulsive to take this responsibility.*

reckless EG *his reckless driving*

A B C D E F G H I J K L M N O P Q R S T U V W X Y Z

WORD POWER
Synonyms
heedless
injudicious
unthinking

❷ rash NOUN
an irritated area on your skin
EG *I noticed a rash on my leg.*
eruption EG *an unpleasant skin eruption*
outbreak EG *an outbreak of blisters around his mouth*

❸ rash NOUN
a large number of events happening together
EG *a rash of strikes*
epidemic EG *A victim of the recent epidemic of shootings.*
flood EG *a flood of complaints about the programme*
plague EG *Last year there was a plague of burglaries.*
spate EG *a spate of attacks on horses*
wave EG *the current wave of violent attacks*

❶ rate NOUN
the speed or frequency of something
EG *appearing at the rate of one a week*
frequency EG *She phoned with increasing frequency.*
pace EG *at an accelerated pace*
speed EG *moving at the speed of light*
tempo EG *They wanted to speed up the tempo of change.*
velocity EG *changes in wind velocity*

❷ rate NOUN
the cost or charge for something
EG *phone calls at cheap rates*
charge EG *An annual charge will be made for this service.*
cost EG *a low-cost mortgage*
fee EG *The work will be invoiced at the usual fee.*

price EG *falling share prices*
tariff EG *How much you pay depends on your tariff.*

❸ rate VERB
to give an opinion of someone's qualities
EG *He was rated as one of the best.*
appraise EG *She gave me an appraising glance.*
class EG *classed as one of the top ten athletes*
consider EG *I considered myself to be quite good at maths.*
count EG *That would be counted as wrong.*
rank EG *The hotel was ranked as one of the world's best.*
regard EG *a highly regarded member of staff*

WORD POWER
Synonyms
adjudge
esteem
evaluate

rather ADVERB
to a certain extent
EG *We got along rather well.*
fairly EG *Both ships are fairly new.*
pretty INFORMAL EG *I'm pretty tired now.*
quite EG *The cottage looks quite ordinary from the road.*
relatively EG *I think I'm relatively easy to get on with.*
slightly EG *slightly startled by his sudden appearance*
somewhat EG *He said, somewhat unconvincingly, that he would pay.*

rational ADJECTIVE
using reason rather than emotion
EG *to arrive at a rational conclusion*
enlightened EG *enlightened companies who take a pragmatic view*
logical EG *There must be a logical explanation for it.*
reasonable EG *a perfectly*

reasonable decision
sensible EG *The sensible thing is to leave them alone.*

❶ rave VERB
to talk in an uncontrolled way
EG *He started raving about being treated badly.*
babble EG *She babbled on and on about her plans.*
rage EG *He was raging at their lack of response.*
rant EG *She started ranting about her boss's attitude.*

❷ rave VERB; INFORMAL
to be enthusiastic about something
EG *She raved about the facilities there.*
be wild about INFORMAL EG *He was just wild about the play.*
enthuse EG *She enthused about the local architecture.*
gush EG *"It was brilliant", he gushed.*

❶ reach VERB
to arrive somewhere
EG *He did not stop until he reached the door.*
arrive at EG *to arrive at an erroneous conclusion*
attain EG *She worked hard to attain a state of calm.*
get as far as EG *If we get as far as the coast we will be quite satisfied.*
get to EG *You must get to the end before noon.*
make EG *They didn't think they would make the summit.*

❷ reach VERB
to extend as far as something
EG *Her cloak reached to the ground.*
extend to EG *The boundaries extend to the edge of the lake.*
go as far as EG *Try to make the ball go as far as the trees.*
touch EG *I could touch both walls with my arms extended.*

❸ reach VERB

to arrive at a certain stage or level
EG *Unemployment has reached record levels.*
arrive at EG *They planted a flag when they arrived at the top.*
attain EG *He was close to attaining his personal best.*
climb to EG *Attendance climbed to a record level this year.*
fall to EG *Profits are expected to fall to their lowest level.*
rise to EG *She rose rapidly to the top of her profession.*

❶ reaction NOUN
a person's response to something
EG *Reaction to the visit was mixed.*
acknowledgment EG *She made no acknowledgment of my question.*
answer EG *In answer to speculation in the press, she declared her interest.*
feedback EG *Continue to ask for feedback on your work.*
response EG *in response to a request from the members*

❷ reaction NOUN
a response to something unpopular
EG *a reaction against religious leaders*
backlash EG *the male backlash against feminism*
counterbalance EG *an organization set up as a counterbalance to the official group*

❶ read VERB
to look at something written
EG *I love to read in bed.*
glance at EG *He just glanced briefly at the article.*
look at EG *She was looking at the evening paper.*
pore over EG *poring over a dictionary*
scan EG *There's only time to scan through it quickly.*
study EG *I'll study the text more*

A B C D E F G H I J K L M N O P Q **R** S T U V W X Y Z

closely later.

❷ read VERB
to understand what someone means
EG *as if he could read her thoughts*
comprehend EG *Her expression was difficult to comprehend.*
decipher EG *She was still no closer to deciphering the code.*
interpret EG *You have to interpret their gestures, too.*

❶ ready ADJECTIVE
prepared for action or use
EG *The plums are ready to eat now.*
organized EG *Everything is organized for the party tomorrow.*
prepared EG *He was prepared for a tough fight.*
primed EG *The other side is primed for battle.*
ripe EG *Are those strawberries ripe yet?*
set EG *We'll be set to go in five minutes.*

❷ ready ADJECTIVE
willing to do something
EG *She was always ready to give interviews.*
agreeable EG *We can go ahead if you are agreeable.*
eager EG *Children are eager to learn.*
happy EG *always happy to help*
keen EG *He wasn't keen to get involved.*
willing EG *questions which they were not willing to answer*

> **WORD POWER**
> Synonyms
> minded
> predisposed

❸ ready ADJECTIVE
easily produced or obtained
EG *ready cash*
accessible EG *The system should be accessible to everyone.*
available EG *Food is available round the clock.*

convenient EG *a convenient excuse*
handy EG *Keep a pencil and paper handy.*

❶ real ADJECTIVE
actually existing and not imagined
EG *You're dealing with real life now.*
actual EG *She was the actual basis for the leading character.*
authentic EG *containing authentic details of what happened*
factual EG *a factual account*
genuine EG *His worries about the future were genuine ones.*
legitimate EG *These are legitimate concerns.*
true EG *the true story of his life*

> **WORD POWER**
> Antonym
> imaginary

❷ real ADJECTIVE
genuine and not imitation
EG *Is that a real gun?*
authentic EG *an authentic French recipe*
bona fide EG *We are happy to donate to bona fide charities.*
genuine EG *It's a genuine Rembrandt, all right.*
honest EG *It was an honest attempt to set things right.*
rightful EG *the rightful heir to the throne*

> **WORD POWER**
> Antonym
> fake

❶ realistic ADJECTIVE
accepting the true situation
EG *It's only realistic to admit that things will go wrong.*
down-to-earth EG *We welcomed her down-to-earth approach.*
level-headed EG *a sensible, level-headed approach*
matter-of-fact EG *He sounded matter-of-fact and unemotional.*
practical EG *a highly practical attitude to life*

sensible EG *I'm trying to persuade you to be more sensible.*

sober EG *a more sober assessment of the situation*

❷ **realistic** ADJECTIVE
true to real life
EG *His novels are more realistic than his short stories.*

authentic EG *They have to look authentic.*

faithful EG *faithful copies of old household items*

lifelike EG *almost as lifelike as a photograph*

true EG *It gave a true picture of how things were.*

> **WORD POWER**
> Synonyms
> naturalistic
> representational
> vérité

reality NOUN
something that is true and not imagined
EG *Fiction and reality were increasingly blurred.*

authenticity EG *The film's authenticity impressed the critics.*

fact EG *No-one knew how much of what he said was fact.*

realism EG *His stories had an edge of realism.*

truth EG *I must tell you the truth about this situation.*

realize VERB
to become aware of something
EG *People don't realize how serious it is.*

appreciate EG *He appreciates the difficulties we face.*

comprehend EG *They do not comprehend the nature of the problem.*

grasp EG *She still couldn't grasp what had really happened.*

recognize EG *Of course I recognize that evil exists.*

understand EG *I didn't*

understand what he meant until later.

❶ **reason** NOUN
the cause of something that happens
EG *for a multitude of reasons*

cause EG *The true cause of the accident may never be known.*

grounds EG *some grounds for optimism*

incentive EG *There is no incentive to adopt these measures.*

motive EG *Police have ruled out robbery as a motive.*

purpose EG *the purpose of their visit*

❷ **reason** NOUN
the ability to think
EG *a conflict between emotion and reason*

intellect EG *good health and a lively intellect*

judgment EG *His judgment was impaired.*

rationality EG *We live in an era of rationality.*

reasoning EG *a lack of sound reasoning and logic*

sense EG *He should have had more sense.*

❸ **reason** VERB
to try to persuade someone of something
EG *It's better to reason with them than to use force.*

bring round INFORMAL EG *We'll try to bring you round to our point of view.*

persuade EG *I had to persuade him of the advantages.*

win over EG *They still hoped to win him over to their way of thinking.*

reassure VERB
to make someone feel less worried
EG *She reassured me that everything was fine.*

bolster EG *measures intended to*

bolster morale

cheer up EG *I wrote it just to cheer myself up.*

comfort EG *He tried to comfort her as far as he could.*

encourage EG *Investors were encouraged by the news.*

> **WORD POWER**
> Synonyms
> buoy up
> hearten
> inspirit

rebel VERB
to fight against authority and accepted values
EG *I rebelled against everything when I was young.*

defy EG *It was the first time she had defied her mother.*

mutiny EG *Sailors mutinied against their officers.*

resist EG *activists convicted of resisting apartheid*

revolt EG *The islanders revolted against the prince.*

rebellion NOUN
an organized opposition to authority
EG *the ruthless suppression of the rebellion*

insurrection EG *They were plotting to stage an armed insurrection.*

mutiny EG *convicted of mutiny and high treason*

revolt EG *The revolt ended in failure.*

revolution EG *after the French Revolution*

uprising EG *Isolated attacks turned into a full-scale uprising.*

❶ receive VERB
to accept something from someone
EG *Did they receive my letter?*

accept EG *They accepted the parcel gratefully.*

be given EG *We were all given presents.*

get EG *She got some lovely things.*

pick up EG *He picked up an award for his performance.*

take EG *Will you take this parcel for your neighbour?*

❷ receive VERB
to experience something
EG *We received a very warm welcome.*

encounter EG *He encountered some unexpected opposition.*

suffer EG *He suffered some bangs and bumps.*

sustain EG *She had sustained a cut on her arm.*

undergo EG *You may have to undergo a bit of teasing.*

❸ receive VERB
to welcome visitors
EG *You must be there to receive your guests.*

entertain EG *She loved to entertain friends at home.*

greet EG *They greeted the visitors at the door.*

meet EG *I'll come down to meet you.*

take in EG *The country took in many refugees.*

welcome EG *Several people came by to welcome me.*

recent ADJECTIVE
happening a short time ago
EG *his most recent acquisition*

current EG *a sound knowledge of current affairs*

fresh EG *fresh footprints in the snow*

new EG *the subject of a new film*

present-day EG *Even by present-day standards these were large aircraft.*

up-to-date EG *the most up-to-date computers*

> **WORD POWER**
> Synonyms
> contemporary
> latter-day

recession NOUN
a decline in economic
conditions
EG *companies which survived after
the recession*
decline EG *signs of economic
decline*
depression EG *the Great
Depression of the 1930s*
downturn EG *due to a sharp
downturn in the industry*
slump EG *Many jobs were lost
during the slump.*

❶ recognize VERB
to know who or what someone
or something is
EG *I recognized him at once.*
identify EG *She tried to identify the
perfume.*
know EG *You'd know him if you
saw him again.*
place EG *He couldn't place my
voice immediately.*
spot EG *I spotted the house quite
easily.*

❷ recognize VERB
to accept or acknowledge
something
EG *He was recognized as an
outstanding pilot.*
acknowledge EG *Her great
bravery was acknowledged.*
appreciate EG *In time you'll
appreciate his good points.*
honour EG *achievements honoured
with the Nobel Prize*
salute EG *We salute your great
courage.*

❶ reconstruct VERB
to rebuild something that has
been damaged
EG *The city centre has been
completely reconstructed.*
rebuild EG *The task of rebuilding
would be very expensive.*
recreate EG *They try to recreate the
atmosphere of former times.*
regenerate EG *the ability to
regenerate damaged tissues*

renovate EG *The hotel was being
renovated.*
restore EG *experts who specialize
in restoring old furniture*

> **WORD POWER**
> Synonyms
> reassemble
> remodel

❷ reconstruct VERB
to build up from small details
EG *The police reconstructed the
scene of the crime.*
build up EG *They built up an
image of him from several different
descriptions.*
deduce EG *The date can be
deduced from other documents.*
piece together EG *It was easy to
piece together the shattered
fragments.*

❶ record NOUN
a stored account of something
EG *medical records*
account EG *The company keeps
detailed accounts.*
archives EG *Earlier issues are
stored in the archives.*
file EG *the right to inspect company
files*
journal EG *He kept a journal while
he was travelling.*
minute EG *Did you read the
minutes of the last meeting?*
register EG *a register of births,
deaths and marriages*

❷ record NOUN
what someone has done in the
past
EG *You will be rejected if you have a
criminal record.*
background EG *His background
was in engineering.*
career EG *His career spoke for itself.*
curriculum vitae EG *I must
update my curriculum vitae.*
track record INFORMAL EG *Her
track record as a teacher was
impeccable.*

A
B
C
D
E
F
G
H
I
J
K
L
M
N
O
P
Q
R
S
T
U
V
W
X
Y
Z

A
B
C
D
E
F
G
H
I
J
K
L
M
N
O
P
Q
R
S
T
U
V
W
X
Y
Z

❸ record VERB
to note and store information
EG *Her diary records her daily life in detail.*

document EG *All these facts have been well documented.*

enter EG *All the names are entered in this book.*

log EG *They log everyone who comes in or out.*

note EG *I must note your birthday.*

register EG *We registered his birth straight away.*

write down EG *If I don't write it down, I'll forget it.*

❶ recover VERB
to get better again
EG *He has still not fully recovered.*

convalesce EG *those convalescing from illness or surgery*

get better EG *He never really got better again.*

get well EG *Get well soon!*

improve EG *The condition of your hair will soon improve.*

recuperate EG *recuperating from a serious injury*

revive EG *Business soon revived once he came back.*

❷ recover VERB
to get something back again
EG *They took legal action to recover the money.*

get back EG *We got everything back after the burglary.*

recapture EG *trying to recapture the atmosphere of our holiday*

recoup EG *trying to recoup their losses*

regain EG *It took him a while to regain his composure.*

retrieve EG *I retrieved my bag from the back seat.*

❶ recovery NOUN
the act of getting better again
EG *He made a remarkable recovery after his illness.*

healing EG *Adams claims that humour is an integral part of healing.*

improvement EG *Germany is showing a perceptible improvement.*

recuperation EG *great powers of recuperation*

revival EG *little chance of a revival of interest*

WORD POWER
Synonyms
convalescence
rally
---

❷ recovery NOUN
the act of getting something back
EG *a reward for the recovery of the painting*

recapture EG *An offensive was launched for the recapture of the airbase.*

reclamation EG *the reclamation of dry land from the marshes*

restoration EG *She owed the restoration of her sight to this remarkable technique.*

retrieval EG *electronic storage and retrieval systems*

❶ recruit VERB
to persuade people to join a group
EG *He helped to recruit volunteers.*

draft EG *drafted into the armed forces*

enlist EG *I had to enlist the help of six people to move it.*

enrol EG *She enrolled me on her evening course.*

muster EG *trying to muster support for the movement*

❷ recruit NOUN
someone who has recently joined a group
EG *the latest batch of recruits*

beginner EG *The course is suitable for beginners.*

convert EG *a recent convert to their religion*

novice EG *I'm a novice at these things.*

trainee EG *My first job was as a graduate trainee with a bank.*

WORD POWER
Synonyms
neophyte
proselyte
tyro

---

red NOUN OR ADJECTIVE

Shades of red:
burgundy
cardinal
carmine
cerise
cherry
claret
crimson
cyclamen
flame
fuchsia
magenta
maroon
poppy
raspberry
ruby
scarlet
strawberry
vermilion

❶ reduce VERB
to make something smaller in size or amount
EG *Gradually reduce the dosage.*
curtail EG *His powers will be severely curtailed.*
cut EG *The first priority is to cut costs.*
cut down EG *Try to cut down your coffee consumption.*
decrease EG *The government plans to decrease interest rates.*
diminish EG *to diminish the prestige of the monarchy*
lessen EG *a diet that would lessen the risk of disease*
lower EG *a commitment to lower taxes*
shorten EG *taking steps to shorten queues*

WORD POWER

Antonym
increase

---

❷ reduce VERB
to bring to a weaker or inferior state
EG *The village was reduced to rubble.*
degrade EG *I wouldn't degrade myself by going out with him.*
demote EG *The Soviet team have been demoted to second place.*
downgrade EG *The female role has been downgraded in the drive for equality.*
drive EG *an old woman driven to shoplifting to survive*
force EG *The men were so hungry they were forced to eat grass.*

❶ refer VERB
to mention something
EG *In his speech, he referred to a recent trip to Canada.*
allude EG *She alluded to his absence in vague terms.*
bring up EG *Why are you bringing that up now?*
cite EG *She cites a favourite poem by George Herbert.*
mention EG *She did not mention her mother's illness.*

❷ refer VERB
to look at to find something out
EG *I had to refer to the manual.*
consult EG *He had to consult a dictionary.*
look up EG *I looked up your file to get your address.*

❶ refined ADJECTIVE
polite and well-mannered
EG *His speech and manner are very refined.*
civilized EG *the demands of civilized behaviour*
genteel EG *two ladies with genteel manners and voices*
gentlemanly EG *Sopwith behaved in his usual gentlemanly manner.*
ladylike EG *They are models of ladylike decorum.*

A
B
C
D
E
F
G
H
I
J
K
L
M
N
O
P
Q
R
S
T
U
V
W
X
Y
Z

A
B
C
D
E
F
G
H
I
J
K
L
M
N
O
P
Q

R

S
T
U
V
W
X
Y
Z

polite EG *polite and correct behaviour*

> **WORD POWER**
> Antonym
> common

❷ refined ADJECTIVE
processed to remove impurities
EG *refined sugar*
distilled EG *distilled water*
filtered EG *two pints of spring or filtered water*
processed EG *a diet high in processed foods*
pure EG *crisp pure air*
purified EG *freshly purified drinking water*

❶ reform NOUN
a major change or improvement
EG *radical economic reforms*
amendment EG *an amendment to remove the ban on divorce*
correction EG *a correction of social injustice*
improvement EG *She is pressing for improvements to education.*
rehabilitation EG *the rehabilitation of young offenders*

> **WORD POWER**
> Synonyms
> amelioration
> betterment
> rectification

❷ reform VERB
to make major changes or improvements to something
EG *his plans to reform the economy*
amend EG *They want to amend the current system.*
better EG *industrial action to better their working conditions*
correct EG *keen to correct injustices*
rectify EG *measures suggested to rectify the financial situation*
rehabilitate EG *a loan for Bulgaria to rehabilitate its railway system*

> **WORD POWER**

> Synonyms
> ameliorate
> emend
> revolutionize

refresh VERB
to make you feel more energetic
EG *A glass of fruit juice will refresh you.*
brace EG *a bracing walk*
enliven EG *Music can enliven the spirit.*
rejuvenate EG *He was told that the Italian climate would rejuvenate him.*
revive EG *The cold water revived me a bit.*
stimulate EG *a toner to stimulate the skin*

> **WORD POWER**
> Synonyms
> freshen
> invigorate
> revitalize
> revivify

refuge NOUN
a place where you go for safety
EG *a mountain refuge*
asylum EG *political asylum*
harbour EG *Patches of gorse were a great harbour for foxes.*
haven EG *The island is a haven for international criminals.*
sanctuary EG *a sanctuary from the outside world*
shelter EG *an underground shelter*

❶ refuse VERB
to say you will not do something
EG *He refused to speculate about the contents of the letter.*
abstain EG *people who abstain from eating meat*
decline EG *He declined to comment on the story.*
withhold EG *Financial aid for Britain has been withheld.*

❷ refuse VERB
to say you will not allow or accept something

EG *He offered me a drink, which I refused.*
decline EG *He declined their invitation.*
reject EG *The court rejected their petition.*
spurn EG *You spurned his last offer.*
turn down EG *He has turned down the job.*

> **WORD POWER**
> Antonym
> accept

❸ **refuse** NOUN
rubbish or waste
EG *a weekly collection of refuse*
garbage EG *rotting piles of garbage*
junk INFORMAL EG *What are you going to do with all that junk?*
litter EG *If you see litter in the corridor, pick it up.*
rubbish EG *They had piled most of their rubbish into yellow skips.*
trash EG *I forgot to take out the trash.*
waste EG *a law that regulates the disposal of waste*

region NOUN
a large area of land
EG *a remote mountainous region of Afghanistan*
area EG *The area is renowned for its cuisine.*
district EG *I drove around the business district.*
land EG *a land permanently cloaked in mist*
locality EG *All other factories in the locality went on strike.*
quarter EG *We wandered through the Chinese quarter.*
sector EG *the northeast sector of Bosnia*
territory EG *the disputed territory of Kashmir*
tract EG *They cleared large tracts of forest.*
zone EG *a different time zone*

❶ **regret** VERB

to be sorry something has happened
EG *I gave in to him, and I have regretted it ever since.*
be sorry EG *I'm sorry you feel that way about it.*
grieve EG *grieving over the death of his wife*
lament EG *We lament the loss of a fine novelist.*
mourn EG *to mourn the loss of a loved one*
repent EG *He repents his past sins.*

> **WORD POWER**
> Synonyms
> bemoan
> bewail
> rue

❷ **regret** NOUN
the feeling of being sorry about something
EG *He expressed regret that he had caused any offence.*
grief EG *his guilt and grief over the failed relationship*
pang of conscience EG *He need not feel any pangs of conscience over his decision.*
penitence EG *an abject display of penitence*
remorse EG *He expressed remorse over his own foolishness.*
repentance EG *an apparent lack of genuine repentance*
sorrow EG *I feel real sorrow that my dad did this.*

> **WORD POWER**
> Synonyms
> compunction
> contrition
> ruefulness
> self-reproach

❶ **regular** ADJECTIVE
even or equally spaced
EG *soft music with a regular beat*
consistent EG *a consistent heart-rate*
constant EG *a constant temperature*

A
B
C
D
E
F
G
H
I
J
K
L
M
N
O
P
Q
R
S
T
U
V
W
X
Y
Z

397

A
B
C
D
E
F
G
H
I
J
K
L
M
N
O
P
Q
R
S
T
U
V
W
X
Y
Z

even EG *an even level of sound*
periodic EG *Periodic checks are carried out.*
rhythmic EG *the rhythmic beating of the drum*
steady EG *a steady pace*
uniform EG *The Earth rotates on its axis at a uniform rate.*

> *WORD POWER*
> Antonym
> irregular

❷ **regular** ADJECTIVE
usual or normal
EG *I was filling in for the regular bartender.*

customary EG *her customary place at the table*
everyday EG *part of everyday life*
habitual EG *habitual practices*
normal EG *a normal day*
ordinary EG *It was just an ordinary weekend.*
routine EG *a routine knee operation*
typical EG *My typical day begins at 8.30.*
usual EG *In a usual week I watch about 15 hours of television.*

reject VERB
to refuse to accept or agree to something
EG *We reject any suggestion that the law needs amending.*

decline EG *They declined his proposal.*
deny EG *He denied our offer of assistance.*
rebuff EG *She rebuffed his advances.*
refuse EG *He offered me a drink, which I refused.*
renounce EG *She renounced her parents' religion.*
say no to EG *Just say no to drugs.*
spurn EG *He spurned the advice of management consultants.*
turn down EG *She turned down his offer of marriage.*

> *WORD POWER*

> Synonyms
> disallow
> repudiate
> Antonym
> accept

rejoice VERB
to be very happy about something
EG *Today we can rejoice in our success.*

be overjoyed EG *I was overjoyed to see him.*
celebrate EG *We should celebrate our victory.*
delight EG *He delighted in her success.*
glory EG *glorying in the achievement of his troops*

> *WORD POWER*
> Synonyms
> exult
> revel

❶ **relation** NOUN
a connection between two things
EG *This theory bears no relation to reality.*

bearing EG *Diet has an important bearing on your general health.*
bond EG *the bond between a mother and child*
connection EG *a possible connection between BSE and human disease*
correlation EG *the correlation between unemployment and crime*
link EG *a link between obesity and heart problems*
relationship EG *the relationship between success and effort*

❷ **relation** NOUN
a member of your family
EG *I was staying with relations in Atlanta.*

kin EG *She has gone to live with her husband's kin.*
kinsman or **kinswoman** EG *the prince who murdered his father and*

kinsmen
relative EG *Get a relative to look after the children.*

❶ relationship NOUN
the way people act towards each other
EG *He has a friendly relationship with his customers.*
affinity EG *the natural affinity between the female members of the community*
association EG *the association between the two countries*
bond EG *The experience created a bond between us.*
connection EG *He felt a personal connection with her.*
rapport EG *He has a terrific rapport with kids.*

❷ relationship NOUN
a close friendship, especially a sexual one
EG *I found myself in a relationship I couldn't handle.*
affair EG *an affair with a married man*
liaison EG *Nobody knew of their brief liaison.*

❸ relationship NOUN
the connection between two things
EG *the relationship between humans and their environment*
connection EG *the connection between age and ill-health*
correlation EG *the correlation between unemployment and crime*
link EG *the link between smoking and lung cancer*
parallel EG *the parallel between painting and music*

relax VERB
to be calm and become less worried
EG *I never have any time to relax.*
laze EG *I'm just going to laze around and do nothing.*
rest EG *Try to rest as much as you can.*

take it easy EG *the chance to just take it easy for a week or two*
unwind EG *It helps them to unwind after a busy day at work.*

❶ release VERB
to set someone or something free
EG *negotiations to release the hostages*
deliver EG *I thank God for delivering me from that pain.*
discharge EG *He may be discharged from hospital today.*
extricate EG *They managed to extricate the survivors from the wreckage.*
free EG *Israeli is set to free more Lebanese prisoners.*
let go EG *They held him for three hours and then let him go.*
liberate EG *liberated under the terms of the amnesty*
set free EG *birds set free into the wild*

WORD POWER
Synonyms
emancipate
manumit

❷ release VERB
to make something available
EG *The new album is released next week.*
issue EG *He has issued a press statement.*
launch EG *The company has just launched a new range of products.*
publish EG *His latest book will be published in May.*
put out EG *putting out a series of novels by Nobel prize winners*

❸ release NOUN
the setting free of someone or something
EG *his release from prison*
discharge EG *a discharge from the army*
emancipation EG *the emancipation of slaves in the 19th*

A B C D E F G H I J K L M N O P Q R S T U V W X Y Z

A
B
C
D
E
F
G
H
I
J
K
L
M
N
O
P
Q

R

S
T
U
V
W
X
Y
Z

century
freedom EG *Hinckley campaigned for his freedom.*
liberation EG *their liberation from a Nazi concentration camp*
liberty EG *her television appearances pleading for his liberty*

> **WORD POWER**
> Synonyms
> deliverance
> manumission

relentless ADJECTIVE
never stopping or becoming less intense
EG *The pressure was relentless.*
incessant EG *incessant rain*
nonstop EG *nonstop background music*
persistent EG *in the face of persistent criticism*
sustained EG *a sustained attack*
unrelenting EG *unrelenting protests*
unremitting EG *the unremitting demands of duty*

relevant ADJECTIVE
connected with what is being discussed
EG *We have passed on all relevant information.*
applicable EG *These fees are not applicable to mortgages in Scotland.*
apposite EG *He could not think of anything apposite to say.*
appropriate EG *The name seemed very appropriate.*
apt EG *an apt comment*
pertinent EG *She had asked some pertinent questions.*

> **WORD POWER**
> Synonyms
> appurtenant
> germane
> material
> Antonym
> irrelevant

reliable ADJECTIVE
able to be trusted

EG *You have to demonstrate that you are reliable.*
dependable EG *dependable information*
faithful EG *a faithful friend*
safe EG *It's all right, you're in safe hands.*
sound EG *sound advice*
staunch EG *a staunch supporter*
sure EG *a sure sign of rain*
true EG *a true account*
trustworthy EG *a trustworthy and level-headed leader*

> **WORD POWER**
> Antonym
> unreliable

religion NOUN

> Religions:
> animism
> Baha'ism
> Buddhism
> Christianity
> Confucianism
> Hinduism
> Islam
> Jainism
> Judaism
> Rastafarianism
> shamanism
> Shinto
> Sikhism
> Taoism
> Zen
> Zoroastrianism or Zoroastrism

❶ **religious** ADJECTIVE
connected with religion
EG *religious worship*
devotional EG *an altar covered with devotional pictures*
divine EG *a request for divine guidance*
doctrinal EG *their doctrinal differences*
holy EG *To Tibetans, this is a holy place.*
sacred EG *Bach's sacred music*
scriptural EG *scriptural and theological references*

spiritual EG *We've got no spiritual values.*

theological EG *theological studies*

❷ religious ADJECTIVE
having a strong belief in a god or gods
EG *They are both very religious.*

devout EG *She is a devout Catholic.*

God-fearing EG *They brought up their children to be God-fearing Christians.*

godly EG *a learned and godly preacher*

pious EG *He was brought up by pious female relatives.*

righteous EG *struggling to be righteous and chaste*

❶ remain VERB
to stay somewhere
EG *You'll have to remain in hospital for the time being.*

be left EG *He was left in the car.*

linger EG *I lingered for a few days until he arrived.*

stay behind EG *I was told to stay behind after the class.*

wait EG *Wait here until I come back.*

❷ remain VERB
to stay the same
EG *The men remained silent.*

continue EG *This state of affairs cannot continue.*

endure EG *Somehow their friendship endures.*

go on EG *The debate goes on.*

last EG *Nothing lasts forever.*

stay EG *They could stay afloat without swimming.*

survive EG *companies which survived after the recession*

remains PLURAL NOUN
the parts of something left over
EG *the remains of an ancient mosque*

debris EG *screws, bolts and other debris from a scrapyard*

dregs EG *Colum drained the dregs from his cup.*

leftovers EG *Refrigerate any leftovers.*

relics EG *a museum of war relics*

remnants EG *Beneath the present church were remnants of Roman flooring.*

residue EG *Discard the milky residue left behind.*

scraps EG *the scraps from the dinner table*

vestiges EG *an attempt to destroy the last vestiges of evidence*

> **WORD POWER**
> Synonyms
> detritus
> leavings

❶ remark VERB
to mention or comment on something
EG *She had remarked on the boy's improvement.*

comment EG *So far, he has not commented on these reports.*

mention EG *I mentioned that I didn't like jazz.*

observe EG *"You're very pale," he observed.*

say EG *"Well done," he said.*

state EG *We stated that he had resigned.*

❷ remark NOUN
something you say
EG *a vulgar remark*

comment EG *his abrasive wit and caustic comments*

observation EG *a few general observations*

statement EG *That statement puzzled me.*

utterance EG *admirers who hung on her every utterance*

word EG *No-one had an unkind word to say about him.*

remember VERB
to bring to mind something from the past
EG *I do not remember the exact words.*

A B C D E F G H I J K L M N O P Q **R** S T U V W X Y Z

A
B
C
D
E
F
G
H
I
J
K
L
M
N
O
P
Q
R
S
T
U
V
W
X
Y
Z

call to mind EG *He invited the congregation to call to mind their sins.*

recall EG *He tried to recall the layout of the farmhouse.*

recognize EG *I don't recognize that name.*

retain EG *information which can be retained in the memory*

> **WORD POWER**
> Synonyms
> recollect
> reminisce
> Antonym
> forget

remind VERB
to make someone remember something
EG *He reminds me of myself at that age.*

bring back to EG *Talking about the accident brought it all back to me.*

jog someone's memory EG *See if this picture helps jog your memory.*

make someone remember EG *Your article made me remember my own traumas.*

put in mind EG *His eagerness to please put her in mind of a puppy.*

refresh someone's memory EG *I read through the list to refresh my memory.*

remove VERB
to take something off or away
EG *I removed the splinter from her finger.*

delete EG *He deleted files from the computer system.*

detach EG *Detach and keep the bottom part of the form.*

eject EG *He was ejected from the restaurant.*

eliminate EG *Eliminate dairy products from your diet.*

erase EG *She had erased the message.*

extract EG *She is having a tooth extracted today.*

get rid of EG *to get rid of raw sewage by pumping it out to sea*

take away EG *She took away the tray.*

take off EG *I won't take my coat off, I'm not staying.*

take out EG *Take that dog out of here.*

withdraw EG *She withdrew her hand from Roger's.*

> **WORD POWER**
> Synonyms
> efface
> excise
> expunge

renew VERB
to begin something again
EG *Syria renewed diplomatic relations with Egypt.*

begin again EG *The audience began the slow handclap again.*

recommence EG *He recommenced work on his novel.*

re-establish EG *He had re-established his close friendship with Anthony.*

reopen EG *It is feared that this issue could re-open the controversy.*

resume EG *Rebels have refused to resume peace talks.*

❶ **repair** NOUN
something you do to mend something that is damaged
EG *The landlord carried out the repairs himself.*

darn EG *a sock with a big darn in it*

mend EG *Spray the area with paint to make the mend invisible.*

patch EG *jackets with patches on the elbows*

restoration EG *the restoration of a war-damaged building*

❷ **repair** VERB
to mend something that is damaged
EG *The money will be used to repair faulty equipment.*

fix EG *If something is broken, get it*

fixed.

mend EG *They mended it without charge.*

patch EG *They patched the barn roof.*

patch up EG *Patch up those holes.*

renovate EG *They spent thousands renovating the house.*

restore EG *experts who specialize in restoring ancient parchments*

repay VERB

to give back money which is owed

EG *It will take me years to repay the loan.*

pay back EG *I'll pay you back that money tomorrow.*

refund EG *Any extra that you have paid will be refunded to you.*

settle up EG *If we owe you anything we can settle up when you come.*

> ### WORD POWER
> Synonyms
> make restitution
> recompense
> reimburse
> remunerate
> square

repeat VERB

to say or write something again
EG *Since you didn't listen, I'll repeat that.*

echo EG *"Are you frightened?" "Frightened?" she echoed. "Of what?"*

reiterate EG *The lawyer could only reiterate what he had said before.*

say again EG *"I'm sorry," she said again.*

> ### WORD POWER
> Synonyms
> iterate
> recapitulate
> restate

❶ repel VERB

to horrify and disgust
EG *The thought of spiders repels me.*

disgust EG *He disgusted everyone with his boorish behaviour.*

offend EG *viewers who are easily offended*

revolt EG *The smell revolted him.*

sicken EG *What he saw there sickened him.*

> ### WORD POWER
> Antonym
> attract

❷ repel VERB

to fight and drive back enemy forces

EG *troops along the border ready to repel an enemy attack*

drive off EG *They drove the guerrillas off with infantry and air strikes.*

repulse EG *Cavalry and artillery were sent to repulse the enemy forces.*

resist EG *The tribe resisted the Spanish invaders.*

replace VERB

to take the place of something else

EG *the man who replaced him as England skipper*

succeed EG *He was succeeded by his son.*

supersede EG *Horses were superseded by cars.*

supplant EG *Anger supplanted all other feelings.*

take over from EG *the man taking over from Mr Berry as chairman*

take the place of EG *Debit cards are taking the place of cash and cheques.*

replacement NOUN

a person or thing that takes the place of another

EG *He has nominated Adams as his replacement.*

proxy EG *They must nominate a proxy to vote on their behalf.*

stand-in EG *He was a stand-in for my regular doctor.*

A
B
C
D
E
F
G
H
I
J
K
L
M
N
O
P
Q
R
S
T
U
V
W
X
Y
Z

substitute EG *an artificial substitute for silk*
successor EG *He recommended him as his successor.*
surrogate EG *They had expected me to be a surrogate for my sister.*

❶ reply VERB
to give someone an answer
EG *He did not even have the courtesy to reply to my fax.*
answer EG *He avoided answering the question.*
counter EG *"It's not that simple," he countered in a firm voice.*
respond EG *'Mind your manners, lady!' I responded.*
retort EG *"Nobody asked you," he retorted.*
return EG *"I can manage," she returned coldly.*

> **WORD POWER**
> Synonyms
> reciprocate
> rejoin
> riposte

❷ reply NOUN
an answer given to someone
EG *There was a trace of irony in his reply.*
answer EG *She could not give him a truthful answer.*
response EG *His response was brusque.*
retort EG *His sharp retort clearly made an impact.*

> **WORD POWER**
> Synonyms
> rejoinder
> riposte

❶ report VERB
to tell about or give an official account of something
EG *He reported the theft to the police.*
cover EG *The US news media will cover the trial closely.*
describe EG *His condition was described as "improving".*
inform of EG *Inform the police of any suspicious activity.*
notify EG *The skipper notified the coastguard of the tragedy.*
state EG *The police stated that he had been arrested.*

❷ report NOUN
an account of an event or situation
EG *reports of serious human rights violations*
account EG *a dishonest account of events*
description EG *a detailed description of the match*
statement EG *a deliberately misleading statement*

❶ represent VERB
to stand for something else
EG *This rune represents wealth and plenty.*
mean EG *This tarot card means the death of your present situation.*
stand for EG *The olive branch stands for peace.*
symbolize EG *a scene which symbolizes the movie's message*

> **WORD POWER**
> Synonyms
> betoken
> equate with

❷ represent VERB
to describe something in a particular way
EG *The popular press tends to represent him as a hero.*
depict EG *Children's books usually depict farm animals as lovable.*
describe EG *She was always described as an intellectual.*
picture EG *In the American press she was pictured as a heroine.*
portray EG *She was portrayed as a heartless, terrible woman.*
show EG *He was shown as an intelligent and courageous man.*

❶ representative NOUN
a person who acts on behalf of another or others

EG *Employees from each department elect a representative.*
agent EG *You are buying direct, rather than through an agent.*
delegate EG *a union delegate*
deputy EG *I can't make it so I'll send my deputy.*
proxy EG *They must nominate a proxy to vote on their behalf.*
spokesman or **spokeswoman** EG *the party's education spokesman*

❷ **representative** ADJECTIVE
typical of the group to which it belongs
EG *fairly representative groups of adults*
characteristic EG *a characteristic feature*
illustrative EG *an illustrative example*
typical EG *a typical Italian menu*

WORD POWER
Synonyms
archetypal
emblematic

reputation NOUN
the opinion that people have of a person or thing
EG *The college has a good reputation.*
character EG *a man of good character*
name EG *I have disgraced the family's name.*
renown EG *a singer of great renown*
repute EG *a writer and scholar of some repute*
standing EG *This has done nothing to improve his standing.*
stature EG *his stature as the world's greatest cellist*

❶ **request** VERB
to ask for something politely or formally
EG *She requested that the door be left open.*
ask EG *The government is being asked to consider the plan.*
beg EG *May I beg a favour of you?*

seek EG *You should seek a medical opinion.*

WORD POWER
Synonyms
entreat
solicit

❷ **request** NOUN
the action of asking for something politely or formally
EG *France had agreed to his request for political asylum.*
appeal EG *an appeal for witnesses to come forward*
application EG *Their application was vetoed.*
call EG *calls to decrease income tax*
plea EG *his plea for help in solving the killing*

WORD POWER
Synonyms
entreaty
petition

❶ **research** NOUN
the act of studying and finding out about something
EG *funds for research into AIDS*
analysis EG *They collected blood samples for laboratory analysis.*
examination EG *a framework for the examination of these topics*
exploration EG *an exploration of classical myths*
investigation EG *Further investigation was hindered by the loss of all documentation.*
study EG *The study demonstrated a link between obesity and heart problems.*

❷ **research** VERB
to study and find out about something
EG *I'm researching for an article on New England.*
analyse EG *We haven't had time to analyse those samples yet.*
examine EG *The spacecraft will examine how solar wind affects Earth's magnetic field.*

A
B
C
D
E
F
G
H
I
J
K
L
M
N
O
P
Q
R
S
T
U
V
W
X
Y
Z

405

explore EG *I would probably be wise to explore the matter further.*

investigate EG *Gas officials are investigating the cause of the explosion.*

study EG *She's been studying chimpanzees for thirty years.*

resemblance NOUN

a similarity between two things
EG *I can see a resemblance between you.*

analogy EG *the analogy between racism and homophobia*

correspondence EG *There's little correspondence between our lifestyles.*

likeness EG *These myths have a startling likeness to one another.*

parallel EG *There were parallels between the two murders.*

similarity EG *similarities between mother and son*

> **WORD POWER**
> Synonyms
> comparability
> parity
> semblance
> similitude

resemble VERB

to be similar to something else
EG *Venison resembles beef in flavour.*

bear a resemblance to EG *She bears a resemblance to Marilyn Monroe.*

be like EG *The ground is like concrete.*

be similar to EG *The gun was similar to an air pistol.*

look like EG *He looks like his father.*

parallel EG *His fate paralleled that of his predecessor.*

take after EG *You take after your grandmother.*

resent VERB

to feel bitter and angry about something
EG *I resent the slur on my integrity.*

be angry about EG *I was angry at the way he spoke to me.*

be offended by EG *She was offended by his comments.*

dislike EG *I dislike his patronizing attitude.*

object to EG *I object to being treated like an idiot.*

take offence at EG *She took offence at the implied criticism.*

resentful ADJECTIVE

bitter about something that has happened
EG *a sullen and resentful workforce*

aggrieved EG *He is still aggrieved at the size of the fine.*

angry EG *I was angry that I wasn't consulted.*

bitter EG *a forsaken and bitter man*

embittered EG *He had grown into an embittered, hardened adult.*

huffy EG *He's so huffy if he doesn't get his own way.*

indignant EG *They were indignant that they had not been consulted.*

offended EG *He was offended at being left out.*

> **WORD POWER**
> Synonyms
> in high dudgeon
> peeved
> piqued

resentment NOUN

a feeling of anger and bitterness
EG *There is growing resentment against newcomers.*

anger EG *Perhaps anger had clouded his vision.*

animosity EG *The animosity between the two men grew.*

bitterness EG *I feel bitterness towards the person who knocked me down.*

grudge EG *It was an accident and I bear no grudges.*

huff EG *She went off in a huff.*

indignation EG *He could hardly contain his indignation.*

rancour EG *There was no trace of*

envy or rancour in her face.

WORD POWER
Synonyms
pique
umbrage

---

❶ reserve VERB
to keep for a particular person or purpose
EG *Hotel rooms have been reserved for us.*
hoard EG *They've begun to hoard food and petrol.*
hold EG *The information is held in a database.*
keep EG *Grate the lemon zest and keep it for later.*
put by EG *She had enough put by for her fare.*
save EG *Save me a seat.*
set aside EG *funds set aside for education*
stockpile EG *People are stockpiling food for the coming winter.*
store EG *potatoes stored for sale out of season*

❷ reserve NOUN
a supply kept for future use
EG *a drain on the cash reserves*
cache EG *a cache of weapons and explosives*
fund EG *a pension fund*
hoard EG *a hoard of food and petrol*
stock EG *stocks of paper and ink*
stockpile EG *stockpiles of chemical weapons*
store EG *a secret store of sweets*
supply EG *food supplies*

❶ resign VERB
to leave a job
EG *Scott resigned from the firm.*
abdicate EG *The King abdicated to marry an American divorcee.*
hand in your notice EG *I handed in my notice on Friday.*
leave EG *I am leaving to become a teacher.*
quit EG *He quit his job as an office boy.*

step down INFORMAL EG *He headed the government until he stepped down in 1990.*

❷ resign
resign oneself VERB
to accept an unpleasant situation
EG *She had resigned herself to losing her home.*
accept EG *You've got to accept the fact that he's left you.*
bow EG *He bowed to the inevitable and allowed her to go.*
reconcile oneself EG *She had reconciled herself to never seeing him again.*

resist VERB
to refuse to accept something and try to prevent it
EG *They resisted our attempts to modernize.*
defy EG *arrested for defying the ban on street trading*
fight EG *He vigorously fought the proposal.*
oppose EG *Many parents oppose bilingual education in schools.*
refuse EG *The patient has the right to refuse treatment.*
struggle against EG *nations struggling against Communist takeovers*

WORD POWER
Antonym
accept

---

❶ respect VERB
to have a good opinion of someone
EG *I want him to respect me as a career woman.*
admire EG *I admire him for his honesty.*
have a good opinion of EG *Nobody seems to have a good opinion of him.*
have a high opinion of EG *He had a very high opinion of Neil.*
honour EG *the Scout's promise to honour God and the Queen*

look up to EG *He looks up to his dad.*

think highly of EG *His boss thinks very highly of him.*

venerate EG *My father venerated General Eisenhower.*

> ### WORD POWER
> Synonyms
> esteem
> revere
> reverence
> set store by
> Antonym
> disrespect

❷ **respect** NOUN
a good opinion of someone
EG *We have no respect for him at all.*

admiration EG *I have always had the greatest admiration for him.*

esteem EG *We have to win the trust and esteem of our clients.*

regard EG *I hold him in high regard.*

reverence EG *We did it out of reverence for the dead.*

> ### WORD POWER
> Antonym
> disrespect

❶ **respectable** ADJECTIVE
considered to be acceptable and correct
EG *respectable families*

decent EG *They married after a decent interval.*

good EG *He comes from a good family.*

honourable EG *His colleagues were honourable people.*

proper EG *It was not proper for women to go on the stage.*

reputable EG *a reputable firm*

upright EG *an upright and trustworthy man*

worthy EG *worthy citizens*

❷ **respectable** ADJECTIVE
adequate or reasonable
EG *a respectable rate of economic growth*

appreciable EG *making appreciable progress*

considerable EG *a considerable amount*

decent EG *a decent standard of living*

fair EG *She had a fair command of English.*

reasonable EG *He couldn't make a reasonable living from his writing.*

❶ **responsibility** NOUN
the duty to deal with or take care of something
EG *The garden is your responsibility.*

duty EG *My duty is to look after the animals.*

obligation EG *You have an obligation to help him.*

onus EG *The onus was on him to make sure he didn't fail.*

❷ **responsibility** NOUN
the blame for something which has happened
EG *We must all accept responsibility for our mistakes.*

blame EG *I'm not going to take the blame for this.*

fault EG *This is all your fault.*

guilt EG *He was not completely free of guilt.*

liability EG *He admitted liability for the crash.*

> ### WORD POWER
> Synonyms
> accountability
> culpability

❶ **responsible** ADJECTIVE
being the person in charge of something
EG *The Cabinet is collectively responsible for policy.*

in charge EG *I wish someone else was in charge of this inquiry.*

in control EG *Who is in control of the operation?*

❷ **responsible** ADJECTIVE
being to blame for something
EG *I hold you responsible for this*

mess.

at fault EG *I was not at fault as my vehicle was stationary.*

guilty EG *I still maintain that I am not guilty.*

to blame EG *Television is possibly to blame for this.*

❸ **responsible** ADJECTIVE
sensible and dependable
EG *He had to show that he would be a responsible parent.*

dependable EG *a dependable, trustworthy teacher*

level-headed EG *a sensible, level-headed approach*

reliable EG *You have to demonstrate that you are reliable.*

sensible EG *She's a sensible girl, if a bit headstrong.*

sound EG *sound advice*

trustworthy EG *He is a trustworthy leader.*

> **WORD POWER**
> Antonym
> irresponsible

❶ **rest** NOUN
the remaining parts of something
EG *Take what you want and leave the rest.*

balance EG *You pay half now and the balance on delivery.*

others EG *She took one and put the others back.*

remainder EG *He gulped down the remainder of his coffee.*

surplus EG *Coat with seasoned flour, shaking off the surplus.*

❷ **rest** NOUN
a period when you relax and do nothing
EG *I'll start again after a rest.*

break EG *He needs to take a break from work.*

holiday EG *I could really do with a holiday.*

leisure EG *We get no leisure, no time off, no overtime pay.*

relaxation EG *Make time for a bit of relaxation.*

respite EG *a respite from the rush of everyday life*

❸ **rest** VERB
to relax and do nothing for a while
EG *He rested briefly before going on.*

have a break EG *Paul felt he had to have a break.*

idle EG *He sat idling in his room.*

laze EG *lazing on the beach*

put your feet up EG *Nobody's home, so I can put my feet up for a while.*

relax EG *Guests can relax in the cosy bar.*

sit down EG *I'll have to sit down for a minute.*

take it easy EG *the chance to just take it easy for a couple of weeks*

restless ADJECTIVE
unable to sit still or relax
EG *She had been restless and irritable all day.*

edgy EG *She was nervous and edgy, still chain-smoking.*

fidgety EG *bored, fidgety youngsters*

fretful EG *The whole family was fretful and argumentative.*

jumpy EG *If she can't smoke she gets jumpy and irritable.*

on edge EG *She's been on edge for weeks.*

unsettled EG *The staff were unsettled and demoralized.*

❶ **restore** VERB
to cause something to return to its previous state
EG *He was anxious to restore his reputation.*

re-establish EG *an attempt to re-establish diplomatic relations*

reinstate EG *the failure to reinstate the ceasefire*

reintroduce EG *the plan to reintroduce wolves to the Highlands*

return EG *their attempts to return the country to an agrarian economy*

A
B
C
D
E
F
G
H
I
J
K
L
M
N
O
P
Q
R
S
T
U
V
W
X
Y
Z

A
B
C
D
E
F
G
H
I
J
K
L
M
N
O
P
Q
R
S
T
U
V
W
X
Y
Z

❷ restore VERB
to clean and repair something
EG *experts who specialize in restoring ancient parchments*
fix up EG *It took us months to fix this house up.*
mend EG *They finally got round to mending the roof.*
rebuild EG *plans to rebuild the opera house*
reconstruct EG *reconstructing paintings by old masters*
refurbish EG *The city is refurbishing the cathedral's facade.*
renovate EG *The hotel was being renovated in expectation of a tourist boom.*
repair EG *The money will be used to repair faulty equipment.*

> **WORD POWER**
> Synonyms
> recondition
> retouch

restrain VERB
to hold someone or something back
EG *He had to be restrained by his friends.*
contain EG *He could hardly contain his rage.*
control EG *She tried to control her excitement.*
curb EG *You must curb your extravagant tastes.*
hamper EG *I was hampered by a lack of information.*
hinder EG *Research is hindered by lack of cash.*
hold back EG *He could no longer hold back his laughter.*
inhibit EG *factors which inhibit growth*

> **WORD POWER**
> Synonyms
> constrain
> rein
> straiten

restrict VERB

to limit the movement or actions of someone or something
EG *laws to restrict foreign imports*
confine EG *Keep your dog confined to the house.*
contain EG *The curfew had contained the violence.*
hamper EG *I was hampered by a lack of information.*
handicap EG *handicapped by the terms of the contract*
impede EG *Their work was being impeded by shortages of supplies.*
inhibit EG *factors which inhibit growth*
limit EG *He limited payments on the country's foreign debt.*
restrain EG *the need to restrain wage rises*

> **WORD POWER**
> Synonyms
> circumscribe
> demarcate
> straiten

restriction NOUN
a rule or situation that limits what you can do
EG *a speed restriction*
constraint EG *financial constraints*
control EG *a call for stricter gun control*
curb EG *support for a curb on migration from neighbouring countries*
limitation EG *A slipped disc causes severe limitation of movement.*
regulation EG *regulations outlawing child labour*
restraint EG *new restraints on trade unions*
stipulation EG *The only dress stipulation was "no jeans".*

❶ result NOUN
the situation that is caused by something
EG *the result of lengthy deliberation*
consequence EG *This could have disastrous consequences for industry.*

effect EG *the intended effect of the revised guidelines*

outcome EG *The ultimate outcome will be different.*

product EG *the product of five years' work*

upshot EG *The upshot is that our employees are all unhappy.*

❷ **result** VERB

to be caused by something
EG *The crash resulted from a defect in the aircraft.*

arise EG *the publicity that arises from incidents of this kind*

derive EG *Poor health often derives from poverty.*

develop EG *a determination which has developed from his new-found confidence*

ensue EG *If the system collapses, chaos will ensue.*

follow EG *the consequences which followed his release from prison*

happen EG *What will happen if the test proves positive?*

stem EG *Her hatred of cars stems from her mother's death in a crash.*

result in VERB

to cause something to happen
EG *50% of road accidents result in head injuries.*

bring about EG *The Suez crisis brought about petrol rationing.*

cause EG *The play caused a stir here.*

lead to EG *brain damage which leads to paralysis*

retaliate VERB

to do something to someone in return for what they did
EG *The militia said it would retaliate against any attacks.*

get back at EG *a desire to get back at our enemies*

get even with INFORMAL EG *He wanted to get even with his former employers.*

get your own back INFORMAL EG *the opportunity to get your own back on your husband*

hit back EG *In this article he hits back at his critics.*

pay someone back EG *I'll pay him back for what he's done.*

take revenge EG *taking revenge for his father's murder*

❶ **retreat** VERB

to move away from someone or something
EG *damage inflicted by the rebels as they retreated from the town*

back away EG *He put up his hands in protest and began to back away.*

back off EG *I stood up for myself and they backed off.*

draw back EG *They drew back in fear.*

pull back EG *Their forces have pulled back in all areas.*

withdraw EG *Troops withdrew from the country last month.*

> **WORD POWER**
> Antonym
> advance

❷ **retreat** NOUN

the action of moving away from someone or something
EG *the long retreat from Moscow*

departure EG *the departure of all foreign forces from the country*

evacuation EG *the evacuation of British troops from Dunkirk*

flight EG *my panicked flight from London*

withdrawal EG *French withdrawal from Algeria*

> **WORD POWER**
> Antonym
> advance

❸ **retreat** NOUN

a quiet place you can go to
EG *He spent the day hidden away in his country retreat.*

haven EG *The hotel is a haven of tranquillity.*

refuge EG *a refuge from the harsh realities of the world*

A B C D E F G H I J K L M N O P Q R S T U V W X Y Z

A
B
C
D
E
F
G
H
I
J
K
L
M
N
O
P
Q
R
S
T
U
V
W
X
Y
Z

sanctuary EG *a sanctuary located on an island*

❶ **return** VERB
to go back to a place
EG *The plane failed to return at the scheduled time.*
come back EG *He said he'd come back later.*
go back EG *I love going back home.*
reappear EG *He reappeared two nights later.*
turn back EG *We've come too far now to turn back.*

❷ **return** VERB
to give something back
EG *They guarantee to return your original investment.*
give back EG *He is refusing to give the dog back.*
pay back EG *You have to pay back the loan, plus an arrangement fee.*
refund EG *The company will refund the full cost.*
repay EG *I can afford to repay the loan.*

> *WORD POWER*
> Synonyms
> recompense
> reimburse

❶ **reveal** VERB
to tell people about something
EG *They were not ready to reveal any of the details.*
announce EG *She was planning to announce her engagement.*
disclose EG *He will not disclose the name of his patient.*
divulge EG *I do not want to divulge where the village is.*
get off your chest INFORMAL EG *I feel it's done me good to get it off my chest.*
let on EG *She never let on that anything was wrong.*

❷ **reveal** VERB
to uncover something that is hidden
EG *The carpet was removed to reveal*

the original pine floor.
bring to light EG *The truth is unlikely to be brought to light.*
lay bare EG *His real motives were laid bare.*
uncover EG *Auditors said they had uncovered evidence of fraud.*
unearth EG *Quarry workers have unearthed the skeleton of a mammoth.*
unveil EG *The statue will be unveiled next week.*

❶ **revenge** NOUN
vengeance for wrongs or injury received
EG *acts of revenge*
reprisal EG *Witnesses are unwilling to testify through fear of reprisals.*
retaliation EG *The attack was in retaliation for his murder.*
retribution EG *They did not want their names used for fear of retribution.*
vengeance EG *He swore vengeance on everyone involved in the murder.*

❷ **revenge** VERB
to take vengeance on someone
EG *to revenge himself on the press*
avenge EG *He was trying to avenge the death of his friend.*
get even EG *I'm going to get even with you for this.*
get your own back INFORMAL EG *I simply want to get my own back on him.*
hit back EG *He hit back at those who criticized him.*
pay someone back EG *Some day I'll pay you back for this.*
retaliate EG *I was sorely tempted to retaliate.*

❶ **reverse** VERB
to change into something different or contrary
EG *They won't reverse the decision to increase prices.*
change EG *They should change the law to make this practice illegal.*

invalidate EG *A contract signed now might be invalidated at a future date.*

overrule EG *In 1998 the Court of Appeal overruled the decision.*

overturn EG *When the parliament overturned his decision, he backed down.*

retract EG *He was asked to retract his comments but refused.*

> ### WORD POWER
> Synonyms
> countermand
> negate
> rescind
> revoke

❷ **reverse** NOUN
the opposite of what has just been said or done
EG *The reverse seldom applies.*

contrary EG *I'm not a feminist, quite the contrary.*

converse EG *In fact, the converse is true.*

opposite EG *When I told him to do something he always did the opposite.*

❶ **review** NOUN
a critical assessment of a book or performance
EG *We've never had a good review in the music press.*

commentary EG *He'll be writing a weekly commentary on American culture.*

criticism EG *literary criticism*

notice EG *Richards's solo work received good notices.*

❷ **review** NOUN
a general survey or report
EG *a review of safety procedures*

analysis EG *an analysis of American trade policy*

examination EG *an examination of the top 250 companies*

report EG *the committee's annual report*

study EG *a recent study of treatments for back pain*

survey EG *a survey of 250 businessmen*

revise VERB
to alter or correct something
EG *The second edition was completely revised.*

amend EG *They voted unanimously to amend the constitution.*

correct EG *time spent correcting his students' work*

edit EG *We have the right to edit this book once it's finished.*

revamp EG *It is time to revamp the system.*

update EG *He was back in the office, updating the work schedule.*

revive VERB
to make or become lively or active again
EG *an attempt to revive the Russian economy*

rally EG *Markets began to rally worldwide.*

resuscitate EG *a bid to resuscitate the weekly magazine*

> ### WORD POWER
> Synonyms
> invigorate
> reanimate
> rekindle
> revitalize

reward NOUN
something given in return for a service
EG *As a reward for good behaviour, treat your child to a new toy.*

bonus EG *We don't get a Christmas bonus any more.*

bounty EG *They paid bounties to people to give up their weapons.*

payment EG *Players now expect payment for interviews.*

prize EG *He won first prize.*

rhythm NOUN
a regular movement or beat
EG *His body twists and sways to the rhythm.*

beat EG *the thumping beat of rock*

music
pulse EG *the repetitive pulse of the drum beat*
tempo EG *Elgar supplied his works with precise indications of tempo.*
time EG *A reel is in four-four time.*

❶ **rich** ADJECTIVE
having a lot of money and possessions
EG *You're going to be a very rich man.*

affluent EG *an affluent neighbourhood*
loaded SLANG EG *Of course he can afford it. He's loaded.*
opulent EG *his opulent lifestyle*
prosperous EG *the youngest son of a relatively prosperous family*
wealthy EG *a wealthy international businessman*
well off EG *My grandparents were quite well off.*

> **WORD POWER**
> Antonym
> poor

❷ **rich** ADJECTIVE
abundant in something
EG *Bananas are rich in vitamin A.*
abundant EG *the Earth's most abundant natural resources*
fertile EG *a fertile imagination*
plentiful EG *a plentiful supply of vegetables*

> **WORD POWER**
> Synonyms
> fecund
> plenteous

rid
get rid of VERB
to remove or destroy something
EG *a senior manager who wanted to get rid of him*
dispose of EG *He disposed of the murder weapon.*
dump EG *We dumped our bags at the hotel.*
eject EG *Officials used guard dogs to eject the protestors.*

jettison EG *The crew jettisoned excess fuel.*
remove EG *Most of her fears had been removed.*
weed out EG *We must weed these people out as soon as possible.*

ridiculous ADJECTIVE
very foolish
EG *It is ridiculous to suggest we are having a romance.*
absurd EG *absurd claims to have met big stars*
laughable EG *He claims the allegations are "laughable".*
ludicrous EG *It's a completely ludicrous idea.*
preposterous EG *their preposterous claim that they had unearthed a plot*

❶ **right** ADJECTIVE
in accordance with the facts
EG *That clock never tells the right time.*
accurate EG *an accurate record of events*
correct EG *The correct answers can be found at the bottom of the page.*
precise EG *Officials did not give precise figures.*
true EG *The true cost often differs from that.*

> **WORD POWER**
> Synonyms
> unerring
> veracious
> Antonym
> wrong

❷ **right** ADJECTIVE
most suitable
EG *The time is right for our escape.*
appropriate EG *an appropriate outfit for the occasion*
desirable EG *This goal is neither achievable nor desirable.*
fitting EG *a fitting end to an exciting match*
suitable EG *the most suitable man for the job*

❸ right NOUN
what is just and fair
EG *At least he knew right from wrong.*
fairness EG *a decision based not on fairness but on expediency*
justice EG *He has no sense of justice or fair play.*
morality EG *standards of morality and justice in society*
virtue EG *Virtue is not confined to the Christian world.*

| WORD POWER |
| Synonyms |
| lawfulness |
| rectitude |
| righteousness |
| uprightness |

right-wing ADJECTIVE
believing in capitalist policies
EG *some right-wing politicians*
conservative EG *the conservative manifesto*
reactionary EG *reactionary army people*
Tory BRITISH EG *a senior Tory peer*

❶ ring VERB
to make a loud clear sound
EG *He heard the school bell ring.*
chime EG *The clock chimed three o'clock.*
clang EG *A little later the church bell clanged.*
peal EG *Church bells pealed at the stroke of midnight.*
resonate EG *a strap hung with bells and resonating gongs*
toll EG *The pilgrims tolled the bell.*

❷ ring NOUN
an object or group of things in the shape of a circle
EG *a ring of blue smoke*
band EG *a black arm-band*
circle EG *Cut out four circles of pastry.*
hoop EG *a steel hoop*
loop EG *a loop of garden hose*
round EG *small fresh rounds of goats' cheese*

❸ ring NOUN
a group of people involved in an illegal activity
EG *a drug-trafficking ring*
band EG *a small band of plotters*
cell EG *a cell of neo-Nazis*
clique EG *A small clique of people is trying to take over the party.*
syndicate EG *a major crime syndicate*

❶ riot NOUN
a disturbance made by an unruly mob
EG *a prison riot*
anarchy EG *a decade of civil war and anarchy*
disorder EG *mass public disorder*
disturbance EG *Three fans were injured in a violent disturbance outside a pub.*
mob violence EG *last week's mob violence in Bucharest*
strife EG *communal strife in Los Angeles*

❷ riot VERB
to take part in a riot
EG *They rioted in protest against the Government.*
go on the rampage EG *Rock fans went on the rampage after a concert.*
rampage EG *A curfew was imposed as gangs rampaged through the streets.*
run riot EG *hooligans running riot in the streets*
take to the streets EG *Workers and students took to the streets in protest.*

❶ rise VERB
to move upwards
EG *Wilson watched the smoke rise from his cigar.*
ascend EG *He held her hand as they ascended the steps.*
climb EG *We climbed up the steps on to the bridge.*
go up EG *He went up the ladder quickly.*

move up EG *They moved up to second place after their win.*

❷ rise VERB
to increase
EG *House prices are expected to rise this year.*

go up EG *Life expectancy has gone up from 50 to 58.*

grow EG *The Chinese economy continues to grow.*

increase EG *the decision to increase prices*

intensify EG *The conflict is bound to intensify.*

mount EG *For several hours the tension mounted.*

> **WORD POWER**
> Antonym
> fall

❸ rise NOUN
an increase in something
EG *a rise in prices*

improvement EG *a major improvement in standards*

increase EG *a substantial increase in workload*

upsurge EG *an upsurge of interest in books*

> **WORD POWER**
> Antonym
> fall

❶ risk NOUN
a chance that something unpleasant might happen
EG *That's a risk I'm happy to take.*

danger EG *the dangers of smoking*

gamble EG *Booking a holiday can be a gamble.*

peril EG *the perils of starring in a TV commercial*

pitfall EG *the pitfalls of working abroad*

❷ risk VERB
to do something knowing that something unpleasant might happen
EG *If he doesn't play, he risks losing his place in the team.*

chance EG *No assassin would chance a shot from amongst that crowd.*

dare EG *Few people dared go anywhere on foot.*

gamble EG *gambling his life savings on the stock market*

jeopardize EG *The talks may still be jeopardized by disputes.*

put in jeopardy EG *A series of setbacks have put the whole project in jeopardy.*

❶ rival NOUN
the person someone is competing with
EG *He is well ahead of his nearest rival.*

adversary EG *political adversaries*

antagonist EG *Greece's key rival and chief antagonist, Turkey*

challenger EG *his only challenger for the presidency*

opponent EG *He's a tough opponent but I'm too good for him.*

❷ rival VERB
to be the equal or near equal of
EG *As a holiday destination, South Africa rivals Kenya for weather.*

be a match for EG *On our day we are a match for anyone.*

equal EG *The victory equalled Portugal's best in history.*

match EG *I think we matched them in every department.*

river NOUN

> **Types of river:**
> beck
> brook
> burn (*Scottish*)
> creek
> estuary
> rivulet
> stream
> tributary
> watercourse
> waterway

road NOUN

a route used by travellers and vehicles
EG *There was very little traffic on the roads.*
motorway EG *Britain's first motorway, the M1*
route EG *the most direct route to the town centre*
street EG *He walked briskly down the street.*
track EG *a rough mountain track*

rob VERB
to take something from a person illegally
EG *He was beaten senseless and robbed of all his money.*
burgle EG *He admitted that he was trying to burgle the surgery.*
con INFORMAL EG *The businessman had conned him of $10,000.*
defraud EG *charges of conspiracy to defraud the government*
loot EG *thugs who have looted shops*
steal from EG *trying to steal from a woman in the street*
swindle EG *two executives who swindled their employer*

romantic ADJECTIVE
connected with sexual love
EG *a romantic relationship*
amorous EG *The object of his amorous intentions is Wendy.*
loving EG *a loving husband*
passionate EG *a passionate love affair*
tender EG *They embraced and kissed. It was a tender moment.*

❶ room NOUN
a separate section in a building
EG *You can stay in my spare room.*
chamber EG *the council chamber*
office EG *I'm in the office at the end of the corridor.*

❷ room NOUN
unoccupied space
EG *There wasn't enough room for his gear.*
capacity EG *a seating capacity of 17,000*

elbow room EG *There wasn't too much elbow room in the cockpit.*
space EG *the high cost of office space*

❶ rot VERB
to become rotten
EG *The grain started rotting in the silos.*
decay EG *The bodies buried in the fine ash slowly decayed.*
decompose EG *The debris slowly decomposes into compost.*
fester EG *The wound is festering and gangrene has set in.*
spoil EG *Fats spoil by becoming rancid.*

❷ rot NOUN
the condition that affects things when they rot
EG *The timber frame was not protected against rot.*
decay EG *tooth decay*
deterioration EG *gum deterioration*
mould EG *He scraped the mould off the cheese.*

WORD POWER
Synonyms
putrefaction
putrescence

❶ rotten ADJECTIVE
decayed and no longer of use
EG *The front bay window is rotten.*
bad EG *That milk in the fridge is bad.*
decayed EG *teeth so decayed they need to be pulled*
decomposed EG *The body was too badly decomposed to be identified at once.*
mouldy EG *mouldy bread*
sour EG *sour milk*

❷ rotten ADJECTIVE; INFORMAL
of very poor quality
EG *It's a rotten idea.*
inferior EG *overpriced and inferior products*
lousy SLANG EG *The menu is limited*

and the food is lousy.
poor EG *The wine was very poor.*
unsatisfactory EG *if you have obtained unsatisfactory goods or services*

❶ **rough** ADJECTIVE
uneven and not smooth
EG *My bicycle bumped along the rough ground.*
bumpy EG *bumpy cobbled streets*
craggy EG *craggy mountains*
rocky EG *a bleak and rocky shore*
rugged EG *a remote and rugged plateau*
uneven EG *The ball bobbled awkwardly on the uneven surface.*

> **WORD POWER**
> Antonym
> smooth

❷ **rough** ADJECTIVE
difficult or unpleasant
EG *Teachers have been given a rough time.*
difficult EG *It's been a difficult month for us.*
hard EG *I've had a hard life.*
tough EG *She had a pretty tough childhood.*
unpleasant EG *The last few weeks here have been very unpleasant.*

❸ **rough** ADJECTIVE
only approximately correct
EG *At a rough guess it is five times more profitable.*
approximate EG *The times are approximate only.*
estimated EG *There are an estimated 90,000 gangsters in the country.*
sketchy EG *a sketchy account of the incident*
vague EG *She could only give a vague description of the intruder.*

> **WORD POWER**
> Synonyms
> imprecise
> inexact

❶ **round** ADJECTIVE
shaped like a ball or a circle
EG *She has a round attractive face.*
circular EG *a circular hole twelve feet wide*
cylindrical EG *a cylindrical container*
rounded EG *a low rounded hill*
spherical EG *gold spherical earrings*

❷ **round** NOUN
one of a series of events
EG *After round three, two Americans shared the lead.*
lap EG *the last lap of the race*
period EG *the second period of extra time*
session EG *The World Champion was ahead after the first two sessions.*
stage EG *the second stage of the Tour de France*

❶ **row** NOUN
several things arranged in a line
EG *He was greeted by a row of glum faces.*
bank EG *a bank of video screens*
column EG *a column of figures*
line EG *a sparse line of spectators*
queue EG *a queue of shoppers*
rank EG *a rank of taxis*

❷ **row** NOUN
a serious disagreement
EG *This could provoke a major diplomatic row with France.*
altercation EG *He had an altercation with the umpire.*
argument EG *an argument about money*
quarrel EG *I had a terrible quarrel with my brother.*
squabble EG *There have been minor squabbles about phone bills.*

rowdy ADJECTIVE
rough and noisy
EG *He complained to the police about rowdy neighbours.*
boisterous EG *Most of the children were noisy and boisterous.*

noisy EG *My neighbours are a noisy bunch.*

unruly EG *a mother accompanied by her ghastly unruly child*

wild EG *They loved fast cars and wild parties.*

> **WORD POWER**
> Synonyms
> obstreperous
> uproarious

royal ADJECTIVE
concerning a king or a queen or their family
EG *the royal yacht*

imperial EG *the Imperial palace in Tokyo*

regal EG *Never has she looked more regal.*

sovereign EG *the Queen's sovereign authority*

❶ rubbish NOUN
unwanted things or waste material
EG *tons of rubbish waiting to be dumped*

garbage EG *I found all kinds of garbage left behind by the tide.*

litter EG *fines for dropping litter*

refuse EG *The Council made a weekly collection of refuse.*

trash EG *The yards are overgrown and covered with trash.*

waste EG *the safe disposal of toxic waste*

❷ rubbish NOUN
foolish words or speech
EG *Don't talk rubbish!*

drivel EG *mindless drivel*

garbage EG *I personally think this is complete garbage.*

hot air INFORMAL EG *His justification was just hot air.*

nonsense EG *all that poetic nonsense about love*

rot EG *What a load of pompous rot!*

❶ rude ADJECTIVE
not polite
EG *He is rude to her friends.*

disrespectful EG *They shouldn't treat their mother in this disrespectful way.*

impertinent EG *I don't like being asked impertinent questions.*

impudent EG *his rude and impudent behaviour*

insolent EG *a defiant, almost insolent look*

> **WORD POWER**
> Synonyms
> churlish
> discourteous
> peremptory
> Antonym
> polite

❷ rude ADJECTIVE
unexpected and unpleasant
EG *a rude awakening*

abrupt EG *The recession brought an abrupt end to his happiness.*

unpleasant EG *an unpleasant surprise*

violent EG *violent mood swings*

❶ rule NOUN
a statement of what is allowed
EG *This was against the rules.*

decree EG *a decree lifting sanctions against China*

guideline EG *Are there strict guidelines for animal experimentation?*

law EG *inflexible moral laws*

order EG *He was sacked for disobeying orders.*

regulation EG *new safety regulations*

> **WORD POWER**
> Synonyms
> dictum
> ordinance
> precept

❷ rule
as a rule ADVERB
usually or generally
EG *As a rule, I eat my meals in front of the TV.*

generally EG *It is generally true*

A
B
C
D
E
F
G
H
I
J
K
L
M
N
O
P
Q
R
S
T
U
V
W
X
Y
Z

that the darker the fruit the higher its iron content.

mainly EG *Mainly I work alone.*

normally EG *Normally, the transport system carries 50,000 passengers a day.*

on the whole EG *Their wines are, on the whole, of a very high standard.*

usually EG *She is usually a calm and diplomatic woman.*

❸ rule VERB
to govern people
EG *For four centuries, he says, foreigners have ruled Angola.*

administer EG *calls for the UN to administer the country until the election*

be in power EG *They were in power for eighteen years.*

govern EG *The citizens are thankful they are not governed by a dictator.*

lead EG *He led the country between 1949 and 1984.*

reign EG *Henry II reigned from 1154 to 1189.*

ruler NOUN
a person who rules or commands
EG *He was a weak-willed and indecisive ruler.*

commander EG *He is commander of the US Fifth Fleet.*

governor EG *He was governor of the province in the late 1970s.*

head of state EG *the heads of state of all the countries in the European Union*

leader EG *the leader of the German Social Democratic Party*

monarch EG *the coronation of the new monarch*

sovereign EG *the first British sovereign to set foot on Spanish soil*

rumour NOUN
a story which may or may not be true
EG *persistent rumours of quarrels within the movement*

gossip EG *We spent the first hour exchanging gossip.*

hearsay EG *Much of what was reported to them was hearsay.*

whisper EG *I've heard a whisper that the Bishop intends to leave.*

word EG *What's the latest word from Washington?*

❶ run VERB
to move on foot at a rapid pace
EG *I excused myself and ran back to the telephone.*

bolt EG *The pig rose, squealing, and bolted.*

gallop EG *The horses galloped away.*

jog EG *He could scarcely jog around the block that first day.*

sprint EG *She sprinted to the car.*

❷ run VERB
to manage
EG *He ran a small hotel.*

administer EG *the authorities who administer the island*

be in charge of EG *He is in charge of public safety.*

control EG *He now controls a large retail development empire.*

direct EG *Christopher will direct day-to-day operations.*

look after EG *I look after his finances for him.*

manage EG *Within two years he was managing the store.*

Ss Ss

❶ sack VERB; INFORMAL
to dismiss from a job
EG *sacked for punching his boss*
discharge EG *discharged from the army*
dismiss EG *the power to dismiss employees*
fire INFORMAL EG *He was fired for poor timekeeping.*

❷ sack
the sack NOUN; INFORMAL
dismissal from a job
EG *He got the sack after three months.*
discharge EG *He plans to appeal his discharge.*
dismissal EG *the case for his dismissal*
termination of employment EG *wrongful termination of employment*

❶ sacrifice VERB
to give something up
EG *She sacrificed her family life for her career.*
forego EG *If we forego our summer holiday we can afford a car.*
forfeit EG *The company is forfeiting safety for the sake of profit.*
give up EG *I gave up my job to be with you.*
surrender EG *We have surrendered our political authority for economic gain.*

❷ sacrifice NOUN
the action of giving something up
EG *He was willing to make any sacrifice for peace.*
renunciation EG *religious principles of renunciation and dedication*
self-denial EG *an unprecedented act of self-denial*

❶ sad ADJECTIVE
feeling unhappy about something
EG *The loss of our friendship makes me sad.*
blue EG *I don't know why I'm feeling so blue today.*
dejected EG *Everyone has days when they feel dejected.*
depressed EG *She's depressed about this whole situation.*
down EG *The old man sounded really down.*
downcast EG *a downcast expression*
glum EG *a row of glum faces*
low EG *He used to listen when I was feeling low.*
melancholy EG *melancholy thoughts*
unhappy EG *I hate to see you so unhappy.*

> **WORD POWER**
> Synonyms
> disconsolate
> doleful
> lugubrious
> woebegone
> Antonym
> happy

❷ sad ADJECTIVE
making you feel unhappy
EG *a sad song*
depressing EG *a depressing film*
dismal EG *a dark, dismal day*
heart-rending EG *heart-rending pictures of the victims*
moving EG *a deeply moving account of her life*
pathetic EG *the pathetic sight of oil-covered sea birds*
poignant EG *a poignant love story*
tragic EG *his tragic death*

sadness NOUN
the feeling of being unhappy
EG *I said goodbye with a mixture of sadness and joy.*
dejection EG *a feeling of dejection*

421

and despair

depression EG *plunged into the deepest depression*

despondency EG *Deep despondency set in again.*

melancholy EG *Dean had shaken off his melancholy.*

unhappiness EG *His unhappiness shows in his face.*

> **_WORD POWER_**
> Synonyms
> cheerlessness
> dolefulness
> Antonym
> happiness

❶ safe ADJECTIVE
not causing harm or danger
EG *This is not a safe place for a woman on her own.*

harmless EG *harmless substances*

innocuous EG *Both mushrooms look innocuous but are in fact deadly.*

wholesome EG *fresh, wholesome ingredients*

> **_WORD POWER_**
> Antonym
> dangerous

❷ safe ADJECTIVE
not in any danger
EG *I felt warm and safe with him.*

all right EG *I'll be all right on my own.*

in safe hands EG *It's all right, you're in safe hands.*

okay or **OK** INFORMAL EG *Could you check that the baby's okay?*

out of danger EG *We were not out of danger yet.*

out of harm's way EG *I'm keeping him well out of harm's way.*

protected EG *Keep the plants dry and protected from frost.*

safe and sound EG *I'm hoping he will come home safe and sound.*

secure EG *I would like to feel financially secure.*

safety NOUN

the state of being safe from harm or danger
EG *I was very anxious about her safety.*

immunity EG *natural immunity to the disease*

protection EG *protection from harmful rays*

security EG *a false sense of security*

> **_WORD POWER_**
> Antonym
> danger

salty ADJECTIVE
tasting of or containing salt
EG *a good rasher of salty bacon*

brak SOUTH AFRICAN EG *the brak shallow water near the dam wall*

briny EG *the flow of the briny water*

salted EG *8 ounces of slightly salted butter*

same ADJECTIVE
exactly like one another
EG *The two words sound the same but have different spellings.*

alike EG *No two families are alike.*

equal EG *Mix equal quantities of soy sauce and rice vinegar.*

equivalent EG *One unit is roughly equivalent to a glass of wine.*

identical EG *Nearly all the houses were identical.*

indistinguishable EG *symptoms indistinguishable from those of AIDS*

> **_WORD POWER_**
> Antonym
> different

❶ sane ADJECTIVE
having a normal healthy mind
EG *This was not the act of a sane person.*

lucid EG *She was lucid right up until her death.*

normal EG *the question of what constitutes normal behaviour*

rational EG *He seemed perfectly rational to me.*

WORD POWER
Synonyms
compos mentis
in your right mind
of sound mind
Antonym
mad

❷ **sane** ADJECTIVE
showing good sense
EG *a sane and practical policy*
judicious EG *the judicious use of military force*
level-headed EG *a sensible, level-headed approach*
rational EG *a rational analysis*
reasonable EG *a reasonable course of action*
sensible EG *the sensible thing to do*
sound EG *sound advice*

sarcastic ADJECTIVE
saying the opposite of what you mean to make fun of someone
EG *A sarcastic remark was on the tip of her tongue.*
caustic EG *his abrasive wit and caustic comments*
ironic EG *an ironic remark*
sardonic EG *a sardonic sense of humour*
satirical EG *a satirical TV show*

WORD POWER
Synonyms
derisive
mordacious
mordant

satisfactory ADJECTIVE
acceptable or adequate
EG *a satisfactory explanation*
acceptable EG *The air pollution exceeds acceptable levels.*
adequate EG *One in four people are without adequate homes.*
all right EG *The meal was all right, but nothing special.*
good enough EG *He's not good enough for you.*
passable EG *She speaks passable French.*

sufficient EG *One teaspoon of sugar should be sufficient.*

WORD POWER
Antonym
unsatisfactory

satisfied ADJECTIVE
happy because you have got what you want
EG *We are not satisfied with these results.*
content EG *I'm perfectly content where I am.*
contented EG *She led a quiet, contented life.*
happy EG *I'm not happy with the situation.*
pleased EG *He seemed pleased with the arrangement.*

WORD POWER
Antonym
disappointed

❶ **satisfy** VERB
to give someone as much of something as they want
EG *a solution which I hope will satisfy everyone*
gratify EG *He was gratified by the audience's response.*
indulge EG *I don't believe in indulging children.*
please EG *Our prime objective is to please our customers.*

WORD POWER
Synonyms
assuage
pander to
sate
satiate
slake

❷ **satisfy** VERB
to convince someone of something
EG *He had to satisfy the doctors that he was fit to play.*
convince EG *trying to convince the public that its product is safe*
persuade EG *I had to persuade him*

A B C D E F G H I J K L M N O P Q R S T U V W X Y Z

of the advantages.

put someone's mind at rest EG *He has done his best to put my mind at rest.*

reassure EG *I tried to reassure them, but they knew I was lying.*

❸ satisfy VERB

to fulfil a requirement
EG *Candidates must satisfy the conditions for admission.*

fulfil EG *All the minimum requirements were fulfilled.*

meet EG *The current arrangements are inadequate to meet their needs.*

❶ save VERB

to rescue someone or something
EG *He saved my life.*

come to someone's rescue EG *His uncle came to his rescue.*

deliver EG *I thanked God for delivering me from the pain.*

redeem EG *to redeem souls from purgatory*

rescue EG *rescued from the flames*

salvage EG *salvaging equipment from the wreckage*

❷ save VERB

to keep someone or something safe
EG *a new machine which could save babies from cot death*

keep safe EG *to keep my home safe from germs*

preserve EG *preserving old buildings*

protect EG *What can we do to protect ourselves from heart disease?*

safeguard EG *measures to safeguard the ozone layer*

❸ save VERB

to keep something for later use
EG *They are saving for a house.*

hoard EG *They've begun to hoard food and petrol.*

keep EG *Grate the lemon zest and keep it for later.*

put by EG *He's putting his money by in a deposit account.*

reserve EG *Drain the fruit and*

reserve the juice.

set aside EG *£130 million would be set aside for repairs to schools.*

WORD POWER
Synonyms
economize
husband
retrench
Antonym
waste

❶ say VERB

to speak words
EG *She said they were very impressed.*

announce EG *"I'm going to bed," she announced.*

declare EG *He declared that he would fight on.*

mention EG *Did I mention that I'm a vegetarian?*

remark EG *"Some people have more money than sense," he remarked.*

speak EG *There is no evidence that he actually spoke those words.*

state EG *We stated that he had resigned.*

utter EG *They left without uttering a word.*

❷ say NOUN

a chance to express your opinion
EG *voters who want a say in the matter*

voice EG *parents are given a voice in decision-making*

vote EG *Every employee felt he had a vote in the company's future.*

saying NOUN

a well-known sentence or phrase
EG *the saying, "charity begins at home"*

adage EG *the old adage, "the show must go on"*

axiom EG *the long-held axiom that education leads to higher income*

maxim EG *I believe in the maxim, "If it ain't broke, don't fix it".*

proverb EG *an old Chinese proverb*

WORD POWER

Synonyms
aphorism
apophthegm
dictum
saw

scarce ADJECTIVE
rare or uncommon
EG *Jobs are becoming increasingly scarce.*

few EG *Our options are few.*

rare EG *Puffins are now rare in this country.*

uncommon EG *an extreme but by no means uncommon case*

unusual EG *To be appreciated as a parent is quite unusual.*

> **WORD POWER**
> Antonym
> common

scatter VERB
to throw or drop things all over an area
EG *She scattered the petals over the grave.*

shower EG *The bomb exploded, showering shrapnel over a wide area.*

sow EG *Sow the seeds in a warm place.*

sprinkle EG *Sprinkle a tablespoon of sugar over the fruit.*

throw about EG *They started throwing food about.*

> **WORD POWER**
> Synonyms
> broadcast
> disseminate
> strew
> Antonym
> gather

❶ **scene** NOUN
a picture or view of something
EG *a village scene*

landscape EG *Arizona's desert landscape*

panorama EG *a panorama of fertile valleys*

view EG *a view of the lake*

> **WORD POWER**
> Synonyms
> outlook
> vista

❷ **scene** NOUN
the place where something happens
EG *the scene of the crime*

location EG *filmed in an exotic location*

place EG *Can you show me the place where the attack happened?*

setting EG *Rome is the perfect setting for romance.*

site EG *the site of the battle*

spot EG *the ideal spot for a picnic*

❸ **scene** NOUN
an area of activity
EG *the music scene*

arena EG *the political arena*

business EG *the potential to revolutionize the publishing business*

environment EG *the Japanese business environment*

world EG *the fashion world*

scold VERB
to tell someone off
EG *She scolded her daughter for being cheeky.*

chide EG *Cross chided himself for worrying.*

lecture EG *My mother always used to lecture me about not eating properly.*

rebuke EG *I turned to him and sharply rebuked him.*

reprimand EG *reprimanded for talking in the corridor*

tell off INFORMAL EG *The teacher really told her off.*

tick off INFORMAL EG *ticked off for being late*

> **WORD POWER**
> Synonyms
> berate
> castigate
> reprove
> upbraid

A B C D E F G H I J K L M N O P Q R S T U V W X Y Z

425

❶ scorn NOUN
great contempt felt for
something
EG *The proposal was greeted with
scorn.*

contempt EG *I treated this remark
with the contempt it deserved.*

derision EG *shouts of derision*

disdain EG *Janet looked at him
with disdain.*

mockery EG *his mockery of all
things English*

❷ scorn VERB
to treat with great contempt
EG *Eleanor scorns the work of others.*

despise EG *She secretly despises
him.*

disdain EG *He disdained politicians.*

look down on EG *I wasn't
successful so they looked down on
me.*

slight EG *He felt slighted by this
treatment.*

> **WORD POWER**
> Synonyms
> be above
> contemn
> hold in contempt

scornful ADJECTIVE
showing contempt for
something
EG *He is deeply scornful of his rivals.*

contemptuous EG *She gave a
contemptuous little laugh.*

disdainful EG *He is disdainful of
politicians.*

scathing EG *He made some
scathing comments about the design.*

sneering EG *a sneering tone*

supercilious EG *His manner is
supercilious and arrogant.*

withering EG *Her mother gave her
a withering look.*

❶ scrape VERB
to rub a rough or sharp object
against something
EG *We had to scrape the frost from
the windscreen.*

graze EG *He had grazed his knees a
little.*

scour EG *Scour the pans.*

scratch EG *The branches scratched
my face and hands.*

scuff EG *scuffed shoes*

skin EG *I found that I had skinned
my knuckles.*

❷ scrape VERB
to make a harsh noise by
rubbing
EG *his shoes scraping across the
ground*

grate EG *His chair grated as he got
to his feet.*

grind EG *Blocks of ice ground
against each other.*

rasp EG *The blade rasped over his
skin.*

scratch EG *He scraped his knife
over the worktop.*

scrounge VERB; INFORMAL
to get something by asking
rather than working for it
EG *He's always scrounging lifts.*

beg EG *They managed to beg a lift
from a passing fisherman.*

bludge AUSTRALIAN AND NEW ZEALAND
INFORMAL EG *They've come here to
bludge food and money.*

cadge EG *Can I cadge a cigarette?*

sponge INFORMAL EG *I got tired of
him sponging off me and threw him
out.*

scruffy ADJECTIVE
dirty and untidy
EG *four scruffy youths*

ragged EG *a ragged band of men*

seedy EG *his seedy clothes*

shabby EG *a shabby, tall man with
dark eyes*

tatty EG *a tatty old cardigan*

unkempt EG *His hair was
unkempt and filthy.*

> **WORD POWER**
> Synonyms
> disreputable
> slovenly
> ungroomed

A B C D E F G H I J K L M N O P Q R **S** T U V W X Y Z

Antonym
smart

❶ **search** VERB
to look for something
EG *The security forces are searching for the missing men.*
comb EG *Police combed the woods for the murder weapon.*
forage EG *foraging for food*
fossick AUSTRALIAN AND NEW ZEALAND EG *to help Gaston fossick for food around the hut*
hunt EG *hunting for a job*
look EG *He's looking for a way out of this situation.*
scour EG *They had scoured the intervening miles of moorland.*
seek EG *the man he had been seeking for weeks*
sift EG *sifting through the wreckage for clues*

❷ **search** NOUN
the action of looking for something
EG *Police will resume the search today.*
hunt EG *the hunt for my lost boy*
quest EG *his quest to find true love*

secret ADJECTIVE
known about by only a few people
EG *a secret location*
closet INFORMAL EG *a closet Fascist*
confidential EG *a confidential report*
covert EG *She gave him a covert glance.*
furtive EG *furtive meetings*
hidden EG *a hidden camera*
undercover EG *undercover FBI agents*
underground EG *the underground communist movement*

> **WORD POWER**
> Synonyms
> cloak-and-dagger
> conspiratorial
> undisclosed

secretive ADJECTIVE
hiding your feelings and intentions
EG *Jake was very secretive about his family affairs.*
cagey INFORMAL EG *He is cagey about what he was paid for the business.*
reserved EG *He was unemotional and reserved.*
reticent EG *She is very reticent about her achievements.*

> **WORD POWER**
> Synonyms
> tight-lipped
> uncommunicative
> unforthcoming

section NOUN
one of the parts into which something is divided
EG *this section of the motorway*
division EG *the company's sales division*
instalment EG *Payment can be made in instalments.*
part EG *the upper part of the body*
piece EG *The equipment was taken down the shaft in pieces.*
portion EG *I had learnt a portion of the Koran.*
segment EG *the third segment of the journey*

❶ **see** VERB
to look at or notice something
EG *Did you see what happened?*
behold EG *She looked into his eyes and beheld madness.*
discern EG *We could just discern the outline of the island.*
glimpse EG *She glimpsed the man's face briefly.*
look EG *She turned to look at him.*
notice EG *She noticed a bird sitting on the roof.*
observe EG *He observed a reddish spot on the planet's surface.*
perceive EG *Infants start to perceive objects at a very early age.*
sight EG *A fleet of French ships was*

A
B
C
D
E
F
G
H
I
J
K
L
M
N
O
P
Q
R
S
T
U
V
W
X
Y
Z

sighted.

spot EG *I think he spotted me but didn't want to be seen.*

WORD POWER
Synonyms
catch sight of
descry
espy

---

❷ see VERB
to realize or understand something
EG *I see what you mean.*
appreciate EG *He appreciates the difficulties.*
comprehend EG *They do not comprehend the nature of the problem.*
follow EG *Do you follow what I'm saying?*
get EG *You don't seem to get the point.*
grasp EG *They have not grasped the seriousness of the crisis.*
realize EG *They realized too late that they were wrong.*
understand EG *I'm not sure I understand.*

❸ see VERB
to find something out
EG *I'll see what's happening outside.*
ascertain EG *Ascertain what services your bank provides.*
determine EG *The investigation will determine what really happened.*
discover EG *Try to discover what you are good at.*
find out EG *Watch the next episode to find out what happens.*

❶ seek VERB
to try to find something
EG *The police were still seeking information.*
be after EG *At last I found what I was after.*
hunt EG *Police are hunting for clues.*
look for EG *I'm looking for a lost child.*

search for EG *searching for answers*

❷ seek VERB
to try to do something
EG *De Gaulle sought to reunite the country.*
aim EG *We aim to raise funds for charity.*
aspire to EG *He aspired to work in music journalism.*
attempt EG *He was forever attempting to arrange deals.*
endeavour EG *They are endeavouring to protect trade union rights.*
strive EG *The school strives to treat pupils as individuals.*
try EG *We are trying to bring about a better world.*

seem VERB
to appear to be
EG *He seemed such a quiet man.*
appear EG *She appeared intoxicated.*
give the impression EG *He gave the impression of being the perfect husband.*
look EG *The cottage looks quite ordinary from the road.*
look like EG *You look like a nice guy.*

❶ seize VERB
to grab something firmly
EG *He seized the phone.*
grab EG *I grabbed him by the neck.*
grasp EG *He grasped both my hands.*
snatch EG *Mick snatched the cards from Archie's hand.*

❷ seize VERB
to take control of something
EG *Rebels have seized the airport.*
annex EG *the plan to invade and annex Kuwait*
appropriate EG *The land was appropriated by Communists.*
confiscate EG *The police confiscated weapons and ammunition.*
hijack EG *Almost 250 trucks were*

hijacked.

impound EG *The ship was impounded under the terms of the trade embargo.*

WORD POWER
Synonyms
commandeer
take possession of

selfish ADJECTIVE
caring only about yourself
EG *his greedy and selfish behaviour*
egoistic or **egoistical** EG *egoistic motives*
egotistic or **egotistical** EG *an intensely egotistic streak*
greedy EG *greedy bosses awarding themselves big rises*
self-centred EG *He was self-centred, but he wasn't cruel.*

WORD POWER
Synonyms
self-interested
self-seeking
ungenerous

sell VERB
to let someone have something in return for money
EG *a tobacconist that sells stamps*
deal in EG *They deal in antiques.*
hawk EG *vendors hawking trinkets*
peddle EG *arrested for peddling drugs*
stock EG *The shop stocks a variety of local craft products.*
trade in EG *They trade in spices and all kinds of grain.*

WORD POWER
Synonyms
market
merchandise
retail
vend
Antonym
buy

❶ **send** VERB
to arrange for something to be delivered

EG *He sent a basket of fruit and a card.*
dispatch EG *He dispatched a telegram of congratulation.*
forward EG *A letter was forwarded from the clinic.*
remit EG *Many immigrants regularly remit money to their families.*

❷ **send** VERB
to transmit a signal or message
EG *The pilot was trying to send a distress signal.*
broadcast EG *to broadcast a message to a whole group of people at once*
transmit EG *the most efficient way to transmit data*

❶ **sense** NOUN
a feeling you have about something
EG *an overwhelming sense of guilt*
consciousness EG *a consciousness of tension*
feeling EG *It gave me a feeling of satisfaction.*
impression EG *The music creates an impression of menace.*

❷ **sense** NOUN
the ability to think and behave sensibly
EG *He had the good sense to call me at once.*
brains INFORMAL EG *At least I had the brains to keep quiet.*
common sense EG *completely lacking in common sense*
intelligence EG *He didn't have the intelligence to understand what was happening.*
judgment EG *I respect his judgment.*
reason EG *a conflict between emotion and reason*
wisdom EG *the wisdom that comes of old age*

WORD POWER
Synonyms
nous

A
B
C
D
E
F
G
H
I
J
K
L
M
N
O
P
Q
R
S
T
U
V
W
X
Y
Z

429

sagacity
wit or wits

❸ sense VERB
to become aware of something
EG *She sensed he wasn't telling her the whole story.*
be aware of EG *He was aware of her anger.*
feel EG *Suddenly, I felt a presence behind me.*
get the impression EG *I get the impression he's lying.*
have a hunch EG *Lowe had a hunch he was on to something.*
realize EG *We realized something was wrong.*

sensible ADJECTIVE
showing good sense and judgment
EG *a sensible, level-headed approach*
down-to-earth EG *the most down-to-earth person I've ever met*
judicious EG *the judicious use of military force*
practical EG *practical suggestions*
prudent EG *It is prudent to start any exercise programme gradually.*
rational EG *a rational decision*
sound EG *sound advice*
wise EG *a wise move*

> **WORD POWER**
> Antonym
> foolish

sensitive ADJECTIVE
easily upset about something
EG *He was sensitive about his height.*
easily offended EG *I am not a feminist, nor am I easily offended.*
easily upset EG *He remained deeply neurotic and easily upset.*
thin-skinned EG *I'm too thin-skinned - I want everyone to like me.*
touchy EG *She is very touchy about her weight.*

sentimental ADJECTIVE
expressing exaggerated sadness or tenderness
EG *sentimental love stories*
maudlin EG *Jimmy turned maudlin after three drinks.*
mushy INFORMAL EG *I go completely mushy when I see a baby.*
nostalgic EG *nostalgic for the good old days*
sloppy INFORMAL EG *I hate sloppy romantic films.*
slushy INFORMAL EG *slushy ballads*

> **WORD POWER**
> Synonyms
> dewy-eyed
> mawkish
> overemotional

❶ separate ADJECTIVE
not connected to something else
EG *The question muddles up two separate issues.*
detached EG *a detached house*
disconnected EG *sequences of disconnected events*
discrete EG *two discrete sets of nerves*
divorced EG *speculative theories divorced from reality*
isolated EG *He lives as if isolated from the rest of the world.*
unconnected EG *The two murders are unconnected.*

> **WORD POWER**
> Antonym
> connected

❷ separate VERB
to end a connection between people or things
EG *Police moved in to separate the two groups.*
detach EG *Three of the carriages on the train became detached.*
disconnect EG *Make sure supply plugs are disconnected from the mains.*
divide EG *This was a ruse to divide them.*

> **WORD POWER**
> Synonyms
> sunder

uncouple
Antonym
connect

❸ **separate** VERB
to end a relationship or marriage
EG *Her parents separated when she was very young.*
break up EG *She hadn't used his name since they broke up.*
divorce EG *We divorced ten years ago.*
part EG *He is parting from his Swedish-born wife Eva.*
split up EG *I split up with my boyfriend last year.*

series NOUN
a number of things coming one after the other
EG *a series of loud explosions*
chain EG *a bizarre chain of events*
run EG *The England skipper is haunted by a run of low scores.*
sequence EG *a sequence of novels*
string EG *a string of burglaries*
succession EG *He had a succession of jobs.*

❶ **serious** ADJECTIVE
very bad and worrying
EG *They survived their serious injuries.*
acute EG *an acute attack of appendicitis*
critical EG *He remains in a critical condition in hospital.*
severe EG *a severe shortage of drinking water*
worrying EG *It is a worrying situation.*

❷ **serious** ADJECTIVE
important and deserving careful thought
EG *I regard this as a serious matter.*
grave EG *a grave situation*
important EG *We've got more important things to worry about now.*
momentous EG *the momentous decision to go to war*

pressing EG *a pressing problem*
significant EG *the most significant question of all*

WORD POWER
Antonym
funny

❸ **serious** ADJECTIVE
sincere about something
EG *I was not quite sure whether he was serious.*
earnest EG *It is my earnest hope that we can work things out.*
genuine EG *a genuine offer*
in earnest EG *I can never tell if he is in earnest or not.*
sincere EG *He's sincere in his views.*

❹ **serious** ADJECTIVE
quiet and not laughing much
EG *He's quite a serious person.*
grave EG *He was looking unusually grave.*
pensive EG *We're both in a pensive mood today.*
sober EG *sad, sober faces*
solemn EG *His solemn little face broke into a smile.*

❶ **set** NOUN
a group of things that belong together
EG *a set of tools*
batch EG *the latest batch of recruits*
kit EG *I forgot my gym kit.*
outfit EG *She was wearing a brand new outfit.*
series EG *a series of books covering the history of aviation*

WORD POWER
Synonyms
assemblage
compendium
ensemble

❷ **set** VERB
to put or place something somewhere
EG *He set his case down on the floor.*
deposit EG *Imagine if you were suddenly deposited on a desert*

431

island.

lay EG *Lay a sheet of newspaper on the floor.*

locate EG *The restaurant is located near the cathedral.*

place EG *She placed a mug of coffee in front of him.*

position EG *Plants were carefully positioned in the alcove.*

put EG *He put the photograph on the desk.*

rest EG *He rested one of his crutches against the rail.*

stick EG *Just stick your bag down anywhere.*

❸ set ADJECTIVE

fixed and not varying
EG *a set charge*

arranged EG *We arrived at the arranged time.*

established EG *the established order*

firm EG *a firm booking*

fixed EG *a fixed rate of interest*

predetermined EG *His destiny was predetermined from the moment of his birth.*

scheduled EG *The plane failed to return at the scheduled time.*

set on ADJECTIVE

determined to do something
EG *She was set on going to the States.*

bent EG *He's bent on suicide.*

determined EG *His enemies are determined to ruin him.*

intent EG *an actress who was intent on making a comeback*

❶ settle VERB

to put an end to an argument or problem
EG *The dispute has been settled.*

clear up EG *Eventually the confusion was cleared up.*

decide EG *None of the cases had been decided.*

dispose of EG *the way in which you disposed of that problem*

put an end to EG *I just want to put and end to this situation.*

reconcile EG *urging the two parties to reconcile their differences*

resolve EG *They hoped the crisis could be resolved peacefully.*

straighten out EG *doing their best to straighten out this confusion*

❷ settle VERB

to decide or arrange something
EG *Let's settle where we're going tonight.*

agree EG *We haven't agreed a date yet.*

arrange EG *Have you arranged our next appointment?*

decide on EG *They decided on an evening to meet.*

determine EG *The final wording had not yet been determined.*

fix EG *He's going to fix a time when I can see him.*

❸ settle VERB

to make your home in a place
EG *refugees settling in Britain*

make your home EG *those who had made their homes in China*

move to EG *His family moved to New Zealand when he was 12.*

people EG *The plateau was peopled by nomadic tribes.*

populate EG *The island was populated by Native Americans.*

WORD POWER
Synonyms
colonize
put down roots
take up residence

set up VERB

to make arrangements for something
EG *setting up a system of communication*

arrange EG *We have arranged a series of interviews.*

establish EG *We have established links with industry and commerce.*

install EG *I'm having cable installed next week.*

institute EG *to institute better*

levels of quality control
organize EG *a two-day meeting organized by the UN*

several ADJECTIVE
indicating a small number
EG *several boxes filled with albums*
assorted EG *overnight stops in assorted hotels*
some EG *some cheers from the gallery*
sundry EG *He has won sundry music awards.*
various EG *a dozen trees of various sorts*

sexy ADJECTIVE
sexually attractive or exciting
EG *a sexy voice*
erotic EG *an erotic film*
seductive EG *I love dressing up to look seductive.*
sensual EG *a wide, sensual mouth*
sensuous EG *his sensuous young mistress*
voluptuous EG *a voluptuous figure*

❶ shabby ADJECTIVE
ragged and worn in appearance
EG *a shabby overcoat*
dilapidated EG *a dilapidated old building*
ragged EG *dressed in a ragged coat*
scruffy EG *a scruffy basement flat in London*
seedy EG *his seedy clothes*
tatty EG *a tatty old cardigan*
threadbare EG *a square of threadbare carpet*
worn EG *a worn corduroy jacket*

WORD POWER
Synonyms
down at heel
run-down
the worse for wear

❷ shabby ADJECTIVE
behaving meanly and unfairly
EG *shabby treatment*
contemptible EG *contemptible behaviour*
despicable EG *a despicable thing*

to do
dirty EG *That was a dirty trick.*
mean EG *It was mean of you to hurt her like that.*
rotten INFORMAL EG *That's a rotten thing to say!*

WORD POWER
Synonyms
dishonourable
ignoble
scurvy

❶ shake VERB
to move something from side to side or up and down
EG *You have to shake the bottle before use.*
agitate EG *Gently agitate the water.*
brandish EG *He appeared brandishing a knife.*
flourish EG *He flourished his glass to make the point.*
wave EG *The crowd were waving flags and cheering.*

❷ shake VERB
to move from side to side or up and down
EG *The whole building shook with the force of the blast.*
jolt EG *The train jolted again.*
quake EG *The whole mountain quaked.*
quiver EG *Her bottom lip began to quiver.*
shiver EG *shivering with fear*
shudder EG *Elaine shuddered with cold.*
tremble EG *The leaves trembled in the breeze.*
vibrate EG *The engine began to vibrate alarmingly.*

WORD POWER
Synonyms
joggle
oscillate

❸ shake VERB
to shock and upset someone
EG *The news shook me quite a bit.*
distress EG *Her death had*

A
B
C
D
E
F
G
H
I
J
K
L
M
N
O
P
Q
R
S
T
U
V
W
X
Y
Z

profoundly distressed me.
disturb EG *dreams so vivid that they disturb me for days*
rattle INFORMAL EG *He was obviously rattled by events.*
shock EG *Pictures of emaciated prisoners shocked the world.*
unnerve EG *unnerved by the sight*
upset EG *I was too upset to speak.*

> **WORD POWER**
> Synonyms
> discompose
> traumatize

shaky ADJECTIVE
weak and unsteady
EG *threatening an already shaky economy*
rickety EG *Mona climbed the rickety wooden stairway.*
tottering EG *the baby's first tottering steps*
trembling EG *She held out one frail, trembling hand.*
unstable EG *an unstable lamp on top of an old tea-chest*
unsteady EG *His voice was unsteady.*
wobbly EG *I'm sorry, this table's a bit wobbly.*

❶ shame NOUN
a feeling of guilt or embarrassment
EG *She felt a deep sense of shame.*
embarrassment EG *He turned red with embarrassment.*
humiliation EG *the humiliation of discussing her husband's affair*
ignominy EG *the ignominy of being made redundant*

> **WORD POWER**
> Synonyms
> abashment
> loss of face
> mortification

❷ shame NOUN
something that makes people lose respect for you
EG *I don't want to bring shame on*

the family.
discredit EG *It was to his discredit that he did nothing.*
disgrace EG *He had to resign in disgrace.*
dishonour EG *his sense of dishonour at his brother's conduct*
scandal EG *They often abandoned their children because of fear of scandal.*

❸ shame VERB
to make someone feel ashamed
EG *Her son's affair had shamed her.*
disgrace EG *I have disgraced my country.*
embarrass EG *It embarrassed him that he had no idea of what was going on.*
humiliate EG *His teacher continually humiliates him in maths lessons.*

> **WORD POWER**
> Synonyms
> abash
> mortify

shameless ADJECTIVE
behaving badly without showing any shame
EG *shameless dishonesty*
barefaced EG *a barefaced lie*
brazen EG *a brazen theft*
flagrant EG *a flagrant violation of the law*
unabashed EG *an unabashed egotist*
unashamed EG *blatant, unashamed hypocrisy*
wanton EG *a wanton woman*

❶ shape NOUN
the outline of something
EG *a round shape*
contours EG *the contours of the mountains*
figure EG *a trim figure*
form EG *the form of the human body*
lines EG *The belt spoilt the lines of her long dress.*

outline EG *the dim outline of a small boat*

❷ **shape** VERB

to make something in a particular form
EG *Shape the dough into a loaf.*
fashion EG *buttons fashioned from bone*
form EG *The polymer is formed into a thin sheet.*
make EG *gold made into wedding rings*
model EG *She began modelling animals from clay.*
mould EG *Mould the cheese into small ovals.*

❶ **share** VERB

to divide something between two or more people
EG *We shared a bottle of champagne.*
divide EG *The prize money was divided between the two winners.*
split EG *We split the bill between us.*

❷ **share** NOUN

a portion of something
EG *a share of the profits*
allotment EG *a daily allotment of three ounces of bread*
portion EG *his portion of the inheritance*
quota EG *a quota of four tickets per person*
ration EG *their daily ration of water*

❶ **sharp** ADJECTIVE

having a fine cutting edge or point
EG *a sharp knife*
jagged EG *jagged rocks*
keen EG *a keen edge*
pointed EG *pointed teeth*
razor-sharp EG *the razor-sharp blade*

> **WORD POWER**
> Antonym
> blunt

❷ **sharp** ADJECTIVE

quick to notice or understand things
EG *a sharp intellect*
alert EG *She is alert and sprightly despite her 85 years.*
astute EG *He made a series of astute business decisions.*
bright EG *an exceptionally bright child*
observant EG *an observant eye*
perceptive EG *a perceptive gaze*
quick EG *His quick mind soon grasped the situation.*
quick-witted EG *He is very alert and quick-witted.*

❸ **sharp** ADJECTIVE

sudden and significant
EG *a sharp rise in prices*
abrupt EG *Her idyllic world came to an abrupt end when her parents died.*
marked EG *a marked increase in crimes against property*
sudden EG *a sudden change in course*

shine VERB

to give out a bright light
EG *The sun is shining.*
beam EG *The spotlight beamed down on the stage.*
gleam EG *The moonlight gleamed on the water.*
glow EG *The lantern glowed softly in the darkness.*
radiate EG *the amount of light radiated by an ordinary light bulb*
shimmer EG *The lake shimmered in the sunlight.*
sparkle EG *Diamonds sparkled on her wrists.*

shining ADJECTIVE

giving out or reflecting light
EG *shining stainless steel tables*
bright EG *a bright star*
brilliant EG *brilliant sunshine*
gleaming EG *gleaming headlights*
luminous EG *the luminous dial on the clock*
radiant EG *He saw a figure*

surrounded by a radiant light.
shimmering EG *a shimmering gold fabric*
sparkling EG *elegant cutlery and sparkling crystal*

❶ shock NOUN
a sudden upsetting experience
EG *The extent of the damage came as a shock.*
blow EG *It was a terrible blow when he was made redundant.*
bombshell EG *His departure was a bombshell for the team.*
distress EG *She wanted to save her mother all the distress she could.*
trauma EG *the trauma of losing a parent*

❷ shock VERB
to make you feel upset
EG *I was shocked by his appearance.*
numb EG *numbed by suffering and terror*
paralyse EG *He stood paralysed with horror.*
shake EG *The news of her death has shaken us all.*
stagger EG *The judge said he was staggered by the defendant's callousness.*
stun EG *Audiences were stunned by the film's violent ending.*
traumatize EG *My wife was traumatized by the experience.*

❸ shock VERB
to offend because of being rude or immoral
EG *She is very easily shocked.*
appal EG *I was appalled by her rudeness.*
disgust EG *He disgusted everyone with his boorish behaviour.*
offend EG *Many people are offended by strong swearwords.*
outrage EG *They were outraged by*

his racist comments.

shop NOUN
a place where things are sold
EG *I had to race round the shops.*
boutique EG *He owns a jewellery boutique.*
market EG *He sold fruit on a small market stall.*
store EG *Within two years he was managing the store.*
supermarket EG *Most of us do our food shopping in the supermarket.*

shore NOUN

Types of shore:
bank
beach
coast
foreshore
front
lakeside
sands
seaboard
seashore
shingle
strand
waterside

❶ short ADJECTIVE
not lasting very long
EG *a short break*
brief EG *a brief meeting*
fleeting EG *a fleeting glimpse*
momentary EG *a momentary lapse of reason*
short-lived EG *a short-lived craze*

❷ short ADJECTIVE
small in height
EG *a short, elderly man*
diminutive EG *a joke about his diminutive stature*
little EG *a dumpy little woman*
low EG *a low table laden with books*
small EG *a small man with a slight build*
wee EG *For a wee guy he has a big mouth.*

> *WORD POWER*
> Antonym
> tall

❸ short ADJECTIVE
not using many words
EG *a short speech*
brief EG *a brief description*
concise EG *a concise summary*
succinct EG *a succinct account*
terse EG *a terse comment*

> *WORD POWER*
> Synonyms
> abridged
> laconic
> pithy

shortage NOUN
a lack of something
EG *a shortage of funds*
dearth EG *the dearth of good fiction by English authors*
deficiency EG *tests for vitamin deficiency*
lack EG *I was hampered by a lack of information.*
scarcity EG *a scarcity of water*
shortfall EG *a shortfall in income*
want EG *a want of manners and charm*

> *WORD POWER*
> Synonyms
> insufficiency
> paucity
> Antonym
> abundance

shorten VERB
to make something shorter

EG *Smoking can shorten your life.*
abbreviate EG *He abbreviated his name to Alec.*
cut EG *The film was cut to two hours.*
trim EG *I need to get my hair trimmed.*

> *WORD POWER*
> Synonyms
> abridge
> downsize
> truncate
> Antonym
> lengthen

❶ shout NOUN
a loud call or cry
EG *I heard a distant shout.*
bellow EG *a bellow of rage*
cry EG *She gave a cry of horror.*
roar EG *a roar of approval*
scream EG *screams of terror*
yell EG *He let out a yell of delight.*

❷ shout VERB
to call or cry loudly
EG *He shouted something to his brother.*
bawl EG *Laura and Peter were bawling at each other.*
bellow EG *He bellowed orders down the phone.*
call EG *He could hear them calling his name.*
cry EG *"You're under arrest!" he cried.*
roar EG *"I'll kill you for that!" he roared.*
scream EG *screaming at them to get out of my house*
yell EG *She pushed him away, yelling abuse.*

❶ show NOUN
to prove something
EG *Tests show that smoking can cause cancer.*
demonstrate EG *The study demonstrated a link between obesity and heart problems.*
prove EG *History will prove him to*

A
B
C
D
E
F
G
H
I
J
K
L
M
N
O
P
Q
R
S
T
U
V
W
X
Y
Z

be right.

❷ show VERB
to do something in order to
teach someone else
EG *I'll show you how to set the video
timer.*
demonstrate EG *She
demonstrated how to make ice
cream.*
instruct EG *He instructed us on
how to give first aid.*
teach EG *She taught me how to ride.*

❸ show VERB
to display a quality or
characteristic
EG *Her sketches showed artistic
promise.*
demonstrate EG *He has
demonstrated his ability.*
display EG *He displayed
remarkable courage.*
indicate EG *Her choice of words
indicated her real feelings.*
manifest EG *Fear can manifest
itself in many ways.*
reveal EG *His reaction revealed a
lack of self-confidence.*

> *WORD POWER*
> Synonyms
> evince
> testify to

❹ show NOUN
a public exhibition
EG *a fashion show*
display EG *a gymnastics display*
exhibition EG *an art exhibition*
presentation EG *Julie's successful
presentation to the board*

❺ show NOUN
a display of a feeling or quality
EG *a show of affection*
air EG *an air of indifference*
display EG *a display of remorse*
pose EG *a pose of injured innocence*
pretence EG *They have given up
all pretence of neutrality.*
semblance EG *trying to maintain
a semblance of order*

shrewd ADJECTIVE
showing intelligence and good
judgment
EG *a shrewd businessman*
astute EG *an astute judge of
character*
canny EG *He was far too canny to
give himself away.*
crafty EG *He is a clever man and a
crafty politician.*
perceptive EG *a perceptive
analysis of the situation*
sharp EG *He is very sharp, and a
quick thinker.*
smart EG *a very smart move*

> *WORD POWER*
> Synonyms
> perspicacious
> sagacious

shrill ADJECTIVE
high-pitched and piercing
EG *the shrill whistle of the engine*
penetrating EG *a penetrating voice*
piercing EG *a piercing squawk*
sharp EG *the sharp cry of a vixen*

shrink VERB
to become smaller
EG *All my jumpers have shrunk in
the wash.*
contract EG *The ribcage expands
and contracts as you breathe.*
diminish EG *The threat of nuclear
war has diminished.*
dwindle EG *The factory's workforce
has dwindled from 4000 to 200.*
get smaller EG *Electronic systems
are getting smaller.*
narrow EG *The gap between the
two parties has narrowed.*

> *WORD POWER*
> Antonym
> grow

❶ shut VERB
to close something
EG *Someone had forgotten to shut
the door.*
close EG *If you are cold, close the
window.*

fasten EG *He fastened the diamond clasp of the necklace.*

slam EG *He slammed the gate shut behind him.*

> **WORD POWER**
> Antonym
> open

❷ **shut** ADJECTIVE
closed or fastened
EG *A smell of burning came from behind the shut door.*

closed EG *All the exits were closed.*

fastened EG *The pockets are fastened with buttons.*

sealed EG *a sealed envelope*

> **WORD POWER**
> Antonym
> open

shy ADJECTIVE
nervous in the company of other people
EG *a shy, quiet-spoken girl*

bashful EG *Offstage, he is bashful and awkward.*

retiring EG *He was the quiet, retiring type.*

self-conscious EG *I felt a bit self-conscious in my swimming costume.*

timid EG *a timid little boy*

> **WORD POWER**
> Synonyms
> diffident
> self-effacing
> Antonym
> bold

❶ **sick** ADJECTIVE
unwell or ill
EG *a ward full of very sick people*

ailing EG *She tenderly nursed her ailing mother.*

poorly INFORMAL EG *I called Julie and she's still poorly.*

under par INFORMAL EG *The flu has left me feeling under par.*

under the weather EG *Are you still a bit under the weather?*

unwell EG *She had been unwell for some time.*

> **WORD POWER**
> Antonym
> well

❷ **sick** ADJECTIVE
feeling as if you are going to vomit
EG *The very thought of food made him sick.*

ill EG *The smell of curry always makes me ill.*

nauseous EG *These drugs may make you feel nauseous.*

queasy EG *The motion of the ship was already making him queasy.*

❸ **sick**
sick of ADJECTIVE; INFORMAL
tired of something
EG *I'm sick of your complaints.*

bored EG *I'm getting bored with the whole business.*

fed up EG *He is fed up with this country.*

tired EG *I am tired of this music.*

weary EG *She was weary of being alone.*

❶ **side** NOUN
the edge of something
EG *Her head hung over the side of the bed.*

edge EG *She fell over the edge of the balcony.*

verge EG *He parked on the verge of the road.*

❷ **side** NOUN
one of two groups involved in a dispute or contest
EG *Both sides began to prepare for battle.*

camp EG *Most of his supporters had now defected to the opposite camp.*

faction EG *leaders of the warring factions*

party EG *the candidates for the three main parties*

team EG *Both teams played well.*

A
B
C
D
E
F
G
H
I
J
K
L
M
N
O
P
Q
R
S
T
U
V
W
X
Y
Z

439

side with VERB
to support someone in an argument
EG *Louise always sided with her sister.*

agree with EG *She's bound to agree with her husband.*

stand up for EG *I was the one who always stood up for my mother.*

support EG *a fellow prisoner who supported her*

take the part of EG *Why do you always take his part?*

❶ sight NOUN
the ability to see
EG *My sight is so bad now that I can't read any more.*

eyesight EG *He suffered from weak eyesight.*

visibility EG *Visibility was very poor.*

vision EG *It can cause blindness or serious loss of vision.*

❷ sight NOUN
something you see
EG *It was a ghastly sight.*

display EG *These flowers make a colourful display in spring.*

scene EG *a bizarre scene*

spectacle EG *an impressive spectacle*

❸ sight VERB
to see something or someone
EG *He had been sighted in Cairo.*

see EG *I saw a deer in the woods today.*

spot EG *I drove round till I spotted her.*

❶ sign NOUN
a mark or symbol
EG *The negative number is preceded by a minus sign.*

character EG *the characters used in the hallmarking system*

emblem EG *a small yellow hammer-and-sickle emblem*

logo EG *the company's logo*

mark EG *Put a tick mark against the statements you agree with.*

symbol EG *the chemical symbol for mercury*

❷ sign NOUN
a notice put up to give a warning or information
EG *a sign saying that the highway was closed*

board EG *He studied the destination board on the front of the bus.*

notice EG *a notice saying "no entry"*

placard EG *The protesters sang songs and waved placards.*

❸ sign NOUN
evidence of something
EG *the first signs of recovery*

clue EG *the only real clue that something was wrong*

evidence EG *there has been no evidence of criminal activity*

hint EG *He showed only the slightest hint of emotion.*

indication EG *All the indications suggest that he is the murderer.*

symptom EG *typical symptoms of stress*

token EG *a token of goodwill*

trace EG *No traces of violence were found on the body.*

❶ signal NOUN
something which is intended to give a message
EG *a distress signal*

beacon EG *an emergency beacon*

cue EG *He gave me my cue to speak.*

gesture EG *She made a menacing gesture with her fist.*

sign EG *They gave him the thumbs-up sign.*

❷ signal VERB
to make a sign as a message to someone
EG *He was frantically signalling to her to shut up.*

beckon EG *I beckoned her over.*

gesticulate EG *He was gesticulating at a hole in the ground.*

gesture EG *I gestured towards the house, and he went in.*

motion EG *He motioned to her to go behind the screen.*
nod EG *They nodded goodnight to the security man.*
sign EG *She signed to me to come near.*
wave EG *He waved the servants out of the tent.*

❶ **silence** NOUN
an absence of sound
EG *There was a momentary silence.*
calm EG *He liked the calm of the evening.*
hush EG *A hush fell over the crowd.*
lull EG *a lull in the conversation*
peace EG *I love the peace of the countryside.*
quiet EG *The quiet of the flat was very soothing.*
stillness EG *An explosion shattered the stillness of the night air.*

> *WORD POWER*
> Antonym
> noise

❷ **silence** NOUN
an inability or refusal to talk
EG *breaking his silence for the first time about the affair*
dumbness EG *a woman traumatized into dumbness*
muteness EG *He retreated into stubborn muteness.*
reticence EG *Fran didn't seem to notice my reticence.*
speechlessness EG *He was shy to the point of speechlessness.*

> *WORD POWER*
> Synonyms
> taciturnity
> uncommunicativeness

❸ **silence** VERB
to make someone or something quiet
EG *The shock silenced her completely.*
deaden EG *We hung up curtains to try and deaden the noise.*
gag EG *I gagged him with a towel.*

muffle EG *You can muffle the sound with absorbent material.*
quiet EG *A look from her husband quieted her at once.*
quieten EG *She tried to quieten her breathing.*
stifle EG *He put his hand to his mouth to stifle a giggle.*
still EG *He raised a hand to still Alex's protest.*
suppress EG *She barely suppressed a gasp.*

❶ **silent** ADJECTIVE
not saying anything
EG *The class fell silent as the teacher entered.*
dumb EG *We were all struck dumb for a moment.*
mute EG *a mute look of appeal*
speechless EG *speechless with rage*
taciturn EG *a taciturn man with a solemn expression*
wordless EG *They exchanged a wordless look of understanding.*

> *WORD POWER*
> Synonyms
> tongue-tied
> uncommunicative

❷ **silent** ADJECTIVE
making no noise
EG *The room was silent except for the ticking of the clock.*
hushed EG *the vast, hushed space of the cathedral*
quiet EG *a quiet engine*
soundless EG *My bare feet were soundless on the carpet.*
still EG *The room was suddenly still.*

> *WORD POWER*
> Antonym
> noisy

silly ADJECTIVE
foolish or ridiculous
EG *I know it's silly to get so upset.*
absurd EG *He found fashion absurd.*
daft EG *That's a daft question.*

A
B
C
D
E
F
G
H
I
J
K
L
M
N
O
P
Q
R
S
T
U
V
W
X
Y
Z

foolish EG *It is foolish to risk injury.*
idiotic EG *What an idiotic thing to say!*
inane EG *He stood there with an inane grin on his face.*
ridiculous EG *a ridiculous suggestion*
stupid EG *a stupid mistake*

> **WORD POWER**
> Synonyms
> asinine
> fatuous
> puerile
> witless

similar ADJECTIVE
like something else
EG *an accident similar to Hakkinen's*
alike EG *You two are very alike.*
analogous EG *a ritual analogous to those of primitive tribal cultures*
comparable EG *paying the same wages for work of comparable value*
like EG *They're as like as two peas in a pod.*
uniform EG *droplets of uniform size*

> **WORD POWER**
> Antonym
> different

similarity NOUN
the quality of being like something else
EG *the similarity of our backgrounds*
analogy EG *the analogy between racism and homophobia*
likeness EG *These myths have a startling likeness to one another.*
resemblance EG *I could see the resemblance to his grandfather.*
sameness EG *He grew bored by the sameness of the speeches.*

> **WORD POWER**
> Synonyms
> comparability
> congruence
> similitude
> Antonym
> difference

❶ simple ADJECTIVE
easy to understand or do
EG *a simple task*
easy EG *This ice cream maker is cheap and easy to use.*
elementary EG *elementary computer skills*
straightforward EG *It was a straightforward question.*
uncomplicated EG *an uncomplicated story*
understandable EG *He writes in a clear, understandable style.*

> **WORD POWER**
> Antonym
> complicated

❷ simple ADJECTIVE
plain in style
EG *a simple but stylish outfit*
classic EG *classic designs which will fit in anywhere*
clean EG *the clean lines of Shaker furniture*
plain EG *Her dress was plain but hung well on her.*
severe EG *hair scraped back in a severe style*

> **WORD POWER**
> Antonym
> elaborate

simplify VERB
to make something easier to do or understand
EG *measures intended to simplify the procedure*
make simpler EG *restructuring the tax system to make it simpler*
streamline EG *an effort to cut costs and streamline operations*

❶ sin NOUN
wicked and immoral behaviour
EG *preaching against sin*
crime EG *a life of crime*
evil EG *You can't stop all the evil in the world.*
offence EG *an offence which can carry the death penalty*
wickedness EG *a sign of human*

wickedness
wrong EG *I intend to right that wrong.*

> **WORD POWER**
> Synonyms
> iniquity
> misdeed
> transgression
> trespass

❷ **sin** VERB
to do something wicked and immoral
EG *I admit that I have sinned.*
do wrong EG *They have done wrong and they know it.*

sincere ADJECTIVE
saying things that you really mean
EG *my sincere apologies*
genuine EG *a display of genuine emotion*
heartfelt EG *heartfelt sympathy*
real EG *the real affection between them*
wholehearted EG *a wholehearted and genuine response*

> **WORD POWER**
> Antonym
> insincere

❶ **single** ADJECTIVE
only one and no more
EG *A single shot was fired.*
lone EG *A lone policeman guarded the doors.*
one EG *I just had one drink.*
only EG *My only regret is that I never knew him.*
sole EG *the sole survivor of the accident*
solitary EG *There is not one solitary scrap of evidence.*

❷ **single** ADJECTIVE
not married
EG *I'm surprised you're still single.*
unattached EG *I only know two or three unattached men.*
unmarried EG *an unmarried*

mother

❸ **single** ADJECTIVE
for one person only
EG *a single room*
individual EG *an individual portion*
separate EG *separate beds*

sinister ADJECTIVE
seeming harmful or evil
EG *There was something cold and sinister about him.*
evil EG *an evil smile*
forbidding EG *a huge, forbidding building*
menacing EG *His dark eyebrows gave him a menacing look.*
ominous EG *A dark and ominous figure stood in the doorway.*
threatening EG *his threatening appearance*

> **WORD POWER**
> Synonyms
> baleful
> bodeful
> disquieting

situation NOUN
what is happening
EG *a serious situation*
case EG *a clear case of mistaken identity*
circumstances EG *I wish we could have met in happier circumstances.*
plight EG *the plight of Third World countries*
scenario EG *a nightmare scenario*
state of affairs EG *This state of affairs cannot continue.*

size NOUN
how big or small something is
EG *the size of the audience*
bulk EG *Despite his bulk, he moved gracefully.*
dimensions EG *He considered the dimensions of the problem.*
extent EG *the extent of the damage*
immensity EG *The immensity of the universe is impossible to grasp.*
proportions EG *In the tropics, plants grow to huge proportions.*

skilful – slang

A B C D E F G H I J K L M N O P Q R S T U V W X Y Z

WORD POWER
Synonyms
magnitude
vastness

skilful ADJECTIVE
able to do something very well
EG *the country's most skilful
politician*
able EG *a very able businessman*
accomplished EG *an
accomplished pianist*
adept EG *an adept diplomat*
competent EG *a competent and
careful driver*
expert EG *He is expert at handling
complex negotiations.*
masterly EG *a masterly
performance*
proficient EG *proficient with
computers*
skilled EG *a skilled wine maker*

WORD POWER
Synonyms
adroit
dexterous
Antonym
incompetent

skill NOUN
the ability to do something well
EG *This task requires great skill.*
ability EG *a man of considerable
abilities*
competence EG *his high
professional competence*
dexterity EG *Reid's dexterity on
the guitar*
expertise EG *the expertise to deal
with these problems*
facility EG *a facility for languages*
knack EG *the knack of getting on
with people*
proficiency EG *basic proficiency in
English*

❶ slander NOUN
something untrue and malicious
said about someone
EG *He is now suing the company for
slander.*

libel EG *defendants seeking
damages for libel*
scandal EG *She loves spreading
scandal.*
slur EG *a vicious slur on his
character*
smear EG *He called the allegation
"an evil smear".*

WORD POWER
Synonyms
aspersion
calumny
defamation
obloquy

❷ slander VERB
to say untrue and malicious
things about someone
EG *He has been charged with
slandering the Prime Minister.*
libel EG *The newspaper which
libelled him had to pay
compensation.*
malign EG *He claims he is being
unfairly maligned.*
smear EG *an attempt to smear their
manager*

WORD POWER
Synonyms
calumniate
defame
traduce
vilify

slang NOUN

Some slang words:
babe
bug
celeb
chill
cool
fave
fit
gimp
goss
grass on
gross
hols
hot
jammy

manky
minging
minted
pants
snazzy
tidy
24/7
wicked
yonks

❶ sleep NOUN
the natural state of rest in which
you are unconscious
EG *They were exhausted from lack of
sleep.*
doze EG *I had a doze after lunch.*
hibernation EG *Many animals go
into hibernation during the winter.*
kip BRITISH SLANG EG *Mason went
home for a couple of hours' kip.*
nap EG *I might take a nap for a
while.*
slumber EG *He had fallen into
exhausted slumber.*
snooze INFORMAL EG *a little snooze
after dinner*

> **WORD POWER**
> Synonyms
> dormancy
> repose
> siesta

❷ sleep VERB
to rest in a natural state of
unconsciousness
EG *The baby slept during the car
journey.*
doze EG *He dozed in an armchair.*
hibernate EG *Dormice hibernate
from October to May.*
kip BRITISH SLANG EG *He kipped on
my sofa last night.*
slumber EG *The girls were
slumbering peacefully.*
snooze INFORMAL EG *Mark snoozed
in front of the television.*
take a nap EG *Try to take a nap
every afternoon.*

❶ sleepy ADJECTIVE
tired and ready to go to sleep

EG *Do you feel sleepy during the day?*
drowsy EG *This medicine may
make you feel drowsy.*
lethargic EG *He felt too lethargic
to get dressed.*
sluggish EG *I was still feeling
sluggish after my nap.*

> **WORD POWER**
> Synonyms
> somnolent
> torpid

❷ sleepy ADJECTIVE
not having much activity or
excitement
EG *a sleepy little village*
dull EG *a dull town*
quiet EG *a quiet rural backwater*

❶ slender ADJECTIVE
attractively thin
EG *a tall, slender woman*
lean EG *Like most athletes, she was
lean and muscular.*
slight EG *She is small and slight.*
slim EG *Jean is pretty, with a slim
build.*

> **WORD POWER**
> Synonyms
> svelte
> sylphlike
> willowy

❷ slender ADJECTIVE
small in amount or degree
EG *He won, but only by a slender
majority.*
faint EG *They now have only a
faint chance of survival.*
remote EG *a remote possibility*
slight EG *There is a slight
improvement in his condition.*
slim EG *a slim hope*
small EG *a small chance of success*

> **WORD POWER**
> Synonyms
> inconsiderable
> tenuous

slight ADJECTIVE
small in amount or degree

A B C D E F G H I J K L M N O P Q R S T U V W X Y Z

A
B
C
D
E
F
G
H
I
J
K
L
M
N
O
P
Q
R
S
T
U
V
W
X
Y
Z

EG *a slight dent*

insignificant EG *an insignificant amount*

minor EG *a minor inconvenience*

negligible EG *The strike will have a negligible impact.*

small EG *It only makes a small difference.*

trivial EG *trivial details*

> ### WORD POWER
> Synonyms
> inconsiderable
> paltry
> scanty
> Antonym
> large

❶ slip VERB
to go somewhere quickly and quietly
EG *Amy slipped downstairs and out of the house.*

creep EG *I crept up to my room.*

sneak EG *Sometimes he would sneak out to see me.*

steal EG *They can steal away at night to join us.*

❷ slip NOUN
a small mistake
EG *There must be no slips.*

blunder EG *an embarrassing blunder*

error EG *a tactical error*

mistake EG *Many people are anxious about making mistakes in grammar.*

> ### WORD POWER
> Synonyms
> faux pas
> indiscretion

slogan NOUN
a short easily-remembered phrase
EG *a poster with the slogan, "Your country needs you"*

jingle EG *a catchy advertising jingle*

motto EG *"Who Dares Wins" is the motto of the Special Air Service.*

❶ slope NOUN
a flat surface with one end higher than the other
EG *The street is on a slope.*

gradient EG *a steep gradient*

incline EG *The car was unable to negotiate the incline.*

ramp EG *There is a ramp allowing access for wheelchairs.*

> ### WORD POWER
> Synonyms
> declination
> declivity
> inclination

❷ slope VERB
to be at an angle
EG *The bank sloped sharply down to the river.*

fall EG *The road fell steeply.*

rise EG *The climb is arduous, rising steeply through thick bush.*

slant EG *His handwriting slanted to the left.*

❶ slow ADJECTIVE
moving or happening with little speed
EG *slow, regular breathing*

gradual EG *Losing weight is a gradual process.*

leisurely EG *He walked at a leisurely pace.*

lingering EG *a lingering death*

ponderous EG *His steps were heavy and ponderous.*

sluggish EG *a sluggish stream*

unhurried EG *She rose with unhurried grace.*

> ### WORD POWER
> Antonym
> fast

❷ slow ADJECTIVE
not very clever
EG *He got hit in the head and he's been a bit slow ever since.*

dense EG *He's not a bad man, just a bit dense.*

dim EG *He is rather dim.*

dumb INFORMAL EG *too dumb to*

realise what was going on
obtuse EG *It should be obvious
even to the most obtuse person.*
stupid EG *He can't help being a bit
stupid.*
thick EG *I can't believe I've been so
thick.*

slow (down) VERB
to go or cause to go more slowly
EG *The car slowed and then stopped.*
check EG *attempts to check the
spread of AIDS*
decelerate EG *He decelerated
when he saw the warning sign.*

slowly ADVERB
not quickly or hurriedly
EG *He turned and began to walk
away slowly.*
by degrees EG *By degrees, the
tension passed out of him.*
gradually EG *Their friendship
gradually deepened.*
unhurriedly EG *The islanders drift
along unhurriedly from day to day.*

> **WORD POWER**
> Antonym
> quickly

sly ADJECTIVE
cunning and deceptive
EG *She is devious, sly and
manipulative.*
crafty EG *a crafty villain*
cunning EG *Some of these kids can
be very cunning.*
devious EG *an extremely
dangerous, evil and devious man*
scheming EG *You're a scheming
little rat, aren't you?*
underhand EG *underhand tactics*
wily EG *a wily politician*

❶ small ADJECTIVE
not large in size, number or
amount
EG *a small child*
diminutive EG *a joke about his
diminutive stature*
little EG *We sat around a little
table.*

miniature EG *a miniature camera*
minute EG *Only a minute amount
is needed.*
petite EG *a petite blonde*
tiny EG *a tiny kitten*
wee EG *Just give me a wee slice.*

> **WORD POWER**
> Synonyms
> Lilliputian
> minuscule
> Antonym
> large

❷ small ADJECTIVE
not important or significant
EG *small changes*
insignificant EG *an insignificant
detail*
minor EG *a minor offence*
negligible EG *a negligible amount*
petty EG *petty disputes*
trifling EG *a trifling sum of money*
trivial EG *a trivial matter*
unimportant EG *an unimportant
piece of evidence*

❶ smart ADJECTIVE
clean and neat in appearance
EG *a smart navy blue outfit*
chic EG *chic Parisian women*
elegant EG *Patricia looked
beautiful and elegant, as always.*
neat EG *a neat grey flannel suit*
spruce EG *Chris was looking spruce
in his uniform.*
stylish EG *stylish white shoes*

> **WORD POWER**
> Synonyms
> modish
> natty
> snappy
> Antonym
> scruffy

❷ smart ADJECTIVE
clever and intelligent
EG *a smart idea*
astute EG *a series of astute
business decisions*
bright EG *She is not very bright.*

A B C D E F G H I J K L M N O P Q R S T U V W X Y Z

canny EG *He was far too canny to give himself away.*
clever EG *Nobody disputed that Davey was clever.*
ingenious EG *an ingenious plan*
intelligent EG *Dolphins are an intelligent species.*
shrewd EG *a shrewd businessman*

> **WORD POWER**
> Antonym
> dumb

❶ **smell** NOUN
the quality of something which you sense through your nose
EG *a smell of damp wood*
aroma EG *the aroma of fresh bread*
fragrance EG *the fragrance of his cologne*
odour EG *a disagreeable odour*
perfume EG *enjoying the perfume of the lemon trees*
pong BRITISH AND AUSTRALIAN INFORMAL EG *What's that horrible pong?*
reek EG *the reek of whisky*
scent EG *flowers chosen for their scent*
stench EG *a foul stench*
stink EG *the stink of stale beer on his breath*

> **WORD POWER**
> Synonyms
> bouquet
> fetor
> malodour

❷ **smell** VERB
to have an unpleasant smell
EG *Do my feet smell?*
pong BRITISH AND AUSTRALIAN INFORMAL EG *She said he ponged a bit.*
reek EG *The whole house reeks of cigar smoke.*
stink EG *His breath stinks of garlic.*

❸ **smell** VERB
to become aware of the smell of something
EG *I could smell liquor on his breath.*
scent EG *The dog had scented*

something in the bushes.
sniff EG *He opened his window and sniffed the air.*

smelly ADJECTIVE
having a strong unpleasant smell
EG *smelly socks*
foul EG *His breath was foul.*
reeking EG *poisoning the air with their reeking cigars*
stinking EG *piles of stinking rubbish*

> **WORD POWER**
> Synonyms
> fetid
> malodorous
> noisome
> Antonym
> fragrant

❶ **smile** VERB
to move the corners of your mouth upwards because you are pleased
EG *When he saw me, he smiled and waved.*
beam EG *She beamed at him in delight.*
grin EG *He grinned broadly.*
smirk EG *The two men looked at me, nudged each other and smirked.*

❷ **smile** NOUN
the expression you have when you smile
EG *She gave me a big smile.*
beam EG *a strange beam of satisfaction on his face*
grin EG *She looked at me with a sheepish grin.*
smirk EG *a smirk of triumph*

smooth ADJECTIVE
not rough or bumpy
EG *a smooth wooden surface*
glassy EG *glassy green pebbles*
glossy EG *glossy dark fur*
polished EG *He slipped on the polished floor.*
silky EG *The sauce should be silky in texture.*
sleek EG *her sleek, waist-length*

hair

smug ADJECTIVE
pleased with yourself
EG *They looked at each other in smug satisfaction.*
complacent EG *an aggravating, complacent little smile*
conceited EG *They had grown too conceited and pleased with themselves.*
self-satisfied EG *a self-satisfied little snob*
superior EG *He stood there looking superior.*

snag NOUN
a small problem or disadvantage
EG *The snag was that he had no transport.*
catch EG *It sounds too good to be true - what's the catch?*
difficulty EG *The only difficulty may be the price.*
disadvantage EG *The disadvantage is that this plant needs frequent watering.*
drawback EG *The flat's only drawback was its size.*
problem EG *The only problem about living here is the tourists.*

❶ sneak VERB
to go somewhere quietly
EG *Sometimes he would sneak out to see me.*
lurk EG *I saw someone lurking outside.*
sidle EG *He sidled into the bar, trying to look inconspicuous.*
slip EG *Amy slipped downstairs and out of the house.*
steal EG *They can steal out and join us later.*

❷ sneak VERB
to put or take something somewhere secretly
EG *I sneaked the books out of the library.*
slip EG *He slipped me a note.*
smuggle EG *We smuggled a camera into the concert.*
spirit EG *treasures spirited away to foreign museums*

snooper NOUN
a person who interferes in other people's business
EG *a tabloid snooper*
meddler EG *a meddler in the affairs of state*
stickybeak AUSTRALIAN AND NEW ZEALAND INFORMAL EG *She's just an old stickybeak.*

soak VERB
to make something very wet
EG *The water had soaked his jacket.*
bathe EG *Bathe the infected area in a salt solution.*
permeate EG *The water had permeated the stone.*
steep EG *green beans steeped in olive oil*
wet EG *Wet the hair and work the shampoo through it.*

sociable ADJECTIVE
enjoying the company of other people
EG *She's usually outgoing and sociable.*

A B C D E F G H I J K L M N O P Q R **S** T U V W X Y Z

friendly EG *The people here are very friendly.*
gregarious EG *I'm not a gregarious person.*
outgoing EG *He was shy and she was very outgoing.*

> **WORD POWER**
> Synonyms
> companionable
> convivial

❶ **society** NOUN
the people in a particular country or region
EG *a major problem in society*
civilization EG *an ancient civilization*
culture EG *people from different cultures*

❷ **society** NOUN
an organization for people with the same interest or aim
EG *the school debating society*
association EG *the Football Association*
circle EG *a local painting circle*
club EG *He was at the youth club.*
fellowship EG *the Visual Arts Fellowship*
group EG *an environmental group*
guild EG *the Screen Writers' Guild*
institute EG *the Women's Institute*
league EG *the World Muslim League*
organization EG *student organizations*
union EG *the International Astronomical Union*

❶ **soft** ADJECTIVE
not hard, stiff or firm
EG *a soft bed*
flexible EG *a flexible material*
pliable EG *a pliable dough*
squashy EG *a squashy tomato*
supple EG *supple leather*
yielding EG *yielding cushions*

> **WORD POWER**
> Synonyms
> bendable

ductile
gelatinous
malleable
tensile
Antonym
hard

❷ **soft** ADJECTIVE
quiet and not harsh
EG *a soft tapping at my door*
gentle EG *a gentle voice*
low EG *She spoke in a low whisper.*
mellow EG *mellow background music*
muted EG *Their loud conversation became muted.*
quiet EG *He always spoke in a quiet tone to which everyone listened.*
subdued EG *His voice was more subdued than usual.*

> **WORD POWER**
> Synonyms
> dulcet
> mellifluous

❸ **soft** ADJECTIVE
not bright
EG *The bedside lamp cast a soft radiance over her face.*
dim EG *The light was dim and eerie.*
faint EG *The stars cast a faint light.*
light EG *The walls were painted a light yellow.*
mellow EG *Their colour schemes tend towards rich, mellow shades.*
pale EG *dressed in pale pink*
pastel EG *delicate pastel hues*
subdued EG *subdued lighting*

> **WORD POWER**
> Antonym
> bright

❶ **soil** NOUN
the surface of the earth
EG *The soil is reasonably moist after the rain.*
clay EG *a thin layer of clay*
dirt EG *The bulldozers piled up huge mounds of dirt.*

earth EG *a huge pile of earth*
ground EG *a hole in the ground*

❷ soil VERB
to make something dirty
EG *He looked at her as though her words might soil him.*
dirty EG *He was afraid the dog's hairs might dirty the seats.*
foul EG *The cage was fouled with droppings.*
pollute EG *chemicals which pollute rivers*
smear EG *The pillow was smeared with makeup.*
spatter EG *Her dress was spattered with mud.*
stain EG *Some foods can stain the teeth.*

WORD POWER
Synonyms
befoul
begrime
besmirch
defile
smirch
sully
Antonym
clean

solemn ADJECTIVE
not cheerful or humorous
EG *a taciturn man with a solemn expression*
earnest EG *Ella was a pious, earnest woman.*
grave EG *He was looking unusually grave.*
serious EG *She looked at me with big, serious eyes.*
sober EG *sad, sober faces*
staid EG *He is boring, old fashioned and staid.*

❶ solid ADJECTIVE
hard and firm
EG *a block of solid wax*
firm EG *a firm mattress*
hard EG *The snow was hard and slippery.*

❷ solid ADJECTIVE

not likely to fall down
EG *a solid structure*
stable EG *stable foundations*
strong EG *a strong fence*
sturdy EG *The camera was mounted on a sturdy tripod.*
substantial EG *The posts are made of concrete and are fairly substantial.*

solitude NOUN
the state of being alone
EG *He went to the cottage for a few days of solitude.*
isolation EG *the isolation he endured while in captivity*
loneliness EG *I have a fear of loneliness.*
privacy EG *the privacy of my own room*
seclusion EG *She lived in seclusion with her husband.*

solve VERB
to find the answer to a problem or question
EG *attempts to solve the mystery*
clear up EG *During dinner the confusion was cleared up.*
crack EG *He finally managed to crack the code.*
decipher EG *trying to decipher the symbols on the stone tablets*
get to the bottom of EG *The police wanted to get to the bottom of the case.*
resolve EG *Scientists hope this will finally resolve the mystery.*
work out EG *I've worked out where I'm going wrong.*

sometimes ADVERB
now and then
EG *Her voice was so low she was sometimes mistaken for a man.*
at times EG *She can be a little common at times.*
every now and then EG *He checks up on me every now and then.*
every so often EG *Every so often he does something silly.*

from time to time EG *I go back to see my mum from time to time.*
now and again EG *I enjoy a day out now and again.*
now and then EG *These people like a laugh now and then.*
occasionally EG *I know that I do put people down occasionally.*
once in a while EG *It does you good to get out once in a while.*

❶ **sophisticated** ADJECTIVE
having refined tastes
EG *a charming, sophisticated companion*
cosmopolitan EG *The family are rich and extremely cosmopolitan.*
cultivated EG *an elegant and cultivated woman*
cultured EG *He is immensely cultured and well-read.*
refined EG *a woman of refined tastes*
urbane EG *a polished, urbane manner*

❷ **sophisticated** ADJECTIVE
advanced and complicated
EG *a sophisticated piece of equipment*
advanced EG *the most advanced optical telescope in the world*
complex EG *complex machines*
complicated EG *a complicated voting system*
elaborate EG *an elaborate design*
intricate EG *intricate controls*
refined EG *a more refined engine*

WORD POWER
Antonym
simple

sore ADJECTIVE
causing pain and discomfort
EG *a sore throat*
inflamed EG *Her eyes were red and inflamed.*
painful EG *a painful knock on the knee*
raw EG *Her hands were rubbed raw by the rope.*
sensitive EG *the pain of sensitive teeth*
smarting EG *My eyes were smarting from the smoke.*
tender EG *My stomach feels very tender.*

❶ **sorry** ADJECTIVE
feeling sadness or regret
EG *I'm terribly sorry to bother you.*
apologetic EG *"I'm afraid I can't help," she said with an apologetic smile.*
penitent EG *He sat silent and penitent in a corner.*
regretful EG *Now I'm totally regretful that I did it.*
remorseful EG *He was genuinely remorseful.*
repentant EG *repentant sinners*

WORD POWER
Synonyms
conscience-stricken
contrite
guilt-ridden
shamefaced

❷ **sorry** ADJECTIVE
feeling sympathy for someone
EG *I was sorry to hear about your husband's death.*
moved EG *I'm moved by what you say.*
sympathetic EG *She gave me a sympathetic glance.*

❸ **sorry** ADJECTIVE
in a bad condition
EG *He was in a pretty sorry state when we found him.*
deplorable EG *living in deplorable conditions*
miserable EG *a miserable existence*
pathetic EG *the pathetic sight of oil-covered sea birds*
pitiful EG *a pitiful creature*
poor EG *the poor condition of the pitch*
sad EG *a sad state of affairs*
wretched EG *the wretched victims of war*

WORD POWER

Synonyms
piteous
pitiable

❶ sort NOUN

one of the different kinds of something

EG *a dozen trees of various sorts*

brand EG *his favourite brand of whisky*

category EG *The topics were divided into six categories.*

class EG *a better class of restaurant*

group EG *Weathermen classify clouds into several different groups.*

kind EG *different kinds of roses*

make EG *a certain make of car*

species EG *400 species of fungi have been recorded.*

style EG *Several styles of hat were available.*

type EG *What type of dog should we get?*

variety EG *many varieties of birds*

> **WORD POWER**
> **Synonyms**
> ilk
> stamp

❷ sort VERB

to arrange things into different kinds

EG *He sorted the material into three folders.*

arrange EG *Arrange the books in neat piles.*

categorize EG *ways to categorize information*

classify EG *Rocks can be classified according to their mode of origin.*

divide EG *The subjects were divided into four groups.*

grade EG *musical pieces graded according to difficulty*

group EG *The fact sheet is grouped into seven sections.*

separate EG *His work can be separated into three main categories.*

❶ sour ADJECTIVE

having a sharp taste

EG *The stewed apple was sour even with sugar added.*

acid EG *The wine had an acid taste.*

bitter EG *a bitter drink*

pungent EG *a pungent sauce*

sharp EG *a clean, sharp flavour*

tart EG *the tart qualities of citrus fruit*

> **WORD POWER**
> **Synonyms**
> acerb
> acetic
> **Antonym**
> sweet

❷ sour ADJECTIVE

unpleasant in taste because no longer fresh

EG *This cream's gone sour.*

curdled EG *curdled milk*

off EG *This meat's gone off.*

rancid EG *rancid butter*

❸ sour ADJECTIVE

bad-tempered and unfriendly

EG *a sour expression*

disagreeable EG *a shallow, disagreeable man*

embittered EG *an embittered old lady*

jaundiced EG *a jaundiced attitude*

tart EG *a tart reply*

> **WORD POWER**
> **Synonyms**
> churlish
> peevish
> waspish

source NOUN

the place where something comes from

EG *the source of his confidence*

beginning EG *the beginning of all the trouble*

cause EG *the cause of the problem*

derivation EG *The derivation of the name is obscure.*

origin EG *the origin of life*

originator EG *the originator of the theory*

A B C D E F G H I J K L M N O P Q R S T U V W X Y Z

A
B
C
D
E
F
G
H
I
J
K
L
M
N
O
P
Q
R
S
T
U
V
W
X
Y
Z

> **WORD POWER**
> Synonyms
> fount
> fountainhead
> wellspring

souvenir NOUN
something you keep as a
reminder
EG *a souvenir of our holiday*
keepsake EG *a cherished keepsake*
memento EG *a memento of the
occasion*
relic EG *the threadbare teddy bear,
a relic of childhood*
reminder EG *a permanent
reminder of this historic event*

❶ **space** NOUN
an area which is empty or
available
EG *a car with plenty of interior space*
accommodation EG *We have
accommodation for six people.*
capacity EG *the capacity of the
airliner*
room EG *no room to manoeuvre*

❷ **space** NOUN
the gap between two things
EG *the space between the two tables*
blank EG *I've left a blank here for
your signature.*
distance EG *the distance between
the island and the mainland*
gap EG *The wind was tearing
through gaps in the window frames.*
interval EG *the intervals between
the trees*

❸ **space** NOUN
a period of time
EG *two incidents in the space of a
week*
interval EG *a long interval of
silence*
period EG *for a limited period only*
span EG *The batteries have a life
span of six hours.*
time EG *At 15 he left home for a
short time.*
while EG *Sit down for a while.*

spacious ADJECTIVE
having or providing a lot of
space
EG *a spacious lounge*
ample EG *the city's ample car parks*
broad EG *a broad expanse of green
lawn*
expansive EG *an expansive play
area*
extensive EG *The palace stands in
extensive grounds.*
huge EG *a huge apartment
overlooking the park*
large EG *a large detached house*
vast EG *a vast chamber*

> **WORD POWER**
> Synonyms
> capacious
> commodious
> roomy
> sizable *or* sizeable

❶ **spare** ADJECTIVE
in addition to what is needed
EG *Luckily I had a spare pair of
glasses.*
extra EG *Allow yourself some extra
time in case of emergencies.*
free EG *I'll do it as soon as I get
some free time.*
superfluous EG *I got rid of all my
superfluous belongings.*
surplus EG *They sell their surplus
produce.*

> **WORD POWER**
> Synonyms
> leftover
> supernumerary

❷ **spare** VERB
to make something available
EG *Can you spare some money for a
cup of tea?*
afford EG *It's all I can afford to
give you.*
give EG *It's good of you to give me
some of your time.*
let someone have EG *I can let
you have some milk and sugar.*

❸ **spare** VERB

to save someone from an unpleasant experience
EG *I wanted to spare her that suffering.*
let off INFORMAL EG *I'll let you off this time.*
pardon EG *Relatives had begged authorities to pardon him.*
relieve from EG *a machine which relieves you of the drudgery of housework*
save from EG *I was trying to save you from unnecessary worry.*

sparkle VERB
to shine with small bright points of light
EG *Diamonds sparkled on her wrists.*
gleam EG *sunlight gleaming on the water*
glisten EG *The wall glistened with frost.*
glitter EG *A million stars glittered in the black sky.*
shimmer EG *In the distance the lake shimmered.*
twinkle EG *The old man's eyes twinkled.*

> **WORD POWER**
> Synonyms
> coruscate
> scintillate

speak VERB
to use your voice to say words
EG *She turned to look at the person who was speaking.*
communicate EG *We communicated in French.*
converse EG *Luke sat behind the driver and conversed with him.*
express EG *Sam was trying to express his thanks.*
pronounce EG *Have I pronounced your name correctly?*
say EG *I won't say a word.*
talk EG *I don't want to talk to him.*
utter EG *They left without uttering a word.*
voice EG *He hadn't expected the stranger to voice an opinion.*

> **WORD POWER**
> Synonyms
> articulate
> discourse
> enunciate

❶ special ADJECTIVE
more important or better than others of its kind
EG *You are very special to me.*
exceptional EG *children with exceptional ability*
important EG *This is an important occasion.*
significant EG *of significant importance*
unique EG *a unique talent*

> **WORD POWER**
> Antonym
> ordinary

❷ special ADJECTIVE
relating to one person or group in particular
EG *the special needs of the chronically sick*
characteristic EG *a characteristic feature*
distinctive EG *the distinctive smell of chlorine*
individual EG *Each family needs individual attention.*
particular EG *Fatigue is a particular problem for women.*
peculiar EG *This is not a problem peculiar to London.*
specific EG *the specific needs of the elderly*

> **WORD POWER**
> Antonym
> general

specify VERB
to state or describe something precisely
EG *Specify which size and colour you want.*
be specific about EG *She was never very specific about her date of birth.*
indicate EG *Please indicate your*

A B C D E F G H I J K L M N O P Q R S T U V W X Y Z

A
B
C
D
E
F
G
H
I
J
K
L
M
N
O
P
Q
R
S
T
U
V
W
X
Y
Z

preference below.

name EG *The victims of the fire have been named.*

spell out EG *He spelled out the reasons why he was leaving.*

state EG *Please state your name.*

stipulate EG *His duties were stipulated in the contract.*

spectator NOUN
a person who watches something
EG *Spectators lined the route.*

bystander EG *an innocent bystander*

eyewitness EG *Eyewitnesses say the police opened fire in the crowd.*

observer EG *a disinterested observer*

onlooker EG *A small crowd of onlookers was there to greet her.*

witness EG *There were scores of witnesses.*

speech NOUN
a formal talk given to an audience
EG *He delivered his speech in French.*

address EG *an address to the American people*

discourse EG *a lengthy discourse on strategy*

lecture EG *a series of lectures on art*

talk EG *a talk on Celtic mythology*

> **WORD POWER**
> Synonyms
> disquisition
> harangue
> homily
> oration

❶ speed NOUN
the rate at which something moves or happens
EG *a top speed of 200 mph*

haste EG *the old saying "more haste, less speed"*

hurry EG *the hurry and excitement of the city*

momentum EG *This campaign is gaining momentum.*

pace EG *He walked at a leisurely pace.*

rapidity EG *My moods alternate with alarming rapidity.*

swiftness EG *Time is passing with incredible swiftness.*

velocity EG *the velocity of light*

❷ speed VERB
to move quickly
EG *The pair sped off when the police arrived.*

career EG *His car careered into a river.*

flash EG *The bus flashed past me.*

gallop EG *galloping along the corridor*

race EG *He raced across town.*

rush EG *He rushed off, closely followed by Kemp.*

tear EG *Miranda tore off down the road.*

spin VERB
to turn quickly around a central point
EG *as the earth spins on its axis*

pirouette EG *She pirouetted in front of the mirror.*

revolve EG *The satellite revolves around the planet.*

rotate EG *rotating propellers*

turn EG *a turning wheel*

whirl EG *The fallen leaves whirled around.*

❶ spirit NOUN
the part of you that is not physical
EG *His spirit had left his body.*

life force EG *the life force of all animate things*

soul EG *praying for the soul of her dead husband*

❷ spirit NOUN
a ghost or supernatural being
EG *a protection against evil spirits*

apparition EG *an apparition of her dead son*

ghost EG *the premise that ghosts exist*

phantom EG *People claimed to*

have seen the phantom.
spectre EG *a spectre from the other world*
sprite EG *a water sprite*

❸ spirit NOUN
liveliness and energy
EG *They played with spirit.*
animation EG *They both spoke with animation.*
energy EG *At 80 her energy is amazing.*
enthusiasm EG *They seem to be lacking in enthusiasm.*
fire EG *His performance was full of fire.*
force EG *She expressed her feelings with some force.*
vigour EG *We resumed the attack with renewed vigour.*
zest EG *He threw himself into the project with typical zest.*

> **WORD POWER**
> Synonyms
> brio
> mettle

❶ spite
in spite of PREPOSITION
even though something is the case
EG *In spite of all the gossip, Virginia stayed behind.*
despite EG *They manage to enjoy life despite adversity.*
even though EG *They did it even though I warned them not to.*
notwithstanding EG *Notwithstanding his age, Sikorski had an important job.*
regardless of EG *He led from the front, regardless of the danger.*
though EG *I enjoy painting, though I am not very good at it.*

❷ spite NOUN
a desire to hurt someone
EG *He just did it out of spite.*
ill will EG *He didn't bear anyone any ill will.*
malevolence EG *a streak of malevolence*
malice EG *There was no malice in her voice.*
spitefulness EG *petty spitefulness*
venom EG *His wit had a touch of venom about it.*

> **WORD POWER**
> Synonyms
> malignity
> rancour

spiteful ADJECTIVE
saying or doing nasty things to hurt people
EG *a stream of spiteful telephone calls*
bitchy INFORMAL EG *It's not just women who are bitchy.*
catty INFORMAL EG *She's always making catty remarks.*
cruel EG *They gave him a cruel nickname.*
malevolent EG *a malevolent stare*
malicious EG *spreading malicious gossip*
nasty EG *What nasty little snobs you all are.*
snide EG *He made a snide comment about her weight.*
venomous EG *a venomous attack*
vindictive EG *How can you be so vindictive?*

❶ splendid ADJECTIVE
very good indeed
EG *I've had a splendid time.*
cracking BRITISH, AUSTRALIAN, AND NEW ZEALAND INFORMAL EG *It's a cracking script.*
excellent EG *The recording quality is excellent.*
fantastic INFORMAL EG *a fantastic combination of colours*
fine EG *a fine little fellow*
glorious EG *a glorious career*
great INFORMAL EG *a great bunch of guys*
marvellous EG *a marvellous thing to do*
wonderful EG *a wonderful movie*

A
B
C
D
E
F
G
H
I
J
K
L
M
N
O
P
Q
R
S
T
U
V
W
X
Y
Z

❷ splendid ADJECTIVE
beautiful and impressive
EG *a splendid old mansion*
gorgeous EG *a gorgeous Renaissance building*
grand EG *a grand hotel*
imposing EG *imposing wrought-iron gates*
impressive EG *an impressive spectacle*
magnificent EG *magnificent views across the valley*
superb EG *The hotel has a superb isolated location.*

❶ split VERB
to divide into two or more parts
EG *The ship split in two.*
diverge EG *Their paths began to diverge.*
fork EG *Ahead of us, the road forked.*
part EG *For a moment the clouds parted.*
separate EG *Fluff the rice with a fork to separate the grains.*

> **WORD POWER**
> Synonyms
> bifurcate
> cleave
> disunite

❷ split VERB
to have a crack or tear
EG *His trousers split.*
burst EG *A water pipe has burst.*
come apart EG *My jacket's coming apart at the seams.*
crack EG *A gas main cracked.*
rip EG *I felt the paper rip as we pulled in opposite directions.*

❸ split NOUN
a crack or tear in something
EG *There's a split in my mattress.*
crack EG *The larvae burrow into cracks in the floor.*
fissure EG *Water trickled out of fissures in the limestone.*
rip EG *the rip in her new dress*
tear EG *the ragged edges of a tear*

❹ split NOUN
a division between two things
EG *the split between rugby league and rugby union*
breach EG *a serious breach in relations between the two countries*
breakup EG *the breakup of the Soviet Union in 1991*
divergence EG *a divergence between France and its allies*
division EG *the conventional division between "art" and "life"*
rift EG *There is a rift between us and the rest of the family.*
schism EG *the schism which divided the Christian world*

❶ spoil VERB
to damage or destroy something
EG *Don't let it spoil your holiday.*
damage EG *This could damage our chances of winning.*
destroy EG *His criticism has destroyed my confidence.*
harm EG *This product harms the environment.*
impair EG *The flavour is impaired by overcooking.*
mar EG *The celebrations were marred by violence.*
mess up EG *He's messed up his life.*
ruin EG *My wife was ruining her health through worry.*
wreck EG *the injuries which nearly wrecked his career*

❷ spoil VERB
to give someone everything they want
EG *Grandparents often spoil their grandchildren.*
cosset EG *We did not cosset our children.*
indulge EG *a heavily indulged youngest daughter*
pamper EG *pampered pets*

> **WORD POWER**
> Synonyms
> coddle
> mollycoddle
> overindulge

spoilsport NOUN
a person who spoils other
people's fun
EG *They made me feel like a
spoilsport for saying no.*
misery BRITISH INFORMAL EG *the
miseries in the government*
wowser AUSTRALIAN SLANG EG *a
small group of wowsers*

❶ **spot** NOUN
a small round mark on
something
EG *a navy blue dress with white
spots*
blemish EG *A small blemish
spoiled the surface.*
blot EG *an ink blot*
blotch EG *His face was covered in
red blotches.*
mark EG *a little red mark on my
neck*
smudge EG *There was a dark
smudge on his forehead.*
speck EG *a speck of dirt*

❷ **spot** NOUN
a location or place
EG *an out-of-the-way spot*
location EG *The hotel is in a
superb isolated location.*
place EG *Jerusalem is Christianity's
most venerated place.*
point EG *the point where the river
had burst its banks*
position EG *She moved the body to
a position where it would not be
seen.*
scene EG *He left a note at the scene
of the crime.*
site EG *plans to construct a temple
on the site*

❸ **spot** VERB
to see or notice something
EG *Her drama teacher spotted her
ability.*
catch sight of EG *I caught sight of
an ad in the paper.*
detect EG *The test should enable
doctors to detect the disease early.*
discern EG *I did not discern any*

change.
observe EG *Can you observe any
difference?*
see EG *I can see a resemblance
between you.*
sight EG *A fleet of French ships was
sighted.*

> *WORD POWER*
> Synonyms
> descry
> espy

staff NOUN
the people who work for an
organization
EG *She made little effort to socialize
with other staff.*
employees EG *a temporary
employee*
personnel EG *An announcement
was made to all personnel.*
team EG *The team worked well
under his direction.*
workers EG *weekend and
night-shift workers*
workforce EG *a sullen and
resentful workforce*

❶ **stage** NOUN
a part of a process
EG *the closing stages of the race*
lap EG *The first lap was clocked at
under a minute.*
period EG *We went through a
period of unprecedented change.*
phase EG *a passing phase*
point EG *a critical point in the
campaign*
step EG *the next step in the process*

❷ **stage** VERB
to organize something
EG *Workers have staged a number of
one-day strikes.*
arrange EG *We're arranging a
surprise party for her.*
engineer EG *He was the one who
engineered the merger.*
mount EG *a security operation
mounted by the army*
orchestrate EG *a carefully*

A
B
C
D
E
F
G
H
I
J
K
L
M
N
O
P
Q
R
S
T
U
V
W
X
Y
Z

459

A
B
C
D
E
F
G
H
I
J
K
L
M
N
O
P
Q
R
S
T
U
V
W
X
Y
Z

orchestrated campaign
organize EG *a two-day meeting organized by the UN*

❶ stain NOUN
a mark on something
EG *grass stains*
blot EG *an ink blot*
mark EG *I can't get this mark to come off.*
spot EG *brown spots on the skin caused by the sun*

❷ stain VERB
to make a mark on something
EG *Some foods can stain the teeth.*
dirty EG *Sheets can be reused until they are damaged or dirtied.*
mark EG *the places where Steve's boots had marked the wood*
soil EG *a soiled white apron*
spot EG *her coat was spotted with blood*

WORD POWER
Synonyms
discolour
smirch

stale ADJECTIVE
no longer fresh
EG *a lump of stale bread*
flat EG *flat beer*
old EG *mouldy old cheese*
sour EG *sour milk*
stagnant EG *stagnant water*

WORD POWER
Synonyms
fusty
musty
Antonym
fresh

star NOUN
a famous person
EG *a film star*
celebrity EG *A host of celebrities attended the premiere.*
idol EG *the city's greatest soccer idol*
luminary LITERARY EG *The event attracted such pop luminaries as Madonna.*

stare VERB
to look at something for a long time
EG *He stared at the floor, lost in meditation.*
gaze EG *gazing at herself in the mirror*
look EG *He looked at her with open hostility.*
ogle EG *ogling the girls as they went past*

WORD POWER
Synonyms
gawp
goggle

❶ start VERB
to begin to take place
EG *School starts again next week.*
begin EG *A typical day begins at 8.30.*
commence EG *The academic year commences at the beginning of October.*
get under way EG *The game got under way.*

WORD POWER
Antonym
finish

❷ start VERB
to begin to do something
EG *Susie started to cry.*
begin EG *He began to groan with pain.*
commence EG *The hunter commenced to skin the animal.*
proceed EG *He proceeded to get drunk.*

WORD POWER
Antonym
stop

❸ start VERB
to cause something to begin
EG *a good time to start a business*
begin EG *The US is prepared to begin talks immediately.*
establish EG *The school was established in 1899.*

found EG *Baden-Powell founded the Boy Scouts in 1908.*
initiate EG *They wanted to initiate a discussion.*
instigate EG *The violence was instigated by a few people.*
institute EG *We have instituted a number of measures.*
set up EG *A committee was set up to arbitrate in the dispute.*

> **WORD POWER**
> Antonym
> stop

❹ **start** NOUN
the beginning of something
EG *His career had an auspicious start.*

beginning EG *the beginning of all the trouble*
birth EG *the birth of modern art*
initiation EG *There was a year between initiation and completion.*
onset EG *the onset of puberty*
opening EG *the opening of the trial*
outset EG *There were lots of problems from the outset.*

> **WORD POWER**
> Antonym
> finish

❶ **state** NOUN
the condition or circumstances of something
EG *the pathetic state of the rail network*

circumstances EG *He's in desperate circumstances.*
condition EG *He remains in a critical condition in hospital.*
plight EG *the plight of Third World countries*
position EG *We are in a privileged position.*
predicament EG *the once great club's current predicament*
shape EG *Her finances were in terrible shape.*
situation EG *a precarious situation*

❷ **state** NOUN
a country
EG *the state of Denmark*

country EG *a country where alcohol is prohibited*
kingdom EG *The kingdom's power declined.*
land EG *in that distant land*
nation EG *a leading nation in world politics*
republic EG *In 1918, Austria became a republic.*

> **WORD POWER**
> Synonyms
> body politic
> commonwealth

❸ **state** VERB
to say something, especially in a formal way
EG *Please state your occupation.*

affirm EG *a speech in which he affirmed his policies*
articulate EG *an attempt to articulate his feelings*
assert EG *He asserted his innocence.*
declare EG *He declared that he would fight on.*
express EG *He expressed regret that he had caused any offence.*
say EG *The police said he had no connection with the security forces.*
specify EG *Please specify your preferences below.*

> **WORD POWER**
> Synonyms
> aver
> expound
> propound

status NOUN
a person's social position
EG *the status of children in society*

position EG *a privileged position*
prestige EG *to diminish the prestige of the monarchy*
rank EG *He was stripped of his rank.*
standing EG *This has done nothing to improve his standing.*

stay VERB
to remain somewhere

A B C D E F G H I J K L M N O P Q R **S** T U V W X Y Z

461

EG *She stayed in bed till noon.*

hang around INFORMAL EG *I can't hang around here all day.*

linger EG *I lingered on for a few days until he arrived.*

loiter EG *We loitered around looking in shop windows.*

remain EG *You'll have to remain in hospital for the time being.*

tarry EG *The shop's aim is to persuade you to tarry and spend.*

wait EG *I'll wait here till you come back.*

❶ steady ADJECTIVE

continuing without interruptions

EG *a steady rise in profits*

consistent EG *consistent support*

constant EG *under constant pressure*

continuous EG *Japanese-style programmes of continuous improvement*

even EG *an even level of sound*

nonstop EG *nonstop background music*

regular EG *a regular beat*

uninterrupted EG *28 years of uninterrupted growth*

❷ steady ADJECTIVE

not shaky or wobbling

EG *O'Brien held out a steady hand.*

firm EG *Make sure the tree is securely mounted on a firm base.*

secure EG *Check joints are secure and the wood is sound.*

stable EG *stable foundations*

❸ steady VERB

to prevent something from shaking or wobbling

EG *Two men were steadying a ladder.*

brace EG *the old timbers which braced the roof*

secure EG *The frames are secured by horizontal rails.*

stabilize EG *gyros which stabilize the platform*

support EG *Thick wooden posts support the ceiling.*

❶ steal VERB

to take something without permission

EG *He was accused of stealing a tin of pineapple chunks.*

appropriate EG *Several other companies have appropriated the idea.*

nick BRITISH, AUSTRALIAN, AND NEW ZEALAND SLANG EG *I nicked that money from the till.*

pilfer EG *Staff were pilfering behind the bar.*

pinch INFORMAL EG *Someone's pinched my wallet.*

swipe SLANG EG *Did you just swipe that book?*

take EG *The burglars took anything they could carry.*

> **WORD POWER**
> Synonyms
> embezzle
> filch
> misappropriate
> purloin
> thieve

❷ steal VERB

to move somewhere quietly and secretly

EG *They can steal out and join us later.*

creep EG *We crept away under cover of darkness.*

slip EG *I wanted to duck down and slip past but they saw me.*

sneak EG *Sometimes he would sneak out to see me.*

tiptoe EG *She slipped out of bed and tiptoed to the window.*

❶ steep ADJECTIVE

rising sharply and abruptly

EG *a steep hill*

sheer EG *a sheer drop*

vertical EG *The slope was almost vertical.*

> **WORD POWER**
> Antonym
> gradual

❷ steep ADJECTIVE
larger than is reasonable
EG *steep prices*
excessive EG *excessive charges*
extortionate EG *an extortionate rate of interest*
high EG *high loan rates*
unreasonable EG *unreasonable interest charges*

> **WORD POWER**
> Synonyms
> exorbitant
> overpriced

❸ steep VERB
to soak something in a liquid
EG *green beans steeped in olive oil*
immerse EG *Immerse the gammon in cold water to remove the salt.*
marinate EG *Marinate the chicken for at least four hours.*
soak EG *Soak the beans overnight.*

❶ sterile ADJECTIVE
free from germs
EG *Protect the cut with a sterile dressing.*
antiseptic EG *an antiseptic hospital room*
germ-free EG *Keep your working surfaces germ-free.*
sterilized EG *a sterilized laboratory*

❷ sterile ADJECTIVE
unable to produce
EG *He found out he was sterile.*
barren EG *a barren mare*
unproductive EG *70 million acres of unproductive land*

> **WORD POWER**
> Synonyms
> infecund
> unfruitful
> Antonym
> fertile

sticky ADJECTIVE
covered with a substance that sticks to other things
EG *She thrust her hand into the sticky mess.*

adhesive EG *adhesive tape*
tacky EG *covered with a tacky resin*

> **WORD POWER**
> Synonyms
> glutinous
> viscid
> viscous

❶ stiff ADJECTIVE
firm and not easily bent
EG *stiff metal wires*
firm EG *a firm mattress*
hard EG *the hard wooden floor*
rigid EG *a rigid plastic container*
solid EG *a block of solid wax*
taut EG *He lifted the wire until it was taut.*

> **WORD POWER**
> Antonym
> limp

❷ stiff ADJECTIVE
not friendly or relaxed
EG *the rather stiff and formal surroundings of the Palace*
cold EG *Sharon was very cold with me.*
forced EG *a forced smile*
formal EG *His voice was grave and formal.*
stilted EG *Our conversation was stilted and polite.*
unnatural EG *a strained and unnatural atmosphere*
wooden EG *a wooden performance*

> **WORD POWER**
> Synonyms
> constrained
> prim
> standoffish

❸ stiff ADJECTIVE
difficult or severe
EG *a stiff exam*
arduous EG *an arduous undertaking*
difficult EG *a difficult job*
exacting EG *exacting standards*
formidable EG *a formidable task*
hard EG *a hard day's work*

A B C D E F G H I J K L M N O P Q R S T U V W X Y Z

A
B
C
D
E
F
G
H
I
J
K
L
M
N
O
P
Q
R
S
T
U
V
W
X
Y
Z

rigorous EG *rigorous military training*
tough EG *a tough challenge*

still ADJECTIVE
not moving
EG *The air was still.*
calm EG *the calm waters of the harbour*
inert EG *He covered the inert body with a blanket.*
motionless EG *He stood there, motionless.*
stationary EG *The train was stationary for 90 minutes.*
tranquil EG *a tranquil lake*

❶ stink VERB
to smell very bad
EG *His breath stinks of garlic.*
pong BRITISH AND AUSTRALIAN INFORMAL EG *She said he ponged a bit.*
reek EG *The whole house reeks of cigar smoke.*

❷ stink NOUN
a very bad smell
EG *the stink of stale beer on his breath*
pong BRITISH AND AUSTRALIAN INFORMAL EG *What's that horrible pong?*
stench EG *a foul stench*

> **WORD POWER**
> Synonyms
> fetor
> malodour

stocky ADJECTIVE
short but solid-looking
EG *a stocky, middle-aged man*
chunky EG *the chunky South African tennis player*
solid EG *a solid build*
sturdy EG *a short, sturdy woman in her early sixties*

> **WORD POWER**
> Synonyms
> stubby
> thickset

stomach NOUN

the front part of the body below the waist
EG *Breathe out and flatten your stomach.*
belly EG *the enormous belly of the Italian foreign minister*
paunch EG *Nicholson surveyed his spreading paunch.*
puku NEW ZEALAND EG *a pain in my puku*
tummy INFORMAL EG *I'd like a flatter tummy, but then who doesn't?*

❶ stop VERB
to cease doing something
EG *I stopped working last year to have a baby.*
cease EG *A small number of firms have ceased trading.*
cut out INFORMAL EG *Will you cut out that racket?*
desist EG *boycotting Norwegian products until they desist from whaling*
discontinue EG *Do not discontinue the treatment without seeing your doctor.*
end EG *public pressure to end the embargo*
quit EG *He's trying to quit smoking.*

> **WORD POWER**
> Antonym
> start

❷ stop VERB
to come to an end
EG *He prayed for the blizzard to stop.*
cease EG *At 1 o'clock the rain ceased.*
come to an end EG *An hour later, the meeting came to an end.*
conclude EG *The evening concluded with dinner and speeches.*
end EG *The talks ended in disagreement.*
finish EG *The teaching day finishes at around 4 pm.*
halt EG *Discussions have halted again.*

WORD POWER
Antonym
start

❸ **stop** VERB
to prevent something
EG *measures to stop the trade in ivory*
arrest EG *trying to arrest the bleeding*
check EG *a policy to check fast population growth*
prevent EG *the most practical way of preventing crime*

WORD POWER
Synonyms
forestall
nip something in the bud

❶ **store** NOUN
a supply kept for future use
EG *I have a store of food and water here.*
cache EG *a cache of weapons and explosives*
fund EG *an extraordinary fund of energy*
hoard EG *a hoard of supplies*
reserve EG *the world's oil reserves*
reservoir EG *the body's short-term reservoir of energy*
stock EG *stocks of paper and ink*
stockpile EG *stockpiles of nuclear warheads*
supply EG *food supplies*

❷ **store** NOUN
a place where things are kept
EG *a grain store*
depot EG *a government arms depot*
storeroom EG *a storeroom filled with furniture*
warehouse EG *a carpet warehouse*

WORD POWER
Synonyms
depository
repository
storehouse

❸ **store** VERB
to keep something for future use

EG *The information can be stored in a computer.*
hoard EG *They've begun to hoard food and petrol.*
keep EG *Grate the lemon zest and keep it for later.*
save EG *His allotment of gas had to be saved for emergencies.*
stash INFORMAL EG *He had stashed money away in a secret offshore account.*
stockpile EG *People are stockpiling food for the coming winter.*

story NOUN
a tale told or written to entertain people
EG *a poignant love story*
account EG *a true account*
anecdote EG *her store of theatrical anecdotes*
legend EG *an old Scottish legend*
narrative EG *a fast-moving narrative*
tale EG *a fairy tale*
yarn EG *a children's yarn about giants*

❶ **straight** ADJECTIVE
upright or level
EG *Keep your arms straight.*
erect EG *The upper back and neck are held in an erect position.*
even EG *to ensure an even hem*
horizontal EG *a horizontal line*
level EG *a completely level base*
perpendicular EG *Position your body perpendicular with the slope.*
upright EG *He sat upright in his chair.*
vertical EG *Keep the spine vertical.*

WORD POWER
Antonym
crooked

❷ **straight** ADJECTIVE
honest, frank and direct
EG *They wouldn't give me a straight answer.*
blunt EG *She is blunt about her personal life.*

A
B
C
D
E
F
G
H
I
J
K
L
M
N
O
P
Q
R
S
T
U
V
W
X
Y
Z

candid EG *I haven't been completely candid with you.*
forthright EG *a forthright reply*
frank EG *a frank discussion*
honest EG *Please be honest with me.*
outright EG *This was outright rejection.*
plain EG *plain talking*
point-blank EG *a point-blank refusal*

❶ **strain** NOUN
worry and nervous tension
EG *the stresses and strains of a busy career*
anxiety EG *Her voice was full of anxiety.*
pressure EG *the pressure of work*
stress EG *the stress of exams*
tension EG *Laughing relieves tension and stress.*

❷ **strain** VERB
to make something do more than it is able to do
EG *You'll strain your eyes reading in this light.*
overwork EG *Too much food will overwork your digestive system.*
tax EG *He is beginning to tax my patience.*

> **WORD POWER**
> Synonyms
> overexert
> overtax
> push to the limit

❶ **strange** ADJECTIVE
unusual or unexpected
EG *A strange thing happened.*
abnormal EG *an abnormal fear of spiders*
bizarre EG *a bizarre scene*
curious EG *a curious mixture of ancient and modern*
extraordinary EG *an extraordinary occurrence*
funny EG *a funny feeling*
odd EG *There was something odd about her.*

peculiar EG *It tasted very peculiar.*
queer EG *I think there's something a bit queer going on.*
uncommon EG *A 15-year lifespan is not uncommon for a dog.*
weird EG *He's a really weird guy.*

> **WORD POWER**
> Synonyms
> out-of-the-way
> outré
> unaccountable

❷ **strange** ADJECTIVE
new or unfamiliar
EG *alone in a strange country*
alien EG *transplanted into an alien culture*
exotic EG *filmed in an exotic location*
foreign EG *This was a foreign country, so unlike his own.*
new EG *I'm always open to new experiences.*
novel EG *a novel idea*
unfamiliar EG *visiting an unfamiliar city*

❶ **strength** NOUN
physical energy and power
EG *an astonishing display of physical strength*
brawn EG *He's got plenty of brains as well as brawn.*
might EG *the full might of the army*
muscle EG *demonstrating both muscle and skill*
stamina EG *The race requires a lot of stamina.*

> **WORD POWER**
> Synonyms
> brawniness
> lustiness
> sinew
> Antonym
> weakness

❷ **strength** NOUN
the degree of intensity
EG *an indication of the strength of feeling among parents*
force EG *the force of his argument*

intensity EG *the intensity of their emotions*

potency EG *the extraordinary potency of his personality*

power EG *the overwhelming power of love*

vehemence EG *I was surprised by the vehemence of his criticism.*

vigour EG *We resumed the attack with renewed vigour.*

> **WORD POWER**
> Antonym
> weakness

❶ strengthen VERB
to give something more power
EG *This move will strengthen his political standing.*

consolidate EG *to consolidate an already dominant position*

encourage EG *encouraged by the shouts of their supporters*

harden EG *evidence which hardens suspicions about their involvement*

stiffen EG *This only stiffened his resolve to quit.*

toughen EG *new laws to toughen police powers*

> **WORD POWER**
> Synonyms
> fortify
> hearten
> invigorate
> Antonym
> weaken

❷ strengthen VERB
to support the structure of something
EG *The builders had to strengthen the joists with timber.*

bolster EG *steel beams used to bolster the roof*

brace EG *tottering pillars braced by scaffolding*

fortify EG *citadels fortified by high stone walls*

reinforce EG *They had to reinforce the walls with exterior beams.*

support EG *the thick wooden posts*

that supported the ceiling

> **WORD POWER**
> Antonym
> weaken

❶ stress NOUN
worry and nervous tension
EG *the stresses and strains of a busy career*

anxiety EG *Her voice was full of anxiety.*

hassle INFORMAL EG *I don't think it's worth the money or the hassle.*

pressure EG *I felt the pressure of being the first woman in the job.*

strain EG *She was tired and under great strain.*

tension EG *Laughing relieves tension.*

worry EG *It was a time of worry for us.*

❷ stress VERB
to emphasize something
EG *The leaders have stressed their commitment to the talks.*

accentuate EG *make-up which accentuates your best features*

emphasize EG *He flourished his glass to emphasize the point.*

repeat EG *We are not, I repeat not, in the negotiating process.*

underline EG *The report underlined his concern about falling standards.*

> **WORD POWER**
> Synonyms
> belabour
> dwell on
> point up
> underscore

❶ strict ADJECTIVE
very firm in demanding obedience
EG *My parents were very strict.*

authoritarian EG *He has an authoritarian approach to parenthood.*

firm EG *the guiding hand of a firm father figure*

A
B
C
D
E
F
G
H
I
J
K
L
M
N
O
P
Q
R
S
T
U
V
W
X
Y
Z

rigid EG *a rigid hospital routine*
rigorous EG *rigorous military training*
stern EG *Her mother was stern and hard to please.*
stringent EG *stringent rules*

❷ **strict** ADJECTIVE
precise and accurate
EG *He has never been a playboy in the strict sense of the word.*
accurate EG *an accurate record of events*
exact EG *I do not remember the exact words.*
meticulous EG *meticulous attention to detail*
particular EG *very particular dietary requirements*
precise EG *precise instructions*
true EG *a true account*

❶ **strong** ADJECTIVE
having powerful muscles
EG *a strong, robust man*
athletic EG *an athletic build*
brawny EG *a brawny sailor*
burly EG *burly shipyard workers*
muscular EG *Like most athletes, she was lean and muscular.*
powerful EG *a powerful physique*
strapping EG *He was a bricklayer - a big, strapping fellow.*

> **WORD POWER**
> Synonyms
> Herculean
> lusty
> sinewy
> stalwart
> Antonym
> weak

❷ **strong** ADJECTIVE
able to withstand rough treatment
EG *a strong casing, which won't crack or chip*
durable EG *Fine bone china is both strong and durable.*
hard-wearing EG *hard-wearing cotton shirts*

heavy-duty EG *heavy-duty scissors*
reinforced EG *windows of reinforced glass*
sturdy EG *The camera was mounted on a sturdy tripod.*

> **WORD POWER**
> Antonym
> fragile

❸ **strong** ADJECTIVE
great in degree or intensity
EG *Despite strong opposition, she was victorious.*
acute EG *an acute attack of appendicitis*
deep EG *the deep attachment between them*
fervent EG *a fervent hope*
fierce EG *He inspires fierce loyalty in his friends.*
intense EG *intense hatred*
vehement EG *vehement criticism*
violent EG *an outburst of violent emotion*

> **WORD POWER**
> Synonyms
> ardent
> fervid
> Antonym
> faint

❶ **structure** NOUN
the way something is made or organized
EG *the structure of this molecule*
arrangement EG *an intricate arrangement of treadles, rods and cranks*
construction EG *The chairs were light in construction but very strong.*
design EG *The shoes were of good design and good quality.*
make-up EG *the chemical make-up of the oceans and atmosphere*
organization EG *the organization of the economy*

> **WORD POWER**
> Synonyms
> configuration
> conformation

❷ structure NOUN
something that has been built
EG *The museum is an impressive structure.*
building EG *an ugly modern building*
construction EG *an impressive steel and glass construction*
edifice EG *historic edifices in the area*

❶ struggle VERB
to try hard to do something
EG *They had to struggle to make ends meet.*
strain EG *straining to lift heavy weights*
strive EG *He strives hard to keep himself fit.*
toil EG *toiling to make up for lost time*
work EG *I had to work hard for everything I've got.*

❷ struggle NOUN
something that is hard to achieve
EG *Life became a struggle for survival.*
effort EG *It was an effort to finish in time.*
labour EG *weary from their labours*
toil EG *another day of toil and strife*
work EG *It's been hard work, but rewarding.*

stubborn ADJECTIVE
determined not to change or give in
EG *a stubborn character who is used to getting his own way*
dogged EG *his dogged insistence on his rights*
inflexible EG *His opponents viewed him as dogmatic and inflexible.*
obstinate EG *a wicked and obstinate child*
tenacious EG *a tenacious and persistent interviewer*
wilful EG *a headstrong and wilful young lady*

| WORD POWER

Synonyms
intractable
obdurate
recalcitrant
refractory

❶ study VERB
to spend time learning about something
EG *He is studying History and Economics.*
learn EG *I'm learning French.*
read up EG *She spent a year reading up on farming techniques.*
swot BRITISH, AUSTRALIAN, AND NEW ZEALAND INFORMAL EG *swotting for their finals*

❷ study VERB
to look at something carefully
EG *He studied the map in silence.*
contemplate EG *He contemplated his hands, frowning.*
examine EG *He examined her passport and stamped it.*
pore over EG *We spent hours poring over travel brochures.*

WORD POWER
Synonyms
peruse
scrutinize

❸ study NOUN
the activity of learning about a subject
EG *the serious study of medieval architecture*
lessons EG *He was lagging behind in his lessons.*
research EG *funds for research into AIDS*
school work EG *She buried herself in school work.*
swotting BRITISH, AUSTRALIAN, AND NEW ZEALAND INFORMAL EG *She put her success down to last-minute swotting.*

❶ stuffy ADJECTIVE
formal and old-fashioned
EG *his lack of stuffy formality*
dull EG *They are nice people but*

A
B
C
D
E
F
G
H
I
J
K
L
M
N
O
P
Q
R
S
T
U
V
W
X
Y
Z

rather dull.
formal EG *an austere and formal family*
old-fashioned EG *She was condemned as an old-fashioned prude.*
staid EG *He is boring, old-fashioned and staid.*
strait-laced EG *She is very strait-laced and narrow-minded.*

> **WORD POWER**
> Synonyms
> fusty
> old-fogeyish
> priggish
> stodgy

❷ **stuffy** ADJECTIVE
not containing enough fresh air
EG *It was hot and stuffy in the classroom.*
close EG *The atmosphere was close.*
heavy EG *The air was heavy, moist and sultry.*
muggy EG *It was muggy and overcast.*
oppressive EG *The little room was windowless and oppressive.*
stale EG *A layer of smoke hung in the stale air.*
stifling EG *the stifling heat of the room*

> **WORD POWER**
> Synonyms
> frowsty
> sultry
> unventilated

stupid ADJECTIVE
lacking intelligence or good judgment
EG *How could I have been so stupid?*
absurd EG *absurd ideas*
daft INFORMAL EG *That's a daft question.*
dim EG *He is rather dim.*
foolish EG *It is foolish to risk injury.*
idiotic EG *What an idiotic thing to say!*
inane EG *She's always asking inane*

questions.
obtuse EG *It should be obvious even to the most obtuse person.*
thick EG *I must have seemed incredibly thick.*

> **WORD POWER**
> Synonyms
> asinine
> crass
> cretinous
> fatuous
> imbecilic
> moronic
> Antonym
> clever

stupidity NOUN
lack of intelligence or good judgment
EG *I was astonished by his stupidity.*
absurdity EG *the absurdity of the suggestion*
folly EG *the danger and folly of taking drugs*
foolishness EG *He expressed remorse over his own foolishness.*
inanity EG *The inanity of the conversation.*
silliness EG *He sounded quite exasperated by my silliness.*

> **WORD POWER**
> Synonyms
> asininity
> fatuity
> imbecility
> obtuseness

❶ **style** NOUN
the way in which something is done
EG *a dictatorial management style*
approach EG *his blunt approach*
manner EG *a satire in the manner of Dickens*
method EG *a new method of education*
mode EG *a cheap and convenient mode of transport*
technique EG *his driving technique*
way EG *He had a strange way of*

talking.

❷ style NOUN

smartness and elegance
EG *She has not lost her grace and style.*

chic EG *French designer chic*

elegance EG *Princess Grace's understated elegance*

flair EG *dressed with typical Italian flair*

sophistication EG *to add a touch of sophistication to any wardrobe*

taste EG *impeccable taste*

> **WORD POWER**
> Synonyms
> élan
> panache
> savoir-faire

subdue VERB

to bring people under control by force
EG *The government have not been able to subdue the rebels.*

crush EG *ruthless measures to crush the revolt*

defeat EG *an important role in defeating the rebellion*

overcome EG *working to overcome the enemy forces*

overpower EG *The police eventually overpowered him.*

quell EG *tough new measures to quell the disturbances*

vanquish EG *his vanquished foe*

❶ subject NOUN

the thing or person being discussed
EG *They exchanged views on a wide range of subjects.*

issue EG *an issue that had worried him for some time*

matter EG *I don't want to discuss the matter.*

object EG *the object of much heated discussion*

point EG *There is another point to consider.*

question EG *the difficult question*

of unemployment

theme EG *The book's central theme is power.*

topic EG *The weather is a constant topic of conversation.*

❷ subject VERB

to make someone experience something
EG *He was subjected to constant interruptions.*

expose EG *people exposed to high levels of radiation*

put through EG *My husband put me through hell.*

submit EG *The old woman was submitted to a terrifying ordeal.*

substance NOUN

a solid, powder, liquid or gas
EG *Poisonous substances should be labelled as such.*

element EG *a chart of the chemical elements*

fabric EG *Condensation will rot the fabric of the building.*

material EG *an armchair of some resilient plastic material*

stuff EG *the stuff from which the universe is made*

❶ substitute VERB

to use one thing in place of another
EG *You can substitute honey for the sugar.*

exchange EG *exchanging one set of problems for another*

interchange EG *Meat can be interchanged with pulses as a source of protein.*

replace EG *We dug up the concrete and replaced it with grass.*

swap EG *Some hostages were swapped for convicted prisoners.*

switch EG *They switched the tags on the cables.*

❷ substitute NOUN

something used in place of another thing
EG *an artificial substitute for silk*

deputy EG *I can't make it so I'll*

A B C D E F G H I J K L M N O P Q R S T U V W X Y Z

send my deputy.

proxy EG *They must nominate a proxy to vote on their behalf.*

replacement EG *He has nominated Adams as his replacement.*

representative EG *Employees from each department elect a representative.*

surrogate EG *They had expected me to be a surrogate for my sister.*

> **WORD POWER**
> Synonyms
> locum
> locum tenens
> makeshift
> stopgap

subtract VERB
to take one number away from another
EG *If you subtract 3 from 5 you get 2.*

deduct EG *Marks will be deducted for spelling mistakes.*

take away EG *Take away the number you first thought of.*

take from EG *Take the 5% discount from the total amount due.*

> **WORD POWER**
> Antonym
> add

❶ **succeed** VERB
to achieve the result you intend
EG *To succeed, you must learn to overcome obstacles.*

be successful EG *We must help our clubs to be successful in Europe.*

do well EG *Their team did well.*

flourish EG *The business flourished.*

make it INFORMAL EG *It is hard for an English actress to make it in Hollywood.*

prosper EG *His team have always prospered in cup competitions.*

thrive EG *The company has thrived by selling cheap, simple products.*

triumph EG *a symbol of good triumphing over evil*

work EG *The plan worked.*

> **WORD POWER**
> Antonym
> fail

❷ **succeed** VERB
to be the next person to have someone's job
EG *David is almost certain to succeed him as chairman.*

replace EG *the man who replaced him as England skipper*

take over from EG *Last year he took over from Bauman as chief executive.*

successful ADJECTIVE
having achieved what you intended to do
EG *Mr Singh was a highly successful salesman.*

flourishing EG *a flourishing business*

lucrative EG *a lucrative career*

profitable EG *a profitable exchange of ideas*

rewarding EG *a rewarding investment*

thriving EG *a thriving housebuilding industry*

top EG *a top model*

sudden ADJECTIVE
happening quickly and unexpectedly
EG *a sudden cry*

abrupt EG *Her idyllic world came to an abrupt end when her parents died.*

hasty EG *his hasty departure*

quick EG *I had to make a quick decision.*

swift EG *a swift blow to the stomach*

unexpected EG *His death was totally unexpected.*

> **WORD POWER**
> Antonym
> gradual

suffer VERB

to be affected by pain or
something unpleasant
EG *I knew he was suffering some
discomfort.*

bear EG *He bore his trials with
dignity and grace.*

endure EG *The writer endured a
harsh life.*

experience EG *Widows seem to
experience more distress than do
widowers.*

go through EG *I wouldn't like to
go through that again.*

sustain EG *He had sustained
massive facial injuries.*

undergo EG *He had to undergo a
body search.*

sufficient ADJECTIVE
being enough for a purpose
EG *He had sufficient time to prepare
his speech.*

adequate EG *an adequate income*
ample EG *an ample supply of petrol*
enough EG *enough cash to live on*

> **WORD POWER**
> Antonym
> insufficient

suffix NOUN

> **Suffixes:**
> -less
> -like
> -logy *or* -ology
> -ness
> -ward *or* -wards

❶ **suggest** VERB
to mention something as a
possibility or recommendation
EG *Clive suggested going out for tea.*

advise EG *I advise you to keep quiet.*

advocate EG *Mr Jones advocates
longer school days.*

propose EG *And where do you
propose building such a huge thing?*

recommend EG *I have no qualms
about recommending this approach.*

❷ **suggest** VERB
to hint that something is the

case
EG *Reports suggested the factory
would close.*

hint EG *The President hinted that
he might make some changes.*

imply EG *The tone of the report
implied that his death was
inevitable.*

indicate EG *She has indicated that
she may resign.*

insinuate EG *an article which
insinuated that he was lying*

intimate EG *He did intimate that
he is seeking legal action.*

❶ **suggestion** NOUN
an idea mentioned as a
possibility
EG *practical suggestions*

plan EG *The government is being
asked to consider the plan.*

proposal EG *the proposal to do
away with nuclear weapons*

proposition EG *a business
proposition*

recommendation EG *a range of
recommendations for change*

❷ **suggestion** NOUN
a slight indication of something
EG *a suggestion of dishonesty*

hint EG *He showed only the
slightest hint of emotion.*

indication EG *He gave no
indication of remorse.*

insinuation EG *The insinuation is
that I have something to hide.*

intimation EG *He did not give any
intimation that he was going to
resign.*

trace EG *No traces of violence were
found on the body.*

❶ **suit** VERB
to be acceptable
EG *They will only move if it suits
them.*

be acceptable to EG *The name
chosen had to be acceptable to
everyone.*

do EG *A holiday at home will do me
just fine.*

A
B
C
D
E
F
G
H
I
J
K
L
M
N
O
P
Q
R
S
T
U
V
W
X
Y
Z

A
B
C
D
E
F
G
H
I
J
K
L
M
N
O
P
Q
R
S
T
U
V
W
X
Y
Z

please EG *I'll leave when it pleases me and not before.*

satisfy EG *Nothing you can do will satisfy him.*

❷ **suit** VERB
to match something else
EG *The battery can be shaped to suit any device.*

agree EG *His statement agrees with those of the other witnesses.*

conform to EG *designed to conform to the new safety requirements*

correspond EG *a number which corresponds to a horse running in the race*

go with EG *Do these shoes go with this dress?*

match EG *tan slacks with a safari jacket to match*

> **WORD POWER**
> Synonyms
> become
> befit
> harmonize

suitable ADJECTIVE
right or acceptable for a particular purpose
EG *Conditions were not suitable for life to flourish.*

acceptable EG *a mutually acceptable new contract*

appropriate EG *an appropriate outfit for the occasion*

apt EG *an apt name*

fit EG *the suggestion that she is not a fit mother*

fitting EG *a fitting background for her beauty*

proper EG *It was not thought proper for a woman to be on stage.*

right EG *He always said just the right thing.*

satisfactory EG *a satisfactory arrangement*

> **WORD POWER**
> Synonyms
> apposite

befitting
pertinent
seemly
Antonym
unsuitable

sulky ADJECTIVE
showing annoyance by being silent and moody
EG *a sulky adolescent*

huffy EG *What are you being so huffy about?*

moody EG *Her husband had become withdrawn and moody.*

petulant EG *He's just being childish and petulant.*

resentful EG *a resentful workforce*

sullen EG *He lapsed into a sullen silence.*

summary NOUN
a short account of something's main points
EG *a summary of the report*

outline EG *an outline of the proposal*

review EG *a film review*

rundown EG *Here's a rundown of the options.*

summing-up EG *The judge concluded his summing-up.*

synopsis EG *a brief synopsis of the book*

> **WORD POWER**
> Synonyms
> abridgment
> digest
> précis
> recapitulation
> résumé

sum up VERB
to describe briefly
EG *He summed up his weekend in one word: "Disastrous".*

recapitulate EG *Let's just recapitulate the essential points.*

summarize EG *The article can be summarized in three sentences.*

❶ **superior** ADJECTIVE
better than other similar things

eg *superior coffee beans*
better eg *I'd like to move to a better area.*
choice eg *the choicest cuts of meat*
de luxe eg *a de luxe model*
exceptional eg *children with exceptional ability*
first-rate eg *a first-rate thriller*
surpassing eg *her surpassing achievements*
unrivalled eg *colour printing of unrivalled quality*

> **WORD POWER**
> Antonym
> inferior

❷ superior ADJECTIVE
showing pride and self-importance
eg *He stood there looking superior.*
condescending eg *I'm fed up with your condescending attitude.*
disdainful eg *She passed along with a disdainful look.*
haughty eg *He spoke in a haughty tone.*
lofty eg *lofty disdain*
patronizing eg *his patronizing attitude to the homeless*
snobbish eg *a snobbish dislike for their intellectual inferiors*
stuck-up INFORMAL eg *She was a famous actress, but she wasn't a bit stuck-up.*
supercilious eg *His manner is supercilious and arrogant.*

❸ superior NOUN
a person in a higher position than you
eg *his immediate superior*
boss INFORMAL eg *Her boss was very supportive.*
manager eg *His plans found favour with his manager.*
senior eg *He was described by his seniors as a model officer.*
supervisor eg *Each student has a supervisor.*

> **WORD POWER**

> Antonym
> inferior

supervise VERB
to oversee a person or activity
eg *He supervised more than 400 volunteers.*
be in charge of eg *He is in charge of the whole project.*
direct eg *Christopher will direct day-to-day operations.*
have charge of eg *He has charge of a three-acre estate.*
keep an eye on eg *I told you to keep an eye on the children.*
manage eg *I manage a small team of workers.*
oversee eg *an architect to oversee the work*
run eg *Each teacher will run a different workshop.*

> **WORD POWER**
> Synonyms
> preside over
> superintend

❶ supplement VERB
to add to something to improve it
eg *I suggest supplementing your diet with vitamin A.*
add to eg *A good bathroom adds to the value of any house.*
augment eg *a way to augment the family income*
complement eg *an in-work benefit that complements earnings*
reinforce eg *measures which will reinforce their current strengths*
top up eg *compulsory contributions to top up pension schemes*

❷ supplement NOUN
something added to something else
eg *a supplement to their basic pension*
addition eg *an addition to the existing system*
appendix eg *The report includes a*

A
B
C
D
E
F
G
H
I
J
K
L
M
N
O
P
Q
R
S
T
U
V
W
X
Y
Z

A
B
C
D
E
F
G
H
I
J
K
L
M
N
O
P
Q
R
S
T
U
V
W
X
Y
Z

six-page appendix.
complement EG *The photographs are a perfect complement to the text.*
extra EG *an optional extra*

supplies PLURAL NOUN
food or equipment for a particular purpose
EG *I had only two pints of water in my emergency supplies.*
equipment EG *vital medical equipment*
provisions EG *provisions for two weeks*
rations EG *Aid officials said food rations had been distributed.*
stores EG *an important part of a ship's stores*

❶ supply VERB
to provide someone with something
EG *an agreement not to supply chemical weapons*
equip EG *plans for equipping the island with water*
furnish EG *They'll be able to furnish you with the details.*
give EG *We'll give you all the information you need.*
provide EG *They'll provide all the equipment.*

> **WORD POWER**
> Synonyms
> endow
> purvey

❷ supply NOUN
an amount of something available for use
EG *a plentiful supply of vegetables*
cache EG *a cache of weapons and explosives*
fund EG *an extraordinary fund of energy*
hoard EG *a hoard of food and petrol*
reserve EG *The Gulf has 65% of the world's oil reserves.*
stock EG *stocks of paper and ink*
stockpile EG *stockpiles of chemical weapons*

store EG *I have a store of food and water here.*

❶ support VERB
to agree with someone's ideas or aims
EG *We supported his political campaign.*
back EG *a new witness to back his claim*
champion EG *He passionately championed the cause.*
defend EG *He defended all of Clarence's decisions, right or wrong.*
promote EG *He continued to promote the idea of Scottish autonomy.*
second EG *The Prime Minister seconded the call for discipline.*
side with EG *accused of siding with terrorists*
uphold EG *We uphold the capitalist free economy.*

> **WORD POWER**
> Antonym
> oppose

❷ support VERB
to help someone in difficulties
EG *Try to support each other when one of you is feeling down.*
encourage EG *When things aren't going well, he encourages me.*
help EG *He'd do anything to help a friend.*

❸ support VERB
to hold something up from underneath
EG *Thick wooden posts support the ceiling.*
bolster EG *steel beams used to bolster the roof*
brace EG *The roll-over bar braces the car's structure.*
hold up EG *Her legs wouldn't hold her up.*
prop up EG *Use sticks to prop the plants up.*
reinforce EG *They had to reinforce the walls with exterior beams.*

WORD POWER
Synonyms
buttress
shore up

❹ **support** NOUN
an object that holds something
up
EG *the metal supports which hold up
the canvas*
brace EG *He will have to wear a
neck brace for several days.*
foundation EG *the foundation on
which the bridge was built*
pillar EG *the pillars supporting the
roof*
post EG *The device is fixed to a post.*
prop EG *a structural part such as a
beam or prop*

WORD POWER
Synonyms
abutment
stanchion

supporter NOUN
a person who agrees with or
helps someone
EG *He is a strong supporter of the
plan.*
adherent EG *Communism was
gaining adherents in Latin America.*
advocate EG *a strong advocate of
free market policies*
ally EG *a close political ally*
champion EG *a champion of
women's causes*
fan EG *fans of this football club*
follower EG *followers of the Dalai
Lama*
sponsor EG *the first sponsor of
Buddhism in Japan*

WORD POWER
Synonyms
patron
protagonist

❶ **suppress** VERB
to prevent people from doing
something
EG *international attempts to
suppress drug trafficking*

crush EG *a plan to crush the
uprising*
quash EG *It may help to quash
these rumours.*
quell EG *The army moved in to
quell the uprising.*
stamp out EG *steps to stamp out
bullying in schools*
stop EG *measures to stop the trade
in ivory*

❷ **suppress** VERB
to stop yourself from expressing
a feeling or reaction
EG *She barely suppressed a gasp.*
conceal EG *Robert could not
conceal his relief.*
contain EG *He could hardly
contain his rage.*
curb EG *He curbed his temper.*
repress EG *people who repress their
emotions*
restrain EG *unable to restrain her
anger*
smother EG *I smothered a chuckle.*
stifle EG *Miller stifled a yawn and
looked at his watch.*

supreme ADJECTIVE
of the highest degree or rank
EG *They conspired to seize supreme
power.*
chief EG *his chief rival*
foremost EG *the world's foremost
scientists*
greatest EG *the city's greatest
soccer idol*
highest EG *the highest academic
achievement*
leading EG *the world's leading
basketball players*
paramount EG *a factor of
paramount importance*
pre-eminent EG *a pre-eminent
political figure*
principal EG *the principal reason*
top EG *the president's top military
advisers*
ultimate EG *the ultimate
international accolade, the Nobel
Prize*

A
B
C
D
E
F
G
H
I
J
K
L
M
N
O
P
Q
R
S
T
U
V
W
X
Y
Z

A
B
C
D
E
F
G
H
I
J
K
L
M
N
O
P
Q
R
S
T
U
V
W
X
Y
Z

❶ sure ADJECTIVE
having no doubts
EG *She was no longer sure how she felt about him.*

certain EG *certain of getting a place on the team*

clear EG *He is not clear on how he will go about it.*

convinced EG *He is convinced it's your fault.*

definite EG *a definite answer*

positive EG *I'm positive it will happen.*

satisfied EG *We must be satisfied that the treatment is safe.*

> **WORD POWER**
> Antonym
> unsure

❷ sure ADJECTIVE
reliable or definite
EG *a sure sign that something is wrong*

definite EG *a definite advantage*

dependable EG *dependable information*

foolproof EG *a foolproof system*

infallible EG *an infallible eye for detail*

reliable EG *a reliable source*

trustworthy EG *trustworthy reports*

undeniable EG *a sad but undeniable fact*

❶ surprise NOUN
something unexpected
EG *The resignation came as a complete surprise.*

bombshell EG *His departure was a bombshell for the team.*

jolt EG *Henderson was jolted by the news.*

revelation EG *Degas's work had been a revelation to her.*

shock EG *I got a shock when I saw her.*

start EG *You gave me quite a start.*

❷ surprise NOUN
the feeling caused by something unexpected
EG *an exclamation of surprise*

amazement EG *He stared in baffled amazement.*

astonishment EG *"What?" Meg asked in astonishment.*

incredulity EG *The announcement has been met with incredulity.*

wonder EG *Cross shook his head in wonder.*

❸ surprise VERB
to give someone a feeling of surprise
EG *I was surprised by the vehemence of his criticism.*

amaze EG *Most of the cast were amazed by the play's success.*

astonish EG *I was astonished to discover his true age.*

astound EG *He was astounded at the result.*

stagger EG *I was staggered by his reaction.*

stun EG *Audiences were stunned by the film's tragic end.*

take aback EG *Derek was taken aback when a man answered the phone.*

> **WORD POWER**
> Synonyms
> flabbergast
> nonplus

❶ surrender VERB
to agree that the other side has won
EG *We'll never surrender to the terrorists.*

capitulate EG *They had no choice but to capitulate.*

give in EG *She gave in to him on everything.*

submit EG *I refuse to submit to their demands.*

succumb EG *The Minister said his country would never succumb to pressure.*

yield EG *The government had to yield to local opinion.*

❷ surrender VERB

to give something up to
someone else
EG *We have surrendered our
political authority for economic
gain.*
cede EG *After the war, Spain ceded
the island to America.*
give up EG *She is loath to give up
her hard-earned liberty.*
relinquish EG *He does not intend
to relinquish power.*
renounce EG *He renounced his
claim to the throne.*
yield EG *He was obliged to yield
territory to France.*

❸ **surrender** NOUN
a situation in which one side
gives in to the other
EG *unconditional surrender*
capitulation EG *the German
capitulation at the end of the First
World War*
submission EG *The army intends
to starve the city into submission.*

surround VERB
to be all around a person or
thing
EG *He was surrounded by
bodyguards.*
encircle EG *A forty-foot-high
concrete wall encircles the jail.*
enclose EG *The land was enclosed
by a fence.*
encompass EG *the largest lake in
Canada wholly encompassed by a
town*
envelop EG *The rich smell of the
forest enveloped us.*
hem in EG *a valley hemmed in by
mountains*

surroundings PLURAL NOUN
the area and environment
around a person or place
EG *He felt a longing for familiar
surroundings.*
background EG *a fitting
background for her beauty*
environment EG *a safe
environment for marine mammals*

location EG *filmed in an exotic
location*
neighbourhood EG *living in an
affluent neighbourhood*
setting EG *Rome is the perfect
setting for romance.*

> **WORD POWER**
> Synonyms
> environs
> milieu

survive VERB
to live or exist in spite of
difficulties
EG *companies which survived after
the recession*
endure EG *Somehow their
friendship endures.*
last EG *Nothing lasts forever.*
live EG *having lived through the
1930s depression*
outlive EG *They have outlived the
horror of the war.*
pull through EG *He should pull
through okay.*

❶ **suspect** VERB
to think something is likely
EG *I suspect they are secretly
planning to raise taxes.*
believe EG *Police believe the
attacks were carried out by
nationalists.*
feel EG *I somehow feel he was
involved.*
guess EG *As you probably guessed,
I don't like him much.*
suppose EG *The problem is more
complex than he supposes.*

❷ **suspect** VERB
to have doubts about something
EG *He suspected her motives.*
distrust EG *I don't have any
particular reason to distrust them.*
doubt EG *Do you doubt my word?*
mistrust EG *He mistrusts all
journalists.*

❸ **suspect** ADJECTIVE
not to be trusted
EG *a rather suspect holy man*

dodgy BRITISH, AUSTRALIAN, AND NEW ZEALAND INFORMAL EG *a dodgy car dealer*

doubtful EG *These details are of doubtful origin.*

dubious EG *dubious practices*

fishy INFORMAL EG *There's something very fishy about it.*

questionable EG *the questionable motives of politicians*

❶ suspicion NOUN
a feeling of mistrust
EG *I was always regarded with suspicion because of my background.*

distrust EG *an instinctive distrust of authority*

doubt EG *I have my doubts about his ability to govern.*

misgiving EG *His first words filled us with misgiving.*

mistrust EG *a deep mistrust of banks*

scepticism EG *The report has been greeted with scepticism.*

> *WORD POWER*
> Synonyms
> dubiety
> qualm

❷ suspicion NOUN
a feeling that something is true
EG *I have a strong suspicion they are lying.*

hunch EG *Lowe had a hunch he was on to something.*

idea EG *I had an idea that he joined the army later.*

impression EG *I get the impression he's hiding something.*

❶ suspicious ADJECTIVE
feeling distrustful of someone or something
EG *He was rightly suspicious of their motives.*

apprehensive EG *She was apprehensive of strangers.*

distrustful EG *Voters are deeply distrustful of all politicians.*

doubtful EG *At first I was doubtful about their authenticity.*

sceptical EG *Other archaeologists are sceptical about his findings.*

wary EG *Many people are wary of lawyers.*

❷ suspicious ADJECTIVE
causing feelings of distrust
EG *suspicious circumstances*

dodgy BRITISH, AUSTRALIAN, AND NEW ZEALAND INFORMAL EG *He was a bit of a dodgy character.*

doubtful EG *selling something of doubtful quality*

dubious EG *This claim seems to us rather dubious.*

fishy INFORMAL EG *There's something fishy going on here.*

funny EG *There's something funny about him.*

questionable EG *the questionable motives of politicians*

shady INFORMAL EG *shady deals*

suspect EG *The whole affair has been highly suspect.*

swap VERB
to replace one thing for another
EG *Some hostages were swapped for convicted prisoners.*

barter EG *bartering wheat for cotton and timber*

exchange EG *exchanging one set of problems for another*

interchange EG *Meat can be interchanged with pulses as a source of protein.*

switch EG *They switched the tags on the cables.*

trade EG *They traded land for goods and money.*

❶ sweet ADJECTIVE
containing a lot of sugar
EG *a mug of sweet tea*

cloying EG *a cloying apricot chutney*

sugary EG *a sugary meringue pie*

sweetened EG *sweetened shortcrust pastry*

> *WORD POWER*

Antonym
sour

❷ sweet ADJECTIVE
having a pleasant smell
EG *the sweet smell of roses*
aromatic EG *a plant with aromatic leaves*
fragrant EG *fragrant clover*
perfumed EG *perfumed soaps*
sweet-smelling EG *cottage gardens filled with sweet-smelling flowers and herbs*

❸ sweet ADJECTIVE
pleasant-sounding and tuneful
EG *the sweet sounds of children's singing*
harmonious EG *harmonious sounds*
mellow EG *mellow background music*
melodious EG *The melodious tones of the organ echoed around the great cathedral.*
musical EG *He had a soft, musical voice.*
tuneful EG *The band were noted for their tuneful backing vocals.*

WORD POWER
Synonyms
dulcet
euphonious

❹ sweet NOUN
a sweet-tasting thing such as a toffee
EG *His sack was full of packets of sweets.*
candy AMERICAN EG *We were sick after eating some syrupy candies she had made.*
confectionery EG *The company specializes in selling confectionery from all over the world.*
lolly AUSTRALIAN AND NEW ZEALAND EG *avoid feeding him too many lollies*
sweetie EG *She presented him with a jar of his favourite sweeties as a thank-you.*

swerve VERB
to change direction suddenly to avoid hitting something
EG *He swerved to avoid a truck.*
swing EG *The car swung off the road.*
turn EG *He turned sharply to the left.*
veer EG *The vehicle veered out of control.*

symbol NOUN
a design or idea used to represent something
EG *the chemical symbol for mercury*
emblem EG *His badge bore a small yellow hammer-and-sickle emblem.*
figure EG *the figure of a five-pointed star*
logo EG *the company's logo*
mark EG *a mark of identification*
representation EG *This rune is a representation of a spearhead.*
sign EG *a multiplication sign*
token EG *He gave her a ring as a token of his love.*

sympathy NOUN
kindness and understanding towards someone in trouble
EG *My heartfelt sympathy goes out to all the relatives.*
compassion EG *I was impressed by the compassion he showed for a helpless old woman.*
empathy EG *They displayed an admirable understanding of the crime and empathy with the victim.*
pity EG *He showed no pity for his victims.*
understanding EG *I'd like to thank you for your patience and understanding.*

system NOUN
an organized way of doing or arranging something
EG *the advantages of the new system over the old one*
arrangement EG *an intricate arrangement of treadles, rods and cranks*
method EG *the methods employed*

A B C D E F G H I J K L M N O P Q R S T U V W X Y Z

in the study
procedure EG *This is now the
standard procedure.*
routine EG *his daily routine*
structure EG *the structure of local
government*
technique EG *a new technique for*

processing sound

WORD POWER

Synonyms
methodology
modus operandi

tact NOUN
the ability not to offend people
EG *He has handled the affair with great tact.*
delicacy EG *Both countries are behaving with rare delicacy.*
diplomacy EG *It took all Minnelli's diplomacy to get him to return.*
discretion EG *I appreciate your discretion.*
sensitivity EG *The police treated the victims with great sensitivity.*

tactful ADJECTIVE
showing tact
EG *Sorry, that wasn't a very tactful question.*
diplomatic EG *She is very direct. I tend to be more diplomatic.*
discreet EG *They were gossipy and not always discreet.*
sensitive EG *his sensitive handling of the situation*

> **WORD POWER**
> Antonym
> tactless

❶ take VERB
to require something
EG *He takes three hours to get ready.*
demand EG *The task of rebuilding would demand much patience.*
require EG *The race requires a lot of stamina.*

❷ take VERB
to carry something
EG *I'll take these papers home and read them.*
bear FORMAL EG *They bore the hardwood box into the kitchen.*
bring EG *He poured a brandy for Dena and brought it to her.*
carry EG *She carried the shopping from the car.*
convey FORMAL EG *The minibus conveyed us to the city centre.*
ferry EG *A plane arrives to ferry guests to the island.*
fetch EG *Sylvia fetched a towel from the bathroom.*
transport EG *They use tankers to transport the oil to Los Angeles.*

❸ take VERB
to lead someone somewhere
EG *She took me to a Mexican restaurant.*
bring EG *Come to my party and bring a girl with you.*
conduct FORMAL EG *He asked if he might conduct us to the ball.*
escort EG *I escorted him to the door.*
guide EG *a young Egyptologist who guided us through the tombs*
lead EG *She confessed to the killing and led police to his remains.*
usher EG *I ushered him into the office.*

talent NOUN
a natural ability
EG *Both her children have a talent for music.*
ability EG *Her drama teacher spotted her ability.*
aptitude EG *Alan has no aptitude for music.*
capacity EG *people's creative capacities*
flair EG *a dentist with a flair for invention*
genius EG *his genius for chess*
gift EG *a gift for teaching*
knack EG *He's got the knack of getting people to listen.*

❶ talk VERB
to say things
EG *They were talking about American food.*
chat EG *We chatted about old times.*
chatter EG *chattering away in different languages*
converse FORMAL EG *They were conversing in German.*

natter INFORMAL EG *His mother would natter to anyone.*

speak EG *He tried to speak, but she interrupted him.*

❷ **talk** NOUN
a conversation
EG *We had a long talk about her father.*

chat EG *I had a chat with him.*

chatter EG *idle chatter*

conversation EG *We had a long conversation.*

❸ **talk** NOUN
an informal speech
EG *a talk about AIDS*

address EG *an address to the American people*

discourse EG *a lengthy discourse on strategy*

lecture EG *a series of lectures*

sermon EG *a church sermon*

speech EG *He delivered his speech in French.*

> **WORD POWER**
> Synonyms
> disquisition
> oration

tall ADJECTIVE
higher than average
EG *tall buildings*

high EG *a high wall*

lanky EG *He was six foot four, all lanky and leggy.*

lofty EG *lofty ceilings*

soaring EG *the soaring spires of churches like St Peter's*

towering EG *towering cliffs of black granite*

> **WORD POWER**
> Antonym
> short

task NOUN
a job that you have to do
EG *Walker had the task of breaking the bad news.*

assignment EG *written assignments and practical tests*

chore EG *household chores*

duty EG *I carried out my duties conscientiously.*

job EG *He was given the job of tending the fire.*

mission EG *Salisbury sent him on a diplomatic mission to North America.*

undertaking EG *Organizing the show has been a massive undertaking.*

❶ **taste** NOUN
the flavour of something
EG *I like the taste of wine.*

flavour EG *a crumbly texture with a strong flavour*

tang EG *the tang of lemon*

❷ **taste** NOUN
a small amount of food or drink
EG *He swirled the brandy around before taking another small taste.*

bite EG *Chew each mouthful fully before the next bite.*

mouthful EG *She gulped down a mouthful of coffee.*

sip EG *a sip of wine*

❸ **taste** NOUN
a liking for something
EG *a taste for adventure*

appetite EG *his appetite for success*

fondness EG *I've always had a fondness for jewels.*

liking EG *She had a liking for good clothes.*

penchant FORMAL EG *He had a penchant for playing jokes on people.*

> **WORD POWER**
> Synonyms
> partiality
> predilection

❶ **tasteless** ADJECTIVE
having little flavour
EG *The fish was mushy and tasteless.*

bland EG *It tasted bland, like warmed cardboard.*

insipid EG *a rather insipid meal*

WORD POWER
Antonym
tasty

❷ tasteless ADJECTIVE
vulgar and unattractive
EG *a house crammed with tasteless ornaments*
flashy EG *a flashy sports car*
garish EG *garish bright red boots*
gaudy EG *her gaudy floral hat*
tacky INFORMAL EG *tacky holiday souvenirs*
tawdry EG *a tawdry seaside town*
vulgar EG *a very vulgar house*

WORD POWER
Antonym
tasteful

tasty ADJECTIVE
having a pleasant flavour
EG *The food was very tasty.*
appetizing EG *a choice of appetizing dishes*
delicious EG *a wide selection of delicious desserts*
lekker SOUTH AFRICAN SLANG EG *a lekker meal*
luscious EG *luscious fruit*
palatable EG *some very palatable wines*

WORD POWER
Synonyms
flavourful
flavoursome
Antonym
tasteless

❶ tax NOUN
money paid to the government
EG *the tax on new cars*
duty EG *customs duties*
excise EG *These products are excused VAT and excise.*
levy FORMAL EG *an annual motorway levy on all drivers*
tariff EG *America wants to eliminate tariffs on items such as electronics.*

❷ tax VERB

to make heavy demands on someone
EG *They must be told not to tax your patience.*
drain EG *conflicts that drain your energy*
exhaust EG *She has exhausted my sympathy.*
sap EG *The illness sapped his strength.*
strain EG *The volume of flights is straining the air traffic control system.*
stretch EG *The drought there is stretching American resources to their limits.*

teach VERB
to instruct someone how to do something
EG *She taught Julie to read.*
coach EG *He coached the basketball team.*
drill EG *He drills the choir to a high standard.*
educate EG *He was educated at Haslingden Grammar School.*
instruct EG *He instructed family members in nursing techniques.*
school EG *He had been schooled to take over the family business.*
train EG *They train teachers in counselling skills.*
tutor EG *She was tutored at home by her parents.*

teacher NOUN
someone who teaches something
EG *a geography teacher*
coach EG *her drama coach*
don EG *a Cambridge don*
guru EG *a religious guru*
instructor EG *a driving instructor*
lecturer EG *a lecturer in law*
master or **mistress** EG *a retired maths master*
professor EG *a professor of economics*
tutor EG *He surprised his tutors by failing the exam.*

A B C D E F G H I J K L M N O P Q R S **T** U V W X Y Z

A
B
C
D
E
F
G
H
I
J
K
L
M
N
O
P
Q
R
S
T
U
V
W
X
Y
Z

WORD POWER
Synonyms
educator
pedagogue

❶ **team** NOUN
a group of people
EG *the football team*
band EG *a band of rebels*
crew EG *the ship's crew*
gang EG *a gang of workmen*
group EG *The students work in groups.*
side EG *Italy were definitely the better side.*
squad EG *the England under-21 squad*
troupe EG *troupes of travelling actors*

❷ **team** VERB
to work together
EG *A friend suggested that we team up for a working holiday.*
collaborate EG *The two men met and agreed to collaborate.*
cooperate EG *They would cooperate in raising their child.*
join forces EG *The groups joined forces to fight against the ban.*
link up EG *the first time the two armies have linked up*
pair up EG *Men and teenage girls pair up to dance.*
unite EG *The two parties have been trying to unite.*
work together EG *We have always wanted to work together.*

❶ **tear** NOUN
a hole in something
EG *I peered through a tear in the curtains.*
hole EG *the hole in my shoe*
ladder EG *There was a ladder in her tights.*
rip EG *the rip in her new dress*
rupture EG *a rupture in the valve*
scratch EG *I pointed to a number of scratches in the tile floor.*
split EG *the split in his trousers*

❷ **tear** VERB
to make a hole in something
EG *She nearly tore my overcoat.*
ladder EG *after she laddered her tights*
rip EG *I tried not to rip the paper.*
rupture EG *a ruptured appendix*
scratch EG *Knives will scratch the worktop.*
shred EG *They may be shredding documents.*
split EG *I'd split my trousers.*

WORD POWER
Synonyms
rend
sunder

❸ **tear** VERB
to go somewhere in a hurry
EG *He tore through busy streets in a high-speed chase.*
charge EG *He charged through the door.*
dart EG *Ingrid darted across the deserted street.*
dash EG *He dashed upstairs.*
fly EG *She flew to their bedsides when they were ill.*
race EG *He raced across town.*
shoot EG *Another car shot out of a junction.*
speed EG *A low shot sped past Lukic.*
zoom EG *We zoomed through the gallery.*

WORD POWER
Synonyms
bolt
career

tease VERB
to make fun of someone
EG *He used to tease me about wanting to act.*
make fun of EG *The kids at school made fun of me and my Cockney accent.*
mock EG *Don't mock me!*
needle INFORMAL EG *He used to enjoy needling people.*

taunt EG *Other youths taunted him about his clothes.*

tell – tend

❶ tell VERB
to let someone know something
EG *They told us the dreadful news.*
inform EG *My daughter informed me that she was pregnant.*
notify EG *We have notified the police.*

> **WORD POWER**
> Synonyms
> acquaint
> apprise

❷ tell VERB
to give someone an order
EG *A passer-by told the driver to move his car.*
command EG *He commanded his troops to attack.*
direct FORMAL EG *They have been directed to give special attention to the problem.*
instruct EG *The family has instructed solicitors to sue the company.*
order EG *He ordered his men to cease firing.*

> **WORD POWER**
> Synonyms
> call upon
> enjoin

❸ tell VERB
to judge something correctly
EG *I could tell he was scared.*
discern EG *It was hard to discern why this was happening.*
see EG *I could see she was lonely.*

temporary ADJECTIVE
lasting a short time
EG *a temporary loss of memory*
ephemeral EG *a reminder that earthly pleasures are ephemeral*
fleeting EG *a fleeting glimpse*
interim EG *an interim measure*
momentary EG *a momentary lapse*
passing EG *a passing phase*
provisional EG *a provisional*

coalition government
transient EG *Modelling is a transient career.*
transitory EG *the transitory nature of political success*

> **WORD POWER**
> Synonyms
> impermanent
> short-lived
> Antonym
> permanent

tempt VERB
to persuade someone to do something
EG *Children not attending schools may be tempted into crime.*
entice EG *She resisted attempts to entice her into politics.*
lure EG *The company aims to lure smokers back to cigarettes.*
seduce EG *We are seduced into buying all these items.*

❶ tend VERB
to happen usually or often
EG *I tend to forget things.*
be apt EG *She was apt to raise her voice.*
be inclined EG *He was inclined to self-pity.*
be liable EG *equipment that is liable to break*
be prone EG *We know males are more prone to violence.*
have a tendency EG *Shetland jumpers have a tendency to be annoyingly itchy.*

❷ tend VERB
to look after someone or something
EG *the way we tend our cattle*
care for EG *They hired a nurse to care for her.*
look after EG *I love looking after the children.*
nurse EG *In hospital they nursed me back to health.*
take care of EG *There was no one else to take care of the animals.*

A
B
C
D
E
F
G
H
I
J
K
L
M
N
O
P
Q
R
S
T
U
V
W
X
Y
Z

tendency NOUN
behaviour that happens very often
EG *a tendency to be critical*
inclination EG *his artistic inclinations*
leaning EG *their socialist leanings*
propensity EG *his propensity for violence*

> **WORD POWER**
> Synonyms
> predisposition
> proclivity
> proneness

❶ tense ADJECTIVE
nervous and unable to relax
EG *Never had she seen him so tense.*
anxious EG *She had become very anxious and alarmed.*
edgy EG *She was nervous and edgy, still chain-smoking.*
jittery INFORMAL EG *Investors have become jittery about the country's economy.*
jumpy EG *I told myself not to be so jumpy.*
nervous EG *It has made me very nervous about going out.*
uptight INFORMAL EG *Penny never got uptight about exams.*

> **WORD POWER**
> Antonym
> calm

❷ tense ADJECTIVE
causing anxiety
EG *the tense atmosphere at the talks*
anxious EG *They had to wait ten anxious days.*
nerve-racking EG *It was more nerve-racking than taking a World Cup penalty.*
stressful EG *a stressful job*

❸ tense ADJECTIVE
having tight muscles
EG *She lay, eyes shut, body tense.*
rigid EG *Andrew went rigid whenever he saw a dog.*
strained EG *His shoulders were*

strained with effort.
taut EG *when muscles are taut or cold*
tight EG *It is better to stretch the tight muscles first.*

> **WORD POWER**
> Antonym
> relaxed

❶ terrible ADJECTIVE
serious and unpleasant
EG *a terrible illness*
appalling EG *an appalling headache*
awful EG *an awful crime*
desperate EG *a desperate situation*
dreadful EG *a dreadful mistake*
frightful OLD-FASHIONED EG *He got himself into a frightful muddle.*
horrendous EG *horrendous injuries*
horrible EG *a horrible mess*
horrid OLD-FASHIONED EG *What a horrid smell!*
rotten EG *What rotten luck!*

❷ terrible ADJECTIVE
of very poor quality
EG *Paddy's terrible haircut*
abysmal EG *The standard of play was abysmal.*
appalling EG *Her singing is appalling.*
awful EG *Jeans look awful on me.*
dire EG *Most of the poems were dire.*
dreadful EG *My financial situation is dreadful.*
horrible EG *a horrible meal*
rotten EG *I think it's a rotten idea.*

> **WORD POWER**
> Antonym
> excellent

❶ test VERB
to find out what something is like
EG *travelling to Holland to test a British-built boat*
assess EG *The test was to assess aptitude rather than academic achievement.*

check EG *It's worth checking each item for obvious flaws.*
try EG *Howard wanted me to try the wine.*
try out EG *London Transport hopes to try out the system in September.*

❷ **test** NOUN
an attempt to test something
EG *the banning of nuclear tests*
assessment EG *He was remanded for assessment by doctors.*
check EG *regular checks on his blood pressure*
trial EG *clinical trials*

texture NOUN
the way that something feels
EG *Her skin is pale, the texture of fine wax.*
consistency EG *Mix the dough to the right consistency.*
feel EG *Linen raincoats have a crisp, papery feel.*

theft NOUN
the crime of stealing
EG *the theft of classified documents*
robbery EG *The man was serving a sentence for robbery.*
stealing EG *She was jailed for six months for stealing.*
thieving EG *an ex-con who says he's given up thieving*

> **WORD POWER**
> Synonyms
> larceny
> pilfering

theory NOUN
an idea that explains something
EG *Darwin's theory of evolution*
conjecture EG *That was a conjecture, not a fact.*
hypothesis EG *Different hypotheses have been put forward.*
supposition EG *As with many such suppositions, no one had ever tested it.*
surmise FORMAL EG *His surmise proved correct.*

thesaurus NOUN

Parts of a dictionary or thesaurus:
antonym
definition
entry
example
homonym
homophone
pronunciation
root word
synonym
word derivation

❶ **thick** ADJECTIVE
measuring a large distance from side to side
EG *a thick stone wall*
fat EG *a fat book*
wide EG *a desk that was almost as wide as the room*

> **WORD POWER**
> Antonym
> thin

❷ **thick** ADJECTIVE
containing little water
EG *thick soup*
clotted EG *clotted cream*
concentrated EG *a glass of concentrated orange juice*
condensed EG *tins of condensed milk*

> **WORD POWER**
> Antonym
> watery

❸ **thick** ADJECTIVE
grouped closely together
EG *thick dark hair*
bristling EG *a bristling moustache*
dense EG *a large dense forest*
lush EG *the lush green meadows*
luxuriant EG *the luxuriant foliage of Young Island*

> **WORD POWER**
> Antonym
> sparse

thicken VERB
to become thicker
EG *The clouds thickened.*

A B C D E F G H I J K L M N O P Q R S T U V W X Y Z

A
B
C
D
E
F
G
H
I
J
K
L
M
N
O
P
Q
R
S
T
U
V
W
X
Y
Z

clot EG *The patient's blood refused to clot.*
condense EG *Water vapour condenses to form clouds.*
congeal EG *The blood had started to congeal.*
set EG *as the jelly starts to set*

> **WORD POWER**
> Synonyms
> coagulate
> jell
> Antonym
> thin

thief NOUN
someone who steals something
EG *a car thief*
burglar EG *Burglars broke into their home.*
crook INFORMAL EG *a petty crook*
mugger INFORMAL EG *after being threatened by a mugger*
pickpocket EG *a gang of pickpockets*
robber EG *armed robbers*
shoplifter EG *a persistent shoplifter*

> **WORD POWER**
> Synonyms
> housebreaker
> pilferer

❶ **thin** ADJECTIVE
measuring a small distance from side to side
EG *The material was too thin.*
fine EG *the fine hairs on her arms*
narrow EG *a narrow strip of land*
slim EG *a slim volume of verse*

> **WORD POWER**
> Antonym
> thick

❷ **thin** ADJECTIVE
not carrying a lot of fat
EG *a tall, thin man with grey hair*
bony EG *bony hands*
emaciated EG *emaciated prisoners*
lean EG *Like most athletes, she was lean and muscular.*

scrawny EG *a scrawny woman*
skinny EG *a skinny little boy*
slender EG *a tall slender woman*
slight EG *She is smaller and slighter than Christie.*
slim EG *The young woman was tall and slim.*
spare EG *She was thin and spare with not an ounce of excess fat.*

> **WORD POWER**
> Synonyms
> skeletal
> spindly
> undernourished
> underweight
> Antonym
> fat

❸ **thin** ADJECTIVE
containing a lot of water
EG *thin soup*
dilute or **diluted** EG *a dilute solution of bleach*
runny EG *a runny soft cheese*
watery EG *watery beer*
weak EG *a cup of weak tea*

> **WORD POWER**
> Antonym
> thick

thing NOUN
a physical object
EG *What's that thing doing here?*
article EG *household articles*
object EG *everyday objects such as wooden spoons*

things PLURAL NOUN
someone's clothes or belongings
EG *Sara told him to take all his things with him.*
belongings EG *He was identified only by his personal belongings.*
effects EG *His daughters were collecting his effects.*
gear EG *They helped us put our gear back into the van.*
possessions EG *People had lost all their possessions.*
stuff EG *Where have you put all your stuff?*

A B C D E F G H I J K L M N O P Q R S T U V W X Y Z

❶ think VERB
to consider something
EG *Let's think what we can do next.*
consider EG *The government is being asked to consider the plan.*
contemplate EG *He cried as he contemplated his future.*
deliberate EG *She deliberated over the decision for a good few years.*
meditate EG *He meditated on the problem.*
mull over EG *I'll leave you alone so you can mull it over.*
muse LITERARY EG *Many of the papers muse on the fate of the President.*
ponder EG *I'm continually pondering how to improve the team.*
reflect EG *I reflected on the child's future.*

> *WORD POWER*
> Synonyms
> cogitate
> ruminate

❷ think VERB
to believe something
EG *I think she has a secret boyfriend.*
believe EG *Experts believe that the drought will be extensive.*
consider EG *He considers that this is the worst recession this century.*
deem FORMAL EG *Many people have ideas that their society deems to be dangerous.*
hold EG *The theory holds that minor events are the trigger for larger events.*
imagine EG *I imagine he was just showing off.*
judge EG *He judged that this was the moment to say what had to be said.*
reckon EG *Toni reckoned that it must be about three o'clock.*

thorough ADJECTIVE
careful and complete
EG *a thorough examination*
complete EG *a complete overhaul of the engine*

comprehensive EG *a comprehensive guide to the region*
exhaustive EG *exhaustive enquiries*
full EG *Mr Primakov gave a full account of his meeting with the President.*
intensive EG *four weeks of intensive study*
meticulous EG *A happy wedding day requires meticulous planning.*
painstaking EG *a painstaking search*
scrupulous EG *Observe scrupulous hygiene when preparing and cooking food.*

> *WORD POWER*
> Synonyms
> all-embracing
> in-depth

❶ thought NOUN
an idea or opinion
EG *his thoughts on love*
idea EG *his ideas about democracy*
notion EG *We each have a notion of what kind of person we'd like to be.*
opinion EG *most of those who expressed an opinion*
view EG *Make your views known to your MP.*

❷ thought NOUN
the activity of thinking
EG *After much thought I decided to end my marriage.*
consideration EG *There should be careful consideration of the BBC's future role.*
contemplation EG *He was lost in contemplation of the landscape.*
deliberation EG *the result of lengthy deliberation*
meditation EG *He stared at the floor, lost in meditation.*
reflection EG *after days of reflection*
thinking EG *THis is definitely a time for decisive action and quick thinking.*

A
B
C
D
E
F
G
H
I
J
K
L
M
N
O
P
Q
R
S
T
U
V
W
X
Y
Z

> **WORD POWER**
> Synonyms
> cogitation
> introspection
> rumination

❶ thoughtful ADJECTIVE
quiet and serious
EG *He was looking very thoughtful.*
contemplative EG *a quiet, contemplative sort of chap*
pensive EG *He looked unusually pensive before the start.*
reflective EG *I walked on in a reflective mood.*

> **WORD POWER**
> Synonyms
> introspective
> meditative
> ruminative

❷ thoughtful ADJECTIVE
showing consideration for others
EG *a thoughtful and caring man*
attentive EG *an attentive husband*
caring EG *a caring son*
considerate EG *the most considerate man I've ever known*
kind EG *She is warmhearted and kind to everyone.*

> **WORD POWER**
> Synonyms
> solicitous
> unselfish
> Antonym
> thoughtless

thoughtless ADJECTIVE
showing a lack of consideration
EG *It was thoughtless of her to mention it.*
insensitive EG *My husband is very insensitive about my problem.*
tactless EG *a tactless remark*

> **WORD POWER**
> Synonyms
> inconsiderate
> undiplomatic
> Antonym
> thoughtful

❶ threat NOUN
a statement that someone will harm you
EG *death threats*
menace EG *demanding money with menaces*
threatening remark EG *He was overheard making threatening remarks to the couple.*

❷ threat NOUN
something that seems likely to harm you
EG *the threat of tropical storms*
hazard EG *a health hazard*
menace EG *a menace to the public*
risk EG *a fire risk*

❶ threaten VERB
to promise to do something bad
EG *He threatened her with a knife.*
make threats to EG *despite all the threats he'd made to harm her*
menace EG *She's being menaced by her sister's latest boyfriend.*

❷ threaten VERB
to be likely to cause harm
EG *The newcomers threaten the livelihood of the workers.*
endanger EG *Toxic waste could endanger lives.*
jeopardize EG *He has jeopardized the future of his government.*
put at risk EG *If they have the virus, they are putting patients at risk.*
put in jeopardy EG *A series of setbacks have put the whole project in jeopardy.*

thrifty ADJECTIVE
careful not to waste money or resources
EG *Britain become a nation of thrifty consumers and bargain hunters.*
careful EG *He's very careful with his money.*
economical EG *a very economical way to travel*
frugal EG *a frugal lifestyle*
prudent EG *the need for a much*

more prudent use of energy

❶ thrill NOUN
a feeling of excitement
EG *the thrill of waking up on Christmas morning*
high INFORMAL EG *the high of a win over New Zealand*
kick INFORMAL EG *I got a kick out of seeing my name in print.*

❷ thrill VERB
to cause a feeling of excitement
EG *It thrilled me to see her looking so happy.*
excite EG *I only take on work that excites me.*
give a kick INFORMAL EG *It gave me a kick to actually meet her.*

thrive VERB
to be successful
EG *His company continues to thrive.*
do well EG *Connie did well at school.*
flourish EG *Racism and crime still flourish in the ghetto.*
prosper EG *His team have always prospered in cup competitions.*

throw VERB
to make something move through the air
EG *throwing a tennis ball against a wall*
cast EG *He cast the stone away.*
chuck INFORMAL EG *He chucked the paper in the bin.*
fling EG *Peter flung his shoes into the corner.*
hurl EG *Groups of angry youths hurled stones at police.*
lob EG *Thugs lobbed a grenade into the crowd.*
pitch EG *Simon pitched the empty bottle into the lake.*
sling EG *He took off his anorak and slung it into the back seat.*
toss EG *She tossed her suitcase onto one of the beds.*

thug NOUN
a very violent person
EG *a gang of armed thugs*
bandit EG *terrorist acts carried out by bandits*
hooligan EG *severe measures against soccer hooligans*
tough EG *The neighbourhood toughs beat them both up.*
tsotsi SOUTH AFRICAN EG *Many are too terrified of local tsotsis to protest.*

❶ tidy ADJECTIVE
arranged in an orderly way
EG *a tidy desk*
neat EG *She put her clothes in a neat pile.*
orderly EG *a beautiful, clean and orderly city*

> **WORD POWER**
> Synonyms
> shipshape
> spick-and-span
> Antonym
> untidy

❷ tidy VERB
to make something neat
EG *He tidied his garage.*
spruce up EG *Many buildings have been spruced up.*
straighten EG *straightening cushions and organizing magazines*

> **WORD POWER**
> Antonym
> mess up

❶ tie VERB
to fasten something
EG *They tied the ends of the bag securely.*
bind EG *Bind the ends of the cord together with thread.*
fasten EG *instructions on how to fasten the strap to the box*
knot EG *He knotted the laces securely together.*
lash EG *The shelter is built by lashing poles together.*
rope EG *I roped myself to the chimney.*
secure EG *He secured the canvas*

A
B
C
D
E
F
G
H
I
J
K
L
M
N
O
P
Q
R
S
T
U
V
W
X
Y
Z

straps as tight as they would go.
tether EG *tethering his horse to a tree*
truss EG *She trussed him quickly with stolen bandage.*

> **WORD POWER**
> Antonym
> untie

❷ tie VERB
to have the same score
EG *Rafferty tied with Nobilo.*
be level EG *At the end of 90 minutes the teams were level.*
draw EG *Holland and Ireland drew 1-1.*

❸ tie NOUN
a connection with something
EG *I had very close ties with the family.*
affiliation EG *They asked her what her political affiliations were.*
affinity EG *He has a close affinity with the landscape.*
bond EG *The experience created a special bond between us.*
connection EG *The police say he had no connection with the security forces.*
relationship EG *family relationships*

❶ tight ADJECTIVE
fitting closely
EG *The shoes are too tight.*
constricted EG *His throat began to feel swollen and constricted.*
cramped EG *families living in cramped conditions*
snug EG *a snug black T-shirt*

> **WORD POWER**
> Antonym
> loose

❷ tight ADJECTIVE
firmly fastened
EG *a tight knot*
firm EG *He managed to get a firm grip of it.*
secure EG *Check joints are secure*

and the wood is sound.

❸ tight ADJECTIVE
not slack or relaxed
EG *Pull the elastic tight.*
rigid EG *I went rigid with shock.*
taut EG *The clothes line is pulled taut and secured.*
tense EG *A bath can relax tense muscles.*

> **WORD POWER**
> Antonym
> slack

❶ tilt VERB
to raise one end of something
EG *Leonard tilted his chair back on two legs.*
incline EG *Jack inclined his head.*
lean EG *Lean the plants against a wall.*
slant EG *The floor slanted down to the window.*
slope EG *The bank sloped down sharply to the river.*
tip EG *She had to tip her head back to see him.*

> **WORD POWER**
> Synonyms
> cant
> list

❷ tilt NOUN
a raised position
EG *the tilt of the earth's axis*
angle EG *The boat is now leaning at a 30 degree angle.*
gradient EG *a gradient of 1 in 3*
incline EG *at the edge of a steep incline*
slant EG *The house is on a slant.*
slope EG *The street must have been on a slope.*

> **WORD POWER**
> Synonyms
> camber
> list

❶ time NOUN
a particular period
EG *I enjoyed my time in Durham.*

interval EG *a long interval of silence*
period EG *a period of calm*
spell EG *a brief spell teaching*
stretch EG *an 18-month stretch in the army*
while EG *They walked on in silence for a while.*

❷ time VERB
to plan when something will happen
EG *We had timed our visit for March 7.*
schedule EG *The space shuttle had been scheduled to blast off at 04:38.*
set EG *A court hearing has been set for December 16.*

timid ADJECTIVE
lacking courage or confidence
EG *a timid child*
bashful EG *Offstage, he is bashful and awkward.*
cowardly EG *I was too cowardly to complain.*
diffident EG *Helen was diffident and reserved.*
nervous EG *a very nervous woman*
shy EG *a shy, quiet-spoken girl*

WORD POWER
Synonyms
faint-hearted
pusillanimous
timorous
Antonym
bold

tiny ADJECTIVE
very small
EG *The living room is tiny.*
diminutive EG *a diminutive figure standing at the entrance*
microscopic EG *a microscopic amount of the substance*
miniature EG *He looked like a miniature version of his brother.*
minute EG *Only a minute amount is needed.*
negligible EG *The pay that the soldiers received was negligible.*

wee SCOTTISH EG *a wee boy*

WORD POWER
Synonyms
infinitesimal
Lilliputian
Antonym
huge

tire VERB
to use a lot of energy
EG *If driving tires you, take the train.*
drain EG *My emotional turmoil had drained me.*
exhaust EG *Walking in deep snow had totally exhausted him.*
fatigue EG *He is easily fatigued.*

WORD POWER
Synonyms
enervate
wear out
weary

tired ADJECTIVE
having little energy
EG *She was too tired to take a shower.*
drained EG *as United stalked off, stunned and drained*
drowsy EG *He felt pleasantly drowsy.*
exhausted EG *She was too exhausted and distressed to talk.*
fatigued EG *Winter weather can leave you feeling fatigued.*
sleepy EG *I was beginning to feel sleepy.*
tuckered out AUSTRALIAN AND NEW ZEALAND INFORMAL EG *You must be tuckered out after that bus trip.*
weary EG *a weary traveller*
worn out EG *He's just worn out after the drive.*

❶ together ADVERB
with other people
EG *We went on long bicycle rides together.*
collectively EG *The Cabinet is collectively responsible for policy.*
en masse EG *The people marched en masse.*

A B C D E F G H I J K L M N O P Q R S T U V W X Y Z

495

in unison EG *Michael and the landlady nodded in unison.*

jointly EG *an agency jointly run by New York and New Jersey*

shoulder to shoulder EG *They could fight shoulder to shoulder against a common enemy.*

side by side EG *areas where different nationalities live side by side*

❷ together ADVERB
at the same time
EG *Three horses crossed the finish line together.*

as one EG *The 40,000 crowd rose as one.*

at once EG *You can't do two things at once.*

concurrently EG *There were three races running concurrently.*

simultaneously EG *The two guns fired almost simultaneously.*

with one accord EG *With one accord they turned and walked back.*

❶ tolerable ADJECTIVE
able to be tolerated
EG *The pain was tolerable.*

acceptable EG *a mutually acceptable new contract*

bearable EG *A cool breeze made the heat bearable.*

> **WORD POWER**
> Antonym
> unbearable

❷ tolerable ADJECTIVE
fairly satisfactory
EG *a tolerable salary*

acceptable EG *We've made an acceptable start.*

adequate EG *The level of service was adequate.*

okay or **OK** INFORMAL EG *For a fashionable restaurant like this the prices are okay.*

passable EG *Ms Campbell speaks passable French.*

reasonable EG *able to make a reasonable living from his writing*

so-so INFORMAL EG *Their lunch was only so-so.*

tolerant ADJECTIVE
accepting of different views and behaviour
EG *more tolerant attitudes to unmarried couples having children*

broad-minded EG *a very fair and broad-minded man*

liberal EG *She is known to have liberal views on divorce.*

open-minded EG *I am very open-minded about that question.*

understanding EG *Fortunately for John, he had an understanding wife.*

> **WORD POWER**
> Synonyms
> forbearing
> latitudinarian
> Antonym
> narrow-minded

❶ tolerate VERB
to accept something you disagree with
EG *We will not tolerate such behaviour.*

accept EG *Urban dwellers often accept noise as part of city life.*

put up with EG *You're late again and I won't put up with it.*

❷ tolerate VERB
to accept something unpleasant
EG *She can no longer tolerate the position that she's in.*

bear EG *He can't bear to talk about it.*

endure EG *unable to endure the pain*

stand EG *He can't stand me smoking.*

tomb NOUN
a burial chamber
EG *Carter discovered Tutankhamun's tomb.*

grave EG *They used to visit her grave twice a year.*

mausoleum EG *the elaborate*

mausoleums of the Paris cemetery
sarcophagus EG *an Egyptian sarcophagus*
sepulchre LITERARY EG *the ornate lid of the sepulchre*
vault EG *the family vault*

tool NOUN
a hand-held instrument for doing a job
EG *The best tool for the purpose is a pair of shears.*
implement EG *knives and other useful implements*
instrument EG *instruments for cleaning and polishing teeth*
utensil EG *cooking utensils*

❶ **top** NOUN
the highest part of something
EG *I waited at the top of the stairs.*
crest EG *the crest of the hill*
head EG *A different name was placed at the head of the chart.*
height EG *at the height of his career*
peak EG *at the peak of the morning rush hour*
pinnacle EG *the pinnacle of sporting achievement*
summit EG *the summit of the mountain*
zenith LITERARY EG *His career is now at its zenith.*

> **WORD POWER**
> Synonyms
> acme
> apex
> apogee
> **Antonym**
> bottom

❷ **top** NOUN
the lid of a container
EG *a bottle top*
cap EG *She unscrewed the cap of her water bottle.*
lid EG *the lid of the jar*

❸ **top** VERB
to be greater than something
EG *The temperature topped 90 degrees.*

exceed EG *Its research budget exceeds $700 million a year.*
surpass EG *He was determined to surpass the achievements of his brothers.*

❶ **total** NOUN
several things added together
EG *The companies have a total of 1776 employees.*
aggregate EG *three successive defeats by an aggregate of 12 goals*
sum EG *the sum of all the angles*
whole EG *taken as a percentage of the whole*

❷ **total** ADJECTIVE
complete in all its parts
EG *a total failure*
absolute EG *absolute beginners*
complete EG *a complete mess*
out-and-out EG *an out-and-out lie*
outright EG *an outright rejection of the deal*
unconditional EG *unconditional surrender*
undivided EG *You have my undivided attention.*
unmitigated EG *an unmitigated failure*
unqualified EG *an unqualified success*
utter EG *utter nonsense*

> **WORD POWER**
> Synonyms
> all-out
> thoroughgoing

❸ **total** VERB
to reach the sum of
EG *Their debts totalled over 300,000 dollars.*
add up to EG *Profits can add up to millions of dollars.*
amount to EG *Spending on sports-related items amounted to £9.75 billion.*
come to EG *That comes to over a thousand pounds.*

❶ **touch** VERB
to put your hand on something

A
B
C
D
E
F
G
H
I
J
K
L
M
N
O
P
Q
R
S
T
U
V
W
X
Y
Z

A
B
C
D
E
F
G
H
I
J
K
L
M
N
O
P
Q
R
S
T
U
V
W
X
Y
Z

EG *Don't touch that dial.*

feel EG *The doctor felt his head.*

finger EG *He fingered the few coins in his pocket.*

handle EG *Wear rubber gloves when handling cat litter.*

❷ touch VERB
to come into contact with
EG *Annie lowered her legs until her feet touched the floor.*

brush EG *Something brushed against her leg.*

graze EG *A bullet had grazed his arm.*

meet EG *when the wheels meet the ground*

❸ touch VERB
to emotionally affect someone
EG *I was touched by his kindness.*

affect EG *Jazza was badly affected by his divorce.*

move EG *These stories surprised and moved me.*

stir EG *She stirred something very deep in me.*

touching ADJECTIVE
causing sadness or sympathy
EG *a touching tale*

affecting LITERARY EG *an affecting memorial to Countess Rachel*

moving EG *It was a moving moment for Marianne.*

poignant EG *a poignant love story*

touchy ADJECTIVE
easily upset
EG *She is very touchy about her past.*

easily offended EG *viewers who are easily offended*

sensitive EG *Young people are very sensitive about their appearance.*

toey NEW ZEALAND SLANG EG *Don't be so toey.*

> **WORD POWER**
> Synonyms
> oversensitive
> thin-skinned

❶ tough ADJECTIVE
able to put up with hardship

EG *She is tough and ambitious.*

hardened EG *hardened criminals*

hardy EG *a hardy race of pioneers*

resilient EG *a good soldier, calm and resilient*

robust EG *Perhaps men are more robust than women?*

rugged EG *Rugged individualism forged America's frontier society.*

strong EG *Eventually I felt strong enough to look at him.*

❷ tough ADJECTIVE
difficult to break or damage
EG *beans with a rather tough outer skin*

durable EG *Fine bone china is both strong and durable.*

hard-wearing EG *hard-wearing cotton shirts*

leathery EG *leathery skin*

resilient EG *an armchair of some resilient plastic material*

robust EG *very robust machinery*

rugged EG *You need a rugged, four-wheel drive vehicle.*

solid EG *The car feels very solid.*

strong EG *a strong casing, which won't crack or chip*

sturdy EG *The camera was mounted on a sturdy tripod.*

> **WORD POWER**
> Antonym
> fragile

❸ tough ADJECTIVE
full of hardship
EG *She had a pretty tough childhood.*

arduous EG *an arduous journey*

difficult EG *We're living in difficult times.*

exacting EG *an exacting task*

hard EG *a hard life*

> **WORD POWER**
> Antonym
> easy

❶ trace VERB
to look for and find something
EG *Police are trying to trace the*

owner.
locate EG *We've simply been unable to locate him.*
track down EG *She had spent years trying to track down her parents.*

❷ **trace** NOUN
a sign of something
EG *No trace of his father had been found.*
evidence EG *He'd seen no evidence of fraud.*
hint EG *I saw no hint of irony on her face.*
indication EG *He gave no indication of remorse.*
record EG *There's no record of any marriage or children.*
sign EG *Sally waited for any sign of illness.*
suggestion EG *a faint suggestion of a tan*
whiff EG *Not a whiff of scandal has ever tainted his private life.*

❸ **trace** NOUN
a small amount of something
EG *to write without a trace of sensationalism*
dash EG *a story with a dash of mystery*
drop EG *a drop of sherry*
remnant EG *Beneath the present church were remnants of Roman flooring.*
suspicion EG *large blooms of white with a suspicion of pale pink*
tinge EG *Could there have been a slight tinge of envy in Eva's voice?*
touch EG *a touch of flu*
vestige EG *the last vestige of a UN force that once numbered 30,000*

> **WORD POWER**
> Synonyms
> iota
> jot
> soupçon

❶ **trade** NOUN
the buying and selling of goods
EG *foreign trade*
business EG *a career in business*
commerce EG *They have made their fortunes from industry and commerce.*

❷ **trade** NOUN
the kind of work someone does
EG *He learnt his trade as a diver in the North Sea.*
business EG *the music business*
line EG *Are you in the publishing line too?*
line of work EG *In my line of work I often get home too late for dinner.*
occupation EG *her new occupation as an author*
profession EG *Harper was a teacher by profession.*

❸ **trade** VERB
to buy and sell goods
EG *They had years of experience of trading with the West.*
deal EG *They deal in antiques.*
do business EG *the different people who did business with me*
traffic EG *those who traffic in illegal drugs*

trader NOUN
someone who trades in goods
EG *a timber trader*
broker EG *a financial broker*
dealer EG *dealers in commodities*
merchant EG *a wine merchant*

tradition NOUN
a long-standing custom
EG *the rich traditions of Afro-Cuban music*
convention EG *It's just a social convention that men don't wear skirts.*
custom EG *an ancient Japanese custom*

traditional ADJECTIVE
existing for a long time
EG *her traditional Indian dress*
conventional EG *conventional family planning methods*
established EG *the established*

A B C D E F G H I J K L M N O P Q R S **T** U V W X Y Z

church

WORD POWER
Antonym
unconventional

tragic ADJECTIVE
very sad
EG *a tragic accident*
distressing EG *distressing news*
heartbreaking EG *a heartbreaking succession of miscarriages*
heart-rending EG *heart-rending pictures of refugees*

transparent ADJECTIVE
able to be seen through
EG *a sheet of transparent plastic*
clear EG *a clear glass panel*
crystalline LITERARY EG *crystalline lakes*
sheer EG *a sheer black shirt*
translucent EG *translucent corrugated plastic*

WORD POWER
Synonyms
diaphanous
see-through
Antonym
opaque

❶ transport NOUN
the moving of goods and people
EG *The prices quoted include transport costs.*
removal EG *the furniture removal business*
shipment EG *transported to the docks for shipment overseas*
transportation EG *the transportation of refugees*

❷ transport VERB
to move people or goods somewhere
EG *They use tankers to transport the oil to Los Angeles.*
carry EG *The ship could carry seventy passengers.*
convey FORMAL EG *a branch line to convey fish direct to Billingsgate*

ship EG *the food being shipped to Iraq*
transfer EG *She was transferred to another hospital.*

❶ trap NOUN
a device for catching animals
EG *a rabbit trap*
net EG *a fishing net*
snare EG *a snare for catching birds*

❷ trap VERB
to catch animals
EG *The locals were encouraged to trap and kill the birds.*
catch EG *an animal caught in a trap*
corner EG *like a cornered rat*
snare EG *He'd snared a rabbit earlier in the day.*

❸ trap VERB
to trick someone
EG *Were you trying to trap her into making some admission?*
dupe EG *a plot to dupe stamp collectors into buying fake rarities*
trick EG *His family tricked him into going to Pakistan.*

WORD POWER
Synonyms
ensnare
entrap

❶ trash NOUN
waste material
EG *He picks up your trash on Mondays.*
garbage EG *rotting piles of garbage*
refuse EG *a weekly collection of refuse*
rubbish EG *They had piled most of their rubbish into yellow skips.*
waste EG *a law that regulates the disposal of waste*

❷ trash NOUN
something of poor quality
EG *Don't read that awful trash.*
garbage INFORMAL EG *He spends his time watching garbage on TV.*
rubbish EG *He described her book as absolute rubbish.*

travel VERB
to make a journey somewhere
EG *You had better travel to Helsinki tomorrow.*
go EG *We went to Rome.*
journey FORMAL EG *He intended to journey up the Amazon.*
make your way EG *He made his way home at last.*
take a trip EG *We intend to take a trip there sometime.*

> **WORD POWER**
> Synonyms
> proceed
> voyage

❶ **treacherous** ADJECTIVE
likely to betray someone
EG *He denounced the party's treacherous leaders.*
disloyal EG *disloyal Cabinet colleagues*
faithless EG *an oppressive father and faithless husband*
unfaithful EG *his unfaithful wife*
untrustworthy EG *Jordan has tried to brand his opponents as untrustworthy.*

> **WORD POWER**
> Synonyms
> perfidious
> traitorous
> Antonym
> loyal

❷ **treacherous** ADJECTIVE
dangerous or unreliable
EG *treacherous mountain roads*
dangerous EG *a dangerous stretch of road*
hazardous EG *hazardous seas*
perilous LITERARY EG *The roads grew even steeper and more perilous.*

treasure VERB
to consider something very precious
EG *He treasures his friendship with her.*
cherish EG *The previous owners had cherished the house.*

hold dear EG *forced to renounce everything he held most dear*
prize EG *one of the gallery's most prized possessions*
value EG *if you value your health*

> **WORD POWER**
> Synonyms
> revere
> venerate

❶ **treat** VERB
to behave towards someone
EG *Artie treated most women with indifference.*
act towards EG *the way you act towards other people*
behave towards EG *He always behaved towards me with great kindness.*
deal with EG *in dealing with suicidal youngsters*

❷ **treat** VERB
to give someone medical care
EG *the doctor who treated her*
care for EG *They hired a nurse to care for her.*
nurse EG *All the years he was sick my mother had nursed him.*

tribute NOUN
something that shows admiration
EG *Police paid tribute to her courage.*
accolade FORMAL EG *To play for your country is the ultimate accolade.*
compliment EG *We consider it a compliment to be called "conservative".*
honour EG *Only two writers are granted the honour of a solo display.*
praise EG *That is high praise indeed.*
testimony EG *a testimony to her dedication*

❶ **trick** NOUN
something that deceives someone
EG *We are playing a trick on a man who keeps bothering me.*

A
B
C
D
E
F
G
H
I
J
K
L
M
N
O
P
Q
R
S
T
U
V
W
X
Y
Z

con INFORMAL EG *Slimming snacks that offer miraculous weight loss are a con.*
deception EG *the victim of a cruel deception*
hoax EG *a bomb hoax*
ploy EG *a cynical marketing ploy*
ruse EG *This was a ruse to divide them.*

> **WORD POWER**
> Synonyms
> stratagem
> subterfuge

❷ **trick** VERB
to deceive someone
EG *They tricked me into giving them all my money.*
con INFORMAL EG *We have been conned for 20 years.*
deceive EG *He deceived me into thinking the money was his.*
dupe EG *I was duped into letting them in.*
fool EG *They tried to fool you into coming after us.*
take in INFORMAL EG *I wasn't taken in for a minute.*

> **WORD POWER**
> Synonyms
> hoax
> hoodwink

❶ **trip** NOUN
a journey to a place
EG *a business trip*
excursion EG *a coach excursion to Trondheim*
jaunt EG *a jaunt in the car*
journey EG *the journey to Bordeaux*
outing EG *a school outing*
voyage EG *Columbus's voyage to the West Indies*

❷ **trip** VERB
to fall over
EG *I tripped on the stairs.*
fall over EG *Plenty of top skiers fell over.*
lose your footing EG *He lost his footing and slid into the water.*

stumble EG *He stumbled and almost fell.*

❶ **triumph** NOUN
a great success
EG *The championships proved to be a personal triumph for the coach.*
success EG *The jewellery was a great success.*
victory EG *a victory for common sense*

> **WORD POWER**
> Synonyms
> coup
> feather in your cap
> tour de force
> Antonym
> failure

❷ **triumph** VERB
to be successful
EG *a symbol of good triumphing over evil*
come out on top INFORMAL EG *The only way to come out on top is to adopt a different approach.*
prevail EG *I do hope he will prevail over the rebels.*
succeed EG *if they can succeed in America*
win EG *The top four teams all won.*

> **WORD POWER**
> Antonym
> fail

❶ **trouble** NOUN
a difficulty or problem
EG *financial troubles*
bother EG *Vince is having a spot of bother with the law.*
difficulty EG *economic difficulties*
hassle INFORMAL EG *We had loads of hassles trying to find somewhere to rehearse.*
problem EG *The main problem is unemployment.*

❷ **trouble** VERB
to make someone feel worried
EG *He was troubled by the lifestyle of his son.*
agitate EG *The thought agitates*

her.

bother EG *Is something bothering you?*

disturb EG *dreams so vivid that they disturb me for days*

worry EG *I didn't want to worry you.*

❸ **trouble** VERB
to cause someone inconvenience
EG *Can I trouble you for some milk?*

bother EG *I don't know why he bothers me with this kind of rubbish.*

disturb EG *a room where you won't be disturbed*

impose upon EG *I was afraid you'd feel we were imposing on you.*

inconvenience EG *He promised to be quick so as not to inconvenience them further.*

put out EG *I've always put myself out for others.*

❶ **true** ADJECTIVE
not invented
EG *The film is based on a true story.*

accurate EG *an accurate assessment of the situation*

correct EG *a correct diagnosis*

factual EG *any comparison that is not strictly factual*

> **WORD POWER**
> Antonym
> inaccurate

❷ **true** ADJECTIVE
real or genuine
EG *She was a true friend.*

authentic EG *authentic Italian food*

bona fide EG *We are happy to donate to bona fide charities.*

genuine EG *There was a risk of genuine refugees being returned to Vietnam.*

real EG *No, it wasn't a dream. It was real.*

> **WORD POWER**
> Antonym
> false

trust VERB
to believe that someone will do something
EG *The president can't be trusted.*

count on EG *I can always count on you to cheer me up.*

depend on EG *You can depend on me.*

have confidence in EG *We have the utmost confidence in your abilities.*

have faith in EG *I have no faith in him any more.*

place your trust in EG *I would never place my trust in one so young.*

rely upon EG *I know I can rely on you to sort it out.*

truth NOUN
the facts about something
EG *Marcel is keen to get to the truth of what happened.*

fact EG *How much was fact and how much fancy no one knew.*

reality EG *Fiction and reality were increasingly blurred.*

❶ **try** VERB
to make an effort to do something
EG *I tried hard to persuade him to stay.*

attempt EG *They are accused of attempting to murder British soldiers.*

endeavour FORMAL EG *I will endeavour to arrange it.*

make an attempt EG *He made three attempts to break the record.*

make an effort EG *He made no effort to hide his disappointment.*

seek EG *We have never sought to impose our views.*

strive EG *The school strives to treat pupils as individuals.*

❷ **try** VERB
to test the quality of something
EG *Howard wanted me to try the wine.*

check out EG *We went to the club to check it out.*

503

A
B
C
D
E
F
G
H
I
J
K
L
M
N
O
P
Q
R
S
T
U
V
W
X
Y
Z

sample EG *We sampled a selection of different bottled waters.*
test EG *The drug was tested on rats.*
try out EG *London Transport hopes to try out the system in September.*

❸ try NOUN
an attempt to do something
EG *After a few tries he pressed the right button.*
attempt EG *a deliberate attempt to destabilize the defence*
effort EG *his efforts to improve*
endeavour FORMAL EG *His first endeavours in the field were wedding films.*
go INFORMAL EG *She won on her first go.*
shot INFORMAL EG *I have had a shot at professional cricket.*

tune NOUN
a series of musical notes
EG *She was humming a merry little tune.*
melody EG *a beautiful melody*
strains EG *She could hear the tinny strains of a chamber orchestra.*

> **WORD POWER**
> Synonyms
> air
> theme

❶ turn VERB
to change the direction or position of something
EG *She had turned the bedside chair to face the door.*
rotate EG *Take each foot in both your hands and rotate it.*
spin EG *He spun the wheel sharply and made a U-turn.*
swivel EG *She swivelled her chair round.*
twirl EG *Bonnie twirled her empty glass in her fingers.*
twist EG *She twisted her head sideways.*

❷ turn VERB
to become or make something different

EG *A hobby can be turned into a career.*
change EG *She has now changed into a happy, self-confident woman.*
convert EG *a table that converts into an ironing board*
mutate EG *Overnight, the gossip begins to mutate into headlines.*
transform EG *the speed at which your body transforms food into energy*

> **WORD POWER**
> Synonyms
> metamorphose
> transfigure
> transmute

❸ turn NOUN
someone's right or duty to do something
EG *Tonight it's my turn to cook.*
chance EG *All eligible people would get a chance to vote.*
go EG *Whose go is it?*
opportunity EG *Now is your opportunity to say what you've always wanted.*

❶ twist VERB
to turn something round
EG *Her hands began to twist the handles of the bag.*
bend EG *Bend the bar into a horseshoe.*
curl EG *She sat with her legs curled under her.*
twine EG *He had twined his chubby arms around Vincent's neck.*
weave EG *He weaves his way through a crowd.*
wring EG *after wringing the chicken's neck*

> **WORD POWER**
> Synonyms
> entwine
> wreathe

❷ twist VERB
to bend into a new shape
EG *The car was left a mess of twisted metal.*

distort EG *A painter may exaggerate or distort shapes and forms.*
mangle EG *the mangled wreckage*
screw up EG *Amy screwed up her face.*

> *WORD POWER*
> **Synonyms**
> contort
> warp

❸ **twist** VERB
to injure a part of your body
EG *I've twisted my ankle.*
sprain EG *He fell and sprained his wrist.*
wrench EG *He had wrenched his back badly from the force of the fall.*

> *WORD POWER*
> **Synonyms**
> rick
> turn

typical ADJECTIVE
having the usual characteristics of something
EG *a typical American child*
average EG *The average adult man burns 1500 to 2000 calories per day.*
characteristic EG *a characteristic feature of the landscape*
normal EG *a normal day*
regular EG *He describes himself as just a regular guy.*
representative EG *fairly representative groups of adults*
standard EG *It was standard practice in cases like this.*
stock EG *He had a stock answer for all problems.*
usual EG *a neighborhood beset by all the usual inner-city problems*

> *WORD POWER*
> **Synonyms**
> archetypal
> archetypical
> stereotypical
> **Antonym**
> uncharacteristic

A
B
C
D
E
F
G
H
I
J
K
L
M
N
O
P
Q
R
S
T
U
V
W
X
Y
Z

Uu Uu

ugly ADJECTIVE
having a very unattractive appearance
EG *She makes me feel dowdy and ugly.*

plain EG *a shy, plain girl with a pale complexion*

unattractive EG *painted in an unattractive shade of green*

unsightly EG *The view was spoiled by some unsightly houses.*

> **WORD POWER**
> Synonyms
> unlovely
> unprepossessing
> Antonym
> beautiful

❶ ultimate ADJECTIVE
being the final one of a series
EG *It is not possible to predict the ultimate outcome.*

eventual EG *Reunification is the eventual aim.*

final EG *the fifth and final day*

last EG *This is his last chance to do something useful.*

❷ ultimate ADJECTIVE
the most important or powerful
EG *the ultimate goal of any player*

greatest EG *Our greatest aim was to take the gold medal.*

paramount EG *His paramount ambition was to be an actor.*

supreme EG *the supreme test of his abilities*

utmost EG *This has to be our utmost priority.*

❸ ultimate NOUN
the finest example of something
EG *This hotel is the ultimate in luxury.*

epitome EG *She was the epitome of the successful businesswoman.*

extreme EG *This was shyness taken to the extreme.*

height EG *the height of bad manners*

peak EG *roses at the peak of perfection*

unaware ADJECTIVE
not knowing about something
EG *Many people are unaware of how much they eat.*

ignorant EG *They are completely ignorant of the relevant facts.*

oblivious EG *John appeared oblivious to his surroundings.*

unconscious EG *totally unconscious of my presence*

unsuspecting EG *The cars were then sold to unsuspecting buyers.*

> **WORD POWER**
> Antonym
> aware

unbearable ADJECTIVE
too unpleasant to be tolerated
EG *Life was unbearable for the remaining citizens.*

intolerable EG *The heat and humidity were intolerable.*

oppressive EG *An oppressive sadness weighed upon him.*

unacceptable EG *She left her husband because of his unacceptable behaviour.*

> **WORD POWER**
> Synonyms
> insufferable
> unendurable
> Antonym
> tolerable

❶ unbelievable ADJECTIVE
extremely great or surprising
EG *He showed unbelievable courage.*

colossal EG *There has been a colossal waste of public money.*

incredible EG *You're always an incredible help on these occasions.*

stupendous EG *It cost a stupendous amount of money.*

❷ unbelievable ADJECTIVE
so unlikely it cannot be believed
EG *He came up with some unbelievable story.*
implausible EG *a film with an implausible ending*
improbable EG *highly improbable claims*
inconceivable EG *It was inconceivable that he'd hurt anyone.*
incredible EG *It seems incredible that anyone would want to do that.*
preposterous EG *The whole idea was preposterous.*
unconvincing EG *In response he was given the usual unconvincing excuses.*

> *WORD POWER*
> Antonym
> believable

❶ uncertain ADJECTIVE
not knowing what to do
EG *For a moment he looked uncertain as to how to respond.*
doubtful EG *He was a bit doubtful about starting without her.*
dubious EG *We were a bit dubious about it at first.*
unclear EG *I'm unclear about where to go.*
undecided EG *Even then she was still undecided about her future plans.*

> *WORD POWER*
> Synonyms
> irresolute
> vacillating
> Antonym
> certain

❷ uncertain ADJECTIVE
not definite
EG *facing an uncertain future*
ambiguous EG *The wording of the contract was ambiguous.*
doubtful EG *The outcome of the match is still doubtful.*
indefinite EG *suspended for an indefinite period*

indeterminate EG *a woman of indeterminate age*

> *WORD POWER*
> Synonyms
> conjectural
> undetermined
> Antonym
> certain

unclear ADJECTIVE
confusing and not obvious
EG *It is unclear how much popular support they have.*
ambiguous EG *in order to clarify the earlier ambiguous statement*
confused EG *The situation remains confused, as no clear victor has emerged.*
vague EG *The description was pretty vague.*

> *WORD POWER*
> Antonym
> clear

❶ uncomfortable ADJECTIVE
feeling or causing discomfort
EG *an uncomfortable bed*
awkward EG *Its shape made it awkward to carry.*
cramped EG *living in very cramped conditions*
disagreeable EG *designed to make flying a less disagreeable experience*
ill-fitting EG *Walking was difficult because of her ill-fitting shoes.*
painful EG *a painful back injury*

> *WORD POWER*
> Antonym
> comfortable

❷ uncomfortable ADJECTIVE
not relaxed or confident
EG *Talking about money made her uncomfortable.*
awkward EG *Offstage, he is bashful and awkward.*
embarrassed EG *an embarrassed silence*
ill at ease EG *I always feel ill at ease in their company.*

unconscious – understand

self-conscious EG *She was always self-conscious about her height.*

uneasy EG *He looked uneasy and refused to answer any more questions.*

> **WORD POWER**
> Antonym
> comfortable

❶ unconscious ADJECTIVE
in a state similar to sleep
EG *By the time the ambulance arrived, he was unconscious.*

asleep EG *They were fast asleep in their beds.*

senseless EG *He was beaten senseless and robbed of all his money.*

stunned EG *stunned by a blow to the head*

> **WORD POWER**
> Synonyms
> comatose
> insensible
> Antonym
> conscious

❷ unconscious ADJECTIVE
not aware of what is happening
EG *quite unconscious of their presence*

oblivious EG *He seemed oblivious of his surroundings.*

unaware EG *He was unaware of the chaos he was causing.*

unknowing EG *unknowing accomplices in his crimes*

unsuspecting EG *She was an unsuspecting victim of his deceit.*

> **WORD POWER**
> Antonym
> aware

under PREPOSITION
at a lower level than something
EG *a labyrinth of tunnels under the ground*

below EG *The sun had already sunk below the horizon.*

beneath EG *the frozen grass*

crunching beneath his feet
underneath EG *people trapped underneath the wreckage*

> **WORD POWER**
> Antonym
> above

undergo VERB
to have something happen to you
EG *He had to undergo major surgery.*

be subjected to EG *She was subjected to constant interruptions.*

endure EG *The company endured heavy losses.*

experience EG *They seem to experience more distress than the others.*

go through EG *I wouldn't like to go through that again.*

suffer EG *The peace process had suffered a serious setback.*

undermine VERB
to make something less secure or strong
EG *You're trying to undermine my confidence again.*

impair EG *Their actions will impair France's national interests.*

sap EG *I was afraid the illness had sapped my strength.*

subvert EG *an attempt to subvert their culture from within*

weaken EG *Her authority had been fatally weakened.*

> **WORD POWER**
> Antonym
> strengthen

❶ understand VERB
to know what someone means
EG *Do you understand what I'm saying?*

catch on INFORMAL EG *I didn't catch on immediately to what he meant.*

comprehend EG *Whenever she failed to comprehend, she just laughed.*

follow EG *I don't follow you at all.*

get EG *Did you get that joke?*

grasp EG *He instantly grasped that they were talking about him.*
see EG *"I see", she said at last.*
take in EG *too much to take in at once*

❷ understand VERB
to know why or how something is happening
EG *too young to understand what was going on*
appreciate EG *You must appreciate how important this is.*
comprehend EG *I just cannot comprehend your viewpoint.*
fathom EG *His attitude was hard to fathom.*
grasp EG *We immediately grasped the seriousness of the crisis.*
realize EG *People just don't realize how serious it could be.*

> **WORD POWER**
> Synonyms
> conceive
> discern

❸ understand VERB
to hear of something
EG *I understand she hasn't been well.*
believe EG *She's coming back tomorrow, I believe.*
gather EG *We gather the report is critical of the judge.*
hear EG *I hear you've been having some problems.*
learn EG *On learning who he was, I wanted to meet him.*

❶ understanding NOUN
a knowledge of something
EG *a basic understanding of computers*
appreciation EG *some appreciation of the problems of consumers*
comprehension EG *completely beyond our comprehension*
grasp EG *a good grasp of foreign languages*
knowledge EG *I have no knowledge of his business affairs.*

perception EG *Her questions showed a shrewd perception.*

❷ understanding NOUN
an informal agreement
EG *There was an understanding between us.*
accord EG *trying to reach an accord*
agreement EG *A new defence agreement was signed last month.*
pact EG *an electoral pact between the parties*

❸ understanding ADJECTIVE
having a sympathetic nature
EG *Fortunately he had an understanding wife.*
compassionate EG *a deeply compassionate man*
considerate EG *They should be more considerate towards the prisoners.*
sensitive EG *He was always sensitive and caring.*
sympathetic EG *a sympathetic listener*

uneasy ADJECTIVE
worried that something may be wrong
EG *I was very uneasy about these developments.*
agitated EG *She seemed agitated about something.*
anxious EG *He admitted he was still anxious about the situation.*
nervous EG *Consumers say they are nervous about their jobs.*
perturbed EG *I am not too perturbed at this setback.*
worried EG *If you're worried about it, just ask for more details.*

> **WORD POWER**
> Synonyms
> apprehensive
> discomposed
> restive
> Antonym
> comfortable

unemployed ADJECTIVE
not having a job

A
B
C
D
E
F
G
H
I
J
K
L
M
N
O
P
Q
R
S
T
U
V
W
X
Y
Z

EG *an unemployed mechanic*
idle EG *He has been idle for almost a month.*
jobless EG *One in four people are now jobless.*
redundant EG *aid for the 30,000 redundant miners*

> **WORD POWER**
> Antonym
> employed

❶ uneven ADJECTIVE
having an unlevel or rough surface
EG *I tripped and fell on an uneven pavement.*
bumpy EG *bumpy cobbled streets*
not level EG *It was hard to walk because the road was not level.*
not smooth EG *The icing isn't smooth enough.*
rough EG *She picked her way across the rough ground.*

> **WORD POWER**
> Antonym
> level

❷ uneven ADJECTIVE
not the same or consistent
EG *six lines of uneven length*
fluctuating EG *a fluctuating temperature*
inconsistent EG *Their performance was inconsistent over the whole season.*
irregular EG *at irregular intervals*
patchy EG *Her career has been patchy.*
variable EG *The potassium content of food is very variable.*

> **WORD POWER**
> Antonym
> even

unexpected ADJECTIVE
not considered likely to happen
EG *His death was completely unexpected.*
astonishing EG *What an astonishing piece of good luck!*

chance EG *a chance meeting*
surprising EG *a most surprising turn of events*
unforeseen EG *The show was cancelled due to unforeseen circumstances.*

> **WORD POWER**
> Synonyms
> fortuitous
> unanticipated

unfair ADJECTIVE
without right or justice
EG *It was unfair that he should suffer so much.*
unjust EG *an unjust decision*
wrong EG *It would be wrong to allow the case to go any further.*
wrongful EG *his claim for wrongful dismissal*

> **WORD POWER**
> Synonyms
> inequitable
> iniquitous
> Antonym
> fair

unfaithful ADJECTIVE
not being faithful to your partner
EG *He was unfaithful to her for years.*
adulterous EG *an adulterous relationship*
two-timing INFORMAL EG *She called him a two-timing rat.*

> **WORD POWER**
> Antonym
> faithful

unfriendly ADJECTIVE
not showing any warmth or kindness
EG *He can expect an unfriendly welcome.*
aloof EG *His manner was aloof.*
antagonistic EG *They were always antagonistic to newcomers.*
cold EG *She was a cold, unfeeling woman.*

disagreeable EG *He may be clever but he's most disagreeable.*
hostile EG *The prisoner eyed him in hostile silence.*
unkind EG *They're always unkind to newcomers.*

> **WORD POWER**
> **Synonyms**
> ill-disposed
> uncongenial
> **Antonym**
> friendly

ungrateful ADJECTIVE
not appreciating the things you have
EG *the most miserable and ungrateful people on earth*
unappreciative EG *He was unappreciative of our efforts.*
unthankful EG *mercenary players and unthankful supporters*

> **WORD POWER**
> **Antonym**
> grateful

unhappy ADJECTIVE
feeling sad or depressed
EG *He was a shy, sometimes unhappy man.*
depressed EG *She's depressed about this whole situation.*
despondent EG *After the interview John was despondent.*
down EG *They felt really down after they spoke to him.*
miserable EG *My job made me really miserable sometimes.*
sad EG *I felt sad to leave our little house.*

> **WORD POWER**
> **Synonyms**
> crestfallen
> disconsolate
> sorrowful
> **Antonym**
> happy

unimportant ADJECTIVE
having little significance or

importance
EG *The difference in their ages seemed unimportant at the time.*
insignificant EG *In 1949, Bonn was a small, insignificant city.*
minor EG *a minor inconvenience*
paltry EG *They had little interest in paltry domestic concerns.*
slight EG *We have a slight problem.*
trivial EG *She waved aside the trivial details.*

> **WORD POWER**
> **Antonym**
> important

❶ union NOUN
an organization of people or groups with mutual interests
EG *a trades union*
association EG *a member of several different associations*
coalition EG *governed by a coalition of three parties*
confederation EG *a confederation of mini-states*
federation EG *a federation of six separate agencies*
league EG *the League of Nations*

❷ union NOUN
the joining together of two or more things
EG *The majority voted for union with Russia.*
amalgamation EG *an amalgamation of two organizations*
blend EG *a blend of traditional charm and modern amenities*
combination EG *the combination of science and art*
fusion EG *fusions of jazz and pop*
mixture EG *a mixture of nuts, raisins, and capers*

> **WORD POWER**
> **Synonyms**
> amalgam
> conjunction
> synthesis

universal ADJECTIVE
relating to everyone or to the

A B C D E F G H I J K L M N O P Q R S T **U** V W X Y Z

whole universe
EG *These programmes have a universal appeal.*

common EG *The common view is that it is a good thing.*

general EG *This project should raise general awareness about the problem.*

unlimited EG *destruction on an unlimited scale*

widespread EG *Food shortages are widespread.*

worldwide EG *the fear of a worldwide epidemic*

> **WORD POWER**
> Synonyms
> catholic
> omnipresent
> overarching

unkind ADJECTIVE
lacking in kindness and consideration
EG *It's very unkind to describe her in those terms.*

cruel EG *Children can be so cruel.*

malicious EG *spreading malicious gossip*

mean EG *I'd feel mean saying no.*

nasty EG *What nasty little snobs you are!*

spiteful EG *How can you say such spiteful things about us?*

thoughtless EG *a small minority of thoughtless and inconsiderate people*

> **WORD POWER**
> Antonym
> kind

unknown ADJECTIVE
not familiar or famous
EG *He was an unknown writer at that time.*

humble EG *He started out as a humble fisherman.*

obscure EG *an obscure Greek composer*

unfamiliar EG *There were several unfamiliar names on the list.*

unsung EG *among the unsung heroes of our time*

> **WORD POWER**
> Antonym
> famous

unlikely ADJECTIVE
probably not true or likely to happen
EG *a military coup seems unlikely*

implausible EG *a film with an implausible ending*

incredible EG *an incredible pack of lies*

unbelievable EG *I know it sounds unbelievable, but I wasn't there that day.*

unconvincing EG *He came up with a very unconvincing excuse.*

> **WORD POWER**
> Antonym
> likely

unlucky ADJECTIVE
having bad luck
EG *He was unlucky not to score during the first half.*

cursed EG *the most cursed family in history*

hapless EG *a hapless victim of chance*

luckless EG *the luckless parents of a difficult child*

unfortunate EG *Some unfortunate person nearby could be injured.*

wretched EG *wretched people who had to sell or starve*

> **WORD POWER**
> Antonym
> lucky

unnecessary ADJECTIVE
completely needless
EG *He frowns upon unnecessary expense.*

needless EG *causing needless panic*

pointless EG *pointless meetings*

uncalled-for EG *uncalled-for rudeness*

> **WORD POWER**

Antonym
necessary

❶ unpleasant ADJECTIVE
causing feelings of discomfort or
dislike
EG *It has a very unpleasant smell.*
bad EG *I have some bad news.*
disagreeable EG *a disagreeable
experience*
distasteful EG *I find her gossip
distasteful.*
nasty EG *This divorce could turn
nasty.*
repulsive EG *repulsive fat white
slugs*
unpalatable EG *Only then did I
learn the unpalatable truth.*

WORD POWER
Antonym
pleasant

❷ unpleasant ADJECTIVE
rude or unfriendly
EG *a thoroughly unpleasant person*
disagreeable EG *He may be clever,
but he's a very disagreeable man.*
horrid EG *I must have been a
horrid little girl.*
objectionable EG *His tone was
highly objectionable.*
obnoxious EG *Clarissa's
obnoxious brother James*
rude EG *He was frequently rude to
waiters and servants.*
unfriendly EG *spoken in a rather
unfriendly voice*

WORD POWER
Antonym
pleasant

unpopular ADJECTIVE
disliked by most people
EG *an unpopular idea*
detested EG *The rebels toppled the
detested dictator.*
disliked EG *one of the most
disliked choices on offer*
shunned EG *the shunned former
minister*

undesirable EG *all sorts of
undesirable effects on health*

WORD POWER
Antonym
popular

unpredictable ADJECTIVE
unable to be foreseen
EG *Britain's notoriously
unpredictable weather*
chance EG *A chance meeting can
change your life.*
doubtful EG *The outcome remains
doubtful.*
hit and miss INFORMAL EG *Farming
can be a very hit and miss affair.*
unforeseeable EG *unforeseeable
weather conditions*

WORD POWER
Antonym
predictable

unsatisfactory ADJECTIVE
not good enough
EG *His work was judged
unsatisfactory.*
disappointing EG *The results were
disappointing.*
inadequate EG *The problem goes
far beyond inadequate staffing.*
mediocre EG *a mediocre string of
performances*
poor EG *Her school record was poor
at first.*
unacceptable EG *The quality of
his work was unacceptable.*

WORD POWER
Antonym
satisfactory

unsuitable ADJECTIVE
not appropriate for a purpose
EG *Her shoes were unsuitable for
walking any distance.*
improper EG *an improper diet*
inappropriate EG *inappropriate
use of the Internet*
unacceptable EG *using completely
unacceptable language*
unfit EG *unfit for human*

A
B
C
D
E
F
G
H
I
J
K
L
M
N
O
P
Q
R
S
T
U
V
W
X
Y
Z

habitation

> **WORD POWER**
> Synonyms
> inapposite
> unseemly
> **Antonym**
> suitable

untidy ADJECTIVE
not neatly arranged
EG *The place quickly became untidy.*
bedraggled EG *My hair was a bedraggled mess.*
chaotic EG *the chaotic mess of papers on his desk*
cluttered EG *There was no space on the cluttered worktop.*
jumbled EG *We moved our supplies into a jumbled heap.*
messy EG *She was a good, if messy, cook.*
unkempt EG *the unkempt grass in front of the house*

> **WORD POWER**
> Synonyms
> disordered
> shambolic
> **Antonym**
> tidy

unusual ADJECTIVE
not occurring very often
EG *many rare and unusual plants*
curious EG *a curious mixture of ancient and modern*
exceptional EG *exceptional circumstances*
extraordinary EG *What an extraordinary thing to happen!*
rare EG *one of the rarest species in the world*
uncommon EG *It's a very uncommon surname.*
unconventional EG *produced by an unconventional technique*

> **WORD POWER**
> Synonyms
> atypical
> unwonted
> **Antonym**
> common

unwilling ADJECTIVE
not wanting to do something
EG *an unwilling participant in school politics*
averse EG *I'm not averse to going along with the suggestion.*
grudging EG *a grudging acceptance of the situation*
loath EG *She is loath to give up her hard-earned liberty.*
reluctant EG *They were reluctant to get involved at first.*

> **WORD POWER**
> **Antonym**
> willing

upkeep NOUN
the process and cost of maintaining something
EG *The money will be used for the upkeep of the grounds.*
keep EG *He does not contribute towards his keep.*
maintenance EG *the regular maintenance of government buildings*
overheads EG *We must cut our overheads or we shall have to close.*
preservation EG *the preservation of historical sites*
running EG *The running of the house took up all her time.*

❶ **upset** ADJECTIVE
feeling unhappy about something
EG *She was very upset when she heard the news.*
agitated EG *in an excited and agitated state*
distressed EG *The animals were distressed by the noise.*
frantic EG *frantic with worry*
hurt EG *I was very hurt when they refused.*
troubled EG *He sounded deeply troubled.*
unhappy EG *The divorce made him very unhappy.*

② upset VERB

to make someone worried or unhappy
EG *The whole incident upset me terribly.*

agitate EG *The thought agitates her.*

bother EG *Don't let his manner bother you.*

distress EG *The whole thing really distressed him.*

disturb EG *These dreams disturb me for days afterwards.*

grieve EG *deeply grieved by their suffering*

ruffle EG *She doesn't get ruffled by anything.*

WORD POWER
Synonyms
discompose
faze
perturb

③ upset VERB

to turn something over accidentally
EG *Don't upset that pile of papers.*

capsize EG *He capsized the boat through his carelessness.*

knock over EG *The kitten knocked over the vase.*

overturn EG *She overturned her glass of wine as she stood up.*

spill EG *The waiter spilled the drinks all over the table.*

① urge NOUN

a strong wish to do something
EG *stifling the urge to scream*

compulsion EG *a compulsion to write*

desire EG *I had a strong desire to help and care for people.*

drive EG *a demonic drive to succeed*

impulse EG *Peter resisted an impulse to smile.*

longing EG *his longing to return home*

wish EG *She had a genuine wish to make amends.*

upset – use

② urge VERB

to try hard to persuade someone
EG *He urged the government to change the law.*

beg EG *I begged him to leave me alone.*

beseech EG *Her eyes beseeched him to show mercy.*

implore EG *He left early, although they implored him to stay.*

plead EG *kneeling on the floor pleading for mercy*

press EG *The unions are pressing him to stand firm.*

WORD POWER
Synonyms
entreat
exhort
solicit

urgent ADJECTIVE

needing to be dealt with quickly
EG *an urgent need for food and water*

compelling EG *There are compelling reasons to act swiftly.*

immediate EG *The immediate problem is transportation.*

imperative EG *It is imperative we end up with a win.*

pressing EG *one of our most pressing problems*

① use VERB

to perform a task with something
EG *Use a sharp knife to trim the edges.*

apply EG *The company applies this technology to solve practical problems.*

employ EG *the methods employed in the study*

operate EG *Can you operate a fax machine?*

utilize EG *The body utilizes many different minerals.*

WORD POWER
Synonyms
avail oneself of
ply

515

A
B
C
D
E
F
G
H
I
J
K
L
M
N
O
P
Q
R
S
T
U
V
W
X
Y
Z

❷ use NOUN
the act of using something
EG *the use of force*
application EG *Her theory was put into practical application.*
employment EG *the employment of completely new methods*
operation EG *the operation of the computer mouse*
usage EG *Parts of the motor wore out because of constant usage.*

❸ use NOUN
the purpose for which something is utilized
EG *of no practical use whatsoever*
end EG *The police force was manipulated for political ends.*
object EG *the object of the exercise*
point EG *I don't see the point of a thing like that.*
purpose EG *It is wrong to use it for military purposes.*

useful ADJECTIVE
something which helps or makes things easier
EG *a great deal of useful information*
beneficial EG *It may be beneficial to study the relevant guidelines.*
effective EG *Antibiotics are effective against this organism.*
helpful EG *a number of helpful booklets*
practical EG *practical suggestions for healthy eating*
valuable EG *Here are a few valuable tips to help you to succeed.*
worthwhile EG *a worthwhile source of income*

> **WORD POWER**
> Antonym
> useless

useless ADJECTIVE
not suitable or useful
EG *We realized that our money was useless here.*
futile EG *It would be futile to make any further attempts.*
impractical EG *A tripod is impractical when following animals on the move.*
unproductive EG *increasingly unproductive land*
unsuitable EG *This tool is completely unsuitable for use with metal.*
worthless EG *The old skills are worthless now.*

> **WORD POWER**
> Synonyms
> disadvantageous
> ineffectual
> unavailing
> Antonym
> useful

usual ADJECTIVE
done or happening most often
EG *sitting at his usual table*
accustomed EG *She acted with her accustomed shrewdness.*
common EG *the commonest cause of death*
customary EG *It's customary to offer guests a drink.*
habitual EG *He soon recovered his habitual geniality.*
normal EG *That's quite normal for a Friday.*
regular EG *samples from one of their regular suppliers*
standard EG *It was standard practice to put them outside.*

vague ADJECTIVE
not clearly expressed or clearly visible
EG *vague promises about raising standards*
hazy EG *Many details remain hazy.*
indefinite EG *at some indefinite time in the future*
indistinct EG *The lettering was worn and indistinct.*
loose EG *a loose translation*
uncertain EG *Students are facing an uncertain future.*
unclear EG *The proposals were sketchy and unclear.*

> **WORD POWER**
> Synonyms
> ill-defined
> indeterminate
> nebulous
> Antonym
> definite

❶ **vain** ADJECTIVE
very proud of your looks or qualities
EG *I think he is shallow and vain.*
conceited EG *They had grown too conceited and pleased with themselves.*
egotistical EG *an egotistical show-off*
ostentatious EG *He was generous with his money without being ostentatious.*
proud EG *She was said to be proud and arrogant.*
stuck-up INFORMAL EG *She was a famous actress, but she wasn't a bit stuck-up.*

> **WORD POWER**
> Synonyms
> narcissistic
> swaggering

❷ **vain** ADJECTIVE
not successful in achieving what was intended
EG *He made a vain effort to cheer her up.*
abortive EG *the abortive coup attempt*
fruitless EG *It was a fruitless search.*
futile EG *their futile attempts to avoid publicity*
unproductive EG *an unproductive strategy*
useless EG *a useless punishment which fails to stop crime*

> **WORD POWER**
> Antonym
> successful

❸ **vain**
in vain ADJECTIVE
unsuccessful in achieving what was intended
EG *Her complaints were in vain.*
fruitless EG *Four years of negotiation were fruitless.*
to no avail EG *His protests were to no avail.*
unsuccessful EG *Previous attempts have been unsuccesful.*
wasted EG *Their efforts were wasted.*

valley NOUN

Types of valley:
canyon
chasm
coomb
cwm (*Welsh*)
dale
defile
dell
depression
dingle
glen
gorge
gulch
gully
hollow
ravine

A B C D E F G H I J K L M N O P Q R S T U **V** W X Y Z

strath (*Scottish*)
vale

❶ valuable ADJECTIVE
having great importance or
usefulness
EG *The experience was very valuable.*
beneficial EG *Using computers has
a beneficial effect on learning.*
helpful EG *a number of helpful
booklets*
important EG *Her sons are the
most important thing in her life.*
prized EG *one of the gallery's most
prized possessions*
useful EG *a mine of useful
information*
worthwhile EG *a worthwhile
source of income*

> **WORD POWER**
> Synonyms
> cherished
> esteemed
> treasured
> Antonym
> useless

❷ valuable ADJECTIVE
worth a lot of money
EG *valuable old books*
costly EG *a small and costly bottle
of scent*
expensive EG *exclusive, expensive
possessions*
precious EG *rings set with precious
jewels*

> **WORD POWER**
> Antonym
> worthless

valuables PLURAL NOUN
the things you own that cost a
lot of money
EG *Leave your valuables in the hotel
safe.*
heirlooms EG *family heirlooms*
treasures EG *The house was full of
art treasures.*

variation NOUN
a change from the normal or
usual pattern
EG *a variation of the same route*
alteration EG *some alterations in
your diet*
change EG *a change of attitude*
departure EG *Her new novel is a
departure from her previous work.*
deviation EG *Deviation from the
norm is not tolerated.*
difference EG *a noticeable
difference in his behaviour*
diversion EG *a welcome diversion
from the daily grind*

❶ variety NOUN
a number of different kinds of
things
EG *a wide variety of readers*
array EG *an attractive array of
bright colours*
assortment EG *an assortment of
pets*
collection EG *a huge collection of
books*
medley EG *a medley of vegetables*
mixture EG *a mixture of sweets*
range EG *a range of sun-care
products*

> **WORD POWER**
> Synonyms
> cross section
> miscellany
> multiplicity

❷ variety NOUN
a particular type of something
EG *a new variety of celery*
category EG *There are three broad
categories of soil.*
class EG *several classes of butterflies*
kind EG *different kinds of roses*
sort EG *several articles of this sort*
strain EG *a new strain of the virus*
type EG *What type of guns were
they?*

various ADJECTIVE
of several different types
EG *trees of various sorts*
assorted EG *swimsuits in assorted
colours*

518

different EG *different brands of drinks*

disparate EG *the disparate cultures of India*

diverse EG *Society is more diverse than ever before.*

miscellaneous EG *a hoard of miscellaneous junk*

sundry EG *sundry journalists and lawyers*

> **WORD POWER**
> Synonyms
> heterogeneous
> manifold

❶ vary VERB
to change to something different
EG *weather patterns vary greatly*

alter EG *During the course of a day the light alters constantly.*

alternate EG *My moods alternate with alarming rapidity.*

change EG *My feelings haven't changed.*

fluctuate EG *Weight may fluctuate markedly.*

❷ vary VERB
to introduce changes in something
EG *Vary your routes as much as possible.*

alternate EG *Alternate the chunks of fish with chunks of vegetable.*

diversify EG *They decided to diversify their products.*

modify EG *The government refuses to modify its position.*

> **WORD POWER**
> Synonyms
> permutate
> reorder

verdict NOUN
a decision or opinion on something
EG *The doctor's verdict was that he was fine.*

conclusion EG *I've come to the conclusion that she's lying.*

decision EG *The editor's decision is*

final.

finding EG *The court announced its findings.*

judgment EG *My judgment is that things are going to get worse.*

opinion EG *You should seek a medical opinion.*

very ADVERB
to a great degree
EG *very bad dreams*

deeply EG *I was deeply sorry to hear about your loss.*

extremely EG *My mobile phone is extremely useful.*

greatly EG *I was greatly relieved when he finally arrived.*

highly EG *Mr Singh was a highly successful salesman.*

really EG *I know her really well.*

terribly EG *I'm terribly sorry to bother you.*

> **WORD POWER**
> Synonyms
> exceedingly
> profoundly
> remarkably

❶ veto VERB
to forbid something
EG *Treasury officials vetoed the plans.*

ban EG *The authorities have banned the advertisement.*

forbid EG *Most airlines forbid the use of mobile phones on their planes.*

prohibit EG *The government intends to prohibit all trade with the country.*

❷ veto NOUN
the act of forbidding or power to forbid something
EG *Dr. Baker has the power of veto.*

ban EG *the arms ban on the Bosnian government*

prohibition EG *a prohibition on nuclear testing*

victory NOUN
a success in a battle or

A B C D E F G H I J K L M N O P Q R S T U V W X Y Z

competition
EG *his 15th consecutive victory in a doubles final*

laurels EG *a former British champion took the laurels in this event*

success EG *league and cup successes*

superiority EG *United Nations air forces won air superiority.*

triumph EG *last year's Republican triumph in the elections*

win EG *eight wins in nine games*

> **WORD POWER**
> Antonym
> defeat

❶ **view** NOUN
a personal opinion
EG *his political views*

attitude EG *other people's attitudes towards you*

belief EG *people's beliefs about crime*

conviction EG *a firm conviction that things have improved*

feeling EG *It is my feeling that Klein is right.*

opinion EG *a favourable opinion of our neighbours*

point of view EG *an unusual point of view on the subject*

❷ **view** NOUN
the things you can see from a particular place
EG *There was a beautiful view from the window.*

aspect EG *the Yorkshire hills which give the cottage a lovely aspect*

landscape EG *Arizona's desert landscape*

panorama EG *a panorama of fertile valleys*

perspective EG *the aerial perspective of St Paul's Cathedral*

scene EG *Wright surveyed the scene from his chosen seat.*

spectacle EG *a sweeping spectacle of rugged peaks*

> **WORD POWER**

> Synonyms
> prospect
> vista

❸ **view** VERB
to think of something in a particular way
EG *They viewed me with contempt.*

consider EG *We consider them to be our friends.*

deem FORMAL EG *His ideas were deemed unacceptable.*

judge EG *His work was judged unsatisfactory.*

regard EG *They regard the tax as unfair.*

viewpoint NOUN
an attitude towards something
EG *We all have our own personal viewpoints.*

attitude EG *other people's attitudes towards you*

belief EG *people's beliefs about crime*

conviction EG *a very personal, political conviction*

feeling EG *What are your feelings on this matter?*

opinion EG *a favourable opinion of our neighbours*

point of view EG *an unusual point of view on the subject*

❶ **violence** NOUN
behaviour which is intended to hurt people
EG *Twenty people were killed in the violence.*

bloodshed EG *The government must avoid further bloodshed.*

brutality EG *the brutality of the war in Vietnam*

cruelty EG *Human beings are capable of such cruelty to each other.*

force EG *If you use any force, I shall inform the police.*

savagery EG *acts of vicious savagery*

terrorism EG *political terrorism in the 19th century*

❷ violence NOUN
force and energy
EG *Amy spoke with sudden violence.*
fervour EG *views he had put forward with fervour*
force EG *She expressed her feelings with some force.*
harshness EG *the harshness of her words*
intensity EG *His voice hoarsened with intensity.*
severity EG *the severity of her scoldings*
vehemence EG *Tweed was taken aback by her vehemence.*

❶ violent ADJECTIVE
intending to hurt or kill people
EG *violent criminals*
bloodthirsty EG *a bloodthirsty monster*
brutal EG *a brutal crime*
cruel EG *He is cruel towards animals.*
murderous EG *a murderous bank-robber*
savage EG *savage warriors*
vicious EG *He was a cruel and vicious man.*

> *WORD POWER*
> Antonym
> gentle

❷ violent ADJECTIVE
happening unexpectedly and with great force
EG *violent storms*
powerful EG *He was caught by a powerful blow.*
raging EG *a raging flood*
rough EG *A wooden ship sank in rough seas.*
strong EG *strong winds and rain*
turbulent EG *the turbulent events of the century*
wild EG *the wild gales sweeping up from the channel*

> *WORD POWER*
> Synonyms
> tempestuous

tumultuous

❸ violent ADJECTIVE
said, felt, or done with great force
EG *the violent reaction to his plans*
acute EG *pain which grew more and more acute*
furious EG *a furious row*
intense EG *a look of intense dislike*
powerful EG *a powerful backlash against the government*
severe EG *a severe emotional shock*
strong EG *strong words*

> *WORD POWER*
> Synonyms
> forcible
> passionate
> vehement

❶ virtue NOUN
the quality of doing what is morally right
EG *He is a paragon of virtue.*
goodness EG *He has faith in human goodness.*
integrity EG *He was praised for his fairness and integrity.*
morality EG *standards of morality and justice in society*

> *WORD POWER*
> Synonyms
> probity
> rectitude
> righteousness

❷ virtue NOUN
an advantage something has
EG *the virtue of neatness*
advantage EG *the advantages of the new system*
asset EG *The one asset the job provided was contacts.*
attribute EG *a player with every attribute you could want*
merit EG *the merits of various football teams*
plus INFORMAL EG *The nutrients in milk have pluses and minuses.*
strength EG *the strengths and*

A B C D E F G H I J K L M N O P Q R S T U V W X Y Z

A
B
C
D
E
F
G
H
I
J
K
L
M
N
O
P
Q
R
S
T
U
V
W
X
Y
Z

weaknesses of our position

❸ virtue

by virtue of PREPOSITION
because of
EG *The article stuck in my mind by virtue of one detail.*

as a result of EG *People will feel better as a result of their efforts.*

because of EG *She was promoted because of her experience.*

by dint of EG *He succeeds by dint of hard work.*

on account of EG *The city is popular with tourists on account of its many museums.*

thanks to EG *Thanks to recent research, new treatments are available.*

❶ visible ADJECTIVE
able to be seen
EG *The warning lights were clearly visible.*

clear EG *the clearest pictures ever of Pluto*

conspicuous EG *He felt more conspicuous than he'd have liked.*

distinguishable EG *colours just distinguishable in the dark*

in sight EG *There wasn't another vehicle in sight.*

observable EG *the observable part of the Universe*

perceptible EG *Daniel gave a barely perceptible nod.*

> **WORD POWER**
> Antonym
> invisible

❷ visible ADJECTIVE
noticeable or evident
EG *There was little visible excitement.*

apparent EG *There is no apparent reason for the crime.*

evident EG *He ate with evident enjoyment.*

manifest EG *his manifest enthusiasm*

noticeable EG *subtle but noticeable changes*

obvious EG *There are obvious dangers.*

plain EG *It is plain a mistake has been made.*

> **WORD POWER**
> Synonyms
> conspicuous
> discernible
> patent

❶ vision NOUN
a mental picture in which you imagine things
EG *my vision of the future*

conception EG *my conception of a garden*

daydream EG *He learned to escape into daydreams.*

dream EG *his dream of becoming a pilot*

fantasy EG *fantasies of romance and true love*

ideal EG *your ideal of a holiday*

image EG *an image in your mind of what you are looking for*

❷ vision NOUN
the ability to imagine future developments
EG *a total lack of vision and imagination*

foresight EG *They had the foresight to invest in technology.*

imagination EG *He had the imagination to foresee dangers.*

insight EG *the development of insight and understanding*

intuition EG *Her intuition told her something was wrong.*

❸ vision NOUN
an experience in which you see things others cannot
EG *She was convinced her visions were real.*

apparition EG *One of the women was the apparition he had seen.*

hallucination EG *The drug can cause hallucinations.*

illusion EG *Perhaps the footprint*

was an illusion.

mirage EG *The girl was a mirage, created by his troubled mind.*

phantom EG *People claimed to have seen the phantom.*

spectre EG *a spectre from the other world*

WORD POWER
Synonyms
chimera
phantasm
wraith

---

❶ **visit** VERB
to go to see and spend time with someone
EG *He wanted to visit his brother in Sydney.*

call on EG *Don't hesitate to call on me.*

go to see EG *I'll go to see him in the hospital.*

look up EG *She looked up friends she had not seen for a while.*

❷ **visit** NOUN
a trip to see a person or place
EG *Helen had recently paid him a visit.*

call EG *He decided to pay a call on Tommy.*

stay EG *An experienced guide is provided during your stay.*

stop EG *The last stop in Mr Cook's tour was Paris.*

vomit VERB
to have food and drink come back up through the mouth
EG *Any product made from milk made him vomit.*

be sick EG *She was sick in the handbasin.*

bring up EG *Certain foods are difficult to bring up.*

chunder AUSTRALIAN AND NEW ZEALAND SLANG EG *the time you chundered in the taxi*

heave EG *He gasped and heaved and vomited again.*

puke INFORMAL EG *They got drunk*

and puked out of the window.

regurgitate EG *swallowing and regurgitating large quantities of water*

❶ **vote** NOUN
a decision made by allowing people to state their preference
EG *Do you think we should have a vote on that?*

ballot EG *The result of the ballot will be known soon.*

plebiscite FORMAL EG *A plebiscite made Hitler the Chancellor.*

polls EG *In 1945, Churchill was defeated at the polls.*

referendum EG *Estonia planned to hold a referendum on independence.*

❷ **vote** VERB
to indicate a choice or opinion
EG *It seems that many people would vote for the opposition.*

cast a vote EG *90% of those who cast a vote*

go to the polls EG *Voters are due to go to the polls on Sunday.*

opt EG *The mass of Spaniards opted for democracy.*

return EG *Members will be asked to return a vote for or against the motion.*

❸ **vote** VERB
to suggest that something should happen
EG *I vote that we all go to Holland.*

propose EG *I propose that we all try to get some sleep.*

recommend EG *I recommend that he be sent home early.*

suggest EG *I suggest we go round the table and introduce ourselves.*

❶ **vulgar** ADJECTIVE
socially unacceptable or offensive
EG *vulgar language*

coarse EG *coarse humour*

crude EG *crude pictures*

dirty EG *dirty jokes*

indecent EG *an indecent suggestion*

rude EG *a rude gesture*
uncouth EG *that oafish, uncouth person*

WORD POWER

Synonyms
improper
ribald
unrefined
Antonym
refined

❷ vulgar ADJECTIVE
showing a lack of taste or quality
EG *I think it's a very vulgar house.*
common EG *She could be a little common at times.*
flashy EG *flashy clothes*
gaudy EG *a gaudy purple-and-orange hat*
tasteless EG *a house with tasteless decor*
tawdry EG *a tawdry seaside town*

WORD POWER

Antonym
sophisticated

vulnerable ADJECTIVE
weak and without protection
EG *vulnerable old people*

exposed EG *The west coast is very exposed to Atlantic winds.*

sensitive EG *Most people are highly sensitive to criticism.*

susceptible EG *an area that is susceptible to attack*

weak EG *He spoke up for the weak and defenceless.*

WORD POWER

Synonyms
assailable
defenceless
unprotected

A
B
C
D
E
F
G
H
I
J
K
L
M
N
O
P
Q
R
S
T
U
V
W
X
Y
Z

① wait VERB
to spend time before something happens
EG *Wait until we get there.*
linger EG *I lingered on for a few days until he arrived.*
pause EG *The crowd paused for a minute, wondering what to do next.*
remain EG *You'll have to remain in hospital for the time being.*
stand by EG *Ships are standing by to evacuate the people.*
stay EG *Stay here while I go for help.*

② wait NOUN
a period of time before something happens
EG *They faced a three-hour wait before they could leave.*
delay EG *The accident caused some delay.*
interval EG *a long interval when no-one spoke*
pause EG *There was a pause before he replied.*

wake VERB
to make or become conscious again after sleep
EG *It was still dark when he woke.*
awake EG *We were awoken by the doorbell.*
come to EG *When she came to she found it was raining.*
rouse EG *We roused him at seven so he would be on time.*
stir EG *She shook him and he started to stir.*
waken EG *wakened by the thunder*

① walk VERB
to go on foot
EG *I walked slowly along the road.*
go EG *Are you going to the shops?*
march EG *He marched right into the office and spoke his mind.*
pace EG *She paced the room nervously.*
stride EG *They strode off down the*

corridor.
tramp EG *tramping the streets*
trudge EG *We had to trudge all the way up the hill.*

> **WORD POWER**
> Synonyms
> perambulate
> promenade

② walk NOUN
a journey made by walking
EG *We'll have a quick walk while it's fine.*
hike EG *a long hike in the country*
march EG *a day's march north of their objective*
ramble EG *They went for a ramble through the woods.*
stroll EG *After dinner we took a stroll around the city.*
trek EG *He's on a trek across the Antarctic.*

> **WORD POWER**
> Synonyms
> constitutional
> perambulation
> saunter

③ walk NOUN
the way someone moves when walking
EG *Despite his gangling walk he was a good dancer.*
carriage EG *her regal carriage*
gait EG *an awkward gait*
pace EG *moving at a brisk pace down the road*
stride EG *He lengthened his stride to catch up with her.*

wander VERB
to move about in a casual way
EG *They wandered aimlessly around the village.*
cruise EG *A police car cruised by.*
drift EG *The balloon drifted slowly over the countryside.*
ramble EG *freedom to ramble*

A
B
C
D
E
F
G
H
I
J
K
L
M
N
O
P
Q
R
S
T
U
V
W
X
Y
Z

across the moors
range EG *They range widely in search of food.*
roam EG *Barefoot children roamed the streets.*
stroll EG *We strolled down the street, looking at the shops.*

❶ want VERB
to feel a desire for something
EG *I want a red car for a change.*
covet EG *He coveted his boss's job.*
crave EG *Sometimes she still craved chocolate.*
desire EG *He could make them do whatever he desired.*
wish EG *I don't wish to know that.*

❷ want VERB
to need something
EG *My hair wants cutting.*
be deficient in EG *Their diet was deficient in vitamins.*
demand EG *The task of reconstruction demanded much sacrifice.*
lack EG *training to give him the skills he lacked*
need EG *My car needs servicing.*
require EG *He knows exactly what is required of him.*

❸ want NOUN
a lack of something
EG *becoming weak from want of rest*
absence EG *a complete absence of evidence*
deficiency EG *They did blood tests for signs of vitamin deficiency.*
lack EG *He got the job in spite of his lack of experience.*
scarcity EG *an increasing scarcity of water*
shortage EG *A shortage of funds is holding them back.*

> **WORD POWER**
> Synonyms
> dearth
> insufficiency
> paucity
> Antonym

abundance

❶ war NOUN
a period of armed conflict between countries
EG *The war dragged on for five years.*
combat EG *men who died in combat*
conflict EG *The conflict is bound to intensify.*
fighting EG *He was killed in the fighting which followed the treaty.*
hostilities EG *in case hostilities break out*
strife EG *The country was torn with strife.*
warfare EG *chemical warfare*

> **WORD POWER**
> Antonym
> peace

❷ war VERB
to fight against something
EG *The two countries had been warring with each other for years.*
battle EG *Thousands of people battled with the police.*
clash EG *The two armies clashed at first light.*
combat EG *measures to combat smuggling*
fight EG *The tribe fought with its rivals.*

❶ warm ADJECTIVE
having some heat but not hot
EG *a warm spring day*
balmy EG *balmy summer evenings*
heated EG *a heated swimming pool*
lukewarm EG *Heat the milk until lukewarm.*
pleasant EG *After a chilly morning, the afternoon was very pleasant.*
tepid EG *a bath full of tepid water*

> **WORD POWER**
> Antonym
> cold

❷ warm ADJECTIVE
friendly and affectionate

EG *a warm and likable personality*

affectionate EG *with an affectionate glance at her children*

amiable EG *He was very amiable company.*

cordial EG *We were given a most cordial welcome.*

friendly EG *All her colleagues were very friendly.*

genial EG *a warm-hearted friend and genial host*

loving EG *He is a loving husband and father.*

> **WORD POWER**
> Antonym
> unfriendly

❸ **warm** VERB
to heat something gently
EG *The sun came out and warmed his back.*

heat EG *Heat the bread in the oven.*

heat up EG *The fire soon heated up the room.*

melt EG *He melted the butter in a small pan.*

thaw EG *Always thaw pastry thoroughly.*

warm up EG *You must begin gently to warm up the muscles.*

> **WORD POWER**
> Antonym
> cool

warn VERB
to give advance notice of something unpleasant
EG *I warned him about those loose tiles.*

alert EG *The siren alerted them to the danger.*

caution EG *Their reaction cautioned him against any further attempts.*

forewarn EG *We were forewarned of what to expect.*

notify EG *The weather forecast notified them of the coming storm.*

> **WORD POWER**
> Synonyms
> admonish
> apprise

warning NOUN
something that tells people of possible danger
EG *advance warning of the attack*

alarm EG *They heard the fire alarm and ran to safety.*

alert EG *a security alert*

caution EG *a note of caution*

notice EG *three months' notice*

premonition EG *He had a premonition of bad news.*

> **WORD POWER**
> Synonyms
> augury
> caveat
> presage

wary ADJECTIVE
showing lack of trust in something
EG *She was wary of marriage.*

cautious EG *His experience has made him cautious.*

distrustful EG *Voters are deeply distrustful of all politicians.*

guarded EG *The boy gave him a guarded look.*

suspicious EG *He was rightly suspicious of their motives.*

vigilant EG *He warned the public to be vigilant.*

> **WORD POWER**
> Synonyms
> chary
> circumspect
> heedful

❶ **wash** VERB
to clean something with water
EG *He got a job washing dishes.*

bathe EG *She bathed her blistered feet.*

cleanse EG *the correct way to cleanse the skin*

launder EG *freshly laundered shirts*

rinse EG *Rinse several times in clear water.*

scrub EG *I was scrubbing the bathroom floor.*

shampoo EG *You must shampoo your hair first.*

❷ wash VERB
to carry something by the force of water
EG *washed ashore by the waves*

carry off EG *The debris was carried off on the tide.*

erode EG *Exposed soil is quickly eroded by wind and rain.*

sweep away EG *The floods swept away the houses by the river.*

❶ waste VERB
to use too much of something unnecessarily
EG *I wouldn't waste my money on something like that.*

fritter away EG *He just fritters his time away.*

squander EG *He had squandered his chances of winning.*

throw away EG *You're throwing away a good opportunity.*

> **WORD POWER**
> Antonym
> save

❷ waste NOUN
using something excessively or unnecessarily
EG *What a complete waste of money!*

extravagance EG *widespread tales of his extravagance*

misuse EG *This project is a misuse of public funds.*

squandering EG *a squandering of his valuable time*

> **WORD POWER**
> Synonyms
> dissipation
> misapplication
> prodigality

❸ waste ADJECTIVE
not needed or wanted
EG *waste paper*

leftover EG *leftover pieces of fabric*

superfluous EG *She got rid of many superfluous belongings.*

unused EG *spoiled or unused ballot papers*

wasteful ADJECTIVE
using something in a careless or extravagant way
EG *wasteful duplication of effort*

extravagant EG *an extravagant lifestyle*

uneconomical EG *the uneconomical duplication of jobs*

> **WORD POWER**
> Synonyms
> improvident
> profligate
> spendthrift
> Antonym
> thrifty

❶ watch NOUN
a period of time when a guard is kept on something
EG *Keep a close watch on the prisoners.*

observation EG *In hospital she'll be under observation night and day.*

supervision EG *A toddler requires close supervision.*

surveillance EG *kept under constant surveillance*

> **WORD POWER**
> Synonyms
> vigilance
> watchfulness

❷ watch VERB
to look at something for some time
EG *I don't watch television very often.*

gaze at EG *gazing at herself in the mirror*

look at EG *They looked closely at the insects.*

observe EG *Researchers observed the behaviour of small children.*

pay attention EG *Pay attention or you won't know what to do.*

see EG *We went to see the*

semi-finals.
view EG *The police have viewed the video recording of the incident.*

❸ watch VERB
to look after something
EG *You must watch the baby carefully.*
guard EG *They were guarded the whole time they were there.*
look after EG *I looked after her cat while she was away.*
mind EG *Can you mind the store for a couple of hours?*
take care of EG *Can you take care of the kids while I get my hair done?*

watch out VERB
to be careful or alert for something
EG *You have to watch out for snakes in the swamp.*
be alert EG *The bank is alert to the danger.*
be watchful EG *Be watchful for any warning signs.*
keep your eyes open EG *They kept their eyes open for any troublemakers.*
look out EG *What are the symptoms to look out for?*

waterfall NOUN

> Types of waterfall:
> cascade
> cataract
> chute
> fall
> linn (*Scottish*)
> rapids
> torrent
> white water

❶ wave VERB
to move or flap to and fro
EG *The doctor waved a piece of paper at him.*
brandish EG *He appeared brandishing a knife.*
flap EG *He flapped his hand at me to be quiet.*
flourish EG *He flourished his glass*

to emphasize the point.
flutter EG *a fluttering white lace handkerchief*
shake EG *Shake the rugs well to air them.*

> ***WORD POWER***
> Synonyms
> oscillate
> undulate

❷ wave NOUN
a ridge of water on the surface of the sea
EG *the sound of the waves breaking on the shore*
breaker EG *The foaming breakers crashed on to the beach.*
ripple EG *gentle ripples on the surface of the lake*
swell EG *We bobbed gently on the swell of the incoming tide.*

❸ wave NOUN
an increase in a type of activity
EG *the crime wave*
flood EG *a flood of complaints about the programme*
movement EG *a growing movement towards democracy*
rush EG *He felt a sudden rush of panic at the thought.*
surge EG *the recent surge in inflation*
trend EG *This is a growing trend.*
upsurge EG *There was an upsurge of business confidence after the war.*

❶ way NOUN
a manner of doing something
EG *an excellent way of cooking meat*
approach EG *different approaches to gathering information*
manner EG *in a friendly manner*
means EG *The move is a means to fight crime.*
method EG *using the latest teaching methods*
procedure EG *He failed to follow the correct procedure when applying for a visa.*
technique EG *The tests were*

performed using a new technique.

❷ way NOUN

the customs or behaviour of a
person or group

EG *Their ways are certainly different.*

conduct EG *People judged him by
his social skills and conduct.*

custom EG *an ancient Japanese
custom*

manner EG *His manner was rather
abrupt.*

practice EG *a public enquiry into
bank practices*

style EG *Behaving like that isn't his
style.*

> **WORD POWER**
> Synonyms
> idiosyncrasy
> wont

❸ way NOUN

a route taken to a particular
place

EG *I can't remember the way.*

channel EG *a safe channel
avoiding the reefs*

course EG *The ship was on a course
that followed the coastline.*

lane EG *the busiest shipping lanes
in the world*

path EG *The lava annihilates
everything in its path.*

road EG *the road into the village*

route EG *the most direct route to
the town centre*

❶ weak ADJECTIVE

lacking in strength

EG *She had a weak heart.*

delicate EG *She was physically
delicate and mentally unstable.*

faint EG *Feeling faint is one of the
symptoms of angina.*

feeble EG *old and feeble and
unable to walk far*

frail EG *in frail health*

puny EG *He was puny as a child
but grew up to be a top athlete.*

sickly EG *a sickly baby with no
resistance to illness*

wasted EG *muscles which were
wasted through lack of use*

> **WORD POWER**
> Synonyms
> debilitated
> decrepit
> enervated
> infirm
> Antonym
> strong

❷ weak ADJECTIVE

likely to break or fail

EG *a weak economy*

deficient EG *The plane had a
deficient landing system.*

faulty EG *The money will be used
to repair faulty equipment.*

inadequate EG *inadequate safety
measures*

❸ weak ADJECTIVE

easily influenced by other
people

EG *He was a weak man who
wouldn't stick his neck out.*

powerless EG *a powerless ruler
governed by his advisers*

spineless EG *bureaucrats and
spineless politicians*

> **WORD POWER**
> Synonyms
> indecisive
> irresolute
> Antonym
> resolute

weaken VERB

to make or become less strong

EG *His authority was weakened by
their actions.*

diminish EG *to diminish the
prestige of the monarchy*

fail EG *His strength began to fail
after a few hours.*

flag EG *Her enthusiasm was in no
way flagging.*

lessen EG *The drugs lessen the risk
of an epidemic.*

reduce EG *Reduced consumer
demand caused the company to*

A B C D E F G H I J K L M N O P Q R S T U V W X Y Z

collapse.

sap EG *I was afraid the illness had sapped my strength.*

undermine EG *They were accused of trying to undermine the government.*

wane EG *His interest in sport began to wane.*

> **WORD POWER**
> Synonyms
> debilitate
> enervate
> mitigate
> Antonym
> strengthen

❶ **weakness** NOUN
a lack of physical or moral strength
EG *His extreme weakness caused him to collapse.*

defect EG *a serious character defect*

flaw EG *His main flaw is his bad temper.*

fragility EG *They are at risk because of the fragility of their bones.*

frailty EG *the triumph of will over human frailty*

imperfection EG *He concedes that there are imperfections in the system.*

vulnerability EG *the extreme vulnerability of the young chicks*

> **WORD POWER**
> Synonyms
> Achilles' heel
> debility
> infirmity
> Antonym
> strength

❷ **weakness** NOUN
a great liking for something
EG *a weakness for chocolate*

fondness EG *a fondness for good wine*

liking EG *a liking for tripe and onions*

passion EG *His other great passion*

was his motorbike.

penchant EG *a stylish woman with a penchant for dark glasses*

> **WORD POWER**
> Synonyms
> partiality
> predilection
> Antonym
> dislike

❶ **wealth** NOUN
a large amount of money
EG *Economic reform brought them wealth.*

affluence EG *the trappings of affluence*

fortune EG *He made a fortune in the property boom.*

means EG *a person of means*

money EG *All that money brought nothing but sadness and misery.*

prosperity EG *Japan's economic prosperity*

riches EG *His Olympic medal brought him fame and riches.*

substance EG *run by local men of substance*

❷ **wealth** NOUN
a lot of something
EG *a wealth of information*

abundance EG *This area has an abundance of safe beaches.*

bounty EG *autumn's bounty of fruits and berries*

plenty EG *He grew up in a time of plenty.*

store EG *She dipped into her store of theatrical anecdotes.*

> **WORD POWER**
> Synonyms
> copiousness
> cornucopia
> plenitude
> profusion
> Antonym
> shortage

wealthy ADJECTIVE
having plenty of money
EG *She came from a very wealthy*

A
B
C
D
E
F
G
H
I
J
K
L
M
N
O
P
Q
R
S
T
U
V
W
X
Y
Z

A
B
C
D
E
F
G
H
I
J
K
L
M
N
O
P
Q
R
S
T
U
V
W
X
Y
Z

background.
affluent EG *living in an affluent neighbourhood*
comfortable EG *from a stable, comfortable family*
opulent EG *Most of the cash went on supporting his opulent lifestyle.*
prosperous EG *The place looks more prosperous than ever.*
rich EG *I'm going to be very rich one day.*
well-to-do EG *a rather well-to-do family in the shipping business*

> **WORD POWER**
> Antonym
> poor

❶ wear VERB
to be dressed in something
EG *He was wearing a brown uniform.*
be clothed in EG *She was clothed in a flowered dress.*
be dressed in EG *The women were dressed in their finest attire.*
don EG *The police responded by donning riot gear.*
have on EG *I had my new shoes on that night.*
put on EG *He had to put on his glasses to read the paper.*
sport INFORMAL EG *sporting a red tie*

❷ wear VERB
to become worse in condition with use or age
EG *The old stone steps were worn in the middle.*
corrode EG *The underground pipes were badly corroded.*
erode EG *Exposed rock is quickly eroded by wind and rain.*
fray EG *fraying edges on the stair carpet*
rub EG *The inscription had been rubbed smooth by generations of hands.*
wash away EG *The topsoil had been washed away by the incessant rain.*

> **WORD POWER**

> **Synonyms**
> abrade
> deteriorate

❸ wear NOUN
the type of use which causes something to be damaged
EG *The tyres showed signs of wear.*
corrosion EG *Zinc is used to protect other metals from corrosion.*
deterioration EG *The building is already showing signs of deterioration.*
erosion EG *erosion of the river valleys*
use EG *The carpet must be able to cope with heavy use.*

> **WORD POWER**
> Synonyms
> abrasion
> attrition

wear out VERB
to make someone tired
EG *The past few days have really worn me out.*
exhaust EG *The long working day exhausted him.*
tire EG *If driving tires you, take the train.*
weary EG *wearied by the constant demands on his time*

weather NOUN

Types of weather:
cloud
drought
frost
hail
haze
heatwave
ice
lightning
sunshine
thaw
thunder

Words used to describe the weather:
balmy
blustery
breezy

clammy
clear
close
cloudy
cold
drizzly
dry
dull
fine
foggy
hot
humid
icy
mild
misty
muggy
overcast
rainy
showery
snowy
stormy
sultry
sunny
thundery
wet
windy

Words for rain and snow:
drizzle
rain
shower
sleet
slush
snow

Words for storm:
blizzard
hailstorm
snowstorm
squall
storm
tempest
thunderstorm

Words for wind:
breeze
cyclone
gale
gust
hurricane
squall
tornado
typhoon

whirlwind
wind

Words for fog:
fog
haar
haze
mist
smog

❶ **well** ADVERB
with skill and ability
EG *He draws well.*
ably EG *He was ably assisted by the other members of staff.*
admirably EG *dealing admirably with a difficult situation*
effectively EG *In the first half he operated effectively in defence.*
expertly EG *Shopkeepers expertly rolled spices up in bay leaves.*
skilfully EG *He skilfully exploited his company's strengths.*

> **WORD POWER**
> Synonyms
> adeptly
> proficiently
> Antonym
> badly

❷ **well** ADVERB
fully and with thoroughness
EG *They should be well washed and well dried.*
amply EG *I was amply rewarded for my trouble.*
completely EG *Make sure you defrost it completely.*
highly EG *one of the most highly regarded authors*
thoroughly EG *Add the oil and mix thoroughly.*

❸ **well** ADJECTIVE
having good health
EG *I'm not very well today.*
fit EG *He keeps himself really fit.*
healthy EG *Most people want to be healthy and happy.*
in good health EG *He seemed to be in good health and spirits.*
sound EG *a sound body*

533

A
B
C
D
E
F
G
H
I
J
K
L
M
N
O
P
Q
R
S
T
U
V
W
X
Y
Z

strong EG *Eat well and you'll soon be strong again.*

> **WORD POWER**
> Synonyms
> able-bodied
> hale
> in fine fettle
> Antonym
> sick

❶ **wet** ADJECTIVE
covered in liquid
EG *Don't get your feet wet.*
damp EG *Her hair was still damp.*
drenched EG *getting drenched by icy water*
moist EG *The soil is reasonably moist after the September rain.*
saturated EG *The filter has been saturated with oil.*
soaked EG *soaked to the skin*
sodden EG *We took off our sodden clothes.*
waterlogged EG *The game was called off because the pitch was waterlogged.*

> **WORD POWER**
> Antonym
> dry

❷ **wet** ADJECTIVE
in rainy weather conditions
EG *It was a miserable wet day.*
humid EG *hot and humid weather conditions*
misty EG *The air was cold and misty.*
rainy EG *The rainy season starts in December.*
showery EG *The day had been showery with sunny intervals.*

> **WORD POWER**
> Antonym
> dry

❸ **wet** VERB
to put liquid on to something
EG *Wet the edges and stick them together.*
dampen EG *You must dampen the*

laundry before you iron it.
irrigate EG *irrigated by a system of interconnected canals*
moisten EG *Take a sip of water to moisten your throat.*
soak EG *The water had soaked his jacket and shirt.*
spray EG *It can spray the whole field in half an hour.*
water EG *We have to water the plants when the weather is dry.*

> **WORD POWER**
> Synonyms
> drench
> humidify
> saturate
> Antonym
> dry

whim NOUN
a sudden fancy for something
EG *We decided to go more or less on a whim.*
craze EG *the latest fitness craze*
fad INFORMAL EG *just a passing fad*
fancy EG *I had a fancy for some strawberries.*
impulse EG *He resisted the impulse to buy a new one.*
urge EG *He had an urge to open a shop of his own.*

> **WORD POWER**
> Synonyms
> caprice
> vagary
> whimsy

white NOUN OR ADJECTIVE

> Shades of white:
> cream
> ecru
> ivory
> magnolia
> off-white
> oyster white
> pearl
> snow-white

❶ **whole** ADJECTIVE
indicating all of something

EG *We spent the whole summer abroad.*

complete EG *The list filled a complete page.*

entire EG *There are only ten in the entire country.*

full EG *a full week's notice*

total EG *The evening was a total fiasco.*

uncut EG *the uncut version of the film*

undivided EG *He has my undivided loyalty.*

❷ **whole** NOUN

the full amount of something
EG *the whole of Asia*

aggregate EG *the aggregate of the individual scores*

all EG *All is not lost.*

everything EG *Everything that happened is my fault.*

lot EG *He lost the lot within five minutes.*

sum total EG *The small room contained the sum total of their possessions.*

total EG *The eventual total was far higher.*

❶ **wicked** ADJECTIVE

very bad or evil
EG *That was a wicked thing to do.*

atrocious EG *He had committed atrocious crimes against the refugees.*

bad EG *Please forgive our bad behaviour.*

depraved EG *the work of depraved criminals*

evil EG *the country's most evil terrorists*

sinful EG *"This is a sinful world",* he said.

vicious EG *He was a cruel and vicious man.*

> **WORD POWER**
> Synonyms
> egregious
> iniquitous
> nefarious

❷ **wicked** ADJECTIVE

mischievous in an amusing or attractive way
EG *She always felt wicked when eating chocolate.*

impish EG *an impish sense of humour*

mischievous EG *like a mischievous child*

naughty EG *little boys using naughty words*

❶ **wide** ADJECTIVE

measuring a large distance from side to side
EG *It should be wide enough to give plenty of working space.*

broad EG *His shoulders were broad and his waist narrow.*

expansive EG *It has swings and an expansive grassy play area.*

extensive EG *The grounds were more extensive than the town itself.*

immense EG *an immense cloud of smoke*

large EG *This fish lives mainly in large rivers and lakes.*

sweeping EG *the long sweeping curve of the bay*

vast EG *The farmers there own vast stretches of land.*

> **WORD POWER**
> Antonym
> narrow

❷ **wide** ADJECTIVE

extensive in scope
EG *a wide range of colours*

broad EG *A broad range of issues was discussed.*

comprehensive EG *a comprehensive guide to the region*

encyclopedic EG *He had an encyclopedic knowledge of drugs.*

extensive EG *The whole question received extensive press coverage.*

inclusive EG *an inclusive system which gives every pupil an equal chance*

vast EG *a vast store of knowledge*

A B C D E F G H I J K L M N O P Q R S T U V **W** X Y Z

WORD POWER
Antonym
narrow

❸ wide ADVERB
as far as possible
EG *Open wide!*
completely EG *He opened the map out completely so we could see.*
fully EG *a fully extended aerial*
right out EG *Spread it right out to the edges.*

widespread ADJECTIVE
existing over a large area
EG *Food shortages are widespread.*
broad EG *The agreement won broad support among the people.*
common EG *the common view that treatment is ineffective*
extensive EG *The bomb caused extensive damage.*
pervasive EG *the pervasive influence of the army in national life*
prevalent EG *Smoking is becoming more prevalent among girls.*
rife EG *Bribery and corruption were rife in the industry.*

❶ wild ADJECTIVE
not cultivated or domesticated
EG *a meadow of wild flowers*
fierce EG *Fierce hyenas scavenged for food after the kill.*
free EG *stunning pictures of wild and free animals*
natural EG *In the natural state this animal is not ferocious.*
uncultivated EG *developed from an uncultivated type of grass*
undomesticated EG *These cats lived wild and were completely undomesticated.*
untamed EG *the untamed horses of the Camargue*
warrigal AUSTRALIAN LITERARY EG *a warrigal mare*

❷ wild ADJECTIVE
in stormy conditions
EG *They were not deterred by the wild weather.*

howling EG *a howling gale*
raging EG *The trip involved crossing a raging torrent.*
rough EG *The two ships collided in rough seas.*
stormy EG *a dark and stormy night*
violent EG *That night they were hit by a violent storm.*

❸ wild ADJECTIVE
without control or restraint
EG *wild with excitement*
boisterous EG *Most of the children were noisy and boisterous.*
rowdy EG *The television coverage revealed their rowdy behaviour.*
turbulent EG *five turbulent years of rows and reconciliations*
uncontrolled EG *His uncontrolled behaviour disturbed the entire group.*
wayward EG *wayward children with a history of emotional problems*

WORD POWER
Synonyms
disorderly
riotous
uproarious

❶ will VERB
to leave something to someone when you die
EG *He had willed his fortune to his daughter.*
bequeath EG *She bequeathed her collection to the local museum.*
leave EG *Everything was left to the housekeeper.*
pass on EG *He passed on much of his estate to his eldest son.*

❷ will NOUN
the strong determination to achieve something
EG *the will to win*
determination EG *Determination has always been a part of his make-up.*
purpose EG *They are enthusiastic and have a sense of purpose.*
resolution EG *He began to form a*

A B C D E F G H I J K L M N O P Q R S T U V W X Y Z

resolution to clear his name.
resolve EG *This will strengthen the public's resolve.*
willpower EG *succeeding by sheer willpower*

❸ **will** NOUN
what someone wants
EG *the will of the people*
choice EG *It's your choice.*
inclination EG *She showed no inclination to go.*
mind EG *You can go if you have a mind to do so.*
volition EG *a product of our volition*
wish EG *done against my wishes*

willing ADJECTIVE
ready and eager to do something
EG *a willing helper*
agreeable EG *We can go ahead if you are agreeable.*
eager EG *Children are eager to learn.*
game INFORMAL EG *He still had new ideas and was game to try them.*
happy EG *That's a risk I'm happy to take.*
prepared EG *I'm not prepared to take orders from her.*
ready EG *ready to die for their beliefs*

> **WORD POWER**
> Synonyms
> amenable
> compliant
> desirous
> Antonym
> unwilling

❶ **win** VERB
to defeat your opponents
EG *The top four teams all won.*
be victorious EG *Despite the strong opposition she was victorious.*
come first EG *They unexpectedly came first this year.*
prevail EG *the votes he must win in order to prevail*
succeed EG *the skills and qualities needed to succeed*

triumph EG *a symbol of good triumphing over evil*

> **WORD POWER**
> Antonym
> lose

❷ **win** VERB
to succeed in obtaining something
EG *moves to win the support of the poor*
achieve EG *We have achieved our objective.*
attain EG *He's half-way to attaining his pilot's licence.*
gain EG *After three weeks the hostages finally gained their freedom.*
get EG *My entry got a commendation this year.*
secure EG *Her achievements helped secure her the job.*

❸ **win** NOUN
a victory in a contest
EG *a run of seven games without a win*
success EG *his success in the Monaco Grand Prix*
triumph EG *their World Cup triumph*
victory EG *the 3-1 victory over Switzerland*

> **WORD POWER**
> Antonym
> defeat

winner NOUN
a person who wins something
EG *The winners will be notified by post.*
champion EG *a former Olympic champion*
conqueror EG *This time they easily overcame their former conquerors.*
victor EG *He emerged as the victor by the second day.*

> **WORD POWER**
> Antonym
> loser

A B C D E F G H I J K L M N O P Q R S T U V **W** X Y Z

wisdom NOUN
judgment used to make sensible decisions
EG *the wisdom that comes from experience*

discernment EG *Her keen discernment made her an excellent collector.*

insight EG *a man of considerable insight and diplomatic skills*

judgment EG *He respected our judgment on this matter.*

knowledge EG *the quest for scientific knowledge*

reason EG *a conflict between emotion and reason*

> *WORD POWER*
> Synonyms
> astuteness
> erudition
> sagacity
> Antonym
> foolishness

wise ADJECTIVE
able to make use of experience and judgment
EG *a wise old man*

informed EG *an informed guess at his wealth*

judicious EG *the judicious use of military force*

perceptive EG *the words of a perceptive political commentator*

rational EG *You must look at both sides before you can reach a rational decision.*

sensible EG *The sensible thing is to leave them alone.*

shrewd EG *a shrewd deduction about what was going on*

> *WORD POWER*
> Antonym
> foolish

❶ **wish** NOUN
a desire for something
EG *She was sincere in her wish to make amends.*

desire EG *her desire for a child of her own*

hankering EG *She had always had a hankering to be an actress.*

hunger EG *a hunger for success*

longing EG *He felt a longing for familiar surroundings.*

urge EG *He had an urge to open a shop of his own.*

want EG *Supermarkets respond to the wants of their customers.*

❷ **wish** VERB
to want something
EG *We wished to return.*

desire EG *He was bored and desired to go home.*

hunger EG *She hungered for adventure.*

long EG *I'm longing for the holidays.*

thirst EG *thirsting for knowledge*

want EG *people who know exactly what they want in life*

yearn EG *The younger ones yearned to be part of a normal family.*

❶ **withdraw** VERB
to take something out
EG *He withdrew some money from the bank.*

draw out EG *I'll have to draw out some of my savings.*

extract EG *She extracted another dress from the wardrobe.*

remove EG *I removed the splinter from her finger.*

take out EG *There was a fee for taking out money from the account.*

❷ **withdraw** VERB
to back out of an activity
EG *They withdrew from the conference.*

back out EG *He backed out of the agreement.*

leave EG *Davis left the game to go to hospital.*

pull out EG *The general pulled out of the talks after two days.*

retire EG *The jury retired three hours ago.*

retreat EG *retreating from the*

harsh realities of life

wither VERB
to become weaker and fade away
EG *Will the company flourish or wither?*
decline EG *The church's influence has declined.*
droop EG *plants drooping in the heat*
fade EG *Prospects for peace have already started to fade.*
shrivel EG *They watched their crops shrivel and die in the drought.*
wilt EG *The roses wilted the day after she bought them.*

❶ **witness** NOUN
someone who has seen something happen
EG *The police appealed for witnesses to come forward.*
bystander EG *Seven other innocent bystanders were injured.*
eyewitness EG *Eyewitnesses say the soldiers opened fire on the crowd.*
observer EG *A casual observer would not have noticed them.*
onlooker EG *a small crowd of onlookers*
spectator EG *carried out in full view of spectators*

❷ **witness** VERB
to see something happening
EG *Anyone who witnessed the attack should call the police.*
be present at EG *Many men are now present at the birth of their children.*
observe EG *We observed them setting up the machine gun.*
see EG *I saw him do it.*

watch EG *She had watched them drinking heavily before the accident.*

woman NOUN
an adult female human being
EG *women over 75 years old*
dame SLANG EG *Who does that dame think she is?*
female EG *The average young female is fairly affluent.*
girl EG *a night out with the girls*
lady EG *Your table is ready, ladies, so please come through.*
lass EG *a lass from the country*
sheila AUSTRALIAN AND NEW ZEALAND INFORMAL EG *his role as a sheila in his own play*
vrou SOUTH AFRICAN EG *Have you met his vrou yet?*

❶ **wonder** VERB
to think about something with curiosity
EG *I wondered what that noise was.*
ask oneself EG *You have to ask yourself what this really means.*
ponder EG *pondering how to improve the team*
puzzle EG *Researchers continue to puzzle over the origins of the disease.*
speculate EG *He refused to speculate about the contents of the letter.*

❷ **wonder** VERB
to be surprised and amazed
EG *He wondered at her anger.*
be amazed EG *Most of the cast were amazed by the play's success.*
be astonished EG *I was astonished to discover his true age.*
boggle EG *The mind boggles at what might be in store for us.*
marvel EG *We marvelled at her endless energy.*

❸ **wonder** NOUN
something that amazes people
EG *one of the wonders of nature*

A B C D E F G H I J K L M N O P Q R S T U V W X Y Z

A
B
C
D
E
F
G
H
I
J
K
L
M
N
O
P
Q
R
S
T
U
V
W
X
Y
Z

marvel EG *a marvel of high technology*

miracle EG *It's a miracle no one was killed.*

phenomenon EG *a well-known geographical phenomenon*

spectacle EG *a spectacle not to be missed*

❶ wonderful ADJECTIVE
extremely good
EG *It's wonderful to see you.*

excellent EG *The recording quality is excellent.*

great INFORMAL EG *a great bunch of guys*

marvellous EG *What a marvellous time we had!*

superb EG *The hotel has a superb isolated location.*

tremendous EG *I thought it was a tremendous book.*

❷ wonderful ADJECTIVE
very impressive
EG *The sunset was a truly wonderful sight.*

amazing EG *containing some amazing special effects*

astounding EG *The results are quite astounding.*

incredible EG *The intensity of colour was incredible.*

magnificent EG *magnificent views across the valley*

remarkable EG *It was a remarkable achievement to complete the course.*

> **WORD POWER**
> Synonyms
> phenomenal
> wondrous

word NOUN

> Parts of a word:
> capital letter
> consonant
> grapheme
> letter
> phoneme
> prefix

suffix
syllable
vowel

❶ work VERB
to do the tasks required of you
EG *I had to work twelve hours a day.*

labour EG *peasants labouring in the fields*

slave EG *slaving over a hot stove*

slog away EG *They are still slogging away at algebra.*

toil EG *Workers toiled long hours in the mills.*

> **WORD POWER**
> Antonym
> laze

❷ work NOUN
someone's job
EG *She's trying to find work.*

business EG *We have business to attend to first.*

craft EG *He learned his craft from an expert.*

employment EG *unable to find employment*

job EG *I got at a job at the sawmill.*

livelihood EG *fishermen who depend on the seas for their livelihood*

occupation EG *Please state your occupation.*

profession EG *a dentist by profession*

> **WORD POWER**
> Synonyms
> calling
> métier
> pursuit

❸ work NOUN
the tasks that have to be done
EG *Sometimes he had to take work home.*

assignment EG *written assignments and practical tests*

chore EG *We share the household chores.*

duty EG *My duty is to look after the*

animals.

job EG *It turned out to be a bigger job than expected.*

task EG *catching up with administrative tasks*

yakka AUSTRALIAN AND NEW ZEALAND INFORMAL EG *a decade of hard yakka on the land*

worker NOUN
a person who works
EG *seeking a reliable research worker*

craftsman EG *furniture made by a local craftsman*

employee EG *Many of its employees are women.*

labourer EG *a farm labourer*

workman EG *Workmen are building a steel fence.*

> **WORD POWER**
> Synonyms
> artisan
> hand
> proletarian

❶ **work out** VERB
to find the solution to something
EG *It took us some time to work out what was happening.*

calculate EG *First, calculate your monthly living expenses.*

figure out EG *You don't need to be a detective to figure that one out.*

resolve EG *They hoped the crisis could be quickly resolved.*

solve EG *We'll solve the case ourselves and surprise everyone.*

❷ **work out** VERB
to happen in a certain way
EG *Things didn't work out that way after all.*

develop EG *Wait and see how the situation develops.*

go EG *Did it all go well?*

happen EG *Things don't happen the way you want them to.*

turn out EG *Sometimes life doesn't turn out as we expect.*

❶ **worn-out** ADJECTIVE

no longer usable because of extreme wear
EG *a worn-out pair of shoes*

broken-down EG *Broken-down cars lined the road.*

tattered EG *tattered clothes*

threadbare EG *a square of threadbare carpet*

worn EG *Worn tyres cost lives.*

❷ **worn-out** ADJECTIVE
extremely tired
EG *You must be worn-out after the journey.*

exhausted EG *too exhausted to do any more*

fatigued EG *Winter weather can leave you feeling fatigued.*

prostrate EG *He lay prostrate with exhaustion.*

tired EG *I need to rest because I'm tired.*

weary EG *a weary traveller*

worried ADJECTIVE
being anxious about something
EG *His parents were worried about his lack of progress.*

anxious EG *I was very anxious about her safety.*

bothered EG *I'm not bothered about it at all.*

concerned EG *a phone call from a concerned neighbour*

nervous EG *Consumers say they are nervous about their jobs.*

troubled EG *He was troubled by the lifestyle of his son.*

uneasy EG *an uneasy feeling that everything was going wrong*

> **WORD POWER**
> Synonyms
> overwrought
> perturbed
> unquiet
> Antonym
> unconcerned

❶ **worry** VERB
to feel anxious about something
EG *Don't worry, it's bound to arrive*

A B C D E F G H I J K L M N O P Q R S T U V W X Y Z

soon.

be anxious EG *They admitted they were still anxious about the situation.*

brood EG *constantly brooding about her family*

feel uneasy EG *I felt very uneasy at the lack of response.*

fret EG *You mustn't fret about someone else's problems.*

❷ **worry** VERB
to disturb someone with a problem
EG *I didn't want to worry the boys with this.*

bother EG *I hate to bother you again so soon.*

hassle INFORMAL EG *Then my boss started hassling me.*

pester EG *I wish they'd stop pestering me for an answer.*

plague EG *I'm not going to plague you with more questions.*

trouble EG *Don't trouble me while I'm working.*

> ### WORD POWER
> Synonyms
> harry
> importune
> perturb

❸ **worry** NOUN
a feeling of anxiety
EG *a major source of worry*

anxiety EG *anxieties about money*

apprehension EG *real anger and apprehension about the future*

concern EG *growing concern for the environment*

fear EG *His fears might be groundless.*

misgiving EG *She had some misgivings about what she was about to do.*

unease EG *a deep sense of unease about the coming interview*

worsen VERB
to become more difficult
EG *My relationship with my mother*

worsened.

decline EG *Hourly output declined in the third quarter.*

degenerate EG *The whole tone of the campaign began to degenerate.*

deteriorate EG *The weather conditions are deteriorating.*

go downhill INFORMAL EG *Things have gone steadily downhill since he left.*

> ### WORD POWER
> Antonym
> improve

❶ **worship** VERB
to praise and revere something
EG *People go to church to pray and worship their god.*

glorify EG *The monks devoted their days to glorifying God.*

honour EG *the Scout's promise to honour God*

praise EG *She asked the church to praise God.*

pray to EG *They prayed to their gods to bring them rain.*

venerate EG *the most venerated religious figure in the country*

> ### WORD POWER
> Synonyms
> deify
> exalt
> revere
> Antonym
> dishonour

❷ **worship** VERB
to love and admire someone
EG *She had worshipped him from afar for years.*

adore EG *an adoring husband*

idolize EG *She idolized her father as she was growing up.*

love EG *He genuinely loved and cherished her.*

> ### WORD POWER
> Antonym
> despise

❸ **worship** NOUN

a feeling of love and admiration for something
EG *the worship of the ancient Roman gods*
admiration EG *Her eyes widened in admiration.*
adoration EG *He had been used to female adoration all his life.*
adulation EG *The book was received with adulation by the critics.*
devotion EG *flattered by his devotion*
homage EG *The emperor received the homage of every prince.*
praise EG *singing hymns in praise of their god*

WORD POWER
Synonyms
deification
exaltation

Places of worship:
altar
basilica (*Christianity*)
cathedral (*Christianity*)
chapel (*Christianity*)
church (*Christianity*)
gurdwara (*Sikhism*)
meeting house (*Quakerism*)
mosque (*Muslim*)
pagoda (*Hinduism or Buddhism*)
shrine
synagogue (*Judaism*)
tabernacle (*Judaism or Christianity*)
temple

worthless ADJECTIVE
having no real value or worth
EG *a worthless piece of junk*
meaningless EG *their sense of a meaningless existence*
paltry EG *a paltry amount*
poor EG *a poor reward for his effort*
trifling EG *We were paid a trifling sum.*
trivial EG *She would go to the doctor for any trivial complaint.*
useless EG *I felt useless and a failure.*

valueless EG *commercially valueless trees*

WORD POWER
Synonyms
negligible
nugatory
Antonym
valuable

write VERB
to record something in writing
EG *Write your name and address on a postcard and send it to us.*
compose EG *Vivaldi composed many concertos.*
correspond EG *We corresponded for several years.*
inscribe EG *Their names were inscribed on the front of the pillar.*
record EG *Her letters record the domestic and social details of her life.*
take down EG *notes taken down in shorthand*

writing NOUN

Types of writing:
autobiography
ballad
biography
column
dissertation
editorial
epitaph
essay
fable
feature
fiction
legend
letter
lyric
memoir
myth
narrative
non-fiction
novel
obituary
parable
play
poem
report

review
rhyme
riddle
script
story
thesis
verse

Styles used in writing:
alliteration
cliché
idiom
metaphor
narrative
parody
pun
satire
simile

Features of writing:
character
dialogue
imagery
motif
plot
setting
subplot
theme

❶ wrong ADJECTIVE
not correct or truthful
EG *That was the wrong answer.*
false EG *We don't know if the information is true or false.*
faulty EG *His diagnosis was faulty from the outset.*
incorrect EG *a decision based on figures which were incorrect*
mistaken EG *a mistaken view of the situation*
unsound EG *The thinking is good-hearted, but muddled and unsound.*
untrue EG *The remarks were completely untrue.*

> **WORD POWER**
> Synonyms
> erroneous
> fallacious
> Antonym
> right

❷ wrong ADJECTIVE
morally unacceptable
EG *It's wrong to hurt people.*
bad EG *I may be a thief but I'm not a bad person.*
crooked EG *crooked business deals*
evil EG *the country's most evil terrorists*
illegal EG *It is illegal to intercept radio messages.*
immoral EG *Many would consider such practices immoral.*
unfair EG *It was unfair that he should suffer so much.*
unjust EG *unjust treatment*

> **WORD POWER**
> Synonyms
> felonious
> iniquitous
> reprehensible
> unethical
> Antonym
> right

❸ wrong NOUN
an unjust action
EG *the wrongs of our society*
abuse EG *controversy over human rights abuses*
crime EG *crimes against humanity*
grievance EG *He had a deep sense of grievance.*
injustice EG *A great injustice had been done to him in the past.*
sin EG *He admitted the many sins of his youth.*

yellow NOUN OR ADJECTIVE

Shades of yellow:
amber
canary yellow
champagne
citrus yellow
daffodil
gold
lemon
mustard
primrose
saffron
sand
straw
topaz

yokel NOUN
a person who lives in the country
EG *a bunch of those yokels*
bushie *or* **bushy** AUSTRALIAN AND
NEW ZEALAND INFORMAL EG *"I'm a bit
of a bushie at heart," she said.*
countryman EG *They are true
old-fashioned countrymen.*
peasant EG *In rural Mexico a
peasant is rarely without his
machete.*

❶ young ADJECTIVE
not yet mature
EG *young people*

adolescent EG *He spent his
adolescent years playing guitar.*
immature EG *an immature female
whale*
infant EG *his infant daughter*
junior EG *a junior member of the
family*
juvenile EG *a juvenile delinquent*

WORD POWER
Antonym
old

❷ young PLURAL NOUN
the babies an animal has
EG *The hen may not be able to feed
its young.*
brood EG *a hungry brood of
fledglings*
family EG *a family of weasels*
litter EG *a litter of pups*
offspring EG *female rats' offspring*

zero NOUN
nothing or the number 0
EG *I will now count from zero to ten.*
nil EG *They beat Argentina one-nil.*
nothing EG *Some weeks I earn
nothing.*
nought EG *How many noughts are
there in a million?*

Wordgames

Synonym Puzzle

The clues are all headwords which appear in the thesaurus.
The answers are all synonyms given for these headwords.
When you have filled in the answers, you will find a hidden
message in the vertical line.

Clues:

1 *sudden* (6)
2 *banish* (6)
3 *casual* (10)
4 *lack* (8)
5 *daring* (8)
6 *passionate* (9)
7 *tendency* (11)
8 *famous* (9)
9 *jail* (11)
10 *genius* (8)
11 *war* (11)
12 *helper* (8)

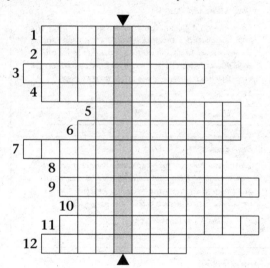

Further activities:

Try making your own puzzle like this, using your thesaurus
to find your synonym clues.

WORDGAMES

EXPRESS YOURSELF

We all tend to overuse some words. The repetition of any word has a boring or annoying effect, and you should try to find alternatives in order to avoid falling into this trap. Another reason for using synonyms is that some words, like "nice", "good" and "bad", have such a general meaning that they do not really add anything to what you are saying or writing, and it is better to use more expressive words in their place.

Try to make these postcards more interesting by substituting words for those underlined.

> Dear Mum and Dad,
>
> I am having a _good_ holiday! The weather is _good_, the food is _good_ and I am managing to get a _good_ tan. There is a lot to do - so many _good_ sights to see and _good_ places to visit. Don't forget to tape Eastenders for me - the next episode is meant to be really _good_.
>
> Best wishes,
>
> Gordon.

> Dear Gordon,
>
> Thank you for your _nice_ postcard! We are glad you had such a _nice_ time on holiday. By the way, your aunt visited us yesterday - she has knitted a _nice_ sweater which I'm sure you'll look very _nice_ in.
>
> See you soon,
>
> Mum and Dad.

Further activities:

What other words can you think of which are overused?

Talk for one minute, or write a short paragraph, about a subject without using any of these words once, and without repeating any of the synonyms you use for them.

FILL IN THE GAPS

The use of expressive words can make a big difference to how effective and interesting your spoken and written English is. Here is a paragraph from which all the descriptive words have been taken out – and you can see how dull and flat it sounds as a result. Choose from the words listed below to fill in the gaps and make the paragraph more expressive and interesting.

> Daphne crept _____ along the _____
> corridor, holding the candle in her _____
> hand. She had the _____ feeling that
> someone or something was watching her.
> A/an _____ noise behind her made her spin
> round, and she gave a/an _____ scream as
> she saw a/an _____ figure approaching. Its
> _____ eyes were fixed on her _____ face
> and it raised its arm and pointed at her
> _____ as it spoke in a/an _____ voice.

dark	unearthly	piercing	terrifying	menacingly
sinister	trembling	chilling	uneasy	glowing
sudden	horrified	ghostly	nervously	silently

Further activities:

Go into pairs. The first person gives a noun and the other has to think of an appropriate adjective beginning with the letter A to describe it. The second person then gives a noun and the first has to give an adjective beginning with the letter B, and so on through the alphabet. The noun given should be different each time. If you are stuck for an adjective, try using your thesaurus to get some ideas.

Alternatively, you can do this as a group in a circle, with each person giving an adjective for their noun and then giving a noun to the next person.

SPECIAL EFFECTS

The way you express yourself makes a big difference to the effect of what you say. You would use a different style of expression if you were :

☆ talking to your friends

☆ writing a letter to apply for a job

☆ making a speech in which you were trying to persuade people to agree with your point of view

☆ writing a story which was meant to be scary or funny or sad

☆ giving instructions on how to do something.

Try writing any three of the following, thinking about the style and language which is most appropriate for each.

1　a postcard or short letter to your best friend (*informal; using descriptive language*)

2　a letter complaining to a shop about poor service or shoddy goods (*formal; avoiding emotive language; brief and to the point*)

3　a short speech for or against something you feel strongly about, for which you are trying to get supporters (*reasonably formal; using emotive and descriptive language*)

4　a set of instructions on how to make or do something (*very factual; no emotive or descriptive language; avoiding big words and long sentences*)

5　a description of a person you want the reader to find funny; a description of a sinister or frightening person; an account of a sad or moving incident (*use of descriptive language is essential here*).

6　a newspaper article reporting on a story of national interest (*may have some emotive language, depending on the subject of the story; avoiding long sentences and big words; sticking to the facts*).

ANTONYM PUZZLE

Here is a word puzzle with a difference – the answers are all *antonyms* of the clues. When you have filled in the answers you will find a hidden message in the horizontal line.

Clues:

1 *approve* (4)
2 *straight* (7)
3 *safe* (9)
4 *temporary* (9)
5 *wasteful* (7)
6 *pessimistic* (10)

7 *changeable* (8)
8 *corrupt* (6)
9 *smart* (7)
10 *grace* (10)
11 *permit* (3)
12 *retreat* (7)

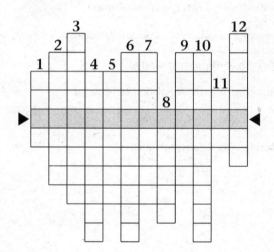

Further activities:

Try making your own puzzle like this using your thesaurus to find your antonym clues.

ODD ONE OUT

Which word is the odd one out in each of these sets? Why is it the odd one out?

1 origin/result/root/source

2 fairly/quite/somewhat/sometimes

3 peace/quiet/stillness/tranquil

4 expand/extend/increase/curtail

5 adjacent/ensuing/following/subsequent

6 exacting/lackadaisical/meticulous/particular

7 balmy/cordial/lukewarm/tepid

8 arrogant/conceited/egotistical/self-effacing

9 distance/duration/period/term

10 build/corpse/figure/physique

CONTEXT MATTERS

Some synonyms can be used in place of a headword in one situation but not in another. Which synonyms work best in these examples? Why don't the others work?

1 My hair was still <u>damp</u>.
   (*dank, humid, moist, soggy, wet*)

2 The cottage sat on the <u>edge</u> of the forest.
   (*border, boundary, brim, fringe, lip, rim*)

3 I could never <u>leave</u> my children.
   (*abandon, depart, desert, forsake, go, quit, withdraw*)

4 She <u>makes</u> all her own clothes.
   (*assemble, build, construct, create, fabricate, fashion, form, manufacture, produce*)

5 The cold <u>numbed</u> my fingers.
   (*dull, freeze, paralyse, stun*)

6 It was <u>plain</u> that he was angry with me.
   (*clear, comprehensible, distinct, evident, obvious, unmistakeable*)

7 The street was <u>empty</u> and silent.
   (*bare, blank, clear, deserted, uninhabited, vacant*)

8 I am not sure I can <u>handle</u> this problem on my own.
   (*administer, conduct, deal with, manage, supervise, take care of*)

9 "Who's there?" she called in a <u>shaky</u> voice.
   (*rickety, tottering, trembling, unstable, unsteady, wobbly*)

10 He has a <u>rare</u> medical condition.
   (*exceptional, few, scarce, sparse, sporadic, uncommon, unusual*)

WORDSEARCH

Red Alert!

All the shades of red listed below can be found in the grid shown. They may read across, up or down, either forwards or backwards, but they are all in straight lines.

Two colours, which are not shades of red, can be made with the letters left over.

```
b z o l a n i d r a c
v e r m i l i o n r h
r c y c l a m e n i e
a r c m a r o o n n r
s i a t n e g a m t r
p m r c e r i s e e y
b s m f l a m e e l p
e o i a m a y b u r p
r n n f u c h s i a o
r n e r t e r a l c p
y r r e b w a r t s e
b u r g u n d y a u q
```

burgundy	crimson	poppy
cardinal	cyclamen	raspberry
carmine	flame	ruby
cerise	fuchsia	scarlet
cherry	magenta	strawberry
claret	maroon	vermilion

CODE GAME 1

In the boxes below, the letters of ten words have been replaced by numbers.

A number represents the same letter each time. Try to crack the code and find the ten words. Here is a clue: all the words you are looking for have something to do with WEATHER.

1 | 1 | 2 | 3 | 4 | 5 | 6 | 7 |
    T   H   U

2 | 10 | 1 | 8 | 7 | 11 | 13 |

3 | 5 | 7 | 9 | 14 | 14 | 12 | 6 |

4 | 1 | 6 | 11 | 17 | 6 | 10 | 1 |

5 | 9 | 15 | 13 |

6 | 10 | 11 | 8 | 16 |

7 | 8 | 18 | 6 | 7 | 15 | 19 | 10 | 1 |

8 | 15 | 13 | 15 | 12 | 8 | 4 | 6 |

9 | 10 | 12 | 6 | 6 | 1 |

CODE GAME II

Can you crack the secret code?

Messages can be sent secretly using a code called the railfence cipher. It works like this. Write down a message, then move every other letter on to the line above, starting with the second letter. The message is then written on two lines, which you divide up into nonsense words. For example:

SUMMER HOLIDAYS SHOULD BE LONGER

U M R O I A S H U D E O G R
S M E H L D Y S O L B L N E

UMRO IAS HUDE OGR
SMEHL DYS OLBLNE

Use the railfence cipher to decode the secret message below.

XM SOL BAOIHD EAS HUD EBLSE

Further activities:

Now that you have cracked the code, try using it on some words from your thesaurus for your class or group to decipher.

ANAGRAMS

Can you rearrange the letters to form parts of a book?

1 PAXEPIND

2 BIG ROYAL PHIB

3 SOYLRAGS

4 SOL TRAIL UNIT

5 TOOT CRUD NINI

6 PEC FEAR

7 PRACHET

8 LET IT

9 ROOF DREW

10 TON SCENT

Further activities:

Choose a list or entry and make up your own scrambled words from it for your class or group to try.

WHAT'S THE CONNECTION?

A single word can be a synonym for more than one headword.
Here are sets of three words which are linked by having one
synonym which can be used for all of them. Look up each
entry to find the linking synonym in each case.

1 fear/panic/warning
2 gap/holiday/crack
3 appear/behave/law
4 cost/blame/accuse
5 comfortable/simple/leisurely
6 beautiful/narrow/splendid
7 easy/fair/soft
8 desire/elaborate/illusion
9 accurate/power/suitable
10 blank/definite/jump

Further activities:

Using the index of your thesaurus, make up some more sets of
linked headwords and try them out on your class or group.

ANSWERS:

Synonym Puzzle:

1 abrupt
2 dispel
3 nonchalant
4 scarcity
5 fearless
6 emotional
7 inclination
8 legendary
9 incarcerate
10 virtuoso
11 hostilities
12 henchman   Hidden message: peace on earth

Antonym Puzzle:

1 veto
2 crooked
3 dangerous
4 permanent
5 thrifty
6 optimistic
7 constant
8 honest
9 scruffy
10 clumsiness
11 ban
12 advance   Hidden message: to err is human

Odd One Out:

1 result
2 sometimes
3 tranquil
4 curtail
5 adjacent
6 lackadaisical
7 cordial
8 self-effacing
9 distance
10 corpse

WORDGAMES

Wordsearch:

```
b  z  o  l  a  n  i  d  r  a  c
v  e  r  m  i  l  i  o  n  r  h
r  c  y  c  l  a  m  e  n  i  e
a  r  c  m  a  r  o  o  n  n  r
s  i  a  t  n  e  g  a  m  t  r
p  m  r  c  e  r  i  s  e  e  y
b  s  m  f  l  a  m  e  e  l  p
e  o  i  a  m  a  y  b  u  r  p
r  n  n  f  u  c  h  s  i  a  o
r     e  r  t  e  r  a  l  c  p
y  r  r  e  b  w  a  r  t  s  e
b  u  r  g  u  n  d  y  a  u  q
```

The remaining letters make up two colours that aren't red:
bronze, aquamarine

Code Game I:	Code Game II:
	Exams should be abolished

Code Game I:

1 thunder
2 stormy
3 drizzle
4 tempest
5 icy
6 smog
7 overcast
8 cyclone
9 sleet

Code Game II:

Exams should be abolished

Anagrams:

1 appendix
2 bibliography
3 glossary
4 illustration
5 introduction
6 preface
7 chapter
8 title
9 foreword
10 contents

What's the Connection?

1 alarm
2 break
3 act
4 charge
5 easy
6 fine
7 light
8 fancy
9 right
10 clear

Index

INDEX

573

I
N
D
E
X

code → law
coerce → force
coerce → make
cogent → convincing
cogent → logical
cogitate → consider
cogitate → think
cogitation → thought
coherent → logical
coin → create
coin → invent
coincidence → chance
cold → callous
cold → cool
cold → impersonal
cold → stiff
cold → unfriendly
cold-blooded → cruel
collaborate → cooperate
collaborate → team
collapse → crash
collapse → downfall
collapse → faint
collapse → fall
collapse → give
colleague → assistant
colleague → associate
collect → concentrate
collect → gather
collected → calm
collected → cool
collection → body
collection → group
collection → number
collection → variety
collectively → together
collide → bump
collide → crash
collide with → hit
collision → crash
colloquial → informal
colloquium → conference
collude → plot
colonize → settle
colossal → big
colossal → great
colossal → huge
colossal → large
colossal → unbelievable
colour → blush
colourless → pale
column → feature
column → line
column → rank
column → row

comatose → unconscious
comb → search
combat → conflict
combat → fight
combat → war
combination → cross
combination → mixture
combination → union
combine → mix
combustion → fire
come about → happen
come about → take place
come across → find
come across → meet
come after → follow
come apart → split
come back → return
come between → divide
come first → win
come into being → appear
come into existence → appear
come into view → appear
come of age → mature
come out → appear
come out on top → triumph
come to → cost
come to → total
come to → wake
come to a decision → decide
come to a head → peak
come to an end → stop
come to grief → fail
come to someone's rescue → save
come up with → invent
come upon → meet
come with → accompany
comedy → humour
comedy → play
comely → attractive
comfort → reassure
comfortable → easy
comfortable → homely
comfortable → leisurely
comfortable → wealthy
comic → funny
comical → funny
comical → hysterical
coming → appearance
coming → future
coming → imminent
command → control

command → direction
command → exact
command → lead
command → manage
command → order
command → tell
commandeer → seize
commander → leader
commander → ruler
commanding → powerful
commemorate → honour
commence → begin
commence → start
commencement → beginning
commencement → opening
commend → advise
commend → honour
commendable → good
commendation → credit
commendation → honour
commendation → praise
comment → remark
commentary → review
commerce → business
commerce → finance
commerce → trade
commercial → advertisement
commercial → economic
commission → employ
commission → hire
committee → council
commodious → spacious
commodity → product
common → frequent
common → general
common → natural
common → popular
common → universal
common → usual
common → vulgar
common → widespread
common sense → sense
commonplace → common
commonwealth → state
commotion → bustle
commotion → excitement
commotion → fuss
commotion → noise
communal → public
communicable → infectious
communicate → express
communicate → inform
communicate → speak

deficient → incomplete
deficient → insufficient
deficient → weak
defile → soil
define → describe
define → explain
definite → clear
definite → final
definite → sure
definition → explanation
definitive → final
deformed → crooked
defraud → cheat
defraud → rob
defunct → dead
defy → challenge
defy → dare
defy → rebel
defy → resist
degenerate → worsen
degrade → reduce
degree → measure
dehumidify → dry
dehydrate → dry
deification → worship
deify → worship
dejected → disappointed
dejected → gloomy
dejected → miserable
dejected → sad
dejection → despair
dejection → disappointment
dejection → grief
dejection → sadness
delay → hinder
delay → pause
delay → postpone
delay → put off
delay → wait
delayed → late
delectable → delicious
delegate → representative
delete → remove
deleterious → harmful
deliberate → consider
deliberate → think
deliberately → on purpose
deliberation → consideration
deliberation → thought
delicacy → tact
delicate → fine
delicate → fragile
delicate → weak

delicious → tasty
delight → charm
delight → ecstasy
delight → entertain
delight → entrance
delight → happiness
delight → joy
delight → please
delight → pride
delight → rejoice
delight in → enjoy
delight in → love
delighted → glad
delighted → happy
delighted → joyful
delighted → pleased
delightful → beautiful
delightful → lovely
delightful → nice
delightful → pleasant
delimit → limit
delineate → outline
delinquent → criminal
delinquent → hooligan
deliquesce → melt
delirium → frenzy
deliver → give
deliver → release
deliver → save
deliverance → freedom
deliverance → release
deluded → fond
deluge → flood
deluge → rain
delusion → dream
delusion → illusion
delusive → deceptive
delusory → fond
demand → ask
demand → command
demand → expect
demand → insist
demand → need
demand → take
demand → want
demanding → difficult
demarcate → limit
demarcate → restrict
demean → degrade
demeanour → appearance
demeanour → manner
demolish → destroy
demolished → broken
demolition → destruction
demonstrate → prove

demonstrate → show
demonstrative → loving
demoralize → discourage
demote → reduce
demotic → colloquial
demur → object
demur → protest
denigrate → belittle
denigration → criticism
denominate → call
denomination → name
denote → indicate
denote → mean
denouement → finish
denounce → accuse
denounce → condemn
denounce → inform on
dense → slow
dense → thick
deny → reject
deny oneself → abstain
depart → leave
departed → dead
departed → late
department → division
department → field
departure → retreat
departure → variation
depend on → trust
dependable → loyal
dependable → reliable
dependable → responsible
dependable → sure
dependence → habit
dependency → colony
depict → describe
depict → represent
deplete → exhaust
deplorable → awful
deplorable → sorry
deplore → disapprove
deport → banish
deportment → manner
deposit → dump
deposit → keep
deposit → payment
deposit → place
deposit → put
deposit → set
depository → store
depot → store
deprave → corrupt
depraved → evil
depraved → perverted
depraved → wicked

depravity → evil
depreciate → fall
depressed → miserable
depressed → sad
depressed → unhappy
depressing → sad
depression → crash
depression → misery
depression → recession
depression → sadness
depth → extreme
depths → bottom
deputy → helper
deputy → representative
deputy → substitute
deranged → mad
deride → belittle
deride → make fun of
deride → mock
derision → abuse
derision → mockery
derision → scorn
derisive → sarcastic
derivation → origin
derivation → source
derive → base
derive → result
derogatory → critical
descend → drop
descendants → family
descent → origin
describe → explain
describe → report
describe → represent
description → explanation
description → report
descry → find
descry → see
descry → spot
desert → abandon
desert → barren
desert → leave
deserted → empty
deserted → lonely
deserve → merit
desiccate → dry
design → intend
design → invent
design → layout
design → pattern
design → plan
design → structure
designate → call
designate → class
designation → name

designed → calculated
desirable → right
desire → longing
desire → passion
desire → urge
desire → want
desire → wish
desirous → willing
desist → abstain
desist → stop
desolate → barren
desolate → lonely
despair → misery
despatch → message
desperate → terrible
despicable → hateful
despicable → shabby
despise → hate
despise → scorn
despite → in spite of
despondency → despair
despondency → disappointment
despondency → sadness
despondent → disappointed
despondent → gloomy
despondent → pessimistic
despondent → unhappy
dessicate → wither
destiny → fate
destiny → luck
destitute → poor
destitution → hardship
destitution → poverty
destroy → bomb
destroy → eat away
destroy → erode
destroy → kill
destroy → spoil
destructive → deadly
destructive → harmful
desultory → random
detach → remove
detach → separate
detached → alone
detached → distant
detached → impersonal
detached → separate
detail → describe
detailed → elaborate
detailed → full
detain → imprison
detain → jail
detect → find

detect → notice
detect → spot
deter → discourage
deteriorate → erode
deteriorate → wear
deteriorate → worsen
deterioration → rot
deterioration → wear
determinant → factor
determination → will
determine → calculate
determine → decide
determine → learn
determine → see
determine → settle
determined → firm
determined → set on
detest → dislike
detest → hate
detestation → hate
detestation → hostility
detested → unpopular
detonate → explode
detonate → fire
detract from → belittle
detriment → cost
detrimental → harmful
detritus → remains
devastate → destroy
devastation → destruction
develop → breed
develop → build
develop → elaborate
develop → enlarge on
develop → expand
develop → expand on
develop → extend
develop → grow
develop → improve
develop → progress
develop → result
develop → work out
development → advance
development → growth
deviant → perverted
deviation → variation
device → bomb
device → gadget
device → machine
devious → cunning
devious → sly
deviousness → cunning
devise → compose
devise → create
devise → invent

disparate → various
disparity → difference
disparity → gap
dispassionate → cool
dispassionate → fair
dispassionate → impersonal
dispassionate → neutral
dispatch → kill
dispatch → message
dispatch → news
dispatch → send
dispel → banish
dispense → distribute
disperse → distribute
disperse → melt
display → show
display → sight
displease → annoy
displeasure → annoyance
dispose of → discard
dispose of → dump
dispose of → get rid of
dispose of → process
dispose of → settle
disposed → prone
disposition → character
disproportionate → excessive
dispute → argument
dispute → challenge
dispute → disagree
dispute → disagreement
dispute → fight
dispute → quarrel
dispute → question
disqualification → ban
disqualify → ban
disquiet → concern
disquieting → sinister
disquisition → speech
disquisition → talk
disregard → ignore
disregard → neglect
disreputable → notorious
disreputable → scruffy
disrespectful → rude
disrupt → disturb
disrupt → interfere
dissembling → lying
disseminate → circulate
disseminate → communicate
disseminate → scatter
dissent → disagree

dissent → disagreement
dissimilar → different
dissimulate → lie
dissimulation → lying
dissipation → excess
dissipation → waste
dissolve → eat away
dissolve → melt
dissuade → discourage
distance → length
distance → space
distant → cold
distant → far
distant → foreign
distaste → dislike
distasteful → unpleasant
distend → enlarge
distilled → refined
distinct → different
distinct → particular
distinct → plain
distinction → difference
distinction → quality
distinctive → characteristic
distinctive → special
distinguishable → visible
distinguished → famous
distinguished → great
distinguishing → characteristic
distort → cloud
distort → colour
distort → misrepresent
distort → twist
distorted → crooked
distorted → deformed
distorted → garbled
distracted → absent-minded
distraction → escape
distress → alarm
distress → concern
distress → disturb
distress → grief
distress → grieve
distress → hurt
distress → pain
distress → shake
distress → shock
distress → upset
distress signal → alarm
distressed → upset
distressing → bad
distressing → painful
distressing → tragic

distribute → circulate
district → area
district → local
district → region
distrust → question
distrust → suspect
distrust → suspicion
distrustful → cynical
distrustful → suspicious
distrustful → wary
disturb → bother
disturb → concern
disturb → distress
disturb → shake
disturb → trouble
disturb → upset
disturbance → riot
disunite → split
dither → hesitate
dive → descend
diverge → split
divergence → difference
divergence → split
divergent → different
diverse → various
diversify → vary
diversion → escape
diversion → hobby
diversion → pastime
diversion → variation
divert → distract
divide → distribute
divide → separate
divide → share
divide → sort
divine → religious
division → department
division → section
division → split
divorce → separate
divorced → separate
divulge → reveal
dizzy → dazed
dizzy → faint
do → accomplish
do → achieve
do → commit
do → practise
do → suit
do away with → abolish
do away with → eliminate
do business → trade
do up → decorate
do well → succeed
do well → thrive

drive into → crash
drive off → repel
drive someone up the
  wall → pester
drivel → garbage
drivel → nonsense
drivel → rubbish
drizzle → rain
droll → funny
drollery → humour
droop → hang
droop → wither
drooping → limp
drop → ball
drop → decrease
drop → drip
drop → dump
drop → fall
drop → lose
drop → lower
drop → trace
drop out of sight →
  disappear
droplet → drip
droplet → drop
drown → flood
drowsy → sleepy
drowsy → tired
drug → medicine
drum → advice
drum → information
dry → barren
dual → double
dub → call
dub → name
dubiety → suspicion
dubious → doubtful
dubious → improbable
dubious → suspect
dubious → suspicious
dubious → uncertain
duck → dodge
duck → escape
duck out of → avoid
ductile → flexible
ductile → soft
duel → fight
dulcet → soft
dulcet → sweet
dull → blank
dull → blunt
dull → boring
dull → cloudy
dull → dim
dull → dreary

dull → fade
dull → flat
dull → gloomy
dull → numb
dull → sleepy
dull → stuffy
dullness → boredom
dumb → dim
dumb → idiotic
dumb → silent
dumb → slow
dumbfound → amaze
dumbness → silence
dummy → mock
dummy → model
dump → discard
dump → get rid of
dunce → fool
dungeon → prison
dupe → cheat
dupe → deceive
dupe → fool
dupe → trap
dupe → trick
duplicate → copy
duplicitous → false
duplicity → dishonesty
duplicity → fraud
duplicity → lying
durable → strong
durable → tough
duration → length
duress → force
dusk → dark
dust → clean
dust → dirt
duty → job
duty → part
duty → responsibility
duty → task
duty → tax
duty → work
dwell → inhabit
dwell → live
dwell on → stress
dwelling → home
dwelling → house
dwindle → decrease
dwindle → fall
dwindle → lessen
dwindle → shrink
dye → colour
dynamic → energetic
eager → enthusiastic
eager → impatient

eager → keen
eager → ready
eager → willing
eagerness → enthusiasm
eagle-eyed → observant
earlier → before
earlier → first
earlier → previous
earliest → first
earmark → intend
earn → deserve
earn → gain
earn → merit
earnest → intense
earnest → serious
earnest → solemn
earnings → income
earnings → pay
earnings → profit
earth → dirt
earth → ground
earth → soil
ease → comfort
ease → moderate
easily offended → sensitive
easily offended → touchy
easily upset → sensitive
easy → comfortable
easy → fluent
easy → informal
easy → leisurely
easy → simple
easy to use → handy
easy-going → mild
eat away → erode
eavesdrop → hear
ebb → fall
echelon → rank
echo → repeat
eclipse → blot out
eclipse → outdo
eco-friendly → green
ecological → green
economic → economical
economic → efficient
economic → financial
economical → cheap
economical → thrifty
economics → finance
economize → save
ecstasy → happiness
ecstasy → heaven
ecstasy → joy
edge → bank
edge → border

eyewitness → witness
fabric → cloth
fabric → material
fabric → substance
fabricate → build
fabricate → invent
fabricate → make
fabricate → make up
fabrication → lie
fabrication → lying
fabrication → making
facade → outside
face → brave
face → expression
face → front
face → look
face → outside
face down → prone
facility → skill
facsimile → copy
facsimile → model
fact → reality
fact → truth
faction → movement
faction → party
faction → side
factor → consideration
facts → information
factual → real
factual → true
fad → craze
fad → fashion
fad → whim
faddish → fussy
fade → die out
fade → disappear
fade → wither
fade away → die
fade out → die
faded → faint
faded → pale
fail → collapse
fail → neglect
fail → weaken
fail to notice → miss
fail to remember → forget
failing → fault
failure → collapse
failure → crash
faint → dim
faint → slender
faint → soft
faint → weak
faint-hearted → cowardly
faint-hearted → timid

fair → all right
fair → beautiful
fair → festival
fair → light
fair → market
fair → moderate
fair → respectable
fairly → pretty
fairly → quite
fairly → rather
fairness → justice
fairness → right
faith → belief
faith → confidence
faithful → accurate
faithful → exact
faithful → loyal
faithful → realistic
faithful → reliable
faithless → treacherous
fake → copy
fake → false
fake → fraud
fake → mock
fake → pretend
fall → descend
fall → downfall
fall → drop
fall → slope
fall apart → disintegrate
fall behind → lag
fall down → collapse
fall out → argue
fall out → quarrel
fall over → trip
fall through → fail
fall to → reach
fall to pieces → disintegrate
fallacious → faulty
fallacious → wrong
fallacy → illusion
false → deceptive
false → fake
false → insincere
false → lying
false → mock
false → wrong
falsehood → lie
falsify → misrepresent
falsify → pretend
fame → glory
famed → great
familiar → accustomed
familiar → informal
familiar with → aware of

family → kin
family → young
famished → hungry
famous → great
famous name → personality
fan → follower
fan → supporter
fancy → desire
fancy → elaborate
fancy → illusion
fancy → imagine
fancy → whim
fantasize → daydream
fantasize → imagine
fantastic → great
fantastic → splendid
fantasy → daydream
fantasy → dream
fantasy → vision
far → distant
far-fetched → improbable
far-fetched → incredible
far-flung → distant
far-off → distant
faraway → distant
fare → do
fare → food
fascinate → appeal
fascinate → entrance
fascination → charm
fashion → craze
fashion → make
fashion → manner
fashion → model
fashion → shape
fashionable → popular
fast → express
fast → quick
fast → quickly
fasten → bond
fasten → connect
fasten → fix
fasten → hang
fasten → join
fasten → link
fasten → shut
fasten → tie
fastened → shut
fastening → connection
fastidious → fine
fastidious → fussy
fastidious → particular
fat → plump
fat → thick
fatal → deadly

INDEX

grace → polish
gracious → good
graciousness → courtesy
grade → class
grade → classify
grade → level
grade → quality
grade → rank
grade → sort
gradient → slope
gradient → tilt
gradual → slow
gradually → slowly
graduate → pass
grain → bit
grain → finish
grand → impressive
grand → splendid
grandeur → glory
grandiloquent → pretentious
grandiose → grand
grandiose → pompous
grant → admit
grant → allow
grant → give
grant → permit
grant → present
graphic → colourful
grapple → fight
grasp → command
grasp → grab
grasp → grip
grasp → handle
grasp → hold
grasp → learn
grasp → master
grasp → realize
grasp → see
grasp → seize
grasp → understand
grasp → understanding
grasping → greedy
grass on → inform on
grate → scrape
gratified → proud
gratify → satisfy
gratis → free
grave → critical
grave → deep
grave → grim
grave → heavy
grave → serious
grave → solemn
grave → tomb

graze → scrape
graze → touch
great → big
great → deep
great → excellent
great → extreme
great → good
great → grand
great → high
great → intense
great → large
great → splendid
great → wonderful
great deal → plenty
greater → better
greatest → supreme
greatest → ultimate
greatly → very
greedy → selfish
green → field
green → ignorant
green → inexperienced
greet → receive
gregarious → sociable
grenade → bomb
grey → dim
grey → drab
grief → misery
grief → pain
grief → regret
grievance → wrong
grieve → distress
grieve → lament
grieve → regret
grieve → upset
grievous → painful
grill → cook
grill → interrogate
grim → horrible
grime → dirt
grimy → dirty
grin → smile
grind → scrape
grip → handle
grip → hold
gripping → interesting
grit → courage
groan → moan
grog → alcohol
gross → disgusting
ground → base
ground → bottom
ground → earth
ground → soil
grounds → argument

grounds → cause
grounds → land
grounds → reason
group → arrange
group → class
group → club
group → collection
group → company
group → grade
group → lot
group → movement
group → organization
group → society
group → sort
group → team
grouping → party
grouse → complain
grow → expand
grow → get
grow → increase
grow → rise
grow up → mature
grown → mature
grown-up → adult
grown-up → mature
growth → gain
growth → increase
grubby → dirty
grudge → resentment
grudging → unwilling
gruesome → horrible
gruff → hoarse
grumble → complain
grumble → moan
grumpy → cross
grunt → moan
guarantee → bond
guarantee → ensure
guarantee → promise
guaranteed → definite
guard → defend
guard → protect
guard → watch
guard against → beware
guarded → cautious
guarded → wary
guess → assume
guess → idea
guess → imagine
guess → suspect
guffaw → laugh
guidance → advice
guidance → direction
guidance → help
guide → direct

hasty → rash
hasty → sudden
hatch → plot
hate → dislike
hate → hatred
hatred → dislike
hatred → hate
hatred → horror
hatred → hostility
haughtiness → pride
haughty → superior
haul → drag
haul → draw
haul → loot
haul → pull
haunt → frequent
hauteur → pride
have → bear
have → experience
have → own
have → possess
have a break → rest
have a go → attack
have a good opinion of → respect
have a hand in → take part in
have a high opinion of → respect
have a hunch → sense
have a meal → eat
have a tendency → tend
have a weakness for → love
have a yen for → fancy
have an accident → crash
have charge of → supervise
have confidence in → trust
have faith in → trust
have fun → play
have on → wear
have power over → control
haven → refuge
haven → retreat
having a liking for → fond
hawk → sell
hazard → danger
hazard → gamble
hazard → guess
hazard → threat
hazardous → dangerous
hazardous → treacherous
haze → cloud
hazy → dim
hazy → vague

head → boss
head → command
head → foam
head → lead
head → leader
head → mind
head → top
head of state → ruler
headlong → quick
headquarters → base
headstrong → obstinate
headway → progress
heal → cure
healing → recovery
healthier → better
healthy → fit
healthy → well
heap → pile
heaps → plenty
hear → gather
hear → learn
hear → listen
hear → understand
hearsay → gossip
hearsay → rumour
heart → basis
heart → centre
heart → essence
heart-rending → sad
heart-rending → tragic
heartache → distress
heartache → grief
heartbreak → grief
heartbreaking → pathetic
heartbreaking → tragic
hearten → encourage
hearten → reassure
hearten → strengthen
heartfelt → passionate
heartfelt → sincere
heartless → callous
heartless → cruel
heartless → merciless
heat → feeling
heat → warm
heat up → warm
heated → hot
heated → warm
heave → raise
heave → vomit
heavy → stuffy
heavy-duty → strong
heckle → interrupt
hectic → busy
heed → hear

heedful → wary
heedless → rash
height → extreme
height → maximum
height → top
height → ultimate
heirloom → legacy
heirlooms → valuables
hellfire → hell
help → benefit
help → blessing
help → comfort
help → encourage
help → support
helper → assistant
helpful → accommodating
helpful → convenient
helpful → handy
helpful → positive
helpful → useful
helpful → valuable
helping hand → help
helpless → powerless
hem → border
hem in → confine
hem in → enclose
hem in → surround
henchman → follower
henchman → helper
herald → messenger
Herculean → strong
here → present
heritage → inheritance
heroic → bold
heroic → brave
heroism → bravery
heroism → courage
heterogeneous → various
hew → carve
hew → chop
hiatus → gap
hiatus → interval
hibernate → sleep
hibernation → sleep
hidden → invisible
hidden → secret
hide → coat
hide → cover
hide → obscure
hidebound → conservative
high → excited
high → steep
high → tall
high → thrill
high point → peak

inflamed → sore
inflexible → firm
inflexible → obstinate
inflexible → stubborn
inflict → bring
inflict → impose
influence → factor
influence → grip
influence → guide
influence → make an
  impression
influential → big
influential → important
influential → powerful
inform → advise
inform → alert
inform → brief
inform → communicate
inform → tell
inform of → report
inform on → betray
informal → colloquial
information → news
informed → aware
informed → wise
infrequent → few
infringe → break
infringe → intrude
infringed → broken
infringement → breach
infuriate → anger
infuriated → mad
ingenious → bright
ingenious → smart
ingenuity → imagination
ingenuous →
  impressionable
ingenuous → innocent
ingenuous → natural
ingenuousness →
  innocence
ingot → block
inhabit → live
inhabitant → local
inhabitants → people
inherent → natural
inheritance → legacy
inhibit → check
inhibit → interfere
inhibit → restrain
inhibit → restrict
inhibited → pent-up
inhumane → cruel
inhumanity → cruelty
inimitable → incomparable

iniquitous → bad
iniquitous → criminal
iniquitous → unfair
iniquitous → wicked
iniquitous → wrong
iniquity → sin
initial → first
initial → opening
initial → original
initially → first
initiate → begin
initiate → start
initiation → beginning
initiation → introduction
initiation → start
injudicious → irrational
injudicious → rash
injunction → command
injure → damage
injure → hurt
injurious → harmful
injury → damage
injury → harm
injustice → wrong
inkling → idea
inlet → bay
inmate → inhabitant
inn → pub
innards → insides
innate → natural
inner → inside
innermost → inside
innocent → ignorant
innocuous → harmless
innocuous → safe
innovative → original
innovatory → original
innumerable → countless
innumerable → many
inordinate → excessive
inquire → ask
inquire into → check
inquiring → curious
inquisitive → curious
inquisitiveness → curiosity
insane → idiotic
insane → mad
inscribe → carve
inscribe → write
insensible → numb
insensible → unconscious
insensitive → callous
insensitive → numb
insensitive → thoughtless
insight → vision

insight → wisdom
insightful → perceptive
insignificant → petty
insignificant → slight
insignificant → small
insignificant → unimportant
insincere → false
insinuate → hint
insinuate → suggest
insinuation → suggestion
insipid → boring
insipid → flat
insipid → mild
insipid → tasteless
insist → claim
insist on → exact
insist upon → exact
insolence → impudence
insolent → cheeky
insolent → rude
insolvency → poverty
insouciant → casual
inspect → check
inspect → examine
inspection → check
inspection → examination
inspire → excite
inspire → motivate
inspired → creative
inspirit → reassure
install → set up
instalment → payment
instalment → section
instance → case
instant → immediate
instant → moment
instantaneous →
  immediate
instantly → immediately
instigate → begin
instigate → incite
instigate → start
instinctive → automatic
instinctive → natural
institute → begin
institute → set up
institute → society
institute → start
institution → introduction
institution → organization
instruct → brief
instruct → order
instruct → show
instruct → teach
instruct → tell

I
N
D
E
X

nonaligned → neutral
nonchalant → careless
nonchalant → casual
nonpartisan → neutral
nonplus → confuse
nonplus → puzzle
nonplus → surprise
nonplussed → confused
nonsense → garbage
nonsense → rubbish
nonsensical → absurd
nonsensical → foolish
nonsensical → irrational
nonstop → constant
nonstop → express
nonstop → relentless
nonstop → steady
nontoxic → harmless
normal → average
normal → natural
normal → ordinary
normal → regular
normal → sane
normal → typical
normal → usual
normally → as a rule
normally → on average
nostalgic → sentimental
nosy → curious
nosy parker → snooper
not be able to abide → dislike
not be able to bear → dislike
not be able to stand → dislike
not dangerous → harmless
not ever → never
not guilty → innocent
not level → uneven
not liable → exempt
not many → few
not quite → almost
not smooth → uneven
not working → dead
notable → important
notable → memorable
notable → particular
note → comment
note → entry
note → message
note → notice
note → record
noted → famous
noteworthy → particular

nothing → zero
notice → advertisement
notice → heed
notice → information
notice → item
notice → review
notice → see
notice → sign
notice → warning
noticeable → visible
notification → notice
notify → advise
notify → alert
notify → inform
notify → report
notify → tell
notify → warn
notion → idea
notion → impression
notion → thought
notwithstanding → despite
notwithstanding → in spite of
nought → zero
nourishing → healthy
nourishment → food
nous → intelligence
nous → sense
novel → original
novel → strange
novelty → curiosity
novice → beginner
novice → recruit
now → immediately
now and again → sometimes
now and then → sometimes
noxious → poisonous
nude → bare
nude → naked
nudge → poke
nugatory → worthless
nuisance → annoyance
nuisance → bother
nuisance → pest
nullify → foil
nullify → frustrate
numb → frozen
numb → shock
numbed → dazed
number → quantity
numeral → number
numerous → many
nurse → look after
nurse → tend

nurse → treat
nurture → breed
nurture → raise
nutritious → healthy
oaf → idiot
obdurate → firm
obdurate → stubborn
obese → fat
obey → follow
object → disagree
object → intention
object → mind
object → point
object → protest
object → purpose
object → subject
object → thing
object → use
object to → resent
objection → disagreement
objection → protest
objectionable → offensive
objectionable → unpleasant
objective → aim
objective → end
objective → intention
objective → object
obligate → force
obligation → bond
obligation → duty
obligation → responsibility
obligatory → compulsory
oblige → force
oblige → make
obliging → accommodating
obliging → good
oblique → indirect
obliterate → blot out
obliterate → destroy
obliteration → destruction
oblivious → ignorant
oblivious → preoccupied
oblivious → unaware
oblivious → unconscious
obloquy → slander
obnoxious → disgusting
obnoxious → hateful
obnoxious → unpleasant
obscene → crude
obscene → naughty
obscure → blot out
obscure → cover
obscure → dim
obscure → unknown
obsequiousness → flattery

outdoors → country
outer → outside
outfit → clothes
outfit → organization
outfit → provide
outfit → set
outgoing → sociable
outing → trip
outlandish → eccentric
outlaw → ban
outlaw → forbid
outlawed → illegal
outlay → cost
outline → shape
outline → summary
outlive → survive
outlook → attitude
outlook → prospect
outlook → scene
outlying → distant
outlying → far
outmoded → old-fashioned
outmoded → out of date
outpost → colony
outrage → anger
outrage → horrify
outrage → offend
outrage → shock
outrageous → impossible
outré → strange
outright → complete
outright → pure
outright → straight
outright → total
outset → beginning
outset → start
outshine → outdo
outspoken → blunt
outstanding → best
outstanding → excellent
outstanding → fine
outstanding → great
outstanding → major
outstanding → prize
outstrip → beat
outstrip → pass
outward → outside
over → above
over → past
over the moon → joyful
overabundance → excess
overall → general
overarching → universal
overbearing → bossy
overcast → cloudy

overcast → dark
overcast → dull
overcome → beat
overcome → crush
overcome → subdue
overdo → exaggerate
overdose → excess
overdue → late
overemotional → sentimental
overestimate → exaggerate
overexert → strain
overflow → flood
overflowing → crowded
overheads → upkeep
overhear → hear
overindulge → spoil
overindulgence → excess
overjoyed → glad
overlay → cover
overlook → excuse
overlook → face
overlook → forget
overlook → ignore
overlook → miss
overlook → neglect
overoptimistic → fond
overpower → subdue
overpriced → expensive
overpriced → steep
override → overrule
override → overturn
overrule → overturn
overrule → reverse
overseas → foreign
oversee → direct
oversee → supervise
oversensitive → touchy
oversight → mistake
overstate → exaggerate
overt → naked
overt → obvious
overtake → pass
overtax → strain
overturn → abolish
overturn → overrule
overturn → reverse
overturn → upset
overweight → fat
overwhelm → beat
overwork → strain
overwrought → hysterical
overwrought → worried
owing to → because
own → have

own → personal
own up → confess
ownership → possession
ozone-friendly → green
pace → rate
pace → speed
pace → walk
pacific → mild
pack → cram
pack → fill
pack → group
pack → load
packed → crowded
packed → full
pact → agreement
pact → understanding
padlock → lock
pagan → heathen
pain → annoyance
pain → distress
pain → grieve
pain → nuisance
pain → pest
pain in the neck → annoyance
pain in the neck → pest
painful → bad
painful → sore
painful → uncomfortable
painless → easy
pains → care
painstaking → careful
painstaking → thorough
paint → colour
paint → draw
painting → picture
pair up → team
pal → friend
palatable → tasty
palatial → grand
palaver → fuss
pale → light
pale → soft
palpable → clear
palpable → obvious
paltry → meagre
paltry → slight
paltry → unimportant
paltry → worthless
pamper → spoil
pamphlet → leaflet
pan → criticize
panache → style
pandemonium → noise
pander to → humour

INDEX

INDEX

INDEX

racket → noise
radiance → light
radiant → bright
radiant → shining
radiate → emit
radiate → shine
radical → drastic
radical → extreme
radical → left-wing
rage → anger
rage → frenzy
rage → rampage
rage → rave
ragged → irregular
ragged → scruffy
ragged → shabby
raging → violent
raging → wild
raid → attack
raid → loot
rail → bar
raiment → clothes
raiment → dress
rainfall → rain
rainy → wet
raise → breed
raise → collect
raise → lift
rally → gathering
rally → recovery
rally → revive
ram → jam
ram → push
ramble → walk
ramble → wander
rambling → indirect
ramp → slope
rampage → rage
rampage → riot
rampart → barrier
rancid → sour
rancorous → bitter
rancour → resentment
rancour → spite
random → absent-minded
random → accidental
random → irregular
randomly → at random
range → area
range → choice
range → variety
range → wander
rank → class
rank → classify
rank → level

rank → line
rank → rate
rank → row
rank → status
ransack → loot
rant → rave
rap → blame
rap → hit
rap someone's knuckles
  → punish
rapid → fast
rapid → hasty
rapid → quick
rapidity → speed
rapidly → fast
rapidly → quickly
rapport → relationship
rapture → ecstasy
rapture → heaven
rapture → joy
rare → scarce
rare → unusual
raring to go → eager
rarity → curiosity
rasp → scrape
rasping → hoarse
rate → class
rate → consider
rate → cost
rate → count
rate → grade
rate → judge
rate highly → appreciate
rather → pretty
rather → quite
ratification → approval
ration → limit
ration → share
rational → logical
rational → sane
rational → sensible
rational → wise
rationale → grounds
rationality → reason
rationalize → cut
rations → supplies
rattle → shake
ratty → irritable
rave → rage
ravenous → hungry
raving → hysterical
raw → cold
raw → inexperienced
raw → sore
raze → destroy

razor-sharp → sharp
re-establish → renew
re-establish → restore
reach → contact
reach → extend
reach a decision → decide
reach adulthood → mature
reach its highest point →
  peak
reactionary → conservative
reactionary →
  narrow-minded
reactionary → right-wing
read up → study
ready → fluent
ready → willing
real → genuine
real → natural
real → sincere
real → true
realism → reality
realistic → actual
reality → fact
reality → truth
realize → accomplish
realize → appreciate
realize → find
realize → see
realize → sense
realize → understand
really → very
reanimate → revive
reap → earn
reap → gain
reappear → return
rear → back
rear → bottom
rear → breed
rear → raise
reason → argue
reason → cause
reason → end
reason → excuse
reason → grounds
reason → purpose
reason → sense
reason → wisdom
reasonable → cheap
reasonable → decent
reasonable → logical
reasonable → moderate
reasonable → rational
reasonable → respectable
reasonable → sane
reasonable → tolerable

rugged → rough
rugged → tough
ruin → crash
ruin → destroy
ruin → downfall
ruin → harm
ruin → spoil
ruined → derelict
rule → control
rule → law
rule → line
rule out → exclude
ruling → decision
ruminate → consider
ruminate → think
rumination → thought
ruminative → thoughtful
rumpus → noise
run → direct
run → flow
run → manage
run → pour
run → race
run → range
run → series
run → supervise
run across → meet
run amok → rampage
run around → associate
run away → escape
run away → flee
run into → hit
run into → meet
run off → escape
run riot → rampage
run riot → riot
run through → exhaust
run-down → shabby
run-of-the-mill → common
run-of-the-mill →
  hackneyed
run-of-the-mill → ordinary
rundown → outline
rundown → summary
runner → candidate
runner → messenger
running → management
running → upkeep
runny → liquid
runny → thin
rupture → breach
rupture → burst
rupture → division
rupture → tear
ruse → manoeuvre

ruse → trick
rush → burst
rush → bustle
rush → flood
rush → fly
rush → hurry
rush → speed
rush → wave
ruthless → harsh
ruthless → merciless
sabbatical → leave
sack → fire
sack → raid
sacred → holy
sacred → religious
sacrosanct → holy
sad → gloomy
sad → miserable
sad → pathetic
sad → sorry
sad → unhappy
sadden → distress
sadden → grieve
sadden → hurt
saddened → disappointed
saddening → painful
sadistic → cruel
sadness → grief
sadness → misery
safe → harmless
safe → immune
safe → reliable
safe and sound → safe
safeguard → defence
safeguard → defend
safeguard → guard
safeguard → precaution
safeguard → protect
safeguard → protection
safeguard → save
sagacious → clever
sagacious → shrewd
sagacity → sense
sagacity → wisdom
sagging → flabby
sail → fly
saintly → holy
salacious → dirty
salacious → obscene
salary → income
salary → pay
salient → important
salient → noticeable
sallow → pale
sally → joke

saloon → pub
salted → salty
salubrious → healthy
salutary → healthy
salute → greet
salute → recognize
salvage → save
same → like
sameness → similarity
sample → example
sample → try
sanction → allow
sanction → approval
sanction → approve
sanction → blessing
sanction → let
sanction → permit
sanctioned → legal
sanctuary → refuge
sanctuary → retreat
sands → beach
sanguine → optimistic
sanitation → hygiene
sap → drain
sap → tax
sap → undermine
sap → weaken
sarcophagus → tomb
sardonic → sarcastic
sate → satisfy
satiate → satisfy
satire → parody
satirical → sarcastic
satirize → make fun of
satisfaction → comfort
satisfaction → happiness
satisfaction → pleasure
satisfaction → pride
satisfactory → decent
satisfactory → good
satisfactory → suitable
satisfied → confident
satisfied → pleased
satisfied → sure
satisfy → convince
satisfy → meet
satisfy → suit
saturate → soak
saturate → wet
saturated → full
saturated → wet
saucy → bold
saunter → walk
savage → violent
savagery → cruelty

INDEX

site – snappy

site → scene
site → spot
situate → place
situation → location
situation → matter
situation → state
sixth sense → instinct
sizable → handsome
sizable → large
sizable → spacious
size → area
size → quantity
sizeable → handsome
sizeable → large
sizeable → spacious
skeletal → thin
skelm → criminal
sketch → draw
sketch → outline
sketch → picture
sketchy → rough
skilful → capable
skilful → expert
skilfully → well
skill → ability
skill → qualification
skilled → expert
skilled → good
skilled → perfect
skilled → practical
skilled → skilful
skim → glance
skimpy → meagre
skin → coat
skin → graze
skin → hide
skin → scrape
skinny → thin
skip → omit
skirmish → fight
skit → parody
skite → boast
skite → braggart
skiter → braggart
skulk → sneak
slack → flabby
slack → lazy
slack → limp
slack → loose
slacken → ease
slacken → loosen
slag → insult
slake → satisfy
slam → shut

slant → colour
slant → slope
slant → tilt
slanted → biased
slap → hit
slapdash → careless
slash → cut
slash → lower
slate → abuse
slaughter → kill
slaughter → murder
slave → labour
slave → work
slay → kill
slay → murder
slaying → murder
sleek → glossy
sleek → smooth
sleepy → tired
slender → narrow
slender → thin
slice → cut
slice → piece
slide → flow
slight → insult
slight → light
slight → minor
slight → scorn
slight → slender
slight → thin
slight → unimportant
slightest → least
slightly → rather
slim → narrow
slim → slender
slim → thin
sling → throw
slink → sneak
slip → mistake
slip → sneak
slip → steal
slipshod → careless
slipshod → inefficient
slit → cut
slog away → work
slope → tilt
sloppy → careless
sloppy → inefficient
sloppy → loose
sloppy → sentimental
slot → opening
slothful → lazy
slovenly → scruffy
slow → dim
slow → gradual

sluggish → sleepy
sluggish → slow
slumber → sleep
slump → drop
slump → fall
slump → recession
slur → slander
slushy → sentimental
sly → cunning
smack → blow
smack → hit
small → fine
small → little
small → modest
small → short
small → slender
small → slight
small-minded → petty
smallest → least
smart → bright
smart → clever
smart → intelligent
smart → neat
smart → shrewd
smarting → sore
smash → break
smash → crash
smash into → hit
smashed → broken
smear → slander
smear → soil
smell → fragrance
smirch → pollute
smirch → soil
smirch → stain
smirk → smile
smooth → easy
smooth → even
smooth → flat
smooth → level
smother → suppress
smoulder → glow
smudge → mark
smudge → spot
smuggle → sneak
smugness → pride
smutty → crude
smutty → dirty
smutty → naughty
smutty → obscene
snag → catch
snag → difficulty
snap → break
snap → crack
snappy → impatient

656

I
N
D
E
X

tell the difference → distinguish
telling → convincing
telling → powerful
temerity → daring
temper → character
temper → humour
temper → moderate
temper → mood
temperament → character
temperamental → moody
temperate → mild
tempestuous → violent
template → pattern
tempo → rate
tempo → rhythm
temporary → brief
tempt → attract
temptation → bait
tenacious → determined
tenacious → stubborn
tenacity → determination
tend → look after
tender → affectionate
tender → gentle
tender → loving
tender → offer
tender → painful
tender → romantic
tender → sore
tenderness → kindness
tenet → belief
tense → nervous
tense → tight
tensile → soft
tension → strain
tension → stress
tentative → cautious
tenuous → slender
tenure → possession
tepid → warm
term → call
term → expression
term → length
term → name
term → period
terminal → fatal
terminate → end
terminate → halt
termination → conclusion
termination → finish
termination → halt
termination of employment → the sack
terminology → language

terms → condition
terrain → ground
terrible → awful
terrible → bad
terribly → very
terrific → grand
terrific → great
terrified → frightened
terrify → frighten
terrifying → frightening
terrifying → horrible
territory → colony
territory → field
territory → habitat
territory → land
territory → region
terror → fear
terror → horror
terror → panic
terror-stricken → frightened
terrorism → violence
terrorize → frighten
terse → abrupt
terse → concise
terse → short
test → check
test → exam
test → examine
test → try
testify to → show
testimony → declaration
testimony → proof
testimony → tribute
testy → cross
testy → moody
tetchy → cross
tetchy → irritable
tetchy → moody
tether → tie
textbook → book
textiles → cloth
texture → finish
thankful → grateful
thanks → credit
thanks → gratitude
thanks to → by virtue of
thaw → melt
thaw → warm
the same → equal
the worse for wear → shabby
theatrical → melodramatic
theme → message
theme → subject

theme → tune
theological → religious
theory → idea
there → present
thick → dim
thick → dumb
thick → slow
thick → stupid
thickset → stocky
thieve → steal
thieving → theft
thin → narrow
thin-skinned → sensitive
thin-skinned → touchy
thing → item
thing → object
thing → obsession
things → possessions
think → assume
think → consider
think → expect
think → feel
think → guess
think → ponder
think about → consider
think highly of → approve
think highly of → respect
thinking → thought
thirst → longing
thirst → wish
thorny → difficult
thorough → careful
thorough → complete
thorough → full
thoroughgoing → total
thoroughly → well
though → in spite of
thought → consideration
thoughtful → kind
thoughtless → irresponsible
thoughtless → unkind
thrash → beat
threadbare → hackneyed
threadbare → shabby
threadbare → worn-out
threat → danger
threaten → endanger
threatening → ominous
threatening → sinister
threatening remark → threat
thrift → economy
thrifty → economical
thrill → excite
thrill → excitement

I
N
D
E
X

usual → average
usual → common
usual → natural
usual → normal
usual → ordinary
usual → regular
usual → typical
usually → as a rule
usually → on average
utensil → gadget
utensil → tool
utilize → employ
utilize → use
utmost → limit
utmost → maximum
utmost → ultimate
utter → complete
utter → emit
utter → express
utter → perfect
utter → pure
utter → rank
utter → say
utter → speak
utter → total
utterance → remark
vacant → bare
vacant → blank
vacant → empty
vacation → holiday
vacation → leave
vacillating → hesitant
vacillating → uncertain
vagary → whim
vague → dim
vague → faint
vague → rough
vague → unclear
vain → conceited
vain → fond
vain → futile
vain → hopeless
vainglorious → conceited
vainglorious → pompous
vainglorious → pretentious
vainglory → conceit
Valhalla → heaven
valiant → bold
valiant → brave
valiant → daring
valid → legal
valid → logical
validate → confirm
valorous → brave
valour → bravery

valour → courage
valuable → precious
valuable → productive
valuable → useful
value → admire
value → appreciate
value → ideal
value → merit
value → price
value → prize
value → quality
value → treasure
valueless → worthless
vandal → hooligan
vanish → die out
vanish → disappear
vanish → melt
vanished → lost
vanity → conceit
vanity → pride
vanquish → beat
vanquish → crush
vanquish → defeat
vanquish → overcome
vanquish → subdue
vapour → cloud
variable → changeable
variable → irregular
variable → uneven
variation → difference
variety → breed
variety → choice
variety → kind
variety → range
variety → sort
various → several
vary → range
vast → big
vast → great
vast → huge
vast → large
vast → spacious
vast → wide
vastness → size
vault → jump
vault → tomb
veer → swerve
vehemence → heat
vehemence → strength
vehemence → violence
vehement → intense
vehement → strong
vehement → violent
vehicle → car
vehicle → medium

velocity → rate
velocity → speed
venal → corrupt
venality → corruption
vend → sell
venerate → admire
venerate → respect
venerate → treasure
venerate → worship
venerated → holy
vengeance → revenge
venom → poison
venom → spite
venomous → poisonous
venomous → spiteful
vent → opening
venture → business
venture → dare
venture → enterprise
venture → gamble
veracious → right
verbal → oral
verbalize → express
verdict → conclusion
verdict → decision
verge → side
verification → proof
verified → actual
verify → confirm
verify → prove
verisimilar → probable
vérité → realistic
verity → principle
vernacular → colloquial
vernacular → language
versed in → familiar
versus → against
vertical → steep
vertical → straight
vertiginous → faint
verve → energy
very much → far
vessel → container
vestige → trace
vestiges → remains
vet → inspect
veteran → practical
veto → forbid
vex → annoy
vexation → anger
vexation → care
vexation → nuisance
viable → economic
viable → possible
vibrant → colourful

I
N
D
E
X

673

wrath → rage
wreak → bring
wreathe → twist
wreck → crash
wreck → destroy
wreck → spoil
wrench → twist
wretched → miserable
wretched → sorry
wretched → unlucky
wring → exact
wring → twist
wrinkle → crumple
wrinkle → fold
write → compose
write down → record
wrong → bad
wrong → crime
wrong → injustice
wrong → sin
wrong → unfair
wrongful → illegal

wrongful → unfair
yakka → work
yank → pull
yarn → story
yawning → deep
yearn → desire
yearn → long
yearn → wish
yearn for → be dying for
yearn for → miss
yearning → desire
yearning → longing
yell → call
yell → cry
yell → shout
yelp → bay
yen → desire
yield → give
yield → give in
yield → surrender
yielding → soft
yob → hooligan

youngster → boy
youngster → child
youth → boy
zeal → energy
zeal → enthusiasm
zeal → passion
zealot → fan
zealot → fanatic
zealous → eager
zealous → enthusiastic
zealous → fanatical
zenith → extreme
zenith → peak
zenith → top
zest → energy
zest → spirit
Zion → heaven
zone → area
zone → region
zoom → tear